Expert Systems

A Decision Support Approach

The Insight Series in Artificial Intelligence

Series Editor: Tony Morgan, SD–Scicon plc.

Associate Editor: Bob Muller, Digital Equipment Corporation.

The series derives its name from the Insight study group sponsored by Systems Designers plc, whose workshops, conferences and study visits promoted international collaboration between companies and other institutions toward the common goal of applying advanced AI technology.

Other titles in the series:

Expert Systems
A Decision Support Approach

With applications in management and finance

Michel Klein
Groupe HEC Graduate School of Management, France

Leif B. Methlie
Norwegian School of Economics and
Business Administration, Norway

▲▼ ADDISON-WESLEY PUBLISHING COMPANY
Wokingham, England · Reading, Massachusetts · Menlo Park, California
New York · Don Mills, Ontario · Amsterdam · Bonn · Sydney
Singapore · Tokyo · Madrid · San Juan

Cover designed by Hybert Design and Type, Maidenhead.
and printed by The Riverside Printing Co. (Reading) Ltd.
Text design by Lesley Stewart.
Typeset by Colset Private Limited, Singapore.
Printed in Great Britain by T.J. Press (Padstow), Cornwall.

First printed 1990

British Library Cataloguing in Publication Data

Klein, Michel
    Expert Systems: A Decision Support Approach
    1. Financial services. Applications of expert systems
    I. Title II. Methlie, Leif B.
    332.1'028'5633

    ISBN 0-201-17562-2

Library of Congress Cataloging in Publication Data

Klein, Michel
    Expert Systems: A Decision Support Approach / Michel Klein, Leif B. Methlie.
        p. cm.
    Includes bibliographical references.
    ISBN 0-201-17562-2
    1. Business enterprises—Finance—Data processing. 2. Finance—Decision making—Data processing. 3. Decision support systems. 4. Expert systems (Computer science) I. Methlie, Leif B. II. Title.
    HG4012.5.K56 1990
    658.15'028'5—dc20

89-77030
CIP

Michel Klein

To my parents and my daughter Emmanuelle

Leif B. Methlie

To my daughters Annike and Linda

Preface

Rationale for the book

An exciting application area is emerging from the field of artificial intelligence – expert systems. In the early 1980s we became aware of the significance of this new technology to business, and ways in which it could change business and improve decision making. However, early research on applying this technology to managerial problems, and financial problems in particular, demonstrated some shortcomings. Firstly, expert systems are reasoning systems. They are not particularly good at dealing with numbers and performing numeric computations. Secondly, they are problem solving systems and are not easily integrated into a decision making environment dealing with ill-structured decisions. Therefore, both of us saw opportunities in integrating the expert systems technology with the decision support systems technology. The new framework resulting from this we have called knowledge-based decision support systems. The paradigm of decision support systems (DSS) remains: to support decision making in ill-structured situations. The system architecture, however, consists of components from DSS and expert systems.

To our knowledge, the idea of such a framework was presented for the first time at a NATO conference 'Decision Support Systems: Theory and Applications' held in Maratea, Italy in 1985. In the Spring semester of 1986 Leif B. Methlie was on sabbatical leave to work with Michel Klein at Centre HEC-ISA, near Paris, on applying this framework to problems in management control and finance. The idea of this book was then created.

Both of us have more than 15 years of experience in academic teaching, research and consulting in the field of DSS. We have taught expert systems and DSS in business schools and in executive seminars for a number of years. In particular, together with Professor Paolo Mottura at SDA Bocconi, Italy, we have organized and run seminars on expert systems and DSS in banks and financial institutions for managers and analysts since 1986. In 1988, seminars of this kind were organized in five different countries in Europe. In our teaching and consulting activities we have felt a need for a comprehensive text on expert systems and problem solving that could deal with these topics from a business perspective. Most textbooks on expert systems take their examples from other fields, such as medicine, science and engineering. This makes the reading rather hard for business students and managers, due to the unfamiliar domain vocabularies that they are confronted with in these examples. After having worked on development tools, prototypes for several financial tasks, and more recently on implementation of such systems in business organizations, we felt that we had enough material to make a comprehensive text on knowledge-based decision support systems for a business-oriented audience.

Readership

This book is particularly designed for students on courses covering DSS, expert systems, or knowledge-based DSS, in a business administration curriculum, in management, in finance, or in information systems. The book gives full coverage of technical aspects together with examples and cases from business.

We think that it is also important for executives and managers, particularly managers of financial institutions, to know about knowledge-based systems, the importance of these systems to their business, and how they can be developed. Business managers may choose to avoid the more fundamental issues developed in Chapters 2–4 as well as the more specific aspects of knowledge modeling described in Chapter 8, and testing and evaluation in Chapter 10. Thus, we recommend business managers to read Chapters 1, 5–7, 9 and 11–13.

For the training of systems personnel in knowledge engineering for business problems, this book should be particularly helpful. In this case, we recommend the reader to study the chapters in the order in which they are presented.

We have presented a comprehensive framework of knowledge-based DSS and shown these concepts partly implemented. Still much has to be done to fully implement this framework. Tool designers and researchers should find this book challenging in this respect.

Acknowledgements

In developing this book over a number of years, we have benefited from discussions with many people.

Michel Klein wishes to thank all the members of the development team on OPTRANS EXPERT at the company SIG. In particular, Alain Manteau for his work on the mainframe version, Pierre Monnier for his work on the PC version, J.L. Dussartre and F. Despoux, Marc Kossa and T. Martin for their work on the expert subsystem, and D. Dollé for his work on the database subsystem.

Michel Klein also wishes to thank: Alain Manteau who made the initial transfer of the FINSIM model under OPTRANS EXPERT, Thierry Villedieu for his work on FINSIM, Eric Briys from the Finance Department of the Groupe HEC for his advice on a first prototype knowledge base. Mr Cabanac and Mr Nicol from the Caisse Régionale du Credit Agricole de Toulouse for their work on one of the FINSIM knowledge base, Mr J.J. Burgun from the SOREFI Champagne Ardenne for his work on another FINSIM Knowledge Base. Mr Derksen (SOREFI Champagne) and Mr Renaudin (CRCAM Toulouse) for their encouragement. Dr Brita Shwartz from the Stockholm School of Economics Research Center for her comments on Chapter 3.

Dr Jacques Pezier for his comments on the rational decision analysis section of Chapter 3. Professor A. Lux from LIFIA-ENSIMAG for his advice on the integration of AI in OPTRANS. Pierre Rosensthiel who encouraged my initial work in this field.

My former professors at the Tuck School of Dartmouth College, Peter Williamson, C. Bower, Vic McGee and W. Carleton who gave me the taste for decision support systems in finance.

My colleagues from the IFIP Working Group 8.3 and 8.1, in particular, Professor R. Traunmuller (J. Kepler Universitat, Linz) and Professor V. Rajkovic (J. Stefan Institute, Ljubljana) with whom I had many discussions in many wonderful European cities.

My partners in the IKB/DSS ESPRIT project, in particular, Dr F. Schmidt (IKE, Universitat, Stuttgart), Professor M. Milanese (Politecnico di Torino), Professor P. Vincke (Université Libre de Bruxelles) with whom I had many discussions on second generation KB-DSS. Hopefully, this project which gave us the opportunity to discuss ideas and collaborate is now financed by the company SIG.

My colleagues from the Information and Decision Support System Department at the Groupe HEC.

Nicole de Saint Aubert, Chantal Boeffard, Micheline Rico and Elisabeth Sartiaux for typing the manuscript.

Leif B. Methlie wishes to thank members of the research team on financial expert systems: Svein O. Båtnes, Heidi Følstad, Per B. Lyngstad, and Helge Lilletvedt and Gunnar A. Dahl, a partner with Ernst and Young in Norway, for making his expertise on financial analysis available for the project. Also he wants to extend his gratitude to the Royal Norwegian Council for Science and Industrial Research for financial support. Furthermore, he wants to thank his colleagues for valuable comments: Gunnar

Christensen, A.M. Fuglseth, Knut Ims and Linda Lai, and, finally, Wenche Mørch for typing and organizing the text.

Both authors wish to thank Professor Paolo Mottura with SDA Bocconi, Italy for valuable collaboration in organizing seminars for financial institutions in Europe.

Availability of the KB-DSS software

The OPTRANS EXPERT development environment is available from the company SIG, as well as the application software presented in the book: FINSIM EXPERT and BANKER, and the exercises LOAN and JIIA-86.

OPTRANS EXPERT is available in English and in French, FINSIM is available in French, however, adaptation to other European accounting has been done. BANKER is available in English. OPTRANS EXPERT is available as a development or run-time version under MS/DOS on PC and under VMS on Digital VAX. Transfer under OS/2 and UNIX are planned. The database and expert subsystem are optional. OPTRANS is also available in English or French, as a junior version for teaching purposes. The junior version has all the functions of the normal version, only the knowledge base is limited to 50 rules and models are limited to 63 variables.

All enquiries concerning the software should be sent to SIG, 4 bis, rue de la Libération, 78350 Jouy en Josas, FRANCE.

Michel Klein
Leif B. Methlie
February 1990

Publisher's Acknowledgements

The publishers would like to thank the following for permission to reproduce the quoted material on the cited pages.

Page 16: reproduced from Winograd T. and Flores F. (1986). *Understanding Computers and Cognition*, © 1987, Addison-Wesley Publishing Co., Inc., Reading, Massachusetts. Reprinted with permission of the publisher. Page 20/21: reproduced from Sowa J.F. (1984). *Conceptual Structures*, © 1984, Addison-Wesley Publishing Co., Inc., Reading, Massachusetts. Reprinted with permission of the publisher. Page 27/28: reproduced from Anderson (1985). *Cognitive Psychology and its Implications*, reprinted by kind permission of the publisher, W.H. Freeman & Co., New York. Page 28: reproduced from Johnson P.E. (1983). What kind of expert should a system be? *The Journal of Medicine and Philosophy* **8**, 77–97. Page 41: reproduced from Cyert R.M. and March J.E. (1963). *A Behavioural Theory of the Firm*, reprinted by kind permission of R.M. Cyert.

Pages 54, 63, 86, 86/7, 87 and 102: reproduced from Holtzman S. (1989). *Intelligent Decision Systems*, © 1989, Addison-Wesley Publishing Co., Inc., Reading, Massachusetts. Reprinted with permission of the publisher. Pages 57 and 199/200: reproduced from Scott Morton M.S. and Keen P.G. (1978). *Decision Support Systems: an Organizational Perspective*, © 1978, Addison-Wesley Publishing Co., Inc., Reading, Massachusetts. Reprinted with permission of the publisher. Pages 58 and 61: reproduced from Watson S.R. and Buede D.M. (1967). *Decision Synthesis*, reprinted by kind permission of Cambridge University Press. Pages 89, 90, 91, 93, 100 and 101: reproduced from Howard R.A. and Matheson J.E. (1968). *An Introduction to Decision Analysis*, reprinted by kind permission of SRI International. Pages 104/105: reproduced from Arrow K.J. (1951). *Social Choice and Individual Values*, © 1951, John Wiley & Sons, Inc. Pages 106 and 107: reproduced from Simon H.A. *et al.* (1987). Decision making and problem solving. *Interfaces* **17** (5), reprinted by kind permission of the publisher.

Page 114: reproduced from Rich E. (1981). *Artificial Intelligence*, reprinted by kind permission of McGraw-Hill, New York. Page 135: reproduced from Minsky M. (1975). A framework for representing knowledge. In *Psychology & Computer Vision* (Winston P., ed.), reprinted by kind permission of McGraw-Hill, New York. Table 4.2: reproduced from Pinson S. (1981). Representation des connaissances dans les systemes expert. *RAIRO*, **15** (4), reprinted by kind permission of the publisher.

Pages 155/156: reproduced from Klein M. and Tixier V. (1971). SCARABÉE: a data and model bank for financial engineering and research. In *Proceedings IFIP Congress*, North-Holland Publishing Co., reprinted by kind permission of Elsevier Science Publishers, Physical Sciences and Engineering Division. Page 170: reproduced from Bonczek R.H. *et al.* (1981). *Foundations of Decision Support*, reprinted by kind permission of Academic Press Inc., Orlando, Florida. Pages 197 and 198: reproduced from Holsapple C.W. and Whinston A.B. (1985). *Managers' Guide to Expert Systems Using Guru*, reprinted by kind permission of Dow Jones-Irwin. Pages 199/200: reprinted by permission of *Harvard Business Review*. An excerpt of

Management Decision Systems: A Computer-based Support of Decision Making by Scott-Morton M.S. (1971). Copyright © 1971 by the President and Fellows of Harvard College. All rights reserved. Pages 213-221: reproduced from Noel J.P., ed, (1986). *Journèes Internationales de l'Informatique et de l'Automatique*, Commissariat JIIA, 16 rue Dufrey noy, 75116 Paris, reprinted by kind permission of the author, and also from Klein M, and Villedieu T. (1986). *The JIIA-86 Case: a Solution with OPTRANS*, SIG Internal Document, reprinted by kind permission of the authors.

Page 224 and Table 6.1: reproduced from Hayes-Roth F. *et al*. (1983). *Building Expert Systems*, © 1983, Addison-Wesley Publishing Co., Inc., Reading, Massachusetts. Reprinted with permission of the publisher. Table 6.3: reproduced from the *PlanPower Manual*, reprinted by kind permission of APEX Inc., Cambridge, Massachusetts.

Page 285: reproduced from Thomas D. (1989). What is an object? *Byte*, reprinted by kind permission of BYTE Publications © McGraw-Hill, Inc.

Page 321: reproduced from Feigenbaum E. (1977). The art of artificial intelligence: themes and case studies of knowledge engineering. In *Proceedings of the Fifth International Joint Conference on Artificial Intelligence*, reprinted by kind permission of MIT Press, Cambridge, Massachusetts. Section 8.5: reproduced from Per Bjarne Lyngstad (1987). Knowledge modeling of expertise in financial diagnostics. *PhD Thesis*, reprinted by kind permission of Per Bjarne Lyngstad.

Page 354: reprinted from The design of man-machine decision systems: an application to portfolio management by Gerrity T.P., Jr., *Sloan Management Review*, 12, Winter 1971, pp. 59–75, by permission of the publisher. Copyright © 1971 by the Sloan Management Review Association. All rights reserved.

Table 10.1 and page 432: reproduced from Weiss S.M. and Kulikowski C.A. (1984). *A Practical Guide to Designing Expert Systems*, reprinted by kind permission of Rowman & Allenheld Publishers, Totowa, New Jersey.

Page 439: reprinted by permission of *Harvard Business Review*. An excerpt from The coming of the new organization, by Drucker P.F. (1988). Copyright © 1988 by the President and Fellows of Harvard College, all rights reserved. Page 445: reproduced from Galbraith J.R. (1977). *Organizational Design*, © 1977, Addison-Wesley Publishing Co., Inc., Reading, Massachusetts. Reprinted with permission of the publisher. Pages 446 and 500/501: reproduced from Gunton T. (1986). *Infrastructure, Building a Framework for Corporate Information Handling*. © 1989, Prentice-Hall International (UK) Ltd., reprinted by kind permission. Section 11.5 and Table 11.1: reproduced from presentations given by Professor Paolo Mottura of SDA-Bocconi, Milan, Italy, reprinted by kind permission of Professor Paolo Mottura.

Page 477: reproduced from Pezier J. (1986). Real time financial trading systems. *Presentation at the SIAD Research Seminar*, Centre HEC-ISA, 78350 Jouy-en-Josas, France, reprinted by kind permission of Michel Klein. Page 478: reproduced from Graham I. (1987). *Knowledge-based Systems in the Dealing Room*. IBM Seminar on Expert Systems in Banking and Insurance, Jouy-en-Josas, France, reprinted by kind permission of Ian Graham.

The publishers would like to thank the following for permission to reproduce the cited figures.

Figure 2.2: reprinted from The structure of 'unstructured' decision processes by Mintzberg H. *et al.* published in *Administrative Science Quarterly* **21** (2), June 1976, by permission of *Administrative Science Quarterly*.

Figures 3.1, 3.12, 13.3 and 13.4: reproduced from Holtzman S. (1989). *Intelligent Decision Systems*, © 1989, Addison-Wesley Publishing Co., Inc., Reading, Massachusetts. Reprinted with permission of the publisher. Figures 3.2 and 3.5: reproduced from Watson S.R. and Buede D.M. (1987). *Decision Synthesis*, reprinted by kind permission of Cambridge University Press and S.R. Watson. Figures 3.13 and 3.16: reproduced from Howard R.A. and Matheson J.E. (1968). *An Introduction to Decision Analysis*, reprinted by kind permission of SRI International and the authors. Figures 3.3, 3.4 and 3.6–3.11: reproduced from Pezier J. and Klein M. (1973). *ARBRE, Manuel d'Utilisation*. SIG, 4 bis rue de la Libération, 78350 Jouy-en-Josas, France, reprinted by kind permission of Michel Klein. Figures 3.14 and 3.15: reproduced from the *FINSIM-EXPERT User Manual*, SIG, 4 bis rue de la Libération, 78350 Jouy-en-Josas, France, reprinted by kind permission of Michel Klein.

Figure 5.1: reproduced from Bonczek R.H. *et al.* (1981) *Foundations of Decision Support Systems*, reprinted by kind permission of Academic Press Inc, Orlando, Florida. Figure 5.6: reproduced from Klein M. and Manteau A. (1983). OPTRANS: a tool for implementation of decision support centers. In *Process and Tools for Decision Support* (Sol H.G., ed.), reprinted by kind permission of Elsevier Science Publishers, Physical Sciences and Engineering Division. Figures 5.2–5.4, 5.7, 5.9, 5.11–5.14: reproduced from the *OPTRANS User Manual*, reprinted by kind permission of Michel Klein. Figure 5.15: reproduced from Noël J.P., ed. (1986). *Journèes Internationales de l'Informatique et de l'Automatique*, Commissariat JIIA, 16 rue Dufrey noy, 75116 Paris, reprinted by kind permission of the author. Figures 5.16 and 5.17: reproduced from Klein M. and Villedieu T. (1986). *The JIIA Case: a Solution with OPTRANS*, SIG Internal Document, reprinted by kind permission of the authors. Figure 5.18: reproduced from *OPTRANS Database User Manual* (1989), reprinted by kind permission of Michel Klein.

Figure 6.10: reproduced from Rich C. and Buchanan B. (1985). Expert Systems – Part 1, Tutorial No. 5. *IJCAI*, 9, reprinted by kind permission of Howard W. Sams & Company, Indianapolis, USA.

Figures 7.1, 7.3 and 7.5: reproduced from the *OPTRANS User Manual*, reprinted by kind permission of Michel Klein. Figures 7.2, 7.4 and 7.7–7.15: reproduced from the *FINSIM-EXPERT User Manual*, SIG, 4 bis rue de la Libération, 78530 Jouy-en-Josas, France, reprinted by kind permission of Michel Klein.

Figure 9.1: reprinted from The design of man-machine decision systems: an application to portfolio management by Gerrity T.P., Jr., *Sloan Management Review*, 12, Winter 1971, pp. 59–75, by permission of the publisher. Copyright © 1971 by the Sloan Management Review Association. All rights reserved. Figure 9.2: reproduced from Keen P.G.W. and Scott Morton M.S. (1978). *Decision Support Systems*, © 1978, Addison-Wesley Publishing Co., Inc., Reading, Massachusetts. Reprinted with permission of the publisher. Figure 9.6: reprinted from Theory of change and the effective use of management science by Zand D.E. and Sorensen R.E. published in *Administrative Science Quarterly* **20** (4), December 1975, by permission of *Administrative Science Quarterly*. Figure 9.7: reprinted from An organization development approach to consulting by Kolb D.A. and Frohman A.L., *Sloan Management Review*, **12** (4), 1970, pp. 51–65, by permission of the publisher. Copy-

Contents

1

Introduction

1.1 From decision support system to knowledge-based decision support system

This is a book about decision making – about understanding how people solve problems and make decisions, and about how they can improve their problem-solving and decision-making capabilities by the use of computers. We shall deal with problems that are characterized as ill-structured because no procedure or algorithm can be prescribed for their solutions. Therefore, there exists no computerized choice procedure. These problems can only be solved by a cooperation between man and computer.

Computer systems for problem solving and decision making have been developed since around the end of the Second World War, when computers became available for non-military tasks. Also, they have been the target of research and application from a multitude of disciplines. Over time, systems have been built on different principles and with different aims. Therefore, investigation of this field, is not a study of one homogeneous area. Despite the diversity of the field, it should be possible to explain continuities and changes and to recognize lines of descent, that is, the genealogy of issues and related concepts and tools.

One concept is central to this book: Decision Support Systems (DSS). This concept is built on the paradigm of *support*. That is, a computer system is placed at the disposal of the decision maker, who may use data or models to recognize, understand, and formulate a problem, and make use of analytical aids to evaluate alternatives. In the complex world in which managerial decision making takes place, we think that this is the only paradigm of computer decision systems that is operational.

The term 'decision support system' was coined at the beginning of the

1

1970s to denote a computer program that could support a manager in making ill-structured decisions. This concept is a result of research in two areas: theoretical studies of human problem solving and decision making done at the Carnegie Institute of Technology during the 1950s and 1960s, and the work on interactive computer systems at the Massachusetts Institute of Technology in the 1960s. As time-sharing systems became available, several business schools in the USA and Europe started to work on computer systems for decision support. At first, this area was dominated by demonstrating the applicability of this new concept to managerial decision making. This was then followed by a great interest in software development. New tools, DSS generators, for easier building of such systems were created. With the introduction of microcomputers, developments in DSS speeded up. Today, software for supporting decision making is available for almost any financial problem. Chapter 5 describes the DSS technology, why it was immediately useful and, in section 5.6, this technology is applied to a particular financial task. Emphasis in the DSS concept is put on information access and display, and on numeric computations by analytical models.

A second important concept to our body of knowledge of computer systems for problem solving and decision making, is the concept of expert systems. Interestingly enough, this concept was created almost at the same time as the DSS concept, with the DENDRAL project at Stanford University in the late 1960s. During the 1970s several research projects were launched in artificial intelligence laboratories. The commercial use of expert systems started at the beginning of the 1980s, but widespread commercial use came with the more powerful microcomputers and cheaper software. Recently, both the cost and the risk of using this technology have been dramatically reduced. This technology is here to be utilized now. Management in general and the financial domain, in particular, is expected to be an important target area of this technology. Chapter 6 discusses the concept of expert systems and shows how it can be applied to a credit decision. Two fundamental results were derived from research on expert systems:

(1)   that it is possible to simulate expert problem solving; and
(2)   that this problem solving can be explained by the system.

When expert systems technology was first applied to management problems, and finance problems in particular, it fell short in several respects. The main problem was that, this technology was not capable of handling the classical DSS functions which are more computational than logical. Also, problem solving in managerial domains is not solely symbolic reasoning, which is the predominant problem-solving method of expert systems. It is not due to just data retrieval and numeric calculations either; which are the functions found in a traditional DSS. What is needed is a system which can process data and numeric relationships and, by reasoning, transform this data into opinions, judgment, evaluations and advice. It turns out that it is not just a matter of interconnecting the existing software tools from the DSS and the expert system areas. Therefore, we shall develop a new framework which is based on the paradigm of decision support, but which also enables us to incorporate specialized knowledge and expertise into the system. This will add the capability of reasoning to the functionality of the DSS and will enable it to give advice on specific problems. We shall call these systems **Knowledge-Based Decision Support Systems** (KB-DSS). This new framework, and the new development tools which come out of this framework, will be described in Chapter 7.

1.2 The scientific background

Decision support systems grew out of the experience of applying quantitative models to management. It became apparent that an *understanding* of the decision situation was a prerequisite to any proposal for improvements. Therefore, in the DSS concept two major scientific developments in the study of decisions merged: the descriptive, behavioral theories, and the prescriptive, rationalistic theories.

To understand how decision making is actually made, we can draw on a body of knowledge developed by psychologists and management researchers. Psychologists have studied human cognition and problem solving. A major contribution on these topics has come from the Carnegie school by researchers such as Herbert Simon and Allan Newell. From empirical studies they developed a theory of the cognitive architecture of the mind – what they call the Human Information Processor System (HIPS). The key characteristic of this theory is that cognitive systems are symbol systems with mental operations on symbol structures which can be in different states (long- and short-term memories). Their theory has methodological consequences for the study of problem solving processes (thinking-aloud protocols). They also gave a description of the problem solving process that holds for a wide range of activities. Problem solving proceeds by **heuristic search** through a large set of possibilities. Heuristics are used to guide the search and in selecting the steps towards the goal. Along with the development of expert systems technology there has been an increase into the research of expert problem solving. What constitutes a good expert system, primarily, is the large amounts of domain knowledge that are stored in memory to which access is gained by pattern recognition.

Also, psychologists have studied decisions by the process used to arrive at a choice. Again, the Carnegie School is central to this research, and to the development of a behavioral theory of decision making. A central concept for designing decision support systems is Simon's description of the *decision making process* – the intelligence-design-choice phases. Simon's work has caused further research on behavioral decision making to be carried out, also by management researchers. We shall report on a framework developed by

Mintzberg and some of his colleagues which is conceptually richer than Simon's description of the decision making process. Another central concept developed by Simon is that of *bounded rationality*. In a situation of incomplete, imprecise and inconsistent knowledge, the decision maker satisfies rather than optimizes in the choice of a decision. We shall deal further with organizational and political decision processes. All of the theories on problem solving and behavioral decision making are collected in Chapter 2. This chapter should be sufficiently rich in conceptions to enable descriptions of specific decision making processes to be made. These descriptions should be sufficiently lucid for a clear understanding of the decision making processes.

In the opening sentence of this chapter we assume that the quality of decision making can be improved. The next issue is 'how this can be accomplished?' Here, we shall rely on the prescriptive decision theories. These are theories that have their roots in economics and mathematical logic. Central to this body of theories is the *utility theory*. It is a formally axiomatized statement of what it means for an agent to behave in a consistent, rational manner. To be rational means to act in a way that is consistent with rules that we have adopted, and to which our actions should conform. The utility theory has been further developed to deal with choice under uncertainty – and the calculus that is used most often to encode uncertainty is the *probability* theory. Furthermore, probability is a subjective concept, it is an individual's perception of uncertainty. Thus, we arrive at a new normative criterion: the subjective, expected utility maximization.

The subjective, expected utility theory is the basis for most of the methods and techniques of modern operations research. Modeling and optimization are the key issues here. Operations research techniques are concerned with choice and they use the assumptions of the subjected, expected utility theory. These techniques work well for decision problems that are relatively well structured.

However, methods have been developed to apply this decision theory to complex, practical situations. These methods include the statistical decision theory, the decision analysis school, and the multi-criteria decision making and preference modeling school. We shall use the term decision methodology to describe the body of techniques that are available for effectively performing analysis of a decision situation. They include: how to structure a problem, and how to model that problem once structured, how to develop an analysis, and how to elicit subjective probabilities and preferences. Normative decision theories are dealt with in Chapter 3. Our objective is to give readers an understanding of the tools (methods and techniques) that are available, and to provide sufficient references to the literature for further studies.

In the spirit of the descriptive tradition and the cognitive studies of human problem solving, the field of artificial intelligence (AI) has been developed. A number of techniques have been developed to imitate intelligent behavior using computers. Today, these computer programs can perform difficult tasks at the same level as professionally-trained humans. These AI programs are usually called **expert systems**. A description of a typical expert system will closely resemble the typical description given to human problem solving, in other words, that of symbolic reasoning and heuristic search. An expert system will rely on the storage and computing power of the machine, while the human being will have a richer set of heuristics, even though the aim is to represent as much heuristics as possible in the computer system. Many AI-techniques have been developed for knowledge representation, reasoning and heuristic search using this computer power. In Chapter 4 we shall deal with these techniques.

Chapters 2, 3 and 4 make up the theoretical foundation for the rest of the book. These chapters are then followed by the three chapters on systems concepts.

The scientific background and the developments that have led to the definitions of the two system concepts, expert systems and DSS are shown, diagramatically, in Figure 1.1. Also, we have shown some key concepts that characterize each major scientific development.

1.3 Development methodology

This book is about applying computer technology to decision making in business organizations. Therefore, we must provide the necessary methods and techniques to put the technology to work in a management environment. The theories on decisions and decision making constitute the conceptual frameworks by which decisions can be studied and understood, and by which improvements can be analysed and proposed. From what has already been said it seems plausible that a development methodology has to be centered on decisions. The first papers on the design of DSS, for instance that by Gerrity (1971), argue strongly for replacing a data-centered approach with that of a decision-centered approach. However, in the DSS field there is some controversy about the decision-centered approach. The argument against it is that it is not compatible with the actual nature of managerial work. Management researchers, like Mintzberg (1973), claim that managers seldom make decisions as part of a deliberate, coherent and continuous decision making process. Instead, managerial work is characterized by brevity, variety and fragmentation. Also, managers are much more than decision makers; they attend to a multitude of roles.

The complexity of the decision making context is also taken as an argument against decision or task analysis. 'Designers literally "cannot get to the first base" because no one, least of all the decision maker or user, can define in advance, what the functional requirements of the system should be' (Sprague and Carlson (1982) p. 15). Adaptive design and prototyping have been the key words. Development has been focused on computer

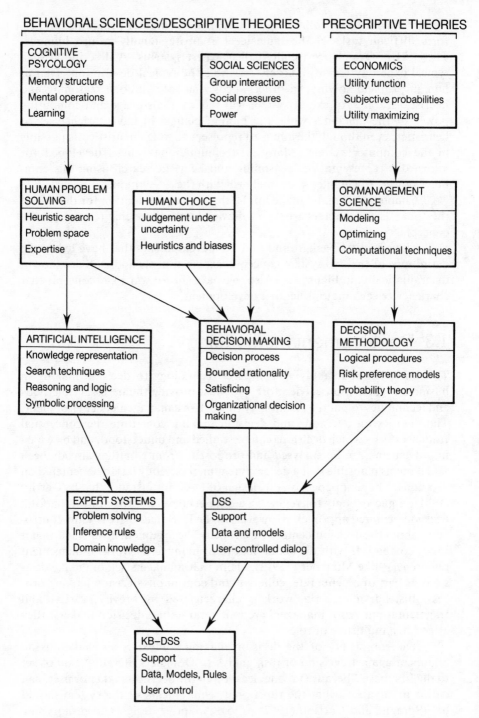

Figure 1.1 The scientific background.

representations and program design. By means of powerful development tools, the so-called DSS generators and expert system shells, rapid prototyping has been the predominating approach. Skill in using these tools has had a greater emphasis than that of methodological competence in performing task analysis. This process can be characterized as a technology-driven process.

Here, we shall adhere to the view that adaptive design and prototyping are important elements in a development methodology for knowledge based DSS. They are important in reducing context complexity by performing successive redefinitions of the functionality of the computer system. However, although difficult to identify, decision making must be understood and described before it can be improved. We shall, therefore, provide a decision-centered methodology for task analysis. This decision-centered methodology includes descriptive and normative aspects as well as knowledge engineering to develop expert problem solving models. A design methodology that we think is needed within the Knowledge-Based DSS (KB-DSS) conceptual framework is presented in Chapter 9. Since knowledge-based functions will be part of this new framework, in Chapter 8, we shall provide a methodology, based on a cognitive approach, to the building of knowledge bases in financial domains. Testing and evaluation of knowledge bases impose problems of validation and verification. These problems will be dealt with in Chapter 10, and in Chapter 11, implementation of knowledge-based DSS in organizations will be discussed.

1.4 Application of the KB-DSS technology

How can decision making take advantage of this new technology? Improved performance can be accomplished by more efficient processes or by better outcomes of decisions. Today, business is, generally, more complex than it was in the past. Almost all sectors of industry experience greater competition, more complex production technology, and more sophisticated market demand. In the financial sector, the environment is even more complex due to deregulation. The result of this is growing diversification and accelerated innovation. The service component of delivered products is increasing, and, in general, service activities are characterized by high-intensity decision making. Supply and demand are more closely interconnected. The gap between production and customers diminishes. More decisions must be made at the front line, and more people are involved in decision making. With a growing number of products to deliver, increased product complexity, more demanding customers, and also greater competition, this puts a heavy burden on the front-line decision makers. Decision making needs to be decentralized, but at the same time, controlled. However, diversification and innovation of the corporation's portfolio of products may lead to rapid obsolescence of front-line knowledge and a problem of specialization. The result of this is a deterioration of services to customers, and a growing risk of ineffective management of customer relationships.

The technology offered by DSS, expert systems, and KB-DSS may improve this situation. Knowledge-based systems can improve quality of decision making throughout the whole organization by making expertise available at the customer level. They can also support decision making which is consistent and in compliance with the rules set by the organization, and can provide a stable service to customers due to easier maintenance of knowledge.

In general, the KB-DSS technology described in this book can be applied to decision making in any organization. However, we have particularly approached the domains of management control and finance. Throughout this book, research, cases, and applications in these areas are reported. To a great extent we are relying on our own research carried out during the last five years, and in almost every chapter we use this research and our practical experience to illustrate concepts and methods. But we are also using selected research and practice from the literature to broaden the scope of the book.

We believe that business opportunities of the KB-DSS framework are infinite. To show this we have surveyed the applications of knowledge-based systems in the area of finance. This survey is presented in Chapter 12. The systems we have found are primarily expert systems. The survey is by no means comprehensive, however, it should give the reader ideas about where to find adequate application domains for this technology. In systematizing this search and in describing these systems we have used a classification scheme based on three major subject types: corporations, individuals, and banks and financial institutions. Within each subject category we have defined financial functions, each of which is described and known systems are presented.

In Chapter 13, we make a survey of present research and developments in this field to see what we can expect to be on the market in the future. This chapter presents some of these expected developments: the second generation of KB-DSS.

1.5 Teaching advice

This book can be used as a textbook in a business administration curriculum at the undergraduate or postgraduate level. The text is intended to be covered in a single-semester course of about 40 lecture hours. The chapters develop the field in a fairly systematic manner from the underlying theories, through an evolution of system concepts, to development and implementation methodologies.

This book can be used in courses on DSS, expert systems, and information systems for management. It should also fit well into more general courses in management and finance as a supplementary text. It should also appeal to specialists, particularly for in-service training courses, for instance, in banks and financial institutions.

A course on knowledge-based decision support systems must, in addition to the study of basic concepts, also include some practical experience in the application of these concepts. Also, it must include the use of a KB-DSS development tool to implement small applications, in order to master the concepts in an operational way. In the appendix we have described a course outline for a single-semester course intended to cover DSS, expert systems, and KB-DSS. In addition to the material covered in this book, the course includes a lecture on the use of a development tool, PC-OPTRANS Expert. Therefore, references are given to the manual of this software product.

Our experience with this course has been that it is difficult to succeed, in a single semester, to get across a thorough understanding of the basic concepts, together with the satisfactory skills that are needed to master the software tool. Therefore, our recommendation is that this text should be supplemented with a project-oriented course, where the students are asked to develop a major application.

2

Human Problem Solving and Decision Processes

2.1 Introduction

2.1.1 Decision making and problem solving

Decision making and problem solving are important tasks in all intelligent activities, and so are of great concern to researchers in a multitude of scientific disciplines. Mathematicians have studied the implications of the axioms of decision theory; statisticians have been concerned with decision making in the face of uncertainty; economists have studied how human decision making determines economic activity. In the behavioral sciences several areas of decision making study can be found: cognitive psychologists study human problem solving; social psychologists study how decisions are reached in organizations; and political scientists study how political processes result in decisions.

The usual image of a decision maker is of someone who evaluates and chooses between decisions. Problem solving, on the other hand, is concerned with the intelligent activities that are performed by a person who is confronted with a situation in which there is a gap between what is desired (the goal) and what is given (the initial state), and in which the steps that need to be taken to reach this goal are unknown. Problem solving has been the concern of cognitive psychologists, some of whom have a managerial perspective. We shall deal with problem solving in the broadest sense taking the definition given above as the basis. This is how it is dealt with in artificial intelligence and expert systems. But we shall also deal with problem solving as part of decision making. This is of concern in decision support systems.

In this book we shall use the term 'decision making' to include all stages of problem solving such as: recognizing situations that call for actions, formulating problems, designing actions and setting goals, as well as final evaluation and choice. We shall call these tasks the *decision making process*.

Two scientific approaches to the study of decisions can be identified:

(1)   the **normative** approach which prescribes optimal behavior, that is, how decisions should be made, and;

(2)   the **descriptive** (or behavioral) approach which is concerned with understanding how people actually behave when solving problems and making decisions.

At the heart of the normative approach lies the rational, 'economic man' decision model. It was first developed in economics and was later applied to management through the fields of operation research and management science. Normative theories are based on a rationality paradigm where rational behavior is prescribed by a formally axiomatized statement. Therefore, normative models of decision making are also called formal models. They define conditions for perfect utility maximization. The decision maker, the economic man, behaves rationally towards this goal by calculating the consequences for each relevant alternative decision, ranking these consequences according to preference, and finally computing the optimal decision, that is, finding the alternative that will maximize utility.

Normative theories are concerned only with how to choose from a set of alternatives. Therefore, we may call them *theories of choice*. They say nothing about how to frame problems, develop alternatives, set goals, or implement decisions.

Rational choice implies that future consequences of current actions are predicted and that guesses are made, about the future preferences for those consequences. Neither prediction is easy. Theories of choice have also been developed to handle uncertainties, usually by assigning probability distributions to the consequences of alternative decisions. In Chapter 3 we shall deal with several methods or schools within this normative tradition of decision making. We shall do this because developing computer aids that are implicit to decision makers implies a normative perspective, in other words, using a DSS makes decision making more effective. Normative theories enable us to analyze the structure of a decision.

However, even though the normative theories are significant in optimizing a decision under certain conditions, they fall short in dealing with the complexity of most real-world decision making. Empirical research carried out on how people make decisions shows that actual human behavior deviates from what should be expected in view of the rationalistic tradition. Simon (1957) by himself, and in collaboration with others, March and Simon (1958) and Newell and Simon (1972), observed that actual decision making is performed under conditions such as:

- lack of information on several aspects such as problem formulation, alternatives and consequences;
- time and cost constraints that inhibit comprehensive search;
- imperfections in perceiving information.

Simon introduced the concept of *bounded* rationality to describe decision making under these conditions. His idea was that the list of technical constraints imposed by the rational models of choice should include the properties of human beings as processors of information and as problem solvers. Bounded rationality is a sensible explanation of the human efforts being undertaken in order to achieve rational information gathering and processing. The theory takes into account the costs of intelligence and information processing. Intelligence is selective; the definition of a situation is oversimplified or subjective; the choices are biased and so on. Simon coined the term 'satisficing' for decision procedures under the bounded rationality paradigm. He made no distinction between individual and organizational decision making. This distinction, however, was made some years later by Cyert and March (1963) in their behavioral theory of the firm.

The theory of bounded rationality is still a rational model. It is based on decision making as a sequential process. A problem has to be decided upon, and there has to be an argument for the alternative chosen. Informational and computational costs are evaluated in light of the benefits that can be achieved. It is assumed that the decision maker will make a rational evaluation of these costs, and thus, bounded rationality still applies, at least as a quasi-rational decision.

Other researchers in organizational decision making have gone even further than Simon in relaxing the rather strong requirements of rational behavior. Lindblom (1959), for instance, argues that, far from making rational decisions, organizations proceed by 'muddling-through'. He explains this decision making behavior as one in which the decision maker moves incrementally, searching for alternatives which are only slightly different from existing situations. Lindblom studied policy making in governmental organizations. His later thoughts on this topic were presented in a paper, after 20 years of discussion of his idea (Lindblom, 1979). He still believes that, as a sensible guide for organizational decision making, incrementalism has much to offer.

So far, we have been primarily concerned with the first implication of rational choice: predicting future consequences. We have assumed that future preferences are exogenous, stable, and are known with enough precision to make the decisions unambiguous. In the beginning of the 1970s researchers started to challenge these assumptions. In the case of collective decision making there is the problem of conflicting objectives that represent the values of different participants. In addition, individual preferences often appear to be fuzzy and inconsistent, and preferences appear to change over time due partly, at least, as a consequence of the actions that were taken (March, 1978). Cohen *et al.* introduced the notion of the 'garbage can' as a model for explaining decision making in organizations (Cohen *et al.*, 1972). This model describes decision situations in terms of 'anarchy', consisting of four loosely-coupled elements: choice opportunities, problems, solutions, and participants. Decisions are made under conditions of ambiguity, that is, situations where goals are vague, problematic, inconsistent or unstable.

Also, social psychologists have studied how decisions are reached in organizations. Janis and Mann (1977) give a good review of the research in this area. They identified the phenomenon of 'group think' that can lead to defective decision making as it inadequately researches the alternative courses of action. It can also lead to a bias in processing the available information. Also, social psychologists have studied how social pressure affects decision making. Two such pressures which have been identified by Janis and Mann (1977) are:

(1)   anticipatory regret, our tendency to worry how disappointed we, and others, might feel after the event, if we take the wrong decision; and

(2)   threats, or constraints, imposed by others.

Finally, we shall mention the study of decision making in the field of political sciences. A subject which is of great interest to political scientists is the way in which the political process results in decisions (see, for instance, Hall and Quinn (1983)). The political science model sees organizational decision making as a result of the interplay of pressure groups who have different views and different powers. The outcome of a decision is determined by negotiation among groups of people, and the exploitation of the influence and power that they have at their command.

Empirical research carried out on actual decision making behavior has modified the classical, formal model in two ways: it has revealed the effects of real-world complexity on rational behavior, and it has shown that most organizational processes cannot be interpreted in the rational framework. The understanding we have gained about decision making behavior is collected in a set of descriptive theories under the label of *behavioral theories of decision making*. These theories are concerned with the process of reaching solutions. Both the behavioral and normative theories are important for recommending better methods and for offering advice on the improvement of decision processes. These theories are the basis for the design of computer aids to be used in decision making.

Simon and his colleagues developed their behavioral theories of decision making into the more general theories of *problem solving*. Rather than concentrating on the kinds of decisions that managers make, psychologists study tasks that can be viewed as problems of choice within a range of alternatives. Human problem solving is usually studied in laboratory settings, using problems that can be solved in relatively short periods of time (theorem proving, puzzles, and so on). From empirical studies, a description can be given of the problem solving process that holds for a rather wide range of activities.

One of the accomplishments of the theory of problem solving has been the understanding of complex problems, and to develop strategies and intelligent processes to deal with them. In the field of artificial intelligence these strategies are developed into formal methods and are computerized. More recently, these methods have been employed in expert systems. The theory of human-problem solving will be studied in more detail in Section 2.2.

2.1.2 What is this chapter about?

Above, we have made a broad exposé of the major developments in the field of decision making and problem solving.

In this chapter, we shall deal in more detail with those theories of behavioral decision making that we think are particularly important to the development of knowledge-based decision support systems. A model of the cognitive architecture of the mind and a theory of human problem solving are presented. These theories are the basis for the artificial intelligence techniques that are applied in expert systems (computer programs that solve problems by heuristic search and symbolic reasoning). They are also the basis for our understanding of expert problem solving and the methods and techniques we shall develop later in this book to elicit knowledge from experts.

Furthermore, we will present conceptual frameworks provided by behavioral theories of decision making; these are a decision process model developed in the Simon tradition of bounded rationality: the Mintzberg decision process model, and an organizational model: the behavioral theory of the firm. These frameworks enable us to describe and analyse behavior and to identify functions for computer support.

Applications of the theories to financial problems are presented throughout this chapter.

2.2 The cognitive architecture of the mind

In this section, a description of the cognitive architecture of the mind will be given, this a model that closely resembles the human mind.

2.2.1 The information processing view

Cognitive psychologists study the human mind and behavior in order to understand the nature of thinking and problem solving. Modern cognitive psychology views human cognition as information processing, and the human mind as an information processing system. The performance of a cognitive task involves a sequence of mental operations (processes) on mental objects (representations). The central hypothesis of the information processing view is that human thinking is governed by programs that organize myriads of simple information processes into orderly, complex sequences.

Advocates of the information processing theory insist that cognitive tasks can best be understood by analogy to programmed computers. The assumptions behind this approach can be summarized as follows (Winograd and Flores, 1986 p. 25):

(1)   All cognitive systems are symbols. They achieve their intelligence by symbolizing external and internal situations and events, and by manipulating those symbols.

(2)   All cognitive systems share a basic underlying set of symbol-manipulating processes.

(3)   A theory of cognition can be couched as a program in an appropriate symbolic formalism such that the program when run in the appropriate environment will produce the observed behavior.

Having stated our information processing view on human cognition we can now proceed to look at the basic components of the human information processing system and the capacities of these components. They will determine the overall cognitive capacity of the mind.

The main components of the human information processing system are a set of memories where representations of knowledge can be stored, and a set of processes which can act upon these representations. We shall deal with these components not in terms of the physiology of the nervous system and neuroscience, but rather in terms of their functionality.

Computers offer an interesting analogy with which to build a functional model of the brain. Due to their ability to interpret, in their memory, sequences of symbols as instructions to perform more complex operations, they are considered to be general-purpose information processing systems. A cognitive theory should be like a computer program. That is, it should be a precise specification of the behavior, but offered in sufficiently abstract terms to provide a conceptually tractable framework for understanding the phenomenon (Anderson, 1985).

Thus, we shall build a model of the human mind that has properties equivalent to real human problem solving. This model defines the functionality of the mind. We call it the cognitive architecture of the mind. The model gives an insight into the limitations of human information processing, and of the specific strategies that people develop in order to deal with complex problems.

The cognitive architecture of the human mind can be described as consisting of:

- *Long-term memory*, which for all practical purposes, has unlimited capacity, permanent storage, instant retrieval times, but fairly long write times.

- *Short-term memory*, or working memory, with instantaneous access and storage, but with a very limited size. Information can only be processed when it is in short-term-memory (in an active state).

- *Mental operations*, or the cognitive processor, which is a serial mechanism capable of executing only a handful of so-called elementary processes, such as retrieving symbols, comparing two symbols and so on.

A fundamental study in cognitive psychology and artificial intelligence is that of human problem solving within the information processing framework which was carried out by Allan Newell and Herbert Simon at the Carnegie-Mellon University in 1972. They developed their theory of human problem solving by observing how subjects solve problems such as theorem proving and puzzles. By asking subjects to explicate their thought processes, the so-called verbal reports (protocols), these cognitive processes are now fairly well understood. More recently, the study of expert problem solving has emerged as an area of specific interest (see, for instance, Anderson, 1985). This is of particular importance to expert systems, and we shall report on the use of verbal reports to study financial experts in Chapter 8.

2.2.2 Long-term memory

In this book we shall be concerned with verbal information for decision making and problem solving. We shall, therefore, look at memory representations of verbal information, and in this section other forms and representations of knowledge such as visual and mental images will be disregarded.

Propositions

It is now well accepted in the field of cognitive psychology that the memory representation of information is meaning-based rather than language-based, in other words, it is the meaning of a sentence that is stored in memory rather than its grammatical form. How then is meaning represented? The theory of propositional representations is supported by experimental evidence. The concept of proposition is borrowed from logic and linguistics and is the simplest complete unit of information. It is complete in the sense that it can be judged to be either true or false.

Consider the following sentence:

Smith, who is a lawyer, sold his car to his colleague Clark

It can be seen that this sentence is composed of the following simpler sentences, each one is represented by a proposition:

(1) Smith is a lawyer
(2) Clark is a colleague of Smith
(3) Smith owns a car
(4) Smith sold this car to Clark

Typically, propositions capture relations such as 'sold', that hold between arguments such as 'Smith', 'car', and 'Clark', in proposition (4). 'Sold' is a three-place relation since it requires three arguments to form a proposition. It is possible to distinguish between types of arguments, such as subjects, objects and so on.

A collection of propositions can be represented graphically by a *propositional network*. In the propositional network each proposition is a unique structural unit built around a node which is denoted by a circle with a number inside it. The value of the number has no other meaning other than to distinguish that particular proposition from other propositions. The propositional node is connected to its constituent nodes (representing the relation and its arguments) by links, which are symbolized by arrows. The composite sentence above can be represented by a propositional network as shown in Figure 2.1, where the relational nodes are denoted by capitals and the argument nodes are denoted by lower case words in angled brackets.

We can think of the nodes in the network as ideas and the links between nodes as associations between ideas. A propositional network then becomes an associated structure that determines the tendency of one idea to lead to another. The closer the concepts in this network are, the better cues they are for each other's recall. We shall return to how nodes are activated and how this activation is spread through the network in Section 4.4.3.

Schemas

So far, the theory of propositional representation of knowledge is incomplete in its development. Facts arise when we attach attributes to objects, for instance, when we attach the attribute of owning a car to the person Smith (the object) as in proposition (3) above. A fact, then, is a type of a conceptual

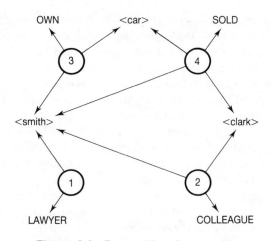

Figure 2.1 Propositional network.

relationship that we can represent by a proposition. However, just to list a set of facts about an object does not capture the interrelational structure, that is, the general information about the object. For instance, we have a general concept of a car: it has generally four wheels, an engine, is driven on roads, carries people, is used for transportation and so on. These general facts can be represented in a propositional network. The cluster of general propositions attached to a concept node (an object or an event) form a conceptual schema for that concept. A **schema** is an abstraction that allows particular objects or events to be categorized (generic concepts) and represented in memory. Our general knowledge, however, seems to go beyond the concepts for discrete objects and events, such as 'car' and 'sell'. There are schemas representing our knowledge about all concepts: that is, those which underlie objects, situations, events, sequences of events, actions and sequences of actions (Rumelhart, 1980).

Schemas, as a formalism for representing knowledge, are used in the field of artificial intelligence for organizing and for reasoning about large knowledge bases (see Chapter 4).

Concepts and categories

Schemas, as described in the previous section, are useful because they represent generalizations about the world that allow us to categorize objects, events, situations and actions. For these categorizations we need concepts. Both concept definitions and conceptual analysis have been of concern to philosophers, linguists and psychologists for many years.

The classical theory of concepts is the **definitional theory**. This theory states that the information content of a concept is a definition that gives the necessary and sufficient conditions that an object must meet in order to fall under the concept (Stillings *et al.*, 1987). For some concepts it may be straightforward to define these necessary and sufficient conditions. For example, a mother would be a female person who has at least one child. However, for most concepts it is hard to find a set of necessary and sufficient conditions that uniquely define each one. Take for instance the concept 'car'. It could be defined as a set of propositions containing the information that a car is a moving vehicle on four wheels, which is powered by an engine, and which transports people and goods. Each proposition is necessary, but is the schema as a whole sufficient to determine the category of objects we call a car? Hardly not. And this is the case with most concepts of everyday life. For the Canadian census, database designers found thorny problems with basic terms like 'building' and 'dwelling'. Since the number of possible forms for buildings was so large, they did not even attempt to give a definition (Sowa, 1984). For most ordinary concepts we do not think in terms of necessary and sufficient conditions, and when we have to describe things we use features that are typical, rather than necessary and sufficient, and we think of typical instances of a concept. We find this more efficient.

The difficulties encountered with the definitional theory of concepts have led philosophers to look for alternative theories that allow for non-necessary features to be included in conceptual schemas. One such philosopher is the Austrian, Ludvig Wittgenstein. In his early work, he adhered to the classical definition of concepts. Later on, however, he developed a new view on concept definitions which was based on family resemblance. When viewed in terms of family resemblance, the instances of a concept resemble each other in the way that members of a family do. Some members of a conceptual family will be very typical because they share many features with many other family members. For example, soccer is a game that shares many features with other games which are played within a finite time, have competition between participants, and in which goals are scored. However, solitaire is also a game, but without the common features just listed. For most of the concepts of everyday life, meaning is determined by family resemblance rather than by definition.

The theory of family resemblance can be developed into a prototype theory. Here, a prototype (the basic structure) is defined by a family resemblance structure that combines all of the most typical features of a concept into one single description. The prototypical description of a game will have all of the most common features of a game. In the prototype theory a concept is defined by an example or prototype if an object, which is an instance of a particular concept, resembles the characteristic prototype of this concept more closely than the prototypes of other concepts (Smith and Medin, 1981).

'When a natural concept is expressed in a computable form, its vague boundaries and continuous shadings are replaced by sharp, precise distinctions. Although precision is usually desirable, it can be misleading when a concept defined by family resemblances is replaced with a concept of

the same that is defined by necessary and sufficient conditions'.
(Sowa, 1984)

Sowa (1984) distinguishes between concepts that are natural types (for example, 'person') and others that are role types (for example, 'pedestrian'). Furthermore, there are concepts of the comparative type like 'big', or the evaluative type like 'good'.

Real world objects can be perceived at several levels of abstraction. For example, the same item can be conceived as an 'asset', a 'fixed asset', a 'factory' or a 'building'. Human memory for natural types of concepts appears to be organized in this kind of hierarchical fashion (Rosch, et al., 1976). Hierarchical organization of object categorization can be described by 'is-a-kind-of' relationships.

Propositional network models for processing structures are often called *semantic networks* because they represent general knowledge about the semantics, or meaning, or concepts rather than facts about specific objects. (See Chapter 4 for a discussion on semantic networks.)

2.2.3 Short-term memory

Short-term memory refers to a capacity for keeping a limited amount of information in a special active state. It is useful to think of short-term memory as a *working memory* holding only the knowledge currently in use. Knowledge in working memory is not thought of as being situated in a different location than long-term memory, but rather as being in a special state. For a long time cognitive psychologists have considered the capacity of working memory to be the major bottleneck in the human information processing system, and numerous attempts have been made to determine the number of items it can hold. Miller (1956) introduced the term **chunk** to describe these units of memory. He argued that memory was not limited by external, physical entities like letters or words, but rather, by meaningful chunks. These chunks are located in long-term memory but are placed in an active state in which they can be used by controlled processes. Spread of activation is one important topic of cognitive psychology.

2.2.4 Mental operations

Above, we have characterized knowledge representation in the human mind. Now it is time to describe the operations we perform in order to manipulate this knowledge. Recent psychological studies have drawn the distinction between *controlled* processes and *automated* processes. Introspectively, this distinction closely coincides with the observation that some mental processes require focused attention, take effort to maintain, and are easily overloaded, while other processes are performed with little or no attention. From every-day life, we have many examples of this, for instance, learning to drive a car compared with being an experienced driver.

Controlled processes are mental processes that require conscious atten-tion in order to be performed. One of the functions of controlled processes is to maintain the goal-directedness of thought and behavior. Achieving a particular goal often requires a series of actions to be carried out that accom-plish a set of subgoals. The controlled process system seems to be designed in such a way that only a very limited number of goals can be maintained in an active state at any one time. Controlled processes are similar to the inter-pretive processes that occur in computers. In the same way that an inter-pretative programming language is able to perform specific data processing on an input statement, controlled processes in the human mind are able to interpret and perform information processing on propositional representa-tions. They are extremely flexible, because they can call on any concept in the vast propositional network of knowledge.

Automated processes, on the other hand, require no interpretation of propositions. Rather, they perform information processing directly, without having to be interpreted by some other process. They can be compared to compiled programs in computers (Stillings *et al.*, 1987). Automated pro-cesses have some key characteristics:

- they make no demands on working memory;
- they are automatically triggered by patterns in the currently activated information;
- they are referred to as data-driven or pattern-driven processes (also called productions (see Chapter 4));
- they are parallel and independent in nature;
- they speed up gradually as the automated sequence is learnt.

2.3 Human problem solving

Problem solving is an intelligent activity performed by a person who is confronted with a situation where there is a gap between what is desired (the goal) and what is given as the initial state. In performing this activity, people employ information processing.

Research has been carried out to explain human behavior in perform-ing poorly-structured tasks and to explain how individuals acquire cognitive skill in a particular domain.

In their theory of human problem solving, Allan Newell and Herbert Simon (1972) developed some key-concepts, such as problem space and heuristic search, which we will describe in the next two sections. Further-more, in Section 2.3.3 we shall deal with a rather new direction in the field of cognitive psychology, this is the novice–expert relation in problem solving, which we will use to derive some key characteristics of expert problem solving.

2.3.1 The problem space and the task environment

Newell and Simon make an important distinction between the two concepts: **problem space** and **task environment**. The problem space is a person's internal (mental) representation of a problem, and the place where the problem-solving activity takes place. The task environment, on the other hand, is the physical and social environment in which problem solving takes place. It contains the task as it exists. The reason for introducing this distinction is that individual behavior influences problem solving; this influence is greater the less structured the task is.

An example may clarify the distinction between the two concepts. A class of business students studying financial statement analysis is given a class assignment to perform a credit evaluation of a company that is asking for a loan. The task is the credit evaluation. The task environment is made up of all the information given about the circumstances of the loan application. That is, financial statements of the company, market information and so on. Thus, everybody in the class has the same assignment and the same information. The task environment is general across all the individuals.

Assuming that the class has not been given a strict, analytical procedure for this task, we can assume that the task is perceived as poorly structured. Consequently, we expect variances in the individual approaches that are taken in order to perform the task. Monitoring the individuals who are solving this problem gives an insight to the problem space; that is, which data from the material provided is used?; in which sequence is it used?; how is new information computed from old?; and so on. All of this is done in the problem space.

Situations which do not influence individual behavior can be studied by only analysing the task environment. For instance, fetching a glass of milk from the refrigerator can be predicted by studying the task environment, that is, the location of the person wanting the milk in relation to the location of the refrigerator. Also, in some modern sciences, for instance, economics, the scientific theory is based on the task environment only, assuming that humans are always motivated to maximize their utility. They behave rationally towards this goal, the economic man, and everything of importance for decision making is given by the task environment (even values and preferences of the performer). Therefore, economics is a science about the structure of the task environment.

We know, however, from empirical findings that behavioral aspects of decision making are closely related to the decision maker and not to the task environment. Decision makers seldom or never behave according to the economic man model. We have to look inside the decision maker's mind to explain this behavior. Therefore, it is of great importance in studying problem solving to analyse the task environment as well as the internal representation of the problem, that is, the problem space.

Newell and Simon (1972) say that examination of behavior leads to two kinds of knowledge: task knowledge and knowledge of the problem space. Task knowledge is obtained if the observed behavior is precisely what is called for by the situation. Knowledge of the problem space is obtained if the observed behavior departs from perfect rationality. Then we gain knowledge about the internal mechanisms for problem solving. The distinction between the task environment and the internal representation in the problem space leads to a study of two complementary aspects of human problem solving:

(1)   the demands of the task environment, and;
(2)   the problem solving behavior in that task environment.

Obviously, there is a close relationship between the task environment and the problem space. We have already mentioned that certain problem situations demand the same behavior (see the milk example above). In other situations, however, the individual's behavior plays a greater role, leading to very different individual problem solving behavior when performing a specific task. It is likely that the degree to which individuals are different is assumed to be a function of the structuredness of the task environment. Highly-structured environments, in which motivation is not a question, will demand similar behavior among performers. Highly unstructured environments, on the other hand, are more open for individual behavior.

According to the theory of human problem solving, the structure of the task environment determines the structure of the problem space, and the structure of the problem space determines the possible programs (strategies) for problem solving. In other words, we see the influence of the task environment on problem solving behavior. Therefore, we must analyse the structure of the task environment as well as the cognitive performance of human problem solvers in order to be able to model and computerize human problem solving.

Given these properties of the task environment and the problem space we will expect problem solving behavior to be very similar among individual performers within domains that deal with fairly well-structured problems.

We shall call the model of the task environment a task model and the model of the problem space a performance model. In reality, they represent two kinds of knowledge.

A **task model** represents generalized concepts (objects, relations, processes and strategies). This model describes a typical high-level problem solving strategy within a domain. It represents an abstract, stereotyped performer within this domain. Task models are sometimes called *epistemological* (Wielinga and Breuker, 1984) or *competence* (Laske, 1986) models.

A **performance** model is a model of the problem space and represents the problem solving behavior of one person who is performing a specific task. Knowledge elicitation by verbal, thinking-aloud protocols leads to performance models. Verbal protocols are discussed in Section 2.3.4 and more extensively in Chapter 8.

Performance models, alone, do not give adequate knowledge for systems development, since they are constrained to a single performer and a single problem. Thus, we are faced with an induction problem: that is, to generalize problem solving behavior from individual cases (performers and problems). Furthermore, elements of performance that are found in protocols do not necessarily reflect the demands of the task environment. Therefore, both task models and performance models are required to enable problem solving behavior to be properly modeled within a specific domain.

To summarize, the cognitive architecture of the mind helps us to understand how problem solving is performed and how we can use this understanding to acquire knowledge of human problem solving behavior. Also, the distinction between the task environment and the problem space helps us to understand and explain individual behavior and how to interpret individual behavior in a broader context, the task environment.

2.3.2 Heuristic problem solving

The theory of human problem solving behavior illustrates the fact that people apply very few general, formal principles and they violate normative rules. Yet, they seem to progress successfully. The answer seems to be that human problem solving is **heuristic**. That is, people employ procedures that are efficient and that work most of the time, even though they sometimes lead to errors. This becomes more apparent as the complexity, that is, the unstructuredness of the task, increases. In highly structured task environments, general, formal principles that are independent of any particular context, for instance, linear programming, can solve problems very effectively. However, in this section we shall describe how people handle ill-structured problems.

Problem solving, as we have seen, is a process of transforming an initial situation into a desired situation, the goal. Problem solving takes place in the problem space, a subjective model of the task is built. Due to the bounded rationality of humans, normally, the problem space is a very simplified model of the task. Problem solving proceeds by a selective search within the problem space, using rules of thumb (heuristics) to guide the search. For most problems, only a selective search will lead to the goal within the time available. We see that problem solving can be described as a *search* for a solution within the problem space. The elements of the space consist of knowledge states.

The first step in solving a problem is that the problem solver must make a representation of the task within the problem space. However, this representation is not trivial. It may turn the problem solving into an obvious, easy, obscure, difficult or unsolvable task depending on the way that the task is represented. The same task may be represented in many different ways by different individuals, depending on experience, values and situations. Different representations may have a large impact on the problem solving process, as well as the solutions that are arrived at.

The second step, following the problem representation, is the selection of a particular problem solving method. Much of the theory of problem solving is concerned with identifying the principles that govern people's search through the problem space. The most general method is called **generate-and-test**.

It consists of two processes:

(1)   *generate* a set of new knowledge states, from a preceding state;
(2)   *test* if one of the generated states is a member of the goal state. If yes stop.

The efficiency of the method will depend on the time to generate states of the problem space, the size of the problem space and the time to test whether a candidate state satisfies the goal state.

Using information about the problem to select states in the problem space to be expanded by the generation process has been known as *heuristic search*. The fundamental heuristic method identified by Newell and Simon is **means-ends** analysis. The available operators or legal moves are the means that will achieve the goal, in other words, the end. The basic principle for operator selection is **difference reduction**; that is, operators are selected that will reduce the difference between the current state of the problem and the goal. Typically, the process is performed as a series of subprocesses where subgoals are subsequently achieved.

Heuristic search by means-ends analysis is a great improvement over general generate-and-test methods (exhaustive search) as we have seen above. Means-ends analysis makes heavy demands on controlled processing. The subgoals that are relevant at that time, and the possible states of the problem being considered must be maintained in an active state. Heuristic search as a formal method for problem solving will be dealt with in more detail in Chapter 4.

So far, we have implicitly assumed that our problem solving method starts with the initial state and proceeds through a generate-and-test procedure working towards the goal state. However, an alternative method can be proposed, that of working backwards. Here, the goal (problem) is decomposed into sub-goals (or sub-problems). The problem solver can then focus on each sub-goal or problem which may either be solved or decomposed further. This procedure is also called problem reduction and is dealt with in Chapter 4.

2.3.3 The nature of expertise

Above, we have focused on a problem solving method which is general enough to hold for a rather wide range of tasks. So far, no attention has been paid to the *semantic content* of the task. Games and puzzles are used for research into problem solving because they involve heuristic search as the major problem solving method. However, when a loan officer in a bank makes a decision about a loan, he or she is not merely exercising a general problem solving method. He or she is also drawing upon a whole body of knowledge about the bank, about the firm, and about the general prospects of the industry in which the firm operates and so on. In his or her work, the loan officer has gained experience. In other words, he or she has become an expert.

Acquisition of expertise

Most complex cognitive skills are thought to require a mixture of automated and controlled processes. When a person is beginning to learn a skill most of the information processing is done by controlled processes where knowledge is interpreted before being processed. The beginner is like an inexperienced cook working from an unfamiliar recipe. Each line of the recipe must be read and interpreted as an instruction before any action can be performed.

Cognitive psychologists agree that the transition process from beginner to expert can be described in terms of three stages. However, the labels given to these stages vary. According to Anderson (1985) we find the following stages:

(1)   *The cognitive stage*, which is characterized by encoding declarative knowledge (propositions) that can be interpreted by general procedures.

(2)   *The associative stage*, which compiles knowledge into procedures that are specific to the performance of the skill. Skill-specific knowledge does not have to be held in a declarative form; thus demanding less on working memory capacity. Even though a procedure is formed, attention is often still required for performance of the skill.

(3)   *The autonomous stage*, which is the final stage. During this stage the procedures become maximally automated, and skill is performed without attention. A procedure, once activated, tends to run to completion without interruption. Verbal reporting on the performance of a task seems to be lost (compare this with unconscious knowledge, below).

The most challenging question now is how people acquire their expertise in various domains. How does a system that stores operators in a declarative form and uses means-ends search discover meaningful configurations and link them to appropriate actions? (Stillings, *et al.*, 1987, p 101). It is interesting to observe the growing awareness and research of problem solving in semantic-rich domains, and on how expertise is developed in these domains. We shall report on some of this research in Section 2.3.4.

Expert characteristics

Paul Johnson (1983) gives the following definition of an expert:

> 'An expert is a person who, because of training and experience, is able to do things the rest of us cannot; experts are not only proficient but also smooth and efficient in the actions they take. Experts know a great many things and have tricks and caveats for applying what they know to problems and tasks; they are also good at plowing through irrelevant information in order to get at basic issues, and they are good at recognizing problems they face as instances of types with which they are familiar (Chi *et al.*, 1981; Larkin *et al.* 1980). Underlying the behaviour of experts is the body of operative knowledge we have termed expertise.'

If we analyse this definition carefully, we can extract certain characteristics of expert behavior.

Performance

Experts are not only proficient but are also efficient. There are two aspects of performance embedded in this. First, we have the aspect of effectiveness. Experts have the ability to reach solutions using incomplete and uncertain knowledge. They use domain-specific knowledge to infer what a correct or plausible conclusion should be. Plausible conclusions are accepted often, they are used as substitutes for certain and provable conclusions in the absence of complete information. Experts utilize the information they have at hand and sometimes resort to 'bricks and caveats' (default reasoning). This may sometimes lead to errors. Furthermore, experts are efficient and reach solutions in the time available (which may depend on the problem situation).

Discrimination

An aspect that is related to efficiency is the expert's ability to 'plow through irrelevant information in order to get at basic issues', that is, experts have highly-developed discrimination mechanisms. Discrimination is similar to the common sense we use in everyday situations. We use common sense when our car has a breakdown. We do not start solving the problem by enumerating all of the possible causes. Dependent on the specific situation, we quickly discriminate among all the causes. This is the capacity which is highly developed in diagnostics where classification criteria are used to prune quickly the search space.

Experts are capable of making finer categorial discriminations (Rosch *et al.*, 1976), and are sensitive to more attributes of domain concepts (Murphy and Wright, 1984) than non-experts are.

Pattern recognition
Experts are good at recognizing the problems they face as instances of types with which they are familiar. They 'learn to perceive recurring patterns in the problem and to associate their problem solutions to these patterns.' (Anderson, 1985)

Domain knowledge
Underlying the behavior of experts is the body of operative knowledge. This knowledge is specific to the knowledge structures of the domain. Through training and experience these structures are compiled into complex schemas and procedures. 'Master chess players are not more intelligent generally than average players; they have achieved their expertise through practice.' (Anderson, 1985). Expertise is, in other words, primarily domain knowledge and is not a general problem-solving strategy and method.

Unconscious knowledge
Following on from the steps involved in acquiring expertise that were described above, another aspect of expert knowledge emerges: that is, the results of the automaticity stage of learning are not usually available to conscious awareness. This is the paradox of expertise. As individuals master more and more knowledge in order to do a task efficiently as well as accurately, they also lose awareness of what they know (Johnson, 1983). In other words, experts can not explicate their full knowledge. In order to make their knowledge conscious it must be contextually stimulated. It will only be called upon in specific problem solving situations. So, the knowledge we want to represent in the knowledge base of a computerized expert system is the knowledge that experts are not able to explicate!

Forward inferencing
Johnson (1983) describes experts as good at plowing through irrelevant information in order to obtain basic facts. This indicates a forward reasoning approach. This view of expert problem solving is supported by John Anderson who has carried out studies in several fields. He observed an interesting feature of expertise acquisition. When people acquire expertise

they tend to reorganize their approach to the problem in order to capitalize on features of the domain. (Anderson, 1985). These observations conform with our own studies of financial experts in action (see Chapter 8).

Theoretical and experiential knowledge
Finally, an expert possesses theoretical knowledge of both conceptual and analytical kinds, and experiential knowledge acquired through training and practice. We want to represent both theoretical and experiential knowledge in computer programs (expert systems) that simulate human problem solving. We should learn from the characteristics of expertise how to acquire the appropriate knowledge.

To summarize, human problem solving is considered as a search for a solution. This search is performed by generating candidates for the solutions which can be tested. Candidates can be disregarded or expanded for further search. The general method is called generate-and-test. Candidates can be generated at random, or by using information that is inherent in the problem domain, in which case it is called heuristic search. Experts have well-developed heuristic problem solving knowledge in specific domains that has been gained through theoretical education and practical experience.

2.3.4 Empirical studies of human problem solving in financial domains

One of the early attempts to simulate human problem solving in financial domains was Clarkson's (1962) model of the decision processes of a bank trust officer who is making investments in stock portfolios. In this information-rich domain, Clarkson showed that the thinking-aloud protocols of a trust officer who is making decisions are indeed capable of capturing the cognitive processes of decision making. Despite the generally favorable reception of this study, it took more than 15 years for follow-up studies of this kind within the financial domain.

Application of the human problem solving theory to financial decision making has been done by Bouwman and his colleagues in a number of studies. The first study used students as subjects (Bouwman, 1983) but more recent studies have employed professional financial analysts and loan officers (Bouwman *et al.*, 1987). These subjects have great experience in the tasks that they perform. Verbal protocol analysis is used to trace and analyse their decision making behavior. Bouwman's studies are what we can call *performance studies*. The purpose of a performance study is to obtain a detailed record of the processes that a decision maker uses in order to arrive at a choice within a decision situation. This trace can be used to explain differences in decision making behavior across several subjects in terms of the frequencies and sequences of operations performed, information search strategies applied, and decision (heuristic) rules used. A key issue, however, is how evidence of differences in observed decision making behavior (descriptive aspects) can lead to improved decision making (normative aspects) in situations which are ill-structured and in which optimal solutions are not evident. The assumption here is that while it may be difficult to assess the correctness of the outcome of the final decision, it may be possible to evaluate the decision's individual components (Biggs, 1983). A performance model is the basis for the design of an expert system that emulates the cognitive behavior of an expert. Performance modeling is discussed in Chapter 8.

2.4 Biases in human decision making

After the normative theories of decisions had been developed, psychologists began asking whether human decision making conformed to these theories. Could they be used as a descriptive theory?

Several experiments were performed and we shall recapitulate the results of these studies in three important areas: the perception of uncertainty, subjective expected utility, and judgment. In so doing, we shall follow closely the review of Watson and Buede (1987).

2.4.1 Uncertainty

Human problem solving and decision-making are performed most often in the context of uncertainty. The normative theories handle uncertainty by means of probabilities. One of the key elements of the probability theory is Bayes's theorem which allows us to compute conditional probabilities (see Chapter 3). In essence, this theorem allows us to compute how the probability of an event is modified due to information about the occurrence of another (conditional) event. The question is then, do people revise their probability judgments according to Bayes's theorem? Clearly, the answer is no.

In 1971, Amos Tversky and Daniel Kahneman published the first of a series of papers on biases which they observed in peoples' judgment of uncertainty. Their work received considerable public notice. More recently, they have republished these articles, and other contributions to this research field, in a set of readings (Kahneman *et al.*, 1982).

Their studies show that people rely on a limited number of heuristic principles, which reduce the complex tasks of assessing probabilities and predicting values to simpler judgmental operations. However, these simple heuristics sometimes lead to systematic and severe errors. A primary goal of their research has been to describe the heuristics that people use, and to predict biases to which these heuristics lead. We shall briefly look at three heuristic strategies that people use in judgment and decision making (see also Kahneman, *et al.*, 1982).

(1)   *Representativeness heuristic.* Many of the probabilistic questions with which people are concerned belong to one of the following types: What is the probability that object *A* belongs to class *B*? What is the probability that event *A* originates from process *B*? In answering such questions people rely on representativeness heuristics, in which probabilities are evaluated by the degree to which *A* is representative of *B*. When *A* is highly representative of *B*, the probability that *A* belongs to *B* is judged to be high, irrespective of information given about prior probabilities. Here is an example: in an experiment, subjects were shown brief personality descriptions of individuals sampled from a population of 100 professionals – engineers and lawyers. One group of subjects was told that the population consisted of 70 lawyers and 30 engineers, while another group was told that there were 30 lawyers and 70 engineers. Given a description of a person, they were asked whether it was a lawyer or an engineer. The results showed that in both cases 50% of the subjects predicted that the person was a lawyer and 50% predicted that they were engineers – even though that the laws of probability dictate that the best forecast for one of the groups would be always to predict that it is a lawyer, and for the other group that it is an engineer.

(2)   *Availability heuristic.* There are situations in which people assess the frequency of a class by the ease with which instances can be brought to mind. In one experiment, subjects heard a list of names of people of both sexes and were later asked to judge whether there were more names of men or women on the list. In the lists presented to some subjects, the men were more famous than the women; in other lists, the women were more famous than the men. In each of the lists, the subjects erroneously judged that the sex that had the more famous personalities was the more numerous. At the time of judgment, easily available recall leads to biases.

(3)   *Adjustment and anchoring heuristic.* In many situations, people make estimates by starting from an initial value that is adjusted to yield the final answer. The initial value can be given, or it may be the result of partial computation. In either case, there is a systematic tendency to underestimate adjustments and to be biased toward the initial values. This tendency is called **anchoring**. In one of the experiments, subjects were asked about the percentage of African countries in the United Nations. Different groups of subjects were given different initial numbers (determined by spinning a wheel) which they were asked to adjust. The median estimates of the

percentage were 25 and 45 for groups that received 10 and 65, respectively, as starting points.

In summary, everyday reasoning seems to be typified by the activation of a schema and the generation of further information within the schema via the heuristic processes we have described above. These tendencies fit in quite well with our general characterization of cognitive architecture (Stillings *et al.*, 1987). Heuristics are necessary for efficient human problem solving as we have seen in Section 2.3. We have, however, to be careful in applying heuristics and to avoid heuristics that violate normative theories.

These findings demonstrate a fundamental failure in human judgmental abilities. However, considerable criticism has been voiced about the generalization of these results (see, for instance, Edwards, 1983).

2.4.2 Subjective expected utility

Central to the body of normative theories of decision making has been the concept of **subjective expected utility**. Therefore, the next research issue that attracted the psychologists' interest was: do decision makers maximize expected utility when they face uncertainty? It should be no surprise to the reader, given the results of the previous section, that we do not naturally conform to the principle of subjective expected utility either.

There has been a considerable amount of interest in this topic; a good review is found in Schoemaker (1980). All of the experiments that have been performed so far show that people appear to violate the subjective expected utility theory. People prefer to gamble on options for which probabilities are more clearly established. Tversky and Kahneman (1981) in yet another sequence of experiments, demonstrated that choices between uncertain options can depend on the way that the problem is *framed*.

The decision maker will need aids to overcome biases in evaluating uncertain options, in the same way as for the biases in the perception of uncertainty.

2.4.3 Judgment

In the previous two sections we have looked at the evidence that psychologists have produced as to the extent to which our perceptions of uncertainty and our decision making in the face of uncertainty follow the prescriptions of the corresponding normative theories. Now we will turn to representation of preferences or value judgments. This is also dealt with in the multi-attribute value theory (see Chapter 3). Does real decision making confirm to this theory? Again, the answer is that it does not. It is easy to find examples of people who take decisions by concentrating on one attribute only, and who only bring others into play if the options are equally good with respect to that attribute. For example, when buying a car, one may first look for candidates within a certain price range, and then use other criteria, in sequence, to discriminate among these candidates until the final choice is made. This is the satisficing choice behavior described by Simon (1957) (see also Section 2.1). It is easy to show that it is not possible to create a value function that is consistent with this choice behavior. Now, despite these observations, it is possible to describe actual decision making as though people were making a decision by maximizing some function of the variables that describe the important attributes. In fact, the linear additive value function (see Chapter 3) has demonstrated considerable descriptive power (see, for example, Fischoff *et al.*, 1982). Can we learn anything about a person's ability to represent his or her preferences in the form of a value function? Are there, for example, biases in representing judgments of relative importance, just as we have seen above with respect to perceptions of uncertainty? Hogarth (1980) provides an extensive discussion on this. The reader is referred to his book for further ideas and results.

2.5 Behavioral decision making

Extensive research has been carried out on behavioral decision making, both by individuals and organizations. These areas will be discussed along with an example that illustrates the decision making processes that occur when a large organization, a bank, grants a loan.

2.5.1 The decision making process

The successful manager is one who is able to choose the right actions at the right time. Thus, our usual image of a decision maker is of a person who makes the right choices. However, a choice is just the final result of a complex process of exploration, analysis and evaluation. This process we call the *decision making process*.

The decision making process can be described by models which form a continuum from the rational models at one end, to irrational models at the other end. Bounded rationality and satisficing are found towards the rational end, while 'garbage can' and ambiguous decisions are located towards the irrational end. The difference is very much determined by the way that the decision maker or the decision making body (in the case of a group) is treated. Rational models regard the decision making body as homogeneous. That is, a person or a group of persons with consistent and non-conflicting objectives. The irrational or anarchistic models, on the other hand, regard the decision making body as an heterogeneous group of people. That is, people have changing and conflicting preferences. There is no doubt that the thrust in decision making research in the 1980s has been in the direction of anarchistic and impressionistic models (Charniawska and Wolff, 1986.) This research is more concerned with the interactions among the participants than the structure of the decision process. It may eventually have some impact on the design of computer support programs, and may be a prosperous approach to group decision support systems which we, however, will not deal with in this book. However, we have already seen a great impact of DSS upon unstructured and semi-structured decisions, these are decisions which can be described within the rationality paradigm of decision making, and for which a structure of the decision process can be identified. In this section we shall, therefore, describe in more detail a framework that describes the unstructured decision processes developed by Mintzberg *et al*. (1976). We have found this framework to be very useful in the diagnosis and evaluation of decision making. Subsequently, we shall move to the organizational level in order to look at a useful framework that was developed by Cyert and March (1963) to study managerial decisions in this context.

Perhaps the most well-known framework for studying decisions by the process is Simon's intelligence-design-choice trichotomy (Simon, 1960). This conceptual framework has been taken as a basis for much of the work that has been carried out on decision support systems (see, for example, Sprague and Carlson, 1982). Simon's framework consists of three phases:

(1)   Searching the environment for conditions that call for a decision – the *intelligence* activity

(2)   Inventing, developing and analysing possible courses of action – the *design* activity

(3)   Selecting a particular course of action from those available – the *choice* activity.

Generally speaking, intelligence activity precedes design, and design precedes choice. The cycle of phases is, however, far more complex than this sequence suggests. For example, in the design phase the decision maker may obtain information that suggests that he or she is working on the wrong problem and so he or she chooses to return to the intelligence phase. This interweaving of the phases of the decision process has been further emphasized by empirical studies. It is believed that human beings cannot gather information without, in some way, simultaneously developing alternatives. They cannot avoid evaluating these alternatives immediately, and in doing this they are forced to a decision (Witte, 1972).

As already mentioned at the very beginning of this chapter, Herbert Simon introduced the concept of bounded rationality in order to describe decision making in an environment of incomplete and inconsistent information. Under these circumstances a decision maker 'satisfices' – he or she looks for a course of action that is 'good enough' rather than one that is optimal. What techniques are available for decision making under satisficing behavior? Simon makes the distinction between *programmed* and *non-programmed* decisions. A task that is programmed is one for which clear rules can be defined. A non-programmed decision, on the other hand, is one for which there is no cut and dried method for handling the problem, and one for which judgment, is essential in reaching a solution. However, Newell and Simon's research on human problem solving showed that, when faced with complex, unprogrammed situations, a problem solver seeks to reduce the problem into subproblems to which he or she applies general-purpose procedures or routines (Newell and Simon, 1972). In other words, a decision maker deals with unstructured situations by factoring them into familiar, structurable elements.

Mintzberg *et al.* (1976) conclude from this that decision processes are programmable even if they are not in fact programmed. Although the processes used are not predetermined and explicit, there is strong evidence that a basic logic or structure underlies what the decision maker does and that this structure can be described by systematic study of this behavior. The behavior that Mintzberg *et al.* studied is that of decision makers dealing with strategic decisions. They developed a decision process model that resembles Simon's model but which is conceptually richer. The model describes the phases slightly differently and uses different terms: identification, development, and selection. Furthermore, these three phases are described in terms of seven activities, called central routines. In addition, three supporting routines: decision control, communication, and political, as well as six sets of dynamic factors that help to explain the relationships among the central and supporting routines, are defined. Figure 2.2 depicts the decision process as envisaged by Mintzberg *et al.*

We shall describe the central routines, supporting routines and dynamic factors in more detail below. In Section 2.5.3 we shall show how this framework is used to study and describe decisions that relate to bank loans. Examples of the various concepts of the framework can also be found in that section.

Central routines

There are seven central routines within the three phases of the decision process which are now discussed.

(1)   *The identification phase.* The identification phase of decision making comprises two routines within Mintzberg *et al.*'s framework: decision *recognition*, in which opportunities, problems, and crises are recognized and evoke decisional activity, and *diagnosis*, in which the decision maker seeks to comprehend the evoked stimuli and determine cause-effect relationships for the decision situation.

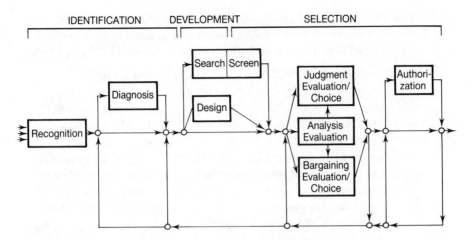

Figure 2.2   A model of the decision process. (Reprinted from The structure of the 'unstructured' decision processes by Mintzberg H. *et al.* published in *Administrative Science Quarterly*, **21** (2) (June 1976) by permission of *Administrative Science Quarterly*.)

(a) *Decision recognition*. Most decisions do not present themselves to the decision maker in convenient ways. Problems and opportunities must be identified in the profusion of information that decision makers receive. A problem is identified as a difference between 'what it is' and 'what it ought to be'; or said in a different way: the actual situation and the desired situation defined by some explicit or implicit norm or standard. Pounds (1969) found that these standards were based on past trends, projected trends, standards in some comparable organization, the expectation of other people, and theoretical models.

Problem, opportunity, and crisis decisions are most clearly distinguished in the recognition routine. While crisis decisions are typically triggered by one single stimulus, problems usually require multiple stimuli.

What initiates decision-making actions? A decision maker is more liable to act when there is a *match* between a problem and an opportunity, that is, when he or she sees an apparent solution, and vice versa. An important aspect is to find the threshold levels of actions.

(b) *Diagnosis*. Once a cumulation of stimuli reaches a threshold level, a decision process is initiated. Symptoms of a problem, opportunity or crisis raised in the recognition routine must be sorted and classified, and further information collected until the real cause is determined. Mintzberg *et al.* are given particular credit to having made the diagnosis routine explicit and adding it to the decision process framework.

(2) *The development phase*. The set of activities that lead to the generation of one or more solutions is called the development phase. Out of the three phases it is the one that put the greatest demand on the resources. Development is described in terms of two basic routines: search and design.

   (a) *Search routine*. Search is evoked to find ready-made solutions. The environment may be scanned for solutions which have been used in previous occasions, or which have been prepared for situations similar to the one now encountered. Four types of search behavior can be identified:

   (i) Memory search is the scanning of the existing memory, human or paper.

   (ii) Passive search is waiting for unsolicited alternatives to appear.

   (iii) Activation of 'search generators' to produce alternatives, such as letting suppliers know that the firm is looking for certain equipment.

   (iv) Active search is the direct seeking of alternatives.

   (b) *Design routine*. The design routine is used either to generate custom-made solutions, or to modify ready-made alternatives identified by the search routine. Mintzberg's study suggests that, with respect to custom-made alternatives, the decision maker designs only one fully-developed custom-made solution. In contrast, decision makers that choose ready-made solutions select them, typically, from among a number of alternatives. Also when relatively little design is involved, as in modified solutions, the decision maker is prepared to develop fully a second solution to compare it with the first.

(3) *The selection phase*. The normative literature prescribes selection in terms of the determination of criteria for choice, the evaluation of the consequences of alternatives, and the making of a choice. Mintzberg's study suggests that selection is, typically, a multi-stage, iterative process, involving a progressively deepening investigation into the alternatives. Three selection routines emerged from this study: screen, evaluation-choice, and authorization.

   (a) *Screen routine*. The screen routine is evoked when search is expected to generate more ready-made alternatives that can be intensively evaluated. Screening is more concerned with what is infeasible than with determining what is appropriate.

(b) *Evaluation-choice routine*. The evaluation-choice routine may
     be considered to use three modes: judgment, bargaining, and
     analysis.

     In *judgment*, an individual makes a choice in his or her
     own mind with procedures that he or she does not, perhaps
     cannot, explain. Judgment seems to be the favored mode of
     selection in ill-structured problems, perhaps because it is fast
     and subjective.

     In *analysis*, factual evaluation is carried out followed by
     managerial choice using judgment or bargaining. The
     normative literature emphasizes the analytic mode, clearly
     distinguishing fact and value in evaluating alternatives. The
     choice is made to maximize expected utility. This normative
     direction is discussed further in Chapter 3.

(c) *Authorization routine*. The final task of the decision process
     when a choice is made, is to commit the organization to the
     course of action that has been chosen. Authorization appears
     to be a typical binary process: acceptance or rejection of the
     whole solution. The authorization routine experiences many
     difficulties. Generally, the time for it is limited. It is a political
     process where the groups involved generally lack the in-depth
     knowledge of the solution and, at the same time, may exercise
     their power to protect their interests.

Supporting routines

Above, we have described the routines that the decision maker executes in
order to reach a solution to a problem. Each routine must be initiated,
resources committed and organized, and progress must be ensured.
Mintzberg *et al.* (1976) define three routines that support the decision
process itself.

(1) *Decision control routines* involve planning the process, selecting the
     correct plan of the process and choosing the sequence of steps that is
     appropriate in the current situation.

(2) *Decision communication routines* involve information processing:
     scanning for general information, searching for specific, special-
     purpose information, and the dissemination of information about
     progress in the decision process.

(3) *Political routines* involve bargaining among those who have some
     control over choices, persuasion and cooperation. Political activities
     reflect the influence of individuals who seek to satisfy their personal
     and institutional needs by using the decision that has been made.

Dynamic factors

Finally, we shall mention the dynamic factors that influence the decision process in a number of ways. They delay the process, stop it, restart it, they cause it to speed up, branch to a new phase, to recycle back, and so on. Mintzberg *et al.* (1976) describe six groups of dynamic factors:

(1)	Interrupts	: are caused by environmental forces.
(2)	Scheduling delays, and	: are effected by the decision
(3)	timing delays and speed-ups	maker.
(4)	Feedback delays,	: are inherent in the decision
(5)	comprehension cycles, and	process itself.
(6)	failure recycles	

The Mintzberg model is general enough to describe any decision process. The general idea is that decisions are made within a process where:

- problems are not given, but are searched for or defined;

- solutions are not given or known, but are searched for or designed;

- the choice situation often comprises alternatives that cannot easily be compared, or where consequences are neither unique nor well known;

- it is not certain that the decided alternative can be implemented or executed as specified, or that consequences will be as anticipated.

Given these constraints, together with the limited cognitive capacity of human beings, the decision maker does not maximize (optimize) but chooses solutions that are satisficing. The model that describes decision making behavior under these constraints is also known as the 'administrative man' model.

2.5.2 Decision making in organizations

The decision making process, as described above, applies, as a *process* model, to individual decision making as well as group decision making. This is the case as long as we do not address the problem of choice under conflict or ambiguity. However, this model lacks a conceptual framework to describe decision making in an organizational context. Decision making in organizations is characterized by the division of tasks among groups of people. Each group attends to a special set of problems and acts in quasi-independence on these problems. To perform complex tasks, the behavior of a large number of individuals must be *coordinated*.

To understand decision making in organizations we need some basic understanding of organization theory. Organization theory is a relatively new theory. It started with several independent studies in the 1940s and was summarized in a logically ordered form by March and Simon (1958) in their book *Organizations*. The third decade (the 1960s) of organization theory gave rise to the monumental *Handbook of Organizations* (March, 1965). The branch of organization theory that takes, as its focus, the *decision making processes* in organizations will now be presented. At the core of this theory lies Herbert Simon's work. His basic idea, the bounded rationality concept, is taken as the point of departure that organizational decision making took from the rational theories of decisions. The decision making behavior that can be observed in the framework of bounded rationality is that of the decision maker searching for a course of action that is satisfactory rather than optimal.

Let us go back to the rational models for a moment. In economics, the classical firm is regarded as a unitary agent. The economic theory of the firm assumes that:

(1)   the firm seeks to maximize its profit, and;
(2)   it operates with perfect knowledge.

With no further assumptions about psychological or organizational constraints, this theory explains the firm's behavior in terms of forces outside the firm. As a challenge to the economic theory of the firm, Cyert and March (1963) who belong, along with Simon, to the Carnegie School developed *A Behavioral Theory of the Firm*. In contrast to the classical, economic theories that explain the firm's behavior in terms of market factors, they focused on the effect of organizational structure upon developing goals, the formulation of expectations, and the execution of choice. Their theory is an extension of Simon's idea of bounded rationality. At the core of this theory are four concepts:

(1)   *Quasi-resolution of conflict*. Organizational subunits may have individual goals that are in conflict. Conflicts that may occur as a result of local rationality are resolved by 'acceptable level' decision rules, and sequential attention to goals.

(2)   *Uncertainty avoidance* by short-run reactions to short-run feedback, or by negotiations with the environment.

(3)   *Problemistic search* which first directs the decision maker to the neighborhood of problem symptoms (local search), and next to the neighborhood of the current alternative.

(4)   *Organizational learning* leads to changing goals, a shift in attention, and the revision of search procedures.

Table 2.1   Check list for diagnosis of the decision-making process.

Aspect of decision situation	Common characteristic
Goal	Local rationality
Uncertainty	Avoidance
Information	Local search
Learning	Simple

The framework presented by Cyert and March provides a theory with empirical support of managerial decision making in organizations. Their four major concepts: 'local rationality', 'uncertainty avoidance', 'local search', and 'organizational learning' provide a guide for what to look for when diagnosing decision making behavior, as summarized in Table 2.1 (Stabell, 1983):

In this section we have touched, briefly, on some of the social science literature on decision making in organizations. Two conclusions can be made. The first is that an organization does not make decisions in the same way that an individual does. The second is that there are many ways in which organizational decision making is inadequate. Support tools are needed to reduce the limitations of the psychological capacity of individuals, as well as to reduce organizational complexity. Prescriptions for how to make better organizational decisions are necessary.

To summarize, the development of decision support systems requires knowledge about the decision making that is to be supported. To model this process we have proposed the conceptual framework of Mintzberg *et al.* (1976). This framework contains concepts for description of activities and cognitive processes. However, to have a complete picture of decision making in organizations, we must understand the organizational constraints under which decision making takes place. Here, we lean on the theories developed in the social sciences, in particular, the theory presented by Cyert and March that is based on organization theory.

The two frameworks of decision making we have presented in more detail above both take a view of decision making that is *process*-oriented within a bounded rationality paradigm. It is beyond the scope of this text to deal with social models of decision making where the interactions among the participants are emphasized. Our focus is determined by the tasks we are aiming to support by a KB-DSS, which are along the central routines in Mintzberg's framework, rather than the communicational aspects of the social models.

2.5.3 Bank loans – a decision process study

Several behavioral studies of decisions that relate to bank loans have been reported in the literature. In this section, we shall report on a study by Ribe (1985), using Mintzberg's framework to describe organizational decision making in the credit department of a commercial bank. This study was part of a program that investigated applications of expert system technology to loan decisions. The purpose of this study was to define the task environment for such decisions and to identify potential tasks for expert systems.

In an early report, Cohen *et al.* (1966) presented a detailed model of the bank loan task that was based on observations of loan officers in two large American commercial banks. The major result of this study was a decision model of the procedures that commercial banks use when evaluating applicants for business loans. It provided a picture of the task environment. They identified eight components of the bank loan task:

(1)   status of the firm's customer relationship;

(2)   evaluation of a new customer relationship;

(3)   credit evaluation;

(4)   check on legal and policy restrictions;

(5)   appraisal of the loan's purpose, amount, maturity, payback, and security;

(6)   detailed recommendations;

(7)   record analyses and recommendations;

(8)   follow-up and review.

Although Cohen *et al.*'s model does not specifically describe decision making behavior, they observed that the loan evaluation process, generally, was handled by heuristics that lead to satisficing behavior. No utility functions incorporating the three possible objectives: minimizing risk, maximizing profit and maximizing service to the community, were apparent in any of the observations.

Empirical research on bank loan decision making indicates that it is a heuristic, satisficing process. Bankers do not optimize. Instead they look for alternatives that meet a set of criteria (Cohen, *et al.* 1966; Stephens, 1980).

Our own observations of bank loan decisions also showed a clear resemblance with a heuristic, satisficing process. Decision makers agree on the goals: to service the customers to the best of their needs under the constraints of high return on capital and minimum risk. No socio-political factors of significance have been observed. The outcome of the decision has impacts on the customer and the bank's profitability but not on the per- formers of the decision making process. This also coincides with the

Stephens' study that the skill of credit evaluation requires the development of similar problem spaces:

> 'Information processing behavior in professional problem solving tasks seems dominated by task requirements, perhaps formulated as professional rules, rather than personality characteristics of individual decision makers.' (Stephens, 1980, p. 69)

In the following, we shall show how bank loan decision making can be described within the Mintzberg model, a conceptual framework which is closer to Cohen's descriptions than the cognitive process description of Stephens. The advantage of using the Mintzberg framework is that there is a set of concepts and a structure to describe seemingly unstructured decision processes.

We can identify four decision situations concerning the bank loan task. The first situation is the credit approval situation, where the decision process is triggered by a customer's application. The second situation occurs during credit monitoring, that is, the credit review situation. Thirdly, we have the credit termination decision, and finally, we have situations where the credit institution itself initiates a process to place credit in the market, with companies, projects, and so on – this is called the credit acquisition situation. Each one of these situations leads to different decision processes. Let us look at how the Mintzberg framework can help us to study two of these situations: credit approval and credit reviews.

Credit applications

Figure 2.3 shows a schematic view of a typical loan application decision process. The following activities (central routines) are triggered:

Central routines
In the case of a credit application the choice situation is easily identified and *problem recognition* is activated by an application.

Diagnosis is concerned with what kind of a problem the credit application constitutes before any credit alternatives are designed and evaluated. For a new customer, a preliminary evaluation of what this customer relationship will bring is made. Furthermore, the diagnosis is concerned with the following tasks:

- information validation (financial statement benchmarks);
- risk exposure;
- evaluation of legal and bank policy constraints.

A judgment is made of risk exposure and other constraints, if the risk exposure is acceptable and these constraints are satisfied then the credit

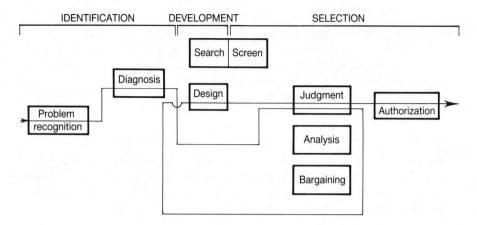

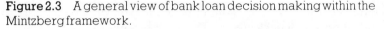

Figure 2.3   A general view of bank loan decision making within the Mintzberg framework.

application is moved back to the design stage. Here, specific alternatives are formulated with detailed conditions relating to each.

The final choice is then made on the basis of risk and profitability. *Evaluation* is based on expected return on the investment. It is not a goal to minimize risk, rather the goal is to maximize expected return over the whole portfolio. Therefore, risk should be appraised: high risk, high interest rate and shorter maturity; smaller risk, lower interest rate and longer maturity. Empirical studies indicate that evaluation is primarily made by judgment rather than by analysis.

Finally, the decision process terminates in the authorization task. The authorization is performed by: the clerk, the branch manager, or a credit committee depending on the amount of credit to be given.

Support routines
Empirical research carried out on credit losses indicates that losses are primarily due to sloppy routines rather than bad credit evaluation. The support routines in the Mintzberg framework are good guidelines here. We shall, however, collect them in one routine called *decision management*. Decision management should attend to the formal procedures that are to be followed in the credit decision process. It should include routines that reveal any involvement in contraventions with the established procedures (protocols, case records, rights to grant credit and so on). It should also include control of the credit agreement: interest rate, amount of credit and covenants. Decision management should establish procedures to be followed in the credit approval process, such as legal validity checks on securities offered.

Furthermore, the decision management routine is responsible for establishing credit policies, that is, how much risk exposure is acceptable, what securities should be required, and for which purposes credit can be obtained.

Also, decision management allocate resources (manpower and skill) to decision processes.

Decision support systems that are aimed at decision management are rather scarce. However, this is a very important target area for computer support where a DSS can *impose* routines to be followed.

Credit review

Central routines
One way to reduce risk is to have short review cycles and good early-warning systems. How do we effectively monitor a large portfolio of loans? The most important routine in the monitoring process is *problem recognition*. Problem recognition can be activated in several ways:

(1)   Predefined periodical reviews (monthly, quarterly, yearly) that are dependent on which risk category the credit belongs to.

(2)   Industrial and economic forecasts.

(3)   External variables, such as changes in the interest rate or changes in supply and demand.

(4)   The debtor's internal variables (income, profitability and so on).

After the problem recognition routine has been activated, the credit is *rediagnosed* to reveal any problems, or to see if the risk exposure has changed. After diagnosis, the credit is passed to the *evaluation* routine for reclassification or termination. In both cases the *design* routine is activated to restructure the agreement.

Two dynamic factors that frequently make an impact on the decision processes are interrupts due to urgent processing of other tasks, and timing delays due to the authorization activity only taking place periodically (for example, once a week).

The purpose of such study could be twofold:

(1)   will expert systems or DSS be of any use in the credit department of the bank; and

(2)   where can these technologies be applied most effectively?

In the Mintzberg model, we divide the decision process into activities or routines in order to analyse which of these routines lend themselves to these technologies. Four routines emerge as potential targets: screen, evaluate, diagnose, and decision management.

(1)   *Screen* is used to search for interesting, potential clients. The purpose of this activity is to screen out all the companies that are of no interest to the bank. This screening is primarily based on

financial analysis. Financial analysis, as we shall see in subsequent chapters, is a well-structured, heuristic process. The benefits of an expert system here are due, partly, to efficiency (saving time) and partly to effectiveness (analysis can be performed by lower-grade clerks with the support of expert systems). Screen is also a good starting point. Since this is not a final decision, an expert system's conclusions are more easily accepted.

(2)   *Evaluation/Choice* is also dominated by financial analysis. However, here additional factors such as management competence, market developments and so on are given more weight than in the screening process. Therefore, an expert system for this activity will be more *supportive* than in the screening activity. More of the knowledge required for the final choice will belong to the user (decision maker).

(3)   *Diagnosis.* Here, the issue is to establish the most accurate picture of the loan applicant and to acquire the right information for evaluation. Expert systems can support this by transforming fiscal statements into true financial statements of the company.

(4)   *Decision Management.* On the meta-decision level, a DSS can be used in the decision management routine, to ensure that the procedures established are followed. Expert systems can be used to establish checklists for these procedures and to give references to previous cases of a similar kind and to give advice on available credit alternatives.

The purpose of this presentation is to show how a theoretical framework, like the Mintzberg model of a decision process, can be used to describe the task environment of a particular type of decision situation. The descriptions are given in terms of central routines, supporting routines and dynamic factors. Each of the routines, together with the pattern of routines that emerge according to the dynamic factors that are activated, can be subjected to computer support: either, a DSS, an expert system, or a KB-DSS.

Exercises

2.1   Define *normative* and *descriptive* as they apply to decision making.

2.2   What is the difference between *problem solving* and *decision making*?

2.3   Explain what is meant by a *symbol system*. Give examples of physical symbol systems.

2.4   Describe the cognitive architecture of the human mind as a symbol system.

2.5   Concepts can be defined in different ways. Explain:

(a)   the classical way;

(b)   by means of family resemblance.

2.6   In their problem solving theories, Newell and Simon define two basic concepts: *task environment* and *problem space*. Explain these two concepts.

2.7   A foreigner is lost in Paris. He had started to walk from his hotel in the direction he thought would take him to the Louvre, but the streets have become unfamiliar. Looking at the map, he observes that it cannot be far away. He could ask the way, but his French is limited and would probably take him a few streets at the time. From his present position he can see a taxi station and a subway station. Define:

(a)   the task environment;

(b)   the problem space.

2.8   Why do people use heuristics in problem solving? Give examples.

2.9   How can expertise be explained in terms of mental processes?

2.10   Two hospitals, *A* and *B*, recorded, for a period of one year, the days on which more than 60% of the babies born were boys. Hospital *A* has a birth rate of 50 babies a day, while in hospital *B* 20 babies a day are born.

Which of the two hospitals do you think recorded the greatest number of days on which more than 60% or the births were boys?

2.11   In a study of practising auditors, subjects were divided into two groups. Subjects in one group were asked:

'It is well known that many cases of management fraud go undetected. We are interested in obtaining an estimate of prevalance of executive-level management fraud as a first step in ascertaining the scope of the problem.

(a)   Based on your audit experience, is the incidence of significant executive-level management fraud more than 10 in 1000 firms (that is, 1%)?

     (i)   Yes, more than 10 in each 1000 firms have significant executive-level fraud.

    (ii)   No, less than 10 in each 1000 firms.

(b)   'What is your estimate of the number of firms per 1000 that have significant executive-level management fraud?'

The second group of subjects were asked the same, except that the fraud incidence was changed to 200 in each 1000 firms audited, rather than 10 in 1000. Subjects in the first group estimated, on average, the incidence of fraud to be 16.52 per 1000, compared with 43.11 per 1000 in the second group.

Explain the results in terms of biases in human decision making.

3

The Normative View of Decision Making

3.1 The importance of the normative view of decision making

In Chapter 2 several descriptive or behavioral theories of decision making were presented. These theories provide frameworks for studying the decision processes as they are actually performed within organizations. A descriptive analysis of a decision situation is the starting point for improvements and for the application of prescriptive methods. Indeed, one of the first means of improvement might be to increase efficiency in the decision process, that is, to provide support for some of the sub-processes by means of DSS.

However, the literature on DSS has always had an emphasis on increased effectiveness of decision making, that is, an increase in *quality* of the decision, as the main benefit of a DSS. This is why it is important to study what has been written by those who have worked on improving our knowledge of *what is a good decision* and how such a decision should be made.

Also, we should keep in mind that if we contend that it is possible to use computers to assist in problem solving performance and decision making we must be able to demonstrate *why* this support should lead to *better decisions*. So we must have a *normative* view to explain why a supported decision is better than an unsupported one. It is interesting to note that the normative point of view, as a guide in designing DSS, is now appearing, once again, in the recent literature on DSS (see, for example, the *Nato Advanced Study Institute Program on Mathematical Models for Decision Support*, held in Val d'Isere, France in 1987).

A designer of a DSS should have design methodologies that include normative methods. Generally, decision makers do not master normative principles for several reasons:

- the presentation is too abstract and complex;
- there is a lack of satisfactory and easy to use software with which to support the method;
- they do not match that real problem that the user has.

However, as we shall see in Chapter 5, a good DSS environment *improves* the decision making process, by *speeding up the learning process* of the user.

We have frequently observed that the user, once he or she has performed the first step (which usually involves performing a task more efficiently than before), will start requesting a more *rigorous* and *effective methodology* as he or she becomes *more conscious* of the weaknesses of the present solution. At least this behavior is observed in domains where there is a motivation to improve results (such as profit in business), or in the search for truth and in the spirit of inquiry found in the scientific field.

Another reason for studying the normative point of view is that, as shown in Chapter 7, it is now much easier to build systems which include *methodological* knowledge and, as a consequence, can provide normative assistance to the user. This possibility is made available through expert system technology.

As a consequence, the decision maker will increasingly look for decision support tools which will provide him or her with a *normative assistance* as and when he or she wishes to use such tools. It is worth noting at this point that, here, we make two important assumptions: firstly that decision making can be studied and secondly that it can be improved. This has been considered to be obvious by most people in the Western world since The Renaissance, but as Howard has pointed out this is not the case in Eastern philosophy.

Before the name DSS was coined, a lot of high quality work had been carried out under the name of Operations Research and Management Science. We have found it useful to recall the point of view of these movements and, also, to study the kinds of problems they have been able to solve for managers. Also in this chapter we shall give a brief review of the quantitative decision methodologies, as they are used in the main schools in this field. We shall end the chapter with a description of the decision analysis cycle which seems to give the most comprehensive normative view.

3.1.1 The difficulty of decision making and the meaning of rationality

In everyday life we usually think of decision making as being good if it is rational, so it will be important to specify the concept of rationality. Each one of us has many examples of decisions that are usually considered to be bad.

It will be argued in this chapter that we should distinguish between the *decision making process* and the *outcome* of the decision. It is quite possible for the outcome that results from a chosen alternative to be good, even though the decision making process is bad and vice versa. Clearly, decisions can be made which are bad, both in process and outcome, one of the usual reasons for this situation occurring is the complexity of the decision. Management problems are full of complex decisions with far-reaching consequences. As we have seen in Chapter 2, there are limitations on a person's ability to take all of the important factors into account. Bad decision making may result from the decision maker's inability to incorporate all of the important factors into his or her thoughts. One of these important factors is uncertainty, and decision making is often difficult just because of the many uncertainties involved.

Another factor which has increased the difficulty of decision problems is the increasingly large number of people involved in a decision. This characteristic may be related to the growing number and size of organizations over the last 50 years.

As a consequence, the people involved in the decision often have different views on the relative importance of various objectives. In the face of complexity, uncertainty, conflicting objectives and multiple decision-makers, the Western culture has developed a rational decision making process. We seek a **rational framework** to help us think through our decisions. The first intuitive approach is to define a good decision as a rational one, which implies the need to clarify this concept of rationality. One of the key characteristics of rationality is, it seems, **consistency**.

For example, if we declare that A implies B, and also that B implies C, then we shall, presumably, declare that A implies C. It would be considered irrational to do otherwise. What we have been doing was just making **inferences** that accord to the classical principle of logic that inferences should be transitive. We would be considered to be inconsistent with this principle if we assert that A does not imply C in this example. Similarly, we might state, as a principle, that our preferences should display transitivity. If we declare that X is preferred to Y, and Y to Z but we do not prefer X to Z, then we may be accused of irrationality. The accusation is probably based on the assumption that we wish our preferences to be consistent.

We notice that, in both these examples, the demonstration of irrationality depended on the *presence of a rule and showing that the statements were inconsistent with that rule*. In other words, we shall make the assumption that the decision maker is willing to make choices that are based on a consistent line of reasoning. We are rational when, having adopted rules which our statements or actions should conform to, we act in a way that is consistent with them. It is to be noted that this definition allows many different kind of rules to be adopted in complex decision making situations. We can then satisfy our need for rationality by conforming to those rules. It is also important to note that for a formal decision methodology to be useful in solving real problems its conclusions must, ultimately, make intuitive sense to the decision maker.

As stated by Holtzman (1989) 'the decision maker must develop an intuitive understanding of the validity of any successful recommendation for action, even if he does not have detailed knowledge of the underlying information that led to the recommendation'.

Section 3.3 is devoted to describing the rules of decision analysis, and we shall argue that they constitute a sensible set of rules to follow.

3.1.2 The nature of formal decision methods and their validity conditions

A formal decision method must provide concepts and a formalism to describe the context of the decision (that is, a formal description of a decision domain and the decision situation, including decision maker's preferences, information and alternatives). The definition of a formal decision method must also include at least one prescriptive axiom (McCarthy 1984) which Holtzman (1989) calls the **action axiom**.

The formal method used to describe the context of a decision is not normative. On the other hand, the action axiom defines a set of conditions that are sufficient for action. The action axiom, being a statement about real action in the terms of a formal system, is an act of faith. In other words, we can give arguments according to which an action axiom such as maximizing expected utility is a valid (that is, sensible) axiom to act upon in the world, but this *cannot be proved*. This raises the problem of validity conditions for formal decision methods. Holtzman (1989) points out that a formal decision method must satisfy two domain-specific conditions: it must be **locally correct**, and capable of **extrapolation**. Local correctness means that the method must yield solutions that are intuitively correct to a representative class of toy problems, that is, simple situations that are solvable 'by inspection' and to which the formal technique is applicable.

> 'When a formal decision method is both locally correct and extrapolable with respect to a decision domain, the method's solutions to large, unintuitive problems can be considered superior to intuitive (and possibly conflicting) alternative solutions, although this superiority can never be proved. In particular, formally derived solutions are superior because there is nothing in a sound formal method (aside from computational limitations) that is adversely affected by the complexity and size of the problem. This cannot be said of intuitive methods, which are subject to our bounded rationality (Simon, 1976, 1982)'. Holtzman, 1989.

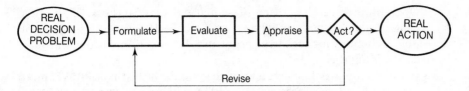

Figure 3.1   Closed-loop decision process. (Reproduced from Holtzman S. (1989). *Intelligent Decision Systems*. Addison-Wesley)

3.1.3 Methodology for using a formal decision method

The purpose of a formal decision method is to tell the decision maker something that, in principle, is already known, in the sense that if the decision maker believes that the model represents his or her decision problem, then he or she should act according to the recommendations of the method's conclusion. In practice, using formal decision methods requires that we formally capture the decision context as a decision model and that we interpret the formal recommendation that results from applying the decision method to the model.

As a consequence, the practical use of formal decision methods is a three-stage process (see Figure 3.1): formulation (that is, development of the formal decision model) evaluation and appraisal (that is, interpretation of the formal recommendation). If a formally derived prescription is unacceptable then a feedback loop is included to remind us that the decision maker should react to any surprising element of the formal prescription by re-evaluating and possibly modifying his or her formulation. Alternatively, if after developing enough insight the decision maker agrees with the suggested strategy or, if he or she determines that his or her disagreements result solely from logical error, he or she may choose to follow the formal prescription.

3.2 The history of quantitative decision making

Management science originated from the failure of operations research to adequately solve management problems, both of these disciplines are now discussed.

3.2.1 Operations research

The French mathematician and philosopher Pascal was probably the first to use a logical and mathematical method to solve certain decisions problems that were met in games.

Operations research is often presented, by some authors, as the first large scale organized activity having, as a goal, the scientific analysis of decisions in complex management problems. To be rational is one thing, to be scientific is another.

In this section we shall give a brief account of the history of this subject and the difficulties it has faced since the 1970s will be discussed. We shall use a definition of the scientific method that was inspired by the Austrian philosopher Karl Popper (1934). To apply a scientific method means to construct a hypothesis about the way the world works, and to collect data to try to falsify this hypothesis. In the absence of such falsification, the hypothesis may be used to explain phenomena.

Engineers take the hypotheses of science and use them to construct artifacts in order to perform useful functions. The procedures of science and engineering are sometimes described as 'scientific rationalism', and this fits with the definition of rationality we have taken: to take the procedures of science as the rules with which we wish to conform.

The application of scientific rationality to the management of organizations is now known as Operations Research (OR) or system analysis.

The best known early operations research study is probably the one carried out for the Air Defence Ministry during the Battle of Britain, and, also, the work in the US Navy to find the best anti-submarine strategy during the Second World War (see Waddington, 1973). Most of the decision problems that were studied by military operational researchers during the Second World War were repetitive problems.

Certain researchers concluded that the only management problems which could be dealt with using a scientific approach were repetitive and, as a consequence, concentrated on the study of repetitive decision processes. Since repetitive decisions are also important in civilian organizations, operational research also made a lot of progress in this environment, particularly in the manufacturing industry.

It is clear that the focus on repetitive problems has led operational researchers to concentrate on operation management. Rarely have higher-level management problems been studied. In the 1970s this led to what has been described by some commentators as an 'intellectual crisis'. Many critical contributions started flourishing in the OR literature, some of them written by well-known pioneers in the field, such as Ackoff (1979a, b), Quade (1975, 1984), Tomlinson and Kiss (1984). The problem was that OR methods were no longer providing the same noticeable improvements to management problems as had been seen in the early years of the subject. Now, it is usually recognized that the mind set of the OR approach, while ideal for solving the logistics problems for which the approach was developed, is inadequate for the higher level management problems.

Checkland (1981) demonstrated that many OR scientists were

more concerned with how to achieve a given end most *efficently*, rather than with what that end should be in the first place. The exploration of goals, their creation, and their expression were not important parts of the analysis made by OR scientists. But, as Checkland pointed out, in many practical problems such as an *investigation of goals* is probably the *most essential* requirement when coping with the problem.

The inadequacies in the attempts to apply the scientific rationality of OR to management were summarized by Watson and Buede (1987):

- 'failure to involve the decision-maker in the experimental and iterative nature of the analysis,
- failure to appreciate the organizational and personnal context of decision making,
- failure to explore ends as well as means'.

3.2.2 The 'management science' movement

In the mid 1950s operations research gave birth to the 'management science' movement. This discipline arose due to the deep concern that management did not receive the attention that could have been expected from operational researchers. The journal *Management Science* published by The Institute of Management Science defined the goal of the Institute as: 'An international society to identify, extend and unify scientific knowledge pertaining to management'.

However, the followers of the management science approach were, just as the OR scientists, quickly accused of having much more interest in problems susceptible to mathematically-elegant solutions, than to the real problems of managers, in particular *top* management, whose problems are more difficult to formalize into quantitative models. This led Michael Scott-Morton and Peter Keen (1978) to characterize the contribution of the OR management science schools in the following way:

- The impact has mostly been on *structured* problems (rather than tasks) where the objective, data, and constraints can be prespecified.
- The pay-off has been in generating better *solutions* for given types of problems.
- The relevance for managers has been the provision of detailed *recommendations* and new technologies for handling complex problems.

Since the OR/management science approach did not provide, in many cases, the adequate methodology for the analysis of management decisions, a certain number of new approaches emerged at the beginning of the 1970s. These new approaches tried to fulfill the following properties which Watson and Buede (1987) considered to be the basic requirements for supporting the decision maker:

(1)   A set of rules for decision making must be defined in order that we may know what it is like to be rational.

(2)   The rules must address the values of the problem owners. It must be possible to articulate their preferences and perceptions.

(3)   The rules must state what it is to be rational in the face of perception of uncertainty.

(4)   The rules must provide a calculus for steering the thinking of the decision makers through complex problems.

Thus, a new discipline, called 'rational decision analysis', emerged, its major facets will be described in the next section.

3.3 Rational decision analysis

Several main directions appeared at the beginning of 1970, roughly at the same time as the DSS concept appeared: the statistical decision theory school, the Stanford school, and the multicriteria school are some of the most well-known examples.

We shall first describe, in this section, the main concepts used by these schools, then the differences in emphasis of each one of these schools will be discussed, followed by a description of the **decision analysis cycle** which seems, to us, to be the most comprehensive of these approaches, and, finally, we shall raise some questions about the normative point of view. We shall follow closely, in this section, the ideas of Watson and Buede (1987).

3.3.1 The problem of conflicting objectives

We make decisions all the time, however, when it comes to 'important' decisions such as which job to choose, or where to live, the stakes at risk are significant, and we find ourselves using more effort to ensure that we choose correctly.

When we have responsibility for decisions that affect many other people we are highly motivated to make the correct decision. It may be the choice between different locations for a factory, the selection of a new computer system, the recruiting of a new employee and so on. In such circumstances we check that the choice we make is consistent with our own beliefs and values, as well as the values of the organization that we serve.

The practical role of the rational decision theory is to provide a framework that assists people in achieving such consistency. In such decisions two important factors can usually be pointed out:

(1)   there exist conflicts between objectives,
(2)   there is uncertainty about the outcomes.

We shall see how the decision theory can provide a framework for thinking about these two factors at once. We shall first see how to handle conflicting objectives when we have no uncertainty about the outcome of our decision making.

Utility and value

Choice is simple if we have only one criterion. For example, if we can buy the same product in several different shops, we usually use cost as the single criterion and we buy the product in the shop where the price is lowest.

If we have several criteria and can establish a single numerical measure which takes all of these criteria into account, then our choice procedure, would again, be straightforward. The difficulty is how to construct such a measure.

The concept of a numerical measure to describe the value of alternative choices has come to be referred to as the **utility theory**, with the **utility function** being the numerical measure itself. The utility theory appears to have been first discussed by the French mathematician Daniel Bernouilli in 1738 when solving a gambling problem. Bernouilli's explanation was that money was not an appropriate measure of value. Instead, he suggested that the *worth*, or the utility of money for each individual, was non linear and had a decreasing slope; marginal utility decreased as wealth increased.

In the 1940s and 1950s the concept was used again, and was made more precise in game theory. Game theory was developed both to describe how people behave when engaged with others in conflicting goals, and to describe how rational people ought to behave in such situations. The game theory was developed by the mathematician John von Neumann and the economist Oskar Morgenstern. In their book *The Theory of Games and Economic Behavior* (1944), they found the need to develop a cardinal theory of utility to describe how people should evaluate options about which they were uncertain.

Decision analysts have made the distinction between two types of utility, which can be characterized as the distinction between value and risk preference. *Value preferences* are made between competing objectives or attributes when *no uncertainty is present*. *Risk preference* addresses the decision maker's aversion to, indifference to, or desire for *risk taking*.

Value functions

We can only recall here the key elements of the value function theory. The reader is referred to Keeney and Raiffa (1976) for an authoritative presentation of this theory. Here, we shall only deal with the properties that a value function should have and why we want to construct one. The problem under consideration can be defined as follows: a set of alternatives has been defined. We assume that we know the attributes (criteria) which discriminate among these alternatives. For example, if the problem is to choose among cars, the alternatives could be: Volvo, Ford, Peugeot, BMW, Mercedes; and the attributes: power, purchase price, mileage, comfort, aesthetics, reliability, maintenance costs and so on. We suppose that there are n such attributes, named $X_1, X_2, \ldots X_n$ and that it is possible to provide a numerical score for each alternative with respect to each attribute. This set of scores will be represented by a vector $x = (x_1, x_2, \ldots x_n)$. The problem is to decide which vector score is most attractive.

Although, at first sight, the formalization above may seem to be a reasonable abstraction, real problems are rarely like this. It is often the case that the set of alternatives is not completely known, or that all the possible alternatives have not been identified. In addition, it may not be clear how to characterize the attributes that distinguish between the alternatives, or how to measure each alternative with respect to some of the attributes. In the preceding example, measuring the reliability of a car is certainly not a simple question! Assuming that this difficulty can be overcome, we introduce the concept of value functions.

A value function v (.) is defined using real numbers that have the following properties:

- $v(x^A) > v(x^B)$ if, and only if, the option whose score vector is x^A is preferred to another with score vector x^B

- $v(x^A = v(x^B))$ if, and only if, there is indifference to the choice between x^A and x^B.

The choice between these alternatives is simple: we choose the alternative with the score vector x for which $v(x)$ is largest. The difficulty will be in constructing this function v (.). If the only way to do so were to elicit from the decision maker, his or her relative preferences for all the possible vector score, then we would not have achieved anything by trying to construct a value function. The choice problem would have been answered by direct intuition.

Fortunately, there are ways of computing v (.) that rely on *general properties* of our preferences structure and just a few simple comparative judgments. As Watson and Buede (1987) point out, the power of the method is that if our preferences obey certain conditions (and they often do) we can synthesize v (.) from an analysis of only part of our set of preferences. In certain cases, we do not even need to completely specify $v(.)$. This is the case when we have *dominance* of one alternative over another. An alternative, A is said to dominate another alternative, B if, for all i, $1 \le i \le n$, $x_i^A \ge x_i^B$ and for at least one i, $x_i^A > x_i^B$. If one alternative dominates all the others, it is rational to choose it. Clearly, dominance rarely occurs with problems that are complex enough to require analysis, and we need to develop a method for those problems.

Existence of the value function

As Watson and Buede (1987) point out, the notion of effecting an explicit construction of a value function to solve a decision problem makes intuitive sense, and this approach is, in fact, widely used for routine decision making such as credit assessment, rating examinations and so on.

If a value function exists then it induces a complete ordering on the vector x, conversely, if we do have a complete preference order, then we can construct a value function by merely placing the vectors in increasing order and attaching any increasing sequence of numbers to the vectors. If we feel confident that, given enough introspection, we could produce a complete ordering on the vector x, then there must be some value function $v(.)$ that can represent our preferences.

Since a partial ordering of our preferences can be inferred from any set of decisions we make, the interest of creating a value function is that it will help us construct preferences between score vectors which we find difficult to compare directly. The problem, then, is to construct our preferences within, and across, the attributes x_i of x in such a way that we have a complete ordering of all vectors x. This theory is *normative*, in that it shows us how we should behave if we want to be rational, rather than being a description of how we actually behave.

> 'The idea is to use value function theory to construct preferences which we find difficult to articulate directly, using only those preferences that we can express easily and adopting the principle of complete transitivity for all our preferences.' (Watson and Buede, 1987)

Once we have assumed the existence of $v(.)$ we now have to measure it. It should be noted that there is no reason to suppose that $v(.)$ will not change from problem to problem or as a function of time. Fortunately, there are properties that our **preference structure** often has that lead to special forms of the value function which can be elicited more easily.

Additive value functions

The most common form of the value function is the additive one:

$$v(x) = \sum_{i=1}^{n} v_i(x_i)$$

This form has the advantage of being very simple, and allows each attribute to be worked on separately. However, it is quite possible for a particular preference structure to lead to a non-additive value function.

We now have to recall what the conditions on our preferences have to be to justify additivity. The essential condition is that of **preference independence**. A pair of attributes X_1, X_2 is said to be preference independent of all the other attributes $\{X_i, i = 3, \ldots n\}$ if preferences between different combinations of X_1, X_2 with the level of all other attributes, being held at constant value, do not depend on what these constant values are.

For example, when buying a car if we say that cost and mileage are preference independent from reliability it means that we prefer a car with cost c_1, mileage m_1 and reliability r to one with cost c_2 mileage m_2 and reliability r, then we prefer a car with cost c_1, mileage m_1 to one with cost c_2 mileage m_2 no matter what r is. This should hold for all possible c_1, c_2, m_1 and m_2.

Clearly, this condition does not hold in certain cases, however, additive value functions can be useful in many circumstances. Several authors have discussed multiplicative or other forms. The reader is referred to Keeney and Raiffa (1976) for an expansion of these functions.

3.3.2 Encoding uncertainty

In the preceding section, we analysed the problem of choosing between alternatives when objectives are in conflict. We assumed that we knew, with certainty, what the results of choosing an alternative would be, so that the only problem was how to cope with the conflict between our objectives.

It is clear that in the problem of choosing which car to buy, to ignore uncertainty is not unreasonable, however, the certainty assumption is obviously unrealistic for most real decision problems. According to authors such as Howard and Matheson (1968) uncertainty is the central problem of decision making. As Watson and Buede (1987) point out that, some years ago, most texts on decision analysis presented the subject as being almost entirely concerned with uncertainty, and generally, there was only one attribute of interest, usually money. The subject has advanced, however, and the analysis of conflicting objectives is now emerging as one which is very useful in practice. Nevertheless, dealing with uncertainty is vital in most applications.

Description of uncertainty

If we are to incorporate uncertainty into our theories of choice, then a calculus for handling uncertainty must be developed. The theory that is most commonly employed for this purpose is that of probability. Probability theory is not very old, and is usually dated back to the French mathematicians and philosophers, Pascal, Bernouilli and Laplace. In fact, contrary to what one may think, there has been considerable controversy about the meaning of probability, and, in particular, its relation to real-world phenomena. The interested reader is referred to Weatherford (1982) and Hacking (1975).

Three main theories of probabilities can be identified. They were developed by their authors to incorporate a satisfactory method for measuring probabilities, and they are: the logical theories of Keynes (1921) and Carnap (1950), the relative frequency theories of Venn, Von Mises (1957) and Reichenbach, and the subjective probabilities theories of Ramsey (1931), de Finetti (1974), and Savage (1954).

The most important conflict has been between the relative frequency theory and the subjective probabilities theory. The relative frequency theory states that the probability of an event is the *long run frequency* with which the event occurs in an infinite repetition of an experiment, thus, it is seen as an objective property of the real world. The subjective theory presents probability as the *degree of belief* which an individual has in a proposition. This is a property of the individual's subjective perception (or state of knowledge) of the real world. The former theory has dominated scientific thinking for many years because it has the appearance of conforming to the empirical objectivity which science is sometimes claimed to need and possess. The relative frequency theory will not be adequate, however, as a theory for helping an individual to model his or her perception of uncertainty when making decisions.

The interpretation of probability which must be adopted for the application of decision theory has to be the subjective probability theory. Alternatives to the probability theory are the subject of much discussion:

> 'interpreting the parameters of nonprobabilistic measures of uncertainty with respect to reality has received much less attention than the interpretation of probabilities' (de Finetti, 1974). These parameters are, at best, poorly defined and essentially unassessable with any degree of reliability. Therefore, although they cannot be completely ruled out, non-probabilistic measures of uncertainty are inferior to probability measures for decision-making.' (Holtzman, 1989).

Events and probability

Probability theory is an obvious construct for describing perceived uncertainty, and has been applied with success during the last fifty years. When we wish to apply this calculus to decision problems we need a set of assumptions about an individual's judgments. This leads us to infer that a set of numbers must exist which describe that individual's perception of uncertainty that is related to a set of possible events and that these numbers should be combined using the rules of probability calculus to infer what numbers should be used to describe other uncertainties.

Numerical estimation of probabilities

The question which has to be raised now is how in the real world, we can set the numerical value of certain probabilities; for example, the probabilities of elementary events need to be set in order that we can compute non-elementary events.

The problem of how to measure probabilities is a practical one which is different from the theoretical problem of their coherence. There are two well-known methods to set the numerical values of probabilities: 'subjective' estimation and experimental estimation. With respect to the experimental method we shall recall, here, the so-called 'law of great numbers': if an event is produced by a process a large number of times, then the relative frequency of event A of probability $p(A)$, converges towards $p(A)$. As a consequence, the observed frequency of occurrence of the event can be used as an estimation for $p(A)$.

As we have pointed out above the interpretation of probability which must be adopted for the application of decision theory has to be the subjective one. The reader should be aware, however, that all scholars are not ready to accept this theory. If the subjective theory of probability is not adopted, the intellectual justification for the procedure of decision analysis is much weakened.

Theoretical background to subjective probabilities

Probability theory is an obvious construct for describing subjectively perceived uncertainty. To apply this calculus in other situations and, in particular, in decision problems requires more than an act of faith. What is required is a set of assumptions about an individual's judgment which, if they are satisfied, lead us to infer that a set of numbers must exist which describe that individual perception of uncertainty, and, moreover, that these numbers should be combined using the rules of the probability calculus to infer what numbers should be used to describe other uncertainties. This work was successfully undertaken by Ramsey (1931), Savage (1954) and most extensively by de Finetti (1974). The behavioral suppositions are set up as axioms as shown in Figure 3.2. The first axiom expresses the idea that given two uncertain events, a person can say which is more likely, or whether they are equally likely. Axioms (2), (3) and (4) are quite easy to accept. Axiom (5) supposes the existence of a set of events which acts as a standard in probability judgment.

With these behavioral assumptions, it can be proved (de Groot, 1970) that a set of numbers exists which correspond to the judgments of relative likelihood, in the sense that if, for two events A and B, A is judged to be more likely than B, then the number for A is larger than the number for B. Furthermore, these numbers must, collectively, satisfy the properties of probabilities such as:

$0 \leqslant p(A) \leqslant 1$

$p(A \text{ or } B) = p(A) + p(B) - p(A \text{ and } B)$

$p(A \text{ and } B) = p(A)\, p(B/A)$

with $p(B/A)$ being the probability of B occurring given A

Axioms for probability

(1) For any two uncertain events, A is more likely than B, or B is more likely than A, or they are equally likely.

(2) If A_1 and A_2 are any two mutually exclusive events, and B_1 and B_2 are any other mutually exclusive events; and if A_1 is not more likely than B_1, and A_2 is not more likely than B_2; then (A_1 and A_2) is not more likely than (B_1 and B_2). Further, if either A_1 is less likely than B_1 or A_2 is less likely than B_2, then (A_1 and A_2) is less likely than (B_1 and B_2).

(3) A possible event cannot be less likely than an impossible event.

(4) Suppose A_1, A_2, ...A_i is an infinite decreasing sequence of events; that is, if A_i occurs, then A_1 occurs, for any i. Suppose further that each A_i is not less likely than some other event B, again for any i. Then the occurrence of all the infinite set of events $A*i = 1, ..., \infty$, is not less likely than B.

(5) There is an experiment, with a numerical outcome, such that each possible value of that outcome, in a given range, is equally likely.

Exhibit 3.1 If an individual is able to, or wishes to, express his or her judgments of likelihood according to these axioms, then numbers must exist which describe his or her perceptions of the uncertainty of any event which satisfy the rules of the probability calculus. Conformity to these rules is our definition of what it means to be rational in evaluating uncertainty.

Figure 3.2   Rationality in evaluating uncertainty. (Reproduced from Watson S.R. and Buede D.M. (1987) *Decision Synthesis: The Principles and Practice of Decision Analysis.* Cambridge University Press)

Despite these results, many scholars reject the notion of subjective probability. They argue that the first assumption (that we can compare the relative likelihood of any two events) is untrue and since the premise is false, the conclusion is false.

However, one of the objectives of developing decision theory is to establish a *framework* to guide rational behavior. For Watson and Buede (1987) the question is whether we choose to behave in such a way that our judgments either have this property or not. What the theory we have described tells us is that if we would like all our judgments of relative likelihood to exist and to exhibit transitivity then subjective probabilities should be used.

Using probabilities

If we accept the idea that our judgment on uncertainty is to be represented by numbers, and that these numbers must satisfy the rules of probability then a question is raised as to how to elicit these numbers in specific cases. Probability elicitation is a difficult problem and much work has been done on this process, for example, by Spetzler and Stael Von Holstein (1975), Seaver *et al.* (1978).

Subjective probabilities have to obey the laws of probability. For example, if we assess the probabilities of events X, Y, X given Y, Y given X

(written as, $p(X)$, $p(Y)$, $p(X/Y)$, $p(Y/X)$) are assessed, we have seen that we must have:

$$p(X) . p(Y/X) = p(Y) . p(X/Y)$$

since both must be equal to the probability that (X and Y) occur. If this relationship is not satisfied with the elicited numbers, then one or more of the four numbers must be changed.

One of the reasons for the observed phenomenon of incoherence in a set of probability estimates may be that the person is suffering from cognitive biases (Hogarth 1980, Kahneman *et al*. 1982). There seems to be considerable evidence that in assessing perception of uncertainty (Section 2.4.1), people are often subject to biases in cases where a norm for comparison exists.

The issue of how to correct biases when accessing subjective probabilities has been explored in the literature about the calibration of probability appraisers. But the literature is controversial, and no general conclusion can yet be derived about the possibilities of correcting for biases. We should also remember that to use probabilities in decision analysis implies familiarity with probability theory. In particular, the following concepts are needed:

- random variables (discrete and continuous);
- cumulative probabilities, probability density functions;
- moments of distributions, means, variances;
- conditional joint and marginal probabilities, independence;
- distribution functions of random variables.

These concepts are classical and the reader should consult one of the many standard instruction texts about probability theory. However, we would like to point out here that since we shall see in Chapters 6 and 7 that it is possible to embed methodological knowledge in a computer system, it is possible to design systems which will take care of most of the tasks of applying the laws of probabilities.

3.3.3 Structuring a problem using a decision tree and risk preference

Since we know how to describe subjectively perceived uncertainty in numerical terms, we have to now describe how this formalism can be used to aid decision makers who face alternative courses of action, each involving uncertainty.

The problem and its representations

The XYZ company has produced a new cosmetic product. Unfortunately, the production cost of this product is 50% higher than ordinary cosmetic products of the same kind. The marketing division of the XYZ company is

Table 3.1   Predicted profit ($000) for a
new product.

	R1	*R2*
A1	800	−300
A2	0	0

discussing the potential market share of the product. After discussion, the
marketing expert of XYZ came to the conclusion that two results are
possible.

R1.   The product very quickly reaches a 10% market share and stays at this
level.

R2.   Total failure.

After careful analysis, the management of the company came to the conclusion that there are two possible courses of action. Either:

A1.   Invest in a production unit able to supply 10% of the market.
A2.   Abandon this product immediately.

The predicted profit (in thousand of dollars) which can be obtained from
these operations is presented in Table 3.1. The management of the company
is rather pessimistic, and uncertain about the future of this product. The
marketing manager estimated that there is a 30% chance of gaining 10% of
the market, but that this estimation could be wrong. The marketing manager
also pointed out that if a market test was done, the uncertainty associated
with this choice could be reduced, and hence, the decision would be
improved. For $50,000 (the cost of the market test and corresponding delays),
the marketing manager thought that it would be possible to identify a good
market with 60% reliability, or a bad market with 80% reliability. If we call
$I1$ and $I2$ the two possible indications of the market test with respect to a
good market ($R1$) or a bad market ($R2$), then:

$P(I1/R1) = 0.6$
$P(I2/R2) = 0.8$

Where $P(I1/R1)$ denotes the probability of having a test indication of a good
market, and the market is good (R_1 and $P(I2/R2)$ denotes the probability of
having a test indicating a bad market, and the market is bad (R_2).

Figure 3.3 illustrates the situation that the manager faces. Such a diagram is referred to as a **decision tree**. It has proved to be useful in describing
decision problems. Indeed, merely describing a problem in this way can
often lead to an appreciation of what the best option ought to be. Three
different kinds of nodes can be distinguished in a decision tree:

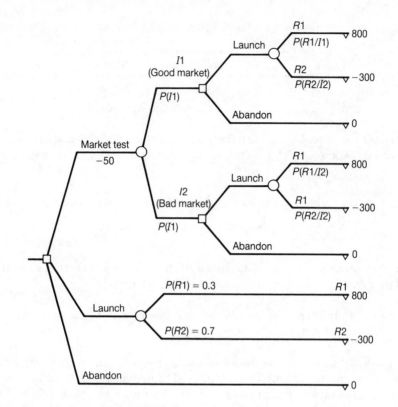

Figure 3.3   A decision tree corresponding to the new product problem.

(1)   decision nodes, denoted by a square (□);
(2)   chance nodes, denoted by a circle (○);
(3)   terminal nodes (outcomes), denoted by a triangle (▽).

and two kinds of branches:

(1)   alternative branches;
(2)   outcome branches.

Emanating from each decision node is a set of branches, each branch representing one of the alternatives available for selection at the corresponding decision node. Each chance node is followed by a set of outcome branches, one branch for each possible outcome that may happen following that chance node. Probabilities of occurrence and values are assigned to each of these outcomes. Costs (resource allocation) are assigned to each decision alternative. Looking at Figure 3.3 we see that the first node (starting with the root of the tree) is a decision node, which represents the three alternatives that are open to the management of the company: (1) abandon, (2) launch, (3) perform a market test.

(1)   If we abandon the product (bottom branch) we come directly to an outcome branch, the end value of which is zero.

(2)   If we launch the product we come to a second node where we have two branches $R1$ and $R2$ corresponding to the two possible conditions of the market (good and bad). At this point, the decision maker can not change anything, he or she can only estimate the probability to move in the direction of each alternative. This is a probabilistic (or chance) node.

(3)   Finally, if the management decides to perform a market test, it will, first of all, be necessary to finance this test (we can consider this cost as a fee the decision maker must pay to move along this branch). Then the decision maker finds his or her self facing a chance node corresponding to possible results from the test. He or she can control the situation again by deciding to launch or abandon the product.

The probability of coming to each of the branches of the tree are not directly known. They depend on the reliability of the market test and can be computed using Bayes's theorem:

$$P(R1/I1) \;=\; \frac{P(R1)\,P(I1/R1)}{P(I1)} \;=\; \frac{(0.3)\,(0.6)}{P(I1)}$$

$$P(R1/I2) \;=\; \frac{P(R1)\,P(I2/R1)}{P(I2)} \;=\; \frac{(0.3)\,(0.4)}{P(I2)}$$

$$\text{with } P(I1) \;=\; P(I1/R1)\,P(R1) \;+\; P(I1/R2)\,P(R2)$$
$$=\; (0.6)\,(0.3) + (0.2)\,(0.7)$$
$$=\; 0.32$$

$$\text{and } P(I2) \;=\; 1 - P(I1) = 0.68$$

$$\text{Thus:} \quad P(R1/I1) = \frac{18}{32} \quad P(R2/I1) = \frac{14}{32}$$

$$P(R1/I2) = \frac{12}{68} \quad P(R2/I2) = \frac{56}{68}$$

The evaluation method

We now seek some way to evaluate the uncertain options (or *lotteries* or *gambles* as we shall refer to them) facing a decision maker.

We want to construct an evaluation method such that, once a problem has been specified, its *decision tree* drawn, and the uncertainties measured using probabilities, we will be able to compute a number that represents its actual value to the decision maker, in a way that is consistent with his or her judgment.

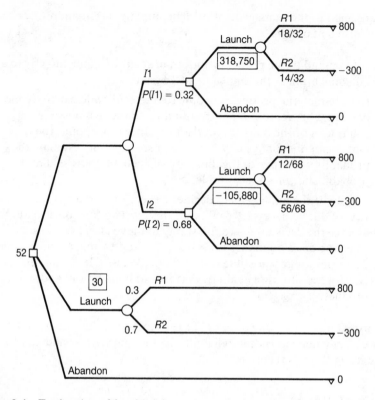

Figure 3.4 Evaluation of the decision tree corresponding to the new product problem.

The simplest and most common evaluation method, at least in problems where the only important attribute is money, is the **expected monetary value** for the option. We multiply the probability of a particular future set of events by the final asset position if that future occurs, and sum it over all possible futures. This method was first explored by Daniel Bernoulli (1738).

The method starts at the end of the branches and moves to the left from node to node. At each chance node, we shall compute the expected value of the tree to the right of the current node. At each decision node we shall select the branch leading to the *maximum expected value*. In our case, the immediate launching of the product leads to an expected value of:

$$800 \, (0.3) - 300 \, (0.7) = \$30,000$$

which is better than immediately abandoning it (value = 0). Similarly, if the result of the market test is favourable (*I*1), the launching of the product leads to an expected value of:

800 (18/32) + 300 (14/32) = $318,750

which is much better than abandoning the project.

On the other hand, if the result of the market test is unfavorable, it is better to abandon the product than to launch it, since the expected value of a launch in this case is:

800 (12/68) − 300 (56/68) = $105,880

Finally, the expected value of the project if we make the market test is equal to:

$318,750 (0.32) + 0 (68) = $102,000 minus the cost of the market test ($50,000) which equals $52,000.

A recording to the criteria of maximum expected value the last strategy is to make a market test since the expected value of this strategy is $52,000 against $30,000 for immediate launching and zero for immediately abandoning it.

Therefore, this method suggests launching the product if the result of the market test is favorable, and abandoning the product if the result of the market test is unfavorable.

Lottery of the project

The expected global value of the project that we have evaluated ($52,000) is just a way to summarize all of the possible consequences when following the best strategy. The details of the consequences take the form of a lottery among the possible outcomes associated with their respective probabilities. In our example, if we follow the best strategy that the company can take then the data shown in Table 3.2 holds.

To understand this lottery, we just have to recall that the best strategy is to make a market test before launching the product (highest expected value), and to launch the product if the market test is good and to abandon if

Table 3.2 Various probabilities and values for the product.

Probability	Value ($)
0.18	750,000
0.68	− 50,000
0.14	− 350,000

the market test is bad. If, after launch, the market is good, we obtain an outcome of:

$$800,000 - 50,000 = \$750,000 \text{ with a probability of } \frac{18}{32} \times 0.32 = 0.18$$

If, after launch, the market is bad: we obtain an outcome of

$$-300,000 - 50,000 = \$-350,000 \text{ with a probability of } \frac{14}{32} \times 0.32 = 0.14$$

If the market test was bad then we abandon the project, the outcome is $\$-50,000$. With a probability of 0.68.

In general, *a decision will be the choice between several lotteries*. The method used above is to replace each lottery by an expected value and to choose the lottery with the highest expected value. This simple rule does not satisfy many people and we must introduce the concept of utility to compare lotteries.

Utility theory

Daniel Bernoulli was the first person to introduce the concept of utility. The *Bernouilli solution* argued that the value (to the individual) of money was not a linear function (Bernouilli suggested that it was a logarithm). However, early writers in this area made no distinction between attitudes towards value differences and attitudes towards risk. It was with the publication of Von Neumann and Morgenstern's theory of games and economic behavior (1944) that modern utility theory can be said to have begun.

The idea behind this theory is to define the utility of an outcome as equal to the probability of winning a given prize in a gamble, such that the individual is indifferent to the choice between receiving the outcome for certain, and accepting the gamble.

We will start by exploring utility for money in a defined range, although the concept can be extended to any amount of money, and also to any non-monetary attribute. A lottery refers to a set of prizes or prospects with probabilities attached, as shown on Figure 3.5. The monetary values are H (high) and L (low). We have assumed that $L < X < H$. Using the symbol $\sim$ to denote the indifference of the decision maker between the options before him or her, we have:

$$X \sim \{L, H; u(X)\}$$

as the definition of the utility function u (.) using a standard notation. We introduce the concept of certain equivalent (X). The certain equivalent is the amount of money that the decision maker is willing to exchange for this lottery.

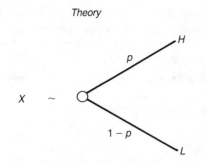

Theory

Figure 3.5   The concept of certain equivalence. For any outcome X which is preferable to L, and not as good as H, there is some probability p such that the decision maker is indifferent between X for sure, and a gamble, giving a chance p of getting H and $1 - p$ of getting L.

Application of the utility theory

The utility concept is now applied to the example of the XYZ company. The management of this company may consider that a probability of 0.3 for a gain of $800,000 and a probability of 0.7 for a loss of $300,000 constitute too risky a prospect to launch the product. On the other hand, if the abandonment had the consequence of leading to a loss of $100,000, the company may still prefer to launch the product.

Their certainty equivalent for this project is somewhere between $0 and $ − 100,000. Where exactly? at − $50,000 if they are obliged to produce an accurate estimate.

One can imagine that instead of computing the expected value we analyse the decision tree by replacing a lottery by a certain equivalent each time it is needed. The advantage of this method over a purely arbitrary method is, perhaps, not very convincing if we are obliged to introduce very subjective and intuitive preferences.

We shall point out, however, that we have reduced the global problem to a series of much simpler smaller experiences and the gain will be more important as the initial problem becomes more complex. In fact, by using some natural coherence axioms, we can define a systematic method to translate our attitude towards any lottery, as complex as it may be, as we had decided to use the expected value of the lottery. The method consists of replacing monetary value by utility for which we shall have to compute an expected value.

In other words, it is possible to demonstrate that utility functions can be built for a decision maker if he or she accepts the following axioms:

U1   **Orderability axiom.** The decision maker can tell if he or she prefers A to B, or B to A, or is indifferent. This preference must be transitive, that is, if A is preferred to B, and B to C, then A must be preferred to C.

U2   Monotonicity axiom. If A is preferred to B, a decision must be made between two lotteries for which the outcomes are A and B with different probabilities, then the lottery giving A with the maximum probability must be preferred.

U3   Decomposability axiom. A superlottery, the outcomes of which are themselves lotteries, is equivalent to a lottery offering the ultimate outcomes with the probabilities computed according to the calculus of probability.

U4   Continuity axiom. If A is preferred to B, and B to C, there must be a probability p such that B is the certain equivalent of the lottery giving outcome A with the probability p, and C with a probability $1 - p$.

U5   Substitutability axiom. It is always possible to replace a lottery by its certain equivalent.

One of the examples of such axiomatization and, perhaps, the most comprehensive one, was done by Savage (1954) who proved that an individual who acts in accordance with these five axioms possesses a utility function that has two important properties:

(1)   He or she can compute the utility for any lottery by computing the utility of each prize, multiplying by the probability of that prize and then summing over all prizes (that is, using the maximum expected utility rule as the action axiom).

(2)   If one lottery is preferred to another, then the utility for it will be higher.

In addition to logic and probability the decision theory requires that the decision maker accepts the set of the five axioms of utility theory, which together imply the Maximum Expected Utility (MEU) action axiom. Thus, MEU is not really an axiom but rather a theorem within the utility theory.

Given our previous discussion (Section 3.1.2) on the validity of formal methods for real decision making, we need to verify that the MEU axiom satisfies the conditions of local correctness and extrapolability in terms of personal decision making.

The orderability axiom (U1) states that the decision maker can consistently and completely rank all of the possible outcomes that could be received as a result of his or her decision. This axiom implicitly requires the decision maker to have a well-defined set of outcomes to consider. By well defined, we mean that the decision maker has successfully circumscribed his or her decision context in order to make the definition of each outcome clear.

Given the many kinds of ignorance we may face, Holtzman (1989) has an interesting classification of types of ignorance, our ability to circumscribe real decision problems is a mixed blessing. One argument to show the local correctness of axiom U1 is known as the 'money pump argument' (Raiffa

1968; Howard *et al.* 1983). This argument demonstrates that a transitive ordering of the decision maker's preference over the outcome set is a direct consequence of the reasonable desire of most decision makers not to voluntarily engage in sure-loss action.

The decomposability axiom (U3) states that the decision maker derives no pleasure (or displeasure) from breaking down an uncertain event into a set of components that together, yield a compound event which has probability of occurring that is equal to that of the original.

The continuity axiom (U4) is the only utility theory axiom subject to controversy. Much of the axiom controversy focused on people's inability to visualize uncertainty effectively (Kahneman *et al.*, 1982). Several areas of research have arisen in response to the difficulty of assessing probabilities in practice.

Extrapolability of the MEU action axiom

The argument here is that the MEU action can be extrapolated to any decision problem which can be represented by a set of well-defined variables (controllable as well as uncertain), by an explicit set of dependence relations between these variables and by a comprehensive utility function. One practical limitation of decision-theoretic calculations is the amount of computation inherent in the methodology. With only rare exceptions, probabilistic descriptions grow exponentially with the number of variables in a problem. As we shall see in Chapter 7 one way to reduce the computational burden is to introduce domain-specific knowledge into the methodology in return for a loss of generality.

Extensive professional experience using decision analysis provides powerful reasons to believe that algorithms based on MEU can be used to solve complex real decision problems (Matheson 1970; Howard 1980, 1983, 1988).

Comparing risky alternatives
Let us imagine that the management of the XYZ company accepts the axioms, let us see how it can take into account its preference for risk and revise the solution to its problem. Let us take two extreme outcomes such as $1,000,000 and $-500,000 and let us suppose that, after an interview with the management, we have established the following equivalents shown in Figure 3.6.

We can now replace the end branches by a lottery between $1,000,000 and $-500,000. For example, the immediate launching of the new product has the equivalent shown in Figure 3.7. The immediate abandonment has the equivalent shown in Figure 3.8. and this seems preferable. The reader can check that the market test leads to the lottery (as shown in Figure 3.9). This is still slightly less satisfactory than immediate abandonment. These answers translate the risk behavior of the company facing certain lotteries. We could

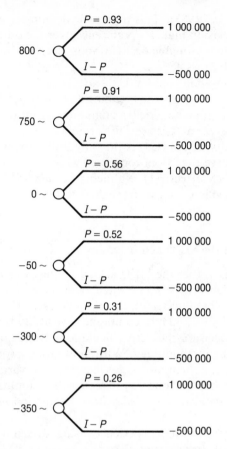

Figure 3.6   The certain equivalents for the management of the XYZ company.

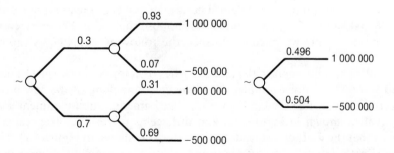

Figure 3.7   Replacing the direct launching alternative.

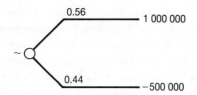

Figure 3.8   Replacing the direct abandon by a lottery.

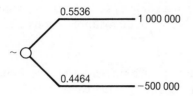

Figure 3.9   Replacing the market test alternative by a lottery.

have asked other questions and plotted the probability, p of the lottery as a function of its certain equivalent x.

We shall denote utility $u(y)$ as the probability p corresponding to a monetary value y. The utility of a lottery will be obtained by computing the weighted mean of utilities of each outcome and the certain equivalent is the monetary value corresponding to this mean utility:

$$u(y_{CE}) = \Sigma\, p_i\, u(y_i)$$

with y_{CE} = certain equivalent

$\quad y_i \quad$ = ith outcome

$\quad p_i \quad$ = probability to obtain the ith outcome.

Implication of the utility theory and use of a utility curve

There are at least three ways to use a utility curve: as a descriptive tool, as a forecasting tool, or as a normative tool. The points obtained when plotting the answers that an individual gives to a series of choices among various lotteries show both the risk behavior and the coherence of the risk behavior. If the points are on a straight line it will imply a general indifference towards risk, a strong curvature indicates an aversion toward risk.

On the contrary, a convex curve will denote the behavior of a player for whom the certain equivalent of a lottery is always greater than its expected value. It is very rare to see a company showing a convex curve. Dispersion of points around a mean curve shows a variability in the decision maker's preference.

We know that for an individual who accepts the five axioms the utility curve must be an increasing monotonous function of monetary outcomes. A person (or a company), having established his or her mean utility curve will be able to delegate his or her decision making power or analyse risks systematically by using just this curve. However, it is common to observe that once this curve is established it turns out to be a normative instrument. The decision maker will reduce the dispersion in this cluster of points answer so as to conform better to the axioms of the theory. Then he or she will try to reduce irregularities in the shape of the curve. From time to time even, he or she will be willing to accept new axioms which will reduce the utility curves to a limited number of reasonable classes of curves. As an example, the following additivity axiom is used in many applications:

Additivity axiom
If all prizes in the lottery are increased by the same amount Δ, then the certain equivalent of the lottery is increased by Δ.

This additional axiom seems quite reasonable, since no matter which prize in the lottery is won, an additional amount of Δ will be won, therefore, the new lottery should be worth more than the original lottery. The counter argument is that having an amount Δ available whatever happens, changes the wealth of the decision maker, and, as a consequence, his or her risk aversion. This axiom is very powerful since it reduces the possible utility curves to exponential functions of the form:

$$u(x) = (1 - e^{-cx})/c$$

Where c is a coefficient called the risk aversion. Figure 3.10 represents three utility functions of the exponential family for positive, null or negative values of the c coefficient, that is, for a risk averse, an indifferent to risk, or a risk-prone person. To understand the meaning of the coefficient, we can note that:

- the asymptote to the utility curve is given for $1/c$ on the utility axis, that is, no profit (no loss) can go beyond the utility of $1/c$ for such a decision maker

- the certain equivalent of a profit distribution following a normal law with mean m and standard error σ is:

$$Ec = m - 1/2c \; \sigma^2$$

We can point out here that any utility function is such that $u^1(x) = au(x) + b$ is equivalent to $u(x)$.

The reader is referred to Howard (1968) and Spetzler (1968) for a more detailed analysis of properties of utility curves and for an example of utility curves used by a company as an element of its policy.

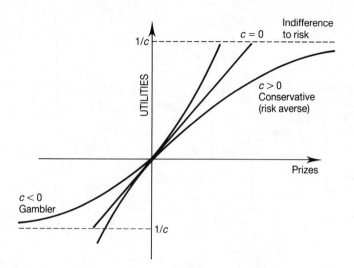

Figure 3.10   Three utility functions of the exponential family.

Stochastic dominance

A utility curve gives an answer to any problem of choice between lotteries, and enables us to compute, for each one, a certain equivalent. However, many problems of choice between lotteries can be solved more simply if circumstances are favorable. For example, we have to choose between the two lotteries $L1$ and $L2$ that are described in Table 3.3

Let us draw the cumulative distribution of the outcomes of the two lotteries that is, the function $F(x)$ = probability for the outcome to be less or equal to x, this is shown in Figure 3.11. As can be seen, the cumulative distribution of lottery $L1$ (solid line) is always below and on the right of $L2$ (dashed line). This means that for any sum x the probability to obtain this outcome with lottery $L2$ is superior or equal to the corresponding probability for $L1$. We say that there is stochastic dominance of lottery $L2$ over lottery $L1$. In these conditions, whatever the user's utility curve he or she will have to prefer lottery $L2$ to lottery $L1$. Let us emphasize the point that this type of

Table 3.3   Outcomes and probabilities for two lotteries.

| | *Probabilites* | |
Outcomes (dollars)	L1	L2
−50	0.25	0.20
0	0.40	0.45
100	0.25	0.20
200	0.10	0.15

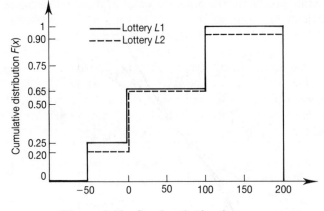

Figure 3.11 Stochastic dominance.

dominance is not absolute but stochastic; it is always possible to win 200 when playing $L1$ or lose 50 when playing $L2$.

Value of information

We shall now introduce a new concept called 'value of information' using the XYZ company case. We shall do this by analysing the value of the information given by the market test, its origin and its limits. First, let us assume that the market test is made in the hope that it will reassure the management. However, due to time constraints it is decided, in advance, to launch the product anyway. The expected value of the project is then:

$$\$318,750 \,(0.32) - \$105,880 \,(0.68) = \$30,000$$

exactly what could have been expected 'a priori' (which is obvious since):

$$[800,000 \,(18/32) - 300,000 \,(14/32)] \,(0.32) + [800,000 \,(12/68) - 300,000 \,(56/68)] \,(0.68)$$
$$= 800,000 \,(0.18 + 0.12) - 300,000 \,(0.14 + 0.56)$$
$$= 800,000 \,(0.3) - 300,000 \,(0.7)$$
$$= 30$$

A piece of information which is not capable of modifying a decision has always a *null value* in the framework of a decision problem. It is also possible to verify that the value of our market test: $\$102,000 - \$30,000 = \$72,000$ is exactly equal to the probable loss that we avoid by abandoning the project (in opposition to the 'a priori' decision) if the market test is unfavorable $= -105,880 \,(0.68) = \$72,000$. It is this Expected Value of Information (EVI) which, compared to its cost (here $\$50,000$), enables the decision maker to decide if it is worthwhile to acquire it or not.

In certain problems, the expected value of a given kind of information can be difficult or costly to compute. In this case, it is useful to use the concept of Expected Value of Perfect Information (EVPI). This quantity is rather easy to compute, and gives a superior limit to the cost of information. In our example, a perfect market test would produce the exact answer to the question: is the market good or bad? (that is, $R1$ or $R2$). With a probability of 0.3 the answer will be 'good', and the project will have a value of $800,000. With a probability of 0.7 the answer will be 'bad', and the project will be abandoned (value 0) the expected value of such a perfect information is:

$$\text{EVPI} = 800,000\,(0.3) + 0\,(0.7) - [800,000\,(0.3) - 300,000\,(0.7)]$$
$$= 210,000$$

No market test, however good it might be, should be undertaken for a cost above this amount.

3.3.4 Risk preference and conflicting objectives

So far we have seen how to construct a calculus for evaluating decision options when the decision maker has conflicting objectives and no uncertainty, or a single objective but considerable uncertainty.

Real decision problems usually involve both. For example, in the problem of choosing which car to buy, it is clear that the characteristics of the cars are uncertain. We shall only really know the cost of maintenance of the car once we have bought it!

If we have to choose vacation destination, we would include more attributes than just the cost of accommodation.

Most problems, which may at first sight appear to be single attributed, may turn out to be better formulated as multi-attribute problems.

All finance courses teach criteria for choice of investment such as net present value, internal rate of return and so on. When studying a new investment, a manager will search to estimate the cash outflows (initial investment, costs and so on) and cash inflows (sales of the product and so on) associated with the investment. Apparently, the outcomes can be measured in monetary terms, so the method of discounting cash flow to obtain a single attribute such as net present value seems appropriate.

It is true that this approach is often a sensible one in commercial organizations, but sometimes it will be useful to use other criteria as well, such as market share or company image, which will be better expressed as separated variables, rather than attempting to give a monetary equivalent for them at the beginning of the analysis. Thus, uncertainty and conflicting attributes need to be handled at the same time. It is possible to extend the single-attribute utility theory, developed in the last section, to the multi-attribute case.

The main difficulty of this approach is its practicability. While there are non-trivial problems in determining satisfactory single-attribute utility functions, these problems are magnified when dealing with multiple attributes.

Part of the power of decision analysis lies in the replacement of complex judgmental tasks by simple ones. Several approaches have been suggested for coping with this difficulty and we will describe two of them in the next sections.

Keeney's approach

The idea initially described by Keeney (1969) in his thesis and in Keeney and Raiffa (1976) is that the assessment of a multi-attribute utility function would be much simplified if it could be written as a simple function of single-attribute utility functions. Then it would be possible to assess the single-attribute functions without reference to the other attributes and, as a consequence, reduce the complexity of the utility assessment task to manageable proportions.

An additive form of the multi-attribute function is the most simple structure which comes to mind. The conditions that would justify using the additive form were a subject of active research for some time, and Keeney has given the conditions for a multi-attribute utility function to have a simple form which is slightly more general than the additive one but which gives additivity in a special case. The conditions stated by Keeney are the following:

- preference independence (see Section 3.3.1)
- utility independence.

An attribute X is said to be utility independent of other attributes Y, Z and so on, if the decision maker's preference between lotteries on X do not depend on the actual level of the other attributes.

Much work was done on this approach for the multi-attribute problem over the last ten years, and there have been many reports of its use on practical problems. (See Kirkwood, 1982 or Bell, 1979a as just two among many examples.) The number of practitioners of decision analysis using these applications has however remained small, and some significant criticisms of this approach can be made. In particular, to carry it out properly, considerable time and effort is required, both from the analyst and from the decision-maker, and in many contexts this is not available (we shall see in Chapter 13 that the development of intelligent DSS may help solve this problem). Another criticism is that some practitioners determine multi-attribute values by asking gambling questions to assess alternatives in situations where there is no uncertainty.

The Stanford approach

The application of decision analysis has a different flavor in different schools of practice. The problem of constructing multi-attribute utility functions which properly reflect risk preference occurs whenever decision theory is applied to a practical problem. Yet it appears that the Stanford school, in which the key figure has been R.A. Howard, has not perceived the need to follow the procedures of Keeney's approach. The procedures followed by the Stanford school are best explained in a series of papers published by Howard *et al.*, 1983.

As a conclusion, we see that there is a theoretically sound definition for the utility of multi-attribute consequences which may be used in the maximization of expected utility. It is difficult to assess this directly, however, and various approaches exist to assist a decision maker in indirect assessment. The approach adopted may be more or less sophisticated, and the analyst will need to exercise judgment, as in many other parts of decision analysis, on the proper balance between accuracy and the resources available (time and money) to solve the problem.

Other normative approaches

The methods which have been presented above are based on what many individuals consider to be reasonable behavioral postulates. These postulates being the preference judgments that the axiomatic development of decision analysis requires. This means that many people consider this framework as a sensible one to adopt when confronting uncertainty and conflicting objectives. Many applications satisfy this requirement. However, this approach is not the only normative one. The other most well-known normative methodologies are: the cost-benefit analysis, and the multi-criterion decision making methods.

Cost-benefit analysis

This technique is a special case of the search for a multi-attribute value function. This method was mainly used for the evaluation of social projects. In the method, all factors of importance are identified, outcomes are measured and a price is determined for each factor, and all the resulting costs are added up. In so doing, an additive multi-attribute value function is constructed. Prices may be interpreted as weight, and the net cost is simply a weighted sum.

The main difference with what we have seen above is that if cost-benefit analysis is used then *society as a whole* will be better off as a result of undertaking the project, in the preceding section we were studying the behavior of an *individual* decision maker. In fact, cost benefit analysis was developed as a tool for the analysis of social desirability of public projects.

However, some writers consider that the method can be criticized in the way that it handles equity and the assumption of additivity (see Fischoff, 1981).

Multi-criteria decision making
The origin of the ideas behind this method can be found in Zeleny's (1982) work. The idea is to use mathematical programming and, in particular, linear programming to solve the multi-criteria problem. The method is usually suited to problems where there is a continuum of options rather than a set of discrete alternatives.

The most important contribution seems to be interactive multi-criterial programming. As we have seen in Section 3.3.1 in applying multi-attribute value theory to a problem, it is necessary to compute weights before the value function can be used. Some people believe that this can be done effectively only when facing real decision options and not hypothetical situations. The interactive versions of multi-criteria programming software are not subject to this criticism since they enable the decision maker to interactively explore the set of good options. In such software, once several conflicting objectives have been presented as (usually linear) objective functions, the interactive system will explore the Pareto optimal boundary, allowing the direction of search to be specified at each stage by the decision maker who is using the system.

Outranking ('surclassement')

This methodology was mainly developed by B. Roy (1973) at the University of Paris-Dauphine and by Philippe Vincke from the University of Brussels.

A good survey of these methods can be found in Roy and Vincke (1981, 1984) and in Brans *et al.* (1986). The method assumes that a well-defined set of alternatives exists, and that each alternative can be unambiguously defined in terms of a set of attributes with respect to which each option can be measured. The method supposes that a weight w_i can be attached to the *i*th attribute.

3.3.5 Influence diagrams

This section introduces the concept of influence diagrams and gives a brief description of them. To conduct a decision analysis, we need an effective means of representing decision problems. A formal representation of a decision problem is a task that reflect someone's perception of the world.

The best known representation language for decision problems is the decision tree. As we have seen in Section 3.3.3 the decision tree representation requires that each decision and each uncertain variable must be made explicit. Also, the end nodes of a decision tree give the value of each of the possible outcomes. However, there are several known drawbacks to using decision trees as a representation language for decision problems:

- They do not allow independence relations to be exploited (as a consequence, they lead the decision maker to describe highly symmetrical structures).

- They grow exponentially with problem size and, as a consequence, can only be used to represent very small problems.

- They lead the decision maker to think in a forward direction about the decision at hand.

Influence diagrams (Howard and Matheson, 1981) have significant theoretical and practical advantages over decision trees (Owen, 1978; Olmsted, 1982). Figure 3.12 (from Holtzman, 1989) gives a comparison between a decision tree and an equivalent influence diagram. The aleatory (uncertain) variables A and B are independent. The distribution of the outcome of B does not depend on the outcome of A – this is not apparent from the tree

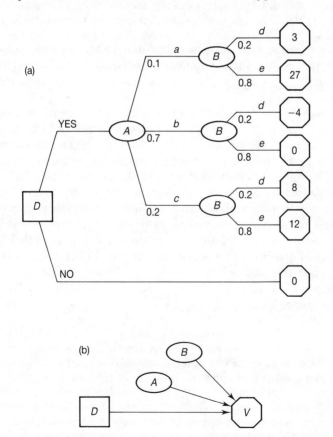

Figure 3.12 Company decision trees and influence diagrams. (a) Sample decision tree. (b) Equivalent influence diagram. (Reproduced from Holtzman S. (1989). *Intelligent Decision Systems*. Addison-Wesley)

structure. It is necessary to examine the numerical distribution to discover the independence. Figure 3.12(b) is much simpler than the decision tree shown in Figure 3.12(a). The absence of an arrow between chance nodes A and B in Figure 3.12(b) indicates, explicitly, their (conditional) independence.

We find in influence diagrams two types of nodes: *decision* and *chance* and two types of arrows *conditioning* and *informational* and typically (although not necessarily) a single sink node of type chance.

'The acyclic, singly connected nature of influence diagrams implies that sets such as predecessors, successors, direct (or immediate) predecessors, and direct (or immediate) successors of a node are defined in the usual manner. Furthermore, for an influence diagram to represent a decision problem for a single decision-maker who does not intentionally forget information (known as the no-forgetting condition), the set of decision nodes in the diagram must be fully ordered, and the direct predecessors of any decision must be direct predecessors of all subsequent decisions.' (Holtzman, 1989)

The decision nodes, in an influence diagram closely resemble those in decision trees, they denote variables under the decision maker's control. Chance nodes usually represented by a circle (or oval), denote probabilistic variables.

Arrows in an influence diagram have a different meaning to the branches in a decision tree. *Conditioning arrows* are always directed towards a chance node and denote probabilist dependence. The aleatory variable represented by a chance node is modeled as being probabilistically dependent on the variables (decision or aleatory) represented by its set of direct predecessors. *Informational arrows*, however, are always directed toward a decision node and denote available information. A decision is assumed to be made using knowledge of the outcomes of its direct predecessors. Furthermore, the no-forgetting condition mentioned above implies that the direct predecessor of a decision that is itself a predecessor (direct or not) of another decision, must also be direct predecessors of the latter decision. In an influence diagram, informational arrows imply a chronological order, where as conditioning ones do not.

'An influence diagram can represent a decision problem completely, not just in terms of its structure. A full description of a decision problem requires that the diagram contain at least one decision node influencing a value node and that consistent, detailed specifications exist for each node in the diagram. For decision nodes, the set of possible outcomes corresponds to the set of decision alternatives; for chance nodes, this set of outcomes corresponds to the sample space of the variable being represented. Furthermore, for chance nodes, a detailed description should also include a probability measure over the set of possible outcomes. An important, yet subtle, fact about probabilistic specifications of chance nodes is that they must be consistent with the set of direct predecessors of the node and their respective outcomes. In addition to containing a list of its direct predecessors (or successors), a node's description should include its name and a label for each of its possible outcomes. Furthermore, because influence diagrams are likely to be implemented in a computer-based environment, it is useful to include a short statement describing each variable being represented.' (Holtzman, 1989)

Manipulating and evaluating influence diagrams

As shown by Olmsted (1982) once a Well-Formed Influence Diagram (WFID) has been defined, we can manipulate it by performing four key elementary operations: reversing an influence, merging two nodes, splitting a node and removing a node and still preserving the state of information embodied in the original WFID.

'Operations that preserve this state of information are very useful, particularly when the WFID includes at least one decision node directly or indirectly influencing a value node; such a diagram is referred to as a **well-formed decision influence diagram (WFDID)**. Since WFDID fully define decision problem in the language of decision theory, the diagram logically entails a recommendation for action.' (Holtzman, 1989)

Goal-directed generation of influence diagrams

The generation of an influence diagram should be viewed as an attempt to represent formally real decision in a progressive manner. As the development proceeds, the diagram will become an increasingly accurate statement about the decision maker's perception of reality. An important feature of the progressive nature of influence diagram generation is that the structural aspect of the diagram is often generated first. Once the structure is reasonably stable, the diagram is defined further in more detail. Using Holtzman's terminology a node which has been fully specified is called an **assessed** node and a node not fully specified is an **unassessed** node. An unassessed node is assessable if the decision maker feels that an actual assessment of a corresponding probability distribution is obtainable with reasonable effort.

'If an outcome space and, in the case of a chance node, an unconditional probability distribution are specified, then the node is said to be directly assessed. It is also possible for a node to be indirectly assessed if, instead of directly specifying an outcome space (and for a chance node, an unconditional probability distribution), a conditional assessment function is given that maps every possible combination of outcomes of its set of direct predecessor variables to a unique outcome space (and for a chance node, a corresponding conditional probability measure) for the node.' (Holtzman, 1989)

An important case of indirect assessment occurs when the assessment function is deterministic. Deterministic assessment functions map sets of direct predecessor values to outcome spaces with a single element that bears the full mass of the associated probability measure (that is, it occurs with unit probability).

We consider the conceptual tool called the influence diagram as one of the most helpful for extracting information in a technically useful form. We shall discuss, in Chapter 13, recent research on delivering this methodology with intelligent software. We must now describe the way to implement the decision analysis methodology. This process is called the decision analysis cycle.

3.3.6 The decision analysis cycle

Our objective in this section is to present the process of applying analysis. We shall use and follow very closely the original presentation made by Howard and Matheson in 1968, which is, in our opinion, the best introduction for managers. The more mathematically-inclined reader is referred to Howard's (1968) paper *Foundation of Decision Analysis*. Decision analysis as a procedure for analysing a decision is described in Figure 3.13. This procedure is a means of ensuring that the essential steps have been consciously considered.

The procedure is iterative and comprises three phases. The first is the **deterministic phase**, during this phase 'the variables affecting the decision are defined and related, values are assigned, and the importance of the variables is measured without any consideration of uncertainty'. (Howard and Matheson, 1968)

During the second, or **probabilistic phase**, the decision analyst introduces probability assignments on the important variables and derives asso-

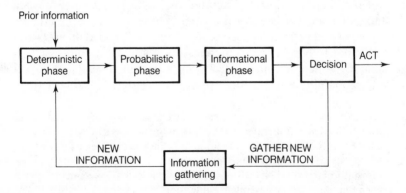

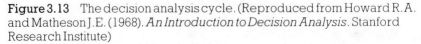

Figure 3.13   The decision analysis cycle. (Reproduced from Howard R.A. and Matheson J.E. (1968). *An Introduction to Decision Analysis*. Stanford Research Institute)

ciated probability assignments on values. This phase also introduces the assignment of risk preference, which provides the solution to take into account uncertainty.

The third, or **informational phase**, 'reviews the result of the last two phases to determine the economic value of eliminating uncertainty in each of the important variables in the problem' (Howard and Matheson, 1968). The third phase is very important because it shows just what it would cost in dollars not to have *perfect information*, a concept which we introduced in Section 3.3.3.

A comparison of the value of information with its costs determines whether additional information should be collected. This is, as we have seen, a very important methodological result because it gives a manager who is facing a decision a guideline on two fundamental questions:

(1) Is it useful to gather additional information?

(2) What is the maximum amount of money I should spend in order to acquire this information?

> 'If there are (profitable) further sources of information, then the decision should be to gather information rather than to make the primary decision at this time. Thereupon will follow the design and execution of the information gathering program, whether it be a market survey, a laboratory test or a military field trial.' (Howard and Matheson, 1968)

The information that results from this program may change the model and the probability assignments on important variables.

> 'Therefore, the original three phases must be performed once more. However, the additive work required to incorporate the modifications should be slight and the evaluation rapid. At the decision point, it may again be profitable to gather new information and repeat the cycle or it may be more advisable to act. Eventually the value of new analysis and information gathering will be less than its costs and the decision to act will then be made.' (Howard and Matheson, 1968)

The deterministic phase

The deterministic phase usually starts with a systematic analysis of the problem. Within this phase, we can distinguish efforts devoted to modeling from efforts devoted to analysis.

Modeling

> 'Modeling is the process of representing the various relationships of the problem in formal, mathematical terms. The first step in modeling is to **bound the decision**, to specify precisely just **what decision must be made**. This requires listing in detail the perceived alternatives. Identification of the alternatives will separate an actual decision problem from a worry.' (Howard and Matheson, 1968)

The next step: finding **new alternatives**, is the most creative part of decision analysis.

'New alternatives can spring from radically new concepts; more often they may be careful combinations of existing alternatives. Discovering new alternatives can never make the problem less attractive to the decision maker; it can only enhance it or leave it unchanged.' (Howard and Matheson, 1968)

Often, the difficulty of a decision problem disappears when a new alternative is generated. Then the decision maker must specify the various *outcomes* that the set of alternatives could produce. These outcomes are the subsequent events that will determine the ultimate desirability of the whole issue. In an investment (a new product introduction, for example) the outcomes might be specified by sales levels and cost of production, or even more simply by yearly profits, computed from the forecasted income statement of the product.

One of the most challenging processes is the selection of the **system variables** for the analysis. System variables are all those variables on which the outcome depends. One could start by having only outcome variables as system variables, but most of the time it is difficult to think directly in terms of outcome variables. In Chapter 7, we described a deterministic model FINSIM that is used to generate financial alternatives for a company. An example of outcome variables a financial manager would consider each year for a given horizon can be:

- the profit level or a measure of return, such as return on assets;
- the debt/equity ratio or another measure of risk.

The direct estimate of these outcomes is difficult. Most of the time it is easier to use other system variables such as level of sales, the growth rate of sales, level of expenses, ratio of expenses to sales, inventory level, ratio of inventory to sales and so on, to compute the profit and the debt/equity ratio.

'The selection of system variables is a process of successive refinement, wherein the generation of new system variables is curtailed by considering the importance of the problem and the contribution of the variables.' (Howard and Matheson, 1968)

Once the selection of system variables is done, the next step is the classification of these variables into *decision* variables and *state* (or environmental) variables. A decision variable is a variable which is under the control of the decision maker, and the selection of an alternative in a decision problem can be defined as the specification of the setting of the decision variables. A state variable is a variable determined by the environment of the problem. Although state variables may have a very important effect on the outcomes, they are autonomous and beyond the control of the decision maker. For example, in the forecast of the sales of a software product marketed by a software company, the increase in the number of computers on which the software products runs, and the number of competitor's software and their associated marketing expenses are state variables.

'The next step (of the modeling process) is to specify the relationships among the system variables. This is the heart of the modeling process, that is, the creation of a structural model that captures the essential interdependances of the problem. This model should be expressed in the language of logical mathematics – typically, by a set of equations relating the system variables.' (Howard and Matheson, 1968)

The decision maker will want to assign values to system variables. In general he or she has a *nominal value* and a *range* of values that the variable may take on. In the case of state variables, the nominal value and range reflects the uncertainty assigned to the variables.

'For convenience, we often think of the nominal value of a state variable as its expected value, in the mathematical sense, and of the range as the 10th percentile and 90th percentile points of the probability distribution.' (Howard and Matheson, 1968)

An important methodological point is that, at this stage, it is better to include a variable that will later prove to be unimportant than to eliminate a variable prematurely. For most decisions of professional interest, the equations will be used to create a computer program that represents the model. It is interesting to note here the importance of defining a *deterministic decision model* as the first step of the decision analysis.

The next step for the decision maker is, as we have seen in Section 3.3.1, to assign *utility values* to the outcomes. (This distinction between utility of an outcome and the outcome itself is fundamental in decision analysis.)

The final step in the deterministic model is to specify the **time preference** of the decision maker. Howard and Matheson are thus using the classical theory of value to relate interest (discount) rate and present value. The market value today of x dollars delivered in period n is called the net 'present value' or worth of the deferred payment.

$$NPV = \frac{x}{(1 + r)^n}$$

where r is the interest (discount) rate. The important point here is that, according to decision analysis, we need a mechanism for describing the time preference of the decision maker, a mechanism that reduces any time stream of money to a single number called worth (NPV).

In the deterministic model the state variables are called S_i and the decision variables d_i. The state variables can be visualized as a set of knobs, the value of which is set by nature. The decision variables are set by the

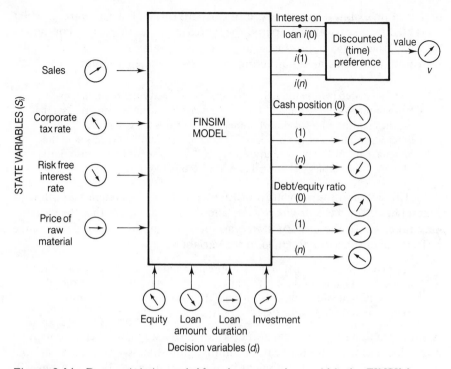

Figure 3.14   Deterministic model for a long-term loan within the FINSIM model.

decision maker (each configuration of these knobs constitutes an alternative). For example, in the case of the FINSIM model (see Chapter 7) used by a credit analyst to decide if a loan will or will not be granted to a company (see Figure 3.14), the state variables (S_i) could be the value, over the lending period of the loan, of the activity level of the company (sales of goods, sales of services and so on), the risk free interest rate, the income tax rate and so on. The decision variables (d_i) are the characteristics of the loan: the loan amount, duration, repayment schedule, interest level and so on. The *outcome* variables are the self-financing capacity of the company to repay the loan (something like the future stream of profit plus depreciation), the flow of interest paid to the bank, the debt to equity ratio at the end of each period (a global measure of risk for the banker), the cash position of the company at the end of each period and so on.

The values developed over time by the model (for example, a stream of interest or profits) are transformed by the time preference function to produce a present value (or worth) v, which is displayed on a present value meter.

Analysis
The analysis which is performed on a deterministic model has several goals:

- To refine the formulation of the problem.
- To generate alternatives and compute criteria for evaluation (values of outcomes) transformed by preference over time, that is, worth.

The analysis is based on the observation of changes in worth due to changes in variables. This type of analysis is well known under the name of **sensitivity analysis**.

The first type of sensitivity analysis is performed on decision variables. The decision maker sets the state variables at their nominal value and then allows one of the decision variables to move in its assigned range and observes how its worth changes. If a particular decision variable has a major effect, then the decision maker knows he or she was correct in including it in the original formulation. On the contrary, if a decision variable has little or no effect, the decision maker is justified in removing it as a decision variable.

The second type of sensitivity analysis is performed on state variables, which are considered to be uncertain by the decision maker, and over which he or she has no control. All other system variables being at their nominal value, the change in worth is observed while sweeping one state variable over its range. If a state variable has a major effect, then the uncertainty in the variable deserves special attention. Such variables are called **aleatory variables**. However, if varying a state variable over its range produces only a minor change in worth, then that variable might well be fixed at its nominal value. The state variable has become a fixated variable.

> 'A state variable may become fixated either because it has an important
> influence on the worth per unit of its range, but an extremely small range,
> or because it has little influence on the worth per unit of its range, even
> though it has a broad range.' (Howard and Matheson, 1968)

There is no reason to conclude that a fixated variable is unimportant in an absolute sense. The corporate tax rate, for example, can be regarded as a fixated variable because the decision maker has no reason to believe it will change over the time period that is considered. Yet, it is possible that a change in government policy could lead to a large change in this variable, which would transform a favorable venture into an unfavorable one.

One difficult problem is raised by *simultaneous* changes in state variables, since the possibility of jointly changing state variables grows rapidly with the number of state variables.

We can suggest how this methodology can by used in the case of a long-term loan decision that is made by the loan officer in a bank. Our hypothesis here is that the loan is issued to the company in order to increase its production capacity. We shall use the FINSIM model (see Chapter 7) but we shall not describe in detail all of the system variables which are represented by that model.

The basic idea of the model is that it should support the decision process of the loan officer by helping him or her to compute the future values of the variable such as: the cash position, over the duration of the loan, of the company that is asking for a loan (*cash t*), the discounted amount of interest paid by the company to the bank for the duration of the loan, the debt equity ratio and so on. The cash position can be computed utilizing a uses and sources of funds statement which gives the cash flow for the period.

The decision for the loan officer is whether he or she should grant a loan or not: in other words, should the investment be financed or not. In fact, the number of alternatives can be much larger if we wish to consider different types of loans, we shall, for the sake of simplification, consider here only one type. The alternatives facing the loan officer can be generated using the FINSIM model. If the loan is granted, the state variables have to be fixed in accordance with this alternative (in particular, the value of the sales variable and of expense variables have to be coherent with the investment which, in our case, is expected to increase the sales). The decision variables are fixed at their nominal amount. The model will then be used to compute the outcomes of interest for the decision maker which are:

- The interest revenue (flow of interest) received by the bank over the duration of the loan.
- The cash position of the company at the end of each period.
- The debt/equity ratio of the company at the end of each period.

The interest revenue will be discounted using a time preference model since it is an important decision criteria for the loan officer. The bank should earn a return for the loan which is higher than the return the bank would receive from an investment in a risk-free asset (government bonds, for example). The cash position of the company is a fundamental outcome. The credit officer wants to check that this variable is positive over the duration of the loan. If it is not, then there is a risk of the company defaulting in its payments. Other important outcomes for the loan officer are the level of debt to equity ratio, if he or she wishes to make a global measure of risk and, also, a 'quick' ratio if he or she wishes to make a short-term measure of risk. The loan officer may not want the debt/equity ratio to go beyond a certain limit, since beyond that limit there is an increase in global risk which he or she may not want to take. The loan officer can now perform a sensitivity analysis. He or she can consider that the estimates of the sales projections, which have been given to him by the company, to be the best known estimates, and the value of the three main outcomes can be completed: the discounted flow of interest, the cash position over the duration of the loan, the global debt/equity rates. The loan can then be granted if the following decision rules hold:

- The discounted value of interest revenue should be positive.

- The cash position should be positive at the end of each period.
- The debt/equity ratio should be below one over the duration of the loan.

If the loan officer is uncertain about the values of the sales estimates, it will be easy to make sensitivity analyses on the sales growth rate given the investment that is to be undertaken. If the above criteria are fulfilled, and the sales growth rate goes down to 10% instead of the 20% which was expected by the company, as a first hypothesis, and the loan officer has good reason to consider that a growth rate of less than 10% has a probability of almost nil, then the decision is, clearly, to make the loan. In the case where one of the outcomes does not fulfill the conditions fixed in the decision rules when the sensitivity analysis is performed on sales growth rate, then a conclusion cannot be reached without going to the next phase, which is the probabilistic phase.

The probabilistic phase

The purpose of the deterministic sensitivity analysis on the state variables is to divide them into aleatory and fixated classes. The probabilistic phase determines the uncertainty in value and worth due to the aleatory variables.

Modeling probability distribution

'The first modeling step in the probabilistic phase is the assignment of probability distributions to the aleatory (stochastic) variables. Either the decision-maker or someone that he or she designates must assign the probability that each aleatory variable will exceed any given value. If any set of aleatory variables is dependent, in the sense that knowledge of one would provide information about the others, then the probability assignment on any one variable must be conditional on the value of the others.' (Howard and Matheson, 1968)

Analysis

Since the deterministic model gives the relation between worth and the state variables, and since we have assigned probability distributions to aleatory variables, it is possible to compute the probability distribution of worth for any setting of the decision variables. This probability distribution is called the 'worth lottery'.

'The worth lottery describes the uncertainty in worth that results from the probability assignments to the aleatory variables for any given alternative (setting of decision variables). Of course the values of the fixated variables are never changed.' (Howard and Matheson, 1968)

To select a course of action, the analyst will generate a worth lottery for each alternative and then select the one that is the more desirable.

Modeling risk preference

If stochastic dominance has not determined the best alternative, the decision analyst must formalize the risk preference of the decision maker. Decision methodology will then request that we encode the risk preference. Decision analysis uses, at this point, the theory of cardinal utility which we have outlined in Section 3.3.3.

The risk preference of the decision maker can be represented as a utility curve as shown on Figure 3.10. This curve assigns a utility to any value of worth. As we have seen, the utility curve provides a practical method of incorporating risk preference into the model. When faced with a choice between two alternatives whose worth lotteries do not exhibit stochastic dominance, the analyst computes the expected utility of each and chooses the one with the highest expected utility. By using the utility curve, the analyst can see what worth corresponds to this expected utility. This quantity is called the 'certain equivalent worth of the worth lottery'. The name 'certain equivalent' comes from the idea that the certain equivalent worth of any lottery is the amount of worth received for certain, so that the decision maker is indifferent between receiving this worth or participating in the lottery (see Figure 3.5). The best alternative is the one whose lottery has the highest certain equivalent worth (see the MEU action axiom in Section 3.3.3.).

Analysis

The first step is to compute the certain equivalent worth of each of the alternatives. Then the alternative with the highest certain equivalent worth is selected. In fact, Howard and Matheson (1968) point out that a careful analyst would not stop there, but would perform sensitivity analysis on:

- decision variables,
- aleatory (stochastic) variables,
- risk.

By setting all of the decision variables but one at their nominal values, and then sweeping this one decision variable through its range, the analyst may find that although this variation changes the worth lottery it does not significantly change the certain equivalent worth. Then the decision variable would be fixed at its nominal value.

Aleatory variables receive the same sensitivity analysis by setting one of the aleatory variables to a trial value within its range, and the other aleatory variables have the appropriate conditional joint probability distribution when all decision variables are set to their nominal value. The model will then give a certain equivalent worth for the trial value. By sweeping the trial value of the stochastic variable over its range the analyst can observe the change in the certain equivalent worth. If this change is small, there is evidence that this aleatory variable can be changed to a fixated variable. This procedure is called measurement of **stochastic sensitivity**. According to Howard and

Matheson (1968) the decision to remove variables from aleatory status on the basis of deterministic sensitivity might be reviewed by measurement of stochastic sensitivity. He also points out that it is possible to test sensitivity of many variables simultaneously. Measurement of stochastic sensitivity appears in the methodology as a powerful tool for locating important variables of a problem and, as a consequence, as a method to focus attention and to validate the model.

The last kind of sensitivity analysis available at this point of analysis of the problem is **risk sensitivity**. As we have seen in Section 3.3.3 it is possible to characterize the utility curve by a single number: which is called the risk aversion constant. When this is possible, the risk aversion constant measures the willingness of the decision maker to accept risk.

If two people share the responsibility for a decision, the less risk tolerant will assign a lower certainty equivalent worth for any given worth lottery than the other will.

> 'The measurement of risk sensitivity determines how the certainty equivalent worths of the most favorable alternative depends on the risk aversion constant.' (Howard and Matheson, 1968)

An example of application of the analysis methodology to the FINSIM case is given in Figure 3.15. The environmental variables are: sales growth rate, risk free interest rate, raw material price. The decision variables are: the equity financing the amount of the loan, the duration of the loan, the interest rate and the amount of the investment. A distribution of the environmental variable is encoded by the decision maker. FINSIM will then produce distributions for the decision variables: interest on loan, cash position, debt/equity ratio.

As can be seen, the best alternative in the problem in derived from the combination of:

- the problem structure,
- the set of alternatives generated,
- the probability assignments to aleatory variables,
- the value assessments,
- the time preference assessment,
- the risk preference.

The overall procedure is presented in Figure 3.16 (from Howard and Matheson, 1968)

Informational phase

The goal of this phase is to help the decision maker decide if it is worthwhile to engage in a possibly expensive information gathering activity before making a decision. One possible result of this experimental design procedure is the decision to perform no experiment at all.

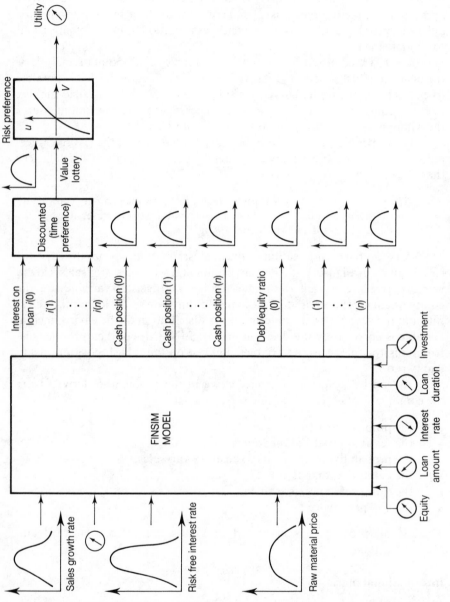

Figure 3.15 The FINSIM model (probabilistic phase).

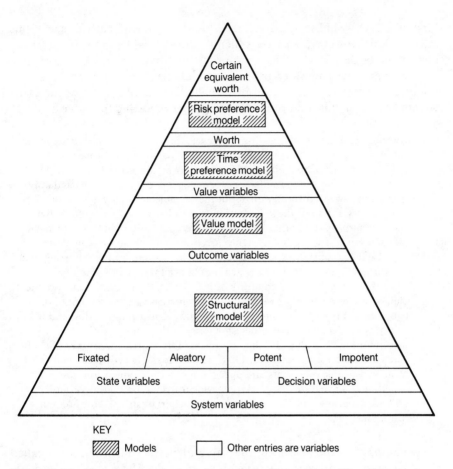

Figure 3.16   The decision analysis hierarchy. (Reproduced from Howard R.A. and Matheson J.E. (1968). *An Introduction to Decision Analysis*. Stanford Research Institute)

Analysis

The fundamental idea in the information phase is that of placing a monetary value on additional information. The concept used here is the idea of perfect information which Howard and Matheson (1968) call 'clairvoyance'. The decision analyst assumes that he can get from a 'clairvoyant' the value of a given aleatory variable. The question is: how much should be paid in order to get this information? To answer this question, recall that the discussion of stochastic sensitivity described how to compute the certain equivalent worth given that an aleatory variable took on a value say, s in this case. In that procedure, the decision variables were set equal to their best values from the probabilistic phase. Suppose now that we engage the clairvoyant at a cost k, and then he or she tells us that the aleatory variable will take on the value s.

First of all, we would set the decision variables to take best advantage of this information. However, since the other aleatory variables are still uncertain, they would be described by the appropriate distributions, given the available information. The computer program would then determine the expected utility of the entire decision problem including the payment to the clairvoyant, which are all conditional on him or her reporting the value of s.

> 'Before engaging the clairvoyant, however, the probability to be assigned to the clairvoyant reporting s as the value of the particular aleatory variable is described by the probability distribution showing the current state of knowledge about this variable. Consequently, we obtain the expected utility of purchasing this information about the variable at a cost k by multiplying the expected utility of the information (given that s and k are reported) by the current probability that he or she will report s, and then summing over all values of s. The analyst uses the current probability in this calculation because if the clairvoyant is reliable, the chance of him or her reporting that the variable falls in any range is just the chance that it will fall in that range.
>
> Knowing the expected utility of purchasing the information from the clairvoyant at a cost of k, we can gradually increase k from zero until the expected utility of purchasing the information is just equal to the expected utility of proceeding with the decision without the clairvoyant's information. The value of k that establishes this equivalence is the value of clairvoyance on the aleatory variable. The value of clairvoyance on an aleatory variable represents an upper bound on the payment for any experimental program designed to provide information on this variable, for no such program could be worth more than clairvoyance.' (Howard and Matheson, 1968)

The process of measuring the value of perfect information is called the measurement of **economic sensitivity**. Clearly, if an aleatory variable exhibits high economic sensitivity, it is a good candidate for an information gathering program. Information gathering programs seldom provide perfect information, so we should not use them for the value of perfect information. An experimental program will provide only a new probability distribution for the aleatory variable under study. In the FINSIM case, it may turn out that the cash position is very sensitive to the price of raw material, or to the sales growth rate, in which case the loan analyst can decide to see if he or she can obtain information to improve his or her knowledge of the probability distribution of these two variables.

> 'The analyst would then determine the best decision, given this new information, and compute the expected utility of the decision problem. He would next multiply the expected utility by the probability that the experimental program would come out in this way and sum over all possible outcomes of the experimental program. The result would be the expected utility of the experimental program at a given cost. The cost that would make the expected utility just equal to the expected utility of the problem

without the experimental program would be the value of the experimental program. If the value is positive, it represents the maximum that one should pay for the program. If the value is negative, it means that the experimental program is expected to be unprofitable. Consequently, even though it would provide useful information, it would not be conducted.'

(Howard and Matheson, 1968)

Modeling

At this stage, the decision maker and the decision analyst must identify the relevant information gathering alternatives, from survey to laboratory experiment, and find which, if any, are expected to make a profitable contribution to the decision problem.

It is important in considering alternatives for information gathering to take into account the negative effect of delay in making the primary decision. In the FINSIM case, if the banker is an investment banker and is studying whether or not he or she should take a partnership in the company, he or she may want to perform a market study in order to check how the new product that he or she might finance is going to perform. But by doing this time may be lost and the probability of competing products improving their market share will increase.

When the preferred information gathering program is performed, it will lead, at least, to new probability assignments on the aleatory variables; it might also result in the structure of the model being changed. Still studying the FINSIM case, it may turn out that sales cannot be analysed properly unless they are broken down by main lines of product, which will mean that the analyst must include new variables.

When all of the changes implied by the information program have been incorporated into the model, the deterministic and probabilistic phases are repeated to check sensitivity. So the decision analyst inserts loops in the process and, at some point, the cost of gathering further information will be more than its worth and the alternative which currently has the highest certain equivalent worth should be selected.

3.4 DSS for supporting the normative point of view

3.4.1 Decision tree compilers

Decision analysts have developed several systems to automate part of the decision analysis process. The first such software were decision tree 'compilers' such as SUPERTREE® (Olmsted, 1982; McNamee and Celona, 1987), ARBRE© (Pezier and Klein, 1973). Then software systems to support the task of defining, checking and evaluating influence diagrams were developed (Korsan and Matheson, 1978; Merckhofer and Leof, 1981) and

Holtzman (1989). We shall see in Chapter 7 that the methodology of decision analysis can take advantage of recent developments in the field of expert systems to give birth to a new kind of decision support environment, including a better support of the normative point of view. This point will be expanded in Chapter 13.

3.4.2 Interactive influence diagram formulation

Holtzman (1989) describes a development environment for 'goal-directed generation' of an influence diagram. The influence diagram is considered as an evolving model whose progress reflects changes in how the decision maker perceives the world. Two tendencies are always present in this process, on the one hand the decision maker wishes to *expand* the diagram in order to increase the accuracy and comprehensiveness of the representation that embodies. On the other hand, the decision maker wishes to *reduce* the diagram to make it more intuitively appealing and more computationally manageable. The other functions must be able to:

- **check** the diagram for mathematical correctness as the development effort proceeds;
- **evaluate** the influence diagram as it progresses.

Once a formal decision model has been defined, and an evaluation algorithm is available, it is possible to compute a strategy. As seen in Section 3.1.3 such a strategy needs to be appraised (that is, interpreted in terms of reality). To appraise a strategy we need to ask two types of questions about the features of the model and about how the model was developed. As we have seen important features of the model are: sensitivity to model variables, profit lotteries and value of information measurement on its uncertain variables. Holtzman calls obtaining information about these features 'mining the model'.

The question about how the model was developed is related to the reasoning that led to the specific model being used. In order to develop an intuitive understanding of a model's recommendation, a decision maker needs to *justify* that model.

'Justifying a model differs from mining it in that the desired information is extralogical (that is, not contained within the model itself). The information needed to justify a model lies primarily in the methodological decisions and trade-offs made to construct it and in the theory (if any) that underlies the methodology.' (Holtzman, 1989)

The development environment proposed by Holtzman to promote the construction of a valid decision model consists of an interactive composition of six tasks: expansion, reduction, checking, evaluation, missing and justification. Holtzman stresses the point that no rigid order should be imposed on applying these tasks within the formulation process.

3.5 The relevance of the normative point of view in DSS

A very strong argument in favor of the normative point of view is that it gives the decision maker a methodology: that is, a series of steps to follow, as a guide, to reaching a decision. This methodology is very useful at the *conceptual* level but also as a guide in *designing* computerized decision support systems. Outcome variables, value functions, value variables, time preference functions, worth (utility of money, present value of money), risk preference functions (utility function) and certain equivalent are all important concepts. The decision analysis cycle is a very fundamental process to guide the decision maker from the certainty model to the probabilistic one, as well as to guide him or her in the methodology of preference and knowledge encoding.

The central concept of the decision methodology maybe is the concept of a decision maker maximizing his or her Subjective Expected Utility (the SEU theory). The major intellectual achievement of the SEU theory is that it provides a formally axiomatized statement of what it means for an individual to behave in a consistent, rational manner.

With respect to the design of a computerized decision support environment it is clear that the environment should provide:

- A language to structure a problem in the form of a deterministic model.
- A language to make different sensitivity analyses on the variables of the model.
- The possibility to convert deterministic variables into probabilistic ones (to move from a deterministic to a probabilistic model).
- The possibility to perform probability calculus (Bayes's theorem).
- A language to structure a problem in the form of a decision tree or, even better, an influence diagram.
- Software to encode risk and time preference for multi-attribute functions.
- Software to encode knowledge on variables (probability elicitation).

3.6 Normative theories for group decision making

Attempts have been made to apply decision theory to organizations. As we have seen, the decision methodology requires that the decision maker expresses a preference order on alternatives and encode his or her knowledge in the form of probabilities. When dealing with organizations and, as a consequence with groups, it is much more difficult to define what the group preferences are. The immediate answer is the method of majority voting. Unfortunately, the majority rule does not lead to a clear-cut group preference as shown originally by the French mathematician Condorcet (1785).

If we consider a group of three people, Michael, Frances and Emma, and they all wish to go on vacation together, there are three alternatives: to go to the mountains (m), to the seaside (s) or on a cruise (c). Their preferences can be displayed as:

Michael	m > s > c
Frances	s > c > m
Emma	c > m > s

If a decision is taken by a vote we can have the following results: Frances and Emma vote in favor of a cruise over a holiday in the mountains, Michael and Frances vote to choose between the seaside and a cruise, and they are two to one in favor of the seaside. Michael, who is not very pleased with this result, suggests that a vote should be made in order to choose between the seaside and the mountains.

The vote on this last alternative results in a majority for the mountains, which were ruled out at first. Thus, by using majority voting the group prefers the mountains to the seaside, the seaside to a cruise but also a cruise to the mountains.

This result, known as the 'Condorcet paradox' shows that if each member of a group displays consistent views, it is perfectly possible for the decisions of the group to be inconsistent. In the above case, majority voting leads to a non-transitive set of preferences.

Since majority voting is not a satisfactory method for determining group preference, it is natural to ask 'what method is satisfactory then?'. This question was studied by Arrow (1951) and the answer came in an astonishing theorem known as 'Arrow's impossibility theorem': there is no satisfactory method.

Arrow established four reasonable conditions that he felt would be fulfilled by a procedure for determining a group's preferences between a set of options, as a function of the preferences of the group members. Arrow's conditions can be stated as follows:†

(1)   Whatever the preferences of the group members, the method must produce a group preference order for the options being compared.

(2)   If every member of the group prefers option *A* to option *B*, then the group must also prefer *A* to *B*.

† (Reproduced from *Social Choice and Individual Values* by Arrow K.J. © 1951, reprinted by permission of John Wiley & Sons, Inc.)

(3)   The group choice between two options, *A* and *B*, depends only on the preferences of the group members between *A* and *B*, and not on their preferences between *A* and *B* and any other option.

(4)   There is no dictator; no individual always gets his way.

Arrow proved that there is no aggregation procedure which satisfies these four conditions. It should be noted, however, that Arrow's result is concerned with the combination of preference orders, and does not use the intensity of preferences of individuals nor interpersonal comparisons of utility. The interested reader can consult Harsanyi (1977) for an in depth treatment of interpersonal comparisons of intensity of preference into account.

As a conclusion we can say that there is still no satisfactory quantitative method for determining group preferences by some mathematical operation on the expressed preferences of individuals.

3.7 Criticism of the normative point of view

As we have seen in the preceding sections, the body of prescriptive knowledge about decision making is well developed. This chapter is a summary of the main concepts and the associated methodology, but anybody who has had a look through the literature on this subject is likely to be impressed by the quality and generality of the concepts and methods associated with decision analysis.

If we start looking for applications of this decision methodology we find interesting cases, such as the ones described by Howard *et al.* (1983) for strategic management decisions, by Tribus (1969) for engineering decisions and by Holtzman for medical decisions and so on, but it would be difficult to argue that the methodology is in widespread use in organizations, nearly twenty years after it was worked out. There are several reasons why this situation has arisen:

(1)   The concepts are not easy to grasp and to put to work.

(2)   There is no adequate low-cost support software to help implement the methodology.

(3)   The concepts themselves are not consistent with reality.

3.7.1 Refinement and complexity of the concepts of decision analysis

The decision maker who is willing to use decision analysis must have mastered the following concepts:

- Model building (the relation between system variables and outcomes).
- Transforming outcomes into values.
- Subjective and objective probability distribution (simple and marginal).
- Updating prior probability with new information (Bayes's theorem).
- Preference function (for risk and time).
- The concept of a lottery to encode risk preference.

It is clear that such a methodology is not for people who have difficulty in formalizing things! A good understanding of the difference between outcome and value, of the Bayes's theorem and so on, implies that the decision maker has some education and an ability to think in abstract terms. We have to recognize that these concepts are well known by the immense majority of decision makers, even after they have been introduced in the curriculum of many graduate Business Schools.

3.7.2 Inexistence of low-cost support software to implement the methodology.

We have seen in Section 3.5 that the implementation of the decision analysis methodology requires computer programs. There have been several attempts to market software, such as decision tree compilers. However, this software has been rather expensive and has only sold in limited numbers. It is interesting to note that we have seen, with the personal computer, a wide distribution of simple decision support software, mainly used for deterministic modeling (such as the spreadsheet, or DSS development tools), but there is no wide distribution of decision analysis software, the only exception maybe of multi-criteria methods. We shall see in Chapters 7 and 13 that these attempts may be developed further in the near future.

3.7.3 Pertinence of the theory

The descriptive view of decision making (Chapter 2) demonstrates that people solve problems by 'selective, heuristic search through large problem spaces and large data bases, using means-ends analysis as a principal technique for guiding the search' Simon et al., 1987. In other words, the empirical research puts the emphasis on the limit of human rationality.

> 'These limits are imposed by the complexity of the world in which we live, the incompleteness and inadequacy of human knowledge, the inconsistency of individual preference and belief, the conflicts of value among people and group of people, and the inadequacy of the computation we can run out.'
> Simon et al., 1987

On the other hand, the normative view assumes that:

> 'A decision maker possessed a utility function (an ordering by preference among all the possible outcomes of choice), that all the alternatives among which choice could be made were known, and that the consequences of choosing each alternative could be ascertained (or, in the version of the theory that treats of choice under uncertainty, it assumed that a subjective or objective probability distribution of consequences was associated with each alternative).'   (Simon *et al.*, 1987).

3.7.4 Limits of rationality

One limit is the computational complexity. The decision analysis methodology makes a high demand on information, even if the influence diagram concept has improved the situation.

In the FINSIM model, we must compute the consequences for each alternative. These consequences are variables associated with a probability distribution. We have to transform these probability distributions (value lotteries) into utilities. We have then, in the case of a multi-attribute decision problem, to convert the utilities into a single number through a multi-attribute utility function. Also, we have in such a model, several exogenous variables which may not be completely independent, which require a marginal assessment of probability to be computed. To perform the complete cycle of formal decision analysis is a formidable task that most people cannot accomplish due to lack of computation power, or more likely, lack of time.

3.7.5 Limited rationality in economic theory

Empirical studies which we have described in Chapter 2 point out that managers are trying to achieve the firm's market share in the industry, rather than trying to maximize profit. New work is being done which still assumes that decision makers seek to maximize utility, but within limits imposed by the incompleteness and uncertainty of the information available to them. In other words, decision makers are seeking to reach specified aspiration levels (satisficing) for goals instead of maximizing them. Empirical studies also seem to point out that economic agents do not follow assumptions made in the decision methodology theory (see Section 2.5). For example, decision makers tend to overact to new information in violation of Bayes's rule. The same idea is conveyed by recent studies which tend to demonstrate that stock prices fluctuate up and down more rapidly and violently than they would if the market were purely rational.

However, we should be careful to acknowledge that a promoter of decision analysis would argue that his or her main task is not just to clarify a decision as a function of the decision maker's criteria and preferences, but also to guide him or her towards more rigorous thinking. In other words, if empirical studies point out that decision makers are not coherent in certain situations, it does not mean that they should not be helped to become conscious of these incoherences in the hope that they will change their mind.

3.7.6 Time constraints

Time is involved in decision making in many ways. Usually through the time preference of a decision maker. However, the subjective expected utility theory assumes a fixed and consistent utility function. It is known that preference changes with time (see Section 2.1). The answer of the decision analyst should be fairly easy: nothing prevents him or her from updating the risk aversion parameter, for example, as it changes with time.

A much more difficult problem arises when decisions have to be taken within time constraints. In such cases, it may not be possible to go through the complete decision analysis cycle. The decision maker may need rules which will help very bad outcomes to be avoided or help him or her to reach a level which he or she considers satisfactory but which is far from maximizing the expected utility. We shall see, in Chapter 7, how such an approach can be implemented.

3.7.7 The ethical point of view

We would like here to point out that there are two families of answers to the question of what the most reasonable course of action is.

- One family is made of theories about **rationality**.
- The other is made of **moral or ethical** theories.

The problem is that when we apply these two classes of theories to some given decisions, we often have different answers (we all know that a sound economic decision may be a moral disaster), so we must decide which is the best theory.

Three main factors are usually considered in order to determine how we look at human conduct from the moral or ethical point of view. The first factor is that we are not alone, but we live in a society and, as a consequence, are confronted by other people who have their own aims and goals, as we do. The second factor is that we live in a world of scarcity. Theft and waste do not matter if there is no limit to the goods available. The third factor is inequality. Even if the division of goods and services was made with perfect equality, in a few days trade, bargaining and different rates of consumption and waste will produce inequality. The problem is to make certain that the unequal distribution of goods and services is not unfair. Equal opportunity to gain advantages is, therefore, a natural provision that must be sought and built into the principle that governs ethical decision making.

The characteristic of a person who looks at his or her life from the moral point of view is that he or she regards him or herself as morally responsible, a creature who is responsible for their actions. Two extreme types of moral behavior can be observed. The first is the nihilist who abdicates all responsibilities on the grounds that nothing matters – we are all in the hands of Fate or God and we have no control over anything, not even our own conduct. Such a person cannot perform any ethical decision making (nor any rational decision making). The other extreme type is the bureaucrat, who dodges responsibility, wherever possible, by acting so that someone else determines how he or she acts and also determines the reasoning for his or her behavior.

The basic problem for ethical decision making is to ensure fair treatment of all concerned, given the fact that there is an irreducible plurality of independent persons to be considered with distinctive and occasionally conflicting and competing interest and rights, situated in a world between extreme scarcity (in which no one's needs could be satisfied) and unlimited resources (in which everyone's whims could be satisfied). So, when a person makes a decision on the grounds of ethics it means that ethical principles are used, and that had he or she not relied on such ethical principles the reason for deciding upon something different would have been due to some other principle such as business efficiency, self interest and so on.

One example of such ethical principle is the following: 'everything possible must be done to avoid causing the innocent to suffer even in a just cause.'

One important question is clearly the objectivity to ethics. 'Are some ethical judgments true and others false?' Most ethical philosophers deny the fact that ethical judgment is a matter of personal preference, opinion or test. They are more likely to claim that ethical decision making can be a rational and objective discipline. This assumption is very important since, if this assumption is not granted, then ethical decision making becomes impossible, or arbitrary, or it turns into something else, such as self interest. The interest in ethics as a discipline is derived from the assumption that not all moral principles and ethical judgments are equally sound.

One very interesting point for us is the following. It seems that people who follow their self interest can be led to contradiction. We would like to refer, here, to the work of philosophers such as Derek Parfit. In his book *Reasons and Persons* (1968) Parfit defines the self interest theory, or *S*, in the following way:

S: for each person, there is one supremely rational ultimate aim: that life goes for him or her as well as possible.

As can be noticed, the S theory is about rationality. Then Parfit introduces the self defeating idea. This idea is that a theory which fails, even in its own terms, and thus condemns itself, is self defeating. Parfit shows that some of the best-known self interest theories are, in certain ways, self defeating.

Exercises

3.1   What does it mean to be rational?

3.2   What methodology is useful for utilizing formal decision methods?

3.3   What are the reasons for studying formal decision methods when designing DSS?

3.4   What are the validity conditions of a formal decision method?

3.5   What is the role of an 'action axiom' in a formal decision method?

3.6   Frances has a job decision to take. She has been offered four jobs. The criteria she is considering are: starting salary, promotion opportunity, location and interest of the job. She is following a course in decision analysis and has structured her decision with the criteria, values and weights shown in Table 3.4

   (a)   Assuming that all pairs of criteria are preference independent of the other criteria, which job maximizes Frances's value function?

   (b)   If Frances changes her weight for the criteria so that starting salary has a weight of 0.2 and promotion opportunity a weight of 0.4, does the job with the highest value change?

   (c)   Do either of these results change if job C is removed from the list?

Table 3.4   Table of criteria, values and weights for a job decision.

Job	Starting salary	Promotion opportunity	Location	Interest of the job
A	100	0	20	60
B	65	100	0	40
C	30	65	100	0
D	0	25	75	100
Weights	0.4	0.2	0.1	0.3

3.7 Select a decision problem of concern to you, such as the choice of a job, or of a vacation destination, and apply the method of multi-attribute analysis to help you think through it (from Watson and Buede).

3.8 We have two bags containing red and blue marbles. One bag contains 70 red marbles and 30 blue marbles, the other bag contains 70 blue marbles and 30 red ones. You select, at random, one bag (it is not possible to distinguish their content) and you pick 12 marbles (putting them back each time), eight red marbles and four blue marbles are picked.

What is the probability for this bag to be the one with 70 red marbles and 30 blue ones? (direct application of the Bayes's theorem).

3.9 In the new cosmetic product case should we consider the proposal made by a market research company who are offering to conduct a more thorough market study: at a cost of $100,000?

$$p(I_1/R_1) = 0.8$$
$$p(I_2/R_2) = 0.9$$

Study the sensitivity of the strategy to change in the 'a priori' probability to obtain a good market.

3.10 Show that the additivity axiom implies the use of an exponential utility curve.

4

Artificial Intelligence

4.1 What is artificial intelligence?

There is no precise and universally accepted answer to the question of what Artificial Intelligence (AI) is. Some people look at AI as the effort made in order to make computers 'think'. Using artificial intelligence we can make machines that have minds. The basic idea is that thinking and computing are the same. After all, they are both performed by symbol manipulation systems (see Chapter 2), whether by men or computers. On the other hand, we find a direction within AI which is concerned with designing computer programs that can imitate human beings, thus creating computer programs that can solve problems that we normally think of as requiring human intelligence.

In both cases, artificial intelligence is more about the abstract principles of symbol manipulation than about computer technology. One way of studying these basic principles is by using tools and techniques from that part of computer science which is concerned with:

> 'designing intelligent computer systems, that is, systems that exhibit the
> characteristics we associate with intelligence in human behavior –
> understanding language, learning, reasoning, solving problems, and so on.'
> (Barr, 1981)

However, a grand interdisciplinary field emerges among AI, psychology, philosophy, and linguistics which is called **cognitive science**. In this sense AI is a branch of cognitive science.

Although, AI has been an active field for almost 30 years, researchers have no idea, as yet, how to create computer programs to be as intelligent as

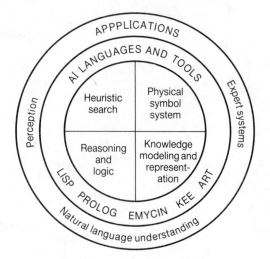

Figure 4.1   The field of artificial intelligence.

the human mind in terms of recalling facts, reasoning, learning, under-standing and so on. However, even if we have not been successful in creating programs that perform all of the tasks that can be associated with intelligent behavior, some progress has been made. In particular, expert systems tech-nology is a major breakthrough in the application of artificial intelligence techniques to solve real world problems.

At the centre of the research into artificial intelligence lies the work carried out by Allan Newell and Herbert Simon at the Carnegie-Mellon University. In 1975 in their Turing Award Lecture, they emphasized two basic concepts that are necessary for intelligent behavior: symbols and search. They were concerned with a physical symbol system that manipu-lated collections of symbolic structures, and that could perform problem solving tasks using heuristic search. They stated the hypothesis that a physical symbol system has the necessary and sufficient means for general intelligent actions (Newell and Simon, 1976). The concept of a physical symbol system is the basis of the belief that it is possible to build computer programs that can perform intelligent tasks.

> 'The importance of the physical symbol system is twofold. It is a significant theory of the nature of human intelligence and so is of great interest to psychologists. It also forms the basis of the belief that it is possible to build computer programs that can perform intelligent tasks now performed by people.' (Rich, 1983, p. 5)

An overview of AI is depicted in Figure 4.1. The inner core consists of the basic theory, methods and techniques. The subject of this chapter is a further treatment of heuristic search, reasoning, and knowledge representation. In the intermediate layer, we find the special languages and tools developed in order to implement AI methods and techniques on computers.

Although it is possible to write any computer program in any language, the field of artificial intelligence has developed its own languages and tools to deal more efficiently with some of the special features of symbolic processing. The two general purpose programming languages in extensive use today are LISP and PROLOG.

LISP is, by far, the most commonly used language to program AI applications. It was developed in the late 1950s (McCarthy, 1960). LISP stands for LIST Processing language. It is a symbol processing language, particularly designed for processing symbolic expressions, for instance, sentences in a natural language. The symbolic expressions are represented as lists which can be linked to each other. Thus, lists can be nested, one within another. To open up nested lists LISP uses **recursion** as a control structure. Both data and programs are represented as lists.

There are only a few basic LISP functions, all other LISP functions are defined in terms of these basic functions.

LISP is no longer a single, unique programming language, due to the ability to easily create new LISP functions from the basic ones. Today, LISP is a generic name for a family of languages (dialects), including MacLISP, FranzLISP, and INTERLISP. Recently, there have been several moves to standardize LISP for commercial purposes. An attempt in this direction is Common LISP.

In Figure 4.2(a) one of the rules used in BANKER is shown in a LISP syntax.

PROLOG stands for PROgramming in LOGic. It is a programming language based on a simplified predicate calculus and is, therefore, a true logical language. It was first developed in France in 1972. But the first really efficient compiler was developed at the University of Edinburgh. PROLOG has enjoyed great popularity in Europe, and, more recently, in the USA. One reason for the recent international popularity can probably be ascribed to the fact that PROLOG has been chosen as the basic programming language in the Japanese fifth generation project for their 'Knowledge Information Processor System', a computer particularly designed for symbolic processing.

PROLOG's control structure is based on *logical deductions*. From a given set of facts PROLOG is able to deduce new facts. One of the most important features of PROLOG is the declarative programming style that is used. Unlike all of the other main computer languages which are procedural, in the sense that the programmer specifies a sequence of steps that must be accomplished by the computer in order to achieve a task, a PROLOG programmer describes the task as a sequence of constraints (given as facts) that must be satisfied. In PROLOG one specifies the *what* and the computer determines the *how*. A small example of a PROLOG program is shown in Figure 4.2(b).

More specialized AI tools also exist. These are, however, closer to a

RULE019

(a) This rule is tried in order to find out how profitable the loan applicant is for the bank.

　　If: (1) The profitability for the bank of the loan applicant is unknown.
　　　　(2) A: The final credit rating of the loan applicant is 1, or
　　　　　　 B: The final credit rating of the loan applicant is 2, and
　　　　(3) The bank is built by 1 by the loan applicant
　　Then: There is suggestive evidence (0.7) that the profitability for the bank of the loan applicant is 1

　　PREMISE:　($and　(NOTKNOWN CNTXT S3)
　　　　　　　　　　　($OR　(SAME CNTXT S1 1)
　　　　　　　　　　　　　　(SAME CNTXT S1 2))
　　　　　　　　　　　(SAME CNTXT S2 1))
　　ACTION:　(CONCLUDE CNTXT S3 1 TALLY 700)

(b)　　Parent(x,y)←Father(x,y).
　　　　Parent(x,y)←Mother(x,y).
　　　　Grandparent(x,z)←Parent(x,y) , Parent(y,z).
　　　　Ancestor(x,z)←Parent(x,z).
　　　　Ancestor(x,z)←Ancestor(x,y) , Ancestor(y,z).
　　　　Sibling(x,y)←Mother(m,x) , Mother(m,y).
　　　　　　　　　　Father(f,x) , Father(f,y).
　　　　Cousin(x,y)←Parent(u,x) , Parent(v,y) , Sibling(u,v).

　　　　Father(Albert,,Jeffrey).
　　　　Mother(Alice,Jeffrey).
　　　　Father(Albert,George).
　　　　Mother(Alice,George).
　　　　Father(John,Mary).
　　　　Mother(Sue,Mary).
　　　　Father(George,Cindy).
　　　　Mother(Mary,Cindy).
　　　　Father(George,Victor).
　　　　Mother(Mary,Victor).

　　　　←Ancestor(x,Cindy) , Sibling(x,,Jeffrey).

Figure 4.2　(a) LISP code of a rule in BANKER. (b) A PROLOG program.

specific application area. We shall deal with special tools for building expert systems in Chapter 6.

　　In the outer layer of Figure 4.1 the major application areas of AI are described. Applications of AI can be dealt with in terms of three broad areas: natural language understanding, robotics, and problem solving using particular expert systems.

(1)　*Natural language understanding* is concerned with developing computer programs that can understand natural languages like English. This is a very complex encoding and decoding problem, given the contextual knowledge required to understand spoken and written sentences.

(2)   *Robotics* is concerned with the problem of controlling physical actions. This area has contributed to the development of several AI techniques, such as, modeling the states of the world and generating plans. A related area to robotics is perception.

(3)   The last broad area of AI application is *expert systems*. Expert systems are computer programs that use knowledge in a particular problem domain to solve problems that are normally carried out by human experts. Expert systems employ basic AI methodology for knowledge representation, reasoning and control strategies. Since expert systems are a major theme of this book we shall deal with these concepts and their applications in much more detail in Chapter 6.

The rest of this chapter will be devoted to the basic AI methods and techniques employed in expert systems. We shall start with a simple example of a search problem to develop the basic architecture of expert systems, known as the production system. Next, we will deal, in turn, with problem solving by heuristic search, knowledge representation and reasoning.

4.2 Production systems

4.2.1 The water jug problem

Many AI applications involve composing a sequence of operations. A simple example of this sort, and one that is useful for illustrating some basic ideas, is the water jug problem.

In this problem there is a four gallon jug and a three gallon jug; neither has any measuring markers on it. There is a pump that can be used to fill the jugs with water. Consider the problem of getting exactly two gallons of water in the four gallon jug. A solution to the problem is an appropriate sequence of moves (actions), such as fill the four gallon jug, empty the three gallon jug and so on.

The first task is to find a problem representation that is appropriate for applying a problem solving technique. Usually, there are several ways of representing a problem. Selecting a good representation is, as we have mentioned in the previous chapter, an important part of the problem solving task. In the water jug problem, the content of the two jugs at any given time is a problem **state**. If we call the content of the four gallon jug x and the content of the three gallon jug y, a problem state can be represented by an ordered pair (x, y). The set of all ordered pairs is the **space** of problem states, also called the **state-space** of the problem.

$$\text{state-space:} \left\{ (x, y) \,\middle|\, \begin{array}{l} x = 0, 1, 2, 3, 4 \\ y = 0, 1, 2, 3 \end{array} \right\}$$

Once the state-space has been defined, one must find a data structure to describe the states, for instance, vectors, sets, arrays, lists and so on. Within the state-space two states are given by the problem statement: (1) the initial state (0, 0), and (2) the goal state (2, y) where y can be any permissible number since the contents of the three gallon jug are irrelevant in the goal state.

A move transforms one state into another state. A move is determined by an operator. What are the operators that determine the set of legal moves in our state-space? Below we have defined these operators:

(1)   Fill the four gallon jug

(2)   Fill the three gallon jug

(3)   Empty the four gallon jug

(4)   Empty the three gallon jug

(5)   Pour water from three gallon jug into four gallon jug until the four gallon jug is full.

(6)   Pour water from four gallon jug into the three gallon jug until the three gallon jug is full.

(7)   Pour all the water from the three gallon jug into the four gallon jug.

(8)   Pour all the water from the four gallon jug into the three gallon jug.

Each of the operators has preconditions that must be satisfied before they can be applied. For instance, operator (1) will only be applied if there is less than four gallons in the four gallon jug. The preconditions, as we can see, are expressed in terms of permissible states at which one particular operator may be applied. If we add the preconditions to operator (1) it looks like this:

> **If** there is less than four gallons in the four gallon jug
> **Then** fill the four gallon jug

When the preconditions are added to the operators, the moves are modeled by production rules. Executing a production rule implies moving from one state to another in the state-space. Therefore, we may express the preconditions as state descriptions and the action part as a conclusion, that is, a description of the state arrived at after having executed the action part. In a more formalized manner, *rule* (1) looks like this:

> IF $(x, y \mid x < 4)$
> THEN $(4, y)$

The formalized set of production rules that generate legal moves in the water jug problem is listed below.

(R1) IF $(x, y \mid x < 4)$ THEN $(4, y)$

(R2) IF $(x, y \mid y < 3)$ THEN $(x, 3)$

(R3) IF $(x, y \mid x > 0)$ THEN $(0, y)$

(R4) IF $(x, y \mid y > 0)$ THEN $(x, 0)$

(R5) IF $(x, y \mid x + y \geqslant 4 \wedge y > 0 \wedge x < 4)$ THEN $(4, y - (4 - x))$

(R6) IF $(x, y \mid x + y \geqslant 3 \wedge x > 0 \wedge y < 3)$ THEN $(x - (3 - y), 3)$

(R7) IF $(x, y \mid x + y \leqslant 4 \wedge y > 0)$ THEN $(x + y, 0)$

(R8) IF $(x, y \mid x + y \leqslant 3 \wedge x > 0)$ THEN $(0, x + y)$

In a certain state, several production rules may be applicable. For instance, the state (4,0) satisfies the preconditions of all of the following rules: (R2), (R3), and (R6). We are then left with a problem of how to select rules from this set of applicable rules. Selecting rules and keeping track of those sequences of rules that have already been tried and the states produced by them constitute what is called the control or search strategy. The search strategy repeatedly applies rules to state descriptions until the goal state is reached. The goal state forms the basis for the termination of the problem solving task.

   In Chapter 2 we saw that problem solving can be described as a *search* for a solution with the problem space. Possible candidate states for a solution are generated by the operators and examined, one after another, by the termination test. How to generate and test candidates is part of the control system. We can apply several search strategies, which we will deal with in Section 4.3.3.

4.2.2 The architecture of production systems

A computational formalism to perform a search problem solving process is known as the **production system**. The major components of the production system are:

(1)   A global database, also known as the workspace, which contains the symbol structures chosen to represent the states of the problem space. In the water jug problem, that will be all of the ordered pairs (x, y) generated and tested, and the initial and goal state descriptions.

(2)   A set of production rules, each consisting of preconditions and actions.

(3)   A control strategy that directs the search by selecting the sequence of rules to be applied.

The production system architecture employs a three-phase **control cycle**. Here, each rule is a separate entity which can be viewed as a small process that monitors the workspace continuously and changes the content of the workspace when it is allowed to execute or 'fire' as it is also called. Execution of a rule requires a **match** between the preconditions of the rule and the content of the workspace. When a pattern of data structures in the workspace matches the preconditions the rule is said to be **applicable**. A pattern-matching facility that can recognize a pattern and modify it is a central feature of the production system. As we have seen above, one particular state of the workspace may match several rules, thus making several rules applicable. We need, therefore, a selection strategy, also called **conflict resolution**, to choose one rule for execution. Executing a rule means to apply the action part, that is, the workspace is **acted** upon and the content is changed. The new state of the workspace gives rise to new patterns and new matches, that is, rules that are eligible for execution. The three-phase control cycle; matching, conflict resolution, and action, is used in most rule-based systems. It is also called the recognize-act cycle.

The recognize-act control cycle is general. However, particular conflict resolution schemes or search strategies may be employed under the control of the general recognize-act cycle. We shall describe specific strategies in more detail in Section 4.3.3. Three things are worth noticing about the production system:

(1)   The *contents* of the workspace determine which production rules are candidates for execution. Which rule to select first is determined by the search strategy applied.

(2)   *Each* rule is an independent entity which constantly surveys the entire workspace. (In practical applications this may be modified by segmenting the workspace in order to increase search efficiency.)

(3)   A rule *activates* itself when the contents of the workspace match the conditions of the rule.

The production system is a good way to model intelligent problem solving behavior. No pre-specified procedure is necessary as in traditional programming. The behavior of the system is determined by the content of the database. Therefore, for a given rule set, alterations in the database will change the behavior of the system. Since each rule is an independent entity and all communication is via patterns in the database, new rules can easily be added to account for new situations without disturbing the rest of the system. Figure 4.3 shows the architecture of the production system as examplified by the water jug problem.

4.3 Search

4.3.1 Introduction to search

Applying the production rules in the water jug example described in the previous section, generates successively new states. Each new state generated

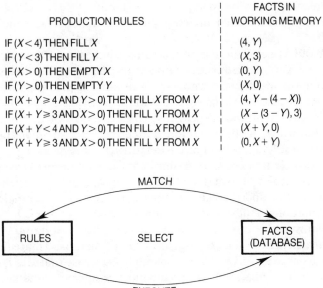

PRODUCTION RULES	FACTS IN WORKING MEMORY
IF $(X < 4)$ THEN FILL X	$(4, Y)$
IF $(Y < 3)$ THEN FILL Y	$(X, 3)$
IF $(X > 0)$ THEN EMPTY X	$(0, Y)$
IF $(Y > 0)$ THEN EMPTY Y	$(X, 0)$
IF $(X + Y \geq 4$ AND $Y > 0)$ THEN FILL X FROM Y	$(4, Y - (4 - X))$
IF $(X + Y \geq 3$ AND $X > 0)$ THEN FILL Y FROM X	$(X - (3 - Y), 3)$
IF $(X + Y < 4$ AND $Y > 0)$ THEN FILL X FROM Y	$(X + Y, 0)$
IF $(X + Y \geq 3$ AND $X > 0)$ THEN FILL Y FROM X	$(0, X + Y)$

Figure 4.3 The production system for the water jug problem.

is tested to see if it is a member of the goal state (see the generate-and-test method in Section 2.3.2.) In this process, we have no information that states that one rule is better than any of the other applicable rules. Only by systematically searching the state-space can we hope to find a solution. When we have no information about which action is better than others, or no information about the progress we are making in finding a solution to the given problem, then we are using a blind search or exhaustive search. Exhaustive search is very impractical when the number of states that must be examined is large.

At this point, we will introduce the standard terminology used in search. Problem solving by search is characterized by an *initial state*, that is, the initial situation given, and a *goal state*, a state satisfying the goal state description. The goal state may be reached by successively applying operators, a single operator transforms a state into another state, called an *intermediate state* if it is not the goal state.

We will use the term **successor** of *i* to mean a state *j* that is reachable from state *i* by a sequence of operator applications. The immediate successor of *i* is a state reached by applying one operator on *i*. The set of all states that can be reached by applying operators in sequence, starting at the initial state is called the **search space**. An exhaustive search proceeds, as we have seen, by each intermediate state generating the exhaustive set of successors. Thus, exhaustive search leads to a **combinatorial explosion**. Combinatorial explosion can be avoided, as we will see below, by having information at each state, about which of the immediate successors is most promising. The three terms: blind search, exhaustive search, and uninformed search have the same meaning and will be used interchangeably in this text depending on the context.

The objective of the search may be to find a goal state, for instance a diagnosis, or to find a sequence of operators (the path) to a goal state, as we have seen in the water jug example. In addition, the problem may be to find just any solution, or an *optimal* solution. To find an optimal solution requires an objective function. Most often we do not optimize a search problem but use heuristics to guide the search. Heuristic search is the principal problem solving technique used in artificial intelligence.

A heuristic is a 'rule of thumb' that is used in problem solving. It constitutes the rules of expertise, the rules of good practice, the judgmental rules of the field, and the rules of plausible reasoning. Heuristics apply to specific situations – they constitute domain-specific knowledge. They point in interesting directions and almost always find a solution. But unlike algorithms, heuristics carry no guarantees of success. Heuristic search is different from exhaustive or blind search in the sense that it is informed. It uses heuristic information to select the most promising candidate (operator or immediate successor) at each intermediate state. Thus, at each state, all new states generated by the applicable operators are sorted according to the heuristic information we use. This sort function is called the (heuristic) **evaluation function**. Evaluation functions will be dealt with in Section 4.3.3.

4.3.2 Search trees

A simple way to implement any search technique is as a tree traversal. In computer science, a tree is a directed graph in which one node has no predecessor, this is the **root**, and some nodes have no successors, these are the **leaves**. The arcs (links) are called **branches**. No one node can have, as its successor, a node which also can be its predecessor. Each node in the tree can be assigned a level. In AI the level number of a node is called its **depth**. The root of the tree has a depth of 0.

A **search tree** shows which paths in a state space have currently been explored. When the search begins the search tree consists of a single node, the initial state description. The search tree grows as the operators are applied to existing nodes. However, this process often leads to regenerating of nodes already in the tree, that is, that the search structure is more like a directed graph than a tree. In Figure 4.4 part of the search graph of the water jug problem is shown. When the search process regenerates a node of the tree, it has found another, new path to this node. This path can either be ignored or old paths can be substituted, and the search tree is correspondingly changed.

It is helpful to classify the nodes of a search tree as either *open* or *closed*. An open node has not yet been examined for possible expansion. A

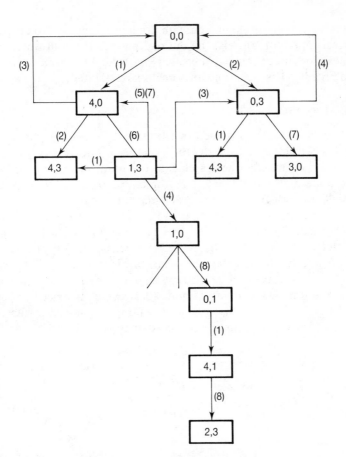

Figure 4.4   Part of the search graph of the water jug problem. ((x) denotes the rule number executed.)

closed node has already been examined. An open node is a leaf if it is the goal node or cannot be expanded otherwise. Usually it is not a leaf. All search techniques proceed by expanding open nodes. The particular search technique being used determines the order in which the open nodes will be expanded.

4.3.3 Search strategies

The fundamental problem in controlling the search procedure is how to select, from the applicable set of operators at a specific node, the operator for execution. The selection criterion is known as the **search strategy**. An important characteristic of this strategy is how much domain knowledge it uses. At one extreme is the completely uninformed search, the blind search, where no information about the problem at hand is used. At the other extreme is a strategy employing enough domain knowledge to always select the 'correct' operator, that is, the optimal path to the goal state. We shall briefly describe three search strategies, two of the uninformed type: depth-first and breadth- first, and one informed search strategy.

Depth-first search

A search which always proceeds in the parent-to-children direction until forced to backtrack is called a **depth-first** search. Backtracking is a general process which means that the search can stop in one direction, go back to a previous node and expand in a new direction. Intervening steps are disregarded. The depth-first strategy orders the open nodes in descending order of their depth in the search tree, that is, nodes on the deepest level are at the front of the list. Computationally, this can be accomplished by organizing open nodes as a **stack** data structure, that is, nodes are placed on, and removed from, the front of the queue (last in, first out).

Figure 4.5 illustrates a depth-first search carried out on the water jug problem. We start with the initial node (0, 0) which is placed on the stack called OPEN. We expand this node by executing all applicable rules, that is, R1 and R2. The expanded nodes are placed on top of the OPEN stack. At the

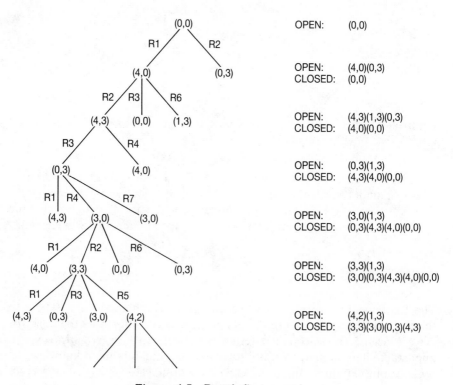

Figure 4.5   Depth-first search.

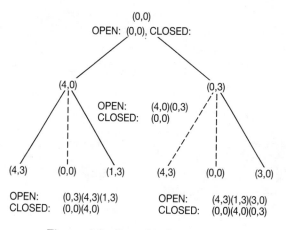

Figure 4.6 Breadth-first search.

same time, we create a list called CLOSED containing parent nodes. Using Figure 4.5 we can see how the search proceeds. Nodes already on the CLOSED list are not placed on the OPEN list to avoid recycling. There is a risk with the depth-first strategy that we may go on forever, deeper and deeper in the search tree. Therefore, we may want to set a bound on the depth in which we want to expand in one direction. This is called the **depth-bound** of the search tree. When this depth is reached, the process will backtrack and expand in a new direction.

Breadth-first search

In the second type of uninformed search, the nodes are examined level by level. This is called a **breadth-first** search. This strategy orders the open nodes in ascending order of their depth, that is, nodes on lowest level of depth are at the front of the list. Computationally, a data structure is established that organizes the open nodes as a queue: first in, first out. A breadth-first search starts with the initial node. When a node is expanded its successors are placed at the end of the queue. Figure 4.6 shows the search tree of the water jug problem using a breadth-first search.

Heuristic search

In principle, the uninformed search methods always eventually find a solution to the problem. However, in searching large problem spaces these methods may not be feasible due to the problem of combinatorial explosion. This problem poses intractable problems to programs which attempt to play games like chess in this way. Since human beings are slower than computers in enumerating and keeping track of all possible alternatives, we can safely assume that chess champions do not work this way. Rather, they apply their

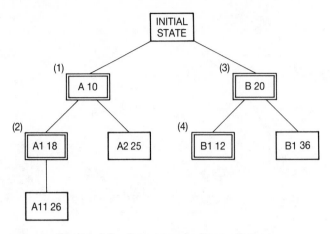

Figure 4.7   An expanded search tree.

experience to evaluate a few, but significant moves. How are these specific moves selected from all of the possible moves? A search which uses information about the current situation to traverse a search tree is called **heuristic search**. Heuristic information increases the efficiency of the search. Introducing the concept of efficiency requires a cost function to be associated with the paths searched. If we can obtain information about which of the open nodes are the most promising, we can order the nodes on the open list according to this. A function is required to estimate the cost from the current node to the goal node. Such a function is called a heuristic evaluation function.

In Figure 4.7 we have expanded a search tree. A node in the tree has an alphanumeric code which is the reference code for that node, and a number which is the value returned by the evaluation function when applied to that node. This number represents an estimated distance to the nearest goal node. Nodes with doubled boxes are those that are expanded. The sequence of expansion is signified by the number outside the box. We can see from this example that search using an evaluation function is significantly different from the uninformed search techniques we have described above.

We can organize heuristic search in two ways:

(1)   *Ordering of successors*, where we can use some heuristic information to estimate which successors look most promising. One very general evaluation function which is used in some expert systems is to expand on a node by applying the rule with the largest number of pre-conditions. One other typical search strategy is known as the A* algorithm. It orders successors according to a measure of their costs (distances) from the initial state, through the successor state and to the goal state. The A* algorithm is regarded as a basic search technique and is described in more detail below.

(2) *Constraining the generation of successors*, where the least promising children are disregarded from further search.

The A* algorithm

The A* algorithm is a heuristic search technique that employs an evaluation function, called h, that measures the cost of going from the node to the goal node. Since this function is not known with complete accuracy, an approximation denoted h^* is used. For this algorithm to work correctly, $h^*(i) < h(i)$ for any node i. The A* algorithm chooses to expand on the node which minimizes the estimated cost function from the starting node to the goal node. Thus, we need to define a new function, f^*, which is the sum of costs from the start node to node i, denoted $g(i)$, and the estimate of the cost of the path from node i to the goal ($h^*(i)$). Thus:

$$f^*(i) = g(i) + h^*(i)$$

Furthermore, we define the cost of going from one node (i) to its immediate successor (j) as $c(i, j)$. The procedure for the A* algorithm can be summarized as follows:

(1) Put the start node S on the OPEN list, set $g(S) = 0$.

(2) If the OPEN list is empty, the search terminates unsuccessfully.

(3) Select from OPEN list the node with the lowest f^*-value. Call it i. Test if the node is a goal node. If it is a goal node, then terminate the search. Otherwise, put node i on the CLOSED list.

(4) Expand node i by applying all applicable operators. If i has no successors, then go to 2.

(5) For all successors, j of i calculate:

$$f^*(j) = g(i) + c(i, j) + h^*(j)$$

Put all successors with their f^* values on the OPEN list. Go to step 2.

Notice that the A* algorithm uses, as its evaluation function, not only the cost of the remaining path from i to the goal, but takes into account how good the path to node i was. This is useful if we care about the path. However, if we are only interested in the solution we can define g to be 0, thus always choosing the node that seems closest to the goal. If we want to find the path involving the minimum number of steps, we can set g to 1.

4.3.4 Problem reduction

In the search trees we have studied so far, the nodes of the trees have represented the alternative states in which the problem may be on its way towards the goal state. In a state-space situation, branches from a node to its successors represent alternative paths. Expanding a node this way is called OR expansion. Many problems can be solved this way.

However, we often solve a problem by decomposing it into two or more subproblems. Each subproblem can, in turn, be broken down into new subproblems. When a problem is solved this way, it is called **problem reduction**. Problem reduction can also be solved by search. In this case, each node in the tree represents a subproblem and branches from a node to its successors designate simultaneous requirements, that is, *all* branches must be searched before a solution is found. In terms of logic, this is called AND expansion. The given problem is the root of the search tree. All other nodes are subproblems. A leaf of the search tree can be:

(1)   A primitive problem which can be solved.

(2)   An unsolvable or a non-decomposable problem.

(3)   A candidate node for further expansion (problem decomposition).

From mathematics we may remember that, in order to find the integral of a complicated expression, we could decompose the original expression into simpler expressions to which we could possibly find standard solutions to the integrals.

Perhaps a more typical example of a problem solved by problem reduction is the credit evaluation procedure employed in the expert system BANKER (see Section 6.6). Here, the credit evaluation problem is decomposed into a number of subproblems: (1) evaluation of management competence, (2) external credit rating, and (3) financial analysis. Some of these subproblems require further reduction: financial analysis can be broken down to a profitability and a solvency rating. Some can be solved in more that one way: for instance, profitability rating may be obtained by using company data only or by a comparison with industry ratios. We continue to break down the credit evaluation problem until a level is reached that can be handled by 'primitive' operations on known data. From this example, we have seen that the major expansion is an AND breakdown, but also that we may encounter alternative branches (OR expansion). The structure needed to represent problem reduction search is called an AND/OR tree. Notationally, the AND expansion is designated by a circular arc across the branches leading from a node to its successors. In an AND/OR tree for problem reduction an OR expansion requires only one of the OR-nodes to be satisfied for the search to proceed, while if one branch under an AND expansion fails, there is no need to explore further.

4.4 Knowledge representation

To solve the water jug problem presented in Section 4.2 we needed to make a symbolic representation of the problem. A symbolic representation of the problem requires both a representation of the contents of the jugs (the states) and of the processes that act upon the states to transform them into new states (actions). Knowledge about states and knowledge about actions occurs as two kinds: declarative and procedural. In order to manipulate a symbol system it is necessary to have knowledge of both kinds. It is like playing a game where you need knowledge about the positions (states) and of the rules of the game (legal moves or actions). **Declarative knowledge** is a description of facts. It is information about real-world objects and their properties, and the relationships among objects. **Procedural knowledge** encompasses problem solving strategies, arithmetical and inferential knowledge. Procedural knowledge manipulates declarative knowledge to arrive at new declarative knowledge. The distinction between declarative and procedural knowledge can be illustrated as follows:

(1)   The contents of the water jugs are x and y and these are facts. We can use the ordered pair (x, y) to symbolize the facts represented in one state. This is declarative knowledge.

(2)   An action which we may make is procedural knowledge, for instance:

   IF $(x < 4)$ THEN FILL x to $x = 4$

It tells us what we can do.

Many of the objects we are concerned with in the real world are composed of elements which are themselves objects. For instance, take a car which is made of components, such as an engine and a gearbox, which again are made up of components. An object, in which we are not interested in finer details, is called a **simple** object. Otherwise, we call it a **structured** object. What is defined as a simple or a structured object is dependent on the context in which it is used. For the taxation authorities a car is a simple object. For a car repair mechanic, the car is a structured object. Facts about simple objects encompass properties of these objects, and facts about structured objects include knowledge about relationships among objects (the structure).

   Knowledge representation means that knowledge is formalized in a symbolic form, that is, to find a symbolic expression that can be interpreted. In AI, we are interested in knowledge representation formalisms that can be manipulated by computer programs. In the following, we shall describe, in more detail, some formalisms developed in the AI area for representing knowledge and which are of particular interest to expert systems. It is required of a formalism that it can represent the knowledge of a domain adequately and efficiently. The representation formalisms we shall deal with are:

- property lists
- rules
- semantic nets
- frames
- logic

4.4.1 Property lists

Simple facts can be described by propositions. A proposition is the smallest unit of knowledge that can stand as a separate assertion, that is, the smallest unit about which a judgment of true or false can be made (see Section 2.2). For instance,

'The company Alpha applies for a loan of $100,000.'

A simple fact has two basic elements: identification of an **object** and a **characterization** (a property) of this object. Objects may be physical entities such as a company, or conceptual entities such as a bank loan. In formal systems it is convenient to split the property element into two: a general characteristic, called an **attribute**, such as interest rate, and a **value**, such as 0.12. Thus the common way to represent a simple fact is as an:

< Object–Attribute–Value > triplet.

In the <O–A–V> triplet the term *object* means a unique reference to (an identification of) a real-world entity. In the proposition stated above, we use the name (Alpha) as a reference to the object of interest. An object belongs to a class, a category, which is usually determined by the context. For a bank dealing with loans (where the context is loan applications), company Alpha belongs to a category called 'company loan applicants'. In a (O–A–V) representation, the proposition above can be formally written as:

<Alpha, loan application, $100,000>

Some representation formalisms allow for the description of structural properties, where, in addition to the basic formalism of <O–A–V> triplets, a context type to which this triplet belongs can be defined.

Usually, an object has several properties. In the example above all of the accounting data such as sales, net profit, debt and so on are properties, that is (attribute–value) pairs, associated with the same object, namely, the

Table 4.1   A property list.

Attributes	Values
Name	Alpha
Loan application	$100,000
Net profit	$25,000
Debts	$1,000,000

company named Alpha. A property list represents this, this is shown in Table 4.1.

   If the object to which a property belongs is obvious from the context, then we may suppress the object reference term from the <O–A–V> triplet, and we are left with (attribute–value) pairs. This representation form is more efficient, and in many cases sufficient. Take, for instance, a credit evaluation system dealing with one loan applicant at each consultation session. We do not have to make the object, that is, the loan applicant, consistently explicit during the processing of one single loan application. Therefore, it is not necessary to specify the company to which the data belong every time it is used. In PC-OPTRANS (see Chapter 5) facts are represented as (attribute–value) pairs, where the values are taken from a defined value set called **scale**. For instance,

   Scale: status (unmarried, married, divorced)
   Fact: civil status (attribute), status (value set).

For instance, we may have the following information on John Smith: civil status (married).

4.4.2 Rules

As shown above, production systems use rules to change the states of the problem space. Each rule consists of two parts: the operator that performs the state change, and the set of conditions that determines when an operator may be executed.

   IF   conditions
   THEN   operation

If the conditions are logically evaluated to true, then the conclusion can be said to be logically true. The rule formalism can be used to encode:

(1)   Inferential knowledge:

   IF   premises   IF   current ratio < 1.5
   THEN   conclusion   THEN   liquidity is bad

(2)   Procedural knowledge:

| IF | situation | IF | days sales outstanding > 30 |
| THEN | action | THEN | check invoicing procedure |

(3)   Declarative knowledge:

| IF | antecedent | IF | X is accounts payable |
| THEN | consequent | THEN | X belongs to current liabilities |

Rules may be composed of a set of conditions and several conclusions, for example:

(1)   IF current assets increase and liquidity is good, THEN, apply for short-term loan

(2)   IF land purchase or building investment, THEN, apply for a mortgage loan.

Conditions and conclusions are propositions which can be evaluated to true or false. Rules (1) and (2) consist of antecedents of several propositions. In rule (1) both propositions must be true for the conclusion to be true. The antecedent of this rule represents a **conjunction** of propositions. In rule (2) it is sufficient that one of the propositions in the antecedent is true for the conclusion to be true. The antecedent represents here a **disjunction**.

If facts are represented as $<$O–A–V$>$ triplets they can look like this:

| IF | (company Alpha, loan size $4,500) |
| THEN | (company Alpha, loan reject) |

This rule signifies that if the amount of loan applied for by the company is $4,500 then it should be rejected (too small). We want to have more general knowledge encoded in the rules, say, for instance, that any company that applies for a loan of the amount less than $5,000 should be rejected. We then have to introduce variables into the rules:

| IF | (loan applicant, loan size $< $5,000) |
| THEN | (loan applicant, loan rejected). |

Here, the variables loan applicant and loan size have to be instantiated before the premise can be evaluated. Next, the two occurrences of the same variable in the premise and the conclusion must take the same value, namely, company Alpha.

Just as uncertainty can be attached to facts, this can also be done with rules, that is, even if the premises are definitely true, the conclusion may be less than definite. We can talk about uncertain facts and uncertain rules. Reasoning with uncertain facts and rules are dealt with in Section 4.5.3.

Rules are used to represent relationships and are used together with some formalism for simple fact representation in the database, for instance, propositions or attribute–value pairs as shown above. In the production system architecture, inferential knowledge is represented as a set of rules. The state of the workspace determines which rules can be activated.

Rules are particularly suitable for representing inferential knowledge of the type that experts use (heuristics). They are simple to understand, and due to the inference methods used the reasoning can be comprehensively explained after a conclusion is drawn. The structure of the rules is uniform, thus permitting good readability of the knowledge. Also, each rule can be regarded as a separate chunk of knowledge. This offers **modularity** and flexible maintenance.

The rule representation formalism, however, has some disadvantages. As the number of rules increases, the processing efficiency decreases rapidly unless some structure is imposed on the rule base, for example, grouping of rules. Also, it is difficult to represent, explicitly, static knowledge about structured objects. For problem domains where it is important to represent this type of knowledge, production rules are used together with representation formalisms more appropriate for this (see Sections 4.4.3 and 4.4.4).

4.4.3 Semantic nets

In Chapter 2 we showed that memory knowledge is represented as propositions, and that a collection of propositions makes up associative structures among concepts which we called propositional networks. These networks were originally called **semantic nets** because they were designed to represent general knowledge about the semantics of concepts, that is, the meaning of words for natural language understanding. They have later proved to be useful to represent facts about specific objects (knowledge representation).

A semantic net is an associative network of concepts. Concepts are represented as nodes and associations are represented as arcs. **Concepts** can be specific (instances) or more general (types). **Arcs** or links can represent any association between concepts. However, the most common structural relationships that we want to deal with, are:

(1)   IS-A links used to define taxonomic relationships (class–subclass–instances), for example, 'A salmon IS-A fish', and 'A fish IS-A animal'. Taxonomic relationships are sometimes called **generalization hierarchies**.

(2)   HAS-A (or IS-PART-OF) links which represent descriptions of objects (components), for example, 'Glass IS-PART-OF a window', and 'A window IS-PART-OF a house'.

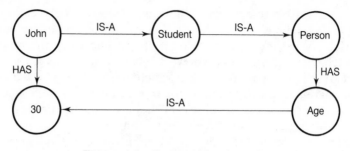

Figure 4.8   A semantic network.

An example of a semantic network is shown in Figure 4.8.

An important property of taxonomic relationships is transitivity. This allows characteristics of higher level more general objects to be associated with lower level more specific objects by an inference mechanism. For example, from the two propositions:

> Jacques is a Parisien
> A Parisien is a Frenchman

we can infer the property that:

> Jacques is a Frenchman.

This procedure is called property inheritance, and is an important aspect of knowledge representation because it saves storing all implied relationships. Of course, this saving of storage space is traded with additional computation.

Several methods exist of reasoning with knowledge that is represented in the semantic net formalism. One of the earliest ones is called *intersection search*, where information is found by activating nodes and searching for the node where all the activation meets. For instance, the question 'What is the age of John?' will start in the Age and the John nodes, and meet in the node with the contents 30. Alternatively, reasoning is performed by *comparison of fragments* of the net. Here, the information required will be formulated as a net (a fragment) and compared to the stored net. For instance, the question posed above, is presented, diagramatically, in Figure 4.9. Semantic nets can also be traversed using rules of inference.

The advantage of semantic nets is the generality to represent any kind of structural knowledge. Also, it gives an integrated view of the knowledge. It is possible to add production rules to a semantic net, thus enabling the combination of the two representation formalisms. A disadvantage of semantic nets is processing efficiency. Also, maintenance can be a problem due to the integration of knowledge by pointers (links). Explanation of reasoning is difficult.

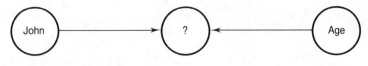

Figure 4.9   A comparison of fragments in a semantic net.

4.4.4 Frames

Rules seem to be the most effective means of representing inferential knowledge. However, they fall short in terms of representing structural, descriptive knowledge. The variables of the propositions are not related to each
other in other ways than through the rules. In the semantic net formalism,
emphasis is put on the integration of knowledge, its elements and relationships. It is frequently very natural to group elements of knowledge around
specific situations, objects or events. Focusing on situations, we can develop
new concepts such as a **stereotyped situation**. We know that people organize
their knowledge according to stereotypes, a standardized mental picture
generally agreed upon, of objects and events. Some examples of such situations are:

- driving a car,
- eating in a restaurant,
- what a bird is.

Stereotypical situations can be objects or events as shown in the examples
above. Here, we shall concentrate on objects. An object-oriented view of
knowledge representation allows the descriptive knowledge to be partitioned
into discrete structures having individual properties. One type of discrete
structures are called **frames**.

> 'A frame is a data-structure for representing a stereotyped situation like a
> being in a certain kind of living room or going to a child's birthday party.
> Attached to each frame are several kinds of information. Some of this
> information is about how to use the frame. Some is about what to do if
> these expectations are not confirmed.' (Minsky, 1975)

Minsky describes frames as a representation of stereotyped situations
or objects that are typical (prototypes) of some category (see the theory of
family resemblance in Chapter 2). A prototypical bird, for instance, will be a
bird that can fly, and not a bird like an emu which cannot fly. Default values
are important properties of frames. The bird prototype is likely to have a
default value: flying. When we describe a particular bird, for instance an
emu, the value of flying will be changed to non-flying. In general, a default
value is a value that we assume to be true unless we are told otherwise.

```
┌─────────────────────────────────────────┐
│  Object:            Mortgage loans       │
│  Superclass:        Loans                │
│  Subclass:                               │
│ ─ ─ ─ ─ ─ ─ ─ ─ ─ ─ ─ ─ ─ ─ ─ ─ ─ ─ ─   │
│  Memberslots                             │
│                                          │
│  Creditor:          Unknown              │
│  Maturity:          Unknown              │
│  Balance:           Unknown              │
│  Interest rate:     Unknown              │
│                                          │
│  Ownslots                                │
│                                          │
│  Total mortgage debt: $25 Million        │
└─────────────────────────────────────────┘
```

Figure 4.10   A general frame for a mortgage loan.

Frames can be used to represent broad concepts, classes of objects, individual instances of objects, or parts of objects. They form structures by joining them together in inheritance hierarchies. That provides for the transmission of common properties among objects in an inheritance hierarchy.

Structural features of frames

Each individual object or class of objects is represented by a frame. Frames can be organized into taxonomies by two constructs:

(1)   membership links representing class membership (classification)

(2)   subclass links representing class specialization (taxonomies).

Frames can also incorporate sets of descriptive information about an object into **slots**. A frame representing a class, for instance, MORTGAGE LOANS, can contain prototype descriptions of members of this class as well as descriptions of the class as a whole. To distinguish these two kinds of information from each other, two kinds of slots may be defined: member slots for attributes of each member of the class, and own slots for attributes of the object represented by the frame.

Let us look at an example. Loan 1 is a specific loan, an instance of the class of credits we may call LOANS. However, we may want to structure our problem domain in such a way that we can distinguish between different kinds of loans, for example, mortgage loans, convertible loans and so on. Figure 4.10 shows a general frame for a mortgage loan. This frame defines the general information that must be specified for this type of loan. Loan 1 is a specific instance of a mortgage loan. Its frame, which is shown in Figure

```
┌─────────────────────────────────────────┐
│  Object:           Loan 1                │
│  Superclass:                             │
│  Member of:        Mortgage loans        │
│  ─ ─ ─ ─ ─ ─ ─ ─ ─ ─ ─ ─ ─ ─ ─ ─ ─ ─    │
│  Own slots                               │
│                                          │
│  Creditor:         City bank             │
│  Maturity:         Dec 31, 1999          │
│  Balance:          12,500,000            │
│  Interest rate:    12%                   │
└─────────────────────────────────────────┘
```

Figure 4.11   Frame for loan 1.

4.11, contains the specific values of the general information described in the mortgage loan frame.

Frames provide structured representations of objects (like loan 1) or classes of objects (like mortgage loans). Through membership and class links a network of frames can be built, each frame representing an object or a class of objects. A procedure can be attached to a slot in a frame which is executed when the value in a slot is missing or should be changed. Each slot can have a number of procedures attached to it. Three typical procedures are:

(1)   If added: the procedure is executed when a value is added to the slot.

(2)   If removed: the procedure is executed when the value is deleted from the slot.

(3)   If needed: the procedure is executed when a value is needed but not existent.

4.4.5 Representations based on logic

There are several formalisms for representing knowledge based on mathematical logic. Here, we will discuss the two most widely-used forms: propositional logic and predicate logic. No detailed technical description will be given.

The use of formal logic in AI provides an interesting contrast with human problem solving. In Chapter 2 we saw that human reasoning was characterized by heuristics which, in many cases, worked well and solved problems efficiently and correctly. However, we also noticed that some of these heuristics violated normative rules and led to biases. One of the reasons that humans do not always use logically correct rules is that deduction often involves too much load on the working memory. Computers can be built without the same constraints. Formal logic systems such as predicate logic were developed with the objectives of being logically sound and complete. There are two major problems with formal logic systems:

(1)   the complexity increases exponentially with the number of propositions, and;

(2)   in everyday situations it is difficult to establish the absolute truth of the propositions involved.

Propositional logic

In logic, a proposition is simply a statement that can be logically true or false. We have seen several examples in the previous sections. A proposition is true if the real world fact that it represents is true, or is supposed to be true. Otherwise, the proposition is false. Propositions are linked together with connectives, such as AND, OR, NOT, IMPLIES and EQUIVALENT. Propositional logic is concerned with the truthfulness of expressions composed of individual propositions and joined by connectives. To evaluate such expressions one uses truth tables, for example:

p	q	p and q
T	T	T
T	F	F
F	T	F
F	F	F

Propositional logic can be used with the rule formalism we have described in the previous sections.

Predicate logic

In propositional logic the smallest unit is a single proposition. This makes it difficult to handle categories of objects by general logical statements. In predicate logic, which is an extension of propositional logic, we represent knowledge by a set of well-formed formulas. For example, the proposition 'Socrates is a man' is written in the predicate logic formalism as:

MAN (Socrates)

Here, MAN( ) is called a **predicate**. A predicate can have one or more arguments, for instance, MARRIED (John, Mary). A predicate has a similar form to a function. However, a function has, as its range, a set of values, while a predicate can take only one value, either TRUE or FALSE.

Predicate logic can also work with variables. The proposition 'All men are mortal' can then be written as:

Forall (x) MAN (x) $\longrightarrow$ MORTAL (x)

'**Forall**' is called the **universal quantifier**. Quantifiers are used to define the range of x for which the proposition is valid.

The inference method used in predicate logic is called **resolution** (theorem proving), where conclusions can be proved valid on a basis of a set of logical propositions. The fundamental mechanism in resolution is the rule of inference applied, for instance, *modus ponens* (see Section 4.5.1). The advantage of logic is its rigorousness due to its strong theoretical foundation. Also, the modularity with which the knowledge can be specified gives a fair amount of flexibility. The disadvantages are the internal coherence required for the methods of reasoning to work, and the processing inefficiency.

4.4.6 Comparison of different representations

In the previous sections we have described several knowledge representation formalisms. We have also discussed advantages and disadvantages of each representation underway. There are no formalisms that are better than the others *per se*. It depends on the problem domain and the task that is to be performed. Table 4.2 is taken from Pinson (1981), slightly modified, and shows a comparison between different knowledge representation formalisms. Figure 4.12 shows how some of these fit together.

Table 4.2 An evaluation table.

	Predicate logic	*Rules*	*Semantic nets*	*Frames*
Declarative knowledge	3	3	3	3
Procedural knowledge	1	2	1	3
Uncertainty	1	3	2	3
Meta-knowledge	2	3	2	3
Explanations	2	3	2	1
Ease of use by expert	2	3	2	1
Modularity	3	3	3	2
Maintenance	3	3	3	2
Processing efficiency	1	2	1	2
Theoretical basis	3	2	3	1

1 = Bad, 2 = Average, 3 = Good

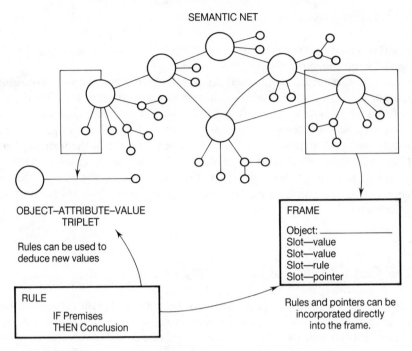

SEMANTIC NET

OBJECT–ATTRIBUTE–VALUE
TRIPLET

Rules can be used to
deduce new values

FRAME

Object: _____
Slot—value
Slot—value
Slot—rule
Slot—pointer

RULE

IF Premises
THEN Conclusion

Rules and pointers can be
incorporated directly
into the frame.

Figure 4.12   Knowledge representation formalisms.

4.5. Reasoning

4.5.1 Hypothetical deductive reasoning

Deductive reasoning allows us to infer new facts from what is already
known. For instance, given the two facts: company A has a current ratio of
2.4 and a quick ratio of 1.2; and also some general knowledge that if a
company has a current ratio >2 and a quick ratio >1, then we can draw the
conclusion that the liquidity of company A is satisfactory. In propositional
logic we can express this as follows:

A1:   company A has a current ratio = 2.4

A2:   company A has a quick ratio   = 1.2

A———→B: IF company X has a current ratio >2

            AND company X has a quick ratio >1
            THEN company X has satisfactory liquidity.

\-

B: COMPANY A has satisfactory liquidity.

A deduction requires a set of premises, also called axioms. These premises
can either be facts (A1 and A2 above) or implications ($A \rightarrow B$). In addition,

logic has some *rules of inference*. The most famous and the basic rule of deductive inferencing is *modus ponens*, which says that if A is true and (A→B) is true, then B is true. As shown in the simple example above, we also need to be able to instantiate general knowledge, that is, given that the implication is true for any company, it must also be true for company A. This rule of inference is called **universal instantiation**: if something is true for everything of a kind, then it is true for any particular instant of that kind.

Using these rules of inferences we can draw logically valid conclusions. Note that a formal logic system works with symbols. We cannot verify the symbolic value of a conclusion. What we know is that if we accept the premises to be true, then we accept the conclusion to be true.

A third rule of inference is *modus tollens*. This rule states that if we are given that the implication (A→B) is true, and that B is false, then we can conclude that A is false. This rule applies to the following situation:

(1)   If the sun is shining tomorrow, then we will go swimming

(2)   we will not be swimming

It follows from (1) and (2) according to *modus tollens* that: the sun is not shining tomorrow. This conclusion, as obvious as it may seem, cannot be reached by a *modus ponens* reasoning system on which most of the expert systems are built.

Chaining and resolution

So far we have shown how the rules of logic, like *modus ponens* and *modus tollens*, can be used to draw conclusions from a simple set of premises. In larger reasoning systems, relationships between facts may be expressed indirectly through logical statements. We need procedures to draw valid conclusions from these larger sets of logical statements. Two procedures used in logical deduction are chaining and resolution.

Chaining is a simple method used in most expert systems based on production rules to form a line of reasoning. Here, the set of rules are organized recursively so that a fact concluded by one rule is used as a premise of another rule. Facts are propagated through the rule set until the ultimate set of facts is inferred. This ultimate set can either be the goal or an initial set of conditions. If the goal state is the ultimate set, the system reasons forward from initial conditions. We call this **forward chaining**. If the system hypothesizes a goal state and works backward to verify this hypothesis, the system is **backward chaining**. We shall return to chaining in Chapter 6 and show the procedure in more detail.

Outside the expert system field almost all computational logic programs use **resolution** (theorem proving and so on). Resolution proves conclusions by refutation, that is, to prove that a statement is true, resolution does this by showing that the negation of this statement is a logical contradiction. Many aspects of resolution are quite technical, and, hence, beyond the scope of this book. It requires using a logic formalism for representation, for example, predicate logic.

Hypothetical deduction means to start with a hypothesis (a conclusion) and then find the premises for that conclusion. If the premises are evaluated to true, then the conclusion is true. One problem with hypothetical deduction is to 'guess' the hypotheses to try and in which order they should be tried. The first version of BANKER (see Chapter 6) worked in a hypothetical deductive manner, where a list of hypotheses are pre-ordered, starting with the reject hypothesis. An alternative method of inferencing is called abduction. Abduction is a method of plausible hypothesis formation.

4.5.2 Plausible reasoning

Unlike deduction, abduction is *not* a legal inference, that is, the conclusion drawn from a set of premises may not be true even if the premises are true. Abduction allows false conclusions. Logically, abduction can be expressed as follows:

$$B$$
$$A \longrightarrow B$$

$$A$$

An example may illustrate this:

B: Socrates is mortal
A ———→ B: All men are mortal

A: Socrates is a man

Socrates could be a dog, in which case the premises are true but the conclusion is wrong. Nevertheless, abduction is a useful method of reasoning, very much used in human reasoning. Typically, in human problem solving, evidences are used to generate plausible solutions which are then verified. For instance, we may know the fact:

If company X has a sales problem, then the net cash flow will be scarce.

This does not mean that observing a reduced cash flow means a sales problem. However, it may be a plausible explanation. We would say that we have *explained* the symptom 'scarce net cash flow' by assuming that there is a problem with sales. Thus, reasoning of this form is a well-controlled form of explanations. A set of symptoms can be used to delimit the search space and to set up an ordered list of hypotheses which can be tried. When one hypothesis is chosen, this hypothesis is used to define the evidence set to be looked for. In certain problem domains, for instance, medical diagnosis, where the solution space (the diseases) is very large, abduction can be used to make good guesses of which disease to hypothesize about first. For further details about abduction, the reader is referred to Charniak (1985).

As we have seen, abduction can lead to wrong conclusions. Put in another way, abduction can give more than one answer. Socrates could be a man or a dog and so on. Abduction introduces uncertainty to the reasoning process. We can look for more and more evidence until we find one hypothesis which is more likely or probable than others.

4.5.3 Reasoning with uncertain information

Deductive reasoning is based on true/false values, so-called two-valued logic, as we have seen above. However, real-world situations are not always such that things are either true or false. On the contrary, nothing in life is certain. Things may be likely, uncertain due to the stochastic nature of the world, or uncertain due to deficient information. Information is deficient because it may be incomplete, inconsistent or not fully reliable. How can we deal with decision making and problem solving in this uncertain world?

To be able to reason with uncertain information we need to *represent* uncertainty, to *combine* uncertain information, and to draw *inferences* from this uncertain information. Various methods or approaches exist, some are numeric and some are non-numeric.

As we have seen in the preceding chapter, the Bayesian approach is the classical method in normative decision theories dealing with uncertainty. The basic element in the Bayesian approach is *probability* – a number that we can use to represent uncertainty. More recently, Schafer (1976) introduced the evidence theory – an extension to the probability theory using the concept of **belief function** to measure uncertainty. Combining evidences based on belief functions is known as the Dempster-Shafer theory of evidence (see, for example, Zadeh, 1981). During the past years, the Dempster-Shafer theory has attracted considerable attention as a promising method of dealing with problems of uncertainty in expert systems. However, problems remain before it can be employed in efficient problem-solving procedures. A third measure of uncertainty – **possibility** – has been proposed by Zadeh (1978). The possibility theory is a development of the Fuzzy Set Theory (Zadeh, 1965) for representing vagueness inherent in linguistic variables.

For instance, the variable AGE takes the values OLD, AVERAGE and YOUNG. Corresponding to each word of this value set is a fuzzy set of values from the universe of discourse of this variable, and there is a mapping function between the two. For instance, if I am 40, how true is it that I am OLD?

$$p((OLD)(x = 40)) = 0.5$$

This proposition states that if x is 40 the possibility (likelihood) of being classified as old is 0.5. We see that in fuzzy logic we deal with non-integer logic and we can deal with logical combinations of propositions. Also we can define fuzzy rules.

These three methods to deal with uncertainty are examined in more detail in Bhatnagar (1986). The strong feature of these methods is their theoretical foundation. Their weakness is, however, the computational inefficiency in drawing inferences with uncertain information. Therefore, several other schemes have been developed under the label of **inexact reasoning**. Their common feature is that they work well but have only a weak theoretical basis. One such scheme is based on what are called certainty factors.

Certainty factors

Let us see how one of the early expert systems, the medical diagnostic system MYCIN, deals with uncertainties. In MYCIN, the numbers attached to facts and rules are called **Certainty Factors** (CF). A certainty factor take values in the range $(-1, 1)$. If the value is positive one believes that the fact is true; if it is negative one believes that the fact is not true, with complete knowledge at each extreme $(-1$ and $+1)$. Certainty factors can be calculated for concluded facts using the following:

(1)   The CF of a conjunction of facts is equal to the minimum CF value of the individual facts.

(2)   The CF of a disjunction of facts is equal to the maximum CF value of the individual facts.

(3)   The CF of the conclusion produced by a rule is the CF of the premise multiplied by the CF of the rule.

(4)   The CF for a concluded fact produced by one or more rules is the maximum of the CFs produced by the individual rules.

An example may clarify these aspects. Consider the two rules:

        R1: IF A AND B THEN E   (CF = 0.5)
        R2: IF C   OR D THEN E   (CF = 0.7)

and the observed (given) facts:

        A(CF = 0.3), B (CF = 0.7), C(CF = 0.5), D(CF = 0.6)

With what certainty factor can we conclude E? A premise consisting of a conjunction of facts is evaluated to:

$$\min (CF_A, CF_B) = \min (0.3, 0.7) = 0.3$$

A premise consisting of disjunctive facts is:

$$\max (CF_C, CF_D) = \max (0.5, 0.6) = 0.6$$

Applying R1 we conclude E with the following certainty factor:

$$CF_E = 0.3 \times 0.5 = 0.15$$

Applying rule 2 we get:

$$CF_E = 0.6 \times 0.7 = 0.42$$

According to (4) above, we conclude E with:

$$\max (CF_E, CF_E) = \max (0.15, 0.42) = \underline{0.42}$$

There are other methods with which we can combine the same concluded fact from several rules. It seems likely that if one arrives at the same conclusion from different reasoning chains, that is, that more positive information emerges, the confidence in the conclusion increases beyond that of the conclusion from any single rule. One way of dealing with this is to define an increment factor which is added for each new rule concluding with the same fact. The increment factor is defined as the remainder to certainty multiplied by the certainty factor for the new fact. The new certainty factor then becomes:

$$CF = CF_1 + (CF_2 (1 - CF_1))$$

In our example above this will give:

$$CF = 0.15 + (0.42 (1 - 0.15))$$
$$\underline{CF} = \underline{0.51}$$

The order in which certainty factors are combined does not matter.

In MYCIN, uncertainties are propagated through the rules of an inference chain. A rule succeeds to draw a conclusion if the certainty factor of the concluded fact is greater than 0.2.

Exercises

4.1   LISP is a functional language and PROLOG is a logic language. What are the key characteristics of the two languages, and what differentiates the two?

4.2   What are the major components of the production system architecture, and what are their functions?

4.3   List advantages of production systems compared to procedural programs.

4.4   Show a search tree for the problem of acquiring a new car. Use a problem reduction solution method and illustrate it by using an AND/OR tree.

4.5   John Smith, who is a financial analyst at Stockbroker Ltd., has just bought a new house in Westend for $250,000. He has financed this property by a mortgage loan of $125,000 by ABC bank, and by a loan from his employer of $60,000. John is 40 years old and is married to Susan. They have three children who are five, eight, and fourteen years old. The house has a beautiful garden, four bedrooms, and garage.

Make a formal representation of this description using the knowledge representation formalisms:
- property lists
- frames
- semantic nets

4.6   What is the difference between propositional logic and predicate logic?

4.7   A problem-solving search can proceed either forward (from a known start state to a desired goal state) or backward (from a goal state to a start state). Describe the difference between the two chaining procedures, and discuss what factors that determine the choice for a particular problem.

4.8   Why are probabilities and Baysian statistics not widely used in production systems?

5

Decision Support Systems

5.1 Requirement for decision support

5.1.1 Origin of DSS research: ill-structured decision processes and man-machine cooperation in problem solving

The origin of DSS as a domain of study and research can be traced back to the end of the 1960s. Initial research work was published by researchers at the Sloan School of Management at the Massachusetts Institute of Technology, the Harvard Business School in the USA, and at the Business School HEC in France.

The concept of a 'management decision system' was described by Scott Morton (1971) in his thesis entitled 'Management decision systems: computer based support for decision making'.

Several professors of the marketing department of the Sloan School published, at the end of the 1960s, some important papers that viewed DSS applied to marketing from a conceptual point of view. The well-known paper of John D.C. Little (1970) on decision calculus was important, with respect to the DSS approach, to solving management decision problems. The concept of DSS, as applied to marketing, was developed by Little and his ideas published several years later (Little, 1979). Even earlier, David B. Montgomery and Glen L. Urban in their book *Management Science in Marketing* (1969), had introduced the concept of decision information systems within a framework including a data bank, a model bank, and a statistical bank, and had stressed the importance of the man–system interaction. However, these works were mainly concerned with marketing information systems and marketing models and not with the design of DSS software itself.

Another interesting work of the same period was the thesis of Gerrity (1970) which concentrated on the design of man–machine decision systems. The methodology developed was applied to portfolio management as described in Gerrity (1971).

At approximately the same time, work was also going on at the Tuck School of Business Administration of Dartmouth College. Several interesting interactive models had been developed by professors of the Finance Department, mainly in financial planning (Carleton, 1970), portfolio performance measurement, Bower (1970) and Williamson (1970), and bank management.

A study of the origin of DSS has still to be written. It seems that the first DSS papers were published by PhD students or professors in business schools, who had access to the first time-sharing computer system: Project MAC at the Sloan School, the Darmouth Time Sharing Systems at the Tuck School. In France, HEC was the first French business school to have a time-sharing system (installed in 1967), and the first DSS papers were published by professors of the School in 1970.

The term DSS (in French, 'Système Interactif d'Aide à la Décision' or SIAD) and the concept of DSS were developed independently in France, in several articles by professors of HEC working on the SCARABÉE project which started in 1969 and ended in 1974. The concept of DSS and a design and implementation strategy for these systems are described in several papers related to this project, Klein and Tixier (1971), Klein (1971), Klein and Girault (1971).

5.1.2 The objective of DSS

A DSS can be defined as:

> A computer information system that provides information in a given
> domain of application by means of analytical decision models and access to
> databases, in order to support a decision maker in making decisions
> effectively in complex and ill-structured (non-programmable) tasks.

DSS are useful when a fixed goal exists but there is no algorithmic solution. The solutions paths can be numerous and user-dependant (Klein and Tixier, 1971). In other words, the goal of a DSS is to improve a decision by better understanding and preparation of the tasks leading towards evaluation and choosing (collectively called the decision making process – see Chapter 2).

The concept of **ill (or semi) structured** problems as opposed to those that are **well structured** is a key concept here. In the literature (Simon, 1973) the latter usually refers to decision making processes that are routine and repetitive, the former to situations where there is no known and clear method of solution because the problem arises for the first time, or because the nature of the problem itself is complex and unclear. The situation is, in fact, slightly more complex. A financial analysis problem which will lead to the decision to grant a loan or not is, for the credit analyst, a **routine task**. However, it is not usually possible to fully automatize the information processing which will be used to reach the conclusion. If an information processing method can be stated as an algorithm then the decision process is structured, and can be incorporated in a computer program. The solution to the problem is then *automated*.The way that the DSS will accommodate the unstructuredness of the problem is expressed by Bonczek *et al.* (1981) in the following way:

> 'The human investigates in the decision-making process and during this investigation the computer supports the process by furnishing pertinent information, thus creating a human–computer decision making system.'

Unstructuredness is accommodated in:

(1)   the nature of and sequencing of requests made on the DSS,

(2)   the manner in which DSS responses are utilized,

(3)   the DSS recognition of alternative methods for satisfying a given request.

Structured problems are routine and repetitive, because they are unambiguous (since each such problem has a single solution method). A less structured problem has more alternative solution methods, and the solutions may not be equivalent. A completely 'unstructured' problem has unknown solution methods or too many solution methods to evaluate effectively.

The number of situations where decisions have to be taken and where the problem is non-programmable is very large in management. In finance, which will be our application domain, we can point out: financial analysis, credit analysis, financial planning and engineering, management control, capital budgeting, investment advising, portfolio management, performance evaluation and so on.

The end users of a DSS application are not always known during its development, but the decisions which it is designed to support must have something in common (see Section 5.5.5 for a consequence of this fact). A credit analysis DSS such as FINSIM which we present in Chapter 7 is designed to support a given decision class. The support provided can include **decision methodology support** (see Chapter 9).

The economic importance of research and development in the field of DSS is directly related to the pervasiveness of ill-structured problems in management (and finance in particular), and the need to provide DSS support to all these decision classes. The development of AI technology has widened the spectrum of application of these systems.

5.1.3 Characteristics of ill-structured problems

Characteristics of situations where the DSS approach is useful are known (Klein and Tixier, 1971). We have defined them above as ill-structured decision problems, in such situations:

- The preferences, judgements, intuition and experience of the decision maker are essential.

- The search for a solution implies a mixture of:

    - search for information,
    - formalization, or problem definition and structuring (system modeling),
    - computation,
    - data manipulation.

- The sequence of the above operations is not known in advance since:

    - it can be a function of data,
    - it can be modified, given partial results,
    - it can be a function of the user preferences.

- Criteria for the decision are numerous, in conflict, and highly dependant on the perception of the user (user modeling).

- The solution must be achieved in limited time.

- The problem evolves rapidly.

As can be noticed from the above description one of the key characteristics of situations where DSS are useful is that modeling of the decision problem (and user) is needed. One of the most obvious examples of time constraint can be found in dealer rooms. Traders working on the money or the stock-market must be able, in certain cases, to make decisions in a few seconds. Here, DSS are a prerequisite. Time is usually an important element in DSS applications.

5.1.4 Requirement for DSS software

Given the above characteristics about the problem class that we wish to support, it is well accepted that certain requirements have to be fulfilled by DSS software. These requirements concern:

- end-user usage and interactivity;
- end-user definition;
- easy access to pertinent information;

- high interaction between users, the system and the learning situation;
- capacity to adapt to fast evolution of user needs;
- portability and peripheral support;
- reliability;
- performance.

We shall outline these requirements below.

End-user usage and interactivity

This requirement states that the end user should not have, during his exploration of the decision process, to use an intermediary (chauffeur) to request information from the system, or to explore some ideas or to compute criteria. This requirement is a direct consequence of the fact that:

- In the search for a solution the next step can be a function of intermediate results obtained. It would not be practical to call for an assistant at each such step. End users wish to test their ideas at once!
- The criteria of choice, preference, risk aversion and so on are specific to the decision maker (user modeling) and are crucial ingredients which cannot be input by a third party. More simply, the decision maker may not wish to communicate these to a third party.
- Some information is highly confidential.

The manager must be able to change inputs (questions, requests and so on) and obtain immediately the corresponding results. Only online systems enable such performance. The necessity of highly interactive systems for successful implementation of computer support was one of the first conclusions of researchers in the DSS field.

It is by studying a problem that the managers learn how to understand the problem better and to find its solution. The concept of a 'decision calculus' (Little, 1970) is related to this idea. As a consequence, the language of interaction and the assistance have to be specifically designed for end users. The assistance is a key point here. The assistance in a DSS can be related to the syntax of the command language, to the resources available in the DSS (data, models, displays) or the problem solving methodology itself. For example, the decision analysis methodology we have seen in Chapter 3.

End-user definition

This requirement was introduced by Klein and Tixier (1971) under the name 'user-designer' principle. In many cases, the DSS is implemented by its user. This is the consequence of the fact that, often, a system for decision support is defined while the user works on his problem. In other words, the system which is given to the user does not solve his problem from the start, but is there to create the environment within which he or she will be able to solve it better than before (Klein and Girault, 1971).

In fact, if there is no discussion about the end-user of DSS, there is much debate about the end-user definition of a DSS. There are several reasons why, frequently, a DSS cannot be implemented by the end users.

The commonest reason is because the end users are just too busy or not motivated enough. End users will use the system to solve problems, they will participate in its definition and evolution, but not in its implementation if the implementation implies too much time and investment. Klein and Villedieu (1987) give a good example of such a situation. The DSS they describe is a DSS for financial analysis and city planning. It is used in many French municipalities and is very successful in terms of number of users and the satisfaction of the users. The final users of the system are, depending on the size of the city, the elected officials in charge of financial problems and/or the administrative staff (General Secretary, Administrative and Financial Manager and so on). The specification and definition of the first version of the system was carried out over a period of one year, during one day meetings held once every month, because the elected officials could not spend more time on the project. In this case, consultants have played the role of 'chauffeur' until the DSS constituted an environment attractive enough for the end users so that they had sufficient interest to have it as a permanent assistant in their office. Starting from this point the user-designer principle has worked. Since then the system has been regularly improved by users and a user group was created.

The second reason which may prevent end users from participating in the definition and design of the DSS is their number. Take, for instance, a DSS for financial analysis and engineering (FINSIM which we describe in Section 7.4 and in Chapter 9 is a good example of such a system). FINSIM is a financial and credit evaluation system used in banks to prepare loan decisions related to companies. Such a system can be used by many people in a bank (in fact, all credit analysts). As a consequence, only a selection of potential users can take part in the definition and design.

One last, classical, reason for users not to participate in the design is that the organization in which they work wishes a certain category of employees to use a given methodology embedded in a DSS, for instance, to ensure homogeneity and consistency in the way the demands for loans is dealt with. As a consequence, the management does not wish to see each employee develop his own system.

Easy access to pertinent information

As we shall see in Section 5.2 a DSS usually includes information about the problem domain and information about the problem processing capabilities of the system:

- data access;
- meaning of data;
- variables;
- decision models;
- statistical, forecasting and optimization tools;
- presentation of information;
- command language syntax and semantics;
- knowledge about the problem (rules – if this form of knowledge representation is used).

We shall briefly discuss below each of these kinds of information.

Data access
In most problems within the DSS class the first step towards a solution is ready access to relevant data since it is through the study of these that, frequently, the problem is recognized and/or diagnosed.

In financial analysis, for instance, within a bank credit department, it is clear that to have an instantaneous and easy access to balance sheets and income statements of client companies requesting a loan is a necessary condition, and a first step to the support of the decisions of the credit analysts. In some banks, the volume of data is such (several thousands of balance sheets) that the data capture is done by specialized personnel and that the analysts only access the information and check it. Increasingly, the raw data is provided on tapes by specialized companies.

If the volume of data is important and the users numerous, data will have to be shared, and may be updated by users. The problem can be further complicated by the fact that the database can be evolving with varying time cycles for various sub-classes of data. For instance, in finance, balance sheets and income statements are annual, semi-annual or quarterly but stock prices can be weekly or daily.

Another difficulty in many DSS situations rises from the fact that information from different origins has to be taken into account and merged. For instance, in a DSS for management control, the support of diagnosis will imply access to accounting information (actual results) as well as budget information so as to compute variance. The accounting information will, most likely, come from the accounting system and the budgets from another system, or directly from the user.

Meaning of data and variables
In many cases it is very important to be able to have access not only to the value of the data but also to its meaning. For instance, an analyst is not only

interested in the numerical value of a price index but also in the origin of the index (who is producing it and publishing it, when it is useful to use it and so on).

The meaning of a variable may have to be specified. The variable 'sales', for example: does it include the sales taxes or not.

As a consequence it is important for a DSS user to have access to texts giving or defining the meaning of the data available in the database of the DSS.

Decision models

As we have seen in Chapter 3, models to support decisions relate environmental, decision and goal variables. We shall call them **decision models**. In other words, a decision model is a formal representation of a **decision class** situation (see Section 13.3.4 for a discussion of this concept).

A DSS may contain several decision models. These models may have been defined and developed over a long period of time by different people. It is essential to have access to the catalogue of these models and to access information on the condition under which each model may be used. Such a situation is described in Klein and Villedieu (1987) for DSS for financial planning in French municipalities. One decision model (STRATEGY) is used to work out and explore the main line of a city strategy, taking into account global variables such as local tax income, debt level and investment level; another model (PLAN) is used to calculate a more detailed financial plan, taking into account a breakdown of local taxes, and a third model (PROJECT) is similar to PLAN but is able to deal with project-by-project information at the investment level in the planning process (the cash inflows and cash outflows associated with each project).

In the case study at the end of this chapter (Exercise 5.14) we present a DSS for management control in a decentralized company within which several decision models are available in the model base.

Statistical, forecasting and optimization tools (toolbox)

In many DSS both statistical routines or forecasting routines may be used to help in a given phase of the decision process to anticipate trends, seasonal factors and so on, to measure causal relationships, to optimize and so on, such a need is presented in the case study for a management control DSS.

The possibility of accessing information using the methodology for short-term forecasting and its underlying hypotheses can be very helpful. Here, the DSS plays the role of a consultant specialized in statistical and/or forecasting techniques. Such a need is described in Gangneux and Rouxell (1988) and its implementations are described in Chapter 7.

Presentation of information

In a given domain, many different displays of information are often used and are standard. For instance, a financial model may be associated with several reports: balance sheets, income statement, ratios and so on. Access to the catalogue of these reports and information on their usage is a necessity, as it is for decision models.

In Section 7.4 we describe the set of standard reports available with the financial model FINSIM, more than 10 reports are used, with three possible transformations of the data for each report.

The user should be able to find out what the available standard presentation of information in the DSS is.

Command language syntax and semantics

All DSS include an end-user language. The syntax of this language may have to be outlined to the user when he or she is working with the system and, in particular, in case of error or abnormal conditions.

Explanations of command semantics should also be on line.

Knowledge about the problem

The information about data, its meaning, and the decision models and displays that are readily available already constitute much knowledge about the problem. However, other forms of knowledge may be used as we have seen in Section 3.4, and this type of information plays a very important role in what is called expert systems and their associated knowledge bases. In particular, we shall propose, in Chapter 7, a new framework to integrate knowledge bases on decision methodologies, for instance decision analysis methods, statistical methods and so on.

High interaction between the users, the system and the learning situation

The DSS user is in a heuristic search situation as described in Chapter 2 (Klein and Tixier, 1971) during his or her problem solving activity. Such a situation has been described in Girault and Klein (1971) for financial analysts working in investment departments. The analysts, for example, have, very often, to make compromises between deepening their search (studying a company in more detail) or widening it (studying other companies). Also, when using decision models for simulation purposes the analyst finds himself in a *learning situation*. This implies a high level of interaction so as to be able to see clearly the consequences of changes in hypotheses. This high interaction implies the existence of a command language to let the user define what he or she wants the system to accomplish.

There is a definite *computer assisted instruction* aspect in the interaction of the user with the DSS.

The reason is that, while quantitative methods and normative models are developing rapidly in these fields, nevertheless intuition, judgment and experience remain essential factors in the process of exploration of alternatives and the search for adequate tools. This implies that the key to success is not to develop better or more numerous quantitative numerical techniques but to continuously improve the search ability of the system user; to help him acquire better heuristics; and to improve his knowledge of the limits and applicability of the tools he has at his disposal (Klein and Tixier 1971)

This point will be developed in Section 5.5.4.

Capacity to adapt to fast evolution of user needs

If a DSS is providing good support it is very likely that users will perceive new problems and needs. As a consequence, the system will have to be able to respond to a fast evolution of user needs. This evolution can be in terms of extensions with respect to:

- new data structure,
- new objects,
- new subsystems,
- new syntactic forms.

This implies that the system must be designed from the start to be able to evolve. This requirement is usually difficult to fulfill, and clearly, compromises have to be done between generality, the capacity to evolve and the delay and cost of producing the system. However, as we shall see in Section 5.3 this requirement is taken into account more and more in DSS development environments, which are able to support a wider spectrum of requirements.

Portability and peripheral support

Software and DSS software, in particular, tend to have a longer life cycle than hardware. As a consequence, it is important to be able to transfer these applications easily. This requirement has consequences on the tools and environment used to develop the DSS development tools themselves: operating system, programming language and so on. With respect to peripheral support, history often leads organizations to have various kinds of terminals, PCs, work stations and printer, it is useful for the system to accommodate a wide range of them.

Reliability

This requirement is well known for on-line systems. Decision situations are usually situations for which users want to use their system when they feel the need for it. They will not use for long the systems which are not readily available. As we shall see, DSS software development environments are large and complex, software reliability is a key issue as for all large software.

Performance

While this requirement is not specific to DSS, it is a very important requirement for interactive systems of the DSS kind. DSS applications are interactive systems of a very different nature than transaction systems where simple requests are made, and where all users are doing the same thing (updating an inventory, making reservations and so on.). On the contrary, when using a DSS a user may easily make requests for information which can necessitate, for its computation, considerable resources in terms of central processing time and disk access. This is the case, for example, for credit or financial analysts requesting some information such as sales or benefit from a financial database containing several hundred companies. These companies fulfill certain conditions (ratio of interest to sales $> x$ and sales $< y$ sorted by the value of the ratio).

Another example in the management control field is the case of a DSS used for financial control of subsidiaries or branches when the number of subsidiaries is large (several tens or hundreds) and when work on consolidated variables has to be done. Such a situation is described in the case study described at the end of the chapter.

DSS are systems with which users can create new objects: models, reports, data files or databases, such operations require powerful machines, which are available as PCs today.

5.2 Functions of DSS

5.2.1 Functions and conceptual structure of DSS

The functions that a DSS should have can be derived from the analysis of the main steps in the decision making process, described in Section 2.6 and from requirements described in Section 5.1.

A decision maker must possess the following abilities: perception, designing or searching for appropriate alternatives, power (that is, the capacity of the decision maker to give orders and to influence the goal which is to be reached), analytic power, planning and implementation, and adaptation to evolution. If these abilities are accepted as being the main facets of a decision maker, then these facets will provide a framework for studying and designing computer-based DSS and will answer questions such as:

- Which of these human abilities are supported by a given DSS?
- To what degree are they supported or performed?
- Which computer-based techniques are used to support each of these human abilities?
- How do capabilities interact with each other in a given DSS?

The number of capabilities incorporated into the machine part of a human–machine system, along with the effectiveness of each, may be taken as a rough measure of the DSS's (artificial) intelligence. We say that the computer-base system *supports* (rather than makes) decisions because some of the facets are not performed within it.

For instance, the system may have no intrinsic power or authority: it has authority only in proportion to the weight that the decision maker attaches to its activities.

For each of the abilities, the machine participates in the joint human–computer decision activity only to the extent that the ability can be *formally* expressed. For example, the facet of evaluation of an alternative may involve some unformalizable subjective processes.

Figure 5.1 taken from Bonczek *et al.* (1981) shows the interaction between the decision maker and the DSS. The language clearly plays a very important role in the passing of messages between the human and computer. The possible behavior of the computer seen as an intelligent assistant is also determined by:

(1)   The language of interaction.

(2)   The degree or mix of capabilities possessed by the software.

(3)   The available information about the decision maker's problem domain.

Following Bonczek *et al.* we shall call the system software of (2) the problem

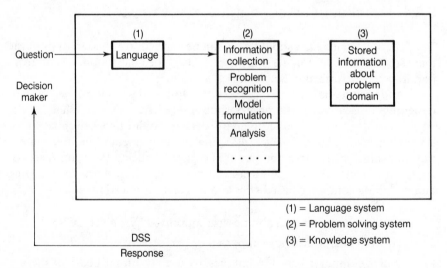

Figure 5.1   Conceptual structure of a DSS. (Reproduced from Bonczek *et al.* (1981). *Foundations of Decision Support Systems*. Academic Press).

processor. The problem processor's information-collecting ability can potentially utilize three sources:

(1)   The decision maker (via the language).

(2)   Knowledge stored in the system (in a database or a model, for example).

(3)   Other persons, through computer-assisted messaging functions.

With respect to the first source, the perception ability involves accepting strings of symbols and converting them into a form that can be used in conjunction with other capabilities (that is, problem recognition) of the processor. With respect to the other sources of information, the perception ability will be supported largely through database management techniques.

When the user's language is identical to a data manipulation language, the only capability possessed by the DSS is that of information collection. Such a DSS is nothing more than a database management system, and all the other capabilities involved in decision making reside with the system users.

Whereas information collecting of some sort is essential to all DSS the other capabilities are usually not. So it is essential that, at the very least, a DSS at its first stage of design is able to collect and display information.

However, after the basic need for decision support: data manipulation, and display have been provided, it is clear that if the system is to be called a DSS it will have to provide at least some sort of support for the task of problem structuring or modeling. We can conclude by saying that the minimum functions a DSS should provide are the following:

- data management,
- display,
- problem analysis and structuring (modeling),
- statistical or other analytical techniques.

We are going now to discuss, briefly, which functions should be given to the user by a DSS. We shall use, from time to time, in this discussion examples taken out of the JIIA-86 case study described at the end of the chapter.

5.2.2 The language of interaction

As we have seen above a DSS user will have to interact with the system using a language. The language is a key element of the DSS since it will be used:

- To interact with the stored information on the problem.
- To interact with the problem processor.

The language should allow the user to define and manipulate the basic resources of the DSS (databases, models, reports, images and so on). At the database level the language will be used to define and manipulate data structures and their relations. At the modeling level the language will be used to define models, relate them to each other, compute, list, and manipulate the models for decision support as we have seen in Chapter 2. At the reporting level the language will be used to define reports, print and list them.

So, two kinds of languages will be needed for each basic resource:

- A language *to define* the *structure* of each basic object: database, model, report.

- A language to *manipulate* the objects as a whole, this language is more likely to be a command language (interpreted rather than compiled).

The importance of the language in the design of DSS was emphasised in Klein and Levy (1974), following Bonczek *et al.* we shall call this part of the DSS the language system. The techniques used to define the language system to interact with the DSS applications can range from non-procedural commands to pull down menus, icons, procedural language, graphical language and so on.

It should be stressed that if pull down menus are efficient in selecting among options, they are highly inefficient when it comes to expressing computation or formulas, there, procedural languages are better adapted.

A good language system should be able to mix different techniques of user–system interaction. For example, in order to help the user keep track of the relationships he or she has defined between variables in a model, it can be useful to provide the user with diagrams showing the inference structure existing between variables.

We have seen, in Chapter 3, the concept of decision trees and influence diagrams. Such structuring tools can be presented to the user in a graphical form with great advantage. Visual language is an important area of development for DSS, we shall deal more with this in Section 13.2.1

5.2.3 The problem processor (solver)

The problem processor part of the DSS will have to support the four main phases of the decision process which are stated below:

(1)   Supporting information collection.
(2)   Supporting problem recognition.
(3)   Supporting economic and financial model formulation.
(4)   Supporting decision analysis.

Each of these are now discussed in turn.

Supporting information collection

Access to information (data collection)
Easy access to the information is the first support a decision maker requests from the DSS. In the JIIA-86 case study described at the end of this chapter, information is about products and branch results but should also be about all the resources of the DSS (data, decision models, statistical tools, displays available and so on). In the JIIA-86 case several users (branch managers) will need to interrogate and update the database at the same time, this will imply the capability of the DSS to provide database management subsystem functions (see Section 5.4.2).

With respect to the access of information in a database context (beyond the simple retrieval of information), two classical functions are the screening and sorting of information. We have pointed out in Section 5.1.4 that a DSS should also provide information about the resources of the system in terms of:

- data available;
- decision models;
- display types;
- analytical or statistical tools;

among other things. The support the DSS provides to its users is here an extension of their memory.

Computer assisted messaging for geographically dispersed users
When decisions have to be taken and the decision implies collecting information between distant decision makers, or negotiation between them (in particular, in conflict situations) it is useful to take advantage of existing networks and use the computer to assist in message transmission. Computer message systems and computer assisted teleconferencing can play a very crucial role in the support of this phase of the process, in particular, when a decision has to be made under pressure of time, and the decision makers are not available at the same time. The importance of this function is well described in Hiltz and Turrof (1978) and Johansen *et al.* (1974).

The message communication function in DSS has, from our point of view, not received the attention it deserves. We believe that one of the main activities of managers is not only to make decisions but *to obtain commitment* from their colleagues and other employees of the organization. This point was stressed by Winograd and Flores (1986).

The existence of a good-quality computer-assisted messaging or teleconferencing system can expand the capacity of a manager to exchange information with others and obtain commitment to get certain tasks done.

Supporting problem recognition

Display of information

Since the essence of problem recognition lies in the ability to detect discrepancies between present state and expected states, the display of information to highlight such discrepancies is essential.

The capacity to present information in different windows and to combine graphics, figures and color is a key element of good display for decision support. For example, in the JIIA-86 case study, the capacity to display trends in sales will help to pinpoint problems on product life cycles. Kahl *et al.* (1977) describe an interesting example of problem recognition through **variance analysis**. This case presents a multinational industrial company at the European headquarters of which the controllers use a DSS. The system enables them to display the global variance of any variable at different levels in the company.

In the database, a variable can be indexed by time, by the subsidiary marketing it, by the currency in which the variable is valued, and by the controller's point of view (is it an actual figure, a budgeted figure or a variance). The controller can decide to display, for instance, the value of a variable (sales, operating margin and so on) for the company (as a whole or a subsidiary) at a given period in a given currency (see Figure 5.2). This value

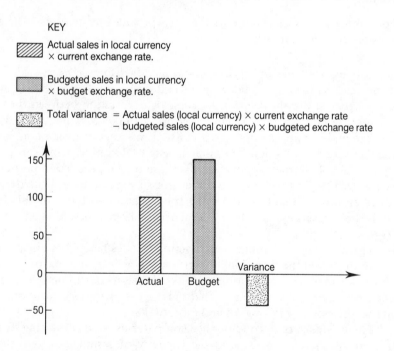

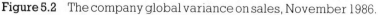

Figure 5.2   The company global variance on sales, November 1986.

can be the actual value or the budgeted value or the variance (management control aspect). In the case described, the actual variables are entered in the system on a monthly basis in local currency using the current exchange rate. The budgeted values are entered once a year during the budget period at the budget exchange rate which is decided as a forecast for the whole of the coming year.

So, the current exchange rate is the exchange rate observed on the money markets each month (in fact the exchange rate is different if the variable is an income statement item or a balance sheet item). The controller may then be interested to break down the global variance at the plant level by country (see Figure 5.3).

Let us imagine that the controller finds out that the negative variance is 80%, at the UK subsidiary. He or she may now be interested to know if this negative variance is due to an exchange rate problem (over which the plant manager has no control) or to an activity-level problem (over which he may have some control). For the French subsidiary, the negative variance can only be due to an activity-level problem since the consolidation currency is the French franc.

To solve this question the controller will ask for a breakdown of variance between the exchange rate variance and activity variance (Figure 5.4), and will see, clearly, that the problem is due to an exchange rate variance.

KEY

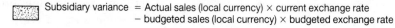

Actual sales in local currency × current exchange rate.

Budgeted sales in local currency × budget exchange rate.

Subsidiary variance = Actual sales (local currency) × current exchange rate − budgeted sales (local currency) × budgeted exchange rate

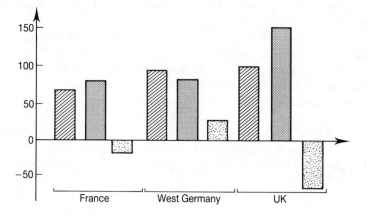

Figure 5.3   Breakdown of sales variance by country, November 1986.

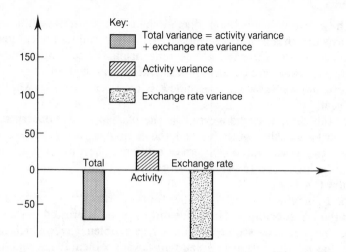

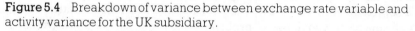

Figure 5.4   Breakdown of variance between exchange rate variable and activity variance for the UK subsidiary.

The controller has progressed considerably and very fast in the diagnosis of the causes of his initial observation. This type of support received from the DSS can be called the capacity to 'mine' a problem.

Alerting
The alerting function of a DSS is a very important function with which to support problem recognition. The idea is that the user should be able to set conditions (predicates and rules) which, if they become true, will trigger the display, or send a message or report, or, eventually, trigger some other action such as the computation of a model. This function is very useful when the decision maker is confronted with a large amount of data which is evolving very fast with time.

This situation is found in trade rooms, where traders have to follow current information on several hundreds or thousands of securities. The trader using a DSS should be able to define conditions which, when fulfilled, will lead the system to flash a signal to him.

An 'intelligent' alerting system must be defined. We shall show (see Chapter 7) that an expert module is a good way to implement such a function.

As a conclusion to the support of the problem recognition phase we can say that the decision maker should be helped by the system during this phase to:

- determine what the questions (decision problems) to be answered are;

- define the hypotheses to be tested;
- define the effects to be estimated.

As can be seen, this kind of support is difficult to provide.

It is easy to display a message if a variable goes beyond a certain threshold, it is more difficult to diagnose what the real problem is. However, we have seen in Chapter 4 that since simulation of human reasoning is possible there is some hope that DSS will become more able to suggest diagnoses, we shall see how in Chapter 7.

Supporting economic and financial model formulation

Importance of model formulation for solution finding
In financial and economic problems a decision maker is very often confronted with the necessity to make calculations. If a loan is made, a repayment schedule has to be computed, if an asset is acquired a depreciation schedule must also be computed according to a given method and so on. This need for computation would, by itself, be sufficient to justify the existence of an end-user language to define calculation.

The widespread use of spreadsheets has shown how large this need is. Its origin is found in the fact that after the information collection phase and problem definition or diagnosis of the decision process, the next step is the need to support transformation of basic information in order to produce more usable information, which will often constitute a criterion for choice. But there is another well-known fundamental reason for defining models. This reason is that the formulation of models is a crucial step in the scientific method applied to economics and social systems. And, since the scientific method has proved to be an efficient method to solve problems, we wish to take advantage of it. This method is based on a four-stage process:

(1)   Observation of the system.
(2)   Formulation of a logical, mathematical model that attempts to explain the observations of the system.
(3)   Prediction of the behavior of the system on the basis of the model using mathematical or logical deduction.
(4)   Performance of experiments to test the validity of the model.

It is clear that the information access function of the DSS will help in the first stage. Since the process of model building is made of two tasks:

(1)   Finding out the variables to include in the model.
(2)   Finding out structural (causal relations) among variables.

The capacity to decide if a variable should be in a model and to define what its relations are with other variables necessitates an *understanding* of the causal relationships in the *real system*, as well as the nature of the decision to be taken (as we have seen in Chapter 3).

Once a model has been formulated and validated we can use it to test alternative hypotheses. The hypotheses can be about:

• Environmental variables on which the decision maker has no control.

• Decision variables (for example, in a financial problem: investment, price, dividend policy and so on) on which the decision maker does have control.

A validated decision model provides us with a tool for tracing out the effect of alternative decision on the behavior of a system. In particular, these effects can be criteria to choose among alternatives. A specific characteristic of model formulation in decision problems is that the modeling function has to be performed on the economic system but also, in certain situations, on the user (preference modeling).

We have summarized the main steps of model formulation and validation in Figure 5.5

Model formulation

The next step in the decision process, after problem recognition, is usually the need to support transformation of basic data to produce more usable information. Such transformation can be done through models. The conceptualization can be done at the data definition level, as well as at the modeling level.

In this section we shall refer to the JIIA-86 case study. We will also use this case study in several other sections to illustrate important points. However, the case will be described in more detail at the end of this chapter.

In this case study the definition of the production cost at the branch level is presented, the definition of commercial cost at the product level and the definition of advertising at the product level are all typical examples of conceptualization at the data level. The computation of the market share is a more sophisticated example of such conceptualization, since market share is defined by a model with two recurring equations. Such a model can then be used to test market share evolution as a function of advertising budget as shown by Little (1970).

A user may be interested to compute forecasted income statement given an hypothesis on activity (sales) level. He or she might be interested to obtain a cumulative margin figure which he or she might consider to be an important criteria.

Choice of model formalism

One of the essential decisions when starting to model a system is the choice of the representation formalism.

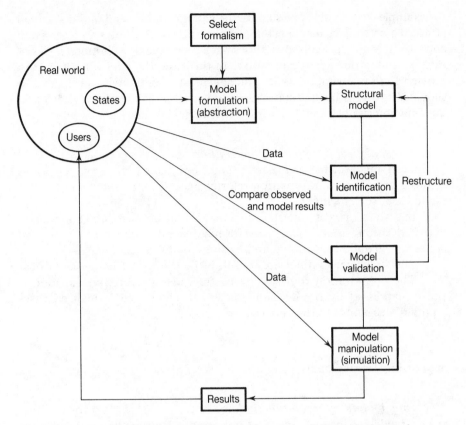

Figure 5.5 The process of model formulation and validation in the study of real-world systems.

Is it an equation type modeling language, a decision tree, an influence diagram formalism, or a mixture of them?

How are uncertainty and time going to be represented in the formalism?

Is the modeling system providing a way to model the user (preference, risk aversion and so on) as well as the economic and financial system?

Model validation

Once a model has been formalized, the user is facing the problem of finding the values of the parameters of behavioral equations of the model. For example, in the FINSIM model described in Section 7.4 the user must provide the structural ratios relating a level of activity (sales variable) and a level of expenses (salary variable, for example). In the JIIA-86 case study the manager wants to use a short-term model for forecasting sales. This implies, for example, that he has to compute the equation of a trend plus a seasonal effect. To do this the user must use special statistical techniques (regression and so on). Many specialized methods have been developed for model identification and parameter computation. In this case, the DSS will attempt to provide the same support that a management scientist who specializes in short-term forecasting and statistics would do. We shall see in Chapter 7 that this function can be extended using artificial intelligence technology.

Access to statistical or optimization routines

When studying information the analyst may be interested to use data analysis methods to structure information (cluster analysis and factor analysis are examples of such methods).

In certain cases an objective function can be defined and an optimization on decision variables can be performed. An interesting case is described in a financial and production planning situation by Jäger *et al.* (1988).

The statistical routines are useful in the process of model identification. The optimization routines are useful when an objective function is clearly expressed by the decision maker. In some well-formalized cases 'optimal' decisions can then be reached.

Supporting decision analysis

Model manipulation for solution finding

Once a model has been defined it is important to be able to use it easily for solution finding. As we have seen in Chapter 3 when studying the normative point of view, it is very useful to distinguish decision variables (instruments), goal variables and exogenous variables (in a model). The usual assistance that a DSS will provide to support solution finding is the following:

- *Computation* of the system variable of the model.
- Assistance in *estimating* the value of certain variables (by using knowledge on the domain).
- *Sensibility analysis* and *impact analysis* on criteria (goal variables) on environmental and decision variables following procedures introduced in the decision analysis cycle (see Chapter 3).

With a formalized model the user can generate alternatives (to which are associated criteria values) and choose among them. For instance, with the model FINSIM, described in Chapter 7, given a projection of financial needs, a financial manager will be able to define and simulate several financial strategies using debt, equity, leasing or a mixture of them.

Alternative evaluation

In the domain of finance, a certain number of classical criteria for evaluating alternatives exist such as the net present value and the internal rate of return. If the decision maker wishes to follow the normative view of decision analysis we shall need functions to encode our knowledge on variables and preference for the outcome, as we have seen in Chapter 3. To decide among several alternatives the manager usually takes into account different criteria (goal variables). These criteria may be numerous and conflictive. Most of the time in real life the selection of one alternative is done intuitively. However, in finance, in particular, the modeling of the relation between risk and return for assets for which a market exists is known (Sharpe, 1963).

Multi-criteria decision and preference modeling

As we have seen in Chapter 3, two rational decision makers can very well take two opposite decisions when facing the same alternatives. The reason is that their preferences for criteria are not the same.

Very often, decision makers do not wish to make their criteria or preferences explicit. They do not separate values and facts but, by judgment, they make a choice (see Section 2.6). However, in complex and non-repetitive situations with high risk they feel the need for support concerning their choice.

Much work has been done on assessement of multi-attribute utility functions as we have seen in Chapter 3, as well as on multi-criteria decision making.

If we wish to support the choice phase of the decision making process it is important to provide preference modeling and algorithms for multi-criteria decision making within the DSS. Even if these functions are not, at present, standard in DSS environments they have attracted more interest recently.

Group decisions: facilitating negotiations

In many cases, the decision problem is faced by one person, in other cases many people are involved and negotiation is required. When many people are involved in a negotiation leading to a decision several types of problems are faced:

- Conflicting criteria and preferences.
- Different information available to each participant.
- Communication problems; in some cases due to the fact that they are geographically dispersed.

The problem of conflicting criteria and goals is a difficult problem. We have dealt with some of the these aspects in Chapter 3.

Several technologies have been developed to support group decision making (see for instance, Kraemer, 1988). These technologies generally tend to provide a DSS kind of environment to members of the group.

When many persons are involved and geographically dispersed it is important that communication process be supported, not only to exchange basic data and share decision models, but also to help them in the negotiation process and to keep contact in between face-to-face meetings. Electronic mail and computer-assisted teleconferencing are very important functions of the DSS in such situations (Johansen *et al.* 1974). The ability to support sharing of models, text, and display is a key characteristic of such environments. However, in contrast with most present electronic mail systems, the communication function must be integrated within the rest of the DSS. De Sanctis (1987) makes a classification of the kinds of support which can be provided to a group. The first level of support being communication, as emphasized above; the second level being decision analysis support; and the third level is providing knowledge bases and expert systems.

5.2.4 Stored information and knowledge about the problem domain

As stated by Bonczek *et al.* (1981):

> 'Unless it contains some knowledge about the decision maker's problem domain, a decision support system is likely to be of little practical value. In fact a good deal of the power of a decision support system derives from its knowledge ability about a problem domain.'

The information embedded in DSS includes, typically:

(1)   **Data**, often in such a large volume that the decision maker has neither the time, nor the inclination, to absorb it in his or her own memory. These data concern attributes of entities.

(2)   **Text**, typically, an explanation of the meaning of concepts and conditions of use of models.

(3)   **Variables**, typically, the names of important variables used in the solution of classical problems of the domain. Such variables may be attributes of entities in the database, but can only be found in models.

(4)   **Models**, much knowledge and knowhow is involved in models: which variables have to be taken into account, what the important relations between variables are and the mathematical structure of these relations.

(5)   **Reports**, knowledge is also involved in the display of information in the form of reports. Reports, suited to help in problem diagnosis,

for example, are complex objects. Just think about the amount of expertise needed to describe a 'uses and sources of funds' report!

(6) **Graphics**, graphics images contain much knowledge. For example, the good graphical presentation of report to follow up consumption of budgeted resources as shown in the JIIA-86 case study implies a specialized knowledge of the problem.

(7) **Rules**, objects or other knowledge representation methods. As we shall see in Chapter 6, knowledge can be stored as rules. This form of knowledge representation is particularly well suited for symbolic knowledge.

5.2.5 Giving assistance

As we have seen, the user interacts with the DSS through a language. This language is of a paramount importance in DSS usage. The user should receive, from the system, assistance on:

- syntax;
- resources available within the system (models, reports, subsystems, data and so on);
- the definition or computation of concepts used in the system;
- explanation of hypotheses on which models rely and their methods of computation;
- possible solutions when using a model for selecting alternatives;
- methodological assistance when defining and using a decision model (we shall see in Chapter 7 that progress in AI has much recently extended this capacity).

5.3 The concept of a DSS generator or DSS development environment

Special software development tools (generators or shells) have had to be designed to implement DSS quickly and easily, and to integrate, with synergy, the several computer technologies required.

In the JIIA-86 case study, the solution to the problem implies the integration of database technology, modeling, display, statistical, and telecommunication software. Such technology cannot be developed in a short time to solve the problem of a user, it must be readily available.

The manager who wishes to use a computer to support a decision rarely has the time to go through the standard steps of a software project of data processing type. These steps are usually known as the project life cycle:

requirements, specifications, design, unit programming, unit testing, integration, integration testing and maintenance. He works under time constraint and the implementation has to be done in a few months or weeks sometimes in a few days! If this constrain is not fulfilled the manager will solve his or her problem by other means and then deal with something else.

Clearly, the user plays a much more important role in the development of a DSS application than in a data-processing application. In a data-processing application the user expresses the specifications of what he or she wishes to a computer specialist, who will design a solution and implement it. In a DSS type of application the situation is different, we wish to supply a tool to support a given decision class, to a user, who will solve his or her particular problem. This tool constitutes an environment which must enable him or her to realize a certain number of functions. The problem is to create this environment in such a way that the tool assists the manager from the start, creating a better supporting environment for the decision class than in the preceding situation. (For example, by giving easier access to data, a better way to display information and the access to decision models to make computations and generate alternatives.) In other words, in certain situations, *the user is the designer* of his or her DSS. He or she may also find himself having to use a DSS which has been implemented for a specific decision class.

The characteristic of DSS situations is that the problem is in frequent evolution. Ill-structured problems usually evolve rapidly with time. Researchers and software companies have concentrated their efforts on developing software that is directly usable by end users after a period of education that is as short as possible.

5.4 Functions of a DSS generator or a DSS development tool

Efficient implementation (fast and at low cost) of DSS implies the use of DSS development tools. We shall now present the conceptual structure of a DSS development tool, then discuss the main functions of such software.

5.4.1 The conceptual structure of DSS development tools

The conceptual structure of a DSS development tool is explained in Figure 5.6 (Klein and Manteau, 1983). The key elements of this structure are found in Klein and Tixier (1971) and were also proposed by Montgomery and

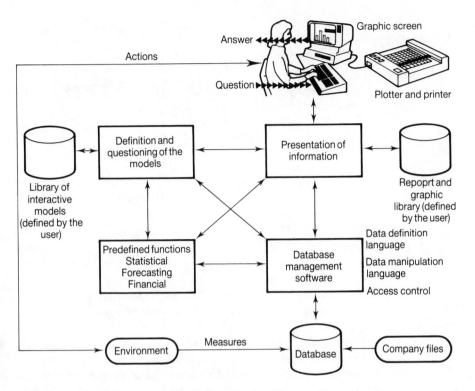

Figure 5.6   The conceptual structure of a DSS development tool.
(Reproduced from Klein M. and Manteau A. (1983). *OPTRANS: a Tool for Implementation of Decision Support Centers in Process and Tools for Decision Support*. Sol H.G., ed.)

Urban (1969) for marketing DSS. As can be seen from Figure 5.6 the user of a Decision Support System Generator (DSSG) will be provided with a language to access the following integrated services or subsystems:

- a data management subsystem,
- a modeling subsystem,
- a display subsystem,
- a toolbox subsystem (statistics, decision analysis techniques and so on).

Clearly, the DSSG must also let the designer define the DSS user interface that he or she finds appropriate to access the software functions, such as window management, menu creation and so on.

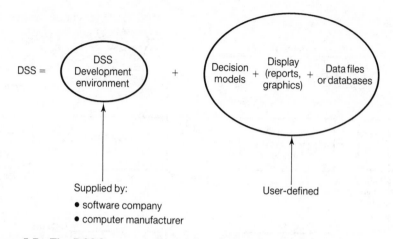

Figure 5.7   The DSSG as an end-user development environment.

The functions to be supported in the DSS are: information collection, problem recognition, economic and financial model formulation, and decision analysis.

The information collection function will be assisted using mainly the technology of data management, and database management systems in particular. Other computer technologies useful here are telecommunications (as soon as distant users are to interact with databases), and computer-assisted messaging or teleconferencing (as soon as message-type information has to be exchanged among widely-dispersed users).

The problem recognition function will be assisted by software tools such as language definition reports and/or graphics.

The economic and financial modeling function will be assisted by specialized modeling languages and statistical software that are used to identify or calibrate relations between variables.

The decision analysis function will be assisted through the language for model manipulation, the preference modeling functions and specialized algorithms for multi-criteria evaluation. As we can see in Figure 5.7 the designer will define three kinds of objects using the three main subsystems of a DSSG: database management, modeling and displays. We shall now describe briefly these subsystems.

5.4.2 Database management subsystem

With respect to the support of this function we find DSS generators which include support from simple data management to advanced database management systems. Methlie describes the data management techniques used in

DSSG. The growing importance of the Database Management Subsystem (DBMS) in DSS is due to the fact that the DBMS technology solves two fundamental problems:

(1) Centralization, coordination, integration and diffusion of information in a community of users.

(2) Logical independence between data and decision models.

With respect to the first problem what has been true, historically, for data processing applications is also true for decision support applications. If the information required by several DSS users has to be shared, the functionality of a DBMS, as described below, is required. This DBMS will prevent the step-by-step creation of a large number of files as the DSS evolves, and keep data integrity.

With respect to the second problem we wish to point out that **data and model independence** is the key to smooth evolution of the system.

Since many DSS situations arise where managers have to make decisions relying on information taken out of a large pool of rapidly evolving data, a DBMS is required in these situations. However, if the DSS uses dedicated data files and performance is critical, then the DBMS is probably undesirable. This is why some DSS development tools such as OPTRANS exist with or without the DBMS component.

General functions of the DBMS

A DBMS is the software that enables the user to organize data on peripheral drives and supply him or her with procedures to search and select that data. To obtain this result the user will describe, in abstract terms, what he or she wishes to do with the data, leaving the system to search as a function of the presentation and organisation on physical support. In brief, a DBMS will provide the following functions.

Data definition
A language called the Data Definition Language (DDL) is provided to describe the data entities and their relationships which will be stored in the database. There are several levels of description of data. When we speak of the *user perception* of the database we shall speak of the *logical* description, if we speak of the organization of data on physical devices we shall speak of the *physical* description. One of the important design problems of DBMS is that the logical description should be as close as possible to the concepts of the users. One of the problems of DBMS for DSS is that users have often to describe fairly complex numerical concepts at the database level. One of the first examples of DBMS design for supporting DSS was described in Klein and Tixier (1971) and Klein and Levy (1974).

Data manipulation

This function provides the user with a language to interact with the database. This interaction takes the form of a dialogue to search, select, sort and modify data.

In database terminology there are three classes of users: end users, application programmers and database administrators. Computer specialists will be able to use algorithmic procedures and end users will use a partially non-procedural command language. However, we have seen that end users, in management and in finance, in particular, wish to define complex models. These models will have to be fed by data coming from the database. As we shall see in Section 7.4 when describing FINSIM, a financial model can be fed by data coming from a database of several hundreds or thousands of companies. In the JIIA-86 case study described at the end of this chapter a model will not only have to be fed by data in the database, but after a series of computations, will have to *update* the database with new data results from that computation. It is also fundamental that new attributes of an entity in the database can be defined using existing attributes.

Data integrity

The more abundant the information in a database the more risky it is to have a piece of data entered that is wrong with respect to the real world. To diminish this risk, the DBMS should allow the user to describe rules to maintain the integrity of the database. These rules are called **integrity constraints**. They correspond to properties that should always be verified in the database whatever the data entered. For instance, in a financial database of annual reports the total assets should always be equal to the total liabilities in the balance sheet.

Control of access rights

If a database is shared among several users, certain subsets of data must only be used by authorized persons. A DBMS must provide procedures to control these access rights. For instance, in the JIIA-86 case study described at the end of this chapter a branch manager should not be allowed to *modify* other branches data, but he may be allowed to *list* other branches data.

The access rights are given by the database administrator who also has the responsibility for defining the logical structure of data, as well as the conceptual data model, and the integrity relations.

Concurrency control

Very often users of decision models or users of statistical routines access the same information in the database at the same time. The DBMS must provide procedures to detect cases when concurrency occurs and deal with it properly. For example, in the case of an inventory database, two users may request a certain quantity of the same item. These two requests have to be dealt with sequentially so as to find out if the first request can be satisfied, then if the second can.

Transaction recovery

In case of hardware failure the database ceases to operate. To make it possible for the system to restart when the incident has been corrected, the DBMS must keep information on transactions at certain control points to enable restarting of the database in a satisfactory state.

Time concepts

The time aspect is so important in management and finance that in most data management subsystems for DSS there are time concepts already in existence in the database. In other words, the system already knows concepts such as year, month, term, semester, week, day, 24 January 1989 and so on. In some systems the user does not have to compute how many calendar days exist between 24 January 1989 and 15 June 1989.

Data extraction

Information required for the decision problem may be represented in many different files. Some of these may be DSS **internal** files, that is, files created and maintained by the DSS data management subsystem itself. However, because of the variety of information requirements for a decision situation, access files managed by other processing systems or external DBMS must also be provided.

These files are called **external** files. External files may be operational, transaction files. They may be accessed through their own database management systems or file management systems; which, in turn, may operate on different computer systems under different operating systems.

Extraction is a technique to access different kinds of source files, operate on these files and produce a target file, called the **extracted database**. Extraction differs from queries in a data management system in two ways. Firstly, a description of the source files, which may be external to the DSS, must be available for the extraction process.

Secondly, while a query is normally displayed to the user, the result of an extraction operation is loaded into a target database.

In a DSS it is of particular importance to be able to collect data from existing data files already stored on computer storage media, since the information required most likely will come from a variety of sources. Data extraction or data conversion as it is sometimes called, is a well-known problem in computer data processing. Software systems have been developed to move data from one file management environment area to another. However, these software systems are not suitable for DSS.

Extraction in one form or another is well known in business data processing. However, most extraction processes are customized to specific applications, and little has been done to describe this process in more general forms. Tools for data extraction should be developed and included in a more comprehensive data management function for DSS (for this point see Methlie (1982).)

5.4.3 Modeling subsystem

The modeling subsystem of a DSSG will have to provide several services: a modeling language to help the user structure his or her problem, define computation of criteria and the definition of the data needed by the models, a command language to manage the model base and a language to manipulate the model for solution finding.

As we have seen in Chapter 2 the modeling language is a key element in the process of supporting the structuring activity of the decision maker. In this book, since we concentrate on financial applications, the dominating modeling paradigm is **equations** modeling. We have seen, in Chapter 3, the concept of decision tree and the more advanced concept of influence diagrams. We think that an ideal modeling subsystem should enable the user to combine decision trees or influence diagrams with a language to model the outcomes. Even in this restricted context it is not obvious what the main characteristics of a 'good' modeling language should be. To support the structuring of a problem by the means of a decision tree or an influence diagram requires that graphical modeling tools be used in other ways to make them easier to use.

The support of the computation of the parameters of the decision tree or the influence diagram (outcome values and so on) requires an equation-oriented language. Several such languages have been developed. As a consequence, several kinds of modeling languages may be needed. A modeling language such as Dynamo is different from standard financial modeling languages in the sense that, for example, it distinguishes between several kinds of variables such as: levels, rates, auxiliaries and so on.

Also, it should be recognized that, generally, the modeling subsystem should include two kinds of modeling tools; a language to perform *corporate* and *financial* modeling and a language to perform *user* modeling (preference function, risk aversion and so on).

First of all we shall recall some important criteria in the classification of economic and financial models and derive some consequences for the modeling language itself. Then we shall study the integration needed between the modeling subsystem and the other subsystems of the DSS and the problem with using these models for decision support.

Types of models

The classification of models is a complex subject. Several taxonomies of models have been suggested such as that by Forrester (1961), here, we shall only emphasize some important aspects of models which can be put in relation to the decision analysis methodology. These aspects are: deterministic versus stochastic, static versus dynamic, and linear versus non-linear (see Figure 5.8).

Deterministic

A deterministic model is a model in which no variable can take more than one value at the same time. Most of the traditional models in microeconomic theory are deterministic models as are most of the financial or corporate planning models described by Warren (1974), Carleton (1970) and so on. The financial analysis and planning system FINSIM which is described in Chapter 7 falls into this category. Analytical solutions are often the most efficient when using these models to compute variable values.

Stochastic

A stochastic model is a model with at least one variable which is uncertain and described by a probability function. Stochastic models are considerably more complex than deterministic. We have seen, when describing the decision methodology in Chapter 3, that when using models for decision analysis the transformation of a deterministic model into a stochastic one may be needed in order to support the decision analysis cycle. The adequacy of analytical techniques for obtaining solutions to these models is quite limited and simulation is often the only efficient solution.

Static

A static model is a model which does not take time explicitly into account. Most of the work carried out in the area of linear programming, non-linear programming and game theory deals with static models. Often, these models are deterministic and solutions can be obtained by analytical techniques such as optimality calculus and mathematical programming. The case of the portfolio problem as described by Markowitz (1959) and Sharpe (1963) falls in this class.

Dynamic

A dynamic model is a model which deals with time-lagging interactions between variables. Simulation has been rather widely used in the area of economic dynamics. Among the well-known applications of the simulation of dynamic systems are:

- Simulation of business cycles and macroeconomic growth models, Samuelson (1939).

- Simulation models of the firm such as Bonini (1968), Cyert and March (1963) and Forrester (1961).

- Financial planning models of the firm such as Warren (1974), Carleton (1970), Alderberger (1976), and Klein and Levasseur (1971).

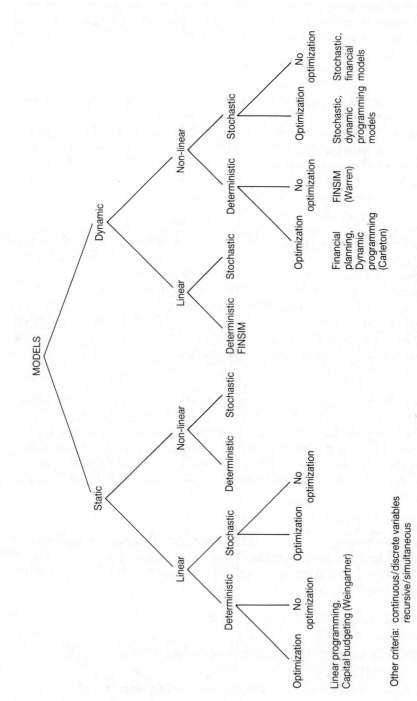

Figure 5.8 A typology of models.

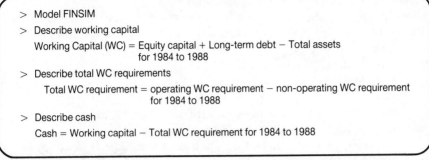

> Model FINSIM
> Describe working capital
> Working Capital (WC) = Equity capital + Long-term debt − Total assets
>   for 1984 to 1988
> Describe total WC requirements
>   Total WC requirement = operating WC requirement − non-operating WC requirement
>   for 1984 to 1988
> Describe cash
>   Cash = Working capital − Total WC requirement for 1984 to 1988

MODEL FINSIM Data Example 500 lines, 32 columns

Figure 5.9   Using the DESCRIBE command of OPTRANS to obtain the definition of variables in the FINSIM model.

In the area of finance, dynamic systems are very important, and it is clear that the real-life systems of the firm that we have to model are dynamic and stochastic.

As we have seen when studying the decision analysis cycle, it is very important to be able to start with a deterministic dynamic model and then transform some of its variables into random variables. In finance, some models have been very important from the theoretical and methodological point of view. Some of them are models, where the goal of the decision maker has been formalized in an objective function that is to be optimized. This the case with the portfolio model (Markowitz, 1959 and Sharpe, 1963), the capital budgeting model (Weingartner) and some long range financial planning models (Carleton, 1970), some others such as Warren's (1974) model or the FINSIM model presented in Chapter 7 have no explicit objective function and, as a consequence, no optimization of decisions.

The modeling language

From what has been described above we can make conclusions about a certain number of characteristics that are suitable for a modeling language.

Natural character of the language
It is very important to be able to define models as a set of equations with the names of variables clearly written. The definition is obtained using the DESCRIBE command (see Figure 5.9.)

Indexing variables in the model
Two types of variable indexing are usually found in DSS: time indexing at the modeling level, and dimension indexing at the database level.

Time indexing variables at the model level
Most models in management and in finance have a time dimension, so it is important to be able to define relations with time-indexed variables, such as:

$$\text{Cash}_t = \text{cash}_{t-1} + \text{cash flow}'_{t-1}$$

or $\text{Cash inflows}_t = \text{sales}\,(t - 1) \times 0.30 + \text{sales}_t \times 0.70$

For DSS generators using a multi-dimensional database, it must be possible to index variables by time but at the database level.

The characteristic of a built-in time dimension is used to automatically link (sum and interpolation) variables having different time frequencies (year, term, month, week and days). When feeding the model from the database a link will be made between the time concept at the database and at the model level. The time dimension enables the user to index variables by time.

Functions and sub-routines in the modeling language
A modeling language should have a wide variety of built-in computational functions: the classical mathematical functions involving numbers (logarithms, integers, exponential, inverse, square root, absolute value, rounding and so on), and, also, vectors: interpolation of steps (to allow the modeling of a discontinuous function), summation, mean, minimum, maximum, variance, standard errors and so on, as well as specialized functions and subroutines:

(1)   Classical financial functions, such as: net present value and internal rate of return.

(2)   Statistical functions, such as: moving average, simple linear regression, multiple linear regression and polynominal fit.

(3)   Financial subroutines, such as: depreciation (straight line, sum of the year digits and declining balance).

There should also be integration between the modeling language and the toolbox. The modeling language must be able to directly access the short-term forecasting subsystem and the statistical subsystem (see Section 5.4.6). Also, the modeling language should provide the user with the capability of calling user-defined functions.

Taking uncertainty into account
One important step in the decision analysis cycle described in Chapter 5 is the encoding of knowledge on uncertain variables. If the modeling language is to support the decision analysis cycle though the probabilistic phase then we should have the possibility to assign probability to variables. This will be done by using several functions such as: normal distribution, uniform distri-

bution, triangular distribution, generalized piecewise distribution, correlation, and so on. These functions will be used to generate values according to the corresponding probability distributions and enables us to generate, through Monte Carlo simulation, a lottery for a goal variable.

Conditional expressions
Often, in a modeling process, the user wishes that certain calculations be done only upon certain conditions being true or false (including time conditions). The general syntax of such a statement is:

> IF (expression) THEN (expression)
> ELSE (expression)

An example of this is:

> taxes = IF taxable income < 0 THEN 0
> ELSE tax rate ∗ taxable income

Procedurality versus non-procedurality
A non-procedural or declarative language enables the user to define a model with relations without having to worry about the sequence of relations in the model. For example, it is possible to write:

> Sales = quantity × unit price
> Unit price = unit production cost + mark up

More generally, a non-procedural language does not request the description of the solution algorithm of the model from the user. A non-procedural modeling system should then be able to recognize what solution method is to be used and use it automatically. Most modeling systems used in commercially-available DSS have only one solution method.

Resolution algorithms available to solve models
A model composed of a set of difference relations between variables over time can be solved in two different ways:

(1) recursively,
(2) simultaneously.

For example, if we have the following models:

Model 1
$$\text{quantity}_t = \text{quantity}_{t-1} \ast 1.15 \tag{1}$$
$$\text{price}_t = \text{price}_{t-1} \ast 1.03 \tag{2}$$

$$sales_t = quantity_t * price_t \tag{3}$$

$$variable\ cost\ t = quantity_t * unit\ cost_t \tag{4}$$

$$total\ cost_t = fixed\ cost + variable\ cost_t \tag{5}$$

$$margin_t = sales_t - total\ cost \tag{6}$$

Model 2

$$quantity_t = C_1 - C_2 * price_t \tag{1}$$

$$price_t = mark\ up_t * total\ cost_t / quantity_t \tag{2}$$

$$sales_t = quantity_t * price_t \tag{3}$$

$$variable\ cost_t = unit\ cost_t * quantity_t \tag{4}$$

$$total\ cost_t = fixed\ cost + variable\ cost_t \tag{5}$$

$$margin_t = sales_t - total\ cost_t \tag{6}$$

It is clear that in Model 1 the quantity sold and price are independent variables. The model can, in fact, be computed variable by variable for the first period, and then computed for the next period. This type of model is easy to solve, recursively.

In Model 2, quantity and price are not independent any more: relation (1) shows that quantity is a linear function of price. The higher the price the smaller the quantity. Relation (2) shows that price is related to quantity. So it is easy to see that these two models may require different solution algorithms. Model 2 necessitates a simultaneous equation algorithm for a non-linear system.

The Gauss-Seidel method is an example of such a solving procedure for a model. But we have seen that some special solution algorithms may be required to solve model where objective functions can be defined.

Loops and control structures

Even if the language is a modeling language and not a programming language it is important that repetition of the computation of a model is possible. For example in the JIIA-86 case at the end of this chapter, the user wishes to make a forecast for the sales of each product in the database, and to update the database. Very often, some repetitive procedure has to be accomplished so that the support of the decision process can proceed.

Sorting

We have seen that in the database, sorting is a classical procedure. It may also be needed in a model. For example, a user may be willing to compute, in a model, the values of variables which have an impact on profit, and then class them with respect to those having a positive impact and those having a negative impact, and display them in decreasing order of importance.

User/model interaction

One of the important functions of the DSS development environment is to integrate different subsystems with synergy as we shall see in Section 5.4.11. This integration will have to be achieved between different subsystems.

Once a model has been defined, it is very important that a user can manipulate the model to interact with it and also to make it usable to other potential users. To achieve this goal the modeling language must allow the user to:

- Manipulate the model during the model design process;
- Input data while the model is running;
- Define sophisticated display for data input and output;
- Manipulate the model for decision support.

Interaction during the model design phase
During the design phase the user needs, mainly, the capacity to check the logic of the model. During the decision support phase it is more a question of supporting the decision analysis cycle such as the one described in Chapter 3.

For example, during the design phase the user must be able to list the model, display the value of any variable (numerical or graphics), trace the computation and so on.

The OPTRANS development environment enables a user to request the definition of any variable through a DESCRIBE command (see Section 5.6).

User/model interaction while the model is running
This interaction should not be limited to inputing data (numerical or alphanumerical) while the model is running but also to select other models, databases, reports and options.

For example, in the OPTRANS development environment which we describe in Section 5.6 it is possible, during the interaction with a model, to pass the control to another model, to select the printing of a report or a graph and so on.

Defining sophisticated display
If we wish the model to be used by somebody who has not defined it, or who is using it only casually we need to guide the user. To achieve this, the modeling language must include statements to define pull down menus, and sophisticated display mixing: such as, menus, reports, and graphics. This means that the window manager and the modeling language are integrated.

In Chapter 7 several examples of such displays in the use of the FINSIM model are given.

Interaction with the model for decision support
The problem here is to support the decision analysis cycle. Commands must be available not only to run or solve the model but also to make:

- impact analysis (WHAT IF),
- sensitivity analysis,
- Monte Carlo analysis (simulation with probability distribution).

If the user is willing to undertake a decision analysis cycle as described by Howard and Matheson (1968) then he or she must be able to access special functions to:

- encode the prior knowledge about variables;
- encode the time preference of money;
- encode the risk aversion;
- make different kinds of sensibility analysis.

If the alternatives studied have multiple outcomes, he or she may be willing to encode his or her preference into a multi-attribute function.

Model interaction with other subsystems

Database/model interaction
One of the important functions of the DSS development environment is to integrate different subsystems with synergy, as we shall see in Section 5.4.11. This integration will have to be achieved between different subsystems.

Feeding the model with data from the database
We have seen that, generally, a DSS integrates decision models with a database management system (see Figure 5.7).

The solution of the JIIA-86 case study provides an example of this integration. The FINSIM model we have described in Chapter 3 also gives a good example of what is needed. In a bank, the management may wish that the credit analysis model FINSIM be fed with data from a database containing all the balance sheets and income statements of clients and/or prospects of the bank. So it is necessary that the designer expresses, in the FINSIM model, with which company data he or she wishes to work. More precisely, it must be possible, in a model, to define which data is needed in the model and access them automatically in a clear way for the user.

The modeling language must then provide statements to give the logical definition of data needed in the model. So a typical model can have the structure shown in Figure 5.10.

As we have seen above that very high interaction must be possible between a model and its user, it must be possible to define the model view of the data interactively during an interaction with the user. For example, the

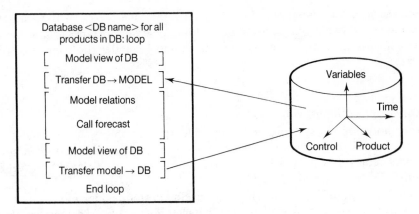

Figure 5.10   Model/database relation (data transfer).

model will request the name of the company to the user, and use the answer (the company name) to complement the view of data needed to feed FINSIM (the list of financial variable and time periods).

It is also necessary that a model can update the database. We have a good example of such a situation in the JIIA-86 case study.

If a model makes a computation, such as a short-term forecast, the computation is applied to the sales variable associated with a list of products stored in the database.

If the user wishes that the model updates the sales forecast in the database each period (monthly, for example) so that sales team or branch managers can use them. The structure of the model must then be like the one shown in Figure 5.10.

Modifying the structure of the database with a model

It must be possible to create new attributes of an entity in the database from the model, and to create and delete entities in the database from the model.

Interface design

To facilitate the use of a DSS it is important to be able to define good user interfaces. For example, when working with a decision model we may wish to see on the same screen:

- the decision variable in a window;
- a goal variable displayed as a graph in another window;
- the relations of the model in a third window;
- the available commands in a fourth window.

So, the modeling language should include statements to call the window manager and the display subsystem. Color is a very important variable in the design of a good interface. The colors should be under the control of the user.

Model/model interaction

The modeling subsystem should provide the possibility for a model to pass control to another model or to a sub-model (in the case of a sub-model, control is passed back to the main model once the sub-model is run).

For example, once a user has developed a financial model such as FINSIM he or she may be interested in developing a sub-model dealing with the production function, or a sub-model which is a market simulation of demand.

Model/display subsystem interaction

The modeling language should contain instructions to call the display subsystem (see Section 5.4.4) so that a model can pass the control to a report or a graph and be back in the model when the display has been done. Communication of variables (numerical and alphanumerical) must be automatic between model and display. In other words, the user should only have to type in a command to the model to obtain the display of a graphics or a report. It should be possible to display reports or graphs automatically, using instructions from the model. The solution provided by OPTRANS is presented in Section 5.6.

Whereas spreadsheets provide one fixed format of report, DSS display subsystem should be capable of supporting as many different types of report as required (see FINSIM, Chapter 7). This interaction is very important to support the decision analysis cycle since we need to display time evolution of model variables, and also probability distribution of variables (environmental or goal variables) and lotteries.

The display of a graphical form of the causal relationship of a model, which is a very interesting way to help the modeling process of the user, implies the integration between the model and the graphical system.

Model/outside software interaction

The modeling language should contain instructions to pass control to software that is outside the DSS development environment, such as operating system commands and/or any other application software. This is a necessity since, in case the modeling language is not well suited for a complex computation, for example, it should be possible to define such a computation in Pascal, C or any other language and call it from within the model.

Model toolbox interaction
The modeling language should give access to existing software for solving problems such as: short-term forecasting, statistical analysis, optimization algorithms and OR methods. For example, it should be possible, when defining a cash management system, to call a short-term forecasting routine or, when defining a planning model, to call a regression to identify a relation.

Language of model base management
The user may develop several decision models as his or her work progresses. If we suppose that there is a community of users then several decision models may also be defined. Each model is usually designed to support a specific problem solving process. The modeling subsystem should provide the command language to create, delete, modify, catalogue and edit the models available. The language should also enable the user to change access rights to the models.

Language to manipulate model for solution finding
This is a key element in the quality of the modeling subsystem. It must be possible to use commands for: sensitivity analysis, impact analysis, moving from a certain variable to a probabilistic one, displaying distributions, encoding knowledge on variables and encoding risk preference.

5.4.4 Display subsystem

The display of information is a key feature of DSS development environments. Two kinds of display are usual in management and finance, in particular, reports and graphics. However, as we have seen above, it is very important to be able to combine these basic elements with a window manager so that the decision process is better supported.

Report generator

The role of a report generator is to enable a user to define structured reports easily and independently from a model. This subsystem is used when the report generated at the model level is not sufficient. The language of the report generator should let the user define the columns and lines of a report with titles, heading zones, variable names, columns, spaces, special characters (£, $ and so on). The important difference between the print commands available at the modeling subsystem level and the statements (or commands) defining a report is that these statements are stored in a file and are executed when the user wishes to print or display the report. There are several reasons for using a report generator:

(1)   The report may be saved in a report library, eliminating the need to re-enter complex print directives.

(2)   The syntax of the report generator allows a number of sophisticated options which are not available at the model subsystem level.

(3)   The report may be generated repetitively by typing one simple command.

Language for report base management

As a user defines new reports he or she will be willing to catalogue them. The display subsystem should provide a command language to save, delete, rename, report and change their access rights.

Report/model interaction

As we have seen above, the model must be able to pass control to the report, and the report must be able to pass back control to the model.

Since communication of data should be possible between model and report, a report should be automatically updated according to changes made at the model level (the model with which it is associated). For example, in the FINSIM model, the title of a report should be updated with the name of the company and the data which it uses.

Graphics

The most usual graphic presentations used in business are curves, bar charts and pie charts. These graphics are usually less complex to define than reports, and the commands needed to generate them are fairly simple. However, in certain cases it can be important to be able to define more complex graphics, for instance, a graphic that mixes curves and bar charts. Graphics are also used to represent the causal relationship in model equations.

Window management

This is a tool that has been recently added to the standard service of a DSSG. A window manager helps in designing much more efficient and ergonomic interfaces between the user and the system. We shall see examples of this in the FINSIM Expert presentation in Chapter 7. In many cases the support of the decision maker is much improved if he or she can have several types of information displayed in front of him or her at the same time. For instance, there will be:

- In one window, the evolution of a variable that is being studied in a graphical form.

- In another window, the numerical values of the variable, the mean and historical values of an explanatory variable.

- In a third window the forecasted value of the variable using given forecasting methods.

- In a fourth window a series of commands available to change the forecast, or move to proceed with the work.

Window management is very useful to define 'forms' when we have to enter data in a system and wish to display, on the screen, the exact form the user is used to filling in.

5.4.5 Editing subsystem

As we have seen, models and reports are in a DSS development environment defined with a modeling language and a reporting language. The user needs very often to modify the text of a model or of a report. This task is made easy when an editor is available. Such a software tool is standard in a programming environment and is also essential in a DSS development environment. Most advanced DSS environments provide a full screen editor. The editor can also be used to document the DSS but these tools are not made to replace advanced text processing software.

5.4.6 Statistical and management science algorithms (toolbox)

On several occasions, the DSS designer may need to access a toolbox of statistical and/or management science algorithms or models. For example, in the process of model building he or she may be willing to identify the relation between variables. This can be done using a regression algorithm. In a DSS for cash management or production planning, the user may wish to use a short-term forecasting algorithm, which should be among the available statistical tools.

Statistics and data analysis

Statistical methods can be subdivided into explanatory methods and descriptive methods. Standard explanatory methods include: segmentation, discriminant analysis, regression analysis, canonical analysis and correlation. Standard descriptive methods include: hierarchical clustering, typology, indscal, multi-dimensional scaling and factorial analysis, and so on.

It is also important to be able to deal with diverse types of data: quantitative, qualitative, ordinal, metric and non metric.

Short-term forecasting

This system provides the user with classical endogenous methods of short-term forecasting: trend fitting, exponential smoothing, multiple regression, Winter's method and box-jenkins.

Optimization and other OR techniques

In certain cases when an objective function may be defined it may be possible to use optimization methods such as linear programming, quadratic programming, or dynamic programming to find 'optimal' decisions. The analyst may be interested in accessing such methods. It is important that these methods can be accessed at the model level.

Database/statistical subsystem interaction

This interaction means that, at the database level, it must be possible to call one of the statistical methods directly. The transfer of information from the database to the statistical subsystem must be totally clear to the user, who for example, when using a regression, should be prompted for the name of the variable to explain, the number of explanatory variables and the name of each explanatory variable, the user should then have only to type the variable names.

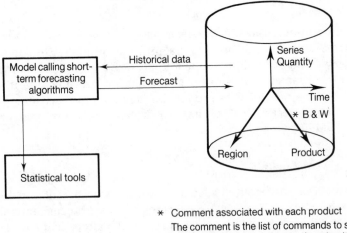

* Comment associated with each product
  The comment is the list of commands to select and run the short-term forecasting algorithm (or methodology) best suited for the product.

Figure 5.11   Use of model-calling statistical routines to update the database with a forecast on each product.

Model/statistical subsystem interaction

This interaction means that at the model level it must be possible to call any of the statistical methods. Such an example of integration is given in the JIIA-86 case study or when a model calls a short-term forecasting routine to make a forecast and then update the database, as shown on Figure 5.11.

Knowledge and preference encoding algorithms

As we have seen it in Chapter 3, we may need to encode the knowledge of the decision maker on uncertain variables. Much work has been done on the assessment of probability and software to do this exists. We also need, if we wish, to support a decision analysis to encode user's preference and we have seen in Chapter 3 the existence of methods for doing this. These algorithms can be made available in the modeling subsystem (in the user modeling part) instead of the toolbox.

5.4.7 Communication function

Two important communication functions should be provided in a DSS environment. One deals with exchange of messages between users of the DSS, particularly when they are geographically dispersed, the other deals with the exchange of data between two copies of the DSS when working in a distributed environment.

Exchange of messages between users

This function is usually provided through some sort of Electronic Mail (EM) or Computer-Assisted Teleconferencing (CAT). The EM subsystem sends and accesses both private and public messages. The difference between an EM and a CAT system is that CAT can support real-time group communication, and allows an electronic conference organizer to specify who will be permitted to participate in the conference. EM does not usually support these functions.

For instance, in the JIIA-86 case study presented at the end of this chapter a conference could be organized to support the exchange of messages between all managers of branches, another one for all controllers and another one for all marketing managers.

One very important feature of the CAT subsystem is that it gives access to all the messages which have been exchanged in the past. These messages constitute a database of messages through which a user can make searches. For instance:

    print all messages sent by M. Davis

    print all messages sent by M. Davis between 1 June 87 and 1 September 87

    print all messages including the word: KB/DSS

with such a communication system users can share a decision model and exchange ideas in real time. Such systems have proved extremely useful in supporting group decision making or group problem solving when users are geographically dispersed, or in 'crisis' management.

Exchange of data between DSS

Most commercially-available DSSG have a mainframe version and a PC or PS version. It is the case for systems such as OPTRANS, EXPRESS, SYSTEM-W and ECS-FPS.

One of the standard situations which will be described in Section 5.6 is where several users are working with the PC version and other users are working with the mainframe version.

In the JIIA-86 case study users of the PC version are located at various branches, the user of the mainframe version is a controller at the headquarters. Clearly, the controller needs to receive data from these branches to make consolidations. Such an application will need an exchange of data between the DSS in these branches and the DSS at the headquarters, using some kind of communication network between the PCs and the mainframe.

In the case of a financial database held in a DSS that is located on a computer at the headquarters of a bank, the financial analysts may need to download financial data on companies or persons from the database of the DSS in the central computer to the PC version of the DSS with which they work. In fact, more and more systems are developed on computers that are interconnected through communication networks. As a consequence, distributed DSS are becoming more and more frequent. Also, the tendency is that the mainframe and PC versions of the DSS environment are identical from the functional point of view, the only major difference being that the mainframe copy is in a multi-user environment. In such a context, the following are required:

- Communication to supply data to (from) a decision model of a DSS from (to) the data management sub-system of another DSS located on another computer.

- Communication to transfer text of models and reports from a DSS on a computer to another DSS on another computer.

- Communication to transfer data from (to) the data management subsystem of a DSS to (from) the data management sub-system of another DSS on another computer.

5.4.8 Assistance to the user

A user-assistant can be implemented by the DSS designer in the decision models themselves, but a very important part of the assistance (in fact the largest) has to be provided automatically (whatever the DSS application) by the DSSG. The types of assistance which must be found in the DSS environment are the following:

- syntax (syntactic aspect),
- meaning of command (semantic aspect),
- definition and description of concepts used in the application system,
- condition of use of models,
- methodological advice.

Assistance on syntax

One of the key design problems of a DSS is the definition of the syntax of the language the user will have at his or her disposal to define and manipulate information and models. The syntax should be simple, powerful and well adapted to the concepts of the users. Systems with hundreds of different commands are certainly not well designed. A key idea is to have a diagnosis of syntax errors with a syntax correction mechanism which is context dependant.

In other words, at any point in the system, the user should be able to request the allowed syntax. Also, in case of error the system should provide a clear diagnosis of the error and the allowed syntax. Such a syntax correction mechanism was introduced in the SCARABEE project by J.P. Levy (1973).

Assistance with the meaning of commands

This is usually implemented using an HELP command. By typing HELP followed by the command name or HELP at any time, the user will be provided will the syntax of the command and explanation of the function of that command. In other words the user manual of the system in on line.

Assistance with the meaning of concepts (note mode)

Concepts are denoted by names in the system, for example: 'sales' clearly means the value which has been billed for a given object or service. However, it may be important to know if the person who has created this variable meant sales including or excluding sales taxes.

One way of providing such information is to have **comments** associated with each entity in the system. A comment is a text associated with an entity, model, or report, which can be accessed whenever needed.

Description of a concept

Some variables (or attributes of an entity) in a database or in a model are not elementary variables, but are computed using other elementary variables (or attributes) or aggregates. It is important to have a command to obtain the expression according to which concept is evaluated. An example of the use of such a command is the DESCRIBE command of OPTRANS (see Figure 5.9).

Conditions of use of models

When DSS are used by a large number of users many decision models and reports are likely to be defined over a period of time. Since the conditions of use of these decision models are not always obvious, it would be useful to be able to have comments related to models or reports in order to explain their conditions of use, as was done with variables. We shall also see in Chapter 7 that a possible solution to this problem is a more intelligent user interface.

5.4.9 Sharing of DSS resources in a multi-user environment

We have seen above (Sections 5.4.2 – 5.4.4) that a DSS designer will create within the DSS environment several kinds of objects: data files or databases, models, reports.

As soon as we are working in a multi-user operating system environment we face a resource-sharing problem with respect to the above objects. For example, several users must be able to use the same decision model, obtain data from the same database, and use the same reports.

If the database is a financial database of income statements and balance sheets on several hundred companies, it must be possible for financial analysts to select the FINSIM model (see Section 7.4) and work with it using either data from the same company (in which case we have problems of concurrency control to solve at the development environment level), or using data from different companies.

The sharing of resources is a more complex problem in a DSS development environment than in a database environment since we do not have to share only data but also models reports and sub-systems.

5.4.10 Control of access to the DSS resources

If we share data, models, reports and subsystems in a community of users we shall need a procedure to control user access rights. A branch manager in the JIIA-86 case study will be allowed to use, for example:

- the income forecast model;
- the market share simulation model and its associated reports;
- the data from his or her branch only.

The controller at headquarters level will be allowed to use all that the branch manager can use, as well as data from the other branches. Classically, three levels of access rights have been defined covering all of the DSS resources:

(1)   use only,
(2)   use and list,
(3)   use, list and modify.

From the user point of view one technique is to associate these rights with each resource (data, model, reports and sub-systems). When the user wishes to use a given resource, an access right control routine is activated to check the rights of the user (asking his name and passwords, for example).

5.4.11 Integration of sub-systems with synergy

The concept of integration in DSS has been analysed by Holsapple and Whinston (1984). Before recalling Holsapple's and Whinston's three levels of integration, let us point out the difference between compatibility and integration: If one program can read a file of data output by another program, then the two programs are compatible. If two programs are able to access the same file, then they are compatible programs. However, if their respective functionalities are not coordinated with each other then they are not integrated.

Integration by coordinating activities

> 'Such integrating software is called an operating environment. Examples of generic operating environments include DesQ, Gem, Top View, and Windows. Others have been designed to work with only a specific collection of programs. An operating environment allows a user to select any of the programs for execution, switch on any other program as desired, and later, resume working with the former program at the point where its execution was interrupted. At any moment, the user is directly interacting with only *one* program, though other programs may be completing processing tasks that were started before switching away from them. Often, each program is assigned to its own window on the screen to help keep track of which programs are available for resumption. The facilities of two separate programs cannot be used together in a single operation.' Holsapple and Whinston, 1986)

Integration by nesting

'The nested (sometimes called inclusive) style of integration nests one or more secondary components within a dominant component. In Lotus 1-2-3, for instance, the dominant component is a spreadsheet processor. The secondary components are a rudimentary graph generator and a pseudo-file management capability. Though this latter capability is sometimes loosely called "database management", it is not even at the level of stand-alone file managers such as pfs-File or dBASE – much less at the level of a real database management system.' (Holsapple and Whinston, 1986)

'Another difficulty with the nested integration approach is that the capabilities and capacities of the secondary components are restricted by the dominant component. This weakness has led various commentators to predict the demise of integrated software's popularity in favor of collections of stand-alone programs. The claim is that as users become more skilled, they need and demand the greater functionality that can be delivered by standalone programs, rather than restricted secondary components. While this claim has merit with respect to nested integration, it ignores the fact that this problem is solved by a different style of integration – without incurring the inconveniences and inefficiencies of trying to coordinate separate programs.' (Holsapple and Whinston 1986)

Integration with synergy

'This third major style of integration is called synergistic integration. The term synergy refers to the integration of multiple components in such a way that no component restricts any other and the total effect of the system is much greater than the sum (individual effects) of its components. If an integrated software package is synergistic, any of its component abilities (spreadsheet, data management, etc.) can be used without even knowing about the existence of the others. In no way does any component restrict or interfere with any other component. On the other hand, there are no barriers between components. Data management, spreadsheet, programming language, and other components blend into each other in such a way that there are really no clear dividing lines between them.' (Holsapple and Whinston, 1986)

Clearly, a DSSG with the components we have described must be designed with a synergistic integration of the components.

5.4.12 Capacity to use the components independently

We would like to remind the reader that it should be possible for a user to use the modeling system without having to define his or her data in the data-base first. Later on, the user must be able to feed the model with data coming from the database of the DSS. Similarly, it must be possible to define data and manipulate them at the database management level without being obliged to go to any other subsystem first.

5.4.13 Peripheral supports

A DSS development environment should support standard peripherals such as: CRT terminals, impact printer, laser printer and plotters. This means that standard drivers should be available for most of these peripherals.

5.5 Improvements expected from DSS usage

The improvements due to DSS usage which have been claimed in the literature can be summarized as follows:

- greater effectiveness of decision making (quality of a decision);
- improved efficiency (delay and cost for certain tasks leading to a decision or the solution of a problem);
- better communication among decision makers;
- improving the learning process.

5.5.1 Improving the effectiveness of decision making

This is the most important claim of DSS literature. Two of the oldest examples are:

(1)   The Laundry Equipment Case (Scott-Morton, 71) where a DSS to support the work of the marketing planning manager is described.
(2)   The evaluation work done in the SCARABEE project on financial analysis with the support of the SCARABEE DSS (Girault and Klein, 1971).

We shall recall some of these results starting with the Laundry Equipment Case. In this case, the task of the marketing planning manager is described and, also, which task combines the sales and production plans into specific production targets for the products for which he or she is responsible. The decision process that was made before the DSS was used was spread over 20 days each month. In his analysis of the situation, Scott-Morton points out that the inadequacies of the existing process were not caused by lack of competence but by 'technical constraints and cognitive limitations, particularly in terms of a lack of capacity to manage large computations and alternatives simultaneously'.

'It was decided to use exactly the same input data that the managers currently had available. In many respects the DSS was an improved methodology for handling the manual spreadsheets; it eliminated bottlenecks that prevented the following type of dialogue in the managers' meetings:

'Why don't we take a quick look at what the inventory will look like 7 months out?'

'I don't like that. Let's try it with 3 months' supply for July through to October.'

'No, go back and adjust June and see if we increase production and get those inventories back in balance.'

Such dialogue was impossible before the DSS. More importantly, because of the bottlenecks, the managers' interactions were mutually defensive, even hostile. With the DSS, this changed to an atmosphere of joint exploration. The managers saw the graphical displays as a communication device. They explained ideas, pointed to supporting data, focused on details, looked ahead rather than concentrating on next month's plan, and made comparisons, and, of course, explored far, far more alternatives. Whereas, with the manual system, there was a large cost involved in considering even one more alternative, the DSS reduced the extra effort almost to zero. The result was that the six days of the manager's time spread over 20 days was reduced to half a day spread over two working days.' (Scott-Morton, 1971)

Analysis of these conclusions shows that a better decision was reached because:

- Problems or potential problems could be identified more easily (support for the problem recognition phase in Minzberg framework).
- Graphical output enables a more rapid assimilation of information (support of the problem recognition phase).
- It was possible to generate many more alternatives (support of the design of alternatives phase).
- It was possible to visualize and compare the consequences/outcomes of the alternatives more easily (support of criteria evaluation).

With respect to the SCARABEE experiment, conducted at the HEC Business School in France, from 1970 to 1974 the main ideas of the system were:

- To provide direct access to a financial database.
- To provide multi-access to this database through an interactive language, giving users the possibility to not only retrieve and sort

information under different conditions, but also to define new financial concepts with the language.

- To give access to a report generator to enable the user to define, very easily, any kind of simple or sophisticated report.
- To give access to a set of statistical tools integrated in the language to make their use extremely easy and comfortable.

Even if the main goal of the project was to develop a methodology of design of DSS software environments, rather than to provide a professional service to financial analysts, several experiments were conducted with professionals. The main results of these experiments were the following:

- Analysts could much more easily identify the companies requesting attention, due to the facility of filtering the database for companies that fulfill certain conditions.
- Graphical output was perceived as much more efficient in coming to conclusions, such as comparing the quarterly return of a portfolio and also of the market.
- It was possible to conduct useful statistical analyses which were impossible before (such as the relation between price and company fundamentals, or industry cross-section analysis to compare performance).
- Better heuristics were developed by professionals improving their problem-solving ability. In fact, the learning process of users was accelerated.
- The fundamental aspect of system interaction, facilitating exploration of new ideas in the acceptance of the system.

As a conclusion, we can say that the improved quality of decisions which is reported in the literature when using DSS is due to the following reasons:

(1) Easier access to information.
(2) Faster and more efficient problem recognition.
(3) Access to computing tools and proven models to compute criteria for choice,
(4) Ability to generate and evaluate a large number of alternatives.

It is interesting to note that if reasons (1) and (2) are directly related to the descriptive view of the decision process, as presented in Chapter 2, then reasons (3) and (4) are more related to the normative view and can be justified on a theoretical basis. We shall now give some hints about efficiency.

5.5.2 Improving efficiency of decision making

This consequence is certainly the one which is the easiest to demonstrate and is so generally accepted that we shall not describe it here at length.

In the Laundry Equipment Case described by Scott-Morton, the length of the decision cycle was reduced by a factor of ten, since instead of using 20 days each month, the decision could be reached in two days.

In recent measures made with FINSIM (Chapter 7) used by credit analysts in banks, the difference is mainly in the level of the quality of the decision, since studies are made in much more depth and with more detailed analysis. The work accomplished with FINSIM is done much quicker (usually divided by a factor of 3 or 4). The three main improvements concerning efficiency when using a DSS are:

(1)   Reduction in the cost of the decision.

(2)   Reduction of the delay to reach the decision for the same level of detail in the analysis.

(3)   Better quality in the printed documents supplied to back the decision.

5.5.3 Improving communication and collaboration among decision makers

This consequence is certainly a very fundamental one. In many situations it can be considered one of the reasons for increased effectiveness. This consequence is very striking in the Laundry Equipment Case since, before the introduction of the DSS, two persons with conflicting goals were involved: the director of marketing and the director of production planning. In fact, a third person, the marketing planning manager, was introduced, whose task was to facilitate the discussion between the two others and help to come to an operational decision and solve conflicts. After the implementation of the DSS the atmosphere 'changed to an atmosphere of joint exploration'. This evolution can be explained easily in terms of decision analysis (see Chapter 3). By using a DSS the two managers had a model in common.

The different levels of knowledge about the problem then tend to disappear since variables and relations are made explicit and their value or nature can be discussed more easily and with precision. Divergences between decision makers can clearly stay, but then, there is precise knowledge on the nature of the difference of opinion, and the methodology of decision analysis can be used to solve it. Also, sharing a model will help separate differences between *facts* and *values* or preferences. As we have already seen the clarification provided by this separation is of fundamental support to the decision makers.

We recognize that certain people may not be willing to make things explicit in a decision and, as a consequence, are not likely to be pleased to see a DSS being used. But, such a situation is usually due to the fact that these people are not interested in the improvement of the decision or a discussion of their real motivations or preferences. The decision was already taken (maybe using the DSS) their goal is to have the alternative they have chosen adopted. This is then a different problem: how do you get your preferences adopted or shared by others?

5.5.4 Improving the learning process of users

This consequence of using DSS is also clearly related to the effectiveness issue. In other words, it is because a DSS improves the learning process of users that the effectiveness of decisions is improved. This consequence has even been considered (Klein and Tixier, 1971) as a design criteria: 'a well-designed DSS is the one which speeds up the learning process of the user'. One of the original ideas of the DSS school is a psychological one. Since, in many cases, the normative computer models were not successful, the recommended approach has been to provide the user with a computer environment within which he or she can accomplish the task more effectively (see Figure 5.12) and become conscious of inconsistency and deficiency in the decision processes:

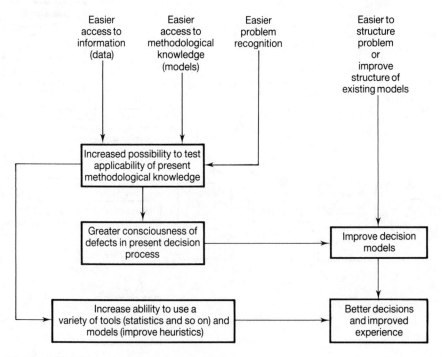

Figure 5.12   Learning process in a DSS environment.

- Easier access to pertinent information through the data management subsystem.
- Easier problem recognition through the display subsystem.
- Easier problem structuring through a modeling language (with emphasis on the clarity of representation of relations).
- Access to knowledge on the problem domain through existing decision models or the possibility to improve and evolve the decision models.
- Easier and faster generation of alternatives through a model manipulation language.

In other words, this provides the user with a starting DSS environment which is better than the one available before.

The assumption is that if the ability to solve a problem relies on two major components: knowledge (in particular, methodological knowledge) and experience, then the environment will provide an easier way to use that knowledge (by making it easier to build models, for example), and, also, a way to speed up the process of building up experience, since it is much easier and faster to study cases. This process is presented in Figure 5.13 which is

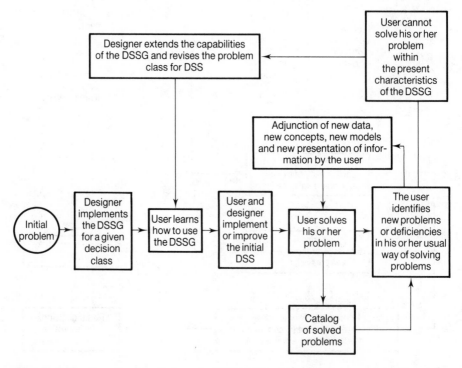

Figure 5.13 Iterative evolution of a DSS and its development enviroment.

derived from an earlier version (Klein and Tixier, 1971). The implementation strategy of the DSS is worked out so as to initialize the learning process of the user and gear it to the evolution process of the DSS itself.

Step 1   The designer designs and implements a DSS development environment (DSSG).

Step 2   The user learns how to use the DSS development environment.

Step 3   The user (or user + designer) implements the starting DSS or improves the existing one.

Step 4   The user works with the DSS to accomplish his tasks and solve problems, so adding to the catalog of solved problems.

Step 5   The user identifies new problems or deficiencies in his actual way of solving problems.

Step 6   If the user can extend the existing DSS by adding new data, new concepts, new models and new presentation then go to Step 3, else go to Step 7.

Step 7   The designer extends the capabilities of the DSS development environment adding a DBMS subsystem, extending the concepts of the modeling language, extending the possibilities of the display generator, adding new data types and adding new subsystems, go to Step 2

5.5.5 Possible drawbacks of DSS usage

We would just like to emphasize here the fact that the availability of a well-designed DSS may also lead to some adverse effects. In our opinion, DSS are there to help managers to make decisions by providing them with a better understanding of the consequences of their decisions, and how they relate to their preference. But, the main task of a manager is to act on his environment to help achieve the goals of his organization in supplying a service or goods to his environment (clients and users). The manager should always be very conscious not to forget to keep a good balance between studying the problem and acting to change the environment. Working with a DSS, as good as it maybe, cannot change the environment. Environments are changed by human beings acting on them! This we can call the **problem of action**.

One of the pertinent criticisms of the DSS concept was made by Winograd and Flores (1986) in their book *Understanding computers and cognition*. The potential problems with DSS, as the authors see them, are the following:

- orientation to choosing,
- assumption of relevance,

- unintended transfer of power,
- unanticipated effects,
- obscuring responsibility,
- false belief in objectivity.

Orientation of choice

The criticism is that

> 'The emphasis implicit in this approach serves to reinforce the decisionist perspective and to support a rigid status quo in organisations, denying the validity of more social, emotive, intuitive, and personalised approaches to the complex process of reaching resolution.' (Winograd and Flores, 1986)

We would like to emphasize here that we recognize that communication is a fundamental task of management, it is useless to try to tell if decision is more important than communication, since both are important and decisions rely on communication.

In some circumstances, the use of computers for communication will be considered as a much more important function than their modeling function. The development of electronic mail and computer-assisted teleconferencing is a good example of this evolution. Also the situation may be such that it is much more difficult to get the commitment of somebody to do a task than to decide that the task has to be done. As we have stated in Section 5.1.2 any DSS application is designed to support a class of decisions. The consequence of this is, simply, that a new user of a DSS must be able, always, to use his or her (natural) intelligence to check that the decision he or she is studying belongs to the class that the DSS was built to support, partially or totally. This capacity of the user is not always easy to apply.

If it is not the case, the user must diagnose whether or not the DSS development environment enables him or her to extend the decision class for which it was built (within the time and budget constraint) to include the new decision. If this extension cannot be done then it is better not to use the system.

Assumption of relevance

'Once a computer system has been installed it is difficult to avoid the assumption that the things it can deal with are the most relevant things for the manager's concern.' (Winograd and Flores, 1986)

As Winograd and Flores point out this behavior is characteristic of people who have not been educated to have 'a permanent attitude of openness to listening'. We could add: who have not understood that any computer application is built under a certain set of assumptions for its use by its designer. If the user is not able to recognize that the condition of use of the system does not fit these assumptions then the system can be harmful.

The problem is that the designer may not be conscious enough of these hypotheses.

Unintended transfer of power

The problem usually arises here if the design made by computer specialists tends to put more emphasis and value on efficiency and to devalue the 'need for human discretion and innovation'. The argument is certainly valid in the case of a full automatization of the decision process, it is much less valid for a DSS since the decision process is only assisted. This argument tends to disappear if the user plays a leading role in the evolution of the system.

Obscuring responsibility

The proposition put forward by Winograd and Flores is that once a computer system is designed and in place, it tends to be treated as an independent entity. For them, the computer's role is not the one of a 'surrogate expert', but the one of an intermediary – a sophisticated medium of communication.

When a computer specialist or a domain expert builds a DSS incorporating a formal representation of their knowledge or discourse (we shall see that this capacity is now much easier to accomplish with expert systems technology), the system will transmit the consequence of this knowledge to the users under the form of advice or statements.

According to Winograd and Flores we should be very careful to remember that the machine is an *intermediary*, the commitment inherent in the conclusion expressed is 'made by those who produce the system'.

We can, of course, only agree with the idea that the DSS is there as a sophisticated means of communication, the responsibility cannot be the one of the machine. However, it is essential to make sure, again, that the future users are properly educated to remember that any DSS or expert system is built within a background of assumptions about how the system will be used, and how its responses will be interpreted.

There is always a risk that a DSS is used in a way which does not fit the assumptions of the expert or designer. The only cure here is education.

5.6 Example of a DSS development environment: OPTRANS

OPTRANS is a DSS development environment, the goal of which was to provide support for all phases of the decision process and which follows closely the conceptual structure shown in Figure 5.14.

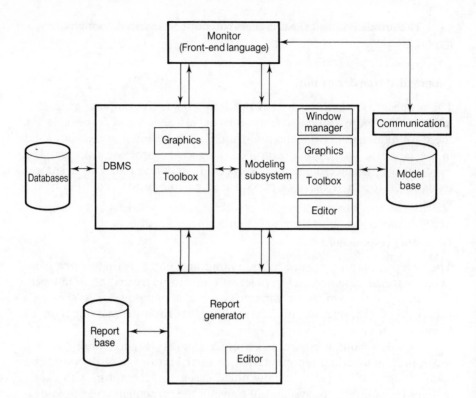

Figure 5.14   OPTRANS overall hierarchical architecture as seen from the user's point of view (version with DBMS component).

5.6.1. Structure of the system

The present system is built as a kernel (nucleus) with extension procedures. The kernel of the system is both modular and hierarchical. Here, we shall only present, briefly, the non-expert version. The expert module is described in Chapter 7.

Modules

The main modules or subsystems are the following:

- a data management or database management system;
- a modeling subsystem;
- a display subsystem (report generator and graphics generator);
- a window manager;

- a toolbox (statistics, short-term forecasting, optimization and MCDM);
- a full screen text editor.

Hierarchical structure

It is possible for the designer to generate different versions of OPTRANS including only those components he or she wishes to use. A structure without the DBMS component (see the FINSIM case study) and a structure with the DBMS component (see Figure 5.14) are both possible, for example. Three levels can be distinguished by a user in the hierarchical structure of OPTRANS when he or she is developing an application:

(1)   a front-end (of monitor) level,
(2)   a modelling, data management, and interface design level,
(3)   a report generator level.

At the front-end level, the user can:

- access the library of resources of the system (directory);
- call any program or file available under the operating system, run it, and return to the OPTRANS environment;
- access other subsystems of the next level: modeling language, DBMS and text editor;
- change some general characteristics of the behavior of the system (output device, number of digits after decimal point and printing default conventions);
- use the communication function to exchange information with other users.

The modeling, data management and communication level

At this level the user can either:

- enter the modeling language to start using it to create decision models;
- enter the data management language to start defining his or her database or data file (if he or she is using the version without the database subsystem);
- communicate with other OPTRANS copies or software using the communication subsystem.

As can be seen in Figure 5.14, such subsystems are synergistically integrated within the modeling subsystem and data management subsystem: window manager, graphics, toolbox, full screen editor.

The report generator level

At this level, the user will access a language to define and display layouts of reports.

5.6.2 Objects managed by the system and their access rights

When using the OPTRANS development environment the user will be able to develop three kinds of objects: databases, models and reports. To obtain the list of the objects' names a command 'directory' is available. The objects are classified by types with the size in number of lines (variables) and columns (time period), and are given with their access rights.

5.6.3 The data management subsystem

Two data management systems are available for OPTRANS. One is a two-dimensional data management system which is adequate for most financial and economic modeling situations, where variables are usually indexed by time. The other is a multi-dimensional database management system which allows the user to deal, with simplicity, with the more complex data structures. The elementary data types used are numbers, strings and dates.

Two-dimensional data management

With the two-dimensional data management system, the user is working with a table that has lines and columns like a spreadsheet. However, this comparison should stop here since the models are not seen as a sequence of 'assignments in cells' but as a sequence of instructions. These instructions being not only assignments (to which a spreadsheet is limited) but are also control types of instruction.

Most financial models do not require more than two dimensions since they are made of relations between variables. These variables being computed over time.

Multi-dimensional data management

OPTRANS provides a six-dimensional DBMS which allows the user to solve, with elegance and simplicity, most financial and management control problems.

Relationship between dimensions

By entering a value of a variable ('sales') for a given year for a given product P produced in a given plant, we implicitly create a relationship between the entities 'sales', 'product' 'plant' and 'date'.

OPTRANS allows two possibilities: either, the user defines the relations between entities, or the relationships are automatically created as he or she enters data. In the first case, the information about the relationships can be used to control the validity of data typed in. In the second case, no control can be made but the use of the system is made simpler.

Memory management of the OPTRANS DBMS

The OPTRANS DBMS is designed to manage an amount of data which cannot be held in the core (as in all real DBMS). If we use the multi-dimensional approach cited above one of the classical problems is to deal with sparse multi-dimensional matrices. OPTRANS will manage the memory in such a way that empty elements are not occupying any space. This is done using binary tree techniques.

The concept of elementary and aggregate variables

In the OPTRANS DBMS the user can define elementary variables (attributes) by using a DEFINE command. It is also possible to define aggregates. An aggregate is a variable (attribute) defined using elementary variables (attributes) or existing aggregates and mathematical or logical symbols. Such aggregate variables can be defined in any dimension. For example, in the time dimension, it is possible to define a moving average in the following way:

定义 define time moving-average = (period (t) + period $(t - 1)$ + period $(t - 2)$))/3

in a control dimension it is possible to define a variance by writing:

define control variance = actual value − budget value

The concept of virtual data and its consequences

An important concept of OPTRANS is that (in the version with the multi-dimensional database) the aggregate variable values are not stored on disk. The definition of aggregate variables is that they are stored on disk and evaluated only when needed. This is the concept of virtual data, originally introduced in Klein and Tixier (1971). The evaluation of elementary data is done by a physical access procedure. It is only at this level that the physical representation of information is used. This access is clear to the rest of the system.

A change in the access mode would only necessitate a modification in this physical procedure. The necessity of the access procedure to elementary data permits an optimization of accesses to auxiliary memories.

Since the evaluation of an aggregate implies the evaluation of aggregates which are used in the definition, this procedure is recursive. This technology has two main consequences:

(1)   It considerably reduces the storage, since only elementary data are physically stored on auxiliary memory (usually disks).

(2)   It provides a mechanism to automatically update any model using this variable and that is connected with the database assuring *consistency* in the model base.

5.6.4 The modeling and display subsystem

The reader is referred to the OPTRANS User Manual (1988).

Exercises

5.1   Do you see similarities between decision problems for which the decision methodology (presented in Chapter 3) seems adequate and those problems which are considered to be 'ill-structured'?

What would be the point of view of a decision analyst on the concept of 'ill-structured problem'?

5.2   Can you describe situations where end-user definition of the DSS seems the appropriate solution? Describe situations where it is unlikely to be the best one.

5.3   Contact somebody in a company which is using a DSS. Study:

(a)   The decision that the system is expected to support.

(b)   The functions in the decision process that the DSS is supporting.

(c)   How the DSS was built (using standard programming language, using a DSS generator or coupling different existing software).

(d)   Which persons were involved in the design and what the tasks of each one were.

5.4   Contact somebody who has been using a DSS generator to develop a DSS. Compare the subsystems (components) of the generator with the list given in Section 5.4.

5.5   (a)   What are the consequences of not having a DBMS component in a DSS generator?

　　　　(b)   What are the suitable characteristics for the DBMS component of a DSS generator?

5.6   (a)   What are the modeling tools suitable in a DSS generator?

　　　　(b)   What are the differences between a standard financial or marketing model and a 'decision model'?

5.7   What are the relations between a decision model and a decision tree or an influence diagram?

5.8   Obtain the documentation of several DSS generators, study and compare the modeling languages available. Is it possible to support user modeling?

5.9   What would you like to find in the toolbox of a DSS generator? Compare with the user manuals of existing DSS generators.

5.10   When is the communication function of a DSS important?

5.11   What is the concept of synergetic integration?

5.12   Select a task involving a decision. Describe the functions a DSS should provide to improve effectiveness of decision making and to improve efficiency of decision making.

5.13   What do you think of the criticisms given by Winograd and Flores in Section 5.5.5?

5.14   A case study for a term project: the JIIA-86 case.

In 1986, during the 'Journées Internationales de l'Informatique et de l'Automatique' (JIIA-86), a bench-mark for DSS development tools was worked out by two researchers. The idea was to ask the companies who were developing and marketing the leading DSS generators in the US and Europe to develop and present a DSS to support the decision processes and tasks which were described in a case called the JIIA-86 case. From an analysis of the solution developed with each system, it was then possible to make a comparative analysis of the main features of each DSS Generator.

We shall give here an adapted translation of the case. The solution which was developed using OPTRANS is available from the authors. On some points, we have extended the text of the case to make it more general and so that we are able to present more advanced features of the OPTRANS DSS. The first part of the case describes the company, its structure and the products sold. The second part describes the tasks to be supported and their associated decision processes. The third part deals with the structure of data in the company data files. The last part of the case lets each software company present the capabilities of their DSS solutions and environments which could not be demonstrated using the case as it is, and that they considered to be both specific and important to their development environment.

We propose this case study being used as a project in a single-semester course.

Description of the company

The case was developed and inspired by the management control DSS needs of a French multinational company. For this test case the structure of the company was simplified.

The company does business in France and in Germany. The sales in Germany are carried out through a subsidiary. In France, the company has four branches: in Paris, Lyon, Nantes and Lille.

A production unit is located in Paris. The products manufactured and sold by the company can be broken down into three product lines: TV sets, hi-fi equipment and video equipment.

(1)   The TV product line is made up of three kind of products: black and white, color and portable.

(2)   The hi-fi product line is made up of four kinds of products: tuners, amplifiers, record players and cassette players.

(3)   The video product line is made up of two kinds of products: recorders and players.

The organizational and product structures are represented in Figure 5.15.

The German subsidiary only markets the hi-fi product line. The exchange rate used is 1 Deutsche Mark = 3 French Francs.

Description of tasks to be supported

The tasks to be supported can be broken down into three domains:

(1)   management control,
(2)   sales and marketing,
(3)   sales forecasting and financial simulation.

Each one of the tasks is now presented.

Organizational structure

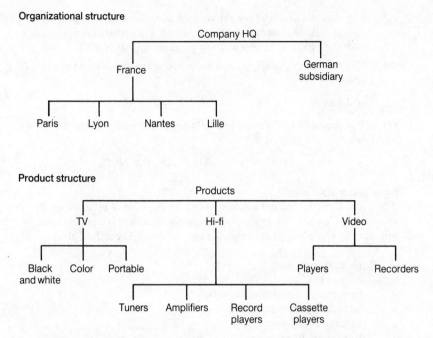

Product structure

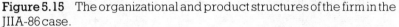

Figure 5.15 The organizational and product structures of the firm in the JIIA-86 case.

Management control

One of the tasks to be supported by the DSS is the computation of monthly income statements. An income statement is defined by the following rules:

(1) For each month, each branch, and each product, a quantity sold (QTE) and a net sale is available (CA.NET).

(2) For each product and each country a unit price is available (PRIX).

(3) The gross sale (CA.BRUT) is computed using the quantity sold and unit price (CA.BRUT = QTE × PRIX).

(4) The percentage of discount (REMISE) is computed using the net and gross sale figures.

$$REMISE = (CA.BRUT - CA.NET)/CA.BRUT$$

(5) For each product and each month a cost of production is given (CT.FAB). The production costs are allocated over the branches in proportion to the CA.BRUT.

(6) For each branch and for each month a marketing cost is given (CT.COM) These costs are allocated over the products in proportion to the CA.NET (net sales).

(7)   For each country and for the year an advertising cost is given (CT.PUB). This annual cost is divided by 12 and is allocated over the products in proportions to quantity sold (QTE).

(8)   The margin (MARGE) is computed using the net sale and the costs.

$$(MARGE = CA.NET - (CT.FAB + CT.COM + CT.PUB)).$$

(7)   The return (RENT) is computed using the margin and the net sale.

$$(RENT = 100 \times MARGIN/CA.NET).$$

Sales and marketing

The French marketing department wants to perform a forecast of the sale of color TV sets for 1987. For that purpose, monthly data are available for the preceding 36 months, for each branch. These data give:

- the quantity sold,
- the unit price,
- the industry market in quantity,
- the industry average price,
- the advertising expense,
- the number of salesmen.

Sales forecasting and financial simulation

The marketing department has computed quantities and sales forecasts for the year 1987. These quantities (NQTE) are given by month, by product and by branches. The pro forma income statement uses the same variables given before. The values of the variables are extrapolated using the following computation rules.

(1)   The unit price (NPRIX) of products increases by 3% in January and by 2% in July for the French branches and by 4% in March for the German subsidiary (compared to 1986 unit price).

(2)   The discount rate (NREMISE) will decrease by 1% compared to 1986.

(3)   The gross sale (NCA.BRUT) is computed as before.

(4)   The net sale (NCA.NET) is computed using the gross sale (NCA.BRUT) and the discount rate.

$$(NCA.NET = NCA.BRUT - (NCA.BRUT \times NREMISE)$$

(5)   The cost of production (NCT.FAB) will be a function of the unit production cost of December 1986, the quantity and an inflation rate of 4%.

$$(NCT.FAB = NQTE \times CT.FAB \ Dec \ 86/QTE \ Dec \ 86 \times 4\%)$$

(6)   The marketing cost (NCT.COM) will be a function of the total marketing cost for the year 1986 and an inflation rate of 3%
$$(NCT.COM = CT.COM \ global \ 86/12 \times 1.03\%)$$

(7)   Advertising costs (NCT.PUB) will be the same as the advertising costs of 1986.

(8)   The margin (NMARGE) and the return (NRENT) will be computed the same way.

ASSIGNMENT

1   Define, for JIIA-86 case:

(a)   The groups of users to be supported.

(b)   The decision processes of each user group:

-    the controller and his or her assistants at headquarters,
-    the marketing manager and his or her assistants at headquarters;
-    the financial manager and his or her assistants at headquarters;
-    the production manager for each plant;
-    the branch managers and the manager of the German subsidiary.

(c)   The possible architectures for the DSS. In particular, an architecture with centralized treatment and an architecture with decentralized treatment.

(d)   The required functions for the DSS (see Figure 5.16). The functions have to be described in the centralized solution and the decentralized solution with respect to:

(e)   The database structure (see Figures 5.17 and 5.18), its definition and its retrieval functions.

(f)   The decision models to implement:
-    margin, sort, max, forecast, income

(g)   The display of information (reports and graphics).

(h)   Which statistical tools should be available to support some of the required tasks.

(i)   The global interface of the system.

The functions have also to be described from the point of view of: the headquarters, the branch, the German subsidiary and the plant manager.

The decentralized solution implies connections between the PCs at branch and plant level, and the mainframe version.

2   Using a DSS development environment such as OPTRANS, implement a DSS to support the computation and display made by the user for any of the concepts described in the text of the case. The system should let the user plot any variable, for any branch and for any product.

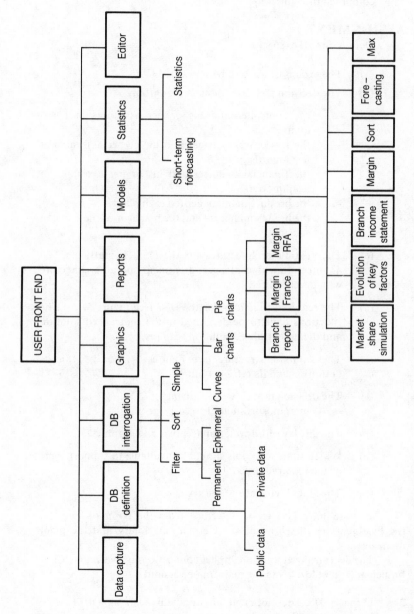

Figure 5.16　Functions of the DSS implemented with OPTRANS to solve the JIIA-86 case (functions at HQ).

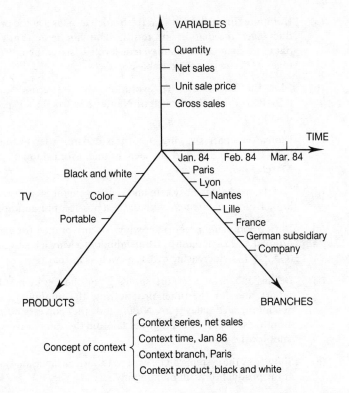

Figure 5.17   Conceptual structure of the database in the JIIA-86 case (HQ Version.)

JIIA–86		Quantity sold	Net sales	Gross sales	Discount
VARIABLE: Quantity sold PRODUCT: Tuner			TIME: JAN 86 .... 5		BRANCH: LILLE .... 6 ....
JANUARY	86	—	—	—	—
FEBRUARY	86	—	—	—	—
MARCH	86	—	—	—	—
APRIL	86	—	—	—	—
MAY	86	—	—	—	—
JUNE	86	—	—	—	—
JULY	86	—	—	—	—
AUGUST	86	—	—	—	—
SEPTEMBER	86	—	—	—	—
OCTOBER	86	—	—	—	—
NOVEMBER	86	—	—	—	—
DECEMBER	86	—	—	—	—
YEAR	86	—	—	—	—

Figure 5.18   Data capture at the database level for a four-dimensional database.

(a)   Compute for each month, at the branch level and at the product level, the margin and return. This can be done at the database or modeling subsystem level. Discuss the advantages of doing it at the database level.

(b)   Plot the curve of the evolution of the gross sales (CA.BRUT) for the branch of Nantes and for the TV product line.

(c)   Plot a pie chart showing, for the video recorder product line, the quantity sold at each branch from January to March 1986.

(d)   Use the modeling subsystem and report generator to show a branch income statement with the best possible presentation.

(e)   Define and print a report showing for any branch for each product and each month, from January to May its net sales (CA.NET) in increasing order, as well as its margin.

(f)   Define and print a report showing for the German subsidiary and for the tuner product line the minimum and maximum net sales (CA.NET) and the corresponding month, as well as the average net sale and the cumulative net sales for the year.

(g)   Show how the system can be used to report variance analysis at the product, branch or company level.

3   Using the toolbox subsystem of the DSS development environment show how to support the needs of the marketing management in term of:

(a)   Statistics, and short-term forecasting (seasonality and trends . . .).

(b)   Simulation of marketing decisions on sales.

(c)   Graphics to support problem recognition and diagnosis.

4   Using the forecasted sales and the computation rules defined in the sales forecasting and financial simulation above:

(a)   Define a model to compute, for 1987, the margin and the return by branch.

(b)   Define and print an associated report showing, by branch, the change, in percentage, between 1986 and 1987 of the quantities sold, of the sales and of the sales margin.

(c)   Use the DSS graphics capabilities to show the change in the sales margin in the following hypotheses:

> –   discounts are cancelled,
> –   catalog prices do not increase,
> –   inflation rate increase of 4% compared to the initial forecast.

(d) Show which command of the DSS you have to use to find out how many color TV sets have to be sold in Paris so that the sales margin is 55.

(e) Show the possibilities of the DSS concerning simulation (goal seeking, sensivity analysis, impact analysis and risk analysis).

5   Evolution of the system. Define the likely evolution of user needs in terms of:

(a) database structure,

(b) model base,

(c) report base.

6

Expert Systems

6.1 Introduction to expert systems

6.1.1 Knowledge-based problem solving

If one looks at any standard textbook in AI one will be amazed at the importance that games and game playing have in this field. In almost any book we find the same problems serving as expository tools: chess, tic-tac-toe, the 8-puzzle and so on. However, you never find games such as football, baseball and billiards. Why? Because chess, tic-tac-toe, and the 8-puzzle all are **formal systems**. Formal systems are characterized by three essential features; firstly, they are token manipulation games like moving a tile in the 8-puzzle; secondly, they are digital in the sense that a tile is either in a correct place or not; and thirdly, that, for any given position, there is a finite, and known number of legal moves that can be performed. Formal systems are self-contained, that is, they carry no references to the outside world which are of relevance to the game, and they cannot be interpreted to have any meaning outside themselves. Thus, formal systems can be studied without introducing the complex concepts of meaning and symbol structures. Formal systems are interesting in the sense that a state–space representation is the basis for problem solving, and that heuristic search is the major problem solving method. Astonishing results have been achieved with computers that can play chess. Games, fascinating as they may be, are, however, fairly unlike most real-world problem solving. Although they may be attractable from a research point of view, due to large state spaces that require effective search algorithms (for example, chess playing), the problem itself is well structured and the domain knowledge limited and easily available. Research in AI on these problems led to the formalization of laws of reasoning, and general methods and strategies for problem solving, as we have seen in Chapter 4. However, these general-purpose problem solving strategies, successful as they may be in the world of games, failed in solving unstructured and uncertain real-world problems, problem areas, for instance, in which we develop expertise.

If you read carefully through the description of experts and expertise given in Chapter 2, you should observe one common thread through all of the features: the importance of domain knowledge in expert problem solving. If the problem solving methods and strategies developed in the field of artificial intelligence should be applied to computerized expert problem solving, more emphasis had to be put on domain knowledge. The person to be given credit for this important observation is Professor E. Feigenbaum at Stanford University. In his work on computerized inferencing of plausible molecular structures of unknown chemical compounds, he experienced the severely limited power of general-purpose problem solving methods and strategies. Human experts, however, rapidly eliminate implausible structures from the solution space by using domain knowledge. This observation led to one of the first computer systems to be labeled an expert system, the DENDRAL System (Buchanan *et al.*, 1969 and Feigenbaum *et al.*, 1971).

Later, at the International Joint Conference on Artificial Intelligence (IJCAI) in 1977, Feigenbaum formulated:

'the paradigm of expert system derives from the knowledge it possesses, and not from the particular formalisms and inference schemes it employs, and further, the expert's knowledge provides the key to expert performance, while the knowledge representation and inference schemes provide the mechanisms for its use.' (Hayes-Roth *et al.*, eds., 1983)

This new paradigm put emphasis on domain knowledge rather than on formal reasoning methods. Hayes-Roth *et al.*, 1983 elaborate further on this and give three reasons. Firstly, most of the difficult and interesting problems do not have tractable algorithmic solutions since many important tasks originate in complex social or physical environments. (This feature of problem solving is also the basis for decision support systems, as described in Chapter 5). Secondly, as we have already elaborated on, human experts achieve their high performance because they are knowledgeable in a specific domain. Thirdly, we have the need for knowledge in an ever-increasingly complex world. The complexity of our world is not created by the means with which we try to solve or reduce this complexity, but by the information technology itself. Using this technology large amounts of data are produced and by telecommunications these data are disseminated throughout organizations and society. We get easier access to more and more information. However, this information has no value unless we are able to utilize it. We need knowledge on *how* to use this information. Knowledgeable persons or experts are a scarce resource of the society. We have shown above that knowledge of a specific problem domain is the key component of expertise. Can we obtain this expertise from human experts and computerize it? If this is possible, then we may develop computer systems which can emulate expert problem solving. Such computer systems we shall call **expert systems**. An expert system is a computer program that uses models of the knowledge and inference procedures of an expert to solve problems. The knowledge consists of facts and heuristics. The Heuristics are mostly private little-discussed rules of experience that characterize expert-level decision making in the field.

6.2 What is an expert system?

6.2.1 An overview

At the beginning of this chapter, we defined an expert system to be a computer program that uses knowledge and procedures to solve difficult problems at the level of professionally-trained humans. We shall now look closer at the functional and structural properties of expert systems. Firstly, we shall introduce the key concepts defining the expert system environment. In subsequent paragraphs we shall develop some of these concepts in more detail. Figure 6.1 shows the main concepts associated with expert systems.

A computer program that employs knowledge and inferencing to solve problems is sometimes called a **knowledge-based system**. When knowledge

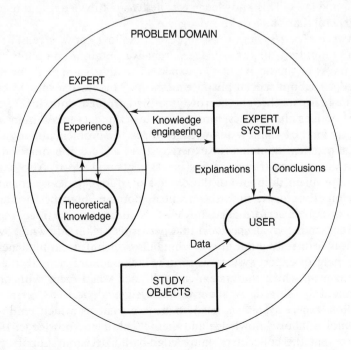

Figure 6.1   The main concepts of an expert system.

and inference procedures are modeled after human experts, we call such a knowledge-based system an expert system. Thus, the knowledge and procedures represented in expert systems are descriptions of the heuristics and search employed by human experts in the field. Two characteristics are particularly important here:

(1)   That the development of expert systems is based on a descriptive theory of human problem solving.

(2)   That focus of development is a representation of expertise, that is, the knowledge acquired by humans through practice and learning.

An expert system is, therefore, built-in dialog with experts in the field. The task of eliciting and modeling this problem solving knowledge and building a computer system is called **knowledge engineering**. This task is carried out by a knowledge engineer; a system designer with some domain knowledge, skill in cognitive methods and techniques, and skill in computer programming. Knowledge engineering will be dealt with in more detail in Chapter 8.

Expertise is developed by training and experience. Sometimes, this knowledge is called *shallow* knowledge because it consists of all the peculiar heuristics and shortcuts that trained professionals have learned to use in order to perform better. However, experts in cognitive domains (which are the only experts we will be interested in) normally have a professional education. Their practice is anchored in a theory, in other words, in first principles, axioms, and laws. This knowledge is called *deep* knowledge and tends to be more general than shallow knowledge.

A true expert system must represent shallow knowledge. The advantage of computing this knowledge is that we obtain a computer program that behaves in similar way to an expert. The disadvantage is that shallow knowledge is about special-purpose methods. Therefore, expert systems are tailor-made for specific and narrowly-defined **problem domains**. A problem domain defines the entities, properties, tasks and events within which a particular kind of shallow knowledge works for problem solving. Typical financial problem domains for expert systems are credit evaluation, financial analysis, option trading, stock investments and so on. Also associated with the problem domain are the objects of study: patients, corporations and so on. By constraining the problem domain, high performance can be obtained. This performance, however, is purchased at a price: the resulting system tends to be a specialist that performs well at a few narrow tasks, but that is helplessly inapt at everything else. Therefore, a tendency in the development of expert systems is to now include more general, theoretical knowledge, on which the system can fall back when faced with problems that cannot be solved by shallow knowledge alone. The term **second-generation expert system** is used to denote systems which employ both experiental, shallow knowledge and theoretical, deep knowledge. It should be noted that the concept of knowledge-based decision support systems, which will be developed in the next chapter, are a kind of second-generation expert system since they employ the combination of algorithmic knowledge usually represented as equational relationships, and inferential knowledge representing heuristics.

Haugeland (1986) has formulated several requirements that a problem domain must fulfill in order to make the development of an expert system practical. Firstly, the decisions must depend on a well-defined set of variables. Secondly, the values of these variables must be known. Thirdly, the exact way in which the decisions depend on the values of the variables must be known, and fourthly, the interrelations among the variables in determining the decision should be complex enough to make the expert system worth the effort to develop.

These stringent conditions may rule out a bulk of ordinary life, but as we have already seen and shall see, many specialized domains are suitable for expert systems developments.

The purpose of an expert system is to computerize the problem solving skill of a highly recognized expert. Thus, this knowledge can be easily accessible and clerks, who have little ability to perform certain tasks can, by consulting an expert system, solve problems which otherwise would have to be handled by experts. Since human experts are scarce, but the need for their expertise high, expert systems can close the skill differentials between experts and problem solvers or decision makers in organizations. For instance, a bank, generally has a few, highly-skilled loan officers, often located at headquarters or large branch offices, but many tellers who serve the customers at all the branch offices. Credit evaluation skill, can by means of an expert system, be replicated to all who need this skill, thus decentralizing the decision responsibility without increasing risk. Furthermore, computerization of expertise is also a documentation of problem-solving knowledge and can be used for feedback to the expert and, thus, leads to improvements in expert skill.

In accordance with computer terminology we shall use the term **user** to denote the problem solver or the decision maker who is consulting an expert system for advice. In the literature about expert systems, much is said about the expert and knowledge acquisition, and little about the user and the user characteristics. Some recent work on user modeling focuses on these latter aspects. We believe that user characteristics impose severe constraints on the design of an expert system. One aspect which has rarely been considered is the extent to which the knowledge gap between the expert and the user imposes constraints on the functionality of the system. A typical assumption in design is that the user is familiar with the vocabulary of the domain. Other aspects are rarely considered.

An expert system has two main functions:

(1)   to draw conclusions, and;
(2)   to explain its reasoning.

A conclusion can be a diagnosis of a disease or a recommendation for a particular financing scheme. It should be noted that the conclusion set always must be fully specified in advance. What the expert system can do is to find the appropriate element of that set, it being a diagnosis or a design. An expert system works in a consulting mode, that is, a user may consult the system for advice. During the consultation the user interacts with the system if the system requires information to perform the reasoning. During these interactions the system, however, is always in control, that is, the system poses the questions and the user provides the answers. The user cannot influence the reasoning process directly. Only the information entered during the consultation influences the reasoning. This is in contrast to a DSS where the user is, at any time, in control and can ask the system for data or calculations.

An important aspect of human problem solving is the capability of a human expert to explain how a particular conclusion has been reached, or to explain why certain questions are asked. We want an expert system to have similar capabilities.

We shall, however, return to consultation and explanation in more detail in the next section.

6.2.2 Consultation

A user may consult an expert system for assistance while performing a task like establishing a diagnosis or designing a plan, or for advice or recommendations in choosing alternatives in decision making. It is important to understand that the task of an expert system may be different from the ultimate task of the user. For instance, an expert system for credit decisions may be designed for alternative tasks such as:

(1)   recommend an accept/reject conclusion;
(2)   advice on creditworthiness;
(3)   make a general financial diagnosis.

In the first task, the expert system almost makes the decision. In this case, decision authority can be transferred to people not particularly skilled in corporate finance and credit decisions. In the second task, the system supports a decision maker who may make the final decision on the basis of additional variables. In the third task, the financial analysis of the system is just one of several reports, on which, for instance, a credit committee may base its decisions.

In designing an expert system we have, therefore, to distinguish between the task of the domain and the task of the expert system.

Hayes-Roth *et al.* (1983) have made a typology of the kind of tasks that

Table 6.1 A typology of tasks for an expert system. (After Hayes-Roth *et al.* (1983).)

Task	Description
Interpretation	Inferring situation descriptions from sensor data.
Prediction	Inferring likely consequences of given situations.
Diagnosis	Inferring malfunctions from observation.
Prescription	Prescribing remedies for malfunctions.
Design	Configuring objects under constraints.
Planning	Designing actions.
Monitoring	Comparing observations to expected outcomes.
Control	Governing overall system behavior.
Instruction	Diagnosing, prescribing and guiding users' behavior.

an expert system can deal with. Summarized and slightly modified, this typology of tasks is shown in Table 6.1.

An expert system can be designed to deal with one or more of these tasks. We have found, as we shall see in more detail later, that financial analysts deal with the interpretation of accounting data, prediction of key variables to estimate a company's future position, diagnoses of causes of potential problems, and prescriptions of actions to remedy for these problems.

Since diagnosis plays an important role in financial domains we shall look, in more detail, at a diagnostic reasoning framework and a particular problem solving method for diagnosis known as classification.

Diagnosis

To make a diagnosis means to determine the cause of a problem on the basis of a set of symptoms or characteristics of the situation. In medical diagnosis, a disease may be determined from a set of symptoms of the patient. In fault diagnosis, malfunctions of equipments may be inferred from observations. In financial diagnosis, something can be said about profitability, liquidity and so on, on the basis of of the financial data of the corporation.

Prior to expert systems, diagnostic computer programs were mainly based on statistical decision theory. More recently, however, diagnosis is more thought of as an inferential process with uncertain information, rather than statistical calculations with probabilities.

Diagnostic problems are solved through a process of hypothesis generation and verification. For small conclusion (problem) sets, possible diagnoses can be tried in a systematic fashion. Each candidate is tried individually and proved to be true or false with some degree of uncertainty. Thus, at the end, a list of diagnoses may be produced ranking the problems in order of uncertainty. How do we handle domains where multiple problems may exist simultaneously? Obviously, we cannot just take the highest-ranking candidate, nor can we take all candidates over a certain threshold. Some diagnostic expert systems work with multiple diagnoses. For large problem sets it is inefficient to make an exhaustive search in a backward process, that is, trying all candidates in the problem set. Hypotheses generation, then, becomes a required process. Here, symptoms may be used to generate plausible hypotheses (see Section 4.5.2) which, in turn, are tried and verified. Information may be collected during the diagnosis process if necessary.

Classification

This is related to diagnosis and is the task of assigning to a particular object, the name of the class to which it belongs (the concept). The possible classes are predetermined. Each one is defined in terms of a set of typical character-istics. To classify a particular object implies finding a match between the characteristics of this particular object and one of the class-typical character-istics. For instance, medical diagnosis implies the assignment of a disease to a set of symptoms displayed by a person. Each disease has a set of class-typical characteristics which are matched against the observed characteristics (symptoms) of the person. When a match is found, the problem, in this case a disease, is classified.

There are many aspects of classification that complicate the inference procedure. There is the problem of necessary and sufficient conditions or typicality for a match (see Section 2.2.2). There is the problem of whether to find just one or all of the possible conclusions in a problem set, and in the case of multiple conclusions, how these conclusions should be interpreted. Are they to be considered conjunctive or disconjunctive sets?

In chapter two, when dealing with heuristic search, we saw that the search can be improved tremendously if we have information to successively exclude parts of the search space. A variation of this approach is called **successive refinements**. This, however, requires that the search space can be hierarchically structured into a class–subclass taxonomy (OR-expansions). Furthermore, we need criteria (class-membership properties) to effectively discriminate among classes on the same level of the hierarchy. A classification algorithm is employed to successively zoom in on the ultimate solution.

6.2.3 Explanation

Generally, explanation means to justify a particular conclusion, that is, to explain the reasoning behavior. Experts can do this. Therefore, we want

```
Please enter the name of the fact to be explained ? >· FINAL_CREDIT_RATING
FINAL_CREDIT_RATING has been changed by Rule number 109
IF MANAGEMENT_COMPETENCE = C;AVERAGE AND OUTSIDE_CREDIT_RATING = A;NOT_BEEN_DONE
AND CREDIT_RATING = MARGINAL
THEN
FACTS_DEDUCED FINAL_CREDIT_RATING IS MARGINAL
CRITERIA_TO_EXAMINE LOAN
MESSAGE FINAL CREDIT RATING is marginal.
COMMENT New 6
FINISH_RULE

        The value of MANAGEMENT_COMPETENCE (C;AVERAGE) The level of this fact has
        already been put in from the keyboard
        The value of OUTSIDE_CREDIT_RATING (A;NOT_BEEN_DONE) The level of this
        fact has already been put in from the keyboard
        CREDIT_RATING has been changed by Rule number 90
        IF LIQUIDITY_OF_CURRENT_ASSETS = AVERAGE AND PROFITABILITY = MINUS_LOW
        THEN
        FACTS_DEDUCED CREDIT_RATING IS MARGINAL
        CRITERIA_TO_EXAMINE FINAL_CREDIT_RATING URGENT
        MESSAGE CREDIT RATING based on financial data is marginal.
        FINISH_RULE
                                        •
                                        •
                                        •
                                        •
```

Figure 6.2   <HOW-example>.

expert systems to have similar capabilities. And most expert systems have some sort of explanation facility.

The most common type of explanation is what is called *retrospective* explanation. *HOW* was a particular conclusion reached? Here the system will display the chain of rules that were executed in order to reach that conclusion (see Figure 6.2).

The second most common explanation facility is *WHY* the program asks the user a particular question during the consultation (see Figure 6.3).

Both HOW and WHY questions are facilities for the user. Sometimes, however, it may be useful to have a complete trace of the inference process. Here, all rules that are tried are displayed, not only those that were executed and shown in a HOW-explanation. A typical command executing this facility is *TRACE*. It is primarily to be used by the knowledge engineer during design and test phases, but also users can take advantage of this (see Figure 6.4).

The three facilities, WHY, HOW and TRACE are provided by most development tools. Explanation mechanisms may also handle hypothetical reasoning, WHAT-IF, where the system explains what will happen if a certain value-set or a rule-set is changed. A value-set change is well known in decision support systems where different scenarios can be built by the WHAT-IF mechanism. An expert system WHAT-IF explanation is different since here a rule set can be the object of hypothetical reasoning.

Is the industry's rate of return (PRE TAX PROFIT TO TANGIBLE ASSETS) higher or
lower than the prime rate of interest
    A;LOWER
    .B;EQUAL_OR_HIGHER

Please put in the level :>
Now being looked at : Rule number 61
IF MEDIAN_PRE_TAX_PROF_RATIO_TO_PRIME_RATE = B;EQUAL_OR_HIGHER AND LOANTYPE = A;
SEASONAL
THEN
FACTS DEDUCED PROFITABILITY IS LOW
CRITERIA _TO_EXAMINE SEASONAL URGENT
MESSAGE PROFITABILITY is low.
FINISH_RULE

—————12:56—————

F1Annul F2Trunc F3Recall F4Stop F5? F6Rule F7Why F8Restart F9Facts F10Zo

Figure 6.3 < WHY-example > .

  1 treatment of the criterion RATIO_NET_WORTH_TO_DEBT
  2 Rule number 1 : RATIO_NET_WORTH_TO_DEBT IS UNKNOWN
  3 .... the user enters YES
  4 Rule 2 verified
  5 the criterion is added to the pile CASH_ACCOUNT with priority URGENT
  6 End of the treatment of the group of rules
  7 treatment of the criterion CASH_ACCOUNT
  8 Rule 4 verified
  9 fact CASH_ACCOUNT <-- POSITIVE
10 the criterion is added to the pile FUNDS_REQUIRED with priority URGENT
11 End of the treatment of the group of rules
12 treatment of the criterion FUNDS_REQUIRED
13 Rule 6 verified
14 fact LAST_YEAR_INCOME_LESS_DEBT_PAYMENT <--POSITIVE
15 fact PROFORMA_INCOME_LESS_DEBT_PAYMENT <--POSITIVE
16 The system EXECUTES the model starting at line 6100
17 the criterion is added to the pile CURRENT with priority URGENT
18 End of the treatment of the group of rules
19 treatment of the criterion CURRENT
20 Rule number 13 : PERCENTILE_CURRENT_RATIO IS UNKNOWN
21 .... the user enters B;BETWEEN_25%_AND_50%
22 Rule number 15 : MEDIAN CURRENT RATIO IS UNKNOWN
23 .... the user enters B;BETWEEN 1.5 AND 2
24 Rule 16 verified
25 fact LEVEL_OF_CURRENT_ASSETS <--- AVERAGE
26 The system EXECUTES the model starting at line 6300

Figure 6.4 < TRACE-example > .

There are alternative implementations of explanation facilities, from simple list of the rule numbers that have been executed, through a display of rules as they are stored in the knowledge base, to a natural language translation. If one is using an expert system development tool, the explanation facility is normally part of that tool.

Another explanation facility developed at the Intelligent System Laboratory at Carnegie-Mellon University by Kosy and Wise (1984), is an explanation of numeric values computed by a model. This explanation facility allows users to ask questions, in English, about observed results, for instance: 'Why did the current ratio go down in 1985?', and queries such as 'What is the formula for current liabilities?' The system responds with the variables that have significantly influenced the change of the value of current ratio, positively or negatively. This explanation facility, however, is more associated with DSS and will be further described in Chapter 7. A more detailed discussion on the explanation facility of expert systems is given in Wick and Slagle (1989).

6.3 How an expert system works

6.3.1 Basic architecture

One of the basic characteristics of expert systems is the separation of knowledge from the problem solving algorithm. Knowledge is specific to a particular problem domain and the tasks to be performed. Problem solving algorithms, on the other hand, can be employed across several domains and tasks. The basic architecture of expert systems is the same as that for production systems (see Section 4.2.2). That is, it consists of three components: working memory (workspace), production rules, and a control strategy.

The main departure of expert systems from production systems is the emphasis on domain knowledge. Thus, the knowledge that is used for problem solving in a particular domain is encoded into the production rules. Since problem solving is performed by heuristic search using inferencing, the term **inference engine** is used for the computer program that perform this inferencing.

Roughly speaking then, an expert system consists of four basic parts: a knowledge base, a working memory (workspace), an inference engine, and a man–machine interface (dialog component) as shown in Figure 6.5.

The *knowledge base* is specific to a particular problem domain and stores all kinds of knowledge that is used by an expert in the domain: descriptions of objects and relationships, description of problem solving behavior, heuristics, constraints, uncertainties, facts and so on. In the production system architecture, production rules constitute the knowledge base.

The *working memory* is the temporary storage of data of the current case or situation that is being processed. It is also called the *workspace*. This

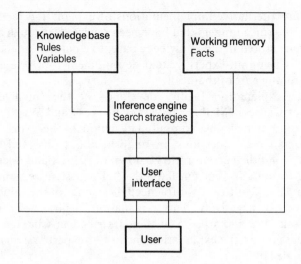

Figure 6.5   Main components of an expert system.

workspace is continually monitored and updated by executing knowledge that is held in the knowledge base.

The component that performs this monitoring and execution is the *inference engine*. Given a situation, that is, a particular state of the work space, it will look for knowledge that can be applied, and according to a control strategy determine a problem solving plan.

In addition to these components we need an *interface* between the user and the computer. This interface enables the knowledge engineer and the user to communicate with the system.

6.3.2 Knowledge base management

Knowledge base management is concerned with how to define and structure the knowledge of a domain, and how this knowledge can be manipulated. Thus, an expert system needs a set of functions in order to perform these tasks. We have already noted that there are two main kinds of knowledge that go into a knowledge base: description of objects and relationships, and description of problem solving. Both kinds of knowledge must be present for an expert system to work. However, we can choose a focus and make one the subordinate of the other. Thus, we have two approaches to knowledge definition:

(1)   The problem-solving behavior approach.
(2)   The object-oriented approach.

The problem-solving behavior approach

The problem-solving behavior approach puts, as the name indicates, emphasis on how a problem is solved: the heuristics and search strategies that are employed to perform inferences on a set of data. This approach is a direct inheritance of the production systems. The main body of knowledge in the knowledge base is encoded into production rules (see Section 4.4.2).

> IF < logical conditions >
> THEN < conclusions >

Rules have proved to be a successful formalism to encode inferential knowledge, and especially knowledge that exhibits intelligent behavior.

Rule-based expert systems are a class of expert systems where the main constituent of the knowledge base is a set of rules. Each rule represents a piece of knowledge, a chunk of know-how. Rules are independent of each other. It is, therefore, easy to extend the scope of the expert system, or increase its power, by adding further rules to the knowledge base.

The other part of the knowledge base, description of objects and relationships, is implicit in the rules. They constitute the antecedents and consequents. According to the terminology used in artificial intelligence, these descriptions are called *facts*. They express assertions about properties and relations. Facts can be observed, that is, entered into the expert system by the user or from a data base, or deduced by the inference engine.

Facts are represented as object–attribute–value triples or as attribute–value propositions, or as property lists (see Section 4.4.1).

> IF (COMPANY X, SALES < $ 5 million)
> THEN (COMPANY X, SIZE = SMALL)

Facts are declared to the knowledge base. In PC-OPTRANS facts are declared by giving them names, and allocating a value scale, that is, a set of legal values of the fact, and an initial value.

> < fact name >   < value scale >   < initial value >

Each fact can be associated with a text, a message or a prompt, which will be displayed by the system when the user is required to input the value. An example is:

> CHILD   NUMBER   UNKNOWN
> 'How many children do you have'

The consequent of an IF-THEN statement can include more than just inferred new facts. The consequent can also contain various actions

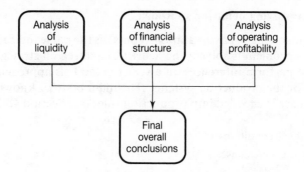

Figure 6.6   An example how to break down financial diagnosis into subproblems.

which should be executed if the antecedent is evaluated to true. These actions could be: where in the knowledge base further search should be directed, calling a model, executing a procedure or displaying a report or a message.

One important feature of knowledge management is to be able to structure the knowledge into **rule sets**. A rule set is a named collection of individual rules pertaining to a defined aspect of a problem. These rule sets aggregate and differentiate rules according to certain defined criteria. For large knowledge bases, segmentation into rule sets may increase the search efficiency considerably. Thus, if the inference engine can receive information about where to look for relevant rules, large parts of the knowledge base can be ignored in the search process. Most complex problems can usually be broken down into a number of subproblems, each of which may concern a single, well-defined aspect of the problem. For example, when we look at how an expert financial analyst works, we find that he or she approaches his or her analysis from a number of different points of view, for example, as shown in Figure 6.6.

If we want this type of logical structure to be imposed on the knowledge base we need the concept of a rule set – a kind of meta-knowledge (rules about how rules are used).

In PC-OPTRANS this concept is called: CRITERIA. An example of this is:

CRITERIA

Synthesis

Liquidity

Financial structure

Operating profitability

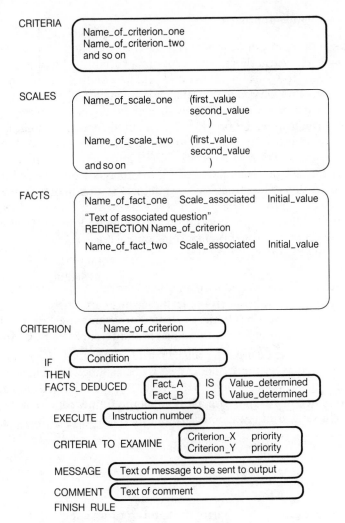

CRITERIA
Name_of_criterion_one
Name_of_criterion_two
and so on

SCALES
Name_of_scale_one   (first_value
                     second_value
)
Name_of_scale_two   (first_value
                     second_value
and so on   )

FACTS
Name_of_fact_one   Scale_associated   Initial_value
"Text of associated question"
REDIRECTION Name_of_criterion
Name_of_fact_two   Scale_associated   Initial_value

CRITERION   Name_of_criterion

IF   Condition
THEN
FACTS_DEDUCED   Fact_A   IS   Value_determined
                 Fact_B   IS   Value_determined
EXECUTE   Instruction number
CRITERIA TO EXAMINE   Criterion_X   priority
                       Criterion_Y   priority
MESSAGE   Text of message to be sent to output
COMMENT   Text of comment
FINISH RULE

Figure 6.7 The different parts of the knowledge base.

The first element of the list will be the first criterion at which the inference engine will look for rules to apply to the facts. The conclusion part of a rule may contain information that will direct the search to other criteria.

We can now summarize the information contained in a rule as shown in Figure 6.7.

The object-oriented approach

The problem domain can be modeled as a set objects and relationships. An object can be a physical thing, a concept or a procedure. An object-oriented approach means to focus on objects and organize all the domain knowledge around objects and classes of objects. Also, elements in a program can be viewed as objects that communicate with each other via messages.

One formalism which provides a structured representation of objects and classes of objects is the frame representation (see Section 4.4.4). A frame provides a representation of a specific object and all the information about that object that we may be interested in, or a class of objects and its associated information. Constructs are available for organizing frames, that represent classes, into taxonomies. The frame representation allows more comprehensive structural description of the problem domain. How can the frame-based representation organize and control reasoning?

Two aspects are important here:

(1)   inferencing is associated with an object and can be treated as a property of that object. Inference procedures are, therefore, attached to the frames (object-oriented programming). Procedural attachments can then be used to perform inferences on those frames;

(2)   frames can also be used to organize production rules. When a rule is represented as a frame, rules can easily be grouped into classes. Just as the rule-set concept described above, this meta-knowledge can be represented in a frame with a link to all the frames representing sub-classes of rules or member-rules of a class.

6.3.3 The inference engine

The inference engine is the control mechanism of an expert system. It puts the knowledge of the knowledge base into work to produce solutions. It is activated when the user initiates a consultation session with the system. The inference engine decides on which rules to execute and in which order. It monitors the workspace, where the initial state description is stored, and where deduced facts are stored during the reasoning process. To perform each elementary deduction, the inference engine applies formal logic to the production rules, also called rules of inference. Most inference engines are based on *modus ponens*, that is, given the fact A and the rule IF A THEN B, the inference engine deduces the fact B (see Section 4.5.1).

A rule-based system reaches its final conclusion by a series of elementary conclusions. When the deduced fact of one rule is put back into the workspace, a new pattern of data is created that may match with other rules. New facts may be deduced, stored in the workspace and so on, until the final conclusion is reached. This procedure of linking rules through premises and conclusions is called chaining (see Section 4.5.1). Two modes of chaining are used in expert systems: forward and backward. Forward and backward chaining refer to the way in which the inference engine examines a rule premise first, or a conclusion first.

Let us see how these two modes of reasoning work in principle. We have the following knowledge base:

R1:   IF A AND B THEN D
R2:   IF B THEN C
R3:   IF C AND D THEN E

and the initial workspace: A, B.

Forward chaining implies that the inference engine will find the rules that have conditions (premises) that match with the data in the workspace. In our case above, we have both rule R1 and R2 that match. The inference engine needs to know which one to execute or in which sequence it should apply all matching rules (see search strategies, Section 4.3.3). If we want to select only one rule (depth first) we still have to resolve the problem of which of rules, R1 or R2, to choose. Several strategies may be applied, for instance, the first found rule or the rule with greatest number of IF conditions. In our case, both strategies lead to the selection of R1. After R1 has been executed, the new fact D is added to the workspace, now containing A, B, D. The next cycle of rule matching gives only one candidate, R2, which when executed, adds C to the workspace. Finally, rule R3 can be executed arriving at the conclusion E.

This way of reasoning is also called *data driven* since new facts, as they are deduced and added to the workspace, drive the rule-matching mechanism.

We can illustrate the reasoning by the inference tree shown in Figure 6.8. Here, arcs represent the applied rules, and the nodes represent the states of the workspace. Solid arcs represent executed rules. Dotted arcs represent candidates, but non-executed rules.

Backward chaining makes the inference engine work backwards from a hypothesized conclusion (the goal state) to all the premises, through chains of rules, which have been verified against the data in the workspace.

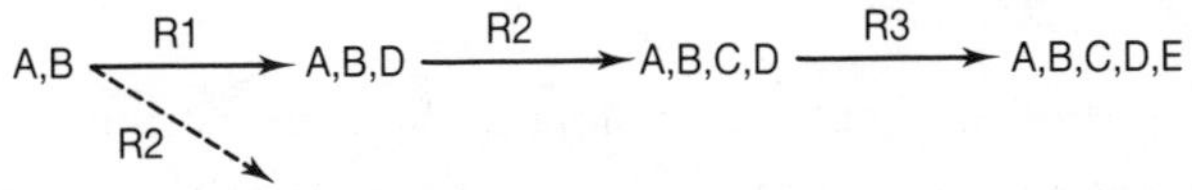

Figure 6.8   An inference tree for forward chaining.

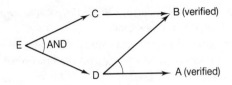

Figure 6.9 An inference tree for backward chaining.

In the example shown in Figure 6.9, the inference engine is told that the goal is E and will, therefore, start with rule R3 which concludes with E. It will replace E with the two subgoals C and D, then substitute D by A and B (rule R1) which are verified against the content of the workspace. Likewise, C is replaced by B (rule R2) and verified. Thus, when C and D are verified, then E is verified. Backward reasoning is also called *goal driven* since it works in a goal-to-subgoal direction.

Note that in drawing the inference trees we have utilized the AND-OR trees described in Section 4.3.4.

The inference engine works according to the control cycle of production systems described in Section 4.2.2 We recall that the control cycle consists of three steps:

(1)   Selection of rule candidates: pattern matching.
(2)   Choice of one of the rules: conflict resolution.
(3)   Execution: action

In forward reasoning, the cycle is as follows:

(1)   Search for the rules whose conditions match the data in the workspace.
(2)   Choose one of the rules according to the search strategy applied.
(3)   Add the concluded fact to the workspace.

This cycle is repeated until the fact that is defined as the goal is added to the workspace. One of the problems of forward chaining is how to focus on the goal, since normally there is no information at the point of choice of rule execution that guides the search in the direction of the goal.

In backward chaining, the cycle becomes:

(1)   Search for rules whose *conclusions* correspond to the current subgoal.
(2)   Choose one of these rules according to the search strategy applied.
(3)   Replace the subgoal with the conjunction of conditions of the rule as new subgoals.

This cycle is repeated until the initial goal is reduced to a set of subgoals that can be verified against the workspace.

One of the advantages of backward chaining is that questions to the user are context dependent, that is, the solution path is dependent on the data given and inferences drawn along the way. Therefore, the sequence of questions can be different in two different consultations.

Sometimes, we want to use a mix of forward and backward chaining. Forward chaining can be used to direct the inference engine to particular rule sets, thus increasing the efficiency of the search. Within a rule set the search can be backward. In PC-OPTRANS a rule set is denoted by 'criteria'. The use of 'criteria' is a means to control the search (see Figure 6.7).

6.3.4 Expert system interfaces

Several kinds of interfaces are required for an expert system at different stages of development. At the building stage the knowledge engineer works with the system; at the consultation stage the system may require inputs from the user or the user may want explanations from the system. Also, at the operational stage the expert system may require interactions with other computer programs and databases. The system interface that can be designed is more a property of the development tool used and will be treated in more detail in Section 6.5. However, some interface features will be briefly described here.

User interface

User interface features include data input, reporting, graphical displays, explanation facilities, on-line help systems and so on.

Two types of dialogues are commonly found: the question–answer dialog, and the menu-driven dialog with windows as shown in the OPTRANS-version of BANKER (see Figure 6.16).

Knowledge engineer interface

The main tool of the knowledge engineer is the editor by which new rules can be entered or existing rules can be modified. Also, a trace facility is required to check reasoning. A graphical view of the knowledge base can give a better view of the reasoning processes. An example of a trace is shown in Section 6.2.3.

System interface

As expert systems move into operational use the need for integration with other computer programs increases. For further detail see Chapter 7.

6.4 Tools for building expert systems

6.4.1 Introduction

To have an expert system performing problem solving within a domain implies having encoded knowledge and reasoning in a form that can be programmed into a computer. This programming is done using a language which can be translated into elementary computer instructions. Over the years, languages have been developed containing constructs that make it easy to write programs for symbolic processing.

However, a more recent development in software programming, is not to have only a language, but to have a package of utilities including editors, window management and so on. Two generic names often used for these packages are 'programming environment' or 'development tool'. They can be found under different labels depending on the application area, for instance, DSS generators, 4 generation languages, application generators, or expert systems shells.

A programming environment provides flexibility in software development which is needed where the problem may change or where the understanding of the problem domain is part of the system development process (prototyping).

There is a need for a variety of support functions during the life cycle of an expert system. For cost-effective use of the expert system technology, expert systems development tools are required.

Primarily, there are three categories of tools for implementing expert systems on computers:

(1)   general programming languages;
(2)   special production systems programming languages;
(3)   expert systems shells.

Moving from general languages to shells implies sacrificing generality and flexibility in choice of solutions. On the other hand, development time is shortened and the programming skill needed is less specialized.

General programming languages

These range from algorithmic languages such as Pascal and C, a functional programming language such as LISP or a logic programming language such as PROLOG. As we have already said, LISP is the dominant computer language in the field of artificial intelligence, at least in the United States, but PROLOG is gaining ground. LISP and PROLOG provide concepts and procedures to deal with representation and control in search-based problem solving. Any control strategy or search procedure can be programmed in LISP. Also, the recursion control structure in LISP allows for easy representation of structural knowledge as well as simple facts. However, the more general the concepts, the more freedom is left to the system designer. It expands the space of problems that the system may be appropriately used for, but it puts more demand on the skill of the designer.

Special production systems programming languages

These are another class of tools that come closer to the programming needs of production systems. Examples of this class of languages are OPS5 and ROSIE. The special characteristic of these languages is their powerful pattern-matching capability. This permits quite complex patterns to be represented and processed and the expert system to be tailored to the characteristics of its problem domain. The generality is restricted compared to LISP, but general enough to deal with most production systems.

Expert system shells

These are highly specialized tools for building expert systems in special domains, for instance, for diagnosis. One of the first shells developed was EMYCIN, basically, it is a domain (knowledge)-independent version of the medical diagnostic system MYCIN. One of the major advantages of an expert system shell is the speed by which an expert system can be built. Utilizing all the general functions of the tool, only the domain knowledge has to be provided. By using EMYCIN, the loan evaluation system BANKER was programmed in a couple of days. The functions of an expert system are illustrated in Figure 6.10.

With built-in representation formalisms for knowledge and facts, and an inference engine to perform reasoning, then time and cost-efficient development must be traded with generality and flexibility. Therefore, expert system shells are developed for more specific problem domains. For

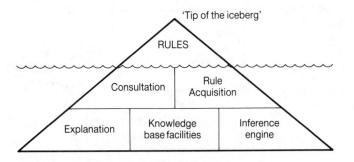

Figure 6.10 Functions of an expert system shell. (Reproduced from Rich C. and Buchanan B. (1985). Expert Systems – Part 1, Tutorial No. 5. *IJCAI*, 9.)

instance, EMYCIN is developed for diagnostic problems where it is appropriate to employ a backward chaining, goal-directed search technique.

Since the days of EMYCIN and other pioneering programming tools for expert systems development, the number of shells in existence has increased greatly. From mini-computers and LISP workstations these tools have expanded into the PC environment. Also, they now exist more and more in two versions, one development and one run-time version. In the early days one could distinguish shells from each other by the knowledge representation formalism they used. However, today, many systems use multiple formalisms, for instance, both frames and rules. Such systems are called **hybrid systems**.

Today we can distinguish better among shells according to the computer environment they reside on. Gilmore and Howard (1986) categorize shells into *small* scale and *large* scale expert system tools.

6.4.2 Functions of expert system tools

The tool used in building an expert system offers a specific perspective on the problem domain. Each tool has a conceptual model or framework for its knowledge representation and reasoning mechanism. On the one hand, these concepts help the designer in representing a problem domain. On the other hand, they constrain the aspects of the knowledge to be modeled.

In discussing the major functions of expert system tools, we shall do this under the following headings (see Figure 6.11):

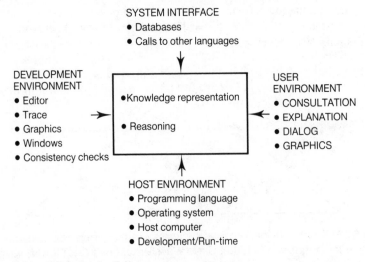

Figure 6.11 Tools for building expert systems.

- knowledge representation languages,
- methods of reasoning,
- development environment,
- user environment,
- host environment,
- system interface.

Knowledge representation languages

A knowledge representation language is, on the one hand, a conceptual framework, and, on the other hand, a coding scheme for knowledge. At the moment, no generally-accepted standard or terminology exists for knowledge representation languages. They must accommodate declarative and procedural knowledge of the types that we have already discussed in Chapter 4. We shall not repeat all aspects of knowledge representation here, only point to some aspects:

- All tools have primitives for representing simple objects and their attributes (facts) either in the form of < object–attribute–value > triplets or attribute–value propositions.

- All tools have primitives for handling inferential knowledge. Most common are rule-based tools that utilize IF-THEN rules and employ the *modus ponens* general logic inferencing rule for deduction.

- Some tools can handle procedural knowledge as procedural attachments to declarative knowledge.

- Some tools can handle structural relationships between objects explicitly and treat complex objects as entities of their own. These tools usually have knowledge, both declarative and procedural, associated with the individual objects (simple and complex). Inheritance mechanisms are found in these tools. Most common are frame-based representations.

- Some tools may handle structural knowledge by subdividing the knowledge base into a hierarchy of partitions.

- Most tools provide primitives for reasoning with uncertainty. Most common is the certainty factor method, first employed by EMYCIN.

- Few tools provide mechanisms for handling algorithmic knowledge or do analytical modeling inside the reasoning system. Some tools allow calls to other languages, such as, Pascal or FORTRAN, where this can be done.

Methods of reasoning

Existing expert systems tools usually use either forward or backward chaining, or both, to control the search for rules in the knowledge base. Some tools do not have a built-in forward or backward chaining procedure. It is merely the ordering of the rules in the rule set that determines the sequence of the search.

Another aspect of the reasoning mechanism is the conflict resolution strategy employed, that is, how to choose the order of rules to be executed when more than one rule has conditions that match the workspace. The most commonly used conflict resolution strategy is the *first found* strategy. Here, the first applicable rule is taken from the applicable rule set.

Development environment

Beyond the knowledge representation language the system designer, or knowledge engineer, needs further aids. To be able to apply the primitives of the representation language effectively, tools can be developed to provide services such as:

- Knowledge base editing. Tools may have their own editor or use external editors (for example, a text editor). External editors may create several problems: they are not adjusted to the specific knowledge representation language of the tool, on-line consistency checking and knowledge base updating cannot be done, thus, the state of the system is lost if a modification has to be done.

- Effective interfaces, for instance, by the use of graphics. Graphics are particularly useful to edit structural relationships.

- Analytical tools to easily find represented knowledge, for instance, which rules are updated by, or related to attributes; consistency checks and so on.

- Inference tracing to help in error findings during execution of a knowledge base. Also, the capability to set interrupts in the reasoning process at critical points is useful in the testing of an expert system. The ability to ask for explanations (HOW and WHY questions) is helpful in the development phase as well as in the usage phase.

- Screen format utilities to design the end-user interface. Most expert systems work in a dialog mode with the end-user, who provides the necessary input data. Window management, screen titles and so on, are facilities that will reduce the design efforts.

User environment

The environment in which the end-user interacts with the system can be of several types:

- line edited question-answer interfaces with natural language parsers;
- menu-driven dialogs with single or multiple answers to prompts;
- graphics.

Also, a help facility is an important part of the end-user environment. Help can be needed for several purposes:

- to use the system facilities;
- to explain the format of the input;
- to explain concepts used;
- to explain protocols used in solving the problem.

Furthermore, end-user access to the knowledge base and the database is provided by some tools. Tools without a special run-time version will have the same facilities available for the developer as well as the user.

Host environment

The host environment includes the computer hardware, the operating system, the programming language, and the version in which systems can be developed and run. The host computer can be of four types:

(1) PCs,
(2) work stations (multi-tasking and large screens),
(3) LISP work stations,
(4) time-sharing on mainframes or minis.

Programming languages will be LISP or PROLOG, the typical AI languages, or algorithmic languages such as Pascal, FORTRAN or C.
      Systems may run in a compiled run-time version or in interpreted development versions.

System interface

The system interface may include data extraction from external databases, procedures to connect to other language or packages (modeling languages, spreadsheet programs and so on).

6.5 Expert systems opportunities

The expert system technology has proved its applicability in many different areas. The technology – also called knowledge technology, establishes an opportunity to computerize knowledge, the ultimate property for better skill, better competence, and better performance. In order to evaluate these opportunities we shall look at this in three steps:

(1)   the feasibility of the technology;
(2)   how to share computerized knowledge;
(3)   what this means in business terms.

6.5.1 Technical feasibility

We have, in our previous description of expert systems, touched upon several of the factors that must be present for an expert systems approach to be feasible. Both the information processing paradigm of human problem solving developed by Newell and Simon, and the knowledge paradigm of expert systems presented by Feigenbaum are important fundamental issues in evaluating tasks and problem domains feasible for expert systems development.
    In general, expert systems can be developed where:

● the task requires symbolic reasoning more than numeric calculations;

● heuristic search is used more than algorithmic procedures;

● domain-specific knowledge is more dominant than common sense;

● the task must have well-defined solutions, that can be specified in advance;

● the inference logic is predetermined;

● the task must be of manageable size, but complex enough to benefit from an expert system.

Furthermore, one or more experts available for knowledge acquisition must exist, that is:

● the expert must be willing to participate;

● the expert must be able to articulate his or her problem solving;

● there exist cases which can be used for knowledge acquisition and validation.

We have found that credit evaluation, for instance, satisfies these characteristics fairly well, as explained in Sections 6.2.1 and 6.6.1.

6.5.2 Knowledge sharing

Replications of expertise is the major driving force for expert systems applications. It affects business in many ways, which we shall look closer at in a moment.

Because of the replication opportunity of expert systems, developments of expertise in new areas can be made cost effective. For instance, the knowledge base of XCON, Digital Equipment's expert system for VAX configurations, was developed by pooling together several knowledgeable persons, such as product designers and sales consultants, to produce the integrated knowledge required to help in this complex task.

Another important factor of computerized knowledge is well-documented know-how in a domain. Knowledge used by experts is rarely available for inspection, evaluation or control. Experts are usually evaluated on their results, not on how they arrive at these results. With a computer system one obtains a detailed documentation of this knowledge. A corollary of this is a better understanding of the task. For example, the application of expert systems to the interpretation of the UK social welfare benefits rules has helped to identify anomalies in the statutes and in the detailed interpretation of the rules (Butler Cox and Partners Ltd., 1987).

One last point about knowledge utilization to be mentioned here is the opportunity to capture and store knowledge. Expert systems have been used in situations where expertise is in danger of being lost, for instance, due to retirement or due to product obsolescence.

We can summarize the advantages of knowledge sharing by the following:

- replication and enhancement of expertise;
- relieve experts of trivial tasks;
- cost-effective expertise development;
- documentation and better understanding of performance knowledge;
- capturing and storing.

Some of these factors are related to a comparison between human experts and artificial expertise. These two types of knowledge are contrasted in Table 6.2.

Table 6.2   Contrast between human and artificial expertise.

Human expertise	Artificial expertise
Perishable	Stable
Difficult to transfer	Multiplicative
Difficult to describe	Documented
Unpredictable	Consistent
Expensive	Cheap
Creative	Monotonic

6.5.3 Business opportunities

The benefits of the expert system technology are to be found in the applications. What are the benefits to be achieved, and how can we express them in business terms? In this section we shall treat this subject more generally, but the reader is referred to Chapter 12 for more examples and cases of the expert system technology applied to financial problems.

Cost reductions

Replicating expertise from the few who have it to the many who need it has cost savings aspects. Experts are expensive, and become more so as they specialize within narrow domains. Therefore, transferring knowledge to lower-skilled personnel also implies that cheaper personnel can perform the tasks. An example of this is found in Coopers & Lybrand, an international audit and accounting firm. This firm decided to develop Expertax, an expert system that would enable less-qualified personnel to handle the simpler tax problems, freeing the experts to concentrate on the difficult problems where their specialist knowledge is of most value. The non-expert can now advise on the simpler tax problems, which form the majority of the cases anyway, without having to refer them to the tax expert. The benefits: *reduced time* and *costs*.

Another important cost factor is increased productivity among clerks or professionals by using support tools such as an expert system. One example is PlanPower, an expert system developed by Applied Expert Systems (APEX) Inc., in the United States. This expert system is developed to produce personal financial plans. The process of providing comprehensive advice to one person, which previously took several days to produce, can now be made in less than one day. In addition, more alternatives are analysed and solutions are more customized to the clients' preferences and needs. Table 6.3 shows the opportunities provided by PlanPower.

One cost reduction factor, as we have just seen, is to use lower-skilled, lower-cost personnel to perform tasks. Another cost reduction factor is the increased automation of services that can be achieved with expert systems. New generations of automatic tellers and telebanking systems will, to a greater extent, incorporate knowledge bases for such tasks as credit granting, stock investments and so on. With expert systems and knowledge bases integrated, more and more, with other computer applications of an organization, one can imagine many places where reasoning can add values to these systems. One example is the recognition and handling of bad debts in a credit institution. American Express has developed an expert system called 'Authoriser's Assistant' running on a Symbolics LISP machine but fully integrated with a mainframe system with databases and statistical models.

Loan or credit management has two cost components. One is related to the cost of processing a loan application. The other is related to the risk

Table 6.3 Opportunities provided by PlanPower.

Change type	Benefit	Valued outcome
Business process change	Eliminate steps in a business process, thereby eliminating key cost elements(s)	Financial analysis costs reduced by 50%
	Eliminate steps in a business process, thereby compressing process time	Financial analysis time reduced from weeks to days
Product change	Create barriers to competitive entry	Financial product/service sales no longer limited by analysis talent
	Raise customer or supplier switching costs	Locks customer and representatives to the company
Work content change	Change work to use less-skilled personnel	Reduction in training costs
	Change work to use fewer skilled personnel	Ability to integrate sub-specialities
	Change work to improve results of process	More consistency, diligence applied to customer service

(Reproduced from the manual of Plan Power, courtesy of APEX Inc.)

of losses due to bad payments. Many financial institutions have experienced, with serious consequences, what insufficient credit evaluation can lead to. Now the situation is changing, and most credit-granting institutions are putting more emphasis on credit evaluation again and are looking for better aids to perform this task. Risk analysis is not only important in granting credit, but can be applied to almost any task in the financial domain.

Added values

It is often said that the expert systems technology is not a typical efficiency technology, that is, applications are not justified primarily on the basis of cost reduction. Improved effectiveness, that is, added values, are more in focus. Since this technology is also called a front-office technology these added values are primarily found in changes in products and services.

Many expert systems are advisory systems. They can provide advice directly to customers, thus creating a new type of products, or they can produce advice in new ways, thus improving customer services.

Let us look at some added value effects of better customer services. Better customer services can be achieved by:

- more consistent services;
- more comprehensive services;
- more decentralized services;
- more customized services.

Multiple expert systems behave consistently. The same conclusion for a given case will be reached in any location using an identical knowledge base. This is particularly important for organizations having a widespread geographical operation dealing with the same tasks everywhere, for example, banks, insurance companies, and auditing firms. People, on the other hand, are less predictable, which means that a loan application, having been rejected in one branch office, may be accepted in another.

More comprehensive services can be accomplished by integrating expertise of different sub-specialities into one system. For instance, until recently, banks had separate departments for bonds, stocks, saving deposits and so on. Advice on bond investments was given by the bonds department, and advice about stocks, from the stocks department. With an expert system, knowledge about different investment alternatives can be integrated into one knowledge base and one system.

More decentralized services follow from replicating and integrating expertise. For instance, decision responsibility for higher credit limits can be granted to branch offices. More customized services are an important benefit of expert systems. Brochures and manuals give general information. For instance, most countries require that their inhabitants must fill in a declaration form of income and wealth for taxation purposes. To help people do this, general instructions are available. However, many people have difficulties in finding the specific rules and statutes that apply for them personally. An expert system can guide in finding these specific rules by intelligent questioning. The final result could be a ready-made declaration form with all the required data filled in.

The increasing level of complexity in society puts more demand on expertise. This is true in all sectors and at all levels, corporations as well individuals. The information technology puts information systems in the market-place with easy access to all kinds of information. The bottlenecks are no longer due to the lack of information, but due to lack of know-how about how to use this information effectively. Information about stock exchange values, foreign currency exchange rates, and so on, has no value unless it can be used in decision making. Directives, instructions, rules, regulations and laws play a greater and greater role in our society. We need help in applying all this correctly. Human expertise is expensive, but expert systems are affordable.

With respect to new products, two aspects are relevant. Expert systems can make customer advice cost-effective in new market areas. For instance, banks can now offer advice to lower-scale customers. Another aspect is that new products can be spin-offs of expert systems developed for other applications. One bank, using an expert system for credit evaluation, found opportunities for marketing the financial analysis necessary for this evaluation as a separate product.

Adding values by expert systems is one way of gaining *competitive advantage*.

Training

Another category of benefits is that of more efficient and effective training by means of expert systems. By using an expert system one can create a complete learning environment in which novices can be trained in expert problem solving, thus transferring knowledge about heuristics as well as theories. A complete learning environment must enable the student to pass smoothly through the different stages of learning:

(1)   the cognitive stage,
(2)   learning methods and,
(3)   practicing.

Training with expert systems is superior to other media such as 'on-the-job' training or classroom teaching, in many respects: it is quick and accurate, there is rapid feedback, uniformity, and there is coherence and so on. Also, the knowledge technology allows us to move from individual learning and expertise to organizational learning and expertise.

Summary of benefits

The following summarizes the major benefits of expert systems that have been described above:

(1)   Cost reduction
    (a)   distribution of expertise to lower-paid personnel;
    (b)   improved productivity of knowledge workers;
    (c)   reduced risks and losses.
(2)   Added values
    (a)   better customer services:
        (i)   more consistent
        (ii)   more comprehensive
        (iii)   more decentralized
        (iv)   more customized
    (b)   New products
        (i)   cost-effective advice in new market areas
        (ii)   new products
    (c)   Competitive advantage
(3)   Training

6.6 BANKER – an expert system for credit evaluation

BANKER is an expert system that makes a credit evaluation of bank loan applicants. It is an expert system because it employs knowledge and inferences to draw conclusions. The set of conclusions consists of ratings of the creditworthiness of a company according to the following scale:

(1) High
(2) Average
(3) Marginal
(4) Low – loan not to be granted

Also, BANKER is an expert system because the knowledge and inference procedures are modeled after human experts, bank loan officers, and they represent heuristics and search strategies employed by these people. Furthermore, BANKER is implemented in a development tool that enables us to separate knowledge from the problem solving program.

BANKER was first developed using EMYCIN (Van Melle and Bennett, 1981) and run on DEC 2060. It was later converted to a PC environment using PC-OPTRANS as the development tool. The PC version of BANKER will be described in this section.

6.6.1 The problem domain

The decision problems that face credit-granting institutions have already been described in Section 2.5.3. BANKER addresses the task of credit analysis in the evaluation phase of this decision making process. There are several criteria on which a bank may base its lending decisions: minimizing risk of losses, maximizing profit, and maximizing services to the community. This multi-criteria decision problem, together with uncertainty of outcomes, incomparable qualities of alternatives and so on, makes it difficult to optimize credit decisions. Empirical observations of actual human behavior show that decisions are made by judgment.

Therefore, it was decided that BANKER should provide expert advice about creditworthiness of a company according to the rating scale: high, average, marginal and low.

Is credit evaluation an appropriate task for an expert system? First of all, genuine experts exist in credit service departments in banks and other credit institutions. These loan officers, with a basic education in business administration and economics, have developed their expertise by performing lending decisions in practice. We have already noticed that this decision making is not appropriate for optimization. Instead, heuristics are used. These heuristics consist of the selection of explanatory variables, their symbolic values, and the reasoning in order to access symbolic values to variables such as profitability, liquidity, credit rating and so on. The task of credit evaluation is of manageable size. The loan applicant will submit the necessary financial statements, which, together with some additional information such as the quality of management, and the availability and value of collateral, make the basis for the evaluation. Also, an expert system for credit evaluation have several important benefits, such as:

- replication of credit skill to customer service departments;
- decentralization of decision making responsibility;
- consistent treatment throughout the organization;
- a general upgrading of skill.

The users of BANKER are the people in credit departments serving the customers.

6.6.2 The domain knowledge of BANKER

To determine creditworthiness of a business loan implies making an evaluation of the loan applicant's capability to service the debts over the time horizon of the loan. With respect to the present and near future (less than one year) this is very much dependent on the current financial situation of the company. With respect to the future, it is dependent on the company's ability to generate earnings, that is, the profitability. The current situation can very much be determined by the data of the balance sheet. However, in the long run, more judgmental factors such as market demand, management and so on, should be included. Since debt management concerns the future, either with a short or a long time-horizon, there are many uncertain factors to be considered. Therefore, the risk of credit granting must be evaluated. The heuristics that experts use take all of these factors into consideration.

Cohen *et al.* (1966) have studied how bankers make decisions. They have presented a decision model of the procedures that commercial banks use in evaluating applications for business loans. Parts of this study have been presented in Chapter 2. Here, we shall focus on the heuristics that they found bankers were using in performing credit analysis. Many of these heuristics are used for interpretation and qualifications of calculated numeric variables and ratios. The bankers do not specify liquidity, for instance, in terms of a number. They do this in qualitative terms such as high, average, low and so on. But how can they? In Cohen *et al.*'s model, qualifications are done by comparing figures of the company with industry. Thus, the heuristics consist of selecting appropriate variables, choosing the right combinations, and making interpretations and comparisons that enable the decision makers to qualify key concepts such as solvency and profitability. There are five parts to this credit evaluation model:

(1)   Is the bank's share of risk clearly unreasonable?
(2)   Does the firm have enough current assets?
(3)   Are the firm's current assets sufficiently liquid?
(4)   Is the firm sufficiently profitable?
(5)   What is the final credit rating of the applicant?

Each of these parts represents a problem to be solved and the conclusion of one subproblem influences the solution of the next.

An important problem for a credit institution is to evaluate the risk, and in case this risk is too high, to reduce the risk, either by reducing the loan, or by asking for collateral. One measure of risk is the net worth to debt ratio. If this ratio is not acceptable the loan should be rejected or reduced to within acceptable limits. If the net worth to debt ratio is acceptable it is still a question of whether the company has enough cash to service the debt. Two calculations on cashflows are made, one based on last year's statements and one on the pro forma data. The knowledge base and the conclusions for this segment are shown in Figure 6.12.

The next two questions that are raised concern solvency. Firstly, a tentative solvency measure is deduced, based on net working capital measures and current ratio. Secondly, the liquidity of the current assets are evaluated by looking at individual items of the current assets. Part (4) is concerned with profitability. The final credit rating of the loan applicant takes into consideration non-financial variables such as management competence. The knowledge base and all conclusions are shown in the figure.

6.6.3 The computer program

Since BANKER operates in the financial domain we may expect the need for numeric calculations as well as reasoning. Numeric calculations are performed to compute aggregated financial ratios and to generate present and future cashflows. Using a particular programming tool, PC-OPTRANS, requires knowledge and reasoning to be formulated in the syntax of the tool. PC-OPTRANS was described in Chapter 5 and will, therefore, not be dealt with here. We shall just note that it is a rule-based expert systems development tool. The knowledge base can be segmented. Reasoning can be forward (data) driven or backward (goal) driven.

We have to define our problem space in such a way that PC-OPTRANS's inference engine can work. This definition is done by specifying a problem solving graph (see Section 4.3) for the problem space, that is, we define the relationships between the final conclusions and the input data. As we have seen, Cohen et al.'s model describes a structure of the problem space. In Figure 6.13 the problem solving graph of BANKER is shown. It is

PART	KNOWLEDGE BASE	CONCLUSIONS
(1) Is the bank's share of risk clearly unreasonable ?	(1) Net worth/total debts < minimally acceptable If yes then reduce loan (2) Cash account < 0 If yes then reject loan application (3) Cashflow to debt service coverage < 1 If yes then reject loan application (4) Cashflow declining	(1) Loan application is processed (2) Loan amount is reduced and processed (3) Loan is rejected. Risk is too high.
(2) Does the firm have enough current assets ?	Heuristics about interpretations of the following variables: (1) Level of net working capital (2) Trend in net working capital (3) Current ratio • Firm • Industry	Tentative solvency rating: • High • Average • Low • Low minus • Reject
(3) Are the firm's current assets sufficiently liquid ?	Heuristics about the interpretation of the following variables: (1) Cash to current liabilities (2) Cash + receivables to current liabilities (percentile value) (3) Trend in inventories (4) Inventories to current assets (percentile value) (5) Tentative solvency rating.	Final solvency rating • High • Average • Low • Low minus • Reject
(4) Is the firm sufficiently profitable ?	Heuristics about the interpretations of the following variables: (1) Net profits (historic and trends) • Level • Trend (percentile value) (2) Debit to assets (3) Debit to assets > prime rate of interest • Firm • Percentile value (4) Type of loan (seasonal or long-term).	Profitability rating: • High • Average • Low • Low minus • Reject
(5) What is the final credit rating of the applicant ?	(1) Credit rating based on financial analysis: • Loan type • Solvency rating • Profitability rating (2) Management competence (3) Outside credit rating	Final credit rating: • High • Average • Marginal • Reject

Figure 6.12 Contents of the knowledge base and the conclusions for different parts of BANKER.

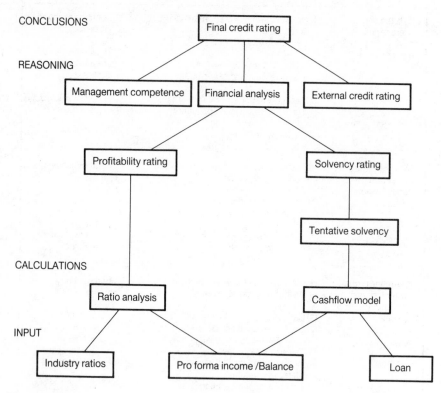

Figure 6.13   Inference structure of BANKER.

divided into four parts:

(1)   input data
(2)   calculations
(3)   reasoning
(4)   final conclusions

Part of the knowledge base of BANKER is shown in Figure 6.14.

6.6.4 Consultation with BANKER

A consultation with BANKER can be divided into four parts:

(1)   preparing the input data
(2)   reasoning
(3)   explanation
(4)   reporting

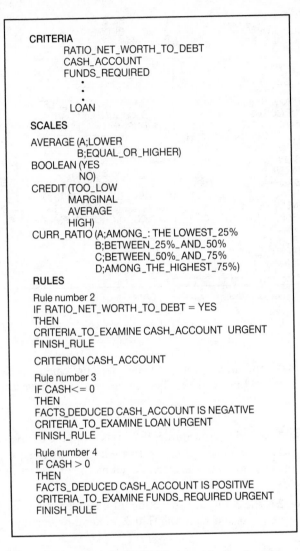

CRITERIA
        RATIO_NET_WORTH_TO_DEBT
        CASH_ACCOUNT
        FUNDS_REQUIRED
           .
           .
           .
        LOAN

SCALES

AVERAGE (A;LOWER
            B;EQUAL_OR_HIGHER)
BOOLEAN (YES
            NO)
CREDIT (TOO_LOW
        MARGINAL
        AVERAGE
        HIGH)
CURR_RATIO (A;AMONG_: THE LOWEST_25%
            B;BETWEEN_25%_AND_50%
            C;BETWEEN_50%_AND_75%
            D;AMONG_THE_HIGHEST_75%)

RULES

Rule number 2
IF RATIO_NET_WORTH_TO_DEBT = YES
THEN
CRITERIA_TO_EXAMINE CASH_ACCOUNT URGENT
FINISH_RULE

CRITERION CASH_ACCOUNT

Rule number 3
IF CASH<= 0
THEN
FACTS_DEDUCED CASH_ACCOUNT IS NEGATIVE
CRITERIA_TO_EXAMINE LOAN URGENT
FINISH_RULE

Rule number 4
IF CASH > 0
THEN
FACTS_DEDUCED CASH_ACCOUNT IS POSITIVE
CRITERIA_TO_EXAMINE FUNDS_REQUIRED URGENT
FINISH_RULE

Figure 6.14   An excerpt from BANKER's knowledge base.

Preparing the input data consists of entering or editing data from financial statements – three years of income and balance sheets – and entering budget data (see Figure 6.15).

When the input data have been entered, a display of some aggregated financial variables are shown in order to check the validity of the data. Next, the computation and reasoning through the parts (1) to (5) of the credit evaluation model can start. Here, the window facilities of PC-OPTRANS

HISTORIC DATA		BUDGET DATA	
L1 C1	YEAR 1	L16 C4	PRO FORMA
TURNOVER	29754	PRIME RATE OF INTEREST	0.16
COST OF GOODS	13489	AMOUNT OF LOAN	1000
OTHER VARIABLE COSTS	1766	CURRENT MATURITIES	1000
FIXED COSTS	12541	LIMIT OVERDRAFT	4500
DEPRECIATION	751	CHANGE IN TURNOVER	0.1
INTEREST PAYMENT	453	RATIO OF CONTRIBUTION MAR	0.48
TAXES	366	INVESTMENTS	1000
CASH	4907	BUDGETED FIXED COSTS	15000
RECEIVABLES	6430	BUDGETED DEPRECIATION	1100
INVENTORIES	3136	CHANGE IN CURRENT ASSETS	0.1
INTANGIBLE ASSETS	650	CHANGE IN SHORT TERM CRED	0.1
FIXED ASSETS	14720		
OVERDRAFT	1949		
SHORT-TERM CREDIT	5275		
LONG-TERM DEBT	1512		

————12:29————

F3Recall   F4Quit   F5Same value   DATA_FILE FIN_DAT   70 lines 5 columns

Figure 6.15   Input screen.

are used to make the interaction with the user convenient. A layout of the screen is shown in Figure 6.16. The three windows have the following purposes:

Window 1 is used to communicate results from the analytical models to the user. Here, calculations performed, that are needed by the user in order to answer questions posed by the expert system, are displayed.

Window 2 is the communication medium between the user and the expert system. As shown in the figure, a menu-driven dialog is used.

Window 3 displays the intermediate conclusions that the system reaches. The system will show conclusions on each of the steps (1) to (5), as shown in Figure 6.17.

BANKER also uses the explanation facilities of PC-OPTRANS. During the consultation, the user can use function keys, as shown on the bottom line of Figure 6.16, to interrupt the reasoning. When the system poses a question to the user, the user can return F5. He or she then asks for a WHY explanation, that is, why does the system pose this question? BANKER will then display the rule on which it is currently working, as in the WHY explanation example shown in Section 6.2.3. At the end of a consultation the user will be asked if

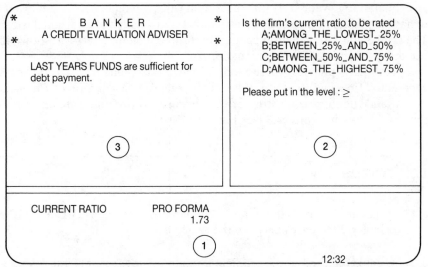

Figure 6.16   User interface and screen layout.

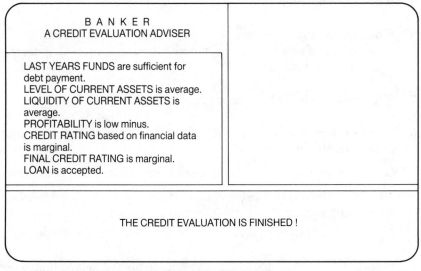

Figure 6.17   An example of BANKER's conclusions.

an explanation is wanted. If yes, the system will ask which fact the user wants to have explained. The most interesting fact is probably the final conclusion: The final credit rating. The explanation of this concluding fact was shown in Section 6.2.3 on the HOW explanation.

BANKER prepares three reports for the user. One report is on some aggregated financial variables. The second one is on a selection of financial ratios, and the third is a listing of the conclusions (intermediate and final) that was shown in Window 3 (see Figure 6.17).

Exercises

6.1 What do expert systems and DSS have in common? What are the primary differences between the two?

6.2. What is required of the problem domain in order to make the development of expert systems practical? How will these requirements constrain the application of the technology?

6.3 Expert systems are formal systems. Explain. Use BANKER to illustrate the criteria of formal systems.

6.4 What are the primary components of expert systems?

6.5 What is the function of the inference engine?

6.6 What are the main features of an expert system shell? What are the advantages and disadvantages compared to general programming languages such as LISP and PROLOG?

6.7 What can be achieved by knowledge sharing?

6.8 Diagnosis is a general task which is found appropriate for the expert systems technology.

    (a)   Give three examples of diagnostic problems in different domains.

    (b)   When is hypothetical deductive reasoning appropriate for diagnosis? Explain.

    (c)   When is it not? Explain.

6.9 Expert systems have been created to assist in tax declaration. Give examples of three facts and three rules that might be part of the knowledge base of an expert system for personal tax declarations.

6.10 The following rule is part of an expert system's knowledge base:

> If product category is automobile, then advertising media is newspaper.

This expert system is designed to help people choose an advertising medium for a particular type of product. Give examples of a rule to which the inference logic would chain forward from the foregoing rule and backward from the foregoing rule.

6.11 Do you see any danger or disadvantages of the expert systems technology?

6.12 Case Study: loan evaluation.

XYZ Bank is a small savings and loan bank with 24 branches. Its customer basis consists largely of medium-income individuals. The bank grants credits for a large range of purposes: real estate, car purchase, various consumer products and so on. The branches employ 52 full-time employees and 24 part-time employees at the teller desks. The policy of the bank has been to authorize the head of the branch to deal with loans without collateral to the amount of $25,000 and secured loans (for example, mortgage loans) to the amount of $85,000.

The bank is currently changing its policy. They want to turn the branch into a more customer-friendly environment where personnel are delegated more functions and are given more customer responsibility. The problem is, however, that the current personnel has rather low skill in dealing with new functions such as credit evaluation. Furthermore, the turnover rate of the employees, especially the part-time employees, is rather high.

To prepare for the change of strategy, you are called upon to develop an expert system for evaluating individual loans. The objective is to make the branch personnel capable of dealing with credits within the limits that the head of the branch earlier.

You have been assigned to one of the credit specialists at headquarters, Dave King. During an interview with Mr King, he told you how to deal with loan applications of this kind. He asks the loan applicant a series of questions. On the basis of the responses to these questions, he evaluates the effects of these factors on risk and repayment capability. On this basis he makes a final conclusion.

Dave King asks the clients about the following aspects:

(1) Size and purpose of the loan.
(2) Age and education.
(3) Family status: married, number of children, age.
(4) Employment: current employer, number of years employed.

(5)   Repayment capability: income, special commitments.

(6)   Risk: wealth and debts.

(7)   Customer relationships: number and types of accounts, payment history.

(8)   Collateral: security, guarantee.

In the interview with Mr King, you agree to use the following scales on all of these factors: 'strong', 'normal', 'weak', and 'poor'. In dealing with repayment capability, Mr King is using a rule-of-thumb which says that total debts should not exceed three times the annual income.

ASSIGNMENTS

1   Define the conclusions you want the system to give.

2   Define the inference structure and draw an AND/OR search tree for the reasoning (hint: employ a problem reduction method).

3   Write the rules (for instance, by using the PC-OPTRANS syntax described in this chapter) that make the reasoning possible. Write at least one rule for each concept node of the inference structure. Make your own assumptions if necessary.

4   Show explicitly the rules that lead to questions to the user (leaves of the search tree).

5   Suggest numerical calculation (analytical models) that may be included in the system.

6   How would you determine the benefits of the system?

7

Knowledge-based Decision Support Systems

7.1 The need for a new framework

We have seen, in Chapters 5 and 6 respectively, the conceptual frameworks of DSS and of Expert Systems (ES) which we can call classical. One of the main conclusions of Chapter 6 is that the technology of expert systems provides us with two new possibilities:

(1)   The ability to build systems which can simulate reasoning.

(2)   The ability to build systems which can explain their reasoning and conclusions.

It is clear that this capacity can be very helpful in a DSS. Zannetos, as far back as 1968, had already foreseen some of the properties of future MIS using AI technology. However, his paper deals mainly with MIS and not DSS and no applications were presented. A conference was held in October 1984 on Expert Database Systems (EDBS). A study of the proceedings shows that the main issue addressed during the conference was the coupling of expert systems and database systems which is, clearly, a key issue in the integration of DSS and ES. EDBS are defined by John Smith (1986) in his keynote paper as 'systems for developing applications requiring knowledge-directed processing of shared information'. To our knowledge, work on the integration of ES technology within the DSS framework began appearing in the literature in June 1985 with the Maratea Advanced Study Institute's conference proceedings on DSS Theory and Applications (Holsapple and Whinston, eds.) We shall study first the enhancement of DSS through expert system technology and then the new KB-DSS paradigm.

7.1.1 Enhancement of DSS through expert systems technology

If we take the classical framework of DSS which was presented in Chapter 5 (see Figure 5.6, in particular), we can extend this framework in six different directions, which we shall describe in the following.

Expert advice on a specific problem domain

This level is very straightforward, expert advice means going beyond the usual capacity of a DSS to ask for an *expert opinion*. This capability requires a KB of *domain* knowledge, for example, financial analysis KB for a DSS to support company credit decisions.

One fundamental aspect to be noted here is that expert advice very often requires a significant amount of symbolic reasoning, this adds a new dimension to the functions of a DSS. We shall present the possibility of expert advice in Section 7.4, in the case of financial analysis.

The idea is simply that, even if present DSS help the user to define concepts, to compute procedures, to run decision models, to present figures in the form of reports or graphics as sophisticated as desired and so on, DSS will not give expert advice as a human being would. Clearly, it is possible with traditional programming to print messages giving conclusions if a series of conditions are fulfilled, but it is not possible to do so with the flexibility derived from the separation of the knowledge and reasoning mechanisms of ES as we have seen in Chapter 6. This expert function adds an expert assistant to the DSS, the opinions of which may or may not be followed by the user.

Integrating the ES component in the DSS conceptual framework will considerably increase the expertise embedded in the DSS and will improve the capacity for the users to enhance this expertise. In fact, the expert system component will increase the learning process of the user and reinforce the user–system feedback loop as described in Section 5.5.

Explanation of the conclusion of the expert

As we have seen, an additional value of the ES technology lies in the capacity of the system to provide an *explanation* of the reasoning process (see Section 6.2.3).

This capacity is very important because it reinforces the idea which has often been promoted by researchers in the DSS field: that a good DSS should improve the learning process of the user (see Section 5.5.4). It is clear that the explanation function is essential because:

- Users tend to have more faith in the result and more confidence in the system.

- Assumptions underlying the system are made explicit rather than staying implicit.
- System development is faster because the system is easier to debug.

Intelligent assistance to support the decision analysis methodology

We consider intelligent assistance to support the decision analysis methodology as one of the most essential consequences of the integration of the DSS and ES technology. As we have seen, decision analysis is a powerful aid in helping individuals to face difficult decisions.

It is now possible to put, in a knowledge base, the methodological knowledge we have described in Chapter 3 to analyse a class of decisions. Such a knowledge base can be used, for example, to help the decision maker to:

- define a decision model or an influence diagram;
- assess a probability distribution;
- assess value functions.

Explanation of a model result and/or model behavior (qualitative reasoning)

Explanation of model behavior is different from using the results of the model with the ES component to conclude something. Instead, we want the expert part of the system to explain the model behavior, that is, to determine the logical structure of the model itself and the causal relationships among variables. Some work in that direction has been published by Kosy and Wise (1984) and more recently by Chidan *et al.* (1988).

This technology was implemented in the 'IFPS Plus' DSS development environment of the Execucom Corporation as reported by King (1986). In this environment the system will give explanations of:

- model definition;
- up/down evolution of a variable;
- no change in the evolution of a variable;
- differential magnitude of peaks/dips;
- trends;
- comparisons of 'what if' cases.

The first step to a good understanding of a model is to be able to read the text of the model (usually a set of equations) and easily understand its logical structure (structural relationships between variables).

Already it is clear that the advantage of a modeling language over spreadsheets is the capability of a modeling language to express, more clearly, not only the relations of the decision models, but also the global logical structure of the models. The capability to have the system find and display the definition of a variable in a model is a feature mostly found in DSS. Such a possibility is available in the OPTRANS system (Chapter 7).

Assistance when using statistical, optimizing or other operations research techniques

It is well known that many managers do not use such techniques properly because they do not have the expertise to master them. For example, many managers do not remember the underlying assumptions for appropriate applications of a multiple regression model. The usefulness of an expert assistant is obvious but in many cases the cost or the non-availability of such an assistant will prevent the use of these methods.

Embedding an expert component in the statistical module of a DSS which uses a specialized methodology knowledge base (in statistics or short-term forecasting or some operation research technique) should improve the situation considerably. In fact, such an intelligent assistance can have three main goals:

- guide a novice user in using the tools properly;
- help the user learn good strategies for using the tools (improve heuristics);
- discover domain knowledge from large database.

The first goal, guiding a novice user was considered by Chambers *et al.* (1981) and attempts have been made to include intelligent interface systems in existing packages (Hajek and Ivanek, 1982), expert software for regression analysis (Gale and Pregibon 1982, 1983) and software which helps user identify an appropriate analysis for the type of data at hand (Portier and Lai, 1983).

The second objective is to teach good strategies for using of the tools. In the statistical domain, data analysis strategies are the result of training and experience. This knowledge can be formalized into rules which constitute specialized KB (Hajek and Ivanek, 1982).

The third goal, discovering domain knowledge from a large database, can be achieved by using, for example, lagged correlations to generate a set of hypotheses which can then be tested. The statistical expert systems cited above incorporate many elements of automatic model building. In general, decision analysts share the same decision process as data analysts except that decision making problems are more complicated and often include the data collection phase. A first step (in this direction) is to provide an intelligent user interface for using the KB-DSS resources.

Guidance in using the DSS resources: Developing intelligent user interfaces

The resources available to DSS users are:

- data bases or data files;
- decision models;
- reports or graphical displays;
- knowledge bases (for a KB-DSS user, as we shall see in this chapter).

Very often, as a system evolves, not only do users increase the number of data files or databases on which they work, but also they develop several decision models to support different decision processes. Such a situation is presented by Klein and Villedieu (1987) who describe KB-DSS for financial planning in French municipalities. The model base of this system contains three different models which support different phases of the decision process of city managers in their planning work, or different levels of details in the planning process.

The system is now being used by about forty municipalities. City planners who have not been trained to use the planning models may encounter difficulties in choosing the appropriate model for each planning situation.

To assist such users, a simple KB can be defined that will ask questions to the user concerning his or her problem, so as to help him or her to select the right model.

When a DSS becomes institutionalized in a company or organization, the number of databases, decision models and reports can increase considerably. We have observed this in a large French company (where the controllers began using OPTRANS in the main division to generate DSS for budgeting, simulations and forecasts). After two years of usage, the number of models increased from zero to one hundred and the number of reports from zero to two hundred.

When time or money constraints make it difficult for users to attend training seminars on the use of DSS, it is clear that some kind of expert assistance to select the appropriate resources is useful. This expert assistance should take the form of an intelligent user interface which helps the user select and use the resources of the system properly.

Assistance in formulating certain questions

When confronted by a large database with complex relationships, the formulation of certain questions can be difficult. An ES could help the user to formulate his or her request.

Intelligent support during the model building process for a specific class of decisions

It was stressed by Klein (1977) that it should be possible to use AI technology to automatically define a financial analysis model such as FINSIM (see Section 7.4) from the definition of the list of variables used in the balance sheet and income statement. This basic list of variables is available to the analyst when he starts his study of a company and needs to define a financial model to generate a pro forma balance sheet and income statement.

The idea of intelligent support of model building is that domain knowledge can be used to support the process of constructing analytical models. Clearly,the problems that could be solved using such assistance are limited to those that can be formalized by the built-in modeling tool. Use of intelligent support in model building has been dealt with by several researchers under the label of *model management*. Elam and Konsynski (1987) provide a review of the main concepts of model management (see Section 13.3.3).

Model management captures knowledge which can assist users in their problem formulation process by providing the right model building blocks for the problem. A commercial implementation of model management is found in the Palladium software, a financial modeling system which incorporates structural and domain-related knowledge about the appropriate use of modeling and analysis techniques. The user interacts with the system to build and use models in a traditional DSS setting.

7.1.2 Contributing disciplines and their roles in the KB-DSS paradigm

As we have seen from the above examples, the goal of KB-DSS is to integrate, with the capabilities of traditional DSS: data management, modeling language, decision methodology, display of numerical data and so on, the new advances of ES with its symbolic reasoning and explanation capabilities.

However, we want to stay within the paradigm of DSS, that is, to *support* decision making. Now, as we have seen, we may, as we perform the decision making task, have to solve very specialized problems requiring expertise for their solutions. We want to be able to provide this expertise in the form of knowledge bases along with reasoning capabilities.

The integration of DSS and ES leads to a new conceptual organization, which we shall call the KB-DSS framework. The basic disciplines, which are the basis of this new framework, are: linguistics, formal logic, cognitive psychology, computer sciences, mathematics, statistics and economics. These basic disciplines have given birth to theories, methods and techniques which are: artificial intelligence, management information systems, behavioral decision making, decision analysis and operations research.

When these methods and techniques have been used in the domain of management decision making they have led to the evolution of two kinds of systems for decision support: DSS and expert systems.

Until recently, the DSS technology relied essentially on the disciplines of management information systems (in particular, for data management subsystems), management (for the domain knowledge) and modeling (from the descriptive, as well as normative point of view), statistics, and other OR techniques.

Integrating expert system technology into DSS technology adds, to this list of disciplines, a reliance upon formal logic, computer science, linguistics and cognitive psychology.

We believe that, in the future, most decision support systems will provide some form of expert system technology to achieve the capabilities listed above and, as a consequence, the DSS development environment will have to supply the ES function in an integrated fashion. The ambition of the new KB-DSS framework is to achieve synergies, as we shall see in this chapter, by integrating the ES technology into the DSS framework.

7.2 The new conceptual framework

The structure of a KB-DSS is defined by the subsystems which comprise it, the integration that exists between the subsystem (communication and control), as well as the hierarchical structure of the system.

We shall first recall the subsystems, then describe the integration needed between them, and finally we shall use the example of the KB-DSS development tool OPTRANS Expert to show how this structure can be organized simply and clearly within a hierarchical system.

7.2.1 Structure: the subsystems

The conceptual framework for a DSS was presented in Figure 5.6, the new KB-DSS framework, is illustrated by Figure 7.1, where we have the following components or subsystems:

- data management or database management,
- display,
- modeling (system and user),
- statistics and optimization,
- user interface,
- inference engine,
- knowledge base management.

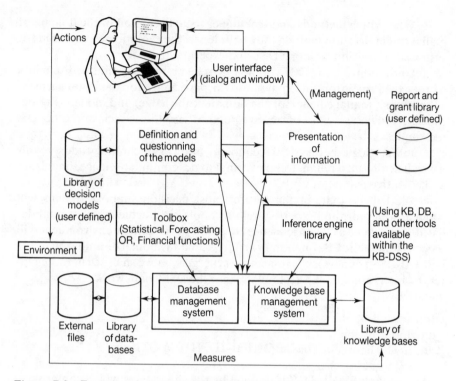

Figure 7.1   Functional structure of a KB-DSS development tool. (Adapted from Klein (1986). *Recent Developments in PC-OPTRANS, a KB-DSS Generator.*)

The figure's main purpose is to present the basic components of the KB-DSS and their relations to the basic resources of the KB-DSS: database files, decision models, displays (reports and graphics) and knowledge bases.

The reader can compare this figure with the basic components of a DSS development tool illustrated in Figure 5.6 and, also, with the OPTRANS architecture shown in Figures 5.14 and 7.5. The modeling, display, and toolbox subsystems (statistics optimization and forecasting algorithms) are present. The new components are: the inference engine, and the knowledge base management system.

The inference engine is represented as a subsystem in itself, since it is a domain-independent inference engine which we must be able to use for several ES functions in the KB-DSS. For example, as we shall see in the financial analysis case presented in Section 7.4 it could be used with different KBs to supply financial analysis diagnosis on a company as well as advice on which financing strategy to use or which estimate to select for the forecast of certain model variables. We shall see that two types of KBs will have to be distinguished: domain KBs and methodological KBs.

One important idea, as we shall see in the following section, is that the rules of the KB should be able to use data which are available in the database (or data file) or in models such as variable values.

The DBMS and KBMS are subsystems with a tight link between them. From the user's point of view they are more likely to appear separated, in that sense the user will call two separate subsystems to work on the database and on the knowledge base; however, transfer of data from one to the other subsystems should be completely clear, in the sense that the user or designer of the system will be allowed to use variables in rules of the KB, the names of which are defined in the database or data file.

A new function also appears in the new framework: *user interface design*. This function may not be embedded in a separate subsystem but is more likely to be implemented using special subsystems which are accessible from the models such as window management, form definition and management of input/output and graphics.

7.2.2 Example of the integration needed between the components in a KB-DSS

Integration is one of the principal problems facing designers of KB-DSS development tools. As we have seen in Chapter 5 there is a fundamental difference between compatibility between two programs (systems or subsystems) and integration between two programs (systems or subsystems).

Several attempts have been made to make existing DBMS or modeling systems and ES compatible through a common file. Many such links have been tried between a spreadsheet and an ES shell, for example, to develop KB-DSS in financial analysis. Usually, these attempts have been doomed to failure since such a file interface can only be useful if the information needed by the expert system is known in advance, which is rarely the case.

The information needed by the ES is changing, according to the initial data available and to the interaction with the user. The KB itself is evolving and, as a consequence, will need information from the DB and the models which are also evolving. Also, acting through a file interface decreases the efficiency of the system.

What is really needed is a KB/DSS development environment (or generator) which is built (designed) from the start to communicate between the expert module and the traditional modules of the DSS development tool. As we shall see later, this raises unusual performance problems.

We shall give a simple example of the kind of interaction which is needed in a KB-DSS generator by using the case of financial analysis, which will then be used to present a real application of the KB-DSS framework. This example, taken from Klein, 1988 will emphasize the main steps of the decision process of a credit analyst as presented in Figure 7.2.

(1) **Gathering information.** The credit analyst must first obtain the basic economic and financial information needed to make the analysis.

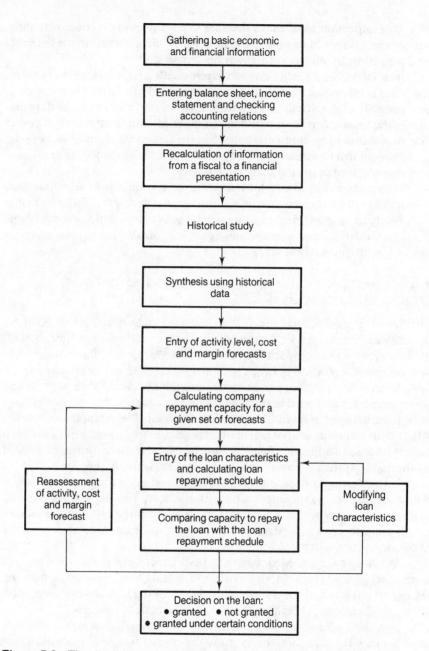

Figure 7.2   The decision process used by a credit analyst when deciding whether or not to grant a loan to a company. (Reproduced from Klein (1988). FINSIM EXPERT: a KB-SS for financial analysis. In *Proceedings Eurinfo* 1988, Bellinger H.J. *et al.*, eds.)

This information is usually found in the annual reports of the company and other sources (industry studies, professional magazines and so on). This step is supported in the traditional DSS framework by the data management module and, eventually, by the data communication function which enables access to a financial data bank. During this stage, the user needs to access the database of financial and general information on a company over time. This information is mainly numerical (value of the accounts of the balance sheet and income statement), but is also alphanumeric (nature of activity, main contacts and name of shareholders). With a DSS generator, the user can design the interface to facilitate the input of data.

(2) **Checking the data**. The credit analyst uses a spreadsheet (paper or computerized) to standardize the data and check basic accounting relations. The data is spread in an homogeneous way. Accounting relations should be used to check errors, which can be done easily with the modeling part of the KB-DSS generator. However, some transformations of the data are complex and imply considerable financial, accounting and fiscal knowledge. These checks are usually supported by the model component, however, if the problem is more complex it could also be supported by an expert module. In this case, an inference engine that reasons on a KB containing accounting knowledge is used to check accounting consistency.

(3) **Aggregation of information**. Basic information, which is usually fiscal information, is compiled and transformed by the analyst into reports suitable for financial analyser. This step can be supported by the data modeling and report components of the KB-DSS generator.

(4) **Historical study**. During this phase the analyst studies the evolution of the company from several points of view, usually: financial structure, return, liquidity and growth potential. To do this, he or she computes diverse financial aggregates (cashflow, ratios, working capital and working capital requirements) and displays them in differents forms (reports and graphics).

This step can be supported by the report generation and graphics subsystem of the KB-DSS generator. Several reports must be available in the report directory. The analyst will, typically, want to display these various reports, such as income statements and balance sheets recalculated for financial analysis and fund flow analysis, as well as financial aggregates, such as ratios. The graphics subsystem is essential at this stage for the display of the various graphics that the user may wish to generate.

(5) **Synthesis and first diagnosis using historical data**. Using the preceding information the analyst makes a tentative conclusion about the credit rating of the company, he or she may include in his

or her reasoning, outside credit ratings and information which would be available if the company is already a client (such as information derived from the history of the cash position of the company).

A synthesis is made by the analyst in order to reach a first conclusion on the basis of criteria such as short-term risk, return and structure, as obtained in step (4).

For this step an *expert module* is needed to infer the conclusions using information calculated in steps (3) and (4).

(6) **Repayment capacity forecast**. When a loan implies a certain risk (given the loan's size relative to the size of the company, or given a long repayment period) the decision cannot be made using only historical data and must consider what is the expected capacity of the company to repay the loan in the future. Therefore, the analyst must make assumptions about the company's activity level, costs and margins in the future, to compute future cashflows.

This step can be supported using a model, window management, and the graphics functions of the KB-DSS generator.

Note that the control is passed *back* from the inference engine to the model, since calculation must now be done on the forecast part of the model.

(7) **Loan characteristics and calculation of the repayment schedule**. Given the loan characteristics (amount, duration, interest rate and start of repayment period) the repayment schedule is calculated. The consequences of the loan have to be taken into account: added interest, modification of financial structure, changes in funds flow statement and so on.

(8) **Comparing capacity to repay** (cashflow available for repayment) **with the loan repayment schedule**. The company must have a future cashflow sufficient to make repayment possible. However, because we are in an uncertain world, this cashflow (capacity to repay the loan) is not certain and the analyst may be inclined to:

   (a)   take a safety margin (use of break-even analysis)
   (b)   use other information to assess the risk

(9) **Reassessment of assumptions to take into account uncertainty**. The analyst is usually given an assumption of future sales levels by the client company. He or she will try to assess the risk by changing some of the assumptions (sales growth rate, costs, margins and so on) to make a sensitivity analysis. He or she will eventually loop on this step as many times as he or she feels are needed.

Steps (7), (8) and (9) can be supported by the modeling subsystem of the KB-DSS generator. We would like to stress the point that the modeling language should provide a certain number of financial functions such as loan repayment schedule and net present value as well as commands to perform impact and sensitivity analyses.

(10) **Final decision on the loan**. The analyst will then use the information and the conclusions obtained by the analysis of past data, together with the information obtained from the forecast study, to conclude his or her decision about the loan.

The support of this step implies the use of the expert module of the KB-DSS. However, it should be noted that the rules of the knowledge base will have to use the forecasted value of the variable and not the historical value as in step (5)

7.2.3 Communication and control between the expert subsystem and the DSS subsystem

Type of communication and control needed

We can see from the above example that in order to reach a conclusion, the expert part of the system must use:

- Observed elementary data (such as elementary accounts from the balance sheet and income statement).
- Data that is calculated from observed elementary data. This calculated data (also called an aggregate), is defined and computed at the database level or in a model. Since the data needed is a function of the way in which the analyst conducts his or her analysis and of the KB rules used by the expert module, the data *are not known in advance.*

The flow of control between modules during the support of the preceding steps can be summarized as follows:

(1) Gathering information. The user calls a model (such as FINSIM see Section 7.4).

(2) Checking the data. The user interacts with the model, which may call upon an expert module by name to check the accounting consistency of data.

(3) and (4) Aggregation and display of information. The user interacts with the model. During his or her work the user will request print outs of various reports and/or graphics. Therefore, the model will pass the control to the report processor, the graphics processor, and to the window manager.

(5) The model calls the artificial expert (that is, the inference engine and the financial KB) having the financial analysis knowledge. The artificial expert provides a first opinion and passes back the control to the model.

(6), (7) and (8) Repayment capacity forecast and repayment schedule and comparison. The user interacts with the model (simulation).

During this phase the user may request access to statistical routines (mainly if working with quarterly data) and printing of various reports and/or graphics. Therefore, the model passes the control to the report processor, graphic processor and window manager.

If the analysis leads the user to simulate different financial policies, the model may pass control to some specialized submodel (evaluation of the price of a share). Final decision on the loan. The model passes control to the inference engine to use a KB containing financial analysis knowledge. (In FINSIM, the KB used is the same as the one used for historical analysis, to enforce consistency in the evaluation.) The inference engine provides its advice and passes back control to the model.

We can see from the above example that, in order to reach a conclusion, the expert system must use observed data which is in the company data file (or database according to the version of the DSSG used). This data is elementary or aggregate. The aggregates are computed in a model. Therefore, rules of the KB will require information (values of variables) from the models and *full communication* is required between models and KB. For example, in the rule concerning liquidity shown in Figure 7.3, we have indicated the location of each variable, both in the model and the database.

The ratio of current assets/current liabilities can be calculated in a model but the elementary variables will often be stored in a file or the database (this is particularly likely where data on large number of companies is stored). Some early technical implementation of such a communication link is described in Klein *et al*. (1987). The integration which must be achieved is represented in Figure 7.3.

7.2.4 New capabilities

The availability of a KB-DSS development environment, of which OPTRANS Expert described in Section 7.3.3 is one of the first examples, leads to the definition of new capabilities (which previously untractable, can now be easily implemented). Some of these capabilities are the following:

- Coupling 'deep knowledge' provided by causal models with 'shallow knowledge' provided by symbolic techniques.
- Developing intelligent user interfaces to select resources available in the system or to interact with a numerical model.
- Designing a more powerful learning environment.
- Supporting the use of the toolbox with intelligent methodological assistance.
- Supporting the decision analysis cycle.

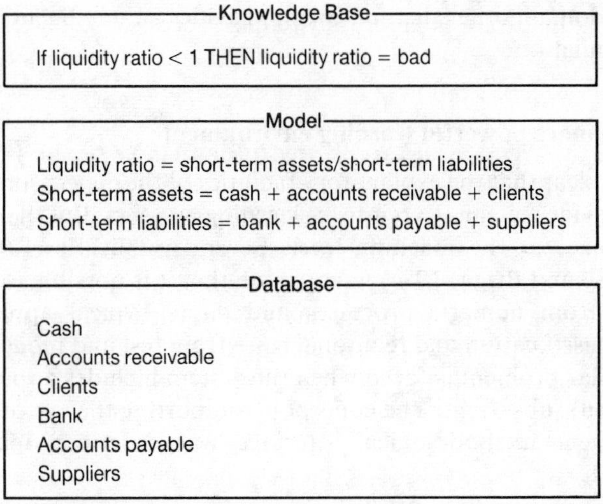

```
┌─────────────── Knowledge Base ───────────────┐
│                                               │
│  If liquidity ratio < 1 THEN liquidity ratio = bad │
│                                               │
└───────────────────────────────────────────────┘

┌───────────────────── Model ──────────────────┐
│                                               │
│  Liquidity ratio = short-term assets/short-term liabilities │
│  Short-term assets = cash + accounts receivable + clients │
│  Short-term liabilities = bank + accounts payable + suppliers │
│                                               │
└───────────────────────────────────────────────┘

┌──────────────────── Database ────────────────┐
│                                               │
│   Cash                                        │
│   Accounts receivable                         │
│   Clients                                     │
│   Bank                                        │
│   Accounts payable                            │
│   Suppliers                                   │
│                                               │
└───────────────────────────────────────────────┘
```

Figure 7.3   Communication: knowledge base ↔ model ↔ database in OPTRANS.

Coupling 'deep knowledge' and 'shallow knowledge'

The development environment corresponding to the KB-DSS framework makes it possible to couple equational or causal models (numeric programs) with symbolic reasoning. The FINSIM system that we present in Section 7.4 is an example of the coupling of a financial simulation model with reasoning, to create a much more powerful decision support tool.

The equation model usually contains causal knowledge of a *theoretical* nature while the rules of the knowledge base contain more experiential knowledge.

As we have seen in the preceding section, during this reasoning we need to use the model to compute criteria and then use it to go on with the reasoning. This is done easily within the KB-DSS framework. We shall describe, briefly, in Chapter 12 other examples of such problems.

Developing an intelligent user interface

As we have pointed out in Section 5.2 decision support problems in management may lead to the development of several decision models integrating numeric algorithms and techniques. It is possible, with the new KB-DSS technology, to define intelligent front ends which will guide the user in selecting and using decision models.

A similar idea is found in Abernathy *et al.* (1985) who describe a system which, in a domain other than business, provides an intelligent interface for numeric simulation.

Designing a more powerful learning environment

It is already clear that the explanatory facilities of the expert component of a KB-DSS provide a means to reinforce learning by users. But the learning can also take place at the machine level. Several publications (Cooper and Kornell, 1986 and Brigg, 1986) have shown that it is possible to extract new knowledge from numeric processes and data. Typical applications are extracting classification and relational rules from test and model data.

A similar problem is faced when the system includes a toolbox (statistics and so on) subsystem. The concept of supporting the use of the toolbox with intelligent methodological interface was described more fully in Section 7.1.1.

Supporting intelligent processing

The goal of such applications is to reduce the computing resources and time associated with expensive numeric processes by substituting simplified algorithms where appropriate.

Supporting the decision analysis cycle

It has already been pointed out (Klein and Pezier, 1975) that one way to reduce the cost and increase the speed of implementing decision analysis has been to build a DSS which would include, not only decision situation structuring aids, but also advice on using the methodology. This was done with the ARBRE software (Klein and Pezier, 1975) but the technology of ES was not widely available then. Recently, this idea was developed markedly by Holtzman (1989) in the medical field.

> 'A rule-based system is an excellent way of implementing the analysis of a
> class of decisions. The goal of this particular system is to constructively
> prove the existence of a formal decision model that represents the decision
> being analyzed.' (Holtzman, 1989)

A KB/DSS is, clearly, a tool to support individual decision within a given decision class. For Holtzman, analysing a class of decisions 'consists of developing a domain-specific knowledge base for a rule-based system that contains a set of assertions designed to guide the analysis of *specific* decisions in a way that reflects the decision maker's unique situation'.

The KB/DSS framework is particularly well suited to implement such a specific KB on decision analysis coupled with influence diagrams or other decision models. This idea will be developed in Section 13.3.4

7.2.5 Is there a need for a definition of a KB-DSS?

We can ask ourselves if a new definition of a KB-DSS is needed or if our previous definition of a DSS (Section 5.1.2) is still sufficient. We think an improvement on the previous definition is made if we make the definition more precise by stating:

> A KB-DSS can be defined as a computer information system that provides information and methodological knowledge (domain knowledge and decision methodology knowledge) by means of analytical decision models (systems and users), and access to data and knowledge bases to support a decision maker in making decisions effectively in complex and ill-structured tasks.

The difference is that the new definition now clearly states that methodological knowledge is one of the resources that the system should provide. This methodological knowledge can be provided using the standard (modeling) technology or the expert system technology, or even better, by coupling the two.

The designer's choice is a pure technical choice. Both technologies are available and he or she should have the competence to decide when one is more appropriate than the other.

The methodological knowledge should be domain knowledge as well as decision methodology knowledge. In other words, a KB-DSS has the clear ambition to improve on the present state of things by providing (on request by the user) domain knowledge as well as decision methodology knowledge. The definition also stresses the point that, in many circumstances, the analytical decision models will include both systems (economic and financial) models and user models (preference function).

7.3 The KB-DSS development tools or generators

7.3.1 Functional requirements for a first-generation KB-DSS development environment for business

We have seen some of the main ideas of the KB-DSS framework in Section 7.2. The goal is to create a development environment which will enable the designer to define KB-DSS which will integrate with **synergy** the DSS capabilities and the ES capabilities. In other words, to define systems that combine the modeling and data management capabilities of DSS with the symbolic processing capabilities needed in complex and ill-structured situations. The environment will have to provide, for the DSS part, the DSS functions we have described in Chapter 5:

- data management or/database management functions;
- modeling (system and user) and model base management;
- report and report base management;
- business graphics;
- toolbox subsystem (statistical, forecasting and optimization functions);
- interface design (window management, forms definition and input/output user interaction during model execution).

and for the ES part, the functions which have been described in Chapter 6:

- knowledge base management;
- inference engine.

as well as the standard support functions of a development environment such as:

- trace (at the modeling level as well as the expert system level);
- coherence testing for the KB;
- editor (full screen as well as specialized editor for rules);
- debuggers.

with the above functions it will be possible to build KB-DSS which will provide many new functions such as:

- giving advice on specific problems;
- assisting the user with methodology on decision analysis;
- intelligent user interface.

In domains such as finance, or management in general, a high level of integration between data access, computation, modeling and symbolic reasoning must be achieved. In a KB-DSS, the situation is more complex than in what has been called Expert Data Base Systems (EDBS).

In expert data base systems, the main problem is the coupling of database management and expert systems. The integration of DBMS and ES is, clearly, a fundamental problem of the KB-DSS architecture. However, the KB-DSS problem is more complex since it requires the integration with synergy of two other main subsystems: the modeling (system and user) and the toolbox subsystems.

Another fundamental constraint of the KB/DSS environment is that we are working with *end users* and we cannot expect end users to use an environment which requires them to express their ideas in a logic programming language such as PROLOG. Exactly as with DSS, we must keep the user/designer concept in the KB/DSS (see Section 5.1.5). The overall integration needed between the components (or subsystems) is represented

	DBMS	MODELING	REPORT GENERATOR	GRAPHICS	WINDOW MANAGER	TOOLBOX	INFERENCE ENGINE	KBMS	COMMUNICATION	EDITOR
DBMS										
MODELING	Yes									
REPORT GENERATOR	Yes	Yes								
GRAPHICS	Yes	Yes	No (1)							
WINDOW MANAGER	Yes	Yes	No	No						
TOOLBOX	Yes	Yes	No	Yes	No					
INFERENCE ENGINE	Yes	Yes	No (2)	No (2)	No	No (2)				
KBMS	Yes	Yes	No	Yes	No	No	Yes			
DATA COMMUNICATION WITH OUTSIDE FILES	Yes	Yes	Yes	N/A	N/A	N/A	N/A	Yes		
EDITOR	Yes	Yes	Yes	N/A	N/A	N/A	N/A	Yes	N/A	

Figure 7.4 Integration (communication and control) between subsystems in a first-generation KB-DSS. (1) Graphics can be integrated in a report using the window manager. (2) Integration can be achieved through the modeling subsystem or directly, in which case we should have a 'Yes'.

by Figure 7.4. The integration between the subsystems of a DSS have been described in Chapter 5. The main new communication and control links in a KB-DSS framework are the following:

- inference engine/DBMS,
- inference engine/modeling subsystem,
- KBMS/DBMS,
- KBMS/modeling subsystem.

7.3.2 Methods concerning subsystems communication

A fundamental point of the KB-DSS architecture is the communication component which allows each subsystem to exchange information with the others. The methods used to provide the communication link between the components (subsystem) can be of different types.

Loose coupling

This can be achieved using a global memory to share variable values and a clear separation between symbolic and numeric functions (model calculation). This type of coupling is sufficient to implement intelligent user interface, interpretation of computed results from models and overall control of the problem solving process. In many circumstances, loose coupling is preferable. This is the case in data interpretation problems.

Between the inference component and the database component a loose coupling will use the database query language. In that case, the communication component will translate the query.

Tight coupling

In the case of the communication between the inference component and the database component, the communication component has direct access to the inner low-level mechanisms of the DBMS, such as the access functions.

For some kinds of problems, governed by numerical formulation, as in finance or marketing, we may want use our knowledge about numerical expressions and mix equations and rules. The solution here may have some analogy with the classical computer-based systems for symbolic manipulation of algebric forms (Macsyma, and Scratchpad II).

The blackboard architecture

When developing a KB-DSS development environment, the so-called 'blackboard' architecture and, also, object-oriented programming have been used.

In a blackboard architecture, a common data structure (the blackboard) is kept. Through this common structure the sources of knowledge (experts) communicate. In other words, the blackboard architecture simulates the resolution of a problem by a group of cooperating experts.

A meta-expert, using strategic knowledge controls the solution process to the problem. The reader can refer to Hayes-Roth (1985) for a presentation of the concept.

Since our purpose, here, is not to deal with the more complex problem of KB-DSS development environment design, we shall just point out that according to Kitzmiller and Kowalik the advantage of the blackboard method is the ability to stratify the problem solving process's knowledge. This ability allows all problem solving and other meta-level information to be uniformly represented in the blackboard, independently of the processes. Individual symbolic and numerical processes can be incorporated as separated multi-level knowledge sources.

Object-oriented programming

Object-oriented programming enables the designer to create software that can be more readily comprehended and shared with others

> 'Unlike more traditional programming methods based on concepts such as data flow or mathematical logic, object oriented programming directly models the application. Programs perform computations by passing messages between active objects, which are computer analogs of entities in the real world.' Thomas (1989)

The object-oriented programming environment provides very interesting characteristics to develop a KB-DSS development environment. Each object is associated with a private memory. The behavior of the object is implemented through a procedure (called **method** in Smalltalk) that has access to the private memory. In other words, an object is viewed by a user as a combination of an entity with its private state and the procedure manipulating it. Only the procedures of an object have access to its states and a procedure can only be involved by sending the object a message.

A characteristic of object-oriented language such as Smalltalk is called **inheritance**. This is the ability to define a new object that is just like an old one except for a few minor differences.

Object-oriented programming techniques can be used to buffer the expert system from the detail of individual processes. The key advantage usually attributed to these techniques is the ability to distribute the system among parallel processors to maintain and comprehend the system operation and to incrementally extend the system capabilities (Kitzmiller and Kowalik, 1985).

7.3.3 Overall structure of a KB-DSS development tool

We shall now describe the structure of the OPTRANS Expert environment which is an attempt to provide an environment which will give the user the capabilities listed above. Figure 7.5 describes the environment. From the user's point of view three layers of software are available:

(1) a front end or monitor level;
(2) a DBMS and/or model level;
(3) a report generator and/or expert system level.

The DBMS is directly connected to the database, the modeling subsystem is directly connected to the model base, the report generator is directly connected to the report base and the expert subsystem is directly connected to the

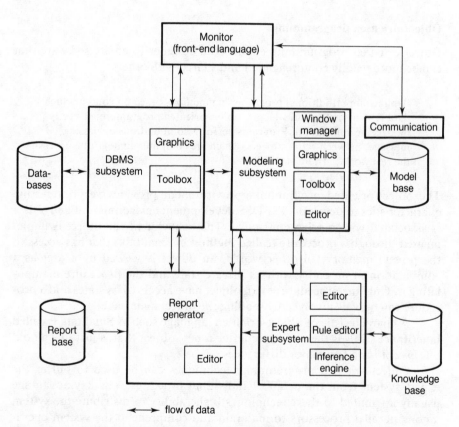

Figure 7.5 OPTRANS overall hierarchical architecture as seen from the user's point of view (version with DBMS component).

knowledge base. Two kinds of knowledge bases are available: a domain specific KB and a decision methodology KB.

At the monitor level the user can:

- access the library of resources of the system (database, models, reports and the KB);
- create, delete, modify and rename objects such as databases and models;
- select a subsystem of the next lower level (DBMS or modeling subsystem);
- access other commands and/or software. For example, it is possible from within OPTRANS to access the operating system commands or any program, run it and return to the OPTRANS environment;
- define general characteristics of the behavior of the system;
- direct the flow of information on several peripherals (screen, printer, plotter, files and modem).

At the second level, the user can define and use a database. The DBMS has a tight link with the graphics and toolbox. In other words, it is possible to use it directly. At the database level, a statistical routine such as a regression can be used. The statistical subsystem uses the access functions of the DBMS.

At the same level, it is possible to use the modeling subsystem either alone or in relation with the DBMS. The model can be fed with data from the database.

The data needed for the model is defined by instructions at the model level. These instructions define a view of the database. This view can also be defined by interaction between a user and the model (or a mix of the two).

At the third level, it is possible to use the report generator or the expert subsystem. Control, as well as data, can be passed from the model to the report. Similarly, control, as well as data, can be passed from the model to the inference engine (such as a knowledge base name, and a time index for example, but also information such as variable values).

Figure 7.5 presents the main subsystems and their relations (control and data exchange). The boxes in each subsystem represent the tools or lower-level subsystems available within it. As can be seen, the level of integration is high since, for example, a model can:

- feed itself from the database or update a database (the view being defined in model instructions or by model–user interaction);
- call one or more 'experts';
- print one or more reports or graphics;
- access tools (statistics);
- call another model and so on.

The inference engine can: call a model, print a report and so on.

7.3.4 Suitable hardware

Several types of hardware are needed to fulfill the need of a large organization in terms of KB-DSS. We can consider five levels of computer hardware on which a KB-DSS can run:

(1)   personal computer,
(2)   workstation,
(3)   departmental computer,
(4)   main frames,
(5)   resource sharing (network or otherwise).

Personal computer

The main characteristics of the personal computer (PC) as a delivery environment are:

* a one user system;
* the standard size screen (23 lines and 80 characters);
* the Disk Operating System (DOS) does not provide multi-tasking.

At the time of writing of this book good examples of such systems are:

* PCs, such as the IBM AT or PS or compatibles with 640 KBytes of main memory on hard disk, under MS/DOS, with graphic card, EGA or VGA.
* Macintosh with 1 MByte of main memory or hard disk under the Finder DOS.

The advantage of this equipment is that it has a low cost, and that it enables the development of professional KB-DSS applications up to a fairly good size, as large disks can be connected to the micro-computer. Knowledge bases of 1500 rules have, for example, been defined and used with OPTRANS Expert on a PC with 640 KBytes of main memory.

These systems support color plotters and laser printers which deliver high-quality paper output.

Workstations

The similarity between the PC and the workstation is that both are **one user** systems. The main differences are due to the hardware used and the operating system: Workstations usually have a larger screen with higher definition, and their operating systems offer multi-tasking.

At the time of writing of this book, Digital Vax and Sun workstations are good examples of such equipment. The more advanced possibilities of the operating system available on these workstations makes it possible to develop KB-DSS application where several processes can coexist. For example, a KB-DSS for a trade room in which computation on historical data can be displayed in one window, while a real-time display of stock prices from several feeders is done in others.

Also, workstations usually take advantage of their larger and higher-resolution screens to use more advanced graphical display. This is also made possible by a larger main memory size or virtual memory OS, which allows larger amounts of data and larger programs to be dealt with.

This can be the case for graphical presentation of rule networks which use large amounts of central memory, and, as a consequence, cannot be run on a PC or a PS. The UNIX operating system is a widely-available OS for these machines.

Departmental computers

The main difference between departmental computers and the PC workstations is that the departmental computers are run under a multi-user operating system. As a consequence, the version of the KB-DSS development environment used on such a machine should be a multi-user version. This has important consequences on the complexity of the KB-DSS development environment. In particular, sharing databases, models, reports, and knowledge bases must be possible under this environment.

The sharing of the resources must be possible in read/write mode for the database and, usually, in read mode only for the knowledge bases. Another standard characteristic of a departmental computer for KB-DSS is that it should be possible to connect the PC or workstation versions of the KB-DSS to the departmental computer.

For example, in a bank, a group of financial analysts may work on their PCs but, by means of the link between the departmental computer and their PC, they can use financial data on companies that they study on the departmental computer. On the departmental computer, a version of the KB-DSS development environment with a DBMS component will compute industry measures. These measures can, themselves, be downloaded to the PC versions.

At the time of writing of this book, the DEC VAX or the IBM AS 400 were good examples of such environments. The UNIX operating system is very often available as standard on departmental computers.

Main frames

From the point of view that we are interested in here, there is no important difference between mainframes and departmental computers. There is, clearly, a difference in terms of the power of the CPU and the disk capacity, but not much, if the operating systems are both of the time-sharing kind. There is an important difference if the operating system of the mainframe, as is often the case, is of a transaction processing type.

KB-DSS applications as we have seen, imply much more computation than transaction-oriented applications. As a consequence, load on the central CPU can be several orders of magnitude higher with KB-DSS applications than with record-keeping applications.

On the other hand, KB-DSS on workstations have, very often, to access transaction-oriented files available on the mainframe. Also, the mainframe can be used to download, to each workstation, updated versions of the KB-DSS application or components of it (that is, an updated knowledge base).

Most of the time, mainframes have operating systems which are specific to the computer manufacturer.

Networks

Workstations can be connected between themselves and to departmental or central computers through a local area network or a long distance network.

In such a network, some computers are used to manage (at the local level) resource sharing between workstations at the local level:

- File servers are specialized computers which print high-quality documents quickly.
- Communication servers are used to give access to other outside networks such as national and international packed switched networks.

The role of specialized software companies developing KB-DSS generators is to provide versions of their software that are able to work on as many of these environments as possible.

7.4 Case study: FINSIM EXPERT, a KB-DSS for financial analysis

We shall now study a KB-DSS for financial analysis in order to show how these concepts can be applied in practice. The system presented, called FINSIM, has been in use for some time, but, in 1986, the system was extended using AI technology (an implementation using the KB-DSS development tool PC-OPTRANS EXPERT).

7.4.1 Goal of the system

FINSIM was designed to provide a user with:

- an in-depth analysis of the financial history of a company;
- a reporting system on the economic and financial performance of a company;
- a simulation of the consequences of the main financial decisions and of the evolution of the environment of the company;
- support of financial diagnosis, using an expert function which can simulate the reasoning of a financial analyst.

Another main objective of the system is to enable the user to adapt the system easily to his or her needs. Examples of such adaptation to particular problems are described in Section 7.4.5.

The version of FINSIM which we shall present here uses a list of variables (accounts and other economic variables) which correspond to the new French accounting plan (Nouveau Plan Comptable or NPC) that has been compulsory for all French companies since 1984.

English, as well as Portuguese and Italian, versions of this system are also available.

7.4.2 The decision process of a financial analyst

Many books on the methodology of financial analysis or credit analysis have been written, some theoretical (such as (Lerner and Carleton, 1966)), others are more practical (Helfert, 1963).

Less work has been published about observed decision processes which lead a financial expert to his or her diagnosis. Some of the first descriptions of this process that have computer support in mind, can be found in Girault and Klein, 1971; Klein and Raphael, 1979; Bouwman, 1978; Bouwman, 1983 and Methlie, 1987. We have described, in Chapter 2, the studies performed by Ribe (1985) and Cohen et al.(1966).

We have seen, in Section 7.2.2, the main tasks that a financial analyst has to perform when facing a credit decision, and pointed out the main requirements of a KB-DSS that are needed to support the process. Figure 7.2 gives an example of such a decision process. This process is clearly divided into four phases: collecting date, historical study, forecast study and final decision. We put ourselves here in the general case, where we consider long-term financing decisions as well as short-term loans.

Collecting and storing data

This phase implies looking for financial and economic information on a company, on its environment (markets) and on its management. Most of the time, the basic information is found in the historical balance sheets and income statements obtained from the fiscal authorities or the company itself. One of the tasks of a KB-DSS is to provide support for entering and checking this information.

The verification of the information can be done, quite simply, using the accounting formulae. In certain countries, such as France, a national accounting plan exists. In other countries, such as the USA and Great Britain, national accounting plans do not exist but all organizations that perform financial analysis on a large scale use some kind of spreadsheet to standardize information.

The basic sources of information are always fiscal documents and the stockmarket (price, price/earnings ratio, and beta coefficients), if the analysis is made for investment purposes.

If there is a generally-accepted structure for the financial and accounting information, there is less standardization of market information, such as demand for main lines of business, sales and market share, price of main products and competitors' prices, cost of production factors and competitors' costs. The quality of management and of key persons in the company both constitute qualitative information of great value.

Historical study

The historical study can usually be divided into four parts:

(1) Calculating the evolution of economic and financial aggregates (ratios) which serve as criteria.

(2) Comparing these ratios with the industry (cross-section analysis).

(3) Studying the business cycle and fund flows associated with it.

(4) Making a synthesis for a first opinion on the company using expert judgment applied to the criteria.

Usually, the analyst recalculates the main financial reports so as to make them better adapted to financial analysis, emphasizing financial aggregates important for the analysis. The recalculated reports are the balance sheet and the income statement. Very often, the analyst wishes to set out figures as a percentage of the total assets for the balance sheet, and as a percentage of total sales or production for the income statement.

No serious financial analysis is completed without some study of the business cycle of the company and of the cashflows associated with it. Usually, a working capital analysis is carried out and a statement of sources and uses of funds is calculated and presented in a multi-period report. Once the analyst has obtained this recalculated information he or she will, in general, start his or her analysis to come to a conclusion concerning important criteria such as: liquidity, profitability, capital structure, growth potential, type of financing for investment and working capital needs. The level of detail and the criteria selected will depend on the goal of the analysis. In the case of FINSIM two important goals were chosen.

One goal was to provide a **synthetic diagnosis** to help the analyst compare his or her own diagnosis with the expert, when the problem is to decide if it is worth doing business with the company under study.

The second goal was to provide the analyst with an in-depth **financial analysis** of the company to facilitate more complex decisions, such as preparing for the financing of an important investment.

To achieve the first goal, the analyst would, essentially, study criteria such as: capital structure, liquidity, activity level and return. The final conclusion being a recommendation on whether the bank should start business with the company being studied (with various levels of warning). To achieve the second goal requires more work from the analyst.

Not only should such an analysis express conclusions on criteria such as: liquidity, return, and capital structure, but it should provide a deeper explanation of what is observed. For example, the rate of profit should be analysed to find out which variables have a positive impact or a negative impact on its variation and their relative importance. Such an analysis cannot be done without a **theoretical structural model** (set of equations) from which the *relationships* between variables can be deduced. This must be done as the analysis has to use hypotheses about the future and not just past data.

Once the main variables explaining the rate of profit have been found it is usually necessary to make a deeper analysis of these variables (margin, salary expense and so on). An in-depth analysis also requires an analysis of the investment policy (in assets and in working capital needs) of the company and an analysis of the financing policy which has been used in the past and is proposed for the forecast hypotheses.

The analysis must lean on a fund flow analysis and is usually a complex task. Here again, the analysis cannot be done without a structural model (set of equations). With respect to the liquidity and capital structure study they are common to the two analyses.

The liquidity analysis is based on a detailed diagnosis of the working capital requirements (inventory, accounts receivable and accounts payable) the main tools are: turnover ratios and cashflow analysis.

The capital structure analysis is based on debt to equity ratio and the maturity structure of the debt. The main tools are ratio and risk analysis.

With respect to profitability analysis it is important to also base this on a diagnosis of return on investment and return on equity, linked by the financial leverage effect.

$$\text{return on equity} = \text{return on investment} + (\text{return on investment} - \text{cost of debt})\, \frac{\text{debt}}{\text{equity}}$$

A comparison is then made between maximum growth and effective growth.

Last, but not least, whenever possible the criteria such as liquidity, capital structure, profitability should be studied in relation with the *industry* and the *size* of the company. When performing such a task the analyst is using databases available outside his or her organization (in France, the 'Centrale des Bilans' of the Bank of France and the industry statistics provided by the Institut National des Etudes Economiques (INSEE) are good examples of such databases) or industry data generated using the data available in his or her own bank.

Forecast study

If the loan being asked for is relatively large compared to the size of the company and if the profitability of the company is low or the debt level of the company has reached a certain point, then no serious risk study can avoid the problem of studying the future capability of the company to repay the loan. In this case, the analyst faces a more complex task. To reach a conclusion he or she must:

- calculate the ability of the company to repay a loan under a certain set of assumptions (usually provided by the company) concerning level of activity, margins and costs;
- compare this loan repayment capacity with the loan repayment schedule;
- study the risk involved in the set of assumptions.

Usually, the analyst must also reach a judgment on the characteristics of the loan the company is asking for and maybe propose another financial 'package'. To do this, he or she must be able to calculate, properly, the company's needs or excess cash, given the investments proposed.

The task is here twofold: on the one hand, the analyst must first check (through a uses and sources of fund statement) that the company is able to repay the loan, given the investment. On the other hand, he or she must try to assess the risk by evaluating the set of assumptions provided and, eventually, reconsider these assumptions and the analysis. But how many times?

It is not possible to do a forecast financial analysis study without an economic and financial model of the company (the model being explicit or not). The situation is best explained by studying Figures 7.2 and 3.14.

The loan decision is made by the analyst, using: industry market evaluations, market share, cost of production parameters and so on, which are given to him or her by the company. With these variables he or she calculates sales forecasts, margins, cashflow, debt, profit/loss, return and liquidity levels. Since some of these variables are uncertain the analyst may wish to make some kind of impact or sensitivity analysis, in order to obtain a distribution of the key variables and assess risk.

Final decision

The final step is the use of the conclusions made after the historical study and of the conclusions made after the forecast study to decide the acceptability of the loan. At this stage, non-numerical information (such as the quality of management) can play an important role.

7.4.3 Functions of the system

The functions of the system can be best explained by Figure 7.6. It is natural to distinguish between the support of historical analysis and the support of forecasting analysis.

Historical analysis

The system provides six main functions for the historical analysis:

(1)   data entry and checking (elementary variables);
(2)   calculation of aggregates as defined in the historical model;
(3)   display of variables (elementary or aggregates) in the form of reports and/or graphics;
(4)   definition of new elementary financial or economic concepts (variables) or aggregates;
(5)   definition and management of knowledge bases for analysis of the historical data;
(6)   display on request of a description of all concepts of the system.

Forecast analysis

The system provides the following eight main functions for the forecast analysis:

(1)   hypotheses entry;
(2)   computing the financial forecast model;
(3)   display of variables in the form of reports and/or graphics;
(4)   commands to use the forecasting model to simulate different decisions and/or evolution of the economic environment;

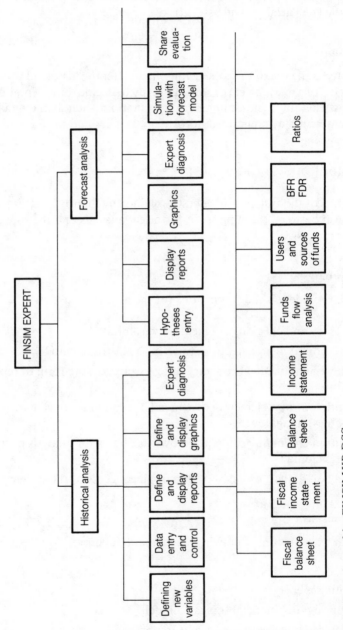

Figure 7.6 Functions of the FINSIM KB-DSS.

(5)   calculation of the excess or need of cash (financing) through the uses and sources of funds equation;

(6)   evaluation of the price of a share;

(7)   definition and management of knowledge bases (expert function);

(8)   display on request of a description of all concepts in the system.

Aspects common to the historical and forecasting models

A certain number of resources and functions are common to the historical and forecasting steps:

(1)   economic and financial reports,
(2)   knowledge bases,
(3)   describe function,
(4)   graphics functions.

With respect of the economic and financial reports the system provides the following possibilities for standard financial reports:

- balance sheet (fiscal presentation);
- income statement (fiscal presentation);
- balance sheet (financial presentation);
- income statement (financial presentation);
- working capital and working capital requirements.

For other economic and financial reports:

- profitability and growth potential;
- liquidity and debt structure;
- uses and sources of funds;
- ratios;
- break-even analysis;
- production and margin analysis;
- investment analysis;
- financing of investment analysis.

The graphical display function is common to the historical and forecasting phase. The knowledge bases are common to the historical and forecasting phase.

As for the display of information, the user can select on which time period he or she wishes to see the rules of the KB being used. The sub-knowledge bases used are:

- profitability,
- liquidity,
- debt/equity structure,
- working capital analysis,
- growth potential,
- analysis of financing for investment and working capital needs,
- investment analysis,
- borrowing capacity.

One of the major aspects of the system and which distinguishes it from similar applications written in a third-generation computer language such as FORTRAN, BASIC, or PASCAL is that it is written using the KB-DSS generator PC-OPTRANS. This means that the end user can not only clearly read the relations but can also easily modify them, if required.

The 'describe' function enables a user to display the definition of any variable (concept) used in the model (historic or forecast) and also to locate any model relationship using the variable (concept) (see Figure 5.9).

Use of the system by an analyst

We shall consider the case of a credit analyst who must decide on whether or not to grant a loan to a company (the case of a financial manager who must decide the best financing policy for an important investment could be another).

If the analyst is studying the company for the first time, he or she will have to obtain the latest annual fiscal forms (or the quarterly financial information if he is the financial manager of the company and has access to internal informations). If this information is stored in the data management part of FINSIM, he or she will just have to check that the last periods (year or quarterly) are in the computer.

The entry of historical data is carried out in a full-page mode, with display on the screen of the fiscal form. This facilitates as much as possible the data entry, and means that a less-qualified person can do the job.

Once the entry of historical data is completed, the system automatically locates possible data errors by using the accounting relations between variables. This check is presently done at the model level but could be done by a specialized KB.

Depending on the problem being tackled the analyst will then print a certain number of reports and/or variables in order to study their development over time. For most situations the existing reports and concepts are sufficient. If not, then the user can define new concepts and present them under the form of reports and graphics.

If an existing concept is not clear to the user, he or she can ask the system to describe the concept. He or she can also ask the system to locate a given variable in a model. The system will send back the list of all relations where the variable is used. If the user defines a new concept, then all the functions of the system can apply to the new concepts (describe, display and so on). The classical function of a DSS stops there.

With the KB-DSS, FINSIM, the analyst can, once the data entry phase is finished, request a diagnosis using the artificial intelligence module. The analyst can ask the expert module to give an opinion on a specific point such as liquidity, profitability or debt structure, or ask for a global diagnosis. The system can recall the definition of any concept being used in the KB. But the system can also *explain* how it came to such and such conclusion (see Figure 6.2). Any output (report or expert advice) of the system can be stored in a file ready for treatment by a wordprocessor. The analysis of the historical data being completed, the user can now switch to the forecasting part of his or her work.

In the case of a new study, the user will have to enter hypotheses or data on:

- activity levels (sales income and volume);
- inventories;
- operating expenses;
- consequences of the past (depreciation on past assets);
- values of short-term assets;
- consequences of past debts (repayment schedule of past debt);
- values of short-term debts;
- exceptional revenues and/or expenses;
- investments (amount, duration and depreciation policy);
- proceeds from sales of assets;
- dividend policy.

During the entry phase the user is supported by the system. For example, when entering data on an expense variable (amount) the system will divide the screen into four windows:

(1) A window to display a graph of the value of the variable (past and forecast values).

(2) A window to present past numerical values of the variable (absolute value and variation, as well as the mean value over the historical period).

(3) A window to present forecast values of the variable.

(4) A window to present possible commands available to the user.

The forecast value of the variable is given by its ratio to an explanatory variable. For example, the forecasted value of salary is a function of production. The analyst can always modify the forecasted value supplied by the system. Once the hypotheses entry phase is finished the analyst has several possibilities:

(1)   print a report and/or graphics (before or after financing);

(2)   ask for the computation of uses or excess cash (before or after financing);

(3)   simulate a financing policy;

(4)   change any hypothesis;

(5)   ask for a diagnosis by the expert module.

Often, the analyst will start printing the forecasted balance sheet, income statement, sources and uses of funds statement before simulating any financing since he or she wishes to see the evolution of the company before financing (given a first set of hypotheses).

By convention, the balance sheet will show, on the cash account, the needed or excess cash.

To explain the evolution of the cash position in the balance sheet statement most analysts will print the uses and sources of funds statement. The cash position for each period is computed using the uses and sources of funds statement according to the relation:

$$\text{cash}_t = \text{cash}_{t-1} + \text{cashflow}'_{t-1}$$

The detailed breakdown of $\text{cashflow}'_{t-1}$ being given by the uses and sources of funds statements.

Usually, the analyst will then either enter the characteristics of the loan which is being asked for (credit problem), or simulate a financing policy. The instruments available within FINSIM to simulate a financing policy are: equity financing, long-term debt, short-term debt, and leasing. At this stage, the analyst can request an expert opinion on the financing policy to follow.

In the case of equity financing the analyst can also request an evaluation of the price of the stock. The financing module recomputes the consequences of the financing policy (interests, dividends, and so on).

It is then possible for the user to:

• print any report and/or graphics after financing;

• ask a diagnosis of uses of excess cash (after financing);

• request an expert evaluation of the company after financing;

• reduce or extend the financing.

7.4.4 An example of the use of the system

We will now set out an example of FINSIM, using it to explain how the system works. The version of FINSIM used is a for a PC or PS.

Selection of the FINSIM model

The user selects the FINSIM model by typing the command: model FINSIM. As soon as this command is typed, the status line indicates that we are using the model FINSIM. To run the model the user types the command CALCU-LATE. Once this command has been typed, a window appears on the right-hand side of the screen and the list of available companies is presented to the user.

Selection of a company from the company database

The user is asked, by the model, to select the company he or she wishes to study. The company may or may not be already included in the database. If the company already exists, the system will display the national code number of the company and the years of historical data that is available. If the company is not in the database, the system asks the user if he or she wishes to create this company in the database. If the answer is YES the menu for data entry is displayed.

Checking the data

Once the company has seen selected the data is checked. The validity checks will eliminate most of the possible errors. For example, in the balance sheet the system checks the equality: total assets = total liabilities. In the income statement, the loss or profit entered is compared with the same variable recalculated from the other variables of the income statement. Relations between inventory levels between periods are also checked and so on.

Main menu of FINSIM

The main menu offers the analyst the possibilities shown in Figure 7.7. The selected option appears on the screen in reverse video.

At this stage, the user having entered historical data, he or she can either make an historical study, ask for a diagnosis with the expert using historical data, or modify some historical data of the company or of the industry.

This last point is very important. It is possible to store, in the system, data on the industry, with statistical measures (mean and standard error) such as, industry ratios, industry balance sheet and industry income statement. This industry information is used in certain reports and in some KB.

Modification of data

After having selected the modification option, the analyst is asked for the year that he or she wants to make a change to. Then a menu is displayed so that he or she can select the screen where the modification must be done.

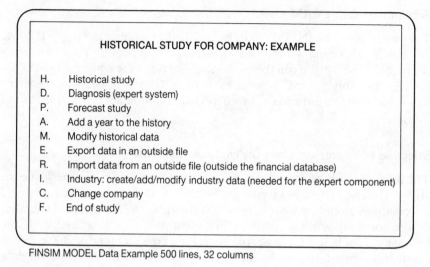

FINSIM MODEL Data Example 500 lines, 32 columns

Figure 7.7   Main menu of FINSIM.

Once a screen has been selected the user can update any number, moving the cursor over the whole screen as in a spreadsheet.

As the user proceeds to enter data, accounting relations will be checked and errors will be located and indicated.

On completion of each screen, the user can interrupt the process, start again at the beginning of the year, move to the next year, return to the preceding screen or stop.

Adding a year of historical data

When the data is entered for the first time, the user is asked how many years of data he or she wishes to enter. However, the user can always add a further year of historical data after the last year recorded.

The user can decide how many years of historical data he or she wishes to enter, and on which horizon (how many future periods) he or she wishes to work on during the forecasting phase.

Historical study

A historical study can be a fairly complex process. The analyst will usually want to obtain a general view of the company. To achieve this he or she will print several multi-period reports and transform them into percentages. If the reports are intelligently designed, then this information will often be sufficient to allow a conclusion to be reached.

In other cases, the analyst may wish to follow one or several variables as they change over time and display them with a variety of different presentations. To do so, he or she must be able to list the variables used in the system, and obtain their definition.

Since it is not possible to define, in advance, all concepts that an analyst may be willing to use during an analysis it must be possible to define *new concepts*, and deal with them as with existing concepts. This kind of extension must be simple.

Here, we will not attempt to present the detail of each of the facilities available for the treatment of the historical data, but we shall try to give an idea of some of the possibilities. The interested reader will find more detailed information in the FINSIM Expert Users Manual.

When the historical option is selected the menu shown in Figure 7.8 is displayed. As can be seen, several multi-period reports are available.

Obtaining the definition of a concept

For example, should the analyst wish to be reminded of the definition of working capital, he or she simply types the command: DESCRIBE FDR and obtains the definition of the three variables which contribute to the concept 'FDR' (see Figure 5.9).

HISTORICAL STUDY: AVAILABLE REPORTS

1.	Fiscal balance sheet	5.	Working capital
2.	Fiscal income statement	6.	Uses and sources of funds
3.	Balance sheet	7.	Ratios
4.	Income statement	8.	Flow of funds
		9.	Committee

A: All reports
OUTPUT to:
      S: Screen ◄— present choice   P: printer

Type of output:

A: Actual value   B: Variation (%)   C: Balance sheet in %
                                                Income statement

E: End (to go back to the main menu)

Report number (or Screen/Printer or A/B/C or End)

FINSIM MODEL Data Example 500 lines, 32 columns

Figure 7.8   Menu of the historical study.

The analyst may then wish to display on the screen the evolution of working capital and of total sales. This information is obtained by the TRACE command.

We now proceed to give an example of the use of the expert part of the system.

Expert diagnosis using historical data

To obtain access to the expert part of the system the user simply selects DIAGNOSIS in the main menu. The system then displays the submenu shown in Figure 7.9.

As we have pointed out above several knowledge bases are available to the user in order to obtain a diagnosis. Here, we shall just briefly describe the following three knowledge bases:

(1)   the working capital KB,
(2)   the synthetic diagnosis KB,
(3)   the detailed analysis KB.

These knowledge bases are useful in that they point out some of the possibilities provided by a KB-DSS development environment.

The KB for working capital
Here, we shall not go through the complete analysis, but we emphasize certain interesting characteristics of the expert system. The analysis made by

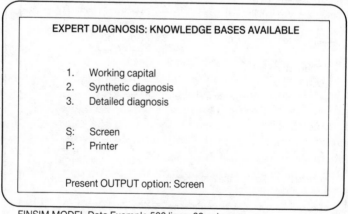

FINSIM MODEL Data Example 500 lines, 32 columns

Figure 7.9   List of knowledge bases (experts) available to the FINSIM user.

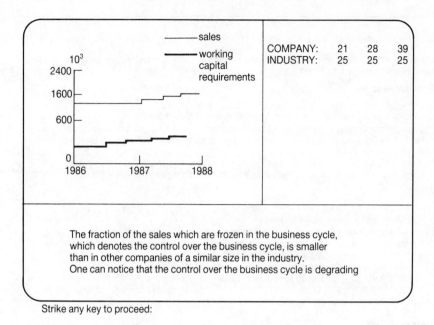

Figure 7.10 Example: the beginning of a comment by the expert analysing the working capital of a company.

the expert using the working capital KB is presented as a series of elementary analyses of each account used in the calculation of the working capital. These analyses use data from the industry to compare each account of the working capital with the industry average. The conclusion of these comparisons is that the variable is a strong, weak or neutral aspect of the company compared to the industry. The first screen provided by the analysis is shown in Figure 7.10.

The main window is subdivided into three windows. In the top left-hand window a graph of the sales and the working capital is displayed. The analyst can thus conveniently follow the evolution of the working capital as a function of sales. In the top right-hand window are the values of the working capital variables in the company, along with the industry average for a company of a similar size. In the bottom window the expert offers its comments about the information displayed.

After examination of each account that makes up the working capital, the system gives a summary of the conclusions.

The KB for synthetic diagnosis
We have recalled in Section 7.4.2 the main objectives of this KB and, in Section 9.4.3, we shall present subproblems and corresponding sub-

---

DIAGNOSTIC

We are studying a company, the industry comparison is made with an average company of the same class-size

Financial structure

The level of equity capital is good given the industry average.
In 1985, the equity capital represented 25.92 % of total balance sheet.
The borrowing capacity is above that of the industry; long and medium-term debts (including deferred taxes) are equal to 50.66 % of the equity capital against 152% of the average in the industry.
The working capital is beyond the industry average; on the average in the industry, it is of eight days of sales, it is of 33 days in the company under study. The financial structure is sound.

Cash

The cash available is close to the level observed in the industry. Two days of sales (sales tax included) against eight in the industry on the average.
Financial needs finding their origin in the business cycle are fully financed by long-term debt.
The suppliers' credit granted by suppliers is very limited; it is likely that the company prefers paying its suppliers faster to take advantage of discount.
The client credit granted by clients is close to the industrial average.
The level of inventory for finished products seem normal.
The cash position is good. From 1984 to 1985, the cash position is improving, moving (−15 to 2 days of sales)

Level of activity

The company being studied is a company of a good size.
It makes a sale of 15089 thousand francs against 2795 thousand on the average in this industry.
In 1985, the growth rate of sales is strong (21.37 %).
Activity is concentrated on production, with some commercial activity.
Productivity measured by the ratio of sales per employee is better than the one observed in the industry. The value added rate (41.96 %) is rather good, compared to the industry.

Return

The profit of the last year available is close to the average in the industry.
The return on equity does not reach the market risk free rate.
Otherwise, the capital financing the working capital cycle is well used and gives a good return.
The company can repay its present loans without difficulty.
The debt outstanding represents the cash flow available in 1985.
The economic break-even point is at 12266, which is at 23.11% of the present sales level.
After taking into account financial costs, the break-even point is still well below the present sale level. We can then conclude a fairly safe situation in case of a decrease in the activity level.

CONCLUSION

Very good advice; the financial situation of this company is sound.

Figure 7.11   Expert conclusion using the 'synthetic diagnosis' knowledge base.

knowledge bases used to solve them. Figure 7.11 shows an example of a diagnosis given by this KB.

This diagnosis is broken down into five parts dealing respectively with financial structure, liquidity, activity level, return and synthesis (see Figure 9.9).

Two types of analysis can be provided, one which does not take into account the industry data and one where each criterion is analysed in the light of industry information. As can be expected the analysis using industry information is more pertinent and rich. The variables being used for each point of view are presented in Figure 9.9 for the financial structure, the level of equity capital, the borrowing capacity and working capital evolution. As can be seen, the level of equity capital, the borrowing capacity and working capital evolution are used in this part of the diagnosis. With respect to liquidity, the system presents an analysis of the level of accounts used in the computation of working capital requirement and working capital.

With respect to activity, an analysis of the sales and production level are given, together with their evolution.

The last point of view that is studied is return, which is measured on equity and on asset. A measure of the reimbursment capacity is provided, as well as a measure of the break-even point. The break-even point analysis is used to assess risk in case of a decrease in the activity level.

The final synthesis is a general advice to the user about the advantage of starting a business relationship with the company from the bank's point of view.

If the analyst wishes to obtain a further explanation of how the conclusions were derived, he or she answers yes to the question 'Explanation of facts?'

The KB for detailed analysis
This KB is used when the user wishes to have a more detailed financial analysis of the company. The diagnosis is broken down into two main parts: a dynamic study and a static study.

The dynamic study is, itself, broken down into five main sections:

Section (1) studies the evolution of activity and profit level;

Section (2) presents the variables (accounts) explaining the profit (loss) level, in other words, the system looks for the causes of the evolution;

Section (3) presents an analysis of the five most important variables that explain the evolution of profitability in the company;

Section (4) studies the impact of the above variations on the income statement, main aggregates;

Section (5) makes an analysis of the flow of funds through the steps now discussed.

Firstly, the investment policy of the company is analysed. Secondly, other flows and their consequence on liquidity are analysed:

- variation of working capital requirement;
- financing of investment and working capital requirement;
- comparing investment and long-term resources.

Thirdly, the impact of these flows on the structure of the balance sheet is presented in a graphical form.

The static study is, itself, broken down into 2 main sections:

(1)   studies the main criteria such as: profit level, self-financing capacity, financial costs and productivity;

(2)   studies the financial structure.

The static study is made in the light of the industry ratios that are available.

This diagnosis is an eight-page text, mixing tables and comments. Here, we shall only make a few remarks on some of the possibilities provided by the KB-DSS framework. The first section of the dynamic study (evolution of activity and profit level) is shown in Figure 7.12.

After the user has chosen a slice of two consecutive years, the expert module starts to display comments on the evolution of sales and production level, as well as profit in absolute value.

Then it provides the evolution of the ratio of profit (loss) to production, the table in Figure 7.12 presents a breakdown of this variation.

The variables listed in the table are the variables which have had an impact on this variation. It should be pointed out here that this list can be provided because the expert module can, during the analysis, access the value of the variables of the historical model which have been used to compute the profit (loss). The analysis of the variation can be used to show which variables have contributed to increase the result or decrease it.

Then, the expert module will sort the variables according to their importance and display them, which immediately tells the user which variables have been important in explaining the result and in which percentage.

The diagnosis provided by any KB can be used with historical as well as forecasted data.

If the diagnosis is requested for a set of forecast hypotheses (a simulation) this means that the expert module will have to perform the same analysis using value of the same variables provided by the forecast model. In the diagnosis of the forecast hypotheses the values of many of the variables used in the expert are provided by the forecast model (simulation results) and are not just values which have been captured.

Also, it should be pointed out that, the sorting of the explanatory variables is done through a sort procedure which is not included in OPTRANS. This shows the advantage of being able to call an outside procedure from the model and pass the control back to the expert.

In the case presented in Figure 7.12 the margin is the most important variable to have contributed to the increased profit, followed by the 'reintegration' of depreciation and provision and salary expenses.

As we have recalled above, Section (3) of the diagnosis will present an analysis of the five most important variables. In our case, the expert module

(1)   DYNAMIC STUDY   YEAR 1986

1.1 EVOLUTION OF THE PROFIT SALE OF COMPANY TANNERY

INTRODUCTION

The net sales are increasing (+12.81%) to 45 201

The production is increasing slightly (+8.94%) to 47 133

The loss went down from −3.06% of production to −6.19% of production

ACCOUNTS RESPONSIBLE FOR THE VARIATION OF PROFIT RATE:

This variation of −3.13% can be broken down according to the following table:

ACCOUNTS	VARIATIONS	
	Positive impact on profit rate	Negative impact on profit rate
Other external expenses (excluding subcontracting)		2.88%
MARGIN	2.80%	
Salary and social charges		1.62%
Total financial costs(excluding exchange rate loss)		1.55%
Total exceptional income	1.46%	0.97%
Total exceptional expenses		0.62%
Taxes, depreciation and provision		
Total financial revenues (excluding exchange rate gains)	0.24%	
Other income		0,09%
Exchange rate gains	0.08%	
Other expenses	0.02%	
TOTAL	4.60%	7.73%

MODEL: Forecast DATA Example 500 lines, 32 columns

Figure 7.12   Beginning of the dynamic study using the EXPERSOC knowledge base.

will print its analysis of the margin. Figure 7.13 illustrates the analysis of the margin.

The French fiscal forms contain information on the production which is sold or put in inventory, the production of assets for the company itself and the commercial activity. Figure 7.13 presents the contribution of each of these types of activities to the total production, the margin on each activity, the contribution of the activity (in %) to the total margin and the evolution of the contribution.

The comments of the expert module on this figure deal with the % of production going into inventory, the eventual bias in computing the evolution of margin, the analysis of the subcontracting policy as an explanation of

————————— BREAKDOWN OF PRODUCTION —————————

	CONTRIBUTION TO TOTAL PRODUCTION		MARGIN RATE		CONTRIBUTION TO TOTAL MARGIN		
	1985	1986	1985	1986	1985	1986	VARIATION
PRODUCTION FOR COMPANY OWN USE	0.00%	0.14%					
PRODUCTION SOLD AND ON INVENTORY	100.00%	99.86%	42.76%	45.56%	42.76%	45.50%	2.74%
SALES OF GOODS	0.00%	0.00%	0.00%	0.00%	0.00%	0.00%	0.00%
			GLOBAL MARGIN RATE		42.82%	45.50%	2.68%

	1985	1986
Production sold	40067	45201
Production on inventory	3197	1868
TOTAL	43264	47069

The variation of the share of the production on inventory in the production sold and on inventory is significant (7.39 % in 1985, 3.97 % in 1986). The variation of the margin rate is, as a consequence, slightly biased in an optimistic way.
The other criteria usually considered do not have any influence here (sub-contracting, export sales and so on).

Figure 7.13   Analysis of the margin using the 'EXPERSOC' knowledge base.

the possible decrease of the industrial margin and so on. The analysis of investment (Section (5) of the diagnosis), is carried out using a table which gives a breakdown of investment by type of assets (non-tangible, tangible and financial) and by type of financing (leasing or full property).

Investment and the variation of the working capital have created a need of cash. The way this need of cash was financed (or is financed in the forecast analysis) is one of the important elements in the diagnosis.

If the analyst wishes to obtain further explanations, he or she answers yes to the question 'Explanation of facts?' If he or she does not remember the names of the facts being used by the expert, he or she can do so by using a function key to obtain this list. He or she then types the name of the fact for which an explanation is needed.

Sub-menu for the forecast study

When the analyst has finished his or her historical analysis, he or she selects the forecast option and moves to the forecast study. The system then displays the submenu shown in Figure 7.14. As we can see, the forecasting phase is divided into 16 possible support functions. The analyst can first enter his or her forecast hypotheses (11 functions).

There are two ways of entering the forecast hypotheses. One method is to enter only the hypotheses on activity level and the data concerning depreciation of existing assets, investment, disvestment (in relation with the

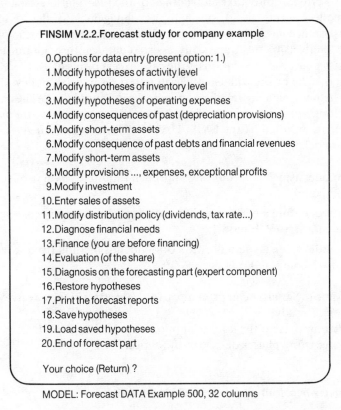

```
FINSIM V.2.2.Forecast study for company example

    0.Options for data entry (present option: 1.)
    1.Modify hypotheses of activity level
    2.Modify hypotheses of inventory level
    3.Modify hypotheses of operating expenses
    4.Modify consequences of past (depreciation provisions)
    5.Modify short-term assets
    6.Modify consequence of past debts and financial revenues
    7.Modify short-term assets
    8.Modify provisions ..., expenses, exceptional profits
    9.Modify investment
   10.Enter sales of assets
   11.Modify distribution policy (dividends, tax rate...)
   12.Diagnose financial needs
   13.Finance (you are before financing)
   14.Evaluation (of the share)
   15.Diagnosis on the forecasting part (expert component)
   16.Restore hypotheses
   17.Print the forecast reports
   18.Save hypotheses
   19.Load saved hypotheses
   20.End of forecast part

Your choice (Return) ?
```

MODEL: Forecast DATA Example 500, 32 columns

Figure 7.14   The submenu of the forecasting part of FINSIM EXPERT.

hypothesis of activity level) and long-term debt repayment schedule. The other method is to enter the hypotheses on each of the subsets of accounts: activity, inventory, expenses, depreciation, debt repayment schedule, investment/disinvestment, dividend policy (see Figure 7.14).

The advantage of the first method is that it requests a minimum of information from the client. In fact, it only requests one hypothesis: the activity level, the two others are pieces of data that are known by the company, since they are either consequences of the past (depreciation of existing assets), or a decision (investment/disinvestment).

All the other accounts will be automatically computed by the system using the historical mean structure ratios.

The analyst is, thus, provided with a robust projection of the financial accounts of the company and can print any of the reports for a first analysis including the expert diagnosis.

It is then possible, in a second step, to make a critical study of the values that were obtained automatically for the accounts using the structured ratios.

This critical study takes advantage of the information the analyst was able to collect during discussions with the management of the company and of the assistance he or she gets from a close examination of the evolution of these accounts using the graphically-assisted data capture option. He or she can then request the calculation of the cash excess or needs. If there is a need for cash then he or she will usually wish to test a financing policy.

Whether financing involves an increase in capital or not, he or she may have to look at the question of the effect on the company's share price. This problem is supported by the EVALUATION function which gives access to several models:

- a model using an accounting approach (liquidative value of the company);
- a model using a performance measure of the company compared to the industry (P/E model);
- a model using an actualization of dividends method (to be used for a growth company).

At any time the analyst can print any of the reports which were available for the historical study.

We now present the kind of support provided by FINSIM during some of the forecasting phases described in Section 7.4.2.

Assistance when studying the evolution of activity

The activity of a company is divided into sales of finished products produced by the company, sales of services, and sales of goods (bought to be resold).

In our example, the company sells only the products which it has manufactured, along with products and services associated with these products (training, consulting and so on). Once the analyst has selected the activity level option of the forecasting phase, then (for each account) a screen will be displayed (see Figure 7.15).

The screen is divided into five windows. The top window reminds the analyst of the name of the variable (here, the activity level is sales) with which he or she is working and the name of the explanatory variable, if one is being used to forecast the variable under study. In our example, the activity variable is 'production of services sold'. The top left-hand window displays the graph of production of services sold as a function of time. The top right-hand window displays the numerical and mean values of the activity values, indicates the name of the explanatory variable, and gives the ratios between these two variables. The bottom right-hand window displays the forecast value of the production of services sold. The bottom left-hand window indicates the command options available, allowing the user to adapt the forecast:

- to modify values;
- to modify the explanatory variable.

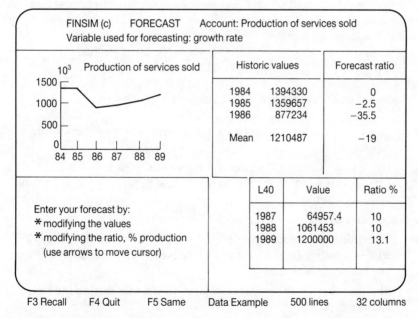

Figure 7.15 Assistance available when studying the evolution of activity level (production of service).

The possible user interactions with the system are as follows: The first time the analyst goes through the forecasting process, the system displays a forecasted value calculated using the last historical values of the explanatory variable.

If the analyst disagrees with this method he or she can either directly change the value of the production of services sold or he or she can alter the explanatory variable. Whichever variable is changed, the other one will be changed accordingly.

Once a set of accounts (variables) has been studied and forecasted the system displays the set of accounts together allowing the user to:

- correct directly in full screen mode;
- return to a previous set of accounts (preceding block);
- review the set, variably by variable;
- proceed to the next set.

The result of these support possibilities is that the analyst can let the system direct the examination of the accounts according to a standardized logical order, and is supplied with estimated forecasts whenever this is possible. If the analyst also wishes to study the accounts in a different order, this is, of course, also possible.

Nonetheless, certain procedures are unacceptable and the system will not permit the user to follow them. For example, it is not possible to compute the excess or need of cash, so long as every set of accounts has been studied.

7.4.5 Future development of FINSIM

The present developments are the following:

- improving the taxation module for detailed fiscal studies on the sale of assets;
- improving present KB or developing new KB (such as a KB for financing policy) which can be plugged in according to the style of analysis wanted;
- embedding marketing models to improve the sales forecast part;
- embedding production models to improve the computation of the cost of goods sold and so that hypotheses on the cost of production variables can be tested.
- developing a KB for giving assistance to the user during the financing phase.

For further details the reader is referred to Klein, 1988 and 1989.

7.5 The epistemological situation of KB-DSS

One interesting question is related to the type of inquiry that persons involved in KB-DSS design are performing.

The goal of the first OR work was clearly empirical: to give a scientific explanation of the facts and make successful predictions of the effectiveness of new weapons.

The goal of a DSS is more prescriptive since it is to assist the decision maker in choosing among alternative courses of action.

Anybody who has been working as a professional in the field of DSS knows that the technology he or she is promoting is used as a vehicle for persuasion and argumentation.

It is well known that in mature disciplines like physics or mathematics, the continuity, what Toulmin (1972) calls a 'genealogy of issues' and related concepts and tools, is maintained by a real process of innovation and selection. This process is performed through a professional 'forum of competition' within which new ideas can be criticized and eliminated to maintain the coherence of the discipline.

In the case of KB-DSS we are facing the case of a clearly composite discipline comprising a stock of theories, conceptual frameworks and techniques for dealing with theoretical and practical problems. We can also view it as a profession comprising a set of institutions, roles and people whose business it is to apply and improve these methods and techniques. For example, the International Federation of Information Processing (IFIP) and its specialized working group on DSS, the DSS International Journal.

When a designer is implementing a KB-DSS, for example for marketing analysis, he or she is looking for facts, he or she usually elaborates a theory to explain the facts (how the market works) and finally he or she uses the facts and theories to make predictions about future operations. This part of the job is, clearly, of a scientific nature. However, as we have seen, the KB-DSS will not only be used for prediction (simulation), it will also be used to provide a normative methodology to compare alternatives be it through decision analysis or a knowledge base.

Here, the designer has translated his or her analysis of a class of decision into a decision analysis methodology which, combined with the knowledge of the user (domain expert) and the specific situation knowledge, should help the user to come to the conclusion concerning what is the 'best' or, at least, a satisfactory decision for him or her.

Exercises

7.1   What is the basic idea underlying the KB-DSS framework?

7.2   What are the basic components (subsystems) of a KB-DSS development environment?

7.3   What are the main communication requirements between the components (subsystems) of a KB/DSS.

7.4   What are the new possibilities offered by KB-DSS over DSS and classical expert system shells

7.5   (a)   Select a spreadsheet and compare its functions in the light of the KB-DSS framework, do the same with an expert system shell.

   (b)   Take the user manual of OPTRANS Expert and study its functions in the light of the KB-DSS framework. Are all kinds of integration between subsystems provided? Do you see reasons why some of them are not provided?

7.6   Make a critical evaluation of FINSIM. In particular consider the functions given to the analyst to support his or her decision. Which KB could be added to the system to improve the support?

7.7   This is a study project for a term's work on a KB-DSS to assist in the completion of private individuals income tax returns. This project has been used with success in the context of French tax regulations. It can be adapted to suit the tax laws applicable in any given country. A KB/DSS must be developed which:

- asks the user for information about his or her family situation and income;
- assists the user in calculating, precisely, the income from property and financial assets to be taken into account;
- assists the user in evaluating the various deductions which he or she is entitled to make from his or her income;
- calculates the number of allowances resulting from the user's family situation;
- calculates the tax payable before deductions;
- assists the user in evaluating the various deductions he or she can make from the tax payable;
- calculates the tax due and payment dates.

For the reductions and allowances, the system must, therefore, look at:

- family situation (married, widowed, divorced, number and age of children);
- income of spouse and children;
- family situation of children and other dependents;
- special conditions: handicaps, war pensions and so on.

The system must be able to deal with incomes from the following situations:

- salaries;
- salaries and other income from companies of which the user is director or shareholder;
- pensions;
- rent of property;
- interest;
- profit from the sale of property or financial assets.

7.8   A case study for a term project: A KB-DSS for personal loan evaluation.

This assignment for a term project is inspired by the loan case in the OPTRANS user manual release 2.

The system to be implemented is made of a model and a knowledge base of 35 to 50 rules. The system can be easily extended to 100 or 150 rules, in which case, the junior version cannot be used any more (the junior version is limited to 50 rules in the KB).

The application to be designed is intended to help a banker decide whether or not to grant a personal loan to a customer. The application is made up of a model called LOAN which is used to compute a certain number of variables, and a KB containing the rules which represent the knowledge the banker is using to decide on the loan.

The loan model

Before considering the loan, the banker needs to know a number of facts about the customer and about the loan being asked for:

- the customer's annual income;
- the amount of the loan being asked for;
- the duration of the loan, in months;
- the annual interest rate applicable.

From this information, he or she will calculate, before going any further:

- the amount of the monthly repayments on the loan (constant payments);
- the total amount to be repaid (capital plus accumulated interest).

The formula used to compute the monthly repayment is the following:

monthly repayment = amount of the loan*(annual interest rate/12)/(1 − (1/coeff))

with coeff = (1 + (annual interest rate /12*loan duration)

In a second step, add a routine to compute another schedule for LOAN repayment (non-constant schedule), and ask the user to choose the one that he or she wishes. This is not to be done in the first simplified version.
The input of this information, the calculations and the display of the figures in a window on the screen are carried out by the model LOAN.
One window is used to enter numerical data about the loan and the customer's annual income, and a second window to display calculated data. In our case, the banker is willing to display the monthly repayment and 1/3 of the customer's monthly income, in the same window.
The first group of instructions sets up and names the numerical variables used by the model and by the rules of the KB. A second group of instructions activates one of the windows and asks the user to input values for the numerical variables. A third group of instructions uses the numerical values entered by the user to calculate a number of aggregate variables. One of these aggregates is the maximum repayment. This variable measures what experience has shown the banker to be the maximum amount of his or her monthly income a person should allocate to payback a loan. In other words, repayments above this amount sharply increase the risk for the banker, from a statistical point of view. A fourth group of instructions display, in another window, the entered and calculated values. Finally, a last block of instructions activates the windows used by the expert and set the expert in motion (specifying the reference column by its header).

The knowledge base LOANEX
We shall outline the structure of the knowledge base used in this very simple example using PC-OPTRANS notation.
The analysis of the problem can be broken down into six subproblems, each dealing with a particular aspect. These are represented in the knowledge base by six rule subsets (or criteria), which are the following:

(1)   LOAN
(2)   INCOME
(3)   ABOVE FIFTY
(4)   BELOW FIFTY
(5)   FAMILY
(6)   GUARANTEE

The rules

In each rule subset or criterion we shall find a set of rules dealing with the knowledge used to solve this subproblem.

Rules of the criterion LOAN

These rules are the first to be examined since the criterion (rule subset) LOAN is the first one declared in the above list. The first criterion LOAN deals with the rules which conclude if the loan is accepted or rejected, or if the first administrative constraint to be accepted is fulfilled.

The rules of the criterion INCOME

These rules cause a second process to be performed:

- Rule 5 expresses the idea that if the monthly repayment is less that 1/10 of the maximum repayment (given by the 1/3 rule) then the loan is granted.

- Rule 6 states that if the monthly repayment is greater than the maximum repayment (given by the 1/3 rule) then the loan is rejected. In other words, the banker does not wish to make the loan if the client will have to spend more than 1/3 of his or her monthly income to pay back the loan.

- Rule 7 states that if the monthly repayment is greater than half of the maximum repayment then the banker wishes to study what kind of guarantee he or she could have.

- Rule 8 states that if the monthly repayment is smaller than half of the maximum repayment then the banker wishes to study the family situation of the client.

According to this analysis, the system will examine either the rules of the criterion ABOVE FIFTY or those of the criterion BELOW FIFTY.

Rules of the criterion ABOVE FIFTY

With these rules the banker attempts to take into account the guarantee he or she can obtain, as well as the family situation when the premise of rule 7 is true.

Rules of the criterion BELOW FIFTY

The rules of this criterion state that the banker will not grant the loan if he or she has no guarantee when the premise of rule 8 is true.

Rules of the criterion FAMILY

In this set of rules, the expert takes into account the family situation of the client (number of children, marital status and so on)

Rules of the criterion GUARANTEE

The rules of this criterion attempt to combine the wealth and profession variables into a judgment on the quality of the guarantee which can be expected.

The value of a certain number of variables will be assigned by the inference engine. These variables are: CHILD, FAMILY, GUARAN-TEE, MARRIED, PROFESSION, WEALTH, LOAN. At the beginning of the reasoning process these variables are set as *undefined*.

At the end of the reasoning process the variable LOAN should take the value either 'granted' or 'rejected'.

ASSIGNMENT

1   In this loan example we wished to improve the KB by introducing several improvements: we wanted to define wealth in terms of assets held by the prospect. The types of assets to be considered are real estate, finances and cash. We also wish to use the profession of the prospect to deduce the stability of his or her job. We shall consider, for example, the following categories: unemployed, manual worker, farmer, employee, middle-management, top management and lawyer.

Define the new rules using OPTRANS syntax, modify the KB, recompile the KB and test the new system. You can also integrate information on the outlook of the industry.

2   In this loan example which knowledge would you like to take into account to make your decision?
Example of such knowledge:

- Is the prospect already a client of the bank? If yes use the information available on his or her bank account (mean level of the account, maximum debit and so on). If not, add a rule stating that his or her salary should be paid into an account at the bank to obtain the loan.

- Take into account the type of asset which is financed. If it is of a real estate kind, then the risk can be reduced through mortgage. The mortgage is compulsory above a given amount.

Define the new rules using OPTRANS syntax, modify the KB, recompile the KB and test the new system.

8

Knowledge Modeling

8.1 Introduction

When Feigenbaum and his colleagues at Stanford University were developing the first expert system they coined the term **knowledge engineering** to describe the process that created an expert system and the term **knowledge engineer** to describe someone who develops an expert system:

> 'The knowledge engineer practices the art of bringing the principles and tools of AI research to bear on difficult application problems requiring experts' knowledge for their solution. The technical issues of acquiring this knowledge, representing it, and using it appropriately to construct and explain lines-of-reasoning, are important problems in the design of knowledge-based systems. . . . The art of constructing intelligent agents is both part of and an extension of the programming art. It is the art of building complex computer programs that represent and reason with knowledge of the world.' Feigenbaum (1977)

Knowledge engineering is a special kind of systems analysis. The purposes of both are the same: to make a specification of an information processing system that can be implemented and run on a computer. The general processes involved are the same: analysing a task in order to specify a problem solving process, designing a computer program, programming and implementation. However, to build a knowledge-based system is different from building conventional information processing systems in several respects. Firstly, the characteristics of typical problem domains are different. An expert system imitates and emulates human expert problem solving. Thus, the problem solving process is very much hidden in the mind of an expert.

Secondly, the target computer system, the knowledge-based system, has a different architecture from conventional information processing systems. A knowledge-based system has a knowledge base and a reasoning system. The focus of the systems analysis process must, therefore, be on knowledge, and in particular, heuristic knowledge.

The task of systems has changed over time as new information technologies and better development tools have been created. These developments have led to new applications and less basic computer skills in the building of such systems. Integration of the computer technology into organizations requires more complex analysis of the application areas, skill in organizational, social and cognitive disciplines, and conceptually richer methodologies for systems analysis. A shift from a dominating technical skill toward contextual skill (organizational, social, business, cognitive and so on) has taken place. Knowledge engineering is a system analysis methodology which requires much contextual skill.

Feigenbaum calls knowledge engineering an *art*. It is true that most expert systems development, until now, has focused on computer representations and program design. By means of very powerful development tools, so-called expert system shells, rapid prototyping has been the dominating approach. Tool skill has been more emphasized than methodological competence in performing problem analysis. As a result, the development of a knowledge engineering methodology has been lagging behind the practice of building expert systems. Lack of concrete methods and techniques of knowledge engineering has led to the common apprehension that the performance of this task is more of an art than a science (see the citation from Feigenbaum above). The practice of building expert systems is very similar to what is found in other areas where computers are applied to ill-structured problems, for instance, in developing decision support systems for complex decision making processes.

In areas where we have highly developed and functionally integrated development tools, like DSS generators or expert system shells, the system development process has been very much driven by the technology.

In a technology-driven process the functionality of the application system grows incrementally. In the context of prototype systems, new ideas are generated and new opportunities are seen in a dialog between the system builder and the user or expert. Thus, application complexity is reduced by successive redefinitions, and the lack of contextual skill is overcome by rapid prototyping.

In a problem-driven approach *analysis* is at the forefront. The problem domain is thoroughly analysed, structured and specified. A conceptual model of problem solving (with knowledge and reasoning) is specified and implemented as a *base version*, from which prototyping can take over for testing, validation and growth of the knowledge base.

A strong critique of rapid prototyping can be found in Laske (1986). He claims that expert systems built by rapid prototyping are built on two 'particularly unhelpful, if not entirely wrong, assumptions'. The first assumption is that the knowledge engineer is a neutral arbiter between the expert and the development tool. The second assumption is that human experts can be tapped directly by verbal retrieval cues (for example, questions) that force the expert to make performance-unrelated observations and comments to his solution process.

Paul Johnson (1983) observed a medical professor in two different situations: (1) actually performing medical diagnosis in clinics, and (2) teaching students how to do the same thing. He discovered that the professor did not teach what he seemed to do clinically. When confronted with this conclusion, the professor explained that he did not know how he actually performed his diagnoses. At the same time, he needed to teach the students and, therefore, created plausible means for doing the task.

The second assumption violates the methodological preconditions for achieving valid verbal reports, that is, reports that really verbalize true performance of the expert. The latter argument is founded on the theory of human problem solving described in Chapter 2. According to Laske (1986) knowledge elicitation based on some form of dialog between the expert and the knowledge engineer (questions, retrospection, rapid prototyping and so on) can only give knowledge about the task environment. He calls these systems **competence systems**. By using concurrent verbal protocols performance knowledge can be elicited. He calls these systems **performance models of expertise**.

It is said that knowledge engineering is the bottleneck of expert systems development. More recently, therefore, we have seen attempts in the literature to present descriptions and models of this process that are theoretically founded and that can be taught.

The influence of cognitive psychology on knowledge engineering methods and techniques seems to be much less than the influence of this field on the architecture of expert systems. The latter is directly derived from the production systems which, as we have seen in Chapters 2 and 4, were an outcome of research on human problem solving.

However, there are some early examples of cognitive approaches, for instance, INTERNIST (Pople, 1982). Also, there is a growth in the area of building, knowledge engineering methodologies more closely on cognitive psychology models, methods and techniques (for example, Breuker and Wielinga (1984), Boose (1984), and Laske (1986)). However, despite the upsurge of interest, cognitive approaches in knowledge engineering are, according to Slatter (1987), more exceptions rather than the rule. He claims that most of the best-known systems, such as MYCIN, PROSPECTOR, DENDRAL and R1/XCON were constructed with little or no explicit aim of modeling expert thinking. In commercial applications of today's expert systems technology the emphasis is firmly on achieving expert-level performance by using formal problem solving methods.

In this chapter, we shall present a cognitive approach to knowledge modeling. It is the process of transferring transcripts of verbalized knowledge into a formalized form that can be processed by a computer. Thus, modeling knowledge is the process of formalizing (and inducing) general task knowledge from individual performance knowledge.

We shall start by giving a brief overview of some approaches to knowledge acquisition, followed by an overview of the knowledge modeling process taken as the basis for our approach. This process description builds on the two basic concepts from Newell and Simon's theory on human problem solving: task environment and problem space (Newell and Simon, 1972). Task analysis gives knowledge about the task environment. Performance modeling is concerned with eliciting, analyzing, and formalizing the knowledge in the problem space of an expert. Most of this chapter will be devoted to performance modeling and the analysis of verbal reports. A methodology is presented which put more emphasis on *conceptual* analysis of such reports than is typically found in other studies of performance using protocol analysis (see for instance, Biggs and Mock (1983) or Bouwman *et al.* (1987)). They are more focused on processes.

Finally, we demonstrate this methodology using a case from financial analysis, and the development of an expert system for financial counselling called SAFIR.

8.2 Knowledge modeling – an overview of the process

8.2.1 Traditional views of the process

One of the first more systematic attempts to structure the process of knowledge engineering was described by Hayes-Roth *et al.* (1983). Here, the term *knowledge acquisition* is used for the process of transferring and transforming knowledge about expert problem solving from the knowledge source to a computer program. Thus, the term knowledge acquisition is used synonymously with knowledge engineering. The process is defined in terms of the following stages:

(1) *Identification* of problem characteristics, that is, what is the problem domain, and who are the experts and the users.

(2) *Conceptualization* of knowledge, that is, the concepts used to describe objects and relations in the problem domain.

(3) *Formalization* which is to put a structure to the knowledge, that is, to map the knowledge into an adequate task framework, for example, a diagnostic framework.

(4) *Implementation* is the mapping of knowledge in a formalized task framework into the knowledge representation formalism of the chosen implementation language, for example, rules or frames.

(5) *Testing* the validation of knowledge and reasoning.

Another attempt to compile our knowledge on knowledge acquisition was done by Welbank (1983). She confirms the opinion given above of this task, that the focus is more on building systems than on knowledge acquisition. Furthermore, it is difficult to find descriptions of actual methods that the knowledge engineers can use and the exact problems that they have encountered. Welbank also describes a staged process of knowledge acquisition. She divides the process into the following three stages:

(1)   obtaining the basic structure of the problem domain;
(2)   producing the first working system;
(3)   testing and debugging.

A more comprehensive text on knowledge acquisition is found in Hart (1986). However, she admits herself that the text is more a collection of ideas. Methods found in other disciplines are brought together with the purpose of being applied to the development of expert systems.

More research-oriented reports on knowledge acquisition are found in Clancey (1984) and Breuker and Wielinga (1984).

8.2.2 A cognitive approach

The methodology for knowledge modeling described in this chapter presumes that the knowledge-based system to be developed is designed to emulate expert problem solving. To adequately understand and represent expertise in a conceptual model, two kinds of knowledge must be present: task and performance knowledge.

A knowledge modeling methodology must provide a way for both kinds of knowledge to be modeled. We shall suggest a two-stage knowledge elicitation process starting with task analysis, followed by a performance study as shown in Figure 8.1.

Task analysis

> 'What is of interest here is the task demands, their interrelationships, the goals or criteria for task completion, and a set of rules that can accomplish the goals given some set of initial conditions.' (Johnson, 1984 p. 369)

The first stage is to develop a model of the task for which we want to build an expert system. The purpose of a task model is as follows:

- to prepare the setting for performance studies of expert problem solving;
- to function as an interpretative framework for protocol analysis;
- to establish user characteristics;

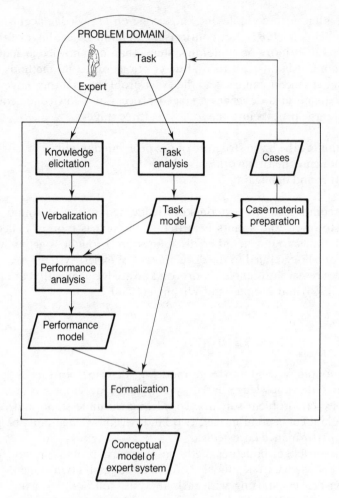

Figure 8.1   A two-stage knowledge elicitation process.

- to establish the criteria for choosing an expert;
- to specify performance criteria for the system.

To prepare the setting for further data collection on performance requires that:

- the task is well defined, which means that the problem is clearly stated, and the conclusion set is well defined;
- a set of relevant cases are available, containing enough information for problem solving.

To develop an interpretative framework for performance analysis, requires a model of the task. A task model is a general, competence model of how a typical expert might perform the task in question. It is a first-order model which will be developed further as more empirical data is available. It is the basic structure of the problem solving process involved and a general model of the reasoning steps. Thus, this task model is a decomposition of the task into subtasks and a specification of the flow of control between the subtasks.

In addition to the task model an interpretative framework must consist of a general *domain description*, usually as found in textbooks, or other reference documents. The domain description consists of:

- a vocabulary of the domain, that is, what are the task-relevant terms that are specific for the domain;
- theories and methods.

To establish the characteristics of a user involve determining:

- the competence level of the users, that is, who are the users and with what methods are they familiar?
- the role of the user in problem solving and decision making.

The final purpose of task analysis is to make an evaluation of the potential costs and benefits of a knowledge-based system for the task. Waterman (1986) has formulated some guidelines for considering expert systems development. He summarizes these guidelines as follows:

> 'Consider expert systems only if expert systems development is possible, justified, and appropriate.' (Waterman, 1987, p. 327)

He develops a set of task attributes for this evaluation.

Performance modeling

Performance modeling is an approach to knowledge engineering which utilizes models, hypotheses, methods and techniques from cognitive psychology in the building process of expert systems. Performance modeling refers to a strategy in expert system design which seeks to elicit real problem solving knowledge from human experts. This knowledge, which is in the mind of the expert, is made explicit through verbalization. Slatter (1987) calls this approach cognitive emulation which, according to him, is both a descriptive concept and a prescriptive principle. As a descriptive concept, it can be argued that expert systems incorporate many features characteristic of human information processing. As a prescriptive principle, it refers to system work in which an explicit strategy of emulating human cognitive processes is followed.

Performance modeling deals with knowledge in the problem space, that is, knowledge about problem representation and problem solving in the mind of the expert. The modeling is executed in two major steps:

(1) knowledge elicitation;
(2) performance analysis.

Using verbalization as our main method for knowledge elicitation, performance analysis starts with verbal reports (protocols) and ends with a performance model of the expert's problem solving process for each case solved. The protocols collected present detailed step-by-step traces of the expert's problem solving behavior. We shall develop a protocol analysis methodology which is particularly suited for knowledge-based system development. Performance analysis is divided into the following tasks:

- concepts identification and classification;
- conceptual structuring;
- qualifications of comparative and evaluative concepts;
- problem solving strategies.

These tasks will be further dealt with in Section 8.4.

8.3 Knowledge acquisition

8.3.1 Modes of knowledge acquisition

According to Kim and Courtney (1988), knowledge acquisition approaches can be classified in terms of two dimensions: strategic and tactical. The **strategic** dimension is concerned with the way the knowledge acquisition processes are driven: knowledge engineer-driven, expert-driven, or machine-driven. The **tactical** dimension is concerned with the techniques that are used for each strategic category. Specific techniques include interviews, protocol analysis, the repertory grid method, visual modeling and so on.

Knowledge engineer-driven knowledge acquisition is the classical approach. Here, the knowledge engineer interacts directly with the expert to model domain knowledge of two kinds: task knowledge and performance knowledge. Necessary skills and requirements for a successful knowledge engineer include good communication skills, empathy and patience, persistence, and intelligence (Hart, 1986). Techniques used in this approach are interviews, protocol analysis, repertory grids, and others.

Expert-driven knowledge acquisition is an approach where the expert encodes his or her own expertise and enters this knowledge directly into the computer. The key assumptions behind this approach are that (Moore and Agongino, 1987):

(1)   The expert can learn and use the encoding interface.

(2)   The expert can identify variables and relationships among them.

(3)   The expert can structure a refinable model by using a structured approach to one's domain.

(4)   The inevitable loss of clarity in encoded knowledge is acceptable if the expert can assure the performance of the model.

Visual modeling techniques are used to construct domain models. The objective of this approach is to give the user the ability to visualize real-world problems, and to manipulate elements of it naturally through the use of graphical entities. Further information on visual modeling is found in (Pracht, 1987).

Machine-driven approaches to knowledge acquisition are associated with a more general field within artificial intelligence, known as **machine learning**. The most widely-used technique in machine learning is learning by examples based on inductive inference. The basic idea here is to present, to the machine, a set of example cases consisting of solutions, along with the attributes which were considered in solving those problems. A computerized algorithm is then used to infer rules from these examples. The research on compiler inductive inference is still at an early stage of development. For more details the reader is referred to Delgrande (1987) and Michalski *et al.* (1986).

In the rest of this chapter we shall only consider the knowledge engineer-driven approach to knowledge acquisition.

8.3.2 Creating the environment for knowledge acquisition

In the knowledge engineer-driven approach, the knowledge engineer works with the expert in the context of solving problems. Welbank (1983) develops a number of problems that one should be aware of in establishing the task environment for knowledge acquisition.

(1)   The expert is inaccessible due to time constraints, and location constraints.

(2)   The expert is unenthusiastic. This is often due to a lack of understanding of what the purpose of knowledge elicitation is.

(3)   Generating enthusiasm can be done by giving information about the task prior to performance, and give the expert feedback on performance as fast as possible, for instance, by prototyping. In this way the expert can get an idea of what the end result looks like.

(4)   Lack of communication between the knowledge engineer and the expert. Our experience is that the knowledge engineer should have a good knowledge of the domain. This will ensure a common frame of reference in terms of the vocabulary and theories between the two. However, the knowledge engineer should be careful not to take over as the expert. This follows from the theory of tacit knowledge dealt with above. Another problem with a knowledge engineer who is very knowledgeable in the domain, is that analysis and interpretation can be biased in the direction of the knowledge engineer's own understanding of the task.

(5)   Lack of domain knowledge. In order to establish a minimum level of frame of reference for adequate communication and feedback for motivation the knowledge engineer should have some domain knowledge.

(6)   The inarticulate expert. This aspect has already been dealt with. It is the paradox of expertise, rephrased, which says that the more of an expert you are, the less able you are to describe your own problem solving, or as Ericsson and Simon (1984) put it: 'as reasoning becomes more practised and faster, it sinks out of consciousness'.

(7)   No awareness at all. There are situations where knowledge is entirely inaccessible to awareness. This seems to be true of learned skills, such as playing a piano. Welbank (1983) reports of this unawareness in computer programming.

(8)   Misleading models. This is phrased in another way by Waterman (1986): 'Don't believe everything experts say!' Therefore, reports by experts must be validated and the problem solving process carefully observed to see that the experts solve the problem according to the task analysis done, that is, that the information given to solve the case is really used.

(9)   The expert becomes a moving target. The expert may not have a consistent way of solving similar problems. Also, the expert may be influenced by feedback from the knowledge engineer in subsequent problem solving.

8.3.3 Knowledge acquisition techniques

In this section, we shall analyse some knowledge acquisition techniques used by the knowledge engineer to elicit human cognition and problem solving behavior. Several techniques exist – each one having both strong and weak properties. Therefore, the techniques described are not mutually exclusive, but should be used complementarily. Furthermore, we shall only give some examples here. The presentation is not meant to be comprehensive.

Interviews

Interviewing experts is the most familiar knowledge acquisition technique used for building knowledge-based systems, together with rapid prototyping. Interviewing is very widely used, probably because it is simple and easy to perform. However, care in the preparation phase is a prerequisite for obtaining useful results. We may distinguish between two types of interviews: unstructured and structured.

Unstructured interviews

These are most akin to normal conversation. The knowledge engineer asks questions and the expert answers. The preparation involved before an unstructured interview is to set up a list of topics one wants to know more about.

The basic structure of unstructured interviews is: addressing and probing. Topics are addressed in a breadth-first or depth-first manner, and probes are used to encourage the expert to talk, to dig deeper into a topic, to specify directions one wants to pursue, or to provide a change in view of a particular topic.

Structured interviews

These are more like an interrogation and are based upon a predefined set and sequence of questions. The knowledge engineer asks for clarifications, explanations, justifications, consequences and so on. The purpose of a structured interview is to obtain a detailed insight into the domain. It may uncover concepts and conceptual structures of the domain, qualifications of variables, justifications and explanations.

According to Welbank (1983), knowledge engineers have mainly used interviews in building expert systems. Interview data tends to be at the level of rules and general principles. It does not elicit performance behavior. On the other hand, interviews produce background knowledge.

Advantages

Knowledge which is explicit to the expert or can be easily probed, can be elicited quickly by interviewing. This technique is useful in early phases to inquire into the basic structure of the domain (task analysis) and in refining a knowledge base.

Disadvantages

Firstly, it is difficult to acquire relevant and correct knowledge. Knowledge elicited is general, inconsistent, incomprehensive, and imprecise. Secondly, it is unsuitable for acquiring performance knowledge. Thirdly, the interviewing process lacks overall structure. This lack of structure makes analysis of interviews difficult (Kim and Courtney, 1988). Fourthly, interviewing is time consuming and tedious.

Verbal protocols

Verbal protocols are used to obtain information about the cognitive processes of a subject dealing with a problem. They are literal transcripts of the expert's verbalization, as recorded on audio tape. There are several techniques for obtaining protocols: retrospective, introspective, interpretative, and concurrent 'thinking aloud' verbalization. Concurrent verbalization causes minimum interference with the problem solving process and will be discussed in more detail below.

In order to collect a concurrent verbal protocol the subject is asked to verbalize his or her thoughts during task performance.

Concurrent verbal protocols directly tap the successive states of heeded information in the mind of the expert. According to Ericsson and Simon (1984) this method comes closest to the reflection of the cognitive processes:

> 'We claim that cognitive processes are not modified by these verbal reports, and that task-directed cognitive processes determine what information is heeded and verbalized.'

Most people cannot verbalize as fast as they can think. People also forget to verbalize, and some repetitive cognitive processes may be automated and thus unavailable for tapping. However, for verbal reasoning tasks such as problem solving and decision making, Ericsson and Simon (1984) conclude that:

> 'the performance may be slowed down, and the verbalization may be incomplete, but . . . the course and structure of the task-performance will remain largely unchanged.'

Although verbal protocols provide a dense trace of cognitive behavior, and the information present is valid, some information is still unavailable, thus leaving out some details of the subject's behavior.

It is important that the setting for concurrent verbal protocols sessions comes as close to the natural task environment as possible. Several preconditions have to be satisfied for a successful session with the expert to be accomplished:

(1)   The sample of cases chosen is crucial and the cases must be representative for the task.

(2)   The task must have a clearly defined conclusion, that is, it must be possible to determine when the task is completed.

(3)   The task must contain sufficient data for completion in one session.

(4)   The data must be presented to the expert in a familiar form.

(5)   The expert should be given a test case in order to become familiar with this experimental technique and to obtain feedback from the knowledge engineer about the verbalization performance.

During a session, as few interruptions as possible should be made by the knowledge engineer. Only when the expert stops verbalizing should the knowledge engineer interfere.

The resulting protocols consist of a continuous string of words expressions of facts and affects, which may, at first glance, look rather disorganized. Protocol analysis is the task of formalizing these chaotic verbalizations into structures and knowledge about problem solving behavior – knowledge that is an accessible representation. We shall deal further with protocol analysis in Section 8.4.

Advantages
It provides a natural setting for problem solving where performance knowledge can be elicited through verbalization of thought processes. The result is a richness of detail and a high temporal density of oral responses. It is particularly useful in obtaining behavioral evidence in complex tasks (Biggs and Mock, 1983).

Disadvantages
Giving protocols can interfere with task performance. Protocol analysis is a skilled and difficult task and is time consuming. Transcripts can be highly ambiguous, requiring much interpretation when analysed (Slatter, 1987). It does not provide assistance to the knowledge engineer in identifying and acquiring deep knowledge of the domain.

Prototyping

The importance of feedback and context has already been mentioned. One means of using feedback is to build a prototype system, once enough knowledge has been collected. This prototype can be used to further elicitate knowledge of two kinds:

(1)   To test already implemented knowledge, and identify missing knowledge.

(2)   To reveal missing patterns in the rules and fill these.

Advantages
Puts the expert in the context of using the system, thus, he or she has a greater realization of the purpose of the knowledge engineering activities.

Disadvantages
No performance knowledge is elicited.

The repertory grid technique

Another well-known technique for knowledge acquisition, which is taken from the field of cognitive psychology, is the repertory grid technique developed by Kelly (1955). Kelly viewed a human as a 'personal scientist' with his or her own personal model of the world. This scientist seeks to predict and control events by forming theories and testing hypotheses. Based on this perspective, Kelly developed a 'personal construct theory'. The model of the world is made up of individual personal constructs. The repertory grid technique is a way to elicit these personal constructs.

A personal model consists of elements and constructs. **Elements** are objects of the domain: cases or examples, that the expert will select. For instance, when studying credit evaluation the expert may be asked to select five cases (loan applications) that are important. These are the elements. Then the expert is asked to compare successive sets of these elements, listing distinguishing characteristics. A **construct** is a bipolar characteristic which each element has to some degree. An example of a construct is management competence: good or bad. A numeric scale is assigned to each construct for subsequent analyses. There are several ways to elicit these constructs from experts, see, for instance, Hart (1986). Having elicited the important constructs, the expert rates each element according to these constructs. A table of constructs and elements with the ratings is referred to as the repertory grid. This grid now represents the expert's view of the world (domain).

Once the grid has been elicited it can be analysed to help the expert identify structures and patterns in the grid. One method of analysis is *cluster analysis* which helps to identify differences and similarities among elements. For more detail, the reader is referred to Hart (1986).

Recently, elicitation and analysis of repertory grids have been made available through interactive computer programs (for example Boose, 1985).

Advantages
Grid techniques are best suited for well-structured problems, like diagnosis and classification, where the elements of the solution space can be enumerated prior to the time of problem solving. They are well suited for elicitation of traits and for building relationships.

Disadvantages
These techniques are not well suited for problems of design and planning where unique solutions are derived from components of the problem. No deep knowledge and no performance knowledge can be elicited.

8.4 Performance modeling: the protocol analysis

We shall adhere to the assumption that performance studies of expert problem solving can best be done by verbal protocols (see Laske (1986) and the above discussion on methodology). The major task in knowledge modeling is, therefore, an analysis of verbal protocols. However, as we shall see in the next section, protocols may be complemented with interviews or other techniques, to acquire as much knowledge as possible.

8.4.1 The protocol methodology

The aim of the protocol methodology is to obtain access to the subject's problem space – that is, the internal or cognitive representation of a task. This problem space provides evidence of information processing and choice behavior of the subject. Such evidence can help to explain problem solving behavior and to explain differences among several individuals.

Protocol analysis is not a uniform technique. How the analysis is done depends upon the focus of the study.

In studying individual problem solving behavior, Newell and Simon's (1972) theory of human problem solving has provided the theoretical foundation for many protocol analysis studies (see, for instance, Biggs and Mock (1983) and Bouwman *et al.* (1987)). The essential task of these studies has been to search for goals, operators and states of knowledge in the subject's problem space. Since the operators represent a subject's processes or actions, they have been of primary concern in many of these studies. In Biggs and Mock's study (1983) 14 operators were defined and classified into four general categories: task structuring, information acquisition, analysis, and action. Similarly, in the study by Bouwman *et al.* (1987) activities were defined (and coded) into 21 types and classified into the following five categories: reading and examination, reasoning, goals, memory access, and comments.

The purpose of our study is to produce the knowledge required to emulate expert behavior. We shall put emphasis on *conceptual analysis*, that is, which concepts are used by the expert, and in which relationships do they enter. After having identified the conceptual relationships we will use interviews and prototyping to qualify these relationships in terms of logical inferences, plausible inferences, numerical relationships and so on.

Our first attempt to produce a rule-based expert system (a production system) for credit evaluation by protocol analysis failed. This analysis was carried out to the level of detail of the Problem Behavior Graphs (PBG), described in Newell and Simon (1972) and to the activity levels as detailed as described in Bouwman *et al.* (1987). These findings may seem contradictory to Newell and Simon's results, who claim that a production system can be induced from the PBG.

The contradiction between our experience and the findings of Newell and Simon may be explained by differences in task complexity. In cryptarithmetic, the kind of problems studied by Newell and Simon, the task is difficult but structured, and the goal state is distinct and definite. In credit evaluation, task complexity is great, there is not one single, definite answer and no normative solution. The process involves evaluation and judgment. Therefore, there is not one distinct path from the initial state to the goal state.

8.4.2 The set-up for data collection

Følstad (1984) has given some practical hints above the collection of verbal protocols. Before the protocols are collected the subject (expert) should be given an explanation of what the experiment is about, what the purpose is, and what is to be expected as the outcome of the experiment. The purpose here is to motivate the subject. Next, the subject is given *instructions* which explain, more specifically, how the experiment is to be accomplished. The first part of these instructions tells the subject what the problem is, for instance, 'based on the given case material make a credit evaluation of this company'. Next, the subject is told how to perform the task, that is, to think aloud, for example, 'think, reason in a loud voice, verbalize everything that passes through your mind as you solve the problem. I am not primarily interested in your final conclusion – but in your thinking behavior, in all your attempts to find a solution, in whatever comes to your mind, no matter whether it is a good or a bad idea, or a question. Don't plan what to say, or think before you speak, but rather let your thoughts speak, as though you were really thinking out loud. Don't let my presence disturb you.'

If the subject does pause, it is necessary to intervene and remind the subject to continue to talk.

The session must be carried out in an environment that is free from external disturbances and with the tape-recording equipment as unobtrusive as possible for the subject. It is important to give the subject a task environment that is as natural as possible. A task analysis must be done prior to the protocol collection where the problems presented to the subject represent relevant cases, have sufficient information for problem solving, and have a clear problem statement.

8.4.3 Conceptual analysis

According to Sowa (1984) the purpose of conceptual analysis is to produce a catalog of concepts, relations, facts, and principles that make up a domain – the **ontology** of a domain. The theoretical foundation of concept definitions is found in Chapter 2.

We shall now describe a protocol analysis method with focus on conceptual analysis, and with the purpose of producing a knowledge base in a computable form. According to what we have said above this means that we must be able to express concepts and concept relations in a precise way, which, for natural concepts, may lead to problems. However, we shall only deal with domains where concepts, to a large extent, are technically defined and expressed in precise terms. For instance, in financial analysis, the vocabulary is given by accounting terminology concerning financial statements and ratio analysis.

We shall divide the task into four subtasks:

(1) concepts identification and classification;
(2) conceptual structuring;
(3) qualifications of comparative and evaluative concepts;
(4) problem solving strategies.

Subsequently, we shall describe the conceptual framework of each subtask. In Section 8.5 we shall illustrate the practical use of the methodology.

Concept identification and classification

Protocols contain information that reveal many aspects of the subject's concern about the task. They not only contain information about cognitive behavior, but also reveal information about the subject's familiarity with the task, uncertainty about how to approach the task, emotions and so on.

We shall only concern ourself with task-specific knowledge, knowledge which describes the subject's *cognitive* behavior.

We shall perform this task in three steps:

(1) identification of natural concepts of the domain;
(2) segmentation;
(3) classification.

Identification of natural concepts of the domain is done by matching terms of the protocol with theoretical concepts of the domain. In financial analysis this is done by matching terms of the protocols with accounting terminology.

For instance, the subject says: 'Let us use as a rule of thumb that if return on investment is between 10 and 15, then it is slightly less than satisfactory'. The object of interest here (the natural concept) is 'return on investment', a term well known in the vocabulary of financial analysis. At this stage of analysis we also have to look for synonyms. Terms that are identified as meaning the same thing may be replaced by synonyms. Some care has to be exercised here in order not to lose semantic content.

Segmentation of a protocol means to split it into parts. The segmentation criterion is an identified object and everything that is said about this object in one sequence. For example:

'Let us use as a rule of thumb that if return on investment is between 10 and 15, then it is slightly below satisfactory. If it is below 10, then it is clearly less than satisfactory. I don't think it is necessary to make any steps below that. But when I see that it moves towards 11–12%, then I say, well, well, this starts to become fair.'

A segment is a paragraph of the protocol concerning *one* object. This object is called the **focus object**. It is described by relations to other objects, verbs, prepositions, and adjectives. A paragraph can be split into **topics**, each one being a description element or argument about the focus object.

Classification of arguments can now be done on the level of a topic of each focus object. The following classifications are used: A focused object is described in terms of evaluative and comparative concepts, or in terms of explanatory concepts and type hierarchies. All these descriptive concepts we call **attributes** of the focused object.

(1)   **Evaluative** attributes are associated with absolute values and explicit norms, for instance, profitability is good. We denote evaluative attributes by the term 'level'.

(2)   **Comparative** attributes are associated with relative values and explicit differentials, for instance, profitability is improving. We shall denote comparative attributes by the term 'trend'.

(3)   **Explanatory** attributes and type hierarchies define concept relations. We shall not, at this stage, define the kind of relation (causal, definitional and so on), but only denote the relation by the name of the object which occurs in a descriptive role. For instance, we may note from the protocol: Return on investment (ROI) has improved due to faster turnover of assets. Here, we shall identify the objects of the relationship, that is, ROI and 'asset turnover', and save the expert's description of this relationship in what we call a **topic line**. A subsequent task, qualification, will formalize and qualify this relationship.

A classified protocol may look like Table 8.1.

A classified protocol, as shown in Table 8.1, can now be used to compile everything that is said about one object (the focus object) and all relational objects to this focused object.

Table 8.1   A classified protocol.

Focus object	Attribute	Topic line	Protocol reference
ROI	Trend	A sizeable dip in 1985	Loan officer 1
ROI	Level	Clearly less satisfactory	•
•	•	•	•
•	•	•	•
ROI	Asset turnover	Improved due to faster turnover	•

Table 8.2 A classified protocol.

Focus object	Attribute
Profitability	Productivity
"	Cost structure
Productivity	Sales per employee
"	Contribution margin per employee
Cost structure	Sales growth
"	Contribution margin
"	Growth in fixed costs
Contribution margin	Sales
"	Contribution
"	Fixed costs

Conceptual structuring

By compiling the set of classified protocols, we have a collection of all that is said about each object and its relations upwards (its role as an explanatory object), and downwards (its role as a focus object). Thus, we can produce a conceptual structure of the domain. This conceptual structure describes *which* objects are related. From this structure knowledge about *how* objects are related can be specified. We shall particularly be concerned with inferential and algorithmic knowledge.

A classified protocol may now look like Table 8.2.

From Table 8.2, we can draw the conceptual structure shown in Figure 8.2.

Qualifications

Descriptive attributes, on the other hand, like level and trend, must be assigned values. Since we are dealing with human reasoning, these attributes will take qualitative values: good, bad, marginal and so on. This process of assigning qualitative values to an attribute is called **qualification**. For example:

Return on investment   level   very good above 20%

Qualification implies defining a value set, also called a **scale**, and defining equivalence among separate scales, for instance, the equivalence between a numeric scale and a qualitative scale.

Return on investment	very good	> 20%
	satisfactory	15–20%
	marginal	10–15%
	very low	< 10%

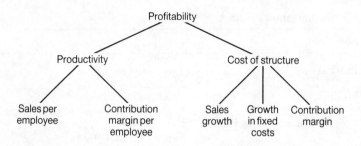

Figure 8.2   A conceptual structure.

Relationships lead to aggregated variables, for instance liquidity, and the relationships are formalized using production rules. The topic lines are the basis for qualification of the relationships. Qualified descriptive objects are entered in the conditional part of the rule, and a qualification of the aggregated variable is made in the conclusion part.

Problem solving strategies

How does the subject approach the problem? We can describe this on two levels, the task level and the performance level. On the task level we arrive at a general model of problem solving. The processes we identify are assumed to be common across several subjects in a domain. This model we have called a task model. For financial analysis we have defined a task model consisting of the following subtasks: financial statements validation and adjustment, ratio analysis, interpretation, diagnosis, and recommendations for change.

On the performance level, individual behavior is identified with respect to information search and reasoning.

In this study we have taken the task model as the basis for the overall design of the expert system. However, within each subtask performance knowledge has been modeled and implemented. No particular problem solving strategies have been defined on this level.

8.4.4 A conceptual model of a KBS

Above, we have considered the process of task analysis and performance analysis. At the end of these processes we arrive at a model of the knowledge and the reasoning process. We shall refer to this model as the *conceptual model* of a knowledge-based system. It represents the knowledge used to solve a particular class of problems in a domain. This knowledge should be organized in such a way that it can be implemented as a knowledge-based system on a computer. This requires that:

(1)   the conclusions or results of the reasoning process are explicitly specified;

(2)   subproblems are identified and further decomposed;

(3)   the input level of observations or findings are determined;

(4)   the relationships between observations and conclusions (the inference structure) are established.

The conceptual model should be free from any tool-specific terminology or computer representation formalisms. Furthermore, the knowledge must be general enough to solve most of the problems in the domain in which the system is going to work. The performance knowledge arrived at by protocol analysis must, therefore, be generalized.

We can now work out a more detailed specification of what this conceptual model should contain:

Task:	conclusions
Facts:	input data (findings/observations)
Algorithmic knowledge:	models, equations
Inferential knowledge:	heuristics, logic, rules
Problem solving strategies:	chaining, conflict resolution

8.5 SAFIR – an example of the knowledge modeling process

We shall now use the methodology described above in the development of SAFIR, a corporate financial adviser in domains dealing with credit evaluation, corporate acquisition, financing of investments, and restructuring of the financing of corporations. SAFIR was developed by extensive task analysis and performance studies of a domain expert. Methods used for knowledge acquisition were interviews, verbal protocols and prototyping.

We shall look at performance modeling of an expert dealing with financial analysis problems. This section is based on a thesis by Lyngstad (1987).

8.5.1 Knowledge elicitation

The first session that was held with the expert was partly an interview and partly a protocol collection. The purpose of this session was for the knowledge engineer to become acquainted with the task and for the expert to gain some experience about concurrent verbal protocols. Methodological aspects about protocol collection were evaluated and the first proposal of a task model was presented.

Altogether, six sessions were performed with the expert. Protocols of eight cases were collected and three unstructured interviews were conducted. Everything said was tape recorded, resulting in 150 pages of type-written reports.

Session (1) Interview: task analysis
Session (2) Protocols of companies 1, 2 and 3
Session (3) Protocol of company 4

      (a)   interview about model specification
      (b)   interview about qualitative variables and
      (c)   their scales.

Session (4) Interviews

      (a)   about financial actions
      (b)   about formalization.

Session (5) Protocols and prototyping

      (a)   companies 5, 6 and 7.

Session (6) Protocols prototyping and interview

      (a)   protocol of company 8
      (b)   review of prototype.

Each of the sessions had two main objectives:

(1)   to test and review knowledge representations
(2)   to identify new knowledge.

8.5.2 Concepts identification and classification

We shall now perform a conceptual analysis of the following sample protocol from the SAFIR project (translated from Norwegian):

> 'I notice that financing costs have fluctuated somewhat. The reason for this is not easy to say. I guess that they have gone up in 1985 due to the dramatic increase in the overdraft. They have gone up by 4.3 million (Norwegian kroner). Long-term debts, I see, have increased sharply in 1985, and dropped strongly in 1984. Why this is so I cannot see immediately from the figures here. It does not look like that the drop in long-term debts is financed by an increase in short-term debts. So, most probably it is a realization of assets.'

This verbalization is a direct transcript of the tape recording of the expert's thinking-aloud protocol (apart from the English translation). This protocol is now analysed for task-relevant knowledge. By using the vocabulary from accounting and financial statements analysis we can identify task relevant objects, like financing costs, overdrafts and so on. Then, we divide the protocol into parts, each part saying something about one particular object. In our case the whole sample protocol says something about financial costs. This part can be further divided into topic lines: statements saying something about the object in focus (properties or relations to other objects).

The protocol now looks like this:

SEGMENT (Focus Object): FINANCING COSTS
Topic 1: – fluctuating

Topic 2: – guess . . . gone up in 1985 due to dramatic increase in OVERDRAFT . . . gone up by 4.3 million (Norwegian kroner)

Topic 3: – LONG-TERM DEBTS . . . sharp increase in 1985 . . . strong drop in 1984. Why . . . I cannot see immediately

Topic 4: – It does not look likely that the decrease in LONG-TERM DEBTS is financed by increase in SHORT-TERM DEBTS

Topic 5: – Probably a REALIZATION.

We have denoted objects of the domain (accounting concepts) by upper-case letters.

Editing a protocol in this way is helpful in order to obtain a better view of the task relevant knowledge in the protocol.

Classification of objects and object relations can now be done on the level of topic lines. Several protocols can now be compiled into one set, the classified set of protocols, containing everything that is said about an object.

The classification of SAFIR protocols resulted in 440 classified statements. Table 8.3 shows all of the classified statements on return on investment (ROI).

Table 8.3 A classified protocol for SAFIR.

Focus object	Relationship	Topic line	Protocol
Return on investment	General	Calculated	1
Return on investment	General	Needs decomposition	2
Return on investment	Level	13.2% improvement	3
Return on investment	Level	Rather hopeless	4
Return on investment	Level	Between 14 and 16, Satisfactory	1
Return on investment	Trend	16.2, definitely better	5
Return on investment	Assets	Kept growth down	5
Return on investment	Assets T – O	Reduced by 50%	2
Return on investment	Profit margin	Not quite satisfactory	6
Times interest earnt	ROI	Too high financial costs	7
Return on equity	ROI	Reasonable relations	1

8.5.3 Conceptual structuring

Conceptual structuring is based on the compiled set of classified protocols. Implicitly, there is a conceptual structure of the domain in the statements. However, to make this structure explicit is not a simple task. Furthermore, taking all the relationships defined by the classified statements probably results in a complex network. To turn this structure into a hierarchy which can form the basis for calculations, logical deductions or plausible inferencing, requires interpretations.

In structuring the domain, the task model is helpful, in addition to the classified protocols. Also, it is helpful to let the expert specify the specific goal states of the diagnosis. The goal states of the financial diagnosis were defined, by our expert, to fall into two categories: (1) operational issues which are primarily related to profitability measures, and (2) status issues which are primarily related to financing measures.

The classified protocols are now turned into the two conceptual structures shown in Figures 8.3 and 8.4, for profitability and financing respectively.

8.5.4 Qualifications

An important task in financial analysis is ratio calculations and ratio analysis. For a ratio to have any meaning it must be interpreted. Here, interpretation means to qualify numeric ratios, that is, what does it mean that return on investment is 14.9%? Our expert interpreted this figure to be 'fairly good'. But what is the equivalent qualitative scale on a numeric scale?

By interviewing the expert it was possible to find one qualitative scale that could be used for level variables and one scale for trends. The two scales are shown below:

Scales

Level	Trend
• very good	• strong growth
• good	• moderate growth
• satisfactory	• stable
• less satisfactory	• moderate decline
• not satisfactory	• strong decline
• bad	

If desirable, a unique scale can be built for one particular ratio. Usually, this scale is a slight modification of one of the scales above. Also, for a ratio it is possible to use only part of the scale.

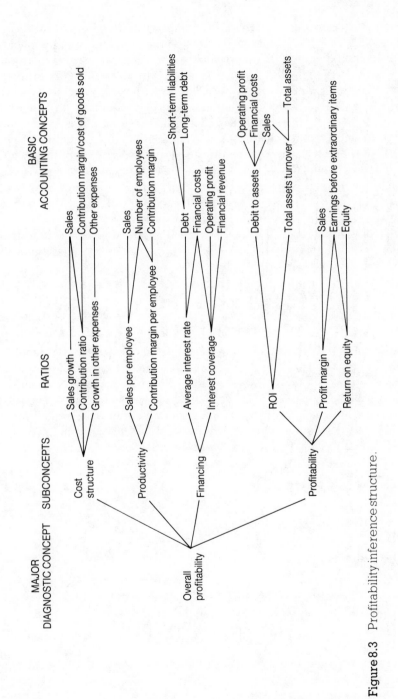

Figure 8.3 Profitability inference structure.

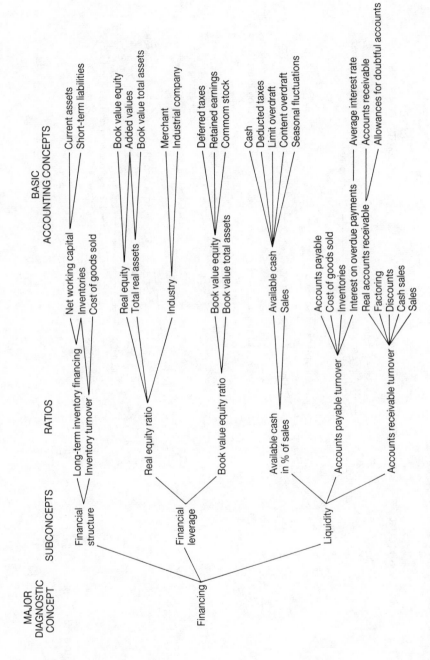

Figure 8.4 Financing inference structure.

Having created the scales, the next step is to assign numerical values (thresholds) to each qualification. For the ratio 'return on investment' it looks like the following:

Scales

Qualitative	Numeric
• very good	> 20%
• good	15–20%
• satisfactory	12–15%
• slightly less than satisfactory	10–12%
• not satisfactory	< 10%

8.5.5 Problem solving strategies

The very first concurrent thinking-aloud protocol gave a good indication of the expert's problem solving process. The expert starts by familiarizing him or herself with the information sources he or she has, that is the income statements and balance sheets. He or she interprets figures and starts to identify problems. Next he or she proceeds to an evaluation of ratios, followed by the other subtasks specified in the task model.

8.5.6 The conceptual model of SAFIR

At this point we can assemble the results of the task analysis and the performance studies under a coherent framework, called the conceptual model of the expert system.

The task is financial diagnosis of a corporation. The components of the diagnosis are:

- profitability
- financial structure
- leverage
- liquidity

The values of the diagnosis 'level' are:

- very bad
- bad
- satisfactory
- good
- very good

The values of the diagnosis 'trend' are:

- strong decline;
- moderate decline;
- stable;
- moderate growth;
- strong growth.

Factual knowledge

- Input data (findings/observations) which are found in financial statements and notes. These data are mainly time-series of data for the accounting periods provided.
- Derived data from the input data, either by inferencing or numeric computations.

Analytical models can be formulated where causal relationships and definitional relationships can be expressed in terms of algorithms or equations. From the task model and the performance studies we have identified the need for two models:

- ratio calculations;
- fund flow statement generation.

Inferential knowledge is particularly present in tasks dealing with interpretation and diagnosis. Using the rule formalism, but not constrained by any computer tool syntax, we could formulate the inferential knowledge as shown in the following rule:

IF   the level of return on investment is very good;
AND   the level of net profit margin is at least good;
THEN   profitability is very good.

Problem solving strategy

The task analysis indicated that the process starts in diagnosis, but moves rather quickly to search for problems in the input data. The search strategy formulated for SAFIR is backward chaining but with a meta-rule that controls reasoning within all the subcomponents of the diagnosis.

SAFIR has been built using the development tool PC-OPTRANS. A print out of the diagnoses is shown in Figure 8.5.

PROFITABILITY

	1984	1985
Return on investment (%)	8.3	14.9
Profit margin (%)	0.7	1.5
Interest coverage (%)	1.1	1.3
Average interest rate (%)	9.1	13.7

Return on investment is satisfactory.
Profit margin is too low.
Interest coverage is less than satisfactory.
Average interest rate is high.
The company has satisfactory operational profitability, but the financing of
capital is expensive. Therefore, the overall profitability is low.

FINANCIAL STRUCTURE

	1984	1985
Long-term inventory financing (%)	31.5	79.5
Inventory turnover (days)	182.9	52.4

Long term financing of inventories is good.
Inventory turnover is average.
The company has a satisfactory relationship between long-term debts and short-term liabilities.
Long-term financing of inventories is increasing sharply.
Inventory turnover is decreasing sharply.
Relationship between short-term liabilities and long-term debt has improved.

FINANCIAL LEVERAGE

	1984	1985
Real equity ratio (%)	18.5	16.9
Accounted equity ratio (%)	1.8	3.4

Real equity ratio is satisfactory.
Financial leverage is satisfactory, but accounted equity is rather low.
Real equity ratio is declining somewhat.
Financial leverage is weakening.

LIQUIDITY

	1984	1985
Available cash (% of sales)	4	14.5
Accounts receivable turnover (days)	53.5	33.5
Accounts payable turnover (days)	121	101

Liquidity is good.
Accounts receivable turnover is normal.
Accounts payable turnover is very high.
Available cash is satisfactory, but accounts payable should be decreased in
order to avoid interest on overdue payments.

Figure 8.5   Financial diagnoses from SAFIR.

Exercises

8.1   What is knowledge engineering? Describe knowledge engineering as a systems analysis task. What distinguishes knowledge engineering from conventional systems analysis?

8.2   Three different modes of knowledge acquisition have been described. Give a short description of these.

8.3   Interviews are used for knowledge acquisition. We distinguish between two types of interviews. Which? Discuss when each type can be appropriate for knowledge acquisition. What are the general advantages and disadvantages of interviews as a knowledge acquisition technique?

8.4   Some people have argued strongly against rapid prototyping. They claim that this technique does not produce a cognitive model of the problem solving process. Why? What are the advantages of prototyping?

8.5   You have been called in as a knowledge engineer to develop a stock investment system. You will start the process by performing a task analysis. Present an analysis of this task, including a task model.

8.6   Describe the set up for concurrent (think-aloud) verbalization.

8.7   The method used for protocol analysis puts emphasis on conceptual analysis. Describe the tasks performed to analyse a protocol.

8.8   Describe the components of a conceptual model of a knowledge-based decision support system.

8.9   Discuss how verbal protocols can be used to study:

   (a)   performance differences between experts and novices in problem solving;

   (b)   categories of behavior displayed by several experts;

   (c)   information acquisition used by experts;

   (d)   decision processes.

8.10   Discuss the pros and cons of using multiple experts in developing an expert system.

8.11   Group work: one knowledge engineer and one domain expert.

   (a)   Provide a city map and select a departure point and a destination point on the map.

   (b)   Assign the roles of knowledge engineer and domain expert.

   (c)   The knowledge engineer should describe the task environment, for instance, which transportation facilities are available, at what time of the day the travel takes place and so on.

(d)   Carry out a performance study on the domain expert who is planning the route from the departure point to the destination point.

(e)   Perform a conceptual study of the verbal protocol.

Material required: road map of a city and recording equipment.

9

Building and Implementing Knowledge-based Decision Support Systems

9.1 History

One of the first papers on the design of DSS was Gerrity's thesis (1970) from the Sloan School of Management, followed by a series of papers (1971) by the same author. At the same time, Segal (1970) was working along the same lines at the Moore School. Some of John Little's papers (1970) were important from the design point of view. Some people working on management information systems had ideas relevant to the use of artificial intelligence in such systems but they were not working specifically on information systems to support decision processes. This was the case for Caroll and Zannetos (1967). Other people working in the field of artificial intelligence saw, clearly, the deep relationship between AI and problem solving. This was the case of Newell (1979) and before this the well-known research of Simon on GPS and the less known work of Teitelman.

Klein (1977) expressed a number of ideas about the introduction of AI technology in DSS, but did not present design methodology and realization. Lee (1983) first defined the concept of KB-DSS.

In fact, until 1985, the AI research community and the DSS research community were working separately. To our knowledge, the topic of integration of AI technology into the DSS framework and the precise concept of the KB-DSS first appeared in the proceedings of the Maratea Conference on DSS Theories and Applications (1985).

Here, we wish simply to recall the methodology of DSS design which was presented by Gerrity in 1971, and some of the design ideas developed during the SCARABEE project where the design problem of the DSS and DSS generator were the main focus of research. We shall then introduce the

353

design methodology that we think is now needed within the KB-DSS conceptual framework.

9.1.1 Gerrity's approach

In his paper Gerrity (1970) points out that the key problems in the design of successful Man–Machine Decision Systems (MMDS was the name then used by Gerrity for DSS) are not technological but rather methodological in nature.

Gerrity presents an approach which is close to the one of Ackoff (1967) in the sense that it also argues strongly for replacing a *data-centered* or machine-centered view of MIS design with a *decision-centered* approach. The steps in the design process advocated by Gerrity are presented in Figure 9.1. This process is highly iterative, with the lines merely indicating particular interactions between phases that are expected to be especially strong. For example, there might, ordinarily, be a number of iterations through normative modeling, system bounding and descriptive modeling in order to reach to a problem definition that can serve as a basis for functional modeling and detailed design.

According to Gerrity (1971):

'during the initial definition and bounding of the decision system it is necessary that a preliminary judgment be made as to the character of the design task and into which of the following categories it falls:

(1)   totally non-programmable;
(2)   totally programmable (either optimally or heuristically);
(3)   a mix of programmable and non-programmable elements.

If it falls in the first or second category, then it may be allocated exclusively to man or machine respectively depending mainly on the economics involved. It is in the third case that a MMDS approach is required'.

Gerrity emphasizes the fact that he adopts a view of design as a process of problem finding and problem solving, as introduced by Pounds (1969). Pounds defines problem finding as the process of defining differences between the actual state of some system and its desired or expected state. Problem solving is defined by Newell and Simon (1972) as the process of finding, selecting and applying operators which will transform or reduce differences between the actual status and some desired or normative status of model.

The methodology proposed by Gerrity follows this pattern with 'normative and descriptive model comparison yielding gaps or problems, which are reduced by application of operators designed into the MMDS'.

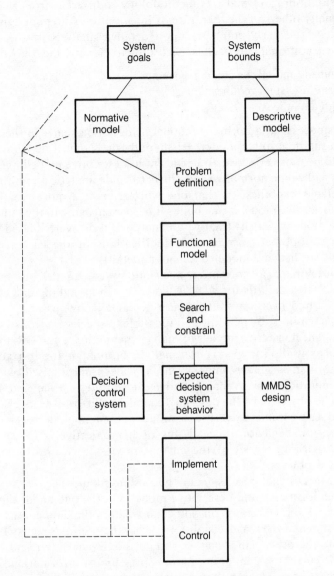

Figure 9.1   MMDS design methodology. (Reprinted from the design of
man-machine decision systems: an application to portfolio management by
Gerrity T. P., Jr., *Sloan Management Review*, 12, 1971, pp. 59–75, by
permission of the publisher. Copyright © 1971 by the Sloan
Management Review Association. All rights reserved.)

Gerrity points out that this methodology is different from that advocated by many others in the literature of information system design 'which places heavy and early emphasis upon detailed analysis of the existing system' the traditional approach is, according to Gerrity, the following:

(1)   define and model the current system;
(2)   determine system requirements;
(3)   design a new system.

Gerrity proposes that a normative model be developed early in the process relative to the descriptive model. His hypothesis is that a decision system analyst will be more effective and efficient in descriptive modelling if he or she begins with some normative constructs to guide analytic attention.

A related hypothesis is that one will arrive at a more creative and effective normative model if one builds it *before* engaging in the bulk of the descriptive modeling effort (that is, an analyst will be overly biased toward suggesting suboptimal, incremental modifications of the current system after having studied and modeled it in great detail).

In developing a normative decision system model, it must be recognized that standards for what is 'good' decision making in a complex and unstructured decision situation are not at all obvious and 'optimal' decision behaviour is, by definition, impossible to specify rigorously in such a situation. The normative models of management science and OR are likely to be useful as guides for what is 'rational' or 'optimal' in the abstract, even if these normative guides must eventually be compromised with real resource limitations on available budget, technology, time and human capacity. The objective of the descriptive modeling effort was, at that time, not to produce a completely verifiable model of the human decision maker's current decision behavior. Instead, his or her objective is to develop a reasonable working model of the current process to use as a basis for recognizing problems.

The MMDS that results from the design should be a compromise between the normative and descriptive model. On the one hand, the result should not be based totally on some abstract optimizing model which neglects so much of the real decision complexity that it proves unworkable in practice. On the other hand, neither should the design only result from a study of the current system and a naive expression of informational needs with the approach of making all such 'desirable' data available on line to the decision maker. (This is the data-centered approach attacked by Ackoff (1967).) In other words, for Gerrity the MMDS design 'should represent a reasonable balance between long-run decision process goals and short-run limitations in resources and capacity for change'.

Given the problems defined by gaps between the normative and descriptive decision models, the MMDS designer should develop approaches to alleviate these problems. These approaches – programmable functions, operators, and their related data structures – constitute the functional model. In other words, the functional model is a concise representation of those decision system components of operators, memory, and plans which should be transferred to the computer in the MMDS in order to improve the decision process.

This phase of associating operators with problems, or gaps, is one of the most creative in the design process. Implied in this process of association is an ability to model and to predict the effects of application of a given operation to a given problem. Such proceses of classification, association, and prognosis have been treated in depth by Gorry (1967, 1969) and related to a formal Bayesian model in his work on the diagnostic process.

9.1.2 The approach developed during the SCARABEE project

In 1969, a research project was started at the Business School Hautes Etudes Commerciales (HEC) the goal of which was:

- To develop a methodology and a development environment for a database-oriented decision support system.

- To experiment with this methodology and this development environment in the field of financial analysis.

Apart from a precise definition of the class of problems relevant to the DSS approach the papers published during the project: Klein and Tixier, 1971; Girault and Klein, 1971 and Klein *et al.*, 1974 put the emphasis on the specific characteristics of DSS:

- Very high interaction between user and system. This interaction being guided by the user during the exploration of hypotheses that he or she considers as he or she obtains intermediary results.

- Need of a language close to the specialized language of the user and with clear non-procedural features.

- Capacity to adapt to fast evolution of user needs, DSS being never finished or perfect.

The contribution of the SCARABEE project was, mainly, to show the importance of two points which had been ignored in the early literature on DSS design: *the language* and *the evolution* which have important implications on the design.

From the point of view of methodological consequences, the requirement of constant evolution is the main problem for the designer. Here, evolution means, in particular:

- extension of the language syntax (to better adapt the language to the user or extend it to take into account new functions);

- creation of new applications;
- extension to new data types.

The steps in the DSS design process which were proposed in the SCAR-ABEE project are the following:

(1) *Study of the task and of the user's decision processes.* At this stage, the designer's job is to identify the main concepts from the user's point of view: how does the user tackle the problem? what are the objects he or she manipulates and their characteristics? what are the procedures or models he or she uses. The goal of this step is to extract the main concepts of the future system.

(2) *Defining the minimum system capabilities.* These minimum capabilities have to be defined with respect to objects and their characteristics, procedures which can be applied to them: user interface and system performance.

(3) *Design of an initial system.* Using base concepts and the minimum system capabilities to define the architecture of the system: an open nucleus with possibilities for extension.

(4) *Implementation.* The importance of professional work was stressed, in particular, with respect to the hierarchical structure and the decomposition into modules. Also, the fact that the design of the system is not sequential but iterative was emphasized.

One of the interesting points of the methodology stresses the idea that it is not suitable to implement a system with all the capabilities identified during the study. Several reasons are given to justify this position:

- The study is theoretical, since users have not yet had the experience of the system. The first version will enable the designer to precise the needs more clearly.
- The user must have an active role in the system's evolution. To achieve this goal, the designer provides him or her with an environment that he or she can extend.

The main problem is to provide users with a starting environment which is sufficiently attractive to convince them of the usefulness of the system and give them the opportunity to improve it.

The last, but maybe the most important contribution of the SCARABEE project was to provide a set of design principles, methodologies and techniques for DSS development environments and not only to contribute to the DSS application design problem. The interested reader is referred to Klein and Tixier (1971). In other words, the strategy was to transform the user into a DSS designer by providing him or her with a software environment of sufficient ease, simplicity and power to enable him or her to develop his or her own applications.

9.1.3 Other normative views of the DSS design process

Scott Morton (1971) has given a description of the DSS design problem which is based on Gerrity's thesis. The same fundamental idea that the design should start with a comparison of the current decision process with the desired process is kept.

A cost-benefit analysis of alternative system design should then take place. Once one alternative is chosen and the system is implemented, the new decision behavior is observed and evaluated (monitoring of decision process) leading to possible changes in the new system.

A more refined view of this process was presented later by Keen and Scott Morton (1978) and is shown in Figure 9.2. Their idea is that a

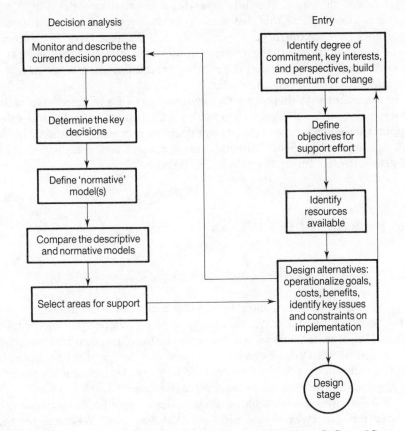

Figure 9.2 The pre-design cycle. (Reproduced from Keen P.G. and Scott Morton M.S. (1978). *Decision Support Systems, An Organizational Perspective*. Addison-Wesley.)

pre-design phase has to be performed before any detailed, more formal definition of the system design is started. The right-hand side of Figure 9.2 relates to 'essential initial steps in the implementation process: building momentum for change and developing a "contract" for action that involves realistic mutual expectations and commitment among the parties involved'. The major aim of the pre-predesign cycle is to make sure that the right problem is worked on.

The rational and normative tradition is represented on the left-hand side of Figure 9.2 together with the descriptive tradition, while the political and behavioral perspectives are represented on the right.

The development of normative models in the pre-design cycle will be used, whereas the descriptive model will be used for discussing improvements. In other words, the 'normative models represent a proposal for change: they define the potential range of designs for an information system'.

Usually, the pay off for implementing a normative model is high, but the risk is also high, as the 'distance' from the present decision process is important. On the contrary, if there is a small distance from the decision maker's current process, the implementation is easier but the pay off is probably low, in the sense that the existing procedures are *reinforced rather than altered*.

The argument that there may be long-term pay-offs if the system facilitates learning and willingness to explore analytical techniques and other computer-based aids even if the present decision process is supported by the DSS, is also used by Scott Morton. This argument was initially presented and demonstrated during the SCARABEE project.

9.2 Building the KB-DSS

9.2.1 The KB-DSS design process

Many of the ideas which have been expressed above are important and useful, most of them have the advantage of being independent of the technology. However, technology has also given birth to new possibilities within the concept of KB-DSS. We need to reassess the design problem given the KB-DSS technology and the existence of new development environments. The 12 steps that we propose are presented in Figure 9.3.

We shall now study each one of these steps. We wish to point out that we have put ourselves in the most general situation. We consider this situation as being the one we are in, when we have to build a KB-DSS for a large community of users. The situation where the designer and the user of the KB-DSS is one and the same person is an easier case to solve.

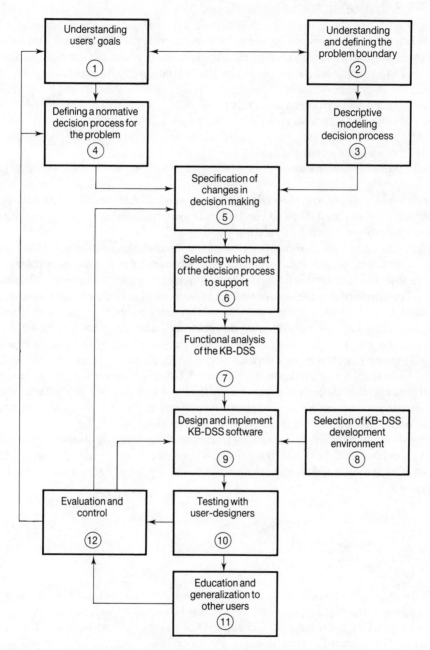

Figure 9.3   Proposed methodology for the KB-DSS implementation process.

9.2.2 Understanding users' goals

When we build a system for ourselves this step is usually not too difficult. Since we wish to build a KB-DSS it usually means that we have an idea of what to expect from such a tool. The usual goals are to be able to:

- recognize a problem situation;
- diagnose a problem;
- generate alternatives;
- evaluate alternatives;
- select one alternative.

easily and quickly, but they can also, more generally, improve the way that a problem is presently solved, or facilitate communication between individuals to ease the reaching of a solution.

If we are in charge of, or involved in the design of a KB-DSS for several potential users and, chiefly, if the number of potential users is large, the task of finding out user goals or principal objectives is more difficult, and conflicts of objectives are possible. We may also be in a situation where users have no goals, except the one of the users doing their tasks as usual (which implies making a decision or proposing a decision for approbation), then the will of their management to change the way this task is being performed may be felt as a threat.

In such a situation, the task of the KB-DSS designer is to understand the motivation of future users and to find out how the introduction of the new system can be felt as an opportunity to achieve their own goals and not to oppose them. It is clear that the motivation of users may be very different from one to another. Since this section is on design and not implementation we shall not go deeper into this question here. We shall study the typology of situations found in implementing KB-DSS and present implementing strategies in Section 9.3.2.

9.2.3 Understanding and defining problem boundaries (problem structuring)

This step is here to acknowledge the well-known fact that a decision maker may not have a clear picture of the problem that he or she is facing. We may have a problem, but no real decision maker has been identified yet. This step will include identification of:

- the decision maker(s);
- the relationship of the decision maker (client) with the decision structure of the organization;

- the decision boundaries that the decision maker must accept as fixed, as well as those that he or she feels he or she can challenge or has control over;
- the problem that will be solved if an alternative other than the *status quo* is chosen;
- the willingness and ability of other decision makers and experts in the organization to cooperate and provide inputs to the analysis.

For example, in the case of the design of a KB-DSS for credit analysis, such as FINSIM, the design of the system is not going to be the same if the problem is to provide the tool to a limited number of credit analysts (say from one to five) of a regional bank or if the problem is to provide a tool for the credit analysts of a large national bank. In large banks, loan decisions can be made in several hundred main branches. Another constraint may be the wish of management to compile a centralized financial data bank of balance sheets and income statements of clients and prospects.

The financial analysis process to be supported may be performed with different perspectives. For example, it can be performed with the goal of supporting a decision to:

- grant a loan;
- invest in a company;
- approach a company to offer banking services (marketing point of view).

It is very important to know if all of these decisions situations have to be supported or only one of them, since the people involved are not going to be the same and the information and criteria used are very likely to be different even if much of the basic information is going to be common to all.

Another example can be to find out if the loan decision to be supported will involve people working at different locations, such as branches and headquarters, in which case support of communication between them will have to be taken into account.

The KB-DSS designer should be in a position, after learning the above information, to suggest and describe, to the decision makers, the benefit that a KB-DSS will have.

However, this last task is not always easy to perform since prediction (for example, the percentage decrease in loans giving rise to repayment problems) is not easy if no experimental measure has been made already somewhere on a similar problem.

A certain number of problem structuring aids have been proposed in the literature. The reader is referred to Kepner and Tregoe (1981). As a conclusion, we can say that the problem structuring and definition or redefinition should lead to the creation of alternatives.

9.2.4 Understanding and defining actual decision processes

If the decision which is studied is repetitive then an understanding of the actual decision process is essential. This is a descriptive step. It is very important to come to a clear understanding of the present decision procedure, since this knowledge will be needed to evaluate what is feasible in terms of progress if the KB-DSS is implemented. If we have to implement a KB-DSS for a large population of users, they are very unlikely to use exactly the same decision process. This is the case of a situation where we wish to support decision for a large group of credit analysts.

The sub-steps for the identification of the decision process are the following:

- describe task within which the decision process occurs;
- describe the decision process itself in terms of:

  - problem diagnosis,
  - alternative generation,
  - selection of decision criteria,
  - evaluation of criteria,
  - constraints to be taken into account.

In fact, each one of these steps defines information and knowledge which is used, and ways of checking the validity of the used information.

The KB-DSS designer can use the Mintzberg *et al.*'s framework described in Section 2.5.1 to help him or herself in the description of the decision process.

Once the major phases of the decision process have been described, the designer will often have to start defining decision models. Three useful tools to structure such models are decision tree influence diagrams and cognitive mapping, we have described them in Chapter 3.

The decision trees and influence diagrams help, in particular, in assessing which are the alternatives, and the type of relations between variables.

9.2.5 Defining a normative decision process for the problem

The task now of the KB-DSS designer is to analyse the decision process, make a diagnosis and define an improved process.

The normative point of view of decision making that we have seen in Chapter 3 is useful here. However, we should not consider that the normative point of view always implies the use of decision analysis methodology (a theoretical norm).

As we have seen in Chapter 6 (on expert systems) the normative point of view can be very well defined by extracting the knowledge from one or more experts and structuring it into a knowledge base (an empirical norm). This knowledge base may not use preference functions and probability and yet will still be acceptable as a good normative process.

Clearly, if the KB-DSS is designed to support the rational decision analysis point of view we shall need a simulation language supporting certain and uncertain variables but also, in the toolbox of the system, algorithms to help the user elicit knowledge and preferences.

As we have seen in Chapter 7 a key new possibility offered by the KB-DSS framework and corresponding development environment is the capacity to couple symbolic and numeric computational processes. In the definition of the normative decision process the designer should define with great care how numeric alogrithms or models can be used in the steps of a reasoning process to reach a solution.

9.2.6 Defining changes in the decision process

Once the normative decision process, indicating how things should ideally be done, has been defined, changes to the actual decision process can be designed.

However, certain other elements must be taken into consideration: for example, the fact that the KB-DSS is going to be used by many decision makers, so we should evaluate to what extent improvement in the decision process can be assimilated by all of them. This implementation problem will be addressed in Section 9.3.

We know that a decision maker, properly supported, will see his or her decision process evolve and is very likely to request new capabilities from the system. The designer should anticipate what is the probable evolution and define a system which will be able to support this evolution in the decision process. For instance, in the loan analysis case, for which FINSIM was implemented, it is possible that the user is not using any kind of formal or explicit evaluation function to combine criteria. The choice is made by judgment.

It may happen that the analyst would like to have a systematic way to evaluate the multiple criteria as we have seen in Section 3.3.4 (such as a score function or other such normative method). Another situation is found when the analyst is using historical data only to make a conclusion and is not using any forecasting hypothesis, or that he or she is not using any fund flow analysis to study the evolution of the cash position of the company when theory can demonstrate that it should be done to improve the decision.

9.2.7 Selecting which part of the decision process to support

The designer will have to define the starting environment of the user. This definition is a skill and is difficult. As pointed out already in the SCARABEE project the starting environment has to be good enough for the user to feel comfortable in it, yet it should not be too sophisticated (so as not to frighten the analyst) and it must be sufficiently powerful (or the analyst will not see the interest of the DSS).

In an early version of FINSIM, for example, it was decided not to support a multicriteria evaluation function neither to support an industry analysis (cross section) but only company analysis (time series). On the other hand it was decided to support the part of the normative decision process using forecasted data.

In other words once the differences between the descriptive model and the normative model have been clearly identified the task of the designer is to evaluate which part of the descriptive model will be combined with which part of the normative model to constitute the starting environment.

9.2.8 Functional analysis of the KB-DSS

The purpose of this step is to define the main functions and the overall architecture of the system. An example of such an analysis was given in Section 5.3.3 for a management control DSS. Another example is given in Section 9.2. At this point it is decided which part(s) of the decision process to support: for instance, make a diagnosis on historical data using a computational model, make a forecast using a simulation model or use an expert module in the system to simulate a given reasoning process and so on.

Constraints of the overall design are also defined at this point. Is the system going to be a distributed system or not? Usually, a first impression of the decision models, type of data structures, presentations, knowledge bases and user interface that are needed are defined at this point.

The main tasks of the functional analysis are shown in Figure 9.4. The designer should at this point decide which subsystem will be needed:

- database management system or data file management system (or both);
- modeling subsystem, or a list of decision models with their functions;
- display subsystem (reports, graphics, maps and so on);
- expert subsystem (list of knowledge bases with their functions);
- toolbox (statistics, forecast, optimization, knowledge, preference and risk modeling).

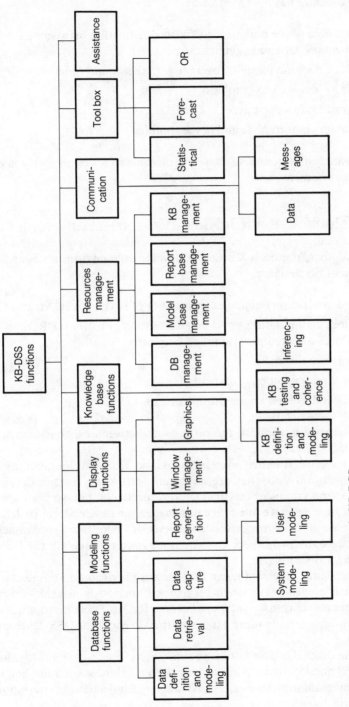

Figure 9.4 Functional analysis of a KB-DSS

This phase should be concluded with:

- a first idea of the data needed. With a distinction between elementary data and aggregates;
- a list of decision models, together with their main functions;
- a list of reports and graphics;
- a list of knowledge bases;
- the algorithms to be found in the toolbox.

Once this analysis is complete, it will be possible to select, properly, a development environment.

9.2.9 Selection of a KB-DSS development environment

We can say that, presently, five main development environments are available for KB-DSS designers.

(1)   Third-generation languages such as FORTRAN, PASCAL and C.
(2)   Symbol manipulation or AI languages such as LISP or PROLOG, or object-oriented programming languages.
(3)   Expert system shells.
(4)   DSS development environments.
(5)   KB-DSS development environments.

We have already introduced the differences between expert systems, DSS and KB-DSS in Chapter 7.

We have listed expert system shells and DSS development environments (generators) since they are important tools to be used in developing classical expert systems or classical DSS, respectively, but we shall not consider them here since we are concentrating on the development of KB-DSS and, also, we have demonstrated, sufficiently, why this new framework should replace the two others as soon as we need to integrate the DSS and expert system functions.

This, clearly, does not mean that the designer should not select a DSS development environment when no expert function is needed – be it for purely economic reasons – software licences for KB-DSS development tools being, naturally, usually more expensive than licences for DSS development tools.

In the context of this book, we shall, therefore, only consider alternatives (1), (2) and (5), that is, the choice between a third-generation language, a symbol manipulation language or AI language and a KB-DSS development environment.

The first criterion for a decision is going to be related to the choice of the designer of the KB-DSS. If the designer is the future user then the important point is to evaluate the capacity of the user to master the development tool and/or to assimilate the concepts used in the tool.

It is clear that most managers do not have the time, competence or motivation to master a third-generation language or a symbol manipulation language such as LISP, PROLOG or Smalltalk.

On the other hand, there is proof that hundreds of thousands of managers or knowledge workers are able to use spreadsheets, DSS or KB-DSS development environments. The reason for this is, simply, that in standard third-generation procedural languages and in symbol manipulation languages the formalism which is used is not coherent with the managers' conceptual view of the world.

Clearly, in some special cases where the user is familiar with languages such as BASIC or PROLOG this argument does not hold, but these cases are unlikely to be very numerous in management circles for some time!

We now consider the other criteria for choosing the KB-DSS development environment, the designer being a manager or a professional in KB-DSS design.

The most important of the other criteria is the availability of standard KB-DSS *components* (subsystems, as we have seen in Chapter 7).

If a third-generation language is used the designer will be facing the formidable task of developing the major subsystems usually found in KB-DSS: the database management subsystem, modeling language, graphics, report generation, inference engine and knowledge base management.

The most obvious cases where the use of third-generation language is useful are cases where special characteristics are needed which are not yet provided by standard development environments, or where the development environment is not available under the required operating system. For example, a trade room or a production management KB-DSS may require real-time capabilities which are not provided by the available generators. With respect to an example that deals with the first case, we know of a bank which decided to write its KB-DSS application in COBOL, since there was no KB-DSS tool available under this real-time monitor at the time of the decision. Here, the operating system was considered to be the constraining factor.

If a symbol manipulation language is used then the most important problem will be the necessity, in a KB-DSS application, to execute a minimum of procedural code as the consequence of a fired rule or slot of an accepted object. Access to external procedures, written in FORTRAN, BASIC, Pascal or C are important for reasons of efficiency and expediency. Computationally intensive procedures will gain from being written in a language which compiles efficient native code on the host machine, and existing subroutine libraries (in statistics, OR, and forecasting) may provide proven code which it is more expedient to use than to rewrite.

Another problem of symbol manipulation languages and PROLOG, in particular, is their inability to represent uncertainty in a natural manner (see Chapter 4).

Finally, the same argument holds for this class of language with respect to the components, all of the standard KB-DSS components will have to be rewritten!

As we can see, in most cases, the use of a KB-DSS development environment will be the right solution. The problem facing the designer will then be to select the right tool within this category.

Here, we shall just recall the main functions that such an environment should provide and integrate:

- model base management,
- report base management,
- database management system (data modeling and data manipulation),
- modeling language,
- report generator,
- graphics,
- window management,
- knowledge base management,
- inference engine,
- toolbox (statistics, forecasting and optimization),
- editor,
- communication (data and messages).

The designer is now facing the problem of designing the initial KB-DSS.

9.2.10 Design and implementation of the initial KB-DSS

The tasks to be performed at this step are outlined in Figure 9.5. They are:

(1)   data analysis and modeling, data loading;
(2)   data verification;
(3)   decision model design and testing;
(4)   display design;
(5)   knowledge base modeling and testing;
(6)   overall user interface design.

Some of these tasks can be subdivided. For example, the decision model design will involve decision modeling, the user decision model interaction,

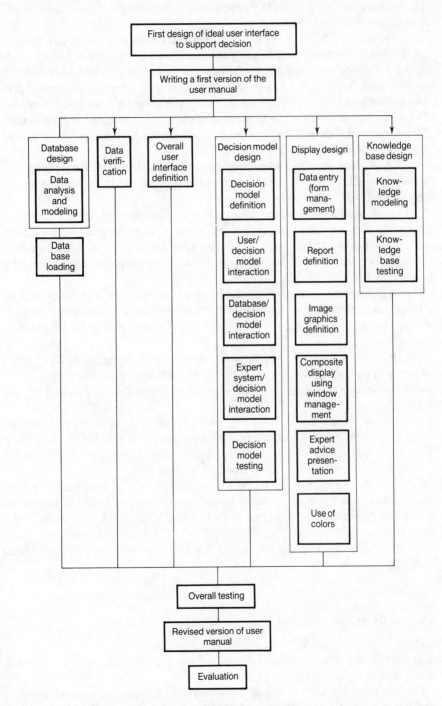

Figure 9.5 Design process using a KB-DSS development environment.

the database/decision model interaction, the expert system/decision model interaction and so on.

The display design can, itself, be broken down into the design of data entry (which often will imply the reproduction, on the screen, of a form), report definition and graphics definition. In fact, often the display will be of a composite kind mixing, for example: text and graphics, computation results and expert advice or reports, graphics and expert advice, and so on. The design of displays is made more complex if the designer wishes to take advantage of color possibilities and to take into account ergonomic and cognitive constraints.

Knowledge base modeling was described, in detail, in Chapter 8. The order in which these design tasks are performed is highly dependent on the decision process that is to be supported.

In some cases, where the first task is to support the problem detection phase of a user working with a large number of entities (products, companies and so on) a database must be defined, with aggregates that compute variance between actual and budgeted data and some reports, including graphics.

In a situation such as the credit analysis case described in BANKER or FINSIM, the first task to support is the computation of alternatives and, as a consequence, a decision model may be the first thing to define and implement.

In other situations, where much knowledge is being used in symbolic reasoning, but where not much computation is performed, the design of the expert system component may be the starting point in the design of the KB-DSS.

A good method with which to start the design is often to imagine the ideal user interface of the system. This user interface will help in writing a first version of the user manual of the future system, this user manual being updated when the first version is finished.

We shall now study each one of these steps. We wish to recall that we put ourselves in the most general situation. We consider this situation as being the one we are in when we have to build a KB-DSS for a large community of users.

The situation where we build the KB-DSS for ourselves is a particular case that is easier to solve.

Data analysis and modeling

Design
The user/designer uses the description of the information used in the decision process to model the data used.

The problem here is to use a classical modeling technique which is as close as possible to the conceptual constructs of the users. The data models available for this purpose are the hierarchical, network, relational and multi-dimensional models.

Our position is that entity-relationship data models and the multi-dimensional models are the best ones for end users since they are usually the closest to the end user's conceptual framework. The object data model is also a good candidate and is, in fact, close to the entity-relationship model.

In the entity-relationship model the real world is viewed as consisting of entities and relationships. With respect to the object model we have introduced some concepts about this model in Section 7.3.2.

We have also explained that many DSSG have adopted what is often called a 'multi-dimensional' database structure. In such models, it is very important to make a distinction between elementary variables and aggregates. An elementary variable is not computed using any other variable. Its value is captured as it is. An aggregate is computed using other elementary variables and/or aggregates. These variables are, in fact, attributes of entities. A data definition language is used to enter data definitions and relationships.

Data loading

The goal of this operation is to enter and store the data in the database, that is, the entities and the values of their attributes. Three different ways of loading the database can be used:

(1) by reading outside static files;
(2) by direct entry at the screen.
(3) by a real-time data feeder

In the first case, the data reader function of the database component will be used. In the second case, it will be necessary to write a model and one or more displays to enter the data. The third case is found in real-time applications.

The data reader will be used to define the structure of the outside file and access methods and read it. Very often it will be necessary to use the capability of the KB-DSS to pass control to an outside procedure since complex testing, aggregation and sorting may be needed to generate a file which can be read directly by the data reader.

The model is used to check relationships in data and avoid data errors. The display is used to guide the user when typing data.

The loading of the database can be a complex and delicate task when the number of entities is large and when it is necessary to update the database from files having a different structure and access methods.

Decision model design

The analysis of the decision process has pointed out the information that is used by the decision maker as he or she studies a problem in order to reach a decision, in particular, the criteria which are specific to the pieces of information that he or she uses.

The user-designer must define the variables and relations which are used in the computation of these criteria.

In the FINSIM example, the user computes'ratios (variable or financial aggregates), in order to measure short-term risk, the return on assets and the leverage of the company. The user will have to define the relations needed to compute these ratios from more elementary system variables for which it is easier to give estimates. According to the kind of modeling system used the user may or may not have to describe the computation procedure.

To compute the criteria (variables) the decision model must, usually, be fed with data coming from two sources:

(1)   the database (or data file);
(2)   the user.

The system variables used in the model will be classified, as we have seen in Chapter 3, between environmental variables, decision variables and goals. The environmental variable may come from the database or be introduced directly by the user during his or her interaction with the system. The same applies for the decision variables.

The designer will, as a consequence, have to define:

• The user/decision model interaction to provide decision variable values and environmental variable hypotheses.

• The database/decision model interaction to provide the user with the analysis of model results.

• The expert system/decision model interaction to provide the user with the analysis of model results.

• The expert system/database interaction to provide the expert component with facts stored in the database. (This last function can be accomplished directly or through the model, as shown in the OPTRANS expert development tool.)

The interaction takes the form of questions and answers between the system and the user, or of a choice in menus by the user.

Of course, all these interactions are defined from a non-procedural point of view and are clear to the user who only works at the logical level.

The designer will have to do this work for all of the models which have been found to be useful at the functional stage and to compute criteria of interest for the decision process studied.

In FINSIM, for example, a model has been defined for the computation of criteria based on historical facts (variables) and another model for the computation of criteria based on forecasted facts (variables). The reader can see that, often, the development of a KB-DSS to support the solution of a problem class will lead to the definition of a set of decision models.

Display design

This task is crucial in the decision support process since information:

- stored in databases and/or files;
- computed by models;
- generated by the inference engine (expert part);
- on available commands and function of the system (assistance);
- coming from the data feeder in real time

have to be displayed in order to let the user:

- assimilate the information;
- analyse the information;
- manipulate the information;
- decide on further action.

It is useful to distinguish between the elementary and composite display of information.

Elementary display design
Such displays are, mainly, composed of:

- one report,
- one graph,
- one menu.

The user-designer will define the reports using the report generator.

Composite display design
Composite displays will integrate, on the same screen, a mixture of:

- reports or results of computation;
- graphics;
- text coming from the expert component and corresponding to advice or answers to questions;
- commands;
- images.

Such composite displays require a window manager to integrate these elements with synergy. We have seen some examples of such display design in the FINSIM and BANKER presentations.

For example, in Figure 7.10 we have a graph in one window, results of computation in a second window, conclusion of the expert (a text in English) in a third window, and the commands available in a fourth window.

On Figure 7.15 we have six windows which display:

- The name of variable under study by the user, the units used and the explanatory variables used for computing the estimation of the variable under study.
- Graphics of the time evolution of the variable.
- Numerical values of the variables and explanatory variables, with a statistical measure of dispersion computed on past periods.
- The forecasted absolute value of the variable and variation rate.
- Commands available in order to proceed with the study.
- Available functions.

Use of color in display
The use of color can improve, considerably, the speed of assimilation of information by the decision maker. In a bar chart such as the one used to demonstrate the diagnosis support of a KB-DSS for management control (Figure 5.2), red could be used to illustrate adverse variance, and black could be used to illustrate positive variance.

Knowledge base design

The methodology required to perform this task was developed in Chapter 8. The designer will have to select one knowledge representation method if the expert component of the KB-DSS development tool provides more than one (in certain cases, he or she may mix several of these).

The application may require several knowledge bases. For example, we have described in Section 7.4.4, a case where different kinds of knowledge bases have been defined to support the different kinds of diagnosis needed, according to the type of financial analysis requested.

Here, we would just like to stress the point that, in our experience, it is very important to have the possibility of demonstrating simplified knowledge bases to the expert in order to help him or her structure his or her knowledge.

Running such a simplified knowledge base helps very much the expert to define his or her ideas.

Overall user interface design

It is very important to develop an overall user interface which informs the user about the possibilities open to him or her and to help in supporting the decision process.

In the FINSIM example, the user calls a model (named FINSIM). The model starts by asking the user on which company he or she wishes to work. The user supplies the company name. If the name is not found in the database then the system assumes that the user wishes to enter the data on this company.

Once the data has been entered, or if the company data was already in the database, then the system displays a menu. This menu is presented in Figure 7.7. As can be seen, the user is presented with a series of options.

One interesting new possibility that is available with a KB-DSS development environment is to build an 'intelligent' overall user interface which will guide the user in selecting the applications adapted to support his or her task.

9.2.11 Testing with designers

Once a KB-DSS has been implemented it is essential to test it thoroughly. The decision models and knowledge bases have to be tested after completion, as well as testing the overall system when it is finished. This testing phase should be done, firstly, with the users who took part in the design.

In the case where the KB-DSS is being implemented by the user for his or her own use the testing period can be reduced, for obvious reasons. The methodology for knowledge base verification and validation is presented in Chapter 10.

During the testing and evaluation phase, it is good practice to write a user manual for the system.

In the case where the KB-DSS is implemented for a larger group of users, the education of these users must be carried out.

9.2.12 Education of users and generalization

The education to be provided to users is largely dependant on their implication in the design, their level of expertise and the goal that the organization is trying to achieve in making the KB-DSS available to them.

The introduction of the KB-DSS to help perform the users' tasks has to be carefully planned. We recommend the organization of a seminar for this purpose. The seminar should cover the following points:

- explain the overall goal of the system;
- discuss the decision process being used by the present decision makers and collect remarks;
- discuss the decision process as management would like to have it performed and collect remarks;

- discuss the function of the KB-DSS and present it for a typical case;
- have the participants analyse a set of carefully-chosen cases and solve them using the system;
- explain how improvements will be integrated in the system, through, for instance, regular meetings to evaluate the support that the system is bringing, and which changes should be integrated into it.

The existence of a user manual is not necessary for the standard use of the system, but it is always very useful in such a seminar, and as a reference document. A user manual should contain not only a commented run of the system but, also, the equations of decision models and an explanation of their workings.

We shall discuss this point, in more detail, in Section 9.3.3, where we discuss implementation problems.

The seminar should be directed by one of the best experts of the organization on the topic of the application, so that there are no questions about competence. Management should be present to, at least, introduce the seminar and to show their commitment to seeing the system in use.

The experts teaching the seminar should be the ones who were leading the design of the KB-DSS.

One important idea that the seminar should get across is that KB-DSS are there to help people *improve themselves from a professional point of view and not replace them*. We shall discuss this further in Section 9.3.3.

The role of users in the evolution of the system should be stressed, in particular, how to monitor its performance, evaluate it and make it evolve. A second seminar, at least, should be planned after a few months as system usage.

9.2.13 Monitoring and evaluation

Results of evaluation of DSS, ES, or, KB-DSSS have not been widely reported in the literature. A framework for results of evaluation is given in Section 10.2.

An example is given by Klein (1977). In the case reported, the evaluation attempted to measure *perception* of improvement on a credit analysis task on two points:

(1)   Capacity of the DSS to deal properly with a variety of examples.

(2)   Perception by the users of the capacity of the DSS to improve the decision.

The experimental design was worked out with two sets of users, some working with the DSS and others with pencils and calculator. The users were given information on companies (including balance sheets and income statements) and had to provide a financial analysis of them and a recommendation for granting a given loan or not. Information on perception was collected using questionnaires. Information on hard data, such as computation of the capacity to refinance a loan over a given horizon using information provided in the case, was also used.

9.2.14 Prototyping and evolutionary design

Figure 9.3 contains a certain number of loops which convey the idea that the design is not linear but iterative. Most of the time it is useful to implement a first version of the system which can be considered as the minimum nucleus.

This nucleus (or starting version) may include only a simple decision model, a first data file or database, or a first simple presentation of the results in a report, and a knowledge base containing only a few rules. The role of this minimum version is to help users define their needs in terms of:

- data;
- type of user interface;
- decision model variables and relationships;
- display of results;
- type of assistance requested from the expert module.

The availability of a KB-DSS development environment makes it possible to have an evolutionary design of the application, in that sense that the initial version is progressively improved to fulfill the needs of users, needs which become more precise as the users interact with the application.

This design method is related to the learning process of users. The method was described in Section 5.5.4 for DSS with the shade that the availability now of KB-DSS development environments makes it less likely that the environment (generator) itself has to be modified during the design.

In this type of design methodology the application is **continuously evolving** from the minimum starting environment to the presently-used version. However, it happens that after an initial version was implemented, experience with users leads to a design that is very different and sometimes incompatible with the initial one. In that case, the designer throws away the initial version, which can be called a prototype and a new one is designed taking into account what was learned.

Problems raised by the design and implementation of the various knowledge bases of a KB-DSS have been dealt with in Chapter 8 (we refer here, mainly, to the domain-specific knowledge base, and not to the methodological knowledge base.)

9.3 Implementing the KB-DSS

The preceding section on building KB-DSS dealt with the design problem independently from real-life constraints. Implementation can be defined as the process of converting an initial conception of a system into a tool that is used effectively.

We shall, in this section, recall the main problems which are found in implementing KB-DSS. As we shall see, the problem of implementing KB-DSS is very intricately related to the introduction of change in organizations, in particular, the introduction of changes related to technological inovation. We shall then recall some theories about how to introduce change and how we can use some of these ideas in introducing KB-DSS.

Section 9.3.3 will deal with the recommendations that have been found useful in order to create the necessary conditions for successful implementation.

9.3.1 Standard problems in implementing KB-DSS

Following Alter (1980) we have classified the problems of implementation into four categories.

Technical problems

The technical problems can be, themselves, broken down into hardware problems, software problems and technical design problems. Also, as pointed out by Alter, we should distinguish a technical *constraint* from a technical *problem*.

If we develop a small financial model associated with a simple knowledge base, for one person, the technology may not be a binding constraint, since we can be sure to find a KB-DSS development environment to develop and run such a small application on a PC. If we face the problem of supporting hundreds of users using the same simple model and simple knowledge base, and that the system must be accessible from the terminals related to, for instance, an IBM mainframe run under the real-time monitor CICS, we may have a severe technical constraint. The technical constraint may be that running a transaction-oriented application under CICS and running a simulation and expert system-oriented application under CICS do not at all imply the same consequences, in terms of CPU speed and transfer rate between the CPU and the terminal. We may find ourselves in a situation where, if this technical constraint is maintained, we shall not find any feasible KB-DSS development environments and will have to do the development in COBOL, and accept a drastic downgrading in terms of the quality of the interface and response time.

Clearly, the situation can turn out to be worse if the application is expected to include more complex simulation models and larger knowledge bases, in which case, the response time can be so bad that the system cannot be used.

Classical hardware problems are characterised by insufficient response time, limited core memory, limited disk space available and physical compatibility between components of the configuration.

One of the classical problems is to decide on the appropriate hardware configuration on which to run a KB-DSS application.

A PC, which was a very good choice for running a financial analysis KB-DSS may be a hardware-limited machine for running the KB-DSS with database components as soon as the user wishes to make an industry analysis involving the manipulation of hundreds of companies data, since the database component requires a machine with capacities that are beyond a typical PC under MS-DOS.

The same database component may require much more disk space than the KB-DSS without the database component in order to store the same amount of data. The ability to deal easily with more complex data structures has to be paid by more complex software using more disk space and more CPU resources.

Software problems

Most KB-DSS software development environments are available under several operating systems. However, they are not available under all operating systems.

Data problems

Most data problems seem to be of two types: problems due to the nature of the data itself, and problems associated with the data feeder.

Problems due to the nature of the data
A non-exhaustive list is the following:

- data is not correct,
- data is not timely,
- data is not measured or structured properly,
- too much data is needed,
- data does not exist.

In the case of non-correct data, the solution can be found, from time to time, in standard techniques of data checking. One classical method is to use redundancy and relations between pieces of data in order to check their validity.

If the data is derived from other sources, a monitoring procedure should be worked out to check the data values. But we should always remember that people are very reluctant to compute data which are the result of a complicated process and, also, are not very good at it.

In the case of non-timely data, it seems that the only way to solve the problem is to modify and simplify the system for generating the data. A system can fail just because it is not updated with timely data. A portfolio management system which is not updated with an acceptable frequency for the portfolio manager will undoubtly fail.

The inadequacy between the structure of the data obtained from data processing applications and KB-DSS applications is a classical problem. This shows the importance of the data reader function of the DSS that we have described in Chapter 5.

A KB-DSS for financial planning in a bank may request, every month, a given list of data from the accounting file of the bank and the values of the balance of the accounts. The accounting system may be able to produce, easily, the balance of the accounts, but not an unchanged list of accounts, since this list is modified nearly every month. As a consequence, an intermediate procedure is required which will aggregate the changing list into a fixed list.

A classical problem related with data structure is due to the incompatibility of the measurement assumptions and periodicities between outside data (such as industry market data) and the data used in the proprietary databases of the KB-DSS.

Some such problems can be solved by using very flexible and simple to use data management components of KB-DSS that develop a procedure to rescale or recombine the improperly indexed data. Some problems cannot be solved, except by regenerating the coherent data at a cost which may be considered prohibitive.

In the case where too much data is being needed then this can be due to a bad model design. The designer has forgotten that variables should be included in the model as long as they are useful in making appropriate decisions (see Chapter 3 for the decision analysis cycle). Then, the solution is to design simpler or more aggregated decision models. If the model design was done properly, then the solution is to develop efficient ways of extracting and combining data, usually from large-scale data processing systems.

If the required data does not exist then this may be due to the fact that the data was never stored in a machine-readable form, or in a data management system.

Before starting the implementation effort the designer should check that the cost of storing and maintaining data will not be too high.

In a more serious situation, the data never existed. In this case, the cost of generating or estimating the data can be studied but it is better to check this once the models are defined, before implementation!

Problems associated with the feeder role
This problem is associated with the fact that, many times, the necessity to generate data was considered a threat by people in a feeder role. The problem to solve here is how to motivate people in supplying data for a model, the interest of which they do not see, or which they see as a tool for overseeing the quality of their work.

Conceptual problems

These problems are related, on one side, to assumptions concerning people and, on the other side, to software and modeling.

Assumptions about people
Usually, designers are over optimistic with regard to users' willingness and/or the ability to figure out how to use systems. One of the consequences of this observation is that it is not sufficient to give the users a good user manual or to design a friendly interface, it is necessary to train users in solving real problems with the system.

One of the interesting new possibilities of the expert component of KB-DSS is that it should allow us to design systems which guide the user from the methodological point of view, however, this is still at the research stage in most cases.

Conceptual design problems related to modeling
The common errors here are to attack the wrong problem, or to try to use an existing model which does not fit the case.

Little (1970) has made a well-known analysis of such difficulties. Stabell (1979) reports on a portfolio management DSS which was designed to support a portfolio-oriented process that determined purchases and sales taking, as a starting point of each, the requirements of an individual's portfolio.

In fact, the real process started with attractive purchases or sales of securities and then searched for a match with portfolios.

The under-utilization of the system was due to the fact that it was not oriented toward the decision process that actually existed, or else that the gap between the existing process was too wide.

The idea here is that you have to be very careful in your design not to implement changes in the decision process that go beyond what will be accepted by users.

Another design error is to attack the 'easy problem'. In particular, many financial planning systems do not contain formal methods for modeling the world outside the firm. For example, one could expect that price, quality of product and advertising would be controllable variables which explain partially, at least, the sales with competitors' actions. The problem is that the modeling of this market mechanism is a difficult problem. Little (1970) gives examples of such models for consumer goods.

People problems

Alter classifies, under this title, what he calls syndromes and manifestation. Syndromes being the things people complain about and the emotions that they feel.

In this category are syndromes such as 'the analysts are scared that the computer would replace them' or 'there is a new person in charge of the system and he is not interested in the system'.

The problem here is to discover if the difficulty is coming from the people, or from real technical problems, as the observer (a consultant or a member of the organization) is always biased by his or her own viewpoint and by knowledge concerning people and technology.

The manifestation of people problems can be revealed by disuse or misuse of the system. As we have seen above, they do not use the KB-DSS because they do not see how to use the system to solve their everyday problems, or they are not willing to make an effort to try to use it.

Fundamental limitations

Another classical problem is found with users which expect too much from KB-DSS. We have seen this problem becoming more accute with the introduction of the AI technology. Some people believe that, with the AI technology, no limitations will remain to the possibilities of DSS.

9.3.2 Introducing change in organizations

It has long been recognized that the process of introducing change is a key determinant of the ultimate success or acceptance of that change. An important literature is devoted to the implementation of computer-based systems and/or management science techniques. Kolb and Frohman (1970), Hammond (1974), Zand and Sorensen (1975) and Ginzberg (1975) are examples.

Since the implementation of a KB-DSS always constitutes some kind of change in a work environment, it is worthwhile studying what sociologists write about the implementation of such systems.

We have described a normative process by which KB-DSS systems projects should take place. This normative description is useful in appreciating the impact on project success of two key variables: the degree to which the user initiated the project, and the degree to which the user participated in the development effort.

The Lewin–Schein theory

According to this theory change consists of three steps:

(1)   *Unfreezing*: creating an awareness of the need for change and a climate of receptivity to change.

(2)   *Moving*: developing new methods and/or learning new attitudes and behaviors.

(3)   *Refreezing*: reinforcing the changes that have occurred, thereby maintaining and stabilizing a new equilibrium situation.

Zand and Sorensen (1975) applied this change theory and list some key issues at each step, these are presented in Figure 9.6.

The Kolb–Frohman model

Kolb and Frohman (1970) propose a seven-step process between the user and the designer of a system (see Figure 9.7).

Typology of situations found in implementing KB-DSS

It is common experience that:

(1)   the degree to which the user *initiated* the system development effort, and;

(2)   the degree to which the user *participated* in the system development effort are key variables explaining successful implementation.

This was considered to be so important that much of the work on DSS and KB-DSS development environments was made with the assumption that, in many cases, the only way to achieve a successful implementation was to have the user work in an environment where he or she could define and implement his or her system. The Lewin–Schein theory and Kolb–Frohman models also imply that these variables are associated with successful implementation.

Alter (1980) has formalized the classical implementation patterns. The initial push to develop a DSS is, according to Alter, of three types: user stimulus, managerial stimulus and entrepreneurial stimulus.

Systems initiated through user stimulus are those in which user perceived the need and pushed for the initial implementation effort. Systems initiated through managerial stimulus are those in which the user's organizational superiors perceived a need for a DSS for the user. Initiation through entrepreneurial stimulus means that a person inside or outside the organization made an effort to sell to people, in the organization, the idea that a DSS or a KB-DSS development environment should be implemented.

Managerial and entrepreneurial stimulus are often intertwined since, in many cases, the DSS or KB-DSS concept is sold to a manager, who will then 'convince' a subordinate as to its merits. This is why, in Alter's presentation,

	Favorable	Unfavorable
Unfreezing	1. Top and unit managers felt the problem was important to company. 2. Top managers became involved. 3. Unit managers recognized a need for change. 4. Top managers initiated the study. 5. Top and unit managers were open, candid. 6. Unit managers revised some of their assumptions.	1. Unit managers could not state their problems clearly 2. Top managers felt the problem was too big. 3. Unit managers did not recognize need for change. 4. Unit managers felt threatened by the project. 5. Unit managers resented the study. 6. Unit managers lacked confidence in the management scientists. 7. Unit managers felt they could do the study alone.
Moving	1. Unit managers and management scientists gathered data jointly. 2. Relevant data were accessible, available. 3. New alternatives were devised. 4. Unit managers reviewed and evaluated alternatives. 5. Top managers were advised of options 6. Top managers helped develop a solution. 7. Proposals were improved sequentially.	1. Management scientists could not educate the unit managers. 2. Needed data were not made available. 3. Unit managers did not help develop a solution. 4. Unit managers did not understand the solution of the management scientists. 5. Management scientists felt the study was concluded too quickly.
Refreezing	1. Unit managers tried the solution. 2. Utilization showed the superiority of the new solution. 3. Management scientists initiated positive feedback after early use. 4. Solution was widely accepted after initial success. 5. Unit managers were satisfied. 6. Solution was used in other areas. 7. The change improved the performance of the unit.	1. Management scientists did not try to support new managerial behaviour after the solution was used. 2. Management scientists did not try to re-establish stability after the solution was used. 3. Results were difficult to measure. 4. Standards for evaluating results were lacking. 5. Top managers ignored the solution recommended by the management scientists. 6. Solution was incompatible with the needs and resources of the unit. 7. Top managers did not encourage other units to use the solution.

Figure 9.6   Key issues in the Lewin–Schein theory of organizational change. (Reprinted from Theory of change and the effective use of management by Dale E., Zand and Richard E. Sorensen published in *Administrative Science Quarterly* Vol. 20 No. 4 by permission of Administrative Science Quarterly.)

1. *Scouting*: User and designer assess each other's needs and abilities to see if there is a match. An appropriate organizational starting point for the project is selected.

2. *Entry*: User and designer develop an initial statement of project goals and objectives. Commitment to the project is developed. User and designer develop a trusting relationship and a 'contract' for conducting the project.

3. *Diagnosis*: User and designer gather data to refine and sharpen the definition of the problem and goals for the solution. User and designer assess available resources (including commitment) to determine whether continued effort is feasible.

4. *Planning*: User and designer define specific operational objectives and examine alternative ways to meet these objectives. Impacts of proposed solutions on all parts of the organization are examined. User and designer develop an action plan that takes account of solution impacts on the organization.

5. *Action*: User and designer put the 'best' alternative into practice. Training necessary for effective use of the system is undertaken in all affected parts of the organization.

6. *Evaluation*: User and designer assess how well the goals and objectives (specified during the Diagnosis and Planning stages) were met. User and designer decide whether to work further on the system (evolve) or to cease active work (terminate).

7. *Termination*: User and designer ensure that 'ownership' of and effective control over the new system rest in the hands of those who must use and maintain it. User and designer ensure that necessary new patterns of behaviour have become a stable part of the user's routine.

Figure 9.7 A normative model of the consulting process in system development activities. (Reprinted from an organization development approach to consulting by Kolb D.A. and Frohman A.L., *Sloan Management Review*, 12(4), 1970, pp. 51–65, by permission of the publisher. Copyright © 1970 by the Sloan Management Review Association. All rights reserved.)

managerial and entrepreneurial stimulus are lumped into one category. From this analysis, Alter defines six implementation situations:

Situation 1 is the ideal situation, the client/user is ready to buy and get involved in a cooperative problem definition and problem solving effort, in addition to buying a product such as a KB-DSS development environment.

Situation 2, the client/user is buying a product (solution) rather than a service. The main issue is to complete the system to specifications within time and budget constraints.

Situation 3, the user was not involved in initiation, but it is possible to convince the client/user that the system is needed and to obtain his or her involvement in its development.

Situation 4, a consultant or salesman attempts to sell the DSS or KB-DSS idea to the user. This is a very common situation, and a situation that any consultant interested in implementing DSS or KB-DSS should master.

This situation is, clearly, a more difficult one to start with, however, many successful innovations have been introduced into organization in this way, since most new ideas often originate outside the settings in which they are applied.

Situation 5 is also a very common situation. The user is obliged to use the system because management wants it. We shall discuss such an implementation pattern in Section 9.5.

Situation 6. In this situation, an OR department or the R&D unit of the computer department develops a prototype to anticipate user needs. This situation is slightly similar to the situation where an outside software or consulting company is attempting to sell the idea of a new system to support a task.

In fact, the situation we are facing is slightly more complex than the one described by Alter. This is due to the fact that between turnkey systems and systems which are fully implemented by users is a wide range of situations where there is a partial implementation by users.

In a KB-DSS, it is easy to involve the user in model, display or knowledge base modification or in implementing new models, we shall see such a situation in Section 9.5.

Decision process required in order to start a KB-DSS project

Experience has shown that, usually, three groups of people are involved in the decision to implement a KB-DSS in an organization. These people are: users, management and computer department representatives.

By users, we mean the people who will use the system, or else someone who is the head of the user department. By computer department representatives, we mean the people whose task it is to keep as coherent as possible the software and hardware equipment of the organization. By management, we mean the group of people that has the responsibility for deciding on a resource allocation which may go beyond the user's authorization.

Clearly, in many organizations, the computer department is not involved in the KB-DSS project if the project has no link (such as data transfer) with the other computer applications under its responsibility.

However, in the most general case, the computer department is involved, in particular, when the head of the computer department has understood that the KB-DSS will play an important role in the organization. Then, it is his or her task to advise users on available development environments and to provide consultants to help users implement their applications.

As shown in Figure 9.8, the user will have to move through a series of stages, starting from ignorance of the concept through to project participation.

Management will have to move from ignorance of the concept of the decision through to allocating resources to a KB-DSS project and monitoring it.

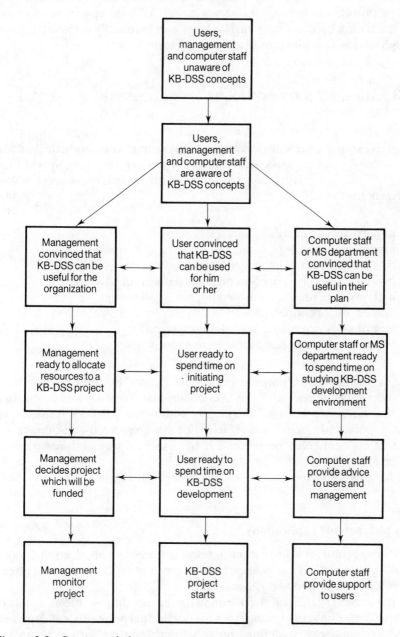

Figure 9.8 Steps made by users, management and the computer department when implementing a KB-DSS project.

The computer department will also have to start from ignorance of the concept through to the task of surveying KB-DSS development environments, advising users on such environment and eventually supporting users through advice, consulting or direct participation.

9.3.3 Creating the conditions for success (key success factors)

As we have seen above, many reasons may make implementation difficult or impossible. As can be expected, ideal situations are very rare in real life. Alter (1977) defines eight main reasons that can reduce the success of the implementation process:

(1)   non-existent or unwilling users;
(2)   multiple users or implementors;
(3)   disappearing users, implementors, or maintainers;
(4)   inability to specify purposes or usage patterns in advance;
(5)   inability to predict and cushion impact on all parties;
(6)   lack or loss of support;
(7)   lack of prior experience with similar systems;
(8)   technical problems and cost-effectiveness issues.

These factors are called 'implementation risk factors' by Alter.

Alter was working with the DSS conceptual framework in mind, but the situation is not changed drastically within the KB-DSS framework, however, some risk factors are greater. For example, a KB-DSS, due to its expert component, may be perceived, by a user, a greater threat than a classical DSS.

We give below some advice to help decrease these risks.

Select high pay-off applications

Whenever possible, it is important to select a domain of application for the KB-DSS where pay-off can be measured (in terms of efficiency and/or effectiveness), demonstrated and is significant.

It will be very difficult to obtain management support for an application, which may be very exciting from the intellectual point of view, but does not lead to some clearly-defined potential improvement for the organization. Criteria for evaluation are described in Section 10.2.

In some domains (such as financial analysis), software or other specialized companies have developed and marketed prototypes or products. It is possible to acquire (or develop) these prototypes which can be used to experiment and define the pay-off and the conditions of success.

Select a competent designer

No good system can be developed without good people to design it. The person in charge of the development should have experience of KB-DSS design. If this is not the case, an experienced consultant can be a major reason for success. The education of the designer with respect to the development environment is also essential.

If the designer is not used to the development tool selected, he or she should follow an educational seminar on the tool and, if possible, start the design with a consultant who is used to the tool.

Select a good user or expert

It is not possible to design a good KB-DSS if the design team is not led. At the very least, it must contain a competent user. If there is no expertise there will be no expert system or KB-DSS.

Obtain user motivation and commitment

It is essential to have not only competent but also motivated users.

The user must be willing to involve him or herself in what can be serious, important and tiring work. The user can see the project as an opportunity to improve his or her knowledge and professional competence. This kind of motivation is particularly suitable because it is very likely to happen and the user will usually be very satisfied. The increase in professional competence usually means promotion and a higher market value of the person. The task may be new and challenging and lead to publication of articles in professional magazines which is another way of improving user image.

The user should commit him or herself to work on the project until it is achieved and, eventually, take part into the maintenance of models and knowledge bases.

One of the classical difficulties is that, if many potential users exist, they cannot all be involved in the design. One solution is to involve them in the evaluation of the system. This will give them the opportunity to improve the system.

Do not start with the most complex application

The reason for this is that a very important learning process occurs during the definition and design of a KB-DSS. As a consequence, it is better to start with a simple application in order to improve the expertise of the organization in mastering this technology.

Once a simple application has been successfully implemented, much has been learned and it will be easier to deal with a more complex one.

Obtain management support

Management support is needed to obtain the funds for the project and the collaboration of users. In particular, it is essential that management decides to enable some of their best experts to spend time on defining the KB-DSS. As we know that most experts are very busy this is one of the most difficult decisions, since management will have to accept that, in the short run, the kind of competence they need the most will be less available, since time will have to be devoted to the definition and design of the application.

It is not sufficient to have management support for the decision to design and implement a KB-DSS, management will be needed to institutionalize the system.

If the management's attitude ranges from indifference to tolerance once the system is implemented, this may lead to low usage except by the users who were involved in the design.

It may be necessary for management, once it has checked that the system is performing well and satisfies some of the best experts, to make its use mandatory.

However, it is always better to organize regular evaluations of the system so that either constructive criticisms are made by non-users or that their 'mauvaise foi' becomes obvious and management can decide on appropriate measures.

Select the appropriate development environment

This decision is also a key one, given the consequences of a bad choice: production of a lower quality product, longer time and cost of development, higher maintenance cost, and lower motivation and service to users.

It is already a great success if the concept of KB-DSS is understood. At the time of writing of this book, most large organizations have only understood the expert system concept or the spreadsheet concept and some of the DSS concepts. A better understanding of the KB-DSS concept can only be achieved through education and demonstration.

Meet user needs and institutionalize the system

Once a good system has been implemented the success is still not certain, if we measure success by the fact that most users will use it and consider that it helps them in making better decisions.

To achieve this goal, good training programs and assistance need to be provided, as well as opportunities for users to participate in the evolution of the system and marketing of the system.

Training programs

The training program is needed for users other than those who took part in the design. Again, the training will be successful only if done by users involved in the design and the competence of whom is not discussed by other potential users.

The training cannot be geared only to provide familiarity with the concepts of the system, it must include cases where the users solve typical problems with the help of the system.

A well-designed training program can turn sceptic users into enthusiastic users if the training program gives them the opportunity to: work on their own problems, check that the system is easy to use, that it will be accessible in their offices, and that it will give them the opportunity to improve their professional competence.

The system, however easy to use, can be a failure if it uses concepts which are too sophisticated for the users. A training program will never solve the problem of a bad design, but a well-designed system can fail due to a bad training program.

Provide on-going assistance

Once a system has been handed over to users it is necessary to support the users. All problems cannot be dealt with during the training sessions. The users must have somebody they can call or interact with in case they need help in using the system to solve their problems. This becomes more important as the system is made compulsory. The on-going assistance should also be provided by updating user manuals, and by notes explaining the evolution of model, reports and knowledge bases.

Provide opportunities to involve users in the evolution of the system

In a KB-DSS application, the system will evolve with respect to the models, the reports, the knowledge base and the interface.

It is very important to have regular meetings with users to give them the opportunity to suggest improvements to the system.

Clearly, this will not solve the problem if the system is too far from users' needs, but it is by making sure that users see that their remarks and criticisms are taken into account that the institutionalization of the system will succeed. In the case of FINSIM, several user groups have been created. These user groups are either internal to a bank or are inter-bank.

A user group that is internal to a bank will discuss the problem of the knowledge base which was developed by the bank and, also, its evolution.

The inter-bank user group will discuss more general questions about the KB-DSS application such as: collaboration on producing industry ratios, the definition of financial concepts used in the DSS part of FINSIM and the evolution of reports.

Tailor the system to people's capabilities

One of the ideas that is found in the literature on DSS is that there are great differences among people with regard to their ability and/or propensity to use analytic techniques. When the number of users is significant it is a major problem to diagnose if the system is not used by some of them due to important differences between the decision methodology used by the designers and most users.

It is also clear that when designing the system, the experts tend to refine and improve their decision methodology. This improvement in the decision methodology may widen the gap between the experts and the more standard users.

Sell the system

It is very important to sell it to users which were not involved in the implementation. We mean here by selling the actions which have, as their purpose, to:

- identify potential new users for the system;
- understand their interests;
- influence their choice by providing them with information;
- work with them to adapt the system to fit their needs.

9.4 Example: the design of FINSIM EXPERT

In this section we shall describe the steps in the design of the KB-DSS, FINSIM, which we have presented in Chapter 7.

In Chapter 7 we have presented the system implemented in OPTRANS EXPERT, as it was at the beginning of 1988.

We shall follow the steps we have outlined above for the design process.

9.4.1 Defining users and understanding user goals

In the case of FINSIM, potential users can be of several categories, and, as a consequence, the user goals can be multiple, we have already pointed out in Chapter 7 that example of types of users are:

- Credit analyst (in a bank) studying a company in order to decide whether to grant a loan or not.

- Investment analyst (in a bank, a broker) studying a company in order to decide whether to buy shares or not.

- Corporate financial manager (in a company) studying how to finance the growth of his or her company.

- A financial adviser (accountant, consultant) interested in an overall financial diagnosis.

- A marketing person (in a bank) studying a company, to find out what kind of financial services should be proposed.

The shared objective here is that all these people need to make a financial analysis in order to support their decision. However, a key point is that all these types of financial analyses will use as a starting point, in France at least, a common source of financial information: the fiscal forms that are used, every year, to make a fiscal declaration to the state authorities.

Clearly, the decision process that they will follow is not the same and will, eventually, give rise to different models to compute different criteria and to different presentations of the information, but there will be a common set of variables that they will use. They will need this information over a certain period of time. Maybe, several periods in the past and several periods in the future.

Some decisions may need information that is not included in the common set. For example, variables to make an economic analysis of the company, its products and its market (position of the company in its industry) and, even, information on the quality of the management.

It is also important to find out if the user will be interested enough to make industry analyses: that is, company comparisons in the same industry or across the industry.

It may be that one of the user's goals is to compute or to use industry data to improve analysis. In the case of FINSIM, it was decided that financial industry data (mean ratios provided by outside organizations) had to be usable or should be computable using the system.

On the other hand, it was decided that in the first version, at least, financial analysis problems requesting data of a higher frequency than the year should not be considered. Very clearly, such a decision rules out certain kind of financial analysis problems for investment purposes.

To conclude on this point, we shall say that for the first version of FINSIM, the decision was to develop a system for a credit analyst who was making medium and long-term loan to companies, with the will to progressively extend the capabilities of the system to support other kind of users.

9.4.2 Understanding requirements and defining problem boundaries

The problem boundaries, in the case of FINSIM, are functions or variables such as:

- Is the analyst having full responsibility for the decision or must he or she interact with a credit manager which will give final approval for his or her recommendation?

- Should the system support five or six analysts in a small regional bank or should the system support the work of hundreds of credit analysts scattered in the two hundred main branches of a large national bank?

- Should the system be able to access a common financial database (inside or outside the bank)?

- Is the system going to be used only for credit analysis or, also, for teaching new analysts?

- Do we have to run it on a given computer or use a given workstation?

The requirement that the decision is of a sequential type, with final approval, may lead, for instance, the designer to provide a communication function between the credit analyst's workstation and the credit manager's workstation.

The need to provide the service to a large number of analysts may imply the support of a larger set of decision procedures and, as a consequence, different knowledge bases.

The will of the management of the bank to constitute a common financial database and not just to provide computational power and expert capabilities to the analysts implies the capacity of the system to provide a multi-user database component.

In the case of FINSIM, a requirement was that each branch dealing with company credit analysis is equipped with a KB-DSS to support its credit analysts but that it is eventually possible to download or upload the financial data of a company from a version of the system located on a multi-users time-sharing computer. If this is the case then the connection between the multi-user and PC version of the system will be crucial.

9.4.3 Understanding the decision process (descriptive phase)

We have pointed out that we concentrate, in the first version of FINSIM, on medium and long-term loan decisions. The study of the decision process of several analysts has shown that the main criteria used for decision making are the following:

- capacity of the company to repay the loan;
- measure of risk for the above variable;
- return of the loan for the bank;
- non-financial considerations (potential of the company to become an important client later, necessity to help avoiding unemployment, quality of relations existing between the company and the bank and so on).

The information used during the decision process is of several types:

- financial, on the company and on its industry;
- economic, on the company and on its industry;
- economic, on the products and markets of the company;
- managerial, on the company.

The financial and economic information on the company is usually historical but is also made up of hypotheses concerning the future. Information is provided by the company or derived from other sources by the credit analyst.

In the case of a company loan analysis it is clear that the variables (accounts) contained in the financial statements (balance sheets, income statements and so on) are very important and used by all analysts.

An examination of the way that the analysts perform their task shows that there will be three phases to support:

(1)   the preliminary phase,
(2)   the historical analysis,
(3)   the forecasting analysis.

Each phase can be ended by deciding to grant the loan, proceeding to the next phase or refusing the loan. Each phase is also characterized by the fact that the analyst gathers some information specific to the company, selects some criteria and concludes.

Criteria used in the first phase are used to filter data rapidly if there is a reason to eliminate the company, or to refuse the loan. For instance, if we find out that this company is already a client and that it has a record of bad payments then the conclusion may be to stop there.

If the preliminary study concludes that we can not accept the loan right away nor reject it but that the question deserves further investigation then we move to the next phase: the historical study.

The analyst may be will gather more or, different, information. For instance, he or she will collect historical balance sheets and income statements, and product and market information on the company.

Then he or she will select criteria to evaluate the company using historical information. Such criteria can be the liquidity level of the company, the debt structure, the activity level, and the return. Differences in criteria used may be observed according to the analyst.

The knowledge used in a financial analysis by one expert is shown in Figure 9.9. The figure shows the knowledge types which are being used by the analyst, and the criteria which are computed during the study. The

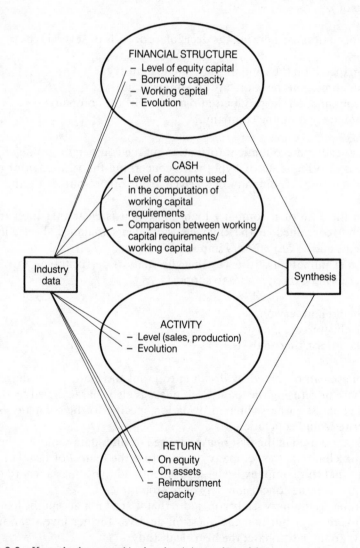

Figure 9.9   Knowledge used in the decision rules of the expert.

reader will notice that industry data are being used in the computation of each criteria. Clearly, each criterion such as return and cash will give birth to a rule subset in the knowledge base.

The next step of the historical study is a multi-criteria evaluation. During this step, the analyst may compare the criteria with normative parameters, some of them taking into account the industry in which the company is operating.

A 'score' is an example of a formal multi-criteria evaluation function. Most of the time the evaluation function is not formalized but the analyst may use statistical data or ratios used as criteria.

The outcome of the historical phase can, once again, be to grant the loan, to refuse the loan, to propose to revise the loan characteristics or to proceed to the next step because the analyst reaches the conclusion that he or she cannot decide using only historical information.

We give, in Figure 9.10, an example of the formalization of the rules used by an analyst to conclude on the financial structure criteria during his or her decision process.

The forecast phase (which may not be used by all analysts) starts with the selection, by the analyst, of what he or she thinks are the relevant criteria. Very often, these criteria are the same as the one used in the historical study. The analyst then:

- generates an hypothesis: for example, an activity-level hypothesis;
- collects information to compute criteria;
- evaluates the alternatives;
- takes the decision to grant the loan, not to grant the loan, generate a new hypothesis (change in activity level or change in loan characteristics) and then loop.

The descriptive analysis of the decision process has shown (using the Mintzberg framework):

- that the decision is reached after a three-phase process;
- that all analysts do not use the third phase (forecast phase);
- which data are used in the analysis (financial data on the company, and economic and industry data when available);
- which are the criteria computed using these data (debt equity ratio, return on assets and cash flow);
- which reasoning is followed in order to come to a conclusion.

As a conclusion, we can say that we have a precise model of the descriptive decision process even if it is clear that there are important differences among

	Insufficient		Correct		Good
Level of Equity Capital (EC)	Insufficient	—	Correct	—	Good
(Equity/Total assets)	< 20%	—	From 20% to 40%	—	>40%
Borrowing Capacity (BC)	Bad	Weak	Mean	Rather good	Good
(LMT resources/Equity)	> 200%	From 100% to 200%	From 80% to 100%	From 50% to 80%	< 50%
Working Capital (WC)	Negative	Zero	—	Weak	Positive
(WK/Sales)	(WC<0)	WC<0 and WK/sales $\geq$ −10	—	WC > 0 and WK/sales < 10	WC > 0 and WK/sales $\geq$ 10
Financial structure	Not balanced (EC $\leq$ insufficient + BC $\leq$ mean level + WC $\leq$ 0) (EC $\leq$ correct + BC > mean + WC $\leq$ 0) (EC > correct + BC $\leq$ mean + WC $\leq$ 0)	—	Correct (EC $\leq$ insufficient + BC $\leq$ mean + WC > 0) (EC $\leq$ correct + BC $\leq$ mean + WC > 0) (EC > correct + BC < mean + WC > 0) (EC > correct + BC > mean + WC $\leq$ 0)	—	Good (EC > correct + BC > mean + WC > 0)

Figure 9.10   Decision rules used by the analyst to conclude on the financial structure criteria.

analysts concerning the way they compute certain variables or reason with them in order to come to a conclusion.

It is also clear that, in the historical analysis, there will be computation of criteria using historical information, and that, in the forecasting analysis, there will be the need for a financial model to generate alternatives and the values of criteria associated with them.

The conclusion of this analysis may be that the decision is made using a certain number of criteria which are financial aggregates such as:

- debt/equity ratio,
- working capital,
- return,
- level of activity.

Once the actual decision process of the analyst is known it is important to study the decision from a normative point of view, to see how it could be improved.

9.4.4 The normative point of view

The designer is confronted with the normative point of view on several issues when he or she considers how to improve the decision process that he or she has observed being used by different analysts. These issues are the following:

- need to eliminate computational errors;
- need to improve the methods of computation of certain concepts (for example, for cash flow);
- need to add new concepts;
- need to improve coherence and consistency in the reasoning (for example contradiction in the ways to deal with two similar situations);
- need to take into account information on the future of the company (important information has to be taken into account even if it is not certain);
- need to eliminate risk of fraud.

We speak here about improvement in the effectiveness of the system, that is, the quality of the decision and not improvement in efficiency which is related with productivity, which we shall deal with in Section 9.4.10.

With respect to the elimination of computational errors this is the most obvious and straight forward consequence of providing a KB-DSS. This is not only the consequence of human errors in computation, but also of errors in data which are avoided by the routine checking of the accounting relations.

Several examples of the need to improve the methods of computation themselves can be given. Many analysts were using the concept of flow of funds to explain the variation of the cash position of the company from one period to the other. There is one good way of computing this variable given the list of accounts used. Many analysts were using an approximation in the computation of this variable. Some were disregarding the impact of accounts belonging to the short-term assets or short-term liability (working capital aspect).

Another example is the computation of long-term debt when moving from the fiscal to the functional presentation of the balance sheet. In the fiscal presentation of the forms used by the French fiscal authorities debts are broken down by types. The financial analyst needs to aggregate the debts by date of maturity. The aggregation process used by most financial analysts was an approximation and was wrong by an important factor in some cases.

One interesting concept in financial analysis is the economic and financial break-even point. This concept is a first attempt to measure the risk involved in case of decrease of activity level. This concept was not used by the analysts of a bank. After the concept was discussed with the designer most financial analysts were willing to use it. This is an example of the need to add a new concept.

The problem of coherence was diagnosed several times. Analysts were using several criteria to come to their conclusion concerning the possibility to make a loan of a given amount. These criteria were measured by ratios or financial aggregates used in the reasoning: the ratio of long-term debt/equity, the working capital and the ratio of equity/total of balance sheet.

In certain circumstances, the analysts were not applying the rules they had defined, by pure mistake and not because of other available information different in each case.

In other circumstances, the rules were different according to the analysts and, as a consequence, a loan which was refused in a branch would have been accepted in another!

However, the most fundamental normative aspect of FINSIM was introduced by making available to the analysts, a model able to use forecast variables such as sales level, cost of raw material and so on, to compute a forecasted aggregate income statement and balance sheet.

From those forecasted income statements and balance sheets it was possible to compute the same criteria used for the evaluation using historical data, and apply the same rules to them to decide on granting the loan or not.

In fact, the necessity of this forecast model was clearly established by the fact that, many times, it could be demonstrated that if the analyst was using the same rules that he or she was using with past data to decide on the loan (coherence principle), his or her decision would be changed when using the criteria computed by using the balance sheet and income statement that was derived from the information available on the evolution of sales (or other key variables) over a one or two year horizon.

Also, it is easy to demonstrate that the use of the flow of funds equations enable the analyst to check, directly, the capacity of the company to repay the loan, and to test the risk by sensitivity analysis.

This model can be easily extended as shown on Figure 3.14 to encode knowledge on environmental variables such as sales growth rate, raw material cost and to compute distribution of criteria. In other words, it is possible to follow the decision analysis cycle of Howard presented in Chapter 3.

With respect to the problem of decreasing the risk of fraud this can be done by using a system such as OPTRANS which allow the analysts to use the models or knowledge bases but not to modify them (control of access to the objects of the system).

9.4.5 Defining changes in the decision process

The changes which exist between the initial decision process used in a bank and the one supported by FINSIM are, clearly, varying each time a version of FINSIM is being defined for use for a given context in a bank.

In the case we have just outlined the differences between the observed decision process and the computer-supported decision process are the following:

- computational errors are eliminated or drastically decreased;
- the methods of computation of variables used in the decision are improved;
- new concepts are added to be used in the decision rules (such as economic and financial break-even points and the leverage effect);
- forecast information is used in the decision process;
- a forecast model is provided to generate alternatives;
- decision rules are made explicit;
- sensitivity analysis is supported;
- uncertainty in environmental variables is taken into account and computation of lotteries on criteria is made possible;
- the user is modeled with respect to his or her preferences.

As we have already suggested, it is not usually a good design principle to introduce, in one step, all the features of an ideal decision process as the designer sees. We shall now examine which part of the normative decision process was, in fact, implemented in FINSIM.

9.4.6 Selecting which part of the decision process to support initially

As for the preceding point, the part of the decision process to support initially will be an important decision for the designer. If the gap between the actual decision process and the new one is too wide then the system may fail because the analysts do not master the concepts and the reasoning which is used in the normative decision process.

If the gap is too narrow, they may not see the interest of using the system which does not, in their opinion, improve the situation sufficiently.

In the case of FINSIM great care is taken in only introducing concepts which have been accepted by the analysts.

However, new concepts are added but freedom is left to the analyst to decide to use them or not. The decision was taken to provide support for the forecasted financial analysis even if most analysts were not using it.

On the other hand, it was not decided to support, in a first step, uncertainty through the possibility of encoding knowledge on variables under the form of probability distribution. It was decided to make explicit decision rules and to provide the conclusion obtained through them to the analyst for examination, as a consultant would do.

9.4.7 Functional analysis of the initial KB-DSS

The functional analysis of FINSIM has been described in Section 7.4.3 to which the reader is referred.

9.4.8 Design an implementation of the initial KB-DSS

From the functional analysis and decision analysis presented above the following objects have to be defined:

- an historical model for the computation of historical criteria;
- a forecast model for the computation of forecasted criteria;
- as many reports as we have financial reports to display;
- as many knowledge bases as types of diagnosis needed.

At first, only one knowledge base was defined and implemented, this was called ANAFIN. However, it was decided to provide, in the starting environment, two small knowledge bases, one of them of approximately 90 rules which was a simplified version of ANAFIN that could be used by the experts of a bank as a structure to work on and improve.

The first professional knowledge base (KB) was defined by an expert of the bank for a detailed analysis of a company return and financing of

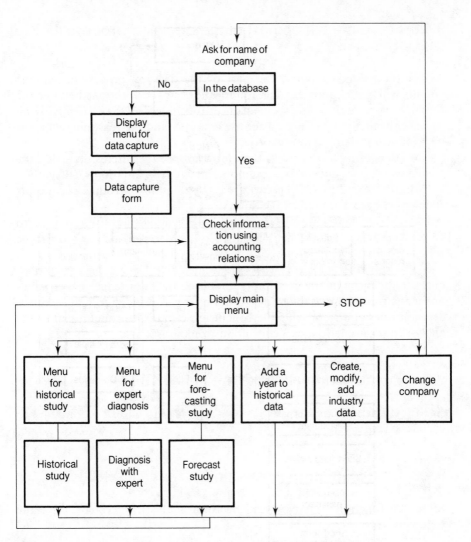

Figure 9.11   User-system interface design in FINSIM.

investment and working capital needs (see Section 7.4.4). A year later, a second knowledge base was defined to support the work of marketing people or analysts whose needs were more a synthetic diagnosis.

The user interface had to be defined in great detail. The definition of part of this interface is given in Figures 9.11 and 9.12.

Figure 9.11 shows the logic of the interaction between the user and the system, at the beginning of KB-DSS use. The user is asked on which company in the database he or she wishes to work. At this point, the system displays the question and, in a window, the list of companies available. The

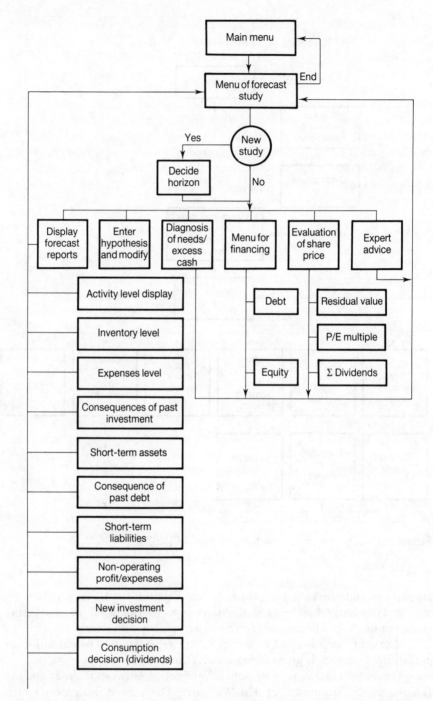

Figure 9.12   User-system interface design in the forecasting model of FINSIM.

user can browse through the list before deciding which name to type. The definition of these menus is given in Section 7.4.4.

Figure 9.12 shows the logic of interaction between the user and the forecast decision model. As we have seen in Section 7.4.4, the user has several options at his or her disposal. Not only with respect to choosing to make an hypothesis concerning the level of activity and letting the model provide estimates of expenses and working capital coherent with what has been observed historically (constant structure hypothesis), but, also, to obtain detailed assistance on the estimation of each account. This design decision was made to take into account the need of the analyst to minimize, in a first phase of his or her work, the amount of data needed to work out a first projection of financial needs or excess cash.

9.4.9 Testing and evaluation with a user-designer

No design of the initial KB-DSS can be considered complete until all of the models, reports and knowledge bases have been thoroughly tested.

In the case of FINSIM several errors were corrected during the testing phase and several changes were made to the interface.

In Chapter 10 we describe a framework for testing and evaluation, as well as knowledge base verification and validation procedures.

9.4.10 Design of documentation and training material

As we have pointed out, a first version of the user manual should be written at the beginning of the design phase. This manual evolves during the design phase and should be rewritten or revised after the testing period.

The FINSIM user manual is a 150 page document, of which 35 pages is devoted to the description of the knowledge base.

In particular, part of the manual should be devoted to the presentation of:

- the use of the system;
- the definition of the models and computation;
- the description of the reports;
- the description of the structure and logic reasoning of the knowledge base.

Several cases should be worked out to show how a decision on a loan is supported. Each case should demonstrate interesting features of the system and clarify the logic of the knowledge base.

These documents play a key role in the seminar during which the system is presented to future users and, later on, as reference manual.

For FINSIM the minimum time for an introductory seminar is two days, when used with two knowledge bases.

One day is spent presenting the historical part (DSS and expert aspects) and one day is spent presenting the forecasting part. During these two days time is used for hands-on exercises on the above mentioned cases.

9.4.11 Monitoring and evaluation

It is extremely important to plan for regular evaluation of the system.

In the case of FINSIM these evaluations are made through a questionnaire. The answers are analysed by the design group (made of the bank's experts in financial analysis and, also, the designers). Proposal for improvements are made at users meetings, where the proposed improvements are discussed and approved after eventual modification.

Updated versions of the user manual are also handed out at these users meetings.

9.5 Implementation of FINSIM EXPERT

At the time of writing this Chapter, FINSIM is being used in many European and, especially, French banks and many implementations have been achieved. Much has been learned about implementing it successfully, from a technical, as well as a person's point of view.

Most banks are running it on stand-alone PCs, others are running it on PC but only with data on the PC, the OPTRANS and FINSIM software being stored on a virtual extension of the PCs disk on the IBM mainframe. Some banks are running it on VAX and PCs which means some work to maintain two compatible versions since, for example, two different graphical subsystems have to be used on these machines and the number of lines on the PC screen and VAX terminals are not the same and so on. With respect to data, some problems were found when checking all of it through accounting relations. For example, to compute, properly, a very important historical variable (long-term debt) a piece of the data which was not in the balance sheet was used. Many errors were observed on using this piece of the data, since it was in the footnotes of the balance sheet, and users were even forgetting to enter it. The situation was relieved when two measures were taken:

(1)   Two more pieces of the data were requested, which had an accounting relation with the first piece. The relation could be checked and a warning message sent to the user.

(2)   An approximation of this data could be computed using other verifiable pieces of the data and substituted with it in case the

additional information was not available. The system keeps track of this approximation.

With respect to the educational and organizational point of view we shall just describe, very briefly, two cases which are interesting from the implementation point of view. The first deals with the implementation in a French regional bank, and the second with the implementation in a group of savings banks.

9.5.1 Implementation in a regional bank

The regional bank has approximately 60 branches. The bank has turned its computer department into a wholly-owned subsidiary. The bank management is proud of the performance of the bank which is considered as one of the most efficient within the national group of 90 banks to which it belongs.

A member of the computer department in charge of DSS applications is willing to provide the financial analysts of the bank an expert system for financial analysis. After a study of what is available on the market he or she decides to acquire a license for FINSIM and for OPTRANS EXPERT. He or she does not, however, acquire a professional knowledge base but only a demonstration copy of a knowledge base for financial analysis. The demonstration knowledge base is made up of 80 rules and is used by the company SIG to introduce users of FINSIM to the concept of a knowledge base. Two programmers of the computer department follow the educational seminar on OPTRANS (for three days). They are not financial analysts. They are expected to play the role of knowledge engineer. During the seminar on OPTRANS, half a day is spent on explaining the structure of FINSIM and the way to use it.

FINSIM is provided to the expert financial analysts of the bank. The designer of FINSIM asks the member of the computer services who is in charge of DSS applications to have the opportunity to present the application to the expert and discuss it with him or her and to explain the model and demonstration knowledge base to him or her.

This proposition, in spite of the insistence of the designer of FINSIM, is not accepted. The official reason is that the expert is very busy (which is true). Apparently, the computer department manager does not wish any direct contact to occur between the FINSIM designer and the expert.

Later on, the programmer tells the designer of FINSIM that the expert of the bank complains that the model does not compute several concepts that he or she would like to have and that the programmer has already made several changes to FINSIM to fit the expert's needs. The situation is felt to be very unsatisfactory by the programmer who has the feeling that the expert is not satisfied by several aspects of the system and is unable to justify these characteristics.

Finally the member of the computer department in charge of DSS applications agrees to a meeting between the expert and the FINSIM designer. During the meeting there is good agreement between the expert and the FINSIM designer: both of them recognize that their counterpart is a good professional, the FINSIM designer discovers (what he or she had forecasted and had been worried about) that, unfortunately, the rationale for the computations of FINSIM had not been explained to the expert by the programmer. In particular, with respect to the forecast phase. This is normal since the computer expert who had to present FINSIM had no knowledge about financial analysis and could only show how to use the commands, but could not explain the financial concepts.

An even more serious problem is discovered by the FINSIM designer: the demonstration knowledge base which was provided, just as an example, to understand the syntax and the way the reasoning mechanism works and as a starting point for development of a financial knowledge base had been taken, by the expert, as a professional and finished knowledge base.

After a few hours of discussion, a certain number of changes in the computation of financial concepts have been defined, as well as an improvement in the procedure to check the validity of the data. Also, the decision is made to implement a specific financial knowledge base for the bank. The development of this knowledge base will require the joint efforts of the expert of the bank, the computer specialist who will formalize the rules and models, and of the FINSIM designer who will play the role of a consultant. The work on the knowledge base will be spread over a six-month period and will require four man months of effort to achieve the first operational version.

After a period of test of four months at headquarters, a decision is taken to decentralize the system in five branches. A training seminar is organized to teach the financial analysts how to use the system. The seminar is half a day long. The FINSIM designer is not invited to take part in the training seminar. The use of FINSIM is not made compulsory by the bank management. The expert who took part in the definition of the knowledge base has, meanwhile, become the head of the credit department, whereas the manager in charge of DSS applications who had pushed the project in the computer department has left the bank.

After a six-month period during which there was no meeting with financial analysts of the branches to evaluate the use of FINSIM, it seems that only two or three branches out of five are using the system. The head of the computer department does not consider this result to be good enough and, since he or she needs the time of the programmer who has been working on FINSIM, he or she puts the programmer on another project.

After two discussions with the FINSIM designer the expert of the bank become conscious of the fact that not enough time has been spent on institutionalizing the system. A meeting is planned in order to discuss and evaluate the use of the system. The FINSIM designer learns that most financial analysts are rather young.

Several conclusions can be drawn from this example:

(1)   When acquiring a KB-DSS application it is very important that the designer (or at least a competent person with excellent knowledge of the application) has the opportunity to present it to the expert of the organization that is acquiring this application.

In this case, once the decision to acquire FINSIM had been made the consultant should have had the opportunity to explain, in detail, the application to the bank's expert. The cost of the consultant would have been nothing compared to the cost of the increased time needed to learn how to master the model and knowledge base.

(2)   If you want a programmer to become a knowledge engineer in a domain of application (finance) you must ask him or her to learn something about the domain, so that he or she can interact more efficiently with experts within domain. Experts have, usually, not much time to teach their domain to knowledge engineers. The knowledge engineer must have adequate knowledge of the application domain.

(3)   Once a knowledge base has been defined and implemented, you cannot expect that half a day is sufficient for an analyst who did not take part in the design to understand and evaluate, properly, a KB-DSS.

(4)   It is not sufficient to deliver a well-designed KB-DSS, even one defined by the best expert, and expect that it will be used by everybody. You must involve future users and institutionalize the system, which needs a lot of work, in particular, training seminars.

9.5.2 Implementation in a group of savings banks

The French savings bank system (Caisses d'Epargne) is made up of several hundred savings banks. Some of the deposits made at the Caisse d'Epargne level are transferred to a centralized organization called 'la Caisse des Dépôts et Consignation'.

Other deposits are transferred at the level of a decentralized regional organization called SOREFI, which usually regroups between 10 and 50 Caisses d'Epargne. Seventeen SOREFI exist in France, one for each of the main regions.

Since a law was passed in 1987, the Caisses d'Epargne are allowed to make loans to companies (their tradition has been, for a long time, to make only loans to people).

Given the deregulation in the French banking system and the new rules within the single European market of 1992, certain privileges of the Caisses d'Epargne are disappearing.

As a consequence, the French network of Caisses d'Epargne is facing a huge problem of lack of expertise in the field of company loan analysis, since they will have to be more involved in company loans and will be competing with the rest of the banking environment.

The analysts of Caisses d'Epargne are not used to making company financial analyses and need to build on or improve their competence in this field.

Most SOREFI are trying to improve the level of competence of their financial analysts in the Caisses d'Epargne and to use, in the best possible way, the available expertise. As a consequence, many SOREFI and Caisses d'Epargne have come to the conclusion that the use of KB-DSS is the way to accelerate the learning process of their analysts and to distribute the knowledge of their experts.

The experience of the SOREFI Champagne-Ardenne is very interesting in this respect. In 1987, the SOREFI Champagne-Ardenne made a survey of expert systems for financial analysis that were available on the market and decided to acquire the license for FINSIM. The acquisition was decided on after the system was presented to the managers of the Caisses d'Epargne that belonged to the Champagne-Ardenne region.

The rationale was that the system was going to improve the education of key people (marketing personnel, credit analysts, credit managers and managers) and to improve the decision making with respect to: the selection of the companies to work with, the decision to make loans and so on.

The system was first acquired by the SOREFI to be evaluated over three months. After some small modifications, the system was considered satisfactory as a starting environment and the decision to supply it to the Caisses d'Epargne taken. However, given the specific market area aimed at by the Caisses d'Epargne, it was decided to develop a simpler knowledge base integrating industry ratios specific to this market area (craftsmen, small businesses and so on).

The knowledge base available by the time the decision was made was considered useful, but it went into too sophisticated an analysis for most cases and, also, for most analysts in the first stage.

A program of education was designed to improve the level of competence of company credit analysts. A three day seminar on the working of a company, followed by a three day seminar on financial analysis methodology were provided to the analysts. A one day seminar on FINSIM was organized, during which two cases were studied. Another one day seminar was organized two months later to discuss the experience of the analysts with FINSIM and to study a new case.

Meanwhile, the expert in charge of FINSIM at the SOREFI had

worked, personally, for half a day with each financial analyst and been at their disposal to answer questions.

The new knowledge base (called synthetic diagnosis) was defined by the expert at the SOREFI level in collaboration with the FINSIM designer. Figure 9.9 shows the structure of this knowledge base which we have described briefly in Section 7.4.4. Figure 9.10 shows the formalization of the rules used by the expert to structure his or her knowledge concerning the evaluation of financial structure. The new knowledge base was presented during a one day seminar which was held six months after the first knowledge base has been provided to the users.

At present, the synthetic diagnosis knowledge base is used, most often, to decide whether or not to work with a company and in simple cases. The detailed analysis knowledge bases is used in more complex cases.

The opinion of the manager of the Caisse d'Epargne is that the decision to use FINSIM has accelerated and helped considerably in improving the education of their analysts, and that the system has helped them to reach a higher level of competence that they would have achieved without it.

The lesson learnt from this example is that the users were better trained than in the regional bank case and, as a consequence, the adoption process was facilitated. However, the difficulty here is that the analysts are isolated, each one in a small bank and they have less opportunities to exchange ideas and problems between themselves. In the regional bank case, several analysts were using the system at the headquarters in the central credit department managed by the expert who developed the knowledge base and who is easily accessible for explanation and help when needed. We believe that regular meetings should be organized to let the users discuss their problems with the experts and application designers.

Exercises

9.1 Recall the steps in the design of a KB-DSS. Contrast it with the steps involved in standard information system development.

9.2 (a) What is the role of the normative point of view in a KB-DSS design?

(b) What is the role of the descriptive point of view?

9.3 What are the classical KB-DSS implementation problems?

9.4 How can a theory of change in organizations such as the Lewin–Schein theory, be used in improving the implementation of KB-DSS?

9.5   Draw a flowchart of events for FINSIM implementation in the bank cases described in Sections 9.5.1 and 9.5.2.

9.6   Define a plan for the implementation of FINSIM in a bank.

9.7   Define a plan to educate the users of a specific DSS. (FINSIM can be used or another system.)

9.8   Select a company that has developed a KB-DSS. Interview the person in charge of the project, a user and a manager who has users of the system under his or her authority. Describe, for each one, the implementation problems they had to face.

9.9   The learning of design methodology can not be achieved at a purely conceptual level. The students must be confronted with the problems of designing a project and the teacher should deal with them in relation to the project. As a consequence, the following questions are related to the term projects defined in Chapters 5 and 7.

   1   Use the methodology defined in this chapter to design the solution of the term project (Exercise 7.8) of a KB-DSS for personal loan evaluation.

   2   Use the methodology defined in this chapter to design the solution of the term project (Exercise 7.7) of a KB-DSS to assist in the completion of a private individual's income tax returns.

   3   Use the methodology defined in this chapter to design a solution for the term project (the JIIA86 case study, Exercise 5.14) of a DSS to assist the controllers of an industrial company with its branches and a foreign subsidiary.

10

Testing and Evaluation

10.1 Introduction

Building a knowledge-based system is an incremental process where the functionality of the system evolves as experience with its use is gained. When a prototype is running, design specifications are tested, revised, and new specifications are added to accomplish needs that were not initially known. Development moves through a series of cycles before the system is finally ready for operation. System development is not a linear process but can best be described as a spiral, as shown in Figure 10.1.

There are two aspects of concern in a revision cycle. Does the system work correctly and does it function well? Correctness can be tested, it is a question of right or wrong. For instance, are the conclusions drawn by the system correct? Functionality must be evaluated, it is a question of good or bad. For instance, is the man–machine interaction well designed?; does the system fit well into the decision making process? what are the benefits and so on. Is the system meeting its original intended requirements and goals?

Testing and evaluation are well-known tasks in model building and computer programming. A computer program is a model of real-world phenomena, where concepts and relationships are mapped into mathematical and logical statements. This process is a stepwise, incremental process where concepts, relationships, and operations are added successively. Before the computer program can be operational we must be sure that it works correctly – that it produces the results that it is supposed to produce, and that it has the intended effects on its environment.

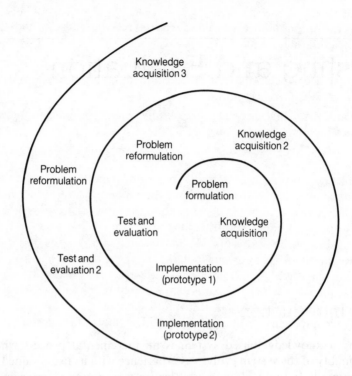

Figure 10.1   Testing and evaluation as a cyclic pattern.

10.1.1 What interesting questions can be asked about BANKER?

Let us take another look at BANKER, the loan evaluation system described in Section 6.6. Having implemented the system on a computer by the development tool PC-OPTRANS, what questions are relevant to ask next? Here are some:

(1)   Are the conclusions given by BANKER correct?

(2)   Is the system reliable and does it give consistent conclusions?

(3)   Is the system robust, not missing vital concepts or concept relationships, and not entering into dead-end reasoning chains?

(4)   Is the input data easily available at the precison level required by BANKER?

(5)   Is the reasoning appropriate, that is, does the system ask for the right information in a natural sequence?

(6)   Is the output (conclusions and reports) relevant, timely, and meaningful?

(7)   Is BANKER easy to use, that is, does the system provide a user interface which is understandable and designed to conform with the user's cognitive capabilities?

(8)   Does BANKER integrate successfully with the organizational setting in which it is going to be used?

A correct conclusion is an output expression, from the system, that can be interpreted as being equivalent to an expert's conclusion in the same situation. Correctness is not only dependent on the internal logic of the program, but also on valid input specifications. Thus, correctness can only be validated against observations outside the system itself.

Reliability and consistency, on the other hand, are a question of representation and logic. A reliable system will yield the same results irrespective of the sequence in which the input data is given. A consistent system behaves in a non-contradictory way. For instance, an increase in the rating of management competence from average to good should not lower the creditworthiness of the firm.

In this chapter, we shall look at a framework for testing and evaluation, how to validate data, knowledge and models, and how to assess the quality of the system. In testing and evaluating a system, we need standards or norms with which we can compare the actual behavior of the system. We have three kinds of norms (see Figure 10.2):

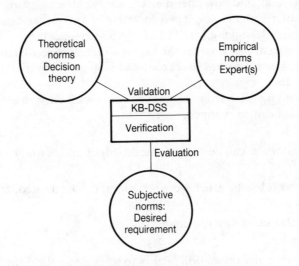

Figure 10.2   Norms as a basis for testing and evaluation.

(1) **Theoretical** norms such as norms prescribed by the normative decision theory

(2) **Empirical** norms such as the norms prescribed by the expert we model for problem solving heuristics

(3) **Subjective** norms, that is, qualitative assessments of system performance, either by the users or the experts.

When we have explicit norms, theoretical or empirical, the system can be validated. In the case of performance, system behavior is evaluated.

Testing and evaluation of models and computer programs have been dealt with in fields such as operations research, data processing and DSS. Many of the issues dealt with in these fields can be of use here. However, developing knowledge-based reasoning systems also introduces new issues. In this chapter, we shall concentrate more on the new issues created by the knowledge technology rather than the more general test and evaluation issues of traditional computer programs. In particular, we shall deal with verification and validation of knowledge-based reasoning systems. In Section 10.2 we shall present techniques to verify the logical correctness of knowledge bases including problems of completeness and consistency. In Section 10.3 we shall deal with what and how to validate. Finally, in Section 10.4, we shall discuss, in more detail, how we can evaluate performance.

Verification and validation of knowledge-based systems are tasks that are closely related to maintenance and learning. As already said, the typical building process of knowledge-based systems is incremental. New knowledge is added to existing knowledge. What is needed to increase the functionality of the system, and how does new knowledge affect existing knowledge? One of the first systems developed to assist in knowledge acquisition and knowledge base debugging was TEIRESIAS. The idea behind TEIRESIAS is to have a system that enables the expert to interactively change a knowledge base. It was developed as a front-end system to the medical diagnosis system MYCIN.

What can we learn from this pioneering work? There are three types of knowledge that can be changed.

(1) *Inference rules* can be deleted, modified, or added to the knowledge base.

(2) *Concepts* (objects, attributes and values) can be deleted, changed, or added.

(3) *Control strategies* can be changed.

TEIRESIAS uses an explanation facility to track down the source of an error in the knowledge base. After a diagnosis is presented, TEIRESIAS allows the expert to comment on it. If the expert does not agree with the diagnosis, a debugging process is initiated and guided by the system.

With the help of TEIRESIAS, the expert can teach the expert system new rules, expressed in terms of known concepts. But TEIRESIAS can also support the expert in teaching the expert system new concepts, and it can modify control strategies. Both of these tasks are complicated and require substantial knowledge. We shall not deal with these tasks, but refer the reader to Davis and Lenat (1982) for more details.

TEIRESIAS is a research system. It provides an interesting environment for studying many of the pertinent issues in knowledge acquisition and knowledge maintenance, in particular, for problems where the expert system development process itself is a way of explicating knowledge in the field. TEIRESIAS illustrates the problems of integrating new knowledge with existing knowledge in a knowledge base.

10.1.2 A framework for testing and evaluation

Our new framework of knowledge-based decision support systems includes expert system features and DSS features under the basic paradigm of decision support. Expert systems and DSSs are different in several respects which make testing and evaluation of these two systems two different tasks.

Expert systems, although evolutionary in development, are designed for well-defined problems with predefined solution sets. This makes it possible to logically verify the knowledge base and to validate the reasoning performed by the system. As we have already seen by the TEIRESIAS example above, changes to an expert system's knowledge base are made in terms of inference rules, concepts, and control strategies. Inference rules form chains of reasoning. Rules must, therefore, be tested for incorrectness, incompleteness, and inconsistencies. Techniques for testing the logic of knowledge bases will be presented in Section 10.2. Furthermore, expert system validation will be discussed in Section 10.3.

The very nature of a DSS, and the situation for which it is designed, makes it a difficult evaluation object. It becomes a moving target. Since there is no predefined solution path, and the environmental context in which it is used may change from time to time, there is no single way or prescribed way of using the system. Instead, the system is a set of resources – data and models, that are placed at the disposal of the decision maker. Thus, individual decision making behavior determines the usage of the system. A DSS may, therefore, be used in different ways by various decision makers. How can we, in these situations, evaluate the system as good or bad? First of all, there is not one single criterion by which a KB-DSS can be evaluated. Unlike expert systems, where we can use the predictive ability (conclusion success) as a measure of good or bad, such a criterion is not found in DSS. One may say that the ultimate objective is to improve the effectiveness of decision making, but when it comes to measurements it remains very much unproven. We can use the verification and validation procedures in Sections 10.2 and 10.3 to test and evaluate the knowledge-based parts of a KB-DSS.

When it comes to the decision support aspects we will lean more on the DSS literature. A review of DSS effectiveness evaluation is found in Sharda *et al.* (1988). Also, in textbooks, like Sprague and Carlson (1982) and Davis and Olson (1985) system evaluation is treated. Sprague and Carlson (1982) is more specifically devoted to DSS, while Davis and Olson (1985) treats evaluation of information systems in general.

We shall deal with performance evaluation in Section 10.4, along the following:

- system performance;
- task performance aspects;
- business opportunities;
- evolutionary aspects.

Three categories of people should be involved:

(1)   the knowledge engineer (system builder),
(2)   the expert,
(3)   the user(s).

Figure 10.3 shows a summary of the test and evaluation framework for a KB-DSS.

10.2 Knowledge base verification

10.2.1 Consistency and completeness

In this section we describe a way of logically verifying the consistency and completeness of a knowledge base. By logic verification we mean a systematic checking of logical statements: IF conditions and conclusions of rules and inference chains. No checking is made as to the validation of the ultimate premises, that is, the meaning of the symbolic expressions. Logic verification, therefore, means to check that a conclusion is logically true, and that the set of rules in an expert system logically spans, completely, the knowledge of the domain.

Logical verification of the rules can detect many potential problems that exist in a knowledge base. These potential problems can be grouped into:

(1)   Consistency problems, which can be caused by redundant rules,

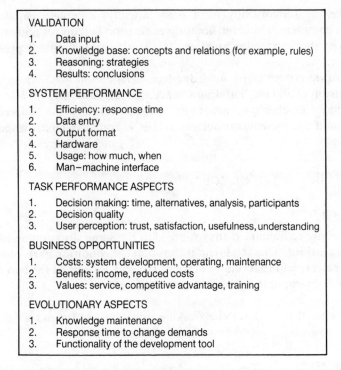

VALIDATION

1. Data input
2. Knowledge base: concepts and relations (for example, rules)
3. Reasoning: strategies
4. Results: conclusions

SYSTEM PERFORMANCE

1. Efficiency: response time
2. Data entry
3. Output format
4. Hardware
5. Usage: how much, when
6. Man–machine interface

TASK PERFORMANCE ASPECTS

1. Decision making: time, alternatives, analysis, participants
2. Decision quality
3. User perception: trust, satisfaction, usefulness, understanding

BUSINESS OPPORTUNITIES

1. Costs: system development, operating, maintenance
2. Benefits: income, reduced costs
3. Values: service, competitive advantage, training

EVOLUTIONARY ASPECTS

1. Knowledge maintenance
2. Response time to change demands
3. Functionality of the development tool

Figure 10.3   A framework for KB-DSS evaluation.

conflicting rules, subsumed rules, unnecessary IF-conditions, and circular rules.

(2) Completeness problems, which can be caused by missing rules due to unreferenced attribute values, or missing combinations of attribute values. Completeness problems can also occur because of control faults, that is, gaps may exist in inference chains.

Logical problems of the kinds described above may not, necessarily, impose reasoning faults. Logical redundancy and subsumed rules may, for instance, not cause problems unless the system is using a scoring mechanism, for aggregating evidence for a conclusion (such as certainty factors in EMYCIN). However, there may be a potential maintenance problem when rules are revised or deleted.

Logical incompleteness occurs when legal values in the value sets of all attributes entering into the IF conditions and conclusions are only partially or not at all covered by rules. Logic completeness spans the value space of all possible combinations of legal values of the attributes of a rule set. Some combinations of legal values may not be meaningful. A rule set may, therefore, be semantically (and pragmatically) complete without being logically complete. However, logical verification will detect potential faults and allow the knowledge engineer to identify which ones represent real problems.

This description of knowledge base verification is based on two articles, Nguyen *et al.* (1987) and Suwa *et al.* (1982). Both articles also describe automated rule-checking programs with algorithms for detecting consistency and completeness problems, CHECK and ONCOCIN respectively.

10.2.2 Checking for consistency

Redundant rules

Two rules are redundant if they succeed in the same situation and have the same conclusions. This statement means that the condition parts of two rules are equivalent, and that one or more of the conclusions of the two rules are the same. For example, consider the two rules:

Rule 1: IF   Firm's net working capital >0, AND trend in net
                 working capital is negative
         THEN   solvency rating is low

Rule 2: IF   Trend in net working capital is not positive, AND firm's
                 net working capital is positive
         THEN   solvency rating is low.

Assuming that the attribute 'trend in net working capital' only takes the two values negative and positive, then these two rules are redundant even if the IF conditions are in different order.

Redundant rules do not necessarily cause logical problems. It may affect efficiency positively, if redundant rules are located in adequate parts of the knowledge base. However, redundant rules may create a maintenance problem. One of the redundant rules may be revised or deleted, while the others are left unchanged.

Conflicting rules

Two rules are conflicting if they succeed in the same situation but with conflicting conclusions.

If we change the conclusion of Rule 2 to be 'solvency rating is low minus', then Rules 1 and 2 become conflicting rules. Note that it is possible that rules with equivalent conditions but different conclusions might not conflict at all. In such a case, the concluding variables belong to a multivalued attribute, for example, a person can be allergic to many different drugs, or can apply for several different types of loans.

For instance, we may have a situation where the conclusion is an advice on which type of loan to apply for: a secured or an unsecured one. In that case, the two following rules are not in conflict even if the conclusions are different. With the given characteristics (conditions) both types of loans are eligible.

IF   Solvency rating is average, AND
        profitability rating is average
THEN   apply for a secured loan

IF   Solvency rating is average, AND
        profitability rating is average
THEN   apply for an unsecured loan.

Subsumed rules

One rule is subsumed by another if the two rules have the same conclusions, but one contains additional constraints on the situation on which it will succeed. Let us define the following rule:

Rule 3: IF   Firm's net working capital > 0, AND
                trend in net working capital is negative, AND
                firm's current ratio < 2
         THEN   solvency rating is low.

In this case, we would say that Rule 1 is subsumed in Rule 3: Whenever Rule 3 succeeds, Rule 1 also succeeds.

Unnecessary IF conditions

Two rules contain unnecessary IF conditions if the rules have the same conclusions, and if an IF condition in one rule is in conflict with an IF condition in the other rule, and all other IF conditions are equivalent. For instance, let us define the following rule:

Rule 4: IF   Firm's net working capital < 0, AND
                trend in net working capital is negative
         THEN   solvency rating is low.

In a rule set consisting of Rules 1, 2, 3 and 4, Rules 1 and 4 will contain unnecessary IF conditions.

Rule 1: Net working capital > 0
Rule 4: Net working capital < 0

In this case, the two rules can be combined into one:

Rule 4:   IF   Trend in net working capital is negative
          THEN   solvency rating is low.

A special case may occur where two rules have the same conclusions, one rule containing a single IF condition that is in conflict with an IF condition of the other rule which has two or more IF conditions. For instance:

Rule 5:   IF   Firm's net working capital < 0
          THEN   solvency rating is low.

If Rule 5 is included in the rule set, Rule 1 should be modified to:

Rule 1:   IF   Trend in net working capital is negative
          THEN   solvency rating is low

(Rule 4 should be omitted).

Circular rules

A set of rules is circular if the chaining of the rules in the set forms a cycle, for example:

Rule 6:   IF   Management competence is good, AND
                    financial credit rating is good
          THEN   overall credit rating is good

Rule 7:   IF   Overall credit rating is good, AND
                    trend in profitability is very good,
          THEN   management competence is good.

Here, the system will move into an infinite loop. In evaluating Rule 6 it will look for rules that conclude with 'management competence is good', it will find Rule 7, which, however, requires that the condition 'overall credit rating is good' is true. This, however, is the conclusion of Rule 6, thus completing a circular chain.

To help detect circular rule chains one may use a dependency chart. A dependency chart is a table with rules displayed as rows and columns. An element (r_i, r_j), where i denotes a row and j denotes a column, determines a dependency if it is marked, for instance by 1. A 1 in the element (r_i, r_j) indicates that one or more IF conditions of rule r_i matches one or more conclusions of rule r_j as illustrated by the example below;

R1   IF A AND B THEN C
R2:   IF B and C THEN D
R3:   IF C and D THEN A

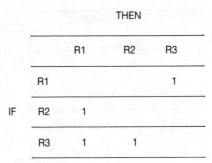

THEN

		R1	R2	R3
	R1			1
IF	R2	1		
	R3	1	1	

Figure 10.4   Rule dependency chart.

Here, we can see that to draw the conclusion C by R1 we need to know A and B. A is determined by R3. Thus R1 is dependent on R3 and we mark this by a 1 in the element (R1, R3). If we continue to analyse the dependencies of the small rule set above we end up with a rule dependency chart as shown in Figure 10.4.

If a dependency is marked in element (r_i, r_j) and in element (r_j, r_i) we have detected circular rules because r_i is dependent on r_j, and r_j is dependent on r_i. The circular rule chain may not always be as direct and apparent as the two rules shown above. However, an algorithm can easily be constructed to detect any implicit circular pattern among rules.

10.2.3 Checking for completeness

Missing rules

Rules may be missing due to:

(1) *Unreferenced attribute values.* Some values in the value set of an attribute are not covered by any rule's IF conditions or conclusions. In other words, the legal values in the value set of the attribute are only covered partially or not at all. Let us look at Figure 10.5. If the value set of creditworthiness is (High, Average, Marginal, Low or Reject), the value 'low' is unreferenced. This might indicate missing rules.

(2) *Missing combinations of condition attribute values* In Figure 10.5 there are two attributes making up the condition parts of rules, each one having the value set (High, Average or Marginal). Two attributes with legal value sets of three elements each, lead to 3×3 possible combinations. To cover the whole set of combinations we need, therefore, nine rules. In general, for *n* attributes, each with a value

| Rule number | CHARACTERISTICS | | CONCLUSIONS |
	Management competence	Financial analysis	Credit worthiness
R1 R2	High Average	High	High
R3	High	Average	Average
R4 R5	Average Marginal	High	
R6 R7	High Average	Marginal	Marginal
R8	Marginal	Marginal	Reject

Figure 10.5   Decision table from BANKER.

set v where v is the number of values for attributes i, logic completeness of the entire value space requires $v_1 \times v_2 \ldots v_i \ldots \times v_n$ combinations (rules). Transferring each row of Figure 10.5 into one rule will give a total number of eight rules. A closer examination shows that there are two conflicting rules (R2 and R4) leaving a rule set of seven legal rules. Thus, two combinations must be missing in the table. A closer inspection uncovers the following missing combinations: (Average, Average) and (Marginal, Average).

The number of rules may be less than the number of possible combinations for two reasons:

(1)   Disjoint conditional parts, for example:

   IF   Management competence is high *or* average AND
           financial analysis rating is high
   THEN   creditworthiness is high

(2)   Meaningless combinations of values. One has to be careful here. If combinations of legal values of attributes lead to meaningless conclusions we must be prepared for those combinations to be inputted. The system must, therefore, be able to detect this fault.

Illegal attribute values

If a rule refers to an attribute value that is not in the set of legal values, an error occurs.

Dead ends

The inference tree of a production system may contain dead ends. These dead ends occur when a conclusion of a rule does not match a goal or an IF condition of another rule. Dead ends are very often caused by terminology errors, for instance, when synonyms are used.

10.3 Validation

A knowledge base may be logically correct without being valid. Validation has to do with how well a model or a measurement conforms to what has been modeled or measured. Thus, validation has to do with something outside the system itself – that the symbolic expressions in the system are true representations of reality.

Three types of faults may be encountered in the validation process:

(1) *Factual* faults: An assertion does not correctly represent the fact (a property of the object studied).

(2) *Inferential* faults: A rule does not correctly represent the domain knowledge. The result is that incorrect conclusions are drawn by the system.

(3) *Control* faults: The rules are correct, but have undesirable control behavior.

The validation procedure is a three-step procedure:

(1) run the program on problems;
(2) identify faults;
(3) modify the program (rules and control strategies).

In the following, we shall first discuss validity more generally, and then describe two specific approaches to expert systems validation.

10.3.1 Validity

Validity refers to relevance, meaningfulness, and correctness. A theory is valid if it is relevant and meaningful and the inferences are correctly derived from premises. A measurement is valid if it correctly measures the right property of the object. Measuring certain physical properties of objects, for instance, weight, length, or temperature, validation is no great problem. However, moving to more abstract entities like intelligence and school achievements, validation becomes more problematic. Firstly, intelligence is not directly measurable. Only through tests can we obtain a measure of

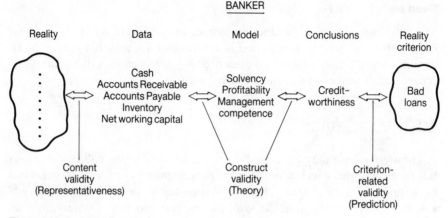

Figure 10.6   Validity types.

intelligence. The question then arises whether the tests performed really measure intelligence. Secondly, having a measure of intelligence, is that measure a good prediction of school achievement?

As we can see, there are several kinds of validity. We shall look at three types: content, construct and criterion related. In discussing these validity types we shall draw on the theory and methods of behavioral research as described in Kerlinger (1973). To explain some of these concepts let us again return to BANKER. Figure 10.6 shows validation points related to BANKER.

Content validity

This is the representativeness or sampling adequacy of the content – the substance, the matter and the topics – of a measuring instrument (Kerlinger, 1973, p. 458). One may ask: Does this item measure what it is supposed to measure? Another term for this concept is **face** validity. According to Kerlinger, content validation is basically judgmental. Each item must be judged for its presumed relevance to the property being measured. For instance, if net working capital is defined as an indicator, do we really measure net working capital by taking the difference of current assets and short-term liabilities from the financial statements? Content validity as it is used here, therefore, is related to data input validity.

Construct validity

This refers to the validation of the theory behind the test (Kerlinger, 1973, p. 461). Applied to knowledge-based systems, construct validity refers to the validity of the models: the knowledge base, the reasoning strategies and the analytical relationships. For instance, are net working capital, acid ratios, and current ratios elements that will explain solvency; and are solvency, profitability, and management competence, constructs or factors that will explain creditworthiness?

A significant point about construct validity is its preoccupation with theory, theoretical constructs, and scientific empirical inquiry involving the testing of hypothesized relations (Kerlinger, 1973, p. 461). Construct validation is dependent on the way a knowledge-based system is built. If the models are built around hypothesized relationships, each relationship can be validated. If the system is built from verbal protocols, that is, we establish a theory of problem solving, then construct validation can be done by the expert's inspection (judgment) of the constructs established. One way of doing this is by a rule trace approach. Here, the system is run on a specific problem. The system behavior is traced as rules are tried, rejected, or fired. The rule trace approach is treated in more detail in Section 10.3.2.

Criterion-related validity

This is studied by comparing test or scale scores with one or more external variables, or criteria, known or believed to measure the attribute under study (Kerlinger, 1973, p. 459). Criterion-related validity is concerned with the predictive ability of the system. When we establish a creditworthiness measure in BANKER we do this to predict the credit taker's ability to service the credit (loan) taken. One external variable, or criterion, to use is 'bad loans', that is, loans where the terms of the loans (interests and instalments) are not fulfilled according to the contract. By measuring, *ex post*, a series of loans, we can validate the predictive ability of BANKER. Criterion-related validation can be performed empirically by measuring the system's success in predicting a criterion. Statistics on overall performance (correct and incorrect conclusions) as well as on individual rules are collected. To measure the overall performance may be easy, but to identify the right and wrong behavior of individual rules is difficult. We shall look at empirical approaches to criterion-related validation in Section 10.3.3.

10.3.2 Rule traces

Running the rules on a problem causes a search tree to be developed. The rule trace is the path through this tree. It is an account of rules that have been tried, those which did not succeed and which did. We have already shown a rule trace of OPTRANS in Chapter 6 (see Figure 6.4). Two types of rule trace analysis can be done: the intuitive and the analytical. In the intuitive approach a rule trace is presented to the expert who will comment on the conclusions and the reasoning. There is no explicit external reference to which the system's performance can be compared. That reference is in the expert's head. There are no systematic and controlled ways of correcting identified faults. One can only hope that changes in the program will not create significant errors in other cases, cases that may have been handled well on a previous occasion.

It is possible to perform a more formal analysis of rule traces. In the AI field, several learning programs have been developed that are based on rule traces. These programs use a more precise conceptual framework and more formal procedures to identify and correct faults. One critical point in a formal analysis is to determine which rules *should* have fired, and in what sequence. An account of this is called the **ideal trace**. Some of the learning programs take the ideal trace as input, others work it out by analysis using problem solving and inference techniques. The ideal trace is compared with the actual trace of the rules, the rule trace, to locate the first point at which the traces differ. If the actual trace differs from the ideal trace it is because the rule that fired in the actual trace, R_i, differs from that in the ideal trace, R_i. Two types of instances may occur:

(1) R_i fired incorrectly because it was insufficiently constrained (this is called an error of commission (Bundy *et al.*, 1985)).

(2) R_i was missing or R_i failed to fire because it was incorrectly constrained (this is called an error of omission (Bundy *et al.*, 1985)).

It is sufficient to concentrate on errors of commission. Correcting these errors will eventually correct errors of omission. When an error of commission is corrected, R_i no longer fires. If another rule, R'_i, now causes an error of commission, this will be corrected. Eventually, R_i must be the most preferred rule (if it exists).

There are several modification techniques associated with rule trace comparisons:

- reordering of rules to correct control faults;
- adding extra conditions to the antecedent of a rule (also called specialization or discrimination);
- concept learning techniques.

A further treatment is beyond the scope of this book. For further details the reader is referred to Bundy *et al.* (1985).

10.3.3 Empirical performance validation

The second approach to system validation is to test the predictive ability of the system by comparing its conclusions with one or more external variables, or criteria. One external variable to use is an expert's conclusions for a set of test cases and test, empirically, how well the system's conclusions match with these.

The critical point in the rule trace approach is to have something with which the rule trace can be compared, for instance, an ideal trace. Here, the critical point is to have enough *representative* coverage for validation. In some domains, it may be possible to gather large numbers of cases for typical decision outcomes, but rare decisions always present a problem. In other domains, for instance, geological exploration, each case is more or less unique, or the cost of obtaining sample cases is very high. In PROS-PECTOR, for instance, special validation techniques were used which were based on sensitivity analysis procedures.

A second critical point in this approach is that the conclusions must be precise for accurate and useful comparisons. A conclusion drawn by the system must be classified as either correct or incorrect. The credit evaluation model, BANKER, lends itself to this type of analysis. On the other hand, the financial adviser SAFIR produces a narrative output (see Figure 8.5) which is composed of several statements that are applicable to conclusions of the case. This narrative output may be difficult to force into a precise conclusion that lends itself to an accurate comparison with an expert's unconstrained narrative statements. For SAFIR, the system was validated by letting the expert inspect the system's conclusions and rule trace. Judgment substitutes statistical performance analysis.

In describing the process of empirical performance validation we shall draw on Weiss and Kulikowski (1984). The process of performance validation is described as iterations through the following steps:

(1)   obtain the performance of rules on a set of stored cases;
(2)   analyse the rules;
(3)   revise the rules.

The first step is to produce a performance summary for all stored cases. There are several cases giving the same conclusions. Measuring the number of cases where the model's conclusions match with that of the expert, gives a performance measure called **true positive**. On the other hand, the model may also falsely infer a conclusion. This performance measure is called **false positive**. Table 10.1 shows a performance summary taken over a set of five types of diagnosis in the domain of rheumatology (taken from Weiss, 1984).

Table 10.1 shows that for the diagnosis 'mixed connective tissue disease', 9 cases out of 33 were correctly diagnosed (true positives) and that no cases were misdiagnosed by the model as 'mixed connective tissue disease' (false positives). For the diagnosis 'rheumatoid arthritis', the model performs quite well (100% positive). However, there are 10 misdiagnosed cases.

This indicates that, with respect to the first diagnosis, the rules are not picking up the disease nearly as well as one would like. The antecedents should be weakened, that is, some conditions may be too strong. Weakening

Table 10.1   A performance study. (Reproduced from Weiss S.M. and Kulikowski C.A. *A Practical Guide to Designing Expert Systems.*)

	True positives		False positives	
Mixed connective tissue disease	9/33	(27%)	0	(0%)
Rheumatoid arthritis	42/42	(100%)	10	(13%)
Systemic lupus erythematosus	12/18	(67%)	4	(0.4%)
Progressive systemic sclerosis	22/23	(96%)	5	(0.4%)
Polymyosities	4/5	(80%)	1	(0.1%)
Total	89/121	(74%)		

the antecedent conditions is called **generalization**. With respect to the second diagnosis, the opposite seems to be the situation. Here the model 'over' diagnoses this disease, 52 cases, of which 42 are correct and 10 are wrong. This calls for strengthening of the antecedent conditions of one or more rules of the inference chains leading to that diagnosis. This is called **specialization** and makes a rule's conditions more difficult to satisfy and, therefore, to execute.

In addition to the results shown above, statistics are gathered about each specific rule as shown in the example below (from Weiss and Kulikowski):

Rule 72:

43 cases: in which this rule was satisfied.

13 cases: in which the greatest certainty in a conclusion was obtained by this rule and it matched the expert's conclusion.

7 cases: in which the greatest certainty in a conclusion was obtained by this rule and it did not match the expert's conclusion.

After performance analysis, the revision of rules, also called rule refinement, is carried out. This is a process of generalizing or specializing rules.

Take a situation where the system arrives at a conclusion C_s and the expert concludes with C_e. Rules leading to the conclusion C_s must have been wrongly fired (errors of commission according to Bundy *et al.* (1985)), or rules which could have led to conclusion C_e can have been incorrectly constrained (errors of omission), thus missing execution. In contrast to the approach described in Bundy *et al.* (1985), where one concentrates on errors of commisison, Weiss and Kulikowski (1984) advocate a combination of the two. Errors of commission can be corrected by specialization, that is, adding constraints to the antecedents of the rules, thus limiting the situations in which it will be fired. At the same time, rules leading to the correct conclusion, C_e, could be generalized, thus being less restrictive. This is, in principle, how rule refinements are done. However, if the system now succeeds in drawing the correct conclusion for a set of cases leading to one particular conclusion, what will be the effect on other conclusions or diagnoses using parts of the same inference chains? By generalizing a rule we may increase the target ratio, that is, the number of correctly concluded cases. However, there is also a potential risk of increasing the number of misconcluded cases. On the other hand, specialization may reduce the number of misconcluded cases, but at the potential risk of reducing the target ratio.

How do we find the right rules for revision? There is no simple answer to this question. Solutions can only be found by performing experiments that incorporate changes into the rule set, and then test the modified rules on the stored cases. A system called SEEK (Politakis, 1985) has been developed to generate suggestions for specific experiments for rule refinements.

The advice generated by SEEK consists of specific generalizations and specializations of rules. Figure 10.7 exemplifies the process of analysing and recommending rule change experiments. In this example, the conclusions of the system and the expert do not match for Case 2. Because Dx2 is the correct answer for Case 2, performance might be improved by generalizing a Dx2 rule or specializing a Dx1 rule. The choice of rules to be refined is based on heuristic knowledge implemented in SEEK.

10.4 Performance evaluation

10.4.1 Aspects of evaluation

In this section, we shall look at aspects (measures) by which we can evaluate the functionality of a KB-DSS. Our ultimate goal is to improve decision making by means of a computer system – a KB-DSS. Evaluation requires an external reference to which the system can be compared. However, we have already described the difficulties in establishing such a reference for a DSS because of the evolutionary nature of these systems, the ill-structuredness of the tasks that they are applied to, and the individual decision making behavior that guides the use of these systems. Instead of being a well-defined goal, this reference point becomes a moving target. Therefore, we present categories of aspects or criteria; no one criterion is likely to be sufficient to evaluate a KB-DSS. We shall follow the categories that were presented in Figure 10.3:

- system performance,
- task performance aspects,
- business opportunities,
- evolutionary aspects.

System performance

We can define several measures to evaluate the quality of a computer system. These include response time, availability, reliability, data entry, dialog, usage time, users, and quality of system support (documentation, training

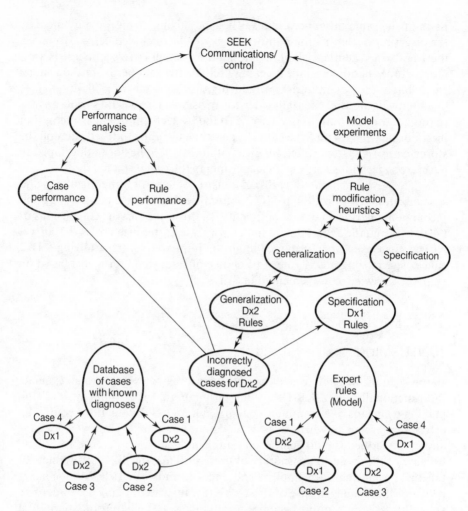

Figure 10.7   Overview of rule definement analysis for diagnosis Dx2.
(Reproduced from Politakis P.G. (1985). *Empirical Analysis for Expert Systems*, copied by kind permission of Pitman Publishing, London.)

and so on). The quality of system performance is of particular importance to the acceptance of the computer program by the users. Measures on system performance can be obtained by observations, event logging, and attitude surveys (these methods are briefly described in Section 10.4.2).

Task performance aspects

These aspects are concerned with the functionality of the computer program in relation to performing the task at hand – the decision. The ideal measure for evaluating a KB-DSS that is aimed at improving decision making is the actual outcome of a decision. In an uncertain world, it is important to distinguish between decisions and outcomes. A good decision does not necessarily lead to a good outcome. The quality of a decision depends on the correctness of the actions taken by the decision maker, given information about the world. Task performance is, therefore, measured by the quality of the decision more than the quality of the outcome. Quality of decision and decision making can be measured in terms of time spent to make a decision, alternatives evaluated, and information searched. Also, some qualitative measures can be done, such as trust (confidence), satisfaction, understanding and so on.

Business opportunities

A decision implies committing resources. The amount of resources can be measured in terms of costs, and the effects of the commitment in terms of added values: added income, reduced costs and so on. However, a KB-DSS may also lead to organizational changes, more cost-effective training, and competitive advantages. In Chapter 6 we discussed the business opportunities of expert systems in terms of cost reduction: distribution of expertise, increased productivity and so on, and also in terms of added values: better customer services, new products, competitive advantages and training.

Methods that can be used to measure business opportunities are cost/ benefit analysis and value analysis.

Evolutionary aspects

A requirement of a computer program that supports decision making in ill-structured tasks is the way that it adapts to changes in environmental factors, problem characteristics, and decision making behavior due to learning and so on. How well the system can adapt to these changes is dependent on the kind of software tool used, the availability of a system builder (knowledge engineer), and the user's own capability to make changes to the system (add data, develop models, and so on).

These measures are more qualitative than quantitative, and evaluation is, primarily, done by judgment.

10.4.2 Methods

Sprague and Carlson (1982) present seven methods that can be used to measure and evaluate the impact of a DSS. We shall briefly describe each method here. These methods are not only general with respect to the kind of information system they apply to, but also general with respect to the particular aspects that one wants to evaluate. The following briefly describes each method. They are not mutually exclusive but can be used in combination to provide a comprehensive evaluation of the system.

Event logging

In event logging, events that might indicate KB-DSS impacts are recorded. An example is keeping a log of bad loans before and after implementation of a loan evaluation system. This is an example of a before/after evaluation. Here, care has to be taken that other external variables have not changed significantly during the measuring period. Also, the system can be evaluated on a continuous basis. For instance, which events trigger the use of the system: periodical review of loans, seeking lending opportunities, environmental events and so on? Event logging is an uninstructed method without a well-defined set of techniques. Judgment is required in selecting the events to be recorded.

Attitude surveys

These are used to evaluate behavioral aspects, in particular, factors that have a positive or negative influence on a person's attitude towards a system. There is a huge amount of literature about users' attitudes (summarized in Christensen (1987)). Some examples of attitude indicators are:

- effect on job performance;
- perceived usefulness;
- motivation for use;
- expectations and so on.

Attitude surveys are performed by using questionnaires and interviews.

Cognitive testing

Cognitive testing is a repertoire of methods to analyse the cognitive processes of decision makers that were developed by cognitive and social psychologists. They range from traces of decision processes to structured conceptual analysis. More specifically, we have verbal protocols, interviews, the repertory grid technique (see also the knowledge acquisition techniques in Section 8.4.3), and others.

Rating and weighting

This is a structured method for a composite numerical evaluation. The method involves developing a set of parameters which are rated according to a given scale and weighted in terms of relative importance. However, care must be taken by the evaluator not to compute a single score by summing up the products of ratings and weights. This measure is undefined theoretically. Only when one system dominates another, that is, the ratings on all para- meters are better for one system than the others, do the scores give an indis- putable answer.

System measurements

Such measurements attempt to quantify effects through measurements of performance of the task (decision making and problem solving) or of the technical system (response time and so on). The measurements may be col- lected automatically by the system, through questionnaires, interviews, or observations, or extracted from documents. This method of evaluation is usually made on a before/after basis. Statistical techniques may be used to analyse the data that has been collected.

Cost/benefit analysis

This produces evaluations in economical and financial terms. Cost/benefit analysis is used more in feasibility studies (in advance) than in retrospective auditing. Care should be taken to include only those costs that are necessary to create the benefits that are measured. Cost/benefit analysis is only useful when you have clearly measurable benefits, that is, the primary objective of the system is increased efficiency. If the objective is improved effectiveness of decision making and problem solving, other methods, for instance, value analysis, should be used.

Value analysis

This has been proposed by Keen (1981). The approach is similar to cost/ benefit analysis with three important differences. Firstly, the emphasis is primarily on benefits and puts costs second. Secondly, the method attempts to reduce risk by requiring that prototyping obtains evaluation data. Thirdly, the method puts emphasis on innovative aspects more than return on investment measurements. Value analysis seems very close to the intuitive approach that many managers use to evaluate a support system.

Exercises

10.1 In the text we have made a distinction between correctness and func- tionality, and validation and evaluation. Discuss these concepts in relation to each other.

10.2 Explain the two concepts validation and verification. How is verification related to validation?

10.3 Describe three types of validity. How is each validity type relevant for expert systems testing?

10.4 Why is evaluation of system performance at the end of a qualitative assessment?

10.5 Given the following rule set:

   (1)   IF A ∪ B THEN D
   (2)   IF A THEN E
   (3)   IF E THEN D
   (4)   IF D ∪ E THEN B

What types of consistency problems do we encounter in this rule set?

10.6 How can you check a knowledge base for completeness?

10.7 Given the following rule:

IF return on investment is better than marginal
AND profit margin is less or equal to marginal
AND average interest rate paid on debts is between 10% and 14%
THEN profitability is marginal.

Show how this rule can be generalized and specialized respectively. What is the purpose of generalizing and specializing the rules of a knowledge base?

10.8 Discuss why a cost/benefit analysis is difficult in DSS evaluation. What kind of analysis is better for evaluating business opportunities of a DSS. Does expert system evaluation exhibit the same problems as DSS evaluation? Discuss.

10.9 Using either BANKER from Chapter 6 or FINSIM from Chapter 7, develop a detailed plan for testing and evaluation of the system, showing which aspects should be tested and evaluated, and which methods you propose to use for the various aspects you plan to test and evaluate.

11

Organizational Impacts of the Knowledge-based Decision Support System Technology

11.1 Introduction

Since modern business enterprise first arose, there have been two major evolutions in the concept and structure of organizations. The first took place in the ten years between 1895 and 1905. It distinguished management from ownership and established management as work and a task in its own right. This happened first in Germany, when Georg Siemens, the founder and head of Germany's premier bank, Deutsche Bank, saved the electrical apparatus company that his cousin Werner had founded, after Werner's sons and heirs had mismanaged it into near collapse. By threatening to cut off the bank's loans, he forced his cousin to turn the company's management over to professionals. A little later, J.P. Morgan, Andrew Carnegie, and John D. Rockefeller Senior followed suit in their massive restructurings of US railroads and industries.

The second evolution took place 20 years later. The development of what we still see as the modern corporation began with Pierre S. du Pont's restructuring of his family company in the early 1920s and continued with Alfred P. Sloan's redesign of General Motors a few years later. This introduced the command-and-control organization of today, with its emphasis on decentralization, central service staff, personnel management, the whole apparatus of budgets and controls, and the important distinction between policy and operations. This stage culminated in the massive reorganization of General Electric in the early 1950s, an action that perfected the model that most big businesses around the world still follow. (This description of administrative history is taken from Peter F. Drucker's article in the *Harvard Business Review* about the coming of the new organization (Drucker, 1988).)

Now we are entering a third period of change: the shift from command-and-control organization, that is, the organization of departments and divisions, to the knowledge-based organization, the organization of specialists and professionals – the knowledge workers. We have little experience, so far, of the knowledge-based organization and what it looks like. In this chapter we make some tentative hypotheses of its main characteristics and requirements. On the basis of an understanding of the developments in the information technology in general, and the knowledge-based technology, represented by expert systems and decision support systems, in particular, we can point to central problems of tasks, values and behavior, organizational change, and technical infrastructure.

There is no doubt that extensive use of the knowledge technology, together with other information technologies, will have an impact on the business organization. We shall start our discussion on this topic by outlining some significant trends in the socio-economic environment of businesses and the organizational structures that businesses will develop to meet these external challenges. We call this section 'Toward a new organization'. This narrative description is followed by a more analytical approach for understanding organizational change. This analysis is based on a conceptual model for organizational change presented by Harold Leavitt. Each of the elements of this model is described with particular emphasis on what is Leavitt's cardinal point, that the key function of management is to maintain a dynamic equilibrium among these elements.

11.2 Toward a new organization

In 1958, Leavitt and Whisler predicted, in an article in the *Harvard Business Review*, that the advent of the computer and management science would significantly change the structure and processes of most corporations. In addition, they suggested that the role of top executives and others would be significantly changed by the new computer technology. Since that time, little has been published to suggest that they were right. In retrospect, this is not surprising. Until the beginning of the 1980s, the information technology had primarily been used to computerize existing procedures in organizations. More recently, however, new applications of the information technology focus more on supporting decision making and customer service, with the aim of increasing effectiveness and developing new business opportunities. The new wave of applications created by the DSS and the expert system technologies, in broader terms, is also called **end-user** computing and penetrates the whole organization in a very different way from that in the past.

Exactly thirty years after the Leavitt–Whisler article was published, Peter Drucker, also in an article in the *Harvard Business Review*, describes the coming of the new organization (Drucker, 1988). He postulates that the typical business in the future will be information-based, an organization composed largely of specialists who direct and discipline their own performance through organized feedback from colleagues, customers, and headquarters. For this reason, it will be what he calls an information-based organization. In the subsequent text, we will call this organization **knowledge-based**. Businesses will have little choice but to become knowledge-based. But a transition to a knowledge-based organization can not only be met by investments in information technology. As we shall see below, fundamental management, structural and cultural changes are needed.

A variety of facts and interpretations of facts lead to the conclusion that future organizational environments will be characterized by more and increasing *information*, more and increasing *complexity*, and more and increasing *turbulence* (Huber and Mcdaniel, 1986). What exactly causes the environment to change? Firstly, the availability of information is changing customer behavior. Customers are becoming more demanding and more sophisticated, and they have more choices in the market because companies will structure their production capabilities to meet specific customer needs. Secondly, competitive advantage is changing. In the 1980s, both product and production technology have been changing at a breath-taking rate. The business of the future will focus on how fast it can bring new products to the market and how flexibly it can shift to new markets. Consequently, it will expend considerable effort finding, forming, and dissolving partnerships. Thirdly, the organization is disintegrating. Today's large organization with a deep functional hierarchy will be broken up and new integration mechanisms will be applied. Here, information technology will play a dominant role.

When the environment changes to a state incompatible with the current organization, the organization may have available a variety of strategies, including (Huber and Mcdaniel, 1986):

- adapting to the changed demands;
- moving to a different environment;
- changing the environment to a more compatible state;
- relying on slack, loose couplings, or other buffers.

It is the knowledge-based organization that will have the required organizational capabilities to meet the environmental challenges. According to Drucker (1988) this organization has the following key characteristics:

- decision making is transformed from opinion into diagnosis;
- knowledge intensive, requiring more specialists located in operations;
- task-focused teams as the basic organizational entity and not functional departments;
- individual responsibility for relationships and for communication, and above all, for information to oneself.

The knowledge-based business organization has many common features within such organizations as a hospital and a symphony orchestra. In a hospital, each speciality has its own knowledge, its own training, its own language. There is a head person who is a working specialist rather than a full-time manager. The head of each speciality reports directly to top management, and there is little middle management. A good deal of work is done in special teams as required by an individual patient's diagnosis and condition. (Similar thoughts can be found in the surgical team idea proposed for organizing computer programming work in Brooks (1970).)

A large symphony orchestra is even more instructive, since for some works there may be a few hundred musicians on stage who are playing together. According to organization theory then, there should be several group vice-president conductors and perhaps half a dozen divisional vice-president conductors. But that is not how it works.

The knowledge-based organization will pose its own special management problems (Drucker, 1988):

- developing rewards, recognition, and career opportunities for specialists;
- creating unified vision in an organization of specialists;
- devising the management structure for an organization of task forces;
- ensuring the supply, preparation, and testing of top management people.

11.3 Understanding long-term organizational changes

11.3.1 Leavitt's model

In the previous section, we have recapitulated some features of the coming organization, the knowledge-based organization, as envisioned by Drucker (1988). The two driving forces of the transformation into this organization are:

(1) the changes in the external socio-economic environment and;
(2) the new integration mechanisms that the information technology provides.

The resulting changes in the internal elements of the organization can best be understood in terms of Leavitt's model. In Chapter 9, we have presented prescriptive models for organizational change as part of the implementation

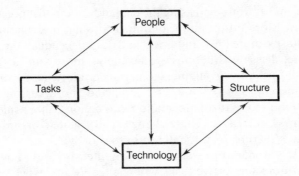

Figure 11.1   Leavitt's model of organizational change.

process of a specific system. In this chapter, on the other hand, we use a descriptive theory of organizational change to anticipate the long-term effects of changes in the business environment.

Leavitt concluded that organizational analysis, particularly one that was trying to match people and organizations to ensure that a given task was to be accomplished effectively, should include four elements: tasks, people, organizational structure and technology (Leavitt, 1965). The significance of the Leavitt's model is that, because of the strong interdependence, a change in one element has effects on all the others. Leavitt saw one of management's key functions as maintaining a dynamic equilibrium among these four elements.

Leavitt's model is presented in Figure 11.1. Many management scientists and information system scientists have used this model as their basis for research. The purpose of this section is to foster the major set of organizational impacts of a widespread use of computer-based information systems in general, and DSS and expert systems, in particular. We shall use Leavitt's model to discuss impacts of knowledge-based systems on tasks, people, management, organizational structure, and technical infrastructure.

11.3.2 The tasks

The greater complexity of the environment, as already discussed, imposes severe changes to the tasks to be performed. *Uncertainty* will increase due to more volatile customer behavior, greater competition, and an increased number of products available in the market-place. Tasks will be less programmed and thus more *decision-intensive*. Decision making becomes more frequent, faster and the complexity increases. The more complex decision making situations require more information and more knowledge. Information about markets, customers, and products must be available for the decision maker, thus increasing the demand for intelligence and information systems. More information, obtained through information networks, can make tasks more self-contained and less dependent on other tasks. Furthermore, decision situations are becoming more *knowledge intensive*. With more information available, greater uncertainty, and a wider range of decisions (more products, more services, and more customization), the knowledge required to turn information into actions, that achieve the goals of the business, increases. These changes call for new organizational and management structures as we shall return to shortly.

With the primary tasks more decision intensive and knowledge intensive, other, more supportive tasks will change. Many experts in organizations will stop providing routine advice, but conduct more research and development instead. In financial institutions, as we have discussed in Chapter 6, employees in branch offices perform tasks that were previously performed by specialists at headquarters. In the knowledge-based organization, many roles will change.

11.3.3 The people

With tasks and the roles changing, one may expect the type of people in the organization to change accordingly. As Drucker (1988) puts it, the information-based organization requires far more specialists than the command-and-control companies we are accustomed to. Moreover, the specialists are found in operations, not at corporate headquarters. Indeed, the operating organization tends to become an organization of specialists of all kinds. These specialists will be knowledge workers, office-based professionals with unique expertise and decision-making power. The new tasks and the new organizational structures will require greater self-discipline and greater emphasis on *individual responsibility* for relationships, for communication, and for information to oneself.

Individual responsibility increases discretion, that is, the power to influence one's own task or absence of influence from anybody else. Attributes that will characterize discretion are timing of actions, methods of problem solving, and dependency on other people (Methlie, 1983). Discretion is, together with influence, one of the two basic concepts that determine the *power* of individuals and the power distribution among individuals. The knowledge-based technology can have an impact on the power base and power distribution in the organization. Expert systems, for example, may reduce the power of certain professional groups because their knowledge becomes public domain. This may shift power from staff units to operational units.

A big challenge to the knowledge-based organization will be to provide *career* opportunities for the knowledge workers. Advancements into 'management' will be the exception, for the simple reason that there will be far fewer management positions to move into. This contrasts sharply with the traditional organization where the main line of advancement in rank is out of the speciality and into general management. Advancement opportunities will have to be created within the speciality. One major problem here is that the compensation structure, in practically all businesses, is heavily biased towards managerial positions and titles.

11.3.4 The organizational structure

Work will be restructured in the knowledge-based organization. According to Huber and Mcdaniel (1986), one may expect that the number of people contributing to a decision from outside the formally appointed decision-making unit will be greater. The basic work unit in the knowledge-based organization will be the **task-focused teams** or task forces. Specialists from different functions will work together as a team.

Heavy reliance on task-focused teams creates a management problem. Who should be a manager? Will it be the task force leader? And what will the management structure look like? We will move from hierarchies based on positions to hierarchies based on competence. Individuals who demonstrate competence are becoming more visible.

Galbraith (1977) describes seven mechanisms which can be used separately, or in combinations, to change organizational structure. Furthermore, he groups these seven mechanisms into three categories: coordinating mechanisms, mechanisms for reduction of information processing needs, and mechanisms for increasing information processing capacity.

The following shows the seven mechanisms allocated to the three categories:

Coordinating mechanisms	(1) Operating procedures and decision rules
	(2) Hierarchy of authority
Mechanisms for reduction of information processing needs	(3) Self-organizing subsystems
	(4) Slack resources
	(5) Self-contained structures
Mechanisms for increasing information processing capacity	(6) Vertical information systems
	(7) Lateral organizational forms

The knowledge technology will have an impact on these mechanisms in many ways. Expert systems may impose more formalized decision rules on some tasks. Task-focused teams, however, will be more self-organized and self-contained. Information will, to a greater extent, be task-related and flow more laterally in the organization than the more control-oriented and vertically flowing information found in today's organizations.

Decision authority will be more *decentralized* to cope with the decision-intensive tasks. Note that it has, for a long time, been a debate whether the information technology enforces centralization or decentralization. The general understanding today of the role of the technology is that it is non-deterministic, that is, the technology can be used in either way. The way that it is used is a management decision. However, we feel that the environmental demands, together with the technological opportunities, force a decentralized decision structure on the knowledge-based organization.

Another point worth noticing is that knowledge-based organizations will not be limited by the physical constraints of an office environment operating between traditional work hours. Information technology will facilitate the relaxing of these physical constraints. The 'office on the move' will become a reality. Here, information access, decision making facilities, and communication are independent of the physical location of the decision maker. The implications of changing definitions of organizational structures in space and time pose new management problems. Organizations can be reorganized according to criteria other than the traditional command-and-control criteria. The task force organization and lateral relationships seem to be the areas of work that can most easily be accommodated in this flexible organizational structure. A further discussion on these aspects can be found in Olson (1982).

11.3.5 The technology

Although we are, primarily, interested in the effects of the knowledge technology, this technology can not be separated from other information technologies when it comes to its impacts because, increasingly, we see knowledge-based systems embedded in the more general information systems of the organizations. Knowledge-based systems can be seen as part of a more generic type of systems – *end-user systems*. In the knowledge-based organization, the real growth area of information technology is that of supporting knowledge work. From a technological point of view, knowledge workers, requirements can best be understood by separating them out into three dimensions (Gunton, 1989):

(1)   In the *information access* dimension, information is obtained from a range of sources.

(2)   In the *services* dimension, a range of processing tools to manipulate and present information is available.

(3)   In the *interworking* dimension, information is distributed to coworkers in their team or organization, or beyond.

In addition to individual support systems, group support systems are needed. These systems have a few additional facilities, such as sharing of information within and between work groups.

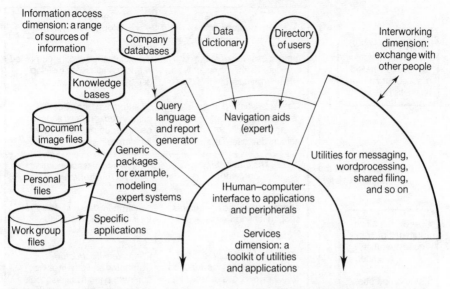

Figure 11.2   An architecture to support knowledge work. (Reproduced from Gunton T. (1989). *Infrastructure. Building a Framework for Corporate Information Handling*.)

The organization requires an *infrastructure* that provides a framework for the systems that have been installed to support knowledge work performed both by individuals and by groups. An architecture serving this purpose is shown in Figure 11.2.

We shall return, more specifically, to an architecture supporting organizational knowledge in Section 11.4.2.

The infrastructure must reflect the underlying needs of the organization. Gunton (1989) has analysed how a range of businesses were organizing their information systems effort. He found that there were, essentially, two dimensions along which their perception of what was best for the business diverged. These two dimensions, or business variables, are:

(1)   **Autonomy** How much freedom should end users have to develop local applications?

(1)   **Coupling** How important is it for end users to have immediate access to operating data on shared computers?

He then proceeds by dividing businesses into two categories along each of the two dimensions, on the basis of either *high* or *low* values on autonomy and coupling respectively, giving four categories altogether. Each category represents a generic strategy and can be depicted in a two-by-two matrix as shown in Figure 11.3.

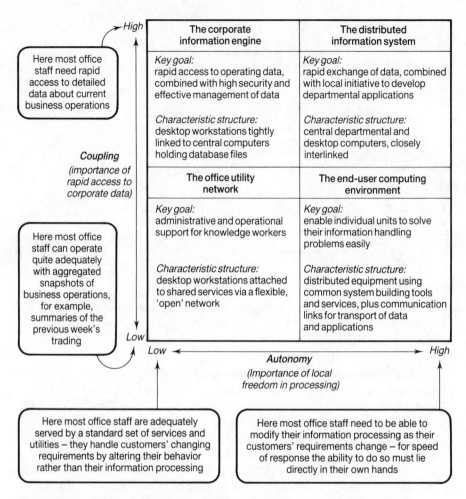

Figure 11.3   Strategies for information systems depend on two business variables. (Reproduced from Gunton T. (1989). *Infrastructure. Building a Framework for Corporate Information Handling.*)

The office utility network places a low emphasis on network performance and on sharing of data. Office workers have administrative and operational support which consists of a standard set of services and utilities.

The corporate information engine favours a hierarchical structure, with end-user systems closely linked via a high-performance communication network to centralized databases. This network provides rapid access to data about current business operations.

The end-user computing environment enables individual knowledge workers to develop their own applications with less emphasis on shared data.

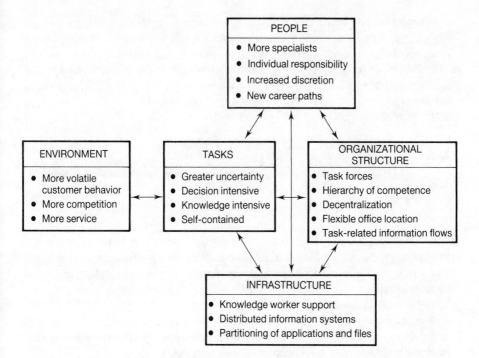

Figure 11.4 The knowledge-based organization in Leavitt's model.

The distributed information system has a high-performance network for sharing of data, as well as local discretion to develop individual solutions to information processing problems.

The infrastructure of knowledge-based organizations must absorb the pressures imposed by the changing business environment due to more demanding customers and greater competition. Also, the infrastructure must absorb the pressures imposed by new technological developments and the growth in end-users' demand.

These business and technology pressures raise new questions about the infrastructure for information systems: It must be *flexible* in order to absorb changes in demand due to environmental and technological pressures for change, and it must support the decentralized need for information processing.

In summary, for the knowledge-based organization to absorb the increasing environmental pressures, tasks will be more decision and knowledge intensive, requiring new organizational structures and new types of work skill. Employees will, generally, be characterized as knowledge workers with increasing demand for information support. The growth area of information systems will be in end-user systems. The infrastructure to provide computing power to individual and organizational needs, as well as accommodate for yesterday's, today's and tomorrow's technologies, must be flexible. Also, the organizational structure will have to be changed from today's command-and-control organization to a task force-oriented organization where information flow is task related and flows laterally along task and competence lines. In Figure 11.4 we have redrawn Leavitt's model, now showing the key characteristics of the knowledge-based organization underneath each element.

11.4 Knowledge as an organizational resource

11.4.1 From individual to organizational knowledge

Once knowledge has been structured into a KB-DSS, it can be replicated throughout the organization and used to increase the performance of knowledge workers. Thus, knowledge and expertise become transferable not only from individual to individual through learning, but also from individuals to the organization as such.

As pointed out in Chapter 6, economy of scale obtained by distributing knowledge bases throughout an organization may justify the investment involved in developing new performance knowledge.

As a consequence, the organization must treat knowledge as a valuable resource, on its own, that can be managed as an entity outside the human brain. A focus on knowledge as a resource implies that the organization ought to make a survey of their experts and decide, in each case, the interest and value of making this expertise available to other persons in the organization under the form of computerized knowledge bases.

During this process, it may appear that the expertise of several persons should be pooled to constitute an improved knowledge base. The sharing of organizational knowledge among knowledge workers is essential from two standpoints. Firstly, it avoids duplication of efforts in knowledge collection and maintenance. Secondly, it enforces consistency in decision making since all users have access to a common pool of knowledge (or several specialized pools).

Management should study if the development of certain non-existing knowledge bases could solve problems which the organization is facing. Such a study must take into account the appropriateness of the storage and distribution of the knowledge that is being looked for. The points which should be emphasized are the following:

- the extent to which the knowledge is domain specific or general;
- maintenance problems of the knowledge;
- sources of the knowledge;
- cost estimates of formalizing the knowledge.

In the database management area a change in focus was observed when the DataBase Management Systems (DBMS) came into use. They provided easier development and maintenance of applications due to data sharing and data independence. Also, as a consequence, a tremendous increase took place in the volume of data formalized and stored in databases. The same effect is expected when knowledge management becomes an explicit function in the organization. Sharing of knowledge and independence among knowledge bases and KB-DSS applications will lead to easier development and maintenance of applications, thus, increasing their numbers and the corresponding volume of knowledge.

11.4.2 Supporting organizational knowledge

The infrastructure to support the activities we have outlined above, will be based on networks. These networks (local area or others) will interconnect workstations, knowledge-based decision support centers, distributed data, models and knowledge bases, and transaction-oriented data processing centers.

On the local workstations, there will be stored local data, knowledge and models. The local workstation will, using its communication functions, enable a user to exchange data with other workstations or KB-DSS, or exchange messages with other users, using electronic mail, or other computer-assisted communication facilities of the local KB-DSS.

A knowledge-based decision support center is running on a computer which is not under the control of a user, but that can provide services to a cluster of workstations. Such a center is equipped to carry out processing which would be inefficient or infeasible to run on an end-user's workstation. Knowledge-based decision support centers are likely to store large amounts of data, knowledge, and/or image bases. Also, the centers can be used to coordinate activities among several workstations.

The data, models and knowledge bases available to users may, in the future, be distributed over the entire organizations. In a bank, for example, financial data on clients could be stored at the workstation level for financial and company loan analysis, but financial data on the client could also be stored on a knowledge-based decision support center to enable industry analysis to be carried out on a large number of companies.

It is likely that personal data on customers in a bank is kept at the transaction processing center. As a consequence, some KB-DSS applications running on workstations will have to access such information from the transaction processing center. As can be seen, in such a structure, data, models and knowledge can be stored in many different places. The location for storage is a function of the size of the data and the knowledge base, the storage access costs, the location of users, and the location of people in charge of creating and maintaining it, and, also, data security.

As a consequence, the ability of the KB-DSS software environment to manage the access rights to the objects (data base, knowledge base, model base) will be a key success factor.

11.4.3. Impact on the information systems department

With end-user computing as one of the major growth areas of information technology, organizations have to provide support functions for these applications. Also, a major trend to be considered is the integration of technologies into the application systems. Knowledge-based systems that proceed beyond the prototype stage will have to be embedded in the more general information systems, in order to share data with other applications, and to provide facilities for communication to other locations of the organization.

These trends will affect the organization and staffing of the information systems departments. When they moved into end-user computing, many organizations created new organizational units to get away from the rather bad image of the information systems department with respect to users' support. These departments were, typically, associated with transaction processing, large databases, low end-user service levels, and huge backlogs of work. The name that is commonly used for these new units is **information center**. Subunits particularly devoted to knowledge-based applications have also been created and called **KB decision support centers**.

An information center helps users to learn how to write their own application programs. They are staffed by people who are specially trained in using the facilities required for end-user computing, such as DSS generators, spreadsheets, knowledge-based development tools, database management and so on. The information center may be organized inside or outside the information systems department. We think that the trend towards more flexible infrastructures to support all kinds of information processing will force the information centers inside the information systems department, in the long run.

Whether inside or outside the information systems department, the organization will have to provide more support for knowledge engineering, knowledge management, and operation of knowledge-based systems. As a consequence, new skills will have to be acquired and developed.

Specialists in KB-DSS software development environments will be needed, as well as knowledge engineers. To achieve maximum flexibility, the information systems department will have to learn how to select the appropriate KB-DSS development tools for the user community.

The trend that already exists for information systems departments to play a consulting role in the implementation of DSS will be accentuated with expert systems and KB-DSS applications. The information system department will receive more and more requests to help in the design and implementation of KB-DSS that are beyond the abilities of individual users.

The information systems department will, in particular, be involved in designing, under the responsibilities of users, the KB decision support center and, probably, the overall KB-DSS infrastructure supporting databases, communication, and KB-DSS. Such an infrastructure must not only be sound from the technical point of view, but, also, from the organizational point of view and consistent with:

- user coordination of activities and incentive plans;
- organizational priorities and goals.

As can be seen, these tasks of creating the knowledge processing infrastructure, are closely related, if not completely intertwined with the evolution of the organization itself. If this becomes true, then management will have to be more and more involved in this technical task, which means either mastering the technology, or losing the ability to influence the evolution of the organization itself. It is particularly important for management to reconceptualize its view of the information systems department from being a cost center to becoming a *result* center.

11.4.4 Impact on information systems

If the trend we have described is confirmed, information systems will have to evolve. Firstly, they will have to interface with KB-DSS more easily than they do today. Classical transaction-oriented information systems will have to incorporate KB-DSS components. For example, the accounting system of a bank will incorporate a KB-DSS component to follow bank liquidity ratios and suggest actions to be taken. Secondly, they will have to incorporate much more information which is relevant for decision purposes. For example, most transaction systems of a bank contain little information on markets and customers, apart from actual transactions. Since this information was not taken into account when the system was initially designed it is much more difficult to develop a KB-DSS for marketing.

11.4.5 Management of knowledge

The management of knowledge-based organizations will have to plan for developing, preserving and maintaining organizational knowledge as a resource. Managers will have to design ways to utilize existing knowledge in a better way, and to develop new knowledge in the organization to achieve organizational goals. Management will have to allocate resources, in terms of money, equipment and time, to KB-DSS applications. In particular, it is not realistic to expect an effort from an already overworked expert to develop a knowledge base, which requires a large investment of time, without having accepted the fact that other tasks that he or she may be responsible for will have less time spent on them. Management will also have to change attitudes with respect to *experimenting*.

It is very rare that a full understanding of the advantages and drawbacks of using a KB-DSS can be obtained without experimenting with it. Hopefully, the cost of developing such an experimental version is very low compared to the cost of deploying fully-developed versions of the system (for example, in all branches of a bank). Management will have to be more receptive to the idea of developing experimental KB-DSS. On the other hand, methods will have to be designed to measure the value of investment in the knowledge technology, to make decisions on acquiring and developing knowledge.

The methodology of decision analysis described in Chapter 3 may be helpful here. But the most important task for management is going to be the change in the value system and in the incentives given to experts so that they take part in the development of KB-DSS applications. These changes must occur if organizations are going to take advantage of this new technology.

11.5 Specific aspects of financial institutions

This section is based on presentations given by Professor Paolo Mottura at SDA-Bocconi, Milan, during seminars on expert systems and DSS for banks and financial institutions in several European countries.

Financial institutions are, today, information-based and are becoming more and more knowledge-based as a consequence of deregulation of financial markets, more competition, and more sophisticated customer demands. The knowledge technology will have significant impacts on organization of work in these institutions and it may, therefore, be worthwhile to look closer at what organizational changes we may expect.

Most financial institutions, and, in particular, banks, face the problem of providing satisfactory skill and competence in branch offices, that is, in customer-related tasks. In order to cope with this problem and to remain competitive, the financial institutions must find ways to transfer knowledge to the market-place – the knowledge technology has this potential and will be used. But introducing new technologies, means, as we have seen from Leavitt's model, that the main characteristics of tasks, personnel, and structure also will have to be changed. Before we look at these variables, let us briefly describe the changing business environments of financial institutions. This enables us to understand more clearly the impacts of the knowledge technology in perspective – more as a totality than in individual systems.

11.5.1 Changing business environment

The environmental forces on financial institutions can be defined in terms of four elements:

(1) The market is, generally, growing fast and the customers are demanding services that are becoming more complex, more diversified, and more sophisticated. The speed of change is increasing.

(2) Deregulation causes a range of new financial services to be delivered to the market-place by new operators.

(3) The many new operators in the financial markets increase competition. Competition from inside and outside the banking industry is increasing, and competitors' reactions to changes in the market-place are quicker.

(4) New technology offers many new opportunities.

These environmental factors collectively force, on each performer, a growing diversification and accelerated pace of innovation. The finance industry becomes, essentially, a service industry. And a service industry is typically *decision intensive* because to produce services means, essentially, to identify and offer convenient solutions to customers' subjective and changing needs. In fact, a sales person selects one solution among many alternative ones in view of the best compromise between:

- customer's satisfaction, and
- bank's convenience (profit or other)

In a competitive environment. Therefore, it should be recognized that the sales person is a decision maker, and focus should be more on decision making than on transaction processing.

However, these decisions have a high content of competitive risk that is growing all the time; they need to be taken at a faster speed, and one has to be prepared for more frequent revisions. Furthermore, they are more complex because an increasing number of variables has to be considered. It should also be recognized that decision making is a complex process that demands skill from several areas. The way that financial institutions have developed highly-specialized skills in the past, will not work in the new business environment. A few specialists within an institution cannot serve the demand in the market-place. To stay competitive the company will have to:

(1) improve its quality of services in the front line and;
(2) reduce costs.

In order to develop a 'service content of high quality', and aim this at individual customer's needs, it becomes necessary to transfer, to the marketplace, at the customer level:

- the knowledge of elementary products and integrated products and;
- the skill and ability to design, select, promote and decide product combinations on a flexible basis.

The organizational impacts of the changes in the business environment are clear. Increasing the service content at the customer level requires:

- decentralization of decision responsibilities;
- new mechanisms for control.

On the other hand, diversification and innovation of the product portfolio generates:

- a rapid obsolescence of peripheral knowledge;
- increasing difficulties in training specialized staff who are delegated to customer contact.

Over time this leads to downgrading and deterioration of services to customers, and increased risk of inefficient and ineffective management of customer relationships.

11.5.2 Structural changes

Financial institutions, facing problems of effectiveness and efficiency with increased emphasis on complex decision making 'up front' at the customer level in the new service-demanding business environment, must find means to stay competitive.

The knowledge technology can provide effective support for:

- Maintaining and improving knowledge and expertise at the branch level.
- Decision making in full coherence with the bank's general policies.
- Monitoring and protecting the level and stability of service quality.

Note, that applications of the knowledge technology expand the capacity of problem solving and decision making beyond the capacity of the few available experts throughout the organization. Also, the knowledge technology provides means and ways to objectify and externalize heuristic knowledge and expertise which, until now, has been subjective and intrinsic to the expert.

How will this have an impact on the organization of companies providing financial services? In general, we will move from the 'top-down' organization we see today to matrix organization.

Top-down organization

Figure 11.5 shows a typical organization of a large financial company like a bank. We find two dominating functions:

(1) *Production* which usually is located at the headquarters. Here, we find the specialists performing the highly-skilled jobs.

(2) *Distribution* which consists of all the branch offices.

In this organization, production is dominant over distribution. Production provides the development of new products and services. The know-how is located at headquarters. As a consequence, the decision authority is also located here. For instance, loans over a certain amount cannot be decided at branch level but need the authorization from the credit department.

Thus, in this type of organization, we have a disconnection between decision authority and customer relationship management.

The traditional solution is to increase the delegation of authority at branch level by providing branches with experts with the unavoidable consequence of increased cost.

The knowledge technology makes it possible to supply *expertise* instead of experts.

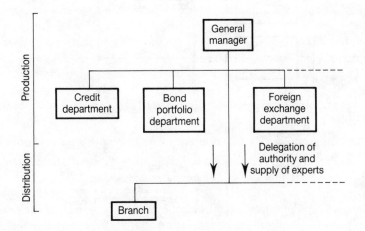

Figure 11.5   A top-down organization.

Matrix organization

Figure 11.6 shows how a matrix organization of a financial company will look like. The main idea is to merge knowledge about:

(1)   products, with
(2)   markets and customers

at the sales level.

This can only be cost effective if expertise is separated from human experts and replicated across the branches.

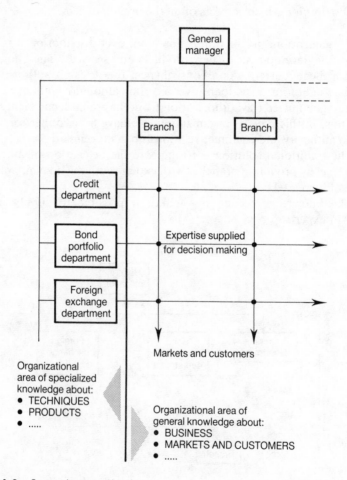

Figure 11.6   A matrix organization.

Table 11.1   Comparative evaluation of alternative learning methodologies

	Apprenticeship 'on the job'	Formal education and training 'class room'	Training assisted by AI applications
Knowledge acquisition and development	• Slow • Inaccurate • Difficult monitoring • Realistic • Acritical	• Quick • Precise • Theoretical • Difficult monitoring • Rational	• Quick • Accurate • Easy monitoring • Realistic • Heuristic
Knowledge application and implementation	• Occasional • Slow • Fragmented • Difficult control and evaluation	• Abstract • Insufficient	• Systematic • Programmable • Easy control and evaluation
Experience accumulation and improvement	• Partial • Slow • Difficult control and evaluation • Acritical and instinctive	• Scarce or none	• Coherent • Systematic • Supervised • Oriented • Exhaustive
Expertise and professional judgment devlopment	• Subjective and heterogenous • Autodidactic • Limited • Unconscious	• None	• Uniform and homogeneous • Objective • Exhaustive • Conscious

11.5.3 Impacts on bank staff training

In Chapter 2 we discussed properties of expert problem solving, and, also, how expertise was developed. Mottura has defined a learning cycle of expertise acquisition which is very similar to the skills learning process described in Chapter 2. Based on this learning cycle, he proceeds to make a comparative evaluation of alternative learning methodologies, one of which is training based on knowledge technology. Table 11.1 shows the attributes of the various learning methods at the various stages of the learning cycle.

Exercises

11.1 In what ways can a symphony orchestra be used as a model of a knowledge-based organization?

11.2 What are the possible career paths of a musician, and how do you see a knowledge-based business organization applying similiar career paths?

11.3 Describe Leavitt's model of organizational change. What is the significance of this model?

11.4 Consider:

(a)   a consulting firm;

(b)   a small bank;

(c)   a small industrial company.

What are the major similarities and differences in view of Leavitt's model?

11.5 Develop a model of a knowledge-based decision support center. What are its main functions and how should it be organized? Use literature about information centers for your analysis.

11.6 Japanese car manufacturers minimize part inventories by locating part suppliers adjacent to the assembly plant. American car manufacturers, on the other hand, select suppliers on criteria other than location. Explain these different organizational policies by Galbraith's coordination mechanisms.

11.7 You have been asked by the general manager of your company to give a proposal on knowledge management for the organization. Write a short note to your manager on the essential issues of organizing and managing knowledge as a resource.

11.8 Why is it important that knowledge-based systems can communicate with other information systems of the organization?

12

Knowledge-based Decision Support Systems Applications in Finance

12.1 Introduction

This chapter surveys the application of knowledge-based systems to problem areas in finance. The area of finance is one of the most advanced users of the knowledge technology. Most problems in finance are well structured and many normative theories exist. However, normative models are not in frequent practical use due to the complexity of the decision environment in which practical decision making is performed. We need prescriptive methods that are based on normative theories as well as practical judgment. This is exactly what knowledge-based systems can do.

This survey is, by no means, comprehensive. One of the major difficulties in surveying financial applications is the secrecy surrounding them. There are two reasons for this. Firstly, financial institutions do not have a tradition for research and development in technological areas. Therefore, there may be some reluctance to speak about things that are still only at an experimental stage, that is, prototypes. But even successfully-operating systems are kept secret. The explanation for this may be that this technology is seen as a competitive tool – therefore, they want to conserve this advantage as long as possible. This, however, is about to change. Since some banks are now using this technology to build an image of a progressive bank in their marketing efforts, other banks do not want to lag behind. Also, since knowledge-based systems now are appearing in the main offices, it is difficult to hide these systems from the competitors.

The sources of this survey are articles and books on expert systems. These sources narrow the applications to a few well-known references appearing frequently in trade journals, as well as at fairs and conferences. In systematizing the information on applications we can use different classification schemes. We can list financial functions by objects:

- private individuals,
- corporations,
- banks and financial institutions.

For banks we can make a classification according to types of activities:

- front office,
- back office,
- services.

And for the financial industry we can make a classification according to the market served:

- retail banking,
- wholesale banking,
- merchant banking,
- securities.

Now, since financial institutions very often span more than one market, and since functions very often span more than one type of activity, we shall use a classification scheme where we differentiate among objects only, and, within each object, list the financial functions that have to be performed. Within corporations, in particular, larger ones, one may find the corporate treasurer or the accountants performing activities which are typical banking activities. These corporate activities are described under the heading of banking functions.

Corporate finance	Financial planning
	Capital budgeting
	Cash management
	Client credit analysis
	Tax planning
	Financial marketing
Personal finance	Financial planning
	Taxation
	Retirement planning
	Real estate
Banks and financial institutions	Company credit assessment
	Personal loans
	Financial advice
	Assets management
	• Assets Evaluation
	• Portfolio Management

Trading
Bank management
- Assets and liability
- Planning and Control
- Compliance and security
- Branch performance analysis
Tax regulations

12.2 Corporate finance

Corporate finance is concerned with evaluating future potential risks and return on investments. The basic tool for this evaluation is the financial statements. All of the firm's investments and strategies, its successes and failures, are reflected in the financial statements.

Three main categories of financial decisions have given rise to DSS and KB-DSS applications:

(1) choice of investment;
(2) cash management;
(3) financial planning and financial engineering.

We shall also add a special section on financial marketing under this heading, since we have seen some interesting developments of the knowledge-based technology to this problem.

12.2.1 Choice of investment

The first important class of decisions deals with managing the portfolio of assets of a company (investment/disinvestment). These decisions are fundamental since they explain the growth and future profitability. They contribute to the progressive development of shareholders' wealth. Such decisions require a rigorous methodology. Most financial managers admit that an acceptable investment is one which will increase shareholders' wealth. This wealth is measured by the Net Present Value (NPV) criterion.

There are a number of different ways to assess the return and to rank the relative value of investments. Normally, we will take into account the time value of money by *discounting*, that is, more value is given to money today than tomorrow. The Net Present Value (NPV) and the Internal Rate of Return (IRR) are two frequently-used techniques that take all cash flows into consideration. These methods, however, are numeric (and usually deterministic). The variables (cash flows) that go into the calculations are single values. Over- or under-estimated values result in lower or higher returns.

A DSS is well adapted to this kind of task, since it will save processing time. Thus, the decision maker will have more time to study alternative hypotheses, and to test how sensitive the NPV is to changes in some of the basic assumptions, such as the stream of cash flows and the discount rate. The choice of discount rate requires experiential knowledge. Introducing knowledge bases is, therefore, particularly helpful here. Several systems of the DSS type have been described in the literature, for instance, Raphael *et al.* (1979). More recently, knowledge-based extensions of these systems have started to appear (see, for instance, Mockler, 1989).

Not many expert systems have been reported for capital budgeting. However, in a recent article Myers (1988) reports on a system for capital budgeting programmed in LISP which runs on a Symbolics computer. The system's basic valuation tool is DCF (Discounted Cash Flow). The knowledge-based part of the system is related to three areas: problem setup and forecasting, interpreting results, and circling back. Forecasting cash flows requires a model of the project. In developing this model, knowledge and insight is required to recognize omitted factors, to cut out unimportant detail, to flush out inconsistent or unlikely assumptions, and to handle important but tricky details, such as the interaction between inflation and taxation. Interpreting results means to give qualitative statements on the basis of numeric values. Sometimes it amounts to highlighting variables or assumptions crucial to the success of the project. Results from complicated numeric calculations, such as option-pricing applications, may need deeper explanations. Finally, circling back is necessary because major decisions are rarely made in one pass. In expert hands, experimentation often generates important surprises.

When the cash flows, NPV, and IRR are calculated, the system enters into a valuation mode. Here are some of the functions available in this mode: explanation of the NPV method; impact on book earnings; and suggestions for further analysis where the following subchoices are available: analysing the margin for error; analysing the use of the project; valuing flexibility; and, finally, analysing the competitors' impact. The knowledge base contains rules that may be executed when one of the above functions is activated. For instance, there is a set of rules for ranking variables on their importance to project NPV. The system then reports critical values for the most important variables. The rules for identifying important variables are built up from common sense. A very simple example is: 'If NPV is negative, and is still negative when S, G & A cost is set to zero, eliminate S, G & A cost from the sensitivity analysis'. This expert system builds a bridge between business knowledge on one side, and the numeric DCF calculations on the other. This is a system that helps and advises, as well as computes. Consequently, the system has knowledge about appropriate relationships to carry out consistency checks and to explain what it does. Furthermore, the system is taught to acquire information about basic economics of the user's business, and to feed that information back into the DCF calculations.

Another system of a similar kind is the **Financial Advisor** developed by Palladian Inc. The system helps managers make capital investment decisions using a wide range of financial techniques, and explains how it arrives at each step in an analysis. Like expert consultants, the system tests every input assumption and conclusion against an extensive knowledge of general business practices, such as the user's company policies, its accounting and management practices, its historical performance, and its competition (according to Turban (1989)).

Klein and Villedieu (1987) describe a capital budgeting and investment planning KB-DSS designed for use in municipalities. Capital budgeting and financial planning of cities raise special problems due to the coexistence of politically-elected decision parties, the mayor and the city council, with the administration. The political and financial planning process to be supported can be characterized by the following steps:

(1)   formulating political goals;

(2)   defining the program of actions (projects) needed to achieve these goals;

(3)   evaluating costs and revenues associated with each project (usually performed by the professional services of the city);

(4)   making a first choice of projects (usually done at the mayoral or city council level);

(5)   simulating the financial consequences of local tax policy and the portfolio of projects selected;

(6)   choosing among the alternatives;

(7)   computing the final plan;

(8)   getting the plan accepted by the city council.

The main functions of the system are presented in Figure 12.1. The system consists of two main decision models: PLAN and PROJECT. PLAN is used to test various policies concerning local tax levels, evolution of other resources, operating expenses, investment level and financing strategies. The decision model PROJECT is similar to PLAN but the user can define a portfolio of projects together with their characteristics (amount of investment, duration, associated operating expenses and revenues) and test the financial impacts of those projects.

The system is presently used by 40 French municipalities. The DSS version was first developed in 1982. The effort to develop knowledge bases was, however, started later than this and the first KB-DSS version was introduced in 1985. The knowledge base contains information on legal aspects of local taxation, and on operating costs associated with standard city investments such as schools and so on.

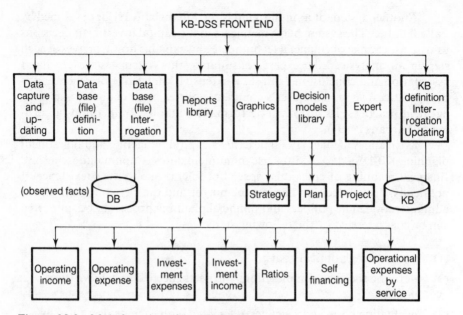

Figure 12.1   Main function of the KB-DSS for city financial planning.

12.2.2 Cash management

With the rise of interest rates, cash management has received increased attention. Companies have seen their financial costs climbing and their profits declining accordingly. As a consequence, financial managers have pushed to keep a closer look at the flow of funds derived from day-to-day transactions. The management of operation dates and value dates was one of the first consequences of this closer monitoring. The option of using over-drafts or discounting letters of credit was addressed.

DSS have been developed to support simulation of interest rates and hypotheses on cash flows. KB-DSS have appeared with new functions to suggest decisions on investments of surplus cash in various financial instruments, or disinvestment from the same. The importance of the cash management function has further increased with trading in foreign currencies, and with a treasurer who is working at a corporate level and not only at a single-entity level.

12.2.3 Financial planning and financial engineering

An important activity in corporate finance is financial planning and financial engineering, a determination of the best financing strategy, and, hence, the best capital structure for a firm. Financial planning is concerned with forecasting and projections of the information in the financial statements. Thus, financial statement analysis is an important part of this activity. Financial statement analysis, also called financial diagnosis in the expert system's terminology, is a study of relationships within a set of financial statements at a specific point in time and with trends in these relationships over time. Financial statement analysis starts with a computation of a set of financial ratios, followed by an individual evaluation of each ratio value at a particular point in time, an evaluation of time series of values of a particular ratio in order to look for trends, and, sometimes cross-sectional evaluations to compare with industry ratios. When this information is combined, more can be learnt about the firm's key performance characteristics such as profitability, financial leverage, financial structure and liquidity. To perform financial planning requires a combination of computing and reasoning. Computations are performed on financial statements to calculate ratios, and analytical models are used to forecast cash positions. Many decision support systems have been developed to perform these tasks. Interactive computing facilities allow for fast responses on the consequences of alternative decision values (what-if and goal seeking).

However, in order to evaluate the meaning of the data produced by these systems and to act adequately on the information that they give, knowledge is needed, knowledge that experienced financial analysts (the experts) use in their practical performance of this task. This knowledge is not available in ordinary textbooks on corporate finance. It is, however, a target for knowledge acquisition and expert systems in corporate finance.

The class of financial tasks addressed can be broken down into a set of financial decisions:

(1) *Choice of the debt/equity ratio.* In financing new investments, the financial manager must decide what percentage of the requirements should be financed with debt versus equity.

(2) *Choice of retained earnings.* How great are the funds that are available from the firm's own operations.

(3) *Choice of financial structure* (equity, debts, leasing, convertibles and so on).

These decisions, which, although presented above as separate entities, are in fact interlinked. For example, if a financial manager looks at self-financing an investment, this will reduce the funds available to provide dividends to shareholders. DSS have been designed to support such decisions for a long time, and optimization models using modern financial concepts to integrate the investment, dividend and financing decisions, have been implemented in a DSS (Carleton, 1970).

Many knowledge-based systems exist to perform financial planning and to support the task of evaluating a financial strategy of a company.

Some of these systems are made for parties outside of the company being studied who may want to make financial evaluation of the company for various reasons. These parties include shareholders, investors and security analysts; lenders and other suppliers; customers; and government/regulatory agencies. We have already described, in great detail, two knowledge-based systems which can support financial diagnosis and financial planning: FINSIM in Chapter 7, and SAFIR in Chapter 8.

Several DSS or KB-DSS are available on the French market to support these decisions: ANALYSIS, developed by Husson, and PREFACE developed by Senicourt (1988) for the financing of new ventures. Several such systems have been presented during the annual international conference on expert systems and management held in Versailles, France, and at the international conference on expert systems held each year in Avignon, France.

In the USA, Arthur Anderson & Co. has developed a prototype called FSA – the Financial Statement Analyser – for the US Securities and Exchange Commission (SEC) in connection with its EDGAR system. EDGAR is a system that electronically receives SEC filings directly from filing companies. FSA analyses the type of financial information contained in EDGAR's filings. The purpose of FSA is to perform consistent financial analysis, despite differences among individual statements. FSA reads the relevant financial tables and footnotes of companies. The system understands a variety of captions and textual notes. It then presents the results of ratio calculations. Ratio calculations are only the first step in automating financial analysis. Once the ratios have been calculated, the results are analysed. A combination of expert system techniques and statistical techniques is used to highlight situations such as:

- companies with ratios significantly higher or lower than average;
- companies with significant increases or decreases in the value of a ratio over a period of years;
- companies with unusual balances in particular accounts;
- companies with no line items for particular accounts.

FSA is developed in KEE and runs on a Symbolics LISP machine. Further details about the system can be found in Mui and McCarthy (1987).

Financial planning systems and financial analysis systems are one of the most developed areas of applications of the KB-DSS technology. Corporate financial managers need tools which enable them, not only to control the past, but, also, to simulate future consequences of possible alternatives, in terms of amount and types of financing, taking into account variables such as activity level, operating expenses, amount of investment and so on. Such systems can provide the user with advice and computations. An interesting system of this kind is described in Buisine (1987).

12.2.4 Financial marketing

Financial marketing is a term used to characterize the financial decision processes used in the marketing of products and services of such a large scale that they can have a significant impact on a company's financial status. A customer interested in buying a high-value product is usually concerned that the financing plan being used to acquire the product is safe, and is attractive from a financial investment point of view. In such cases, financial considerations become an important part of the buying decision.

In two articles, a system called FAME (Financial Marketing Expertise) developed at IBM's Thomas J. Watson Research Center has been described (Kastner *et al.* (1986) and Mays *et al.* (1987)). FAME is an expert system that generates a financial plan. In this respect, it is different from the systems described above which are diagnostic in nature. The system employs a heuristically-guided generate-and-test problem solving procedure for *designing* an acceptable financial plan. The original prototype system consisted of over 700 OPS5 rules. More recently, an object-oriented knowledge representation technique has been incorporated into the system.

12.3 Personal financial planning

In the last decade, the financial environment has undergone tremendous changes in most countries. Deregulation of the financial industry has led to an increase in the number of performers in the market-place, and a growth in number and complexity of financial products. Also, the consumer power of people has increased, resulting in a sophisticated market-place of both the supply and demand of financial services and products.

Financial services are now provided by a multitude of financial institutions and consultant firms. Banks, for instance, have established selling places for these services, sometimes called financial supermarkets. A financial supermarket is a concept that brings together normal banking services, and services traditionally handled by other specialist institutions, with barriers to entry largely created by official regulations. Such services usually include stocks and shares brokerage, insurance, real estate finance, and brokerage services.

In this new and more complex environment, the need for counselling and guidance is also evolving. Individuals need advice on how to manage their personal income and assets. They need financial plans covering areas such as cash management, investment, credits, tax planning, retirement, real estate planning, and insurance. Good financial plans provide coordinated recommendations covering actions to be taken in these areas over time. Providing personal financial plans is a service either charged directly, or is used as a means for promoting other products.

To provide a comprehensive personal financial plan requires expert knowledge in a multitude of domains, such as investment, cash management, taxation, inheritance laws, retirement planning, insurance, real estate assets management and so on. A financial service center can either be composed of experts from different fields to whom the client can be moved, or a financial consultant can use a support system with knowledge bases of different kinds. Systems which offer advice on financial planning have been a target for expert system developers for a long time. Such a system needs certain data on the client such as age, financial status, his or her needs at various stages of the life cycle, risk profile and so on. Such a system should be able to collect data from various sources such as public wire services or company-specific files. The output is a plan providing coordinated recommendations covering actions to be taken in different areas. It should also provide an explanation of the plan, why particular actions have been selected, and how they meet the client's objectives.

We know of many systems available in this area, some more comprehensive than others. The Norwegian company, A/S Ekspertsystemer, has developed a range of products in this area called PC-Tax, PC-Invest and PC-Finance delivered on IBM-PC. The French company SIG has developed KB-DSS to calculate personal tax. The system asks the user for information about his or her family situation and income. It then assists in calculating declarable income from various income sources such as real estates, securities and so on, the system can give advice on tax reduction options. Finally, when a plan is decided, the system calculates taxes and payment dates.

Arthur D. Little has developed the Personal Financial Planning System and the Investment Manager's Assistant. The first is designed to provide personal financial plans for people with incomes between $20,000 and $70,000. It is written in LISP and runs on a Symbolics 3600 machine in batch mode, with connections to databases on an IBM mainframe (Guilfoyle and Jeffcoate, 1987). Another well-known product in this category is Plan Power provided by Applied Expert Systems (APEX). This system provides the client with a comprehensive financial plan ranging from 20 to 120 pages, plus up to 40 tabular and graphic data exhibits. The system also creates an after-planning case representing the client's situation after all recommendations have been simulated on a XEROX LISP machine (see Stansfield and Greenfeld (1987) for more details).

12.4 Banks and financial institutions

12.4.1 Credit assessment

Credit may be obtained in a variety of different forms, covering consumer and business lending, as well as credit cards and leasing. Many types of credit are available. Here are a few examples:

- personal loan (secured or unsecured);
- banks' overdraft facilities;
- corporate loans;
- credit card and credit card applications.

As we can understand from the list, some of the demands are high-volume, small-ticket transactions such as credit card applications, while other types of credit may be demanded far less frequently. This will affect methods for credit assessment. Credit assessment involves predicting a client's or a corporation's, ability to service the debt taken on. This includes questions about solvency and profitability. Credit assessment means establishing credit-worthiness and repayment conditions on the basis of information about the client that is known at this moment, and predicting from this and other, more general, economic and market indicators, the future capability of the client to repay the debt.

The need for credit assessment has increased tremendously in the last decade or two, due to the deregulation in the financial sector in many countries. The supply and demand for credit has grown tremendously. Altogether, this has led to a level of credit in society which is higher than ever before. The ease with which credit has been made available has also led to over-consumption – people take on more credit than they can cope with. In many countries, credit institutions suffer from defaulters – people or companies who cannot fulfill their commitments. Bankruptcy is often the result, with heavy losses for the credit giver. Bad loans have been a real burden on the income statements of many commercial banks. Therefore, better procedures and better techniques for credit assessment are needed, and many developers of expert systems have seen a market for applications in this domain.

Obviously, credit assessment is needed at the time credit is asked for. However, credit assessment may also be pertinent in other situations as well. Screening the credit market for low-risk credit takers is one important task of most credit institutions. Searching actively for credit takers may involve running through computer files, for instance, on companies' annual financial statements, to find prospective borrowers. In this screening process, an expert system can greatly enhance the efficiency.

Also, credit institutions need to continuously monitor their credit takers. This can be done periodically, or for particular purposes when information on key variables change. For instance, changes in interest rates or new tax regulations that affect net income, may lead to problems for the credit takers. To sum up, credit assessment is needed:

- at the time of credit giving;
- in searching and screening for new clients;
- in monitoring clients' abilities to service the credit;

- in predicting clients' problems to meet their commitments due to environmental changes in key variables, for instance, interest rate.

Mottura (1988) has developed a conceptual model of the influencing factors on the loan portfolio quality of a credit institution (see Figure 12.2) from which he deduces a set of benefits of KB-DSS applied to credit evaluation and loan decisions.

Corporate loans

The two types of business lending mainly offered by commercial banks are overdraft lending and term lending. Overdraft lending is designed to meet

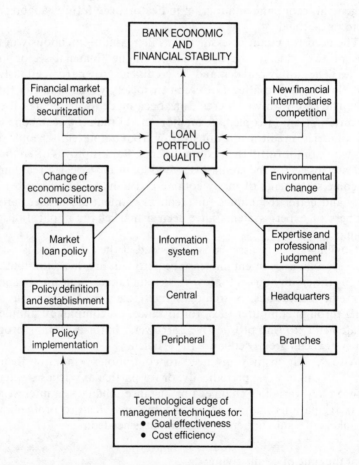

Figure 12.2   Influencing factors on loan portfolio quality. (Reproduced from Mottura P. (1988). *Problem-solving and Decision-making in Banks and the Opportunity of Knowledge Technology*.)

short-term working capital fluctuations. Term loans are usually unsecured and run for a period of three to ten years, depending on the situation. Credit assessment for overdrafts requires the analysis of the current position of the company, while for term loans the analysis of future positions is required.

In Section 6.6 we described an expert system for credit evaluation, called BANKER. Credit evaluation of corporate loans involves:

- financial analysis;
- management evaluation;
- market potential of the corporation;
- general economic outlook;
- benefits for the credit institution.

Financial analysis involves analysis on historical and forecasted data where the credit has been included (pro forma financial statements).

Originally, human experts assessed credit applications using a *judgmental* method based on their own experience (heuristics) and guidelines provided by the credit institution. Carter and Cartlett (1987) have described the following drawbacks of a judgmental method.

- poor performance,
- inflexibility,
- inconsistency,
- low efficiency.

Another method, credit scoring, is one of the widely-used assessment methods.

Do knowledge-based systems perform well in this domain? It is a domain which has attracted a lot of interest in the expert system field, and many systems exist to support credit assessment in part, or as a whole. The journal *Financial Management* has a special issue (Autumn 1988) that is devoted to financial applications of expert systems. Three of the articles in this issue describe loan evaluation systems (Duchessi *et al.* (1988), Shaw and Gentry (1988) and Srinivasan and Kim (1988)).

In Chapter 6, we described the loan evaluation system BANKER in detail. BANKER classifies a corporate loan applicant's creditworthiness. But many systems have been developed for financial analysis, as we have already seen in Section 12.2, that can assist a credit assessor. This is also an area in which many banks have been busy. Many prototypes exist and a few systems are in operation.

In France, knowledge-based systems for company loan evaluation offered by specialized software and consulting companies are competing aggressively on the banking industry market. Due to the deregulation of financial markets, certain bank networks such as the 'Caisses d'Epagne', which, previously, were not allowed to grant loans to companies, can now do so. Because of lack of expertise, they consider expert systems to be a way to save time in the education of their employees, and, also, to make the best use of experts that they had to hire at a very high cost from competing banks. For a middle-sized bank in France, that is, a bank with 50 to 60 branches, it is not unusual to find that more than ten of its branches are equipped with expert systems. Some have nearly all of their branches equipped.

Many banks are using such systems now on a regular basis: Credit Agricole de Toulouse since 1987, Credit Agricole of la Brie since 1988 and Credit Agricole of Midi since 1989. A market for financial analysis knowledge bases has now developed around products such as FINSIM. FINSIM is now in use in more than 60 financial institutions. Also, industry-specific loan evaluation systems have now appeared on the market. An example is a system used by the Credit Agricole to evaluate short- and long-term loans to farmers.

Interested readers can find a comparative study of several loan evaluation systems in Briys (1987).

Credit card authorization

American Express has developed the expert system Authorizer's Assistant in collaboration with Inference Corp, the supplier of the expert system development tool Art. This system supports the authorizer in making decisions on charges to a card holder's account. At American Express they have a policy of not placing a limit on the accounts as long as the card holders clear their accounts at the next billing cycle. However, this policy causes difficulties for the 300 credit authorizers who, from four different locations, may have to access up to 13 different databases in order to make credit authorization.

The authorizers' terminals communicate with an IBM mainframe. The expert system runs on a Symbolics machine which communicates with the IBM computer through a Sun workstation. The system went on line, on a trial basis, in January 1987. It is now reported to support 300 credit authorizers on a 24-hour basis. Tests from the trial period show an 11% better performance by the system over the credit authorizers, and it provides the correct decision in 96% of cases rather than 85% (Butler Cox, 1987).

An interesting approach to credit card assessment was taken by Carter and Cartlett (1987) at the University of Sydney. They used machine-learning techniques based on Quinlan's ID3 algorithm, which takes examples of good decisions from which it forms a general decision procedure.

12.4.2 Product advisers

With the growing number of products and services provided by banks and financial institutions today, there is a need for an advisory system to assist sales personnel with the characteristics of the products. In this section, we shall restrict the systems to those providing information about each product – a kind of product manual. There is a considerable overlap here with financial planning systems dealt with in Section 12.3 and even more with customer support systems which are described in Section 12.4.6.

The advantages offered by product advisers include:

- providing a consistent level of information for the customers;
- covering, in detail, the full range of products on offer;
- more effective maintenance of product information at the front line;
- providing training for the bank staff.

Several banks are developing product advisers on the basis of the expert system technology. In France, the first system appeared in 1985 at Credit Lyonnais (de Langle and Michel, 1985). Many banks are now using such systems to provide more expertise at the branch office level, for instance, Banque Populaire de Loraine (Chapuzot, 1987). Telebanking is another area where product advisers may be useful. Such systems may improve the level of service offered.

12.4.3 Assets management

Portfolio management

The management of investment portfolios in the form of stocks, bonds, mutual funds and so on, is a vital activity in banks and financial institutions. Given the typical magnitude of an institutional portfolio, the investment income of an institution is very sensitive to small improvements in their portfolios.

Portfolio management requires high professional financial and investment expertise. Today, the portfolio managers have access to more or less the same information networks and quantitative analytical techniques. Consequently, what distinguishes one portfolio manager from another is the judgment of economy and market developments, and the ability to couple this knowledge with quantitative analyses.

Given the current number of financial instruments, the number of possible portfolio mixes that can be composed is extremely large. To search for portfolio allocations that match the objectives and constraints of a fund manager is a laborious and time-consuming process, and a highly-skilled task. What complicates portfolio management is that the concern is with the distribution of the return on the portfolio. The characteristics of individual securities are important only in terms of their effect on the distribution of the portfolio return. There exists a highly normative theory on portfolio management which has its roots in Markowitz's (1952) research. This theory is based on probability distributions and that investors are risk averse. It is, however, advantageous to connect qualitative business knowledge to the probablistic models of portfolio theory. Therefore, several knowledge-based systems have been developed to assist in portfolio management.

For example, the Portfolio Management Advisor developed by the Athena Group in USA is an expert system of this type. It assists professional portfolio managers in construction and maintenance of investment portfolios. The system performs portfolio analysis by making use of specific investment information provided by the portfolio manager, and internal investment analysis and portfolio construction heuristics, along with rules for implementing modern portfolio theory both quantitatively and qualitatively. The system evaluates all potential equity investments and their combinations with regard to value, risk and the investment goals and constraints. This process is facilitated by analytical models. The expert system performs asset selection, asset allocation and portfolio construction.

Another security portfolio advisory system is Le Courtier developed by the US firm Cognitive Systems Inc. for Belgium's largest bank, the Generale de Banque. The purpose is to provide high-quality investment advice to customers of the bank. While the Athena Group's system was designed for fund managers, Le Courtier is designed to be used directly by the bank's customers. The system, which accepts both conversational French and English input, offers specific recommendations about stock purchases and portfolio distribution and also answers factual questions about the Belgian stock market. Le Courtier can give detailed investment advice only if it has a detailed financial profile of the customer. It gives the customer the option of completing a brief or an in-depth financial statement questionnaire, including current investments, assets and liabilities, and cash available for investment. From this information, Le Courtier may make stock portfolio recommendations or it may determine that the customer's assets are not large enough to warrant investments in the stock market. The customer may, however, override the system's recommendations.

Le Courtier differs from most other knowledge-based systems in the way it puts emphasis on natural language conversations and the combination of this with Videotex. There is a small step from using natural languages and Videotex to access a database to using the two facilities to access a knowledge base, and that is how Le Courtier was born. The database query system behaves intelligently by not only answering factual questions with facts, but may produce a recommendation along with the factual answer. For example, a customer may ask: 'Should I buy stocks in company A?' and the system may answer: 'Company A may not be a bad investment; however, company B would make a better investment.' (See Digital's management report *Europa* (June 1985) and also Turban (1989).)

12.4.4 Trading

The foreign exchange market is the largest financial market in the world. Approximately $150 billion in currency is traded daily on a world-wide basis. Therefore, the trading function has become a key discipline within many financial institutions. The world's financial markets have undergone a period of radical change. As the range of tools grows, the requirements for efficient information services and decision support systems have increased. An interesting presentation of trading DSS can be found in Peziers (1986). According to this, a DSS for trading should have the following features:

(1)   *Versatility of data acquisition.* The system must be trained to 'read' the required information from the information vendor. This process must be reliable and easily modifiable. Indeed there are very few, if any, constraints imposed on the formats used by information contributors and the contributors may decide to change the formats at almost any time.

(2)   *Possibility of respecifying static assumptions.* New tools are created every month; characteristics of old tools may change. Internal constraints (commission structure, taxes and so on) within user companies may need respecification. All these parameters must, therefore, be easily accessible and modifiable, otherwise, the software would become rapidly obsolete.

(3)   *Exploratory search.* A key advantage of using a DSS or a KB-DSS is to survey a large number of alternative strategies very quickly and identify among these the best strategies that meet various classes of objectives. Thus, a cash multi-currency arbitrage system should be capable of exploring hundreds of possible arbitrage loops in a few seconds and listing the most profitable arbitrages within a class of possible transactions.

(4)   *Dealing pad.* The prices supplied by vendors are for information only. They are not necessarily dealable prices or, at any rate, they may have to be adjusted by a particular user to reflect his or her own constraints. It should, therefore, be possible to override every item of information to reflect the specific circumstances of a deal.

(5)   *Cash flow – monitoring.* Many strategies will have consequences spread over time or will necessitate further transactions at some future date. A dealer needs to know how and when these transactions should be carried out, and when he or she will have a chance to review the situation in the future on the basis of the current information.

Here, we shall concentrate on areas where expert systems can be applied. Front office, back office and some support functions are all potential targets, but the prospect of artificial intelligent systems advising, or in the extreme cases, performing the trading function, is the one that has aroused most speculation (Guilfoyle, 1988). Such artificial intelligent systems would be high risk, and highly visible within the company. Large profits may be made by even a marginal improvement on the success ratio of trading transactions.

Buy and sell decisions

Price forecasting is a major, but difficult task in all trading decisions. Statistical methods have failed to provide accurate price forecasts for securities. Two principal methods are used for buy and sell decisions. They are known as fundamental analysis and technical analysis.

Fundamental analysis is made on the fundamental data of a security. For a stock, for instance, this data may include evaluations of management, product range, sales prospects, financial conditions, industry data and so on.

Technical analysis is a different way of arriving at the same result; a buy and sell signal. The assumption here is that the underlying determinants of security prices are so complicated that the best prediction of market behavior is made by empirically observing the macro behavior of the price curve, or the price action as it also is called, and other indicators.

According to Graham (1987), there are four ways in which artificial intelligence techniques can be brought to bear on technical analysis:

(1)   To permit the effects of a combination of different, recognizable, buy and sell indicators to be analysed.

(2)   To allow the incorporation of non-numerical, subjective or fuzzy factors.

(3)   To carry out pattern matching on price action, or point and figure charts, comparing areas of the charts with prestored templates for recognizable patterns such as head and shoulders, double bottom, flag, pennant and so on.

(4)   To use data on prices and actual deals performed over a period of time to generate optimal trading rules, using some rule induction techniques.

Several systems exist in front office trading.

The Equity Trader from Arthur D. Little is designed to assist security traders by monitoring the state of the stock-market, analysing when a trader should buy or sell, detecting orders which can be carried out without risk, and selecting a broker for a particular transaction. This system had not, apparently, proceeded beyond the prototype stage by May 1987 (Guilfoyle, 1988). A fully-developed system will accept information from on-line sources such as Reuters and Stock Exchange Automatic Quotation system.

The IF-FX (Intelligent Forecaster-Foreign Exchange) from Data Logic in Great Britain provides advice on the sterling/dollar market in the form of buy/sell recommendations based on chart forecasting techniques. The system runs on an IBM mainframe in a service bureau and is available to clients on a PC in their local environment. The system will be extended to other currencies, and to incorporate information from the New York and Tokyo markets.

Many banks and financial institutions have been active in this field. Lehman Brothers is a huge American investment bank which transacts about $15 million worth of fees for interest rate swaps on behalf of its clients. The Lehman Brothers' system, called K:Base, assists in finding the most likely candidate for the other side of the proposed swap. The system runs on IBM PCs which can be optionally connected to a Symbolics machine. Data on actual swaps is entered and the system induces decision rules which are used to query the brokers about new applications for swaps.

Option trading

Options are contracts whose values are contingent upon the values of the underlying assets. Options can be traded for a number of reasons, two of which are speculation and hedging. Speculation occurs when one has confidence in either a rise or fall in an asset's value. Hedging occurs when trading or production activity forces the holding of futures of uncertain value. Options can be used to reduce market risks. Option trading is an interesting domain for expert system applications because traders use heuristics and special techniques widely, basing their theories on many assumptions. Furthermore, complex trading strategies are involved, and the uncertainty of future market prices presents many possibilities for large portfolios.

Graham (1987) describes an option strategy selection system for options on currency futures. It takes, as inputs user opinions on trends in the dollar and the cross rates, volatility and costs. It picks a suitable strategy and optimizes its profile in terms of strike prices, deltas and so on.

The Foreign Exchange Advisory System from the Athena group provides advice for both the initial development of a strategy in foreign currency option trading, as well as suggestions for future modifications to the option strategy as a result of currency price movements in the market-place. The system provides recommendations for a foreign currency option trading strategy based upon market outlook, expected price movements, price volatility and the investor's risk profile. It gives the following advice:

• suggested option pricing;

- selection of optimal option contract type (call and put), and option contract combination strategies (spread and so on);
- strategy choice;
- follow-up strategies based upon price movements.

The future dealing room

Graham (1987) envisages the dealing room of the 1990s. Dealer workstations are networked to information feeds and demon-driven filters. On the network there are expert systems of the types described above. These are controlled by a blackboard system which throws up advice on the dealer screens, alongside price services and price change warnings.

A blackboard system imitates a group of highly-specialized experts sitting around a blackboard in order to solve a problem. When an expert sees that he or she can contribute a new fact, for instance, to confirm or refute an hypothesis already on the board, or to add a new one. The evidence will now be available to the other experts. In this context, our experts are represented by a technical analysis system, a fundamental analysis system, an option strategy adviser and so on. Common storage, as the blackboard and the agenda, is under the control of a specialized inference program.

Furthermore, the systems are demon-driven. The most noticeable thing about a modern trading room is the large number of screens on the dealing desks. Expert systems with 'demons' can reduce the number of screens by having a ready application in the background that can make analysis of price movements, identify significant changes, direct the trader's attention to a particular information entity, and suggest an improved trading strategy.

Back office systems

So far most attention has been focused on front office applications. Expert systems may be employed also to back office functions of trading. Such applications include (Guilfoyle, 1988):

- processing of trades;
- difference research;
- margin questions;
- dividend and interest questions;
- auditing transactions;
- compliance to internal and external regulations;
- monitoring for fraud (insider trading).

12.4.5 Bank management

Bank sheet evaluation

The banking industry has, in most countries, been a regulated activity (limitations to credit authorization, decisions on interest rates, control of international operations and so on). During the 1970s this industry experienced a substantial change in competitive conditions as a result of a deregulation movement, that first started in the USA, then moved to Great Britain, and later spread to most European countries. As a consequence, new capital markets opened which changed the traditional patterns of funding for both banks and corporations. Large percentages of bank deposits were now provided from other banks via the interbank market. Banking authorities had to define liquidity ratios, such as Cooke's ratio and structure ratio, in order to limit risk. The European Commission has defined rules for competition within the unified European Common Community of 1992. For example, a new set of liquidity and structure ratios have been used since 1988 to measure the capacity of banks to cope with large withdrawals made by their clients.

Several French banks have, as a consequence, developed KB-DSS to follow the evolution of these ratios, obtaining diagnoses and suggestions for actions. By the means of a data communication function of the KB-DSS, the account balance from the general ledger is transferred to the workstation on which the knowledge bases are located. The data reader of the KB-DSS is used to aggregate and sort the accounts of the general ledger. These aggregated data are downloaded to the database of the KB-DSS. A model computes a series of ratios which are presented to the financial manager in tabular or graphical forms. The expert module can be used to obtain, automatically, a diagnosis on the bank's liquidity risk. A simulation model can be used to test possible actions suggested by the expert module or the financial manager himself. This system was developed by the company SIG for Caisses de Credit Agricole using the OPTRANS KB-DSS generator.

Global analysis of bank risk

The system described above was implemented to follow and, also, control the liquidity of the bank. In fact, many other operations that create a risk for the bank exist: the exchange rate risk, the base rate risk and so on. The Compagnie Bancaire in France, through its subsidiary STS, has developed a DSS to analyse these kinds of risks. The structure of this system is shown in Figure 12.3.

The basic data used are found in the balance sheet of the bank. These data have to be sorted and aggregated by financial assets and by maturity dates to obtain the global risk. This system simulates operations on financial

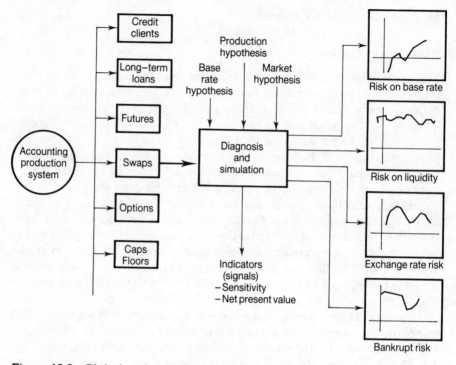

Figure 12.3   Global analysis of bank risk.

markets and computes risk indicators for all balance sheet items. Thus, the management obtains a picture of the risk facing the bank, as well as a simulation tool to define its strategy taking into account:

- the sensitivity of the net present value to changes in base rate;
- forecasts of commercial activities;
- changes in the base rate and so on.

Other systems have been developed to help financial institutions to make better decisions on the interest rate mixes which they offer to savers and borrowers in a highly competitive market. Singh and Cook (1988) describe a hybrid KB-DSS which they have developed to help retail banks to determine optimal interest rates in a competitive environment. Interest rates are determined for both savings and lending products by using a knowledge base comprising the expert knowledge of a number of managers, combined with historical information and market research information.

Management control of branches

One of the main tasks of control in a bank is to follow the activity of each branch. A DSS has been implemented in a medium-sized French bank (50 branches). The system gives access to a database of the balance sheet of each branch. These data are automatically transferred every month from the accounting system. A model is available which enables each branch manager to simulate the balance sheet and income statement. The simulation takes into account a forecast of the commercial activity, as well as the base rate, the margins on different operations and so on. Rates and margins are common for all branches. The controller at headquarters can browse through the database to follow indicators by branch, as well as to consolidate all the branches to obtain an overall picture. The system has, recently, been extended using an expert system module to automatically display messages when certain ratios are not verified.

Compliance and security

Compliance
Along with the tremendous growth and globalization of the financial markets, several incidents have occurred on the exchanges that have raised the issue of better surveillance and compliance. October 19, 1987, or Black Monday, and insider trading scandals on the stock-markets have triggered several studies in this area.

From October 1988, financial institutions in the United Kingdom have been legally required to ensure that their employees comply with good professional practice. The purpose of this legislation is to ensure that rules which constitute this practice are really adhered to. This means that institutions will need to monitor all business transactions made by their employees. The National Westminster Investment Bank in London is developing an automatic monitoring system using an expert system development tool called Vanilla Flavor. The details of the transactions executed by each salesman or trader are matched against a set of rules, and any breaches are brought to the attention of the compliance officer, who can then examine the records in more detail (Butler Cox, 1987).

Nixdorf has developed a system of 700 rules which advises on the import/export restriction on currency. There are 684 paragraphs covering the relevant information, yet the system can access the information required in 30 seconds. This system uses Nixdorf's expert system shell Twaice (Guilfoyle, 1988).

Also, in other countries compliance systems can be found. Banque National de Paris has built a prototype application on the rules governing foreign exchange transactions. Credit Suisse has a prototype system developed for the Swiss brokerage rules covering the commission a broker may charge, together with their own in-house rules.

The national and international laws which govern taxation, brokerage commission and foreign exchange are rule-based systems that lend themselves to the application of the expert system technology. Such systems apply to large groups of institutions. They may be supplemented by knowledge bases that cover the internal and specific rules of an institution.

Security

Most banks and financial institutions experience losses due to intentional fraud. A distinction can be made between *internal* fraud and *external* fraud. Internal fraud refers to fraud committed by the institution's own personnel. External fraud includes bad cheques, credit card fraud, automatic teller machine-related crime, and frauds on wire transfers and loans.

Security Pacific National Bank in Los Angeles has built a fraud detection system for its bank card department. More specifically, the system deals with the problem of fraudulent use of the automated teller machine debit cards. The expert system is linked to two IMS databases residing on two different IBM mainframes. The result is an on-line bank card fraud detection system, which has been in operation since April 1988. The main advantage of the fraud detection system is that the knowledge and experience of the senior fraud investigators are made available on-line to everybody who needs it. It can analyse large amounts of financial and criminal information to prevent fraud, can detect patterns in historical transaction data to detect existing fraud activities, and can explain its decisions to the user (Lecot, 1988).

TRW Information Services has developed Discovery, an expert system to search for recurrent patterns in inquiry data and compare these patterns to daily inquiry activities to detect variances in normal user behavior. Discovery is an attempt to integrate expert system and decision support system features to provide pattern recognition, self-learning capability, and interactive features to detect unsuspected violations. TRW's goal is to review all daily inquiry activities and detect those inquiries made by potentially unauthorized individuals. The system processes 400 000 inquiries per day. A prototype was initially developed for an IBM PC-XT, but is now converted to a COBOL application on an IBM mainframe (Tener, 1988).

12.4.6 Customer support

Banks' information systems are, traditionally, very production-oriented. They are centered around accounts or other entities which comprise the products. Information about markets in general, and customers in particular, are attributes of these accounts more than information objects in themselves.

The volatile financial markets are about to change this situation. What is needed to sell an array of financial services effectively to an increasing discerning client is an understanding of the client's full financial situation.

An approach to customer relationship management has been outlined by Alan Bond of the Santa Monica based firm Expert Software. He believes that the relationship between a financial institution and each individual customer can be modeled. It consists of five types of information:

(1)   the expectations and commitments agreed between the parties;

(2)   the goals of both parties;

(3)   the preferences of each party;

(4)   the policies which are agreed between the parties for normal situations;

(5)   the history of the relationship.

This knowledge forms the basis for three types of expert systems: a product salesman, a financial adviser and a service monitor.

Another system is APEX Client Profiling from Applied Expert Systems in Cambridge, MA. It provides salesmen in the field with the expertise and analytical skills needed to sell an expanding mix of financial products effectively and uses expert systems technology to develop financial strategies for the clients. With the system, financial services firms can:

- understand client needs and match specific product offerings to those needs;
- provide tangible value to clients by offering advice that addresses their expressed needs;
- gather client information to improve customer targeting and product development.

The APEX Client Profiling system analyses information regarding the customer's current financial profile – income, assets, and liabilities, in the context of his or her expressed priorities and attitudes. The system includes both a knowledge base and a product base.

12.4.7 Text interpretation

Many applications in banks involve the handling of large numbers of items of text by clerks. These items have to be identified, read and interpreted. The advantages of applying expert systems technology to these tasks are:

- consistency across the organization;

- reduction in staff costs;
- reformation of messages for input to other data processing systems.

Many banks already have systems to handle telex messages. Chase Manhattan has a prototype system using natural language and expert system technology to read telex messages concerning the transfer of funds, analysing its content and routing it to the appropriate department.

The processing of letters of credit is a competitive international banking function. This seems to be a target area of several banks. The expertise exists in the letter of credit examiner. Therefore, systems for efficient processing of the voluminous documentation which, typically, accompanies a letter of credit application are being developed using the expert system technology.

Also, several systems are being developed based on natural language processing.

Exercises

12.1   What are the judgmental factors involved in capital budgeting and investment analysis? How can knowledge bases be embedded in a KB-DSS using discounted cash flow analysis as the basic tool?

12.2   What can a knowledge-based financial statement analyser give in terms of added values compared to a numeric ratio calculation system?

12.3   Describe the steps required to perform a financial analysis of a company on the basis of available financial statements from an acquisition point of view.

12.4   What are the main parts and functions that a personal financial planning system should have?

12.5   When loan officers, credit analysts, and loan review committees evaluate a commercial loan application, they combine financial projections with qualitative information.

(a)   What kind of financial projections are made and on what kind of data are they based?

(b)   What kind of qualitative data are used?

(c)   How are the qualitative information combined with the financial projections to give a final credit assessment?

12.6   Compare the following three systems for business loan evaluation:

(a)   CLASS (Duchessi *et al.*, 1988);

(b)   MARBLE (Shaw and Gentry, 1988);

(c)   BANKER (Chapter 6).

Describe the similarities and differences between the features of the knowledge bases of these three systems.

12.7   How can artificial intelligence techniques be used in technical analysis for buy and sell decisions of securities?

12.8   Why is option trading an interesting domain for expert system application?

12.9   Name an expert system for foreign currency option trading. Present the main functions of this system.

12.10   Give an example of a financial problem domain where a real-time expert system is appropriate.

12.11   Discuss the problems of compliance in the financial services sector, and give examples of compliance systems.

12.12   Discuss the content of a customer support system for a bank.

12.13   A common finding in many surveys of financial management practice has been that the real-world usage of normative financial models is infrequent. It is widely recognized that this phenomenon is related to the complexity of the decision environment presented in normative models, the lack of attention to such critical details as the availability of necessary information and the difficulty of usage.

Discuss the constraints of normative models and how DSS and expert systems can overcome some of these constraints.

12.14   Develop a knowledge base for one of the following problems by interviewing an expert in the field and/or reading an article on the topic in a practice-oriented finance magazine:

(a)   Financial statements analysis of a bank or an insurance company.

(b)   Corporate credit management.

(c)   Cash management.

(d) Assets and liabilities management.

(e) Financial restructuring of a company.

(f) Foreign exchange risk exposure for a company dealing with international business.

13

Developments and Research in Knowledge-based Decision Support Systems

13.1 Introduction

The integration of the DSS technology with expert systems, and AI technologies in general, is a recent phenomenon. Papers about a coherent knowledge-based framework for DSS were presented and discussed at the NATO Advanced Study Institute on DSS in Maratea, Italy in 1985 (the proceedings are edited by Holsapple and Whinston (1987)). In fact, two papers were presented at this conference which described the architecture of two KB-DSS development tools: Guru and OPTRANS-EXPERT, both of which were released as commercial products shortly afterwards. At the EURO VIII Congress in Lisbon in 1986, a special session on DSS and expert systems debated the integration of DSS, expert systems and OR models. Other research, along the same lines, is the work by DSS researchers on model management systems starting at the beginning of the 1980s, and more recently, the work on intelligent decision systems. We shall return to these issues in Section 13.3.

Another line of development has been the integration of logic in database management systems. The conference on expert database systems in 1986 (Kerchberg, 1986) clearly addresses one of the fundamental problems of the KB-DSS framework: the integration of databases and expert systems. However, the perspective of this conference was not decision making and decision support.

In June 1986, a conference on multi-attribute decision making via OR based expert systems was organized at the University of Passau, Italy. Several papers presented at this conference addressed the problem of integrating AI and DSS (see for instance, Jarke and Radermacher (1988), Keeney (1988), Beulens and van Neurer (1988), and Richter (1988)). These

489

(December 1988) papers were published in a special issue of the *DSS International Journal* under the title of 'Design Issues of Advanced DSS'. In the introduction to this volume, the guest editors develop arguments in favor of the integration of classical DSSs and AI tools, and AI decision analysis methodology, to build enhanced DSSs.

Research and development in KB-DSS is a highly interdisciplinary field, since it draws on research from a range of contributing disciplines, both basic scientific disciplines, as we have seen in Chapter 1, but, also, from other areas of information systems. We do not attempt here even to summarize all of the research and development that will influence the application, design and technology of KB-DSS. However, we shall look at some improvements of the KB-DSS technology that we may expect in the coming years from what we know of the existing state-of-the-art technologies of the various components that make up a comprehensive KB-DSS development tool (as we have defined it in Chapter 7). We shall also look at what we may expect of new software development environments that not only take advantage of the new capabilities of the components, but also integrate these into a coherent and easy to use tool. Finally, as the applications of the expert systems mature, new operating environments are needed, in particular, environments where resources are distributed over several computer systems. All of the directions in improvements that we have indicated above require more demanding algorithms; as a consequence, faster machines and larger memory capacities are needed. For example, the trend in favour of graphical representations of objects and interactive manipulation of these objects requires considerable central memory capacity. From these developments we try to make a specification of what we see as the second generation of a KB-DSS development tool.

With respect to research issues it is not possible to make a comprehensive review in this broad field. We shall outline a framework for research and then select four issues which we deal with in more detail. Extensive references, however, should help the reader to find literature for further studies on the topics mentioned.

13.2 Developments in the KB-DSS technology

13.2.1 Improvements of components

The present KB-DSS development tools integrate components which do not take advantage of the state-of-the-art technology in each component area. A new generation of development tools will emerge as the component technologies are updated. We shall now describe what we can expect of improvements in each component in the near future.

Databases

As we have seen in Chapter 5, most of the DBMS components included in today's business orientated DSS and KB-DSS are of the multi-dimensional type. The multi-dimensional type of DBMS provides, in certain situations, an easier way to deal with data structures as they are perceived by the user: lists, vectors and so on.

It is true that for management control and most financial and marketing problems the multi-dimensional data model (or the relational data model) is well adapted.

Two extensions to the currently-applied database technology in DSS that could be useful are:

- Pictorial images

- Deductive databases.

Pictorial images

Pictorial images are extremely useful in many applications: we already know of expert systems that advise on routes for a walk in a park. Such systems mix logical reasoning with the display of images (scenery and so on), or with maps. Some examples may illustrate the use of images in KB-DSS.

In a travel agency, a KB-DSS for supporting the selection of holiday destinations would be much enhanced if the user could be given the opportunity to see objects and maps of the places which are suggested as vacation destinations. Images can be displayed as the conversation between the travel agent and the client proceeds, where information about budget constraints, number of people travelling, composition of the party, preferences for locations (seaside, countryside or a mountain area) and types of activities are exchanged. An image processing KB-DSS can display information in much the same way as we find in the colourful catalogs in travel agencies today, with the important difference that the system will help the agency to elicit preferences and guide in selecting an appropriate goal.

In a real estate agency, an expert system for selecting housing, a flat or a house should be able to display plans and pictures as the selection process progresses, to support the interaction with the client.

A KB-DSS for supporting a field engineer in charge of maintenance should be able to provide diagrams or plans of parts of the equipment.

Images are graphical objects without an explicit representation structure. They are represented as matrices which describe the pixels of a certain part of the screen. To implement image processing, the pixel matrices will be stored in the database in a condensed way. Once the format of the stored data is known, it is possible to reconstruct the pixel matrices and, at the same time, transform them into forms that are appropriate for the graphics device used.

Deductive database systems

Deductive database systems are database systems with enhanced inference capabilities. Inference capabilities require a knowledge base and an inference mechanism, that is, a knowledge-based system. A typical knowledge-based system has few facts and many rules. Its knowledge base and working memory reside in main memory during reasoning. A typical database system has no rules, but many facts. These facts reside in secondary storage. In a database system, facts are retrieved or derived by a data manipulation language. In knowledge-based systems, facts are deduced by logic reasoning, a recursive process which is done by chaining in rulebased systems. Deductive database systems are, typically, built around relational database systems and logic systems.

Relational databases consist of two parts: stored relations, and data retrieval statements (for instance, written in a query language like SQL). The drawbacks of relational database systems are, firstly that the logic that can be applied is very limited, and secondly, that they can not perform recursions because they do not accommodate rules.

Deductive databases transform tuples in a relational database into facts represented as propositions in the knowledge base. By introducing rules and an inference mechanism, more complex facts can be *derived* from the stored relations.

There are two basic approaches to the design of deductive database systems (Missikoff and Widerhold, 1984). The **homogeneous** approach uses a single integrated system to manage the database, to perform fact retrieval by means of data retrieval statements, and to make inferences on the stored or retrieved facts. The **heterogeneous** approach uses a separate system to manage the relational database and another system, an inference system, to perform deductive reasoning based on retrieved facts.

In the homogeneous approach, the inference system is enhanced with data management functions. These functions manage data that is residing on external storage. Therefore, facts stored in external storage can be accessed from the inference system when needed.

The heterogeneous approach uses two separately-developed technologies, inferencing systems and database management systems, in constructing deductive database systems. The advantage of this approach is obvious. Existing DBMS and databases can be used as subsystems in a deductive database system. However, an interface allowing interaction between the two subsystems must be built.

The various architectures, tools, and techniques used to build deductive database systems draw upon aspects of knowledge-based systems and database management. Logic programming using PROLOG combined with the relational database systems SQL, is one approach. The result is known as PROSQL (Chang and Walker, 1984). Also combining production systems and relational database systems has been done. One example is RPL (the Relational Production Language). Expert systems written in RPL have direct access to conventional databases because RPL relies on a relational query language to express rules (Delcambre, 1988).

Deductive database systems make inferencing possible on large amounts of data that are currently stored in conventional databases and that, until now, have been relatively inaccessible to expert systems.

Decision modeling languages

Present modeling languages are efficient for definition of standard financial and economic relationships. However, equational knowledge (representing knowledge by sets of equations, or relations and constraints) is not the only way to represent task structure knowledge. Decision trees and influence diagrams (introduced in Chapter 3) are useful tools with which to represent causal relationships and should be made available in the modeling component of the KB-DSS. Some of the most obvious improvements in the modeling component seem to be:

Model building aids

The use of AI technology and expert systems to provide methodological knowledge in model building is an emerging issue. The user may interact with the methodology knowledge base to analyse and model a decision. A specific line of research started in the beginning of the 1980s in the DSS field addressing this issue is called **model management**. We shall return to this issue in Section 13.3.

An approach to decision modeling which has proved to be useful in domains characterized by great uncertainty and large consequences, is the decision analysis methodology presented in Chapter 3. This approach is based on formal decision theory and has a firm methodological basis. However, to apply decision analysis requires both time and skill. To make this methodology available for a user, a knowledge-based modeling environment has to be created. This modeling environment should support the decision analysis cycle: deterministic phase, probabilistic phase and informational phase. In agreement with this goal the decision maker should be able to find commands and corresponding procedures to:

- Generate automatic sensitivity analysis for system and decision variables.
- Encode: time preference model, multi-attribute preferences, uncertainty on stochastic variables and risk preferences.
- Compute lotteries and their certain equivalents.
- Measure stochastic sensitivity.
- Measure risk sensitivity.
- Measure economic sensitivity.

These possibilities could be introduced within a standard financial modeling language. Implementing the decision analysis approach enables us to perform **user modeling**, an aspect which is normally not found in traditional KB-DSS. They could also be introduced to support an influence diagram modeling system.

An interesting line of research is the development of knowledge-based decision analysis systems, by Holtzman (1989) called intelligent decision systems. We shall return to this concept in Section 13.3.

Equation reasoning
Traditional DSS have, to a large extent, been applied to domains that can be modeled by systems of simple arithmetic relationships such as finance, control and marketing. These relationships, formulated as equations, represent the structure of the domain. Values of dependent variables are computed from definitional and causal relationships. Expert systems, on the other hand, reason with domain knowledge represented as heuristic rules. The problem with a rule-based system is to make the rule set complete and general enough to handle all situations that may be encountered. Attempts at addressing this shortcoming, have resulted in systems that integrate numerical models of a problem with appropriate heuristic models.

Apté and Hong (1988) describe a general mechanism for the qualitative interpretation of simple arithmetic relations. This mechanism is based on equations and rules. The central component is an Equation Base (EB) where all equations are stored in an unfocused form $(x + y + z = 0)$. The equation base is interrogated by the Equation Reasoner (ER) which has general (domain-independent) qualitative knowledge (rules) about the most common arithmetic operations (addition, subtraction and so on). In a domain-Specific Knowledge base (SK) the current status of the variables are stored. By means of the general knowledge in ER, and the domain knowledge in SK, a problem solver can reason qualitatively with arithmetic equations.

Qualitative reasoning can be very useful while performing financial planning and analysis. Suppose a financial planner of a corporation requires an answer to the problem: If the corporation's concern is its earning per share ratio, what criteria should be used for ranking analyses of several financing alternatives? This query is passed on to the ER. Earning per share will be identified as the focused variable with the constraint 'increase'. ER will attempt to solve the earning per share ratio after having found the relevant equation in the EB and turned it into a focused form:

$$\text{Earning per share} = \frac{\text{Operating income} - \text{Taxes} - \text{Profit/loss impact}}{\text{Total shares}}$$

By applying a particular strategy, ER will deduce a constraint on profit/loss impact to be 'decrease'. When passed back to the problem solver this can infer: If earning per share is of concern, rank alternatives by profit/ loss impact.

The work of Apté and Hong is particularly devoted to domains of simple arithmetic. Research on qualitative reasoning with causal models requiring more complex mathematical representations can be found in a special issue of *Artificial Intelligence*, **24**(1–3).

Decision trees and influence diagram compilers
The best-known decision modeling tool for analysing decisions under uncertainty is the decision tree. Computer programs to describe and evaluate decision trees have been presented in Chapter 3. However, no such program has, to our knowledge, been combined with an equation modeling language and embedded in a DSS to support, in a better way, both the formulation of the decision problem and the calculations necessary for the evaluation of certain parameters of the decision tree.

Influence diagrams are a generalization of decision trees which have been shown, empirically, to have considerable intuitive appeal for a wide class of decision makers, and which are a powerful communication tool for the participants in the decision process. Influence diagrams are acyclic, directed graphs representing the probabilistic, logical and informational relationships between variables in a decision model. As we have seen in Chapter 3, an influence diagram can be used to obtain optimal solutions. The possibility of formulating a problem under the form of an influence diagram and then switching to an equation mode to compute parameter values should be extremely useful in a KB-DSS environment.

Report generation

A first, natural, extension of a report generator is the development of a 'hypertext', including images, graphics and maps. This evolution will follow as soon as images can also be stored in the database (for example in a video disc sub-unit).

Present day report generators included in KB-DSS do not yet even offer the facilities of current modern text processing software (use of various character fonts, sizes and so on). The report description languages used do not allow the user to define the report directly on the screen, as in a standard wordprocessing package.

The present dominating philosophy in KB-DSS is that there is no need to provide sophisticated presentation or text processing. If a user wishes to generate a document of publishable quality then the table of results, graphics or so on, must be transferred to a file which can be further processed by a text processing package.

The integration of the two technologies into one environment would simplify the task of a decision maker who wants to provide a top quality report to justify and explain a decision.

Graphics

Business applications, and financial applications in particular, use rather simple graphics. However, maps can be very useful in certain circumstances when the financial model relies on marketing or logistical types of information. One important development is certainly going to be the capability to input a map easily, using a scanner, display the map, and connect it with data in the database. A graphic component also improves the presentation of inferential knowledge. Certain expert systems, for instance Nexpert, include graphical presentations of the inference network of rules. A DSS product such as Javelin includes a 'diagram' mode which produces a graphical presentation of relationships among variables, as represented by the equations of a model.

Improvements in the graphics component should take advantage of the more advanced graphical processing facilities found in the computer-aided design area. The graphic system should preferably be object oriented, so that objects for different applications can be easily added. Graphical objects must be identified by names which can be indexed. The following procedures should be provided:

- the support of the generation and modification of symbols of an object class;
- the management of a symbol library;
- the support of the construction of more complex objects.

There is a very close connection between the graphics component and the user interface (see Chapter 7).

Inference engine

The inference engine of a KB-DSS may be given improved inferencing capabilities to deal, in a better way, with uncertainty, non-monotonicity and negations and time. Furthermore, the inference engine may be improved with respect to learning and explanation capabilities.

Uncertainty
Several expert systems allow for multiple approaches to dealing with uncertainty. The expert system shell Leonardo from Creative Logic in the UK provides both the fuzzy set approach as well as the probability approach. The KB-DSS developing tool Guru allows several algebraic methods for dealing with uncertainty coefficients.

In the next generation of KB-DSS we may allow for several measures of uncertainty, numeric as well as non-numeric measures. In domains where the result is, at least, potentially verifiable we should use probabilities, or uncertainty coefficients that can be given a probabilistic interpretation. We could argue that most problems in finance and management control fall into this category. However, contexts in which there is 'uncertainty' concerning apparently non-verifiable statements occur frequently in AI. One type of 'uncertainty' here is impreciseness, this is illustrated by the sentence 'Mary is fairly tall'. The fuzzy set approach is often argued to be appropriate in assessing the degree to which a particular case in hand fulfills a loosely defined concept. Reasonableness is another kind of 'uncertainty', for instance, to what extent is a recommended action or conclusion reasonable. In such a case, the theory of endorsement is better suited.

For further reading on this topic, the reader is referred to the book *Uncertainty in Artificial Intelligence*, edited by Kanal and Lemmer (1986).

Non-monotonic reasoning and negation

Most of the recent research in the domain of problem solving has been restricted to systems based on logic, or, more specifically, first order predicate calculus.

Classical symbol logic lacks the tools for describing how to revise a formal theory to deal with inconsistencies caused by new information. In the world of first order predicate calculus, if we have evidence that a variable may have more than one possible value then, by some method, the contradiction must be resolved immediately and some assumption must be made to assign a value to the variable. Researchers in AI have been led to formalize systems where, as new information arises, the description of the world has to be updated and, in particular, contradictory beliefs have to be resolved. In the light of new information, if a contradiction develops, the assumptions are revised so that the consistency of the system is restored.

Inference systems allowing the withdrawals of assumptions, or the absence of knowledge, are called non-monotonic. These systems attempt to simulate the kind of reasoning in which former conclusions are re-evaluated in the light of newly acquired information. Non-monotonic logic provides a theoretical framework for updating descriptions of the world. There are several attempts to extend standard logic in order to incorporate non-monotonicity.

Few inference mechanisms are able to simulate this kind of reasoning which is, nonetheless, fundamental in management. Studies have been made by McDermott and Doyle (1980) and by McDermott (1982), this approach is known as the 'Modal Approach'. Default logic, as presented in Reiter (1978), is an attempt to model the use of general rules subject to exceptions. Default reasoning is possible in OPTRANS by the use of the redirection rule.

The treatment of negation is a complex problem. In automatic theorem proving, treatment of negation may result in combinatorial explosion. Usually, a negative answer is the result because of failure to demonstrate (negation as failure). In order to derive a negative answer within HORN clause-based logic, special rules are needed. The most popular of these special rules is called the closed world assumption introduced by Reiter (1978). This can be written: if $P \rightarrow Q$ and we have non-Q then we have non-P. The closed world assumption is an example of a non-monotonic inference rule.

Time representation

Time representation is a crucial aspect of many reasoning systems. Most DSS have a time dimension at the database level. In DSS many variables are time-tagged by a time variable, t. Also, it is important to be able to tell the system that a given relation is true for certain time periods or dates.

There are, basically, two approaches for handling time in logic. One is to add a time index to each predicate of the language. The other is to use temporal connectives in order to describe behaviour in time. The two approaches can be combined, for example, in a formula like: $P(R(x,y))$ (t) which should be read: in the past at time $t, R(x,y)$ was true. This is very useful in systems having built in time dimension with a calendar, as is the case in the OPTRANS database subsystem.

Some expert system shells, have a real-time capability. This capability is, clearly, fundamental when decisions have to be taken in a real-time context (trade rooms, arms systems, production control and so on).

The extension of the inferencing mechanism to handle real-time situations still have to be implemented in most KB-DSS development environments.

Explanation

The quality of explanations in expert systems can, and should still be, much improved. We have given in Chapters 6 and 7, examples of explanations provided by OPTRANS EXPERT which can be compared to a TRACE of the work of the inference engine. As can be seen, the indentation represents the different levels of explanation. The objective in this area is to obtain more concise and easier to understand explanations for the users than of the TRACE explanation kind. A review of explanation methods in expert systems can be found in Safar (1986).

Learning

When a KB-DSS is working in an environment where there is a regular updating of information then learning mechanisms may be useful. The new information may come from the database component of the system, or from the user or the expert. The toolbox of the system may include statistical learning procedures such as those which can be found in short-term forecasting algorithms. Large financial or marketing databases with frequent updating are examples of domains of application where learning can be important in management.

Knowledge base management

Hybrid systems
Several expert system shells now offer two knowledge representation methods, so-called hybrid systems. Examples are Nexpert (rules and objects), KEE (rules and frames), Art (rules and frames), and Kool, from the French company Bull, which is the result of an Esprit project (mixes rules, frames and objects).

To our knowledge, no KB-DSS presently integrates a knowledge management system supporting several knowledge representation methods at the expert module level. It is desirable to see such a development in order to be able to deal in a better way with problems in highly structured domains, such as, for instance, production.

Knowledge base verification
The problem of testing consistency and completeness in knowledge bases was discussed in Chapter 10. Many aspects of this problem are still research problems, in particular, if the rules are assigned uncertainty coefficients. Consistency and completeness verification algorithms should be added to the management functions of knowledge bases.

Man–machine interaction

There are several lines of development in the man–machine interface area that we expect to see implemented in KB-DSS in the near future. However, some of these features require more powerful end-user equipment – workstations. Some of the features we see are:

- better presentation management;
- multi-tasking;
- natural language interfaces;
- intelligent user assistance;
- contextual fit between users' views and the technology.

Assisting the user in the choice of an appropriate problem solving approach, model-building and other methodological knowledge will be dealt with in Section 13.3 under the headings of model management systems, and intelligent decision systems.

Let us now look at the features listed above in more detail.

Presentation management
Future workstations must integrate all needs of the end-user and, at the same time, be easy to use and to learn. The man–machine interface must be designed to fit the way that office workers think and act. We already have an idea of what a good man–machine interface should look like with the Apple

Macintosh personal computer, which arose at the end of a long line of research and development that began in Xerox Corporation's Palo Alto Research Centre in the 1970s. Also, developments in the more expensive workstations, such as SUN and Apollo, give good indications of the direction that we will be moving in, and, also, in end-user support for decision making.

The Macintosh's special interface features can be summarized as windows, icons, mouse, and pull-down menus. Apple user interface guidelines for the Macintosh (from Gunton, 1989) explain the concept as follows.

The Macintosh is designed to appeal to an audience of non-programmers, including people who have previously feared and mistrusted computers. To achieve this goal, Macintosh applications should be easy to learn and use. To help people feel more comfortable with the applications, the application should build on skills that people already have, not force them to learn new ones. The user should feel in control of the computer, not the other way round.

What distinguishes the Macintosh interface from other similar systems like Windows running under MS/DOS is that the user interface routines are built into the Macintosh operating system. This enables consistency across different applications. The aim of the designers of the Macintosh has been to create a machine which intuition tells you how to drive, rather than an instruction – the initial screen resembles a desktop, the windows simulating overlapping sheets of paper, the icons identifying disks and files.

Multi-tasking

The excellent features of the Macintosh and, to some extent, the packages on the IBM PC, such as Lotus 1-2-3, are derived, to a large extent, from the fact that all of the resources of the machine are dedicated to a single user and a single task. However, in the future, we expect the demands from the users to go in the direction of an environment where it will be easy to perform multiple tasks, share data files with coworkers, interchange documents and so on. The personal computer of today makes this possible, but not easy. Moving from one application to another involves changing the interface structure, data storage and data retrieval and so on.

According to Gunton (1989) we can distinguish three basic ways of overcoming the single-task limitation of a workstation.

(1)   A **virtual screen** routine divides up the memory and shares it between a number of applications, all of which are started up and held in memory, but only one of which controls and occupies the screen and the keyboard at a time. The user can easily switch between applications.

(2)   In **foreground/background** operation, the foreground application controls the keyboard and the screen, while other applications

running in the background share processing power with the foreground application.

(3)   In a full-scale **multi-tasking** both foreground and background applications may have windows on the screen, although only one window can be active at a time. Additionally, each application can start up a number of tasks which run under its control in parallel and which can communicate with one another.

Full multi-tasking may be a luxury for the vast majority of DSS and expert systems for the time being. However, two things are essential from the user's point of view. Firstly, a presentation management system which enforces consistency across applications and makes it possible to switch painlessly between them. Secondly, a network attachment that is integrated into the operating software, so that users can send or receive messages, access shared files, initiate long print runs, or send data files to others, without locking up their workstations for lengthy periods or invoking clumsy procedures (Gunton, 1989).

Natural language interfaces
Natural language processing has been one of the major application areas of AI. The goal is for a user to communicate with the computer through a natural language such as English. Some expert systems employ a natural language like interface. They are restricted to a limited vocabulary, grammar, and meaning. However, even within a limited domain they are not natural language understanding systems. It has often been said that the real breakthrough of end-user computing, in the managerial area, will not come until the computer interaction becomes more natural, that is man-like. Natural language interfaces are one such step. Speech recognition may be the next, and the major step.

Natural language interfaces have been built as front-end systems, for instance, to databases and DSS. An example of a commercial product is Intellect from Artificial Intelligence Corporation in the USA.

Intelligent user assistance
Assistance can be built into a KB-DSS on methodologies, at several levels. As mentioned already, we will deal with methodology knowledge bases later. However, by the use of the expert system technology we can develop intelligent help systems.

Contextual fit between users' views and the technology
Spreadsheet programming has been a great success in promoting end-user computing for managers, despite its limitations as a full-blown DSS tool. What can we learn from this? There needs to be a close fit between the user's framing of a problem and the way the problem solving process is performed

by the computer. To phrase it in another way, the conceptual model that is mapped onto the computer must fit the conceptual model of the problem as perceived by the user.

Normally, the conceptual model taken as basis for the software is more abstract than that of the user. Due to the generic character of a computer program, fewer and more abstract concepts are used. Take, for instance, the area of databases. Data modeling uses a conceptual framework, for example entity-relationships, to describe the reality. Reasoning systems may use rules and control strategies, and analytical modeling may use equation models. They are all rather abstract ways of presenting and analysing a problem. The greater the abstraction gap is between the user and the computer language, the greater is the need for an intermediary to transform problem specifications into the language understood by the computer, unless we can design interfaces that can close this gap.

Object-oriented programming and graphical presentation techniques are areas that offer promises for closing the contextual gap discussed above. For instance, inference networks can be drawn on the screen and the system will develop the rules and the control strategies of the expert system.

Kaltenbach (1987) describes a system that allows interactive graphical description of mathematical proofs. However, one still needs to be a mathematician to use the system. The objective is to extend this system to be capable of specifying the mathematical and logical structures of the problem in non-technical terms. A substantial amount of work goes on in the area of evaluating man–machine interfaces in view of cognitive modeling of the user (Billingsley (1982), Zoeppritz (1986) and Woods (1984)).

Toolbox

The present toolbox component of most KB-DSS provides three kinds of algorithms: statistical, forecasting and financial. Computerized tools like these are generally available in systems supporting decision making in areas such as finance, marketing, and management control. However, in other domains such as production, the usual required methods, such as scheduling algorithms, are lacking.

13.2.2 KB-DSS software environments

The second-generation KB-DSS will have to be improved with respect to the integration of components. Better integration will be needed not only to fulfill the inadequacies of the first generation but also to take advantage of the new component technologies available. Here, we shall offer a few comments on integration improvements.

(1) **DBMS–Model** integration is classical in a first-generation KB-DSS. However, as the DBMS is extended, special control and instructions must be included at the modeling component level to allow the use of new types of representations available in the database (pictures, diagrams and so on). Furthermore, if several modeling paradigms are used (equations, trees, influence diagrams and so on), the integration with the DBMS will have to be extended accordingly.

(2) **DBMS–Report generator** integration is usually found in the first-generation KB-DSS for numerical and alphanumerical information. The integration will have to be extended to take into account images, graphics and maps. For example, it should be possible to display an image or a map in a report or within a window.

(3) **DBMS–Graphics** is a classical integration in the first generation KB-DSS to display numerical information. The integration may be extended to represent, in a graphical or diagrammatic form, the structure of aggregates and/or objects in the database.

(4) **DBMS–Toolbox** is a classical integration in KB-DSS. However, this integration is often limited to elementary statistics and forecasting. The integration should be extended to data analysis and specialized OR algorithms in finance, marketing and production.

(5) **DBMS–Communication**. It must be possible to transfer data between copies of the same KB-DSS stored on computers connected to a network, for example, to feed a model in the first KB-DSS with data from a database of a second KB-DSS located on another computer. The communication software must allow a model of the first KB-DSS to address and describe the needed data stored in the database of a second KB-DSS.

(6) **DBMS–Inference engine** integration is now available in certain expert system shells for standard relational DBMS. The integration with a DBMS which is a component of the KB-DSS should be more easily available in the future.

(7) **Model–Report generator** integration is classical in DSS and KB-DSS. Improvements are needed to accommodate the new objects managed by the extended report generator (pictorial images and graphics).

(8) **Model–Toolbox**. In a first-generation KB-DSS the toolbox was usually limited to statistical and financial functions. In the second generation, a wider spectrum of OR algorithms should be available.

(9) **Model–Inference engine** is one of the fundamental integrations found in a first-generation KB-DSS. In a second generation, several modeling languages will be available, a traditional equation modeling language, plus, for example, an influence diagram modeling subsystem, and a multi-attribute preference modeling

subsystem. Several modeling languages may be needed, dependent on the problem to be modeled: each must integrate separately with the inference engine component. The inference engine will work with a domain-specific KB but also with a methodological KB (rational decision methodology, for example) as we have seen in Chapter 7.

13.2.3 KB-DSS operating environments

Cooperation between a PC version of a KB-DSS and a multi-user version (for example, located on a mainframe) is already available. More complex distribution of resources on networks will have to be defined and developed to allow for the cooperation of KB-DSS located on different machines. A model of the model library of a KB-DSS located on one machine should be able to utilize data stored on databases of KB-DSS on other machines. Several KB-DSS located on different machines may exchange conclusions obtained by their individual expert components.

An example of such a system for an investment application in a trade room was presented in Section 12.4.4.

13.2.4 Second generation of KB-DSS development tools

The first generation of KB-DSS is represented by software having the capabilities described in Chapter 7 (**OPTRANS EXPERT** and Guru are examples of this category even though they do not have all of the functions described in Chapter 7).

As we have seen above, a KB-DSS software environment is defined by the characteristics of each of its components, as well as the degree of integration among them. In Table 13.1 we describe the major improvements required in each of the component areas to move to a second-generation KB-DSS.

Figure 13.1 shows the general structure of a second generation KB-DSS development environment.

A new conceptual framework for KB-DSS needs to be defined as precisely as possible. Therefore, we need a definition of standards. This will lead to easier evaluation of tools and a better diffusion of them. The definition of standards should be done in terms of functions at the KB-DSS conceptual level, and on the tool level with respect to individual components as well as integration among components.

Table 13.1 KB-DSS from first to second generation

Components	First generation	Second generation
Database management system	Multi-dimensional or relational	Multi-dimensional + Objects + Images
Decision modeling	Equation modeling	Full support of decision analysis cycle and influence diagrams Mixing equation and rules
User modeling	Not available	Multi-attribute preference functions, risk preferences
Display	Report with numbers and texts, graphics, composite display	Hypertext: reports mixing: numbers, texts, graphics, images
Inferencing	On rules (forward, backward and mixed) only. No real-time capabilities	Mixing rules and objects (structured objects) properties of objects can be used in rules, actions related to objects have impact on reasoning inheritance
Knowledge base management system	Rules (only one knowledge representation apart from the modeling and database system)	Rules + structured objects (entities related by relations)
Knowledge coherence	Very limited	Extended
Toolbox	Short-term forecasting Optimization Statistics	Short-term forecasting Optimization Statistics OR models
Communication	Transfer of files Electronic mail	Accept real time (event driven) information
Distributed aspect	Limited (relation between PC and mainframe version)	Distribution of data, knowledge, models, display
User interface	Menus Language with assistance on syntax No intelligent assistance	Intelligent assistance (the user is guided in his work in each component from the methodological point of view)
Domain knowledge base	Yes	Yes

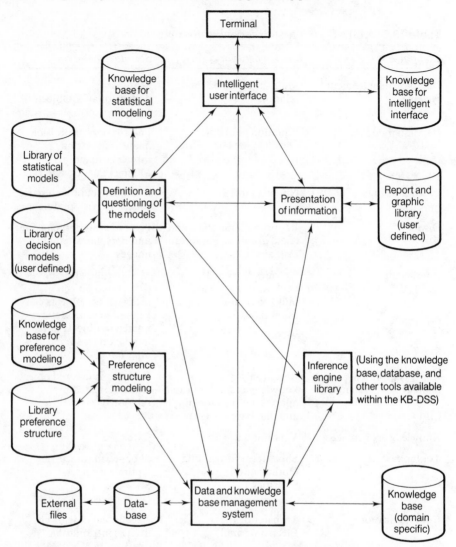

Figure 13.1   General structure of a KB-DSS development tool (second generation). (Reproduced from Klein (1986).)

13.3 General research issues and emerging trends

13.3.1 Introduction

The field of DSS is exceedingly broad, and research issues relate to a wide spectrum of disciplines, from 'hard' to 'soft' sciences, as we have already seen in Chapter 1. In the preceeding section, we have dealt with technological developments that will determine the next generation of computer environments (hardware and software). Most of these developments will come from other related disciplines such as databases, expert systems, decision theory and so on. However, the DSS field itself has, in certain areas, been pushing the technology. The fast growing area of end-user computing started off in the DSS field with interactive systems needed to support ill-structured decisions where flexibility and user control were critical success factors. Also, new developments in workstation technology can be traced back to the needs for interactive computing for decision support.

However, DSS is very much an application-driven field where the focus of research has been on developing tools that can augment the decision making capabilities of the manager. The DSS research has, as its common objective, the developments of the computer technology to improve problem solving and decision making. Research issues are raised in the intersection of decision making and technology: how is a DSS used, what are the effects on the decision making, what are the requirements on the technology, how are systems built and so on?

A framework for research can be built around the three fundamental perspectives: applications, design, and technology (Henderson, 1987).

The application perspective focuses on the use of DSS; the impacts on individual behaviour; and on organizational and social issues. Also, an important part of application research is to study to what extent technological support should be given, from passive to normative support (Keen, 1986). Normative support has been advocated by researchers in the operations research and management science fields. **Decision aiding** is the term used when the DSS provides methodological computer support. We have dealt with model building aids above. Below we shall also deal with two lines of research in this area: model management systems, and intelligent decision systems.

The design perspective puts emphasis on development life cycle methodologies and strategies which span the hold process from problem recognition and analysis, through systems specifications to computer implementation. Normative research focuses on decision modeling; behavioral research develops descriptive frameworks for studying decision making; cognitive sciences concentrates on knowledge acquisition methods and learning; and within the systems analysis tradition, issues such as adaptive design, prototyping design, and participative design are addressed.

The technology perspective have been described in the preceding sections and need not to be repeated here. Much of this research focuses on man–machine interaction and developments of software environments.

In the following text, we shall deal with a few selected issues which we think may have long-term impacts on the DSS field in general, and on KB-DSS development tools, in particular. These issues are:

• decision modeling systems;

- model management systems;
- intelligent decision systems;
- connectionism and neural networks.

13.3.2 Decision modeling

Decision research is a broad area attracting scientists from many different areas, as we pointed out in Chapter 1. This research could be divided into two major directions, the behavioral decision making direction as described in Chapter 2, and the normative direction in Chapter 3. New conceptual frameworks for decision modeling coming from this research will affect the way we support decision making and, thus, the design specifications of a KB-DSS.

Probably the best research briefing on decision making and problem solving in more recent times is the report by a group of very distinguished decision scientists, chaired by Herbert Simon and published in *Interfaces* (Simon *et al.*, 1987). We have referred to this work extensively in the theoretical parts of this book (Chapters 2–4). According to this group, what we need is an augmented normative theory, one that takes into account the gaps and elements of unrealism in the subjective expected utility theory by encompassing problem solving as well as choice, and demanding only the kind of knowledge, consistency and computational power that are attainable in the real world. This approach leads us to conclude that the lines of research which are needed are as follows:

- Extending empirical knowledge of actual human, cognitive processes and methods for dealing with complexity.
- Empirical studies of experts' behavior to find out how the problems that they study are solved. This should give birth to knowledge bases combining empirical knowledge and theoretical knowledge.
- Resolution of conflicts of value (individual and groups) and of inconsistencies in belief.
- Setting agendas and framing problems.

Another completely different area of research is to study the relationship between rationality and goals. Several theories give an answer to the question of what we have most reason to do. The theories we have dealt with in Chapter 3 are theories about rationality. We have pointed out, however, in the section dealing with the criticism of the rationality paradigm, that there are also moral theories. Since we defined rationality as being the ability to abide by given rules, we could equally well consider goals other than the expected utility maximization and still be rational.

13.3.3 Model management systems

Model management is a specific body of research within the DSS field that has focused on identifying those tasks required to build, and on using models in an interactive problem solving environment and, also, on providing a high level of software support for performing these tasks (Elam and Konsynski, 1987). The term Model Management Systems (MMS) has come to denote generalized software environments that offer a wide range of models and allow for flexible access, updating, and changing of the model base.

In order to make use of the analytical capabilities contained in an MMS, the problem must be formulated and analysed and the results interpreted. We can allocate a number of tasks to each of these functions, as shown in Figure 13.2.

To perform these tasks, human intelligence is usually required. They are, therefore, potential candidates for the application of AI techniques. According to Elam and Konsynski (1987), enhancing MMS so that they perform tasks that usually require human intelligence is, in many ways, similar to developing a knowledge-based system.

The availability of generalized MMS that support the formulation,

---

Formulation Tasks
> *Formulate* – Formulate a new decision model if an appropriate one does not exist in the model base
> *Explore* – Explore ideas and analyse issues
> *Choose* – Choose an existing model from the model base

Analysis Tasks
> *Match* – Identify and test (from a base of existing model structures) the applicability of a model and its associated solution approach to a particular problem
> *Expect* – Detect, explain, and suggest solutions for abnormal behavior based on user-supplied expectations about model behavior and/or history of the models utility
> *Plan* – Determine ways to perform analyses to reach predetermined goals
> *Cause* – Identify causal relationships between model entities
> *Recommend* – Identify, evaluate, and choose among potential courses of action
> *Synthesize* – Synthesize new models from model fragments that prove locally successful

Interpretation Tasks
> *Explain* – Generate explanatory models that provide intuitively reasonable explanations for the model's results
> *Interpret* – Interpret the analysis solution or results in the context of the problem semantics
> *Present* – Select appropriate report formats for requested information

---

Figure 13.2 User-model interaction tasks – opportunities for AI application. (Reproduced from Elam J.J. and Konsynski B. (1987). Using artificial intelligence techniques to enhance the capabilities of model management systems. *Decision Sciences*.)

analysis, and interpretation functions through the use of AI techniques will greatly affect the ability to deliver DSS that can be used for interactive problem solving.

13.3.4 Intelligent decision systems

Intelligent Decision Systems (IDS) is the term used by Holtzman (1989) to denote a new computer-based technology for aiding decision makers in complex decision situations. The tool is built upon the discipline of decision analysis, which we have described in Chapter 3. The objective is to make the skill of expert decision analysts available by using the expert system technology. This will significantly reduce the cost, time, and level of training needed to analyse difficult decisions by the decision analysis methodology. An IDS provides both domain knowledge and methodological knowledge. Confronted with a complex decision situation there are both the generic and the unique aspects to consider. Expert systems provide help to deal with the generic aspects by means of domain knowledge. The decision analysis methodology provides help for the decision makers to understand their specific circumstances and preferences, the unique aspects of the decision situations at hand. Therefore, IDS applications can address both the generic and unique aspects of a class of decisions.

The concept of a class of decisions is central to the IDS framework. The decision analysis methodology focuses on unique aspects, specific preferences and circumstances, of a decision situation. Analysing classes of similar decisions as a single unit can greatly reduce the overall expenses and time that are typically associated with the task of decision analysis. Holtzman gives a series of guidelines for designing a class of decisions. He points out that a rule-based system is an excellent way of implementing the analysis of a class of decisions: Analysing a class of decisions consists of developing a domain-specific knowledge base for a rule-based system that contains a set of assertions designed to guide the analysis of *specific* decisions in a way that reflects the decision maker's unique situation (Holtzman, 1989, p. 81) (see also Figure 13.3.). The rule-based system in which the decision class analysis is implemented is an expert system. This expert system, together with a powerful facility for manipulating and evaluating decision theoretic models (such as influence diagrams), constitute, according to Holtzman, an intelligent decision system.

Our position is that the KB-DSS framework is ideal to implement the IDS concept. A domain-specific knowledge base is augmented, together with a decision analysis methodology knowledge base. The decision analysis knowledge base will help the decision maker to formulate and appraise influence diagrams for the problem. An IDS provides the decision maker with several advantages over traditional expert systems which are, according to Holtzman:

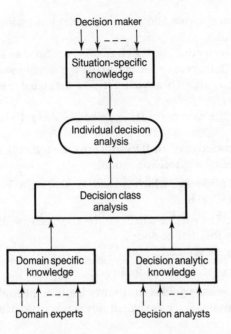

Figure 13.3 Analysing a class of decisions consists of designing a set of rules to guide individual decision analyses. (Reproduced from Holtzman S. (1989). *Intelligent Decision Systems.*)

- normative power;
- ease of representation and use of uncertainty;
- clarity in the acquisition of knowledge.

The normative power of an IDS arises from the maximum expected utility axiom which is the prescriptive action axiom of decision analysis. Guided by the methodology of decision analysis, an IDS can elicit important unanticipated features of the given situation. In contrast, the normative power of traditional expert systems are limited to situations that the heuristics of the knowledge base have encountered.

It has been shown that under very weak and desirable assumptions of normative decision making behavior, the representation of uncertainty must obey the axioms that define a probability measure. Non-probabilistic measures used in knowledge engineering (see Chapter 6) have been developed for either or both of the following two purposes:

(1) to avoid the computational burden often associated with probabilistic calculations, and;

(2) as an attempt to automate the way humans perceive and reason with uncertainty (Holtzman, 1989, p. 94).

Intelligent decision systems address the problem of probability assessments in specific decisions.

Holtzman claims that an IDS based on decision analysis is superior to expert systems with respect to the clarity of the terms used in the knowledge acquisition process, due to a well-defined language to describe decision problems.

The knowledge base of an IDS can be divided into five components:

(1)   Domain knowledge in an IDS concerns the indirect assessment of chance nodes in the decision model.

(2)   Preference knowledge which is used to elicit a preference model from the decision maker.

(3)   Probabilistic knowledge which guides the assessment of probability distributions for chance nodes.

(4)   User data which encompasses the set of facts that define the circumstances of the individual user.

(5)   Process knowledge guides the user of an IDS through the process of decision analysis. We have called this methodological knowledge.

The IDS concept uses expert system technology and the decision analysis methodology in combination. This gives advantages in two ways:

(1)   automating the skills and factual knowledge of the expertise of a few individuals, and;

(2)   the normative power of decision analysis which improves the quality of the decision studied.

Figure 13.4 shows that the IDS fills an important gap in the decision making technology.

13.3.5 Connectionism and neural networks

The theories of cognitive psychology we have described in Chapter 2, the AI-techniques in Chapter 4, expert systems in Chapter 6, and finally, knowledge acquisition methods in Chapter 8, are all based on the fundamental theory known as the **information processing theory**, also called the symbolic paradigm of cognition.

Another paradigm of cognition is known as **connectionism**. It takes, as its basic point of view, that understanding cognition requires an understanding of how the human brain works. There are roughly a hundred billion neurons (neural cells) in the human brain, each one has in the order of 1000 connections with other neurons. These connections are thought to be either

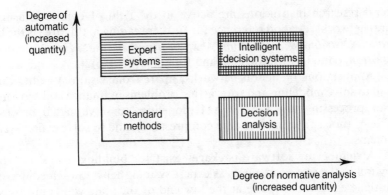

Figure 13.4 Decision makers have a choice of four kinds of decision making technology. (Reproduced from Holtzman S. (1989). *Intelligent Decision Systems*.)

excitatory or inhibitory. That is, the signal reaching a connection serves to excite or inhibit the target unit to a greater or lesser degree. The information processing capacity of a single neuron is extremely limited. The computational significance of a single neuron lies in its pattern of connections with other neurons. The computing power of connections, on the other hand, is truly impressive, resulting in a huge number of operations in a couple of milliseconds. This gives the human brain an interesting property. For tasks such as vision, language and motor control, a brain is more powerful than 1000 supercomputers. The human visual system, for instance, has the power of recognizing complex objects in a very short time. And yet, for simple tasks such as multiplication it is less powerful than a 4-bit microprocessor (Reddy, 1988).

Connectionist theories in cognitive science try to stay reasonably close to the fundamental facts of the brain system. We can state the essential features of connectionism as:

(1) *Parallelism*. A cognitive system consists of a large number of units that work in parallel.

(2) *Distribution*. Representations do not exist explicitly, but are implicit through the connections.

(3) *Harmonizing*. The state of the network is a result of an internal 'harmonizing' of the system, normally a result of an adaption to external stimuli.

(4) *Learning*. The system's connections are modified over time through continuous changes in the internal harmonization as a result of environmental impacts.

Several research institutions are active in the field of connectionism and neural networks. A good reference for further reading in this area is the book *Parallel Distributed Processing: Explorations in the Microstructure of Cognition*, edited by McClelland and Rumelhart (1986).

Applications of neural networks, apart from vision systems, can be found to solve modeling and forecasting problems in finance and economics, sensor processing and CAD/CAM modeling; to solve signal processing problems (noise filtering and data compression); and to solve expert systems problems.

A number of software packages exist for building neural networks. They fall in the same categories as expert system shells: low-, medium-, and high-scale categories. Those at the low end of the scale will comprise software packages under $100, those in the middle of the scale will be software packages around $1000, and those at the high end of the scale around $5000.

Exercises

13.1 What are the directions of research that are useful in the KB-DSS domain?

13.2 Select one example of industrial KB-DSS development software.

Perform an analysis of the functions of each subsystem (DBMS, system modeling, user modeling, display management and knowledge management). Compare each subsystem with the functions that are expected to be available in a second-generation KB/DSS.

13.3 (a)   What are the application domains that you foresee will be feasible as soon as it is possible to store pictorial images in the DBMS component of a KB-DSS?

(b)   Define the specifications of an image extension of a KB-DSS. What are the extensions needed at the modeling language component level, and at the rule syntax level?

(c)   Define a work plan for such an extension of a KB-DSS development environment.

13.4 (a)   What are the application domains where an object extension of the DBMS component of a KB-DSS seems to be particularly useful?

(b)   Define the specifications of an object extension of a first-generation KB-DSS such as OPTRANS-DBMS. Define a work plan for implementing such an extension.

13.5 (a)   Study the interest of coupling an equation modeling language (for a financial application, for example) and a decision tree compiler or, even better, an influence diagram development tool.

(b)   Define the specification of such an extension.

(c)   Define a work plan for implementing the extension.

13.6 Select a KB-DSS being used by several people in an organization.

(a)   Define an experiment to measure:

    (i)   The level of usage of the system.

    (ii)   The impact of user characteristics on system usage (age, education, prior experience with DSS and prior exposure to PCs).

    (iii)   The perception of the assistance given by the system.

    (iv)   Objective measure of productivity.

    (v)   Objective measure of decision quality.

(b)   How would you organise your experiment to collect information on:

    (i)   System usage by users.

    (ii)   Users characteristics.

    (iii)   Productivity in their tasks.

    (iv)   Decision quality.

Appendix A: A Curriculum Proposal for a Course on Knowledge-based Decision Support Systems

Session Theme 2 × 45 minutes		Chapter References
1	**Course presentation** Course material, pedagogics, evaluation and overview	1
2	**Decision making and problem solving** The descriptive view: decision process and heuristics	2
3	**Decision making: The normative view** Basic concepts, risk, decision tree, preferences and so on	3.1–3.5
4	**Decision making: The normative view** Decision analysis cycle and criticism of normative view	3.6–3.7
5	**Artificial intelligence techniques** Production systems, search, knowledge representation and reasoning	4
6	**DSS conceptual framework** Concepts, architectures and demonstration	5.1–5.3
7	**DSS development environment** Components and functions	5.4
8	**Introduction to a development tool (part 1)** (PC-OPTRANS): Hands-on using examples	User manual primer
9	**Introduction to a development tool (part 2)** Interface designs	User manual primer

Session Theme 2 × 45 minutes		Chapter References
10	**Expert systems** Concepts, architectures, opportunities and tools	6
11	**Knowledge-based DSS** Framework and demonstration (BANKER or FINSIM)	7.1–7.4
12	**Expert system development environment (part 1)** (PC-OPTRANS-Expert) Loan example	User manual primer
13	**Development environment (part 2)** Loan example continued	User manual primer
14	**Knowledge modeling** Concepts, methods and case (SAFIR)	8
15	**Design and implementation of KB-DSS** Steps and problems	9.2–9.4
16	**Testing and evaluation**	10
17	**Organizational impacts** Case study: financial institutions	11
18	**Applications in finance** Guest lecture of a practioner	12
19	**Future developments and research in KB-DSS**	13
20	**Presentation of term papers – concluding remarks**	

References

Abernathy, Bernabe, Chandler, Wilkins and Wolfe. (1985). A conceptual design of an Intelligent Front End to Scientific Application Programs. *Coupling Symbolic and Numerical Computing* Workshop 1985

Ackoff R. (1967). Management misinformation systems. *Management Science*, Dec. 1967, pp. 147–56

Ackoff R.L. (1979a). The future of operational research is past. *Journal of the Operational Research Society*

Ackoff R.L. (1979b). Resurrecting the future of operational research. *Journal of the Operational Research Society*

Alderberger O. (1976). *Simulfin, Die Finanzwirtschaft der Onternchmuig als simulations experiment*. S. Toeche-Mittles-Verlag

Alter S. (1980). Decision Support Systems, Current Practice and Continuing Challenges. Reading MA: Addison-Wesley

Amsted S.M. (1983). On representing and solving decision problems. *PhD dissertation*, Engineering-Economic Systems Department, Stanford University, Stanford, California

Anderson J.R. (1985) *Cognitive Psychology*. New York: W.H. Freeman and Company

Apté and Se June Hong (1988). Using qualitative reasoning to understand financial arithmetic: *Engineering*

Arkes H.R. and Freedman M.R. (1984). Demonstration of the cost and benefits of expertise in recognition memory. *Memory and Cognition*, 12, 84–9

Arrow K.J. (1951). *Social Choice and Individual Values*. New York: Wiley

Barr A. and Feigenbaum E.A. (1981). *The Handbook of Artificial Intelligence*. Los Altos CA: Kaufman

Bayes T. (1763). Toward solving a problem in the doctrine of chance. *Essay* (published posthumously by his friends of the Royal Society)

Bell D.E. (1979a). Consistent assessment procedures using conditional utility functions. *Operations Research*, 27, 1054–66

Bell D.E. (1979b). Multiattribute utility functions: decompositions using interpolation. *Management Science*, **25**, 744–53

Bernouilli D. (1738). Specimen theoriae Novae de Mensura Sortis. *Commentarii
Academiae Scientiarum Imperialis Petropolitanae*, tomus V

Beulens A.J.M. and van Neunen (1988). The use of expert system technology in DSS,
in design aspects of advanced DSS. *DSS International Journal*, 4(4)

Bhatnagar R.K. and Kanal L.N. (1986). Handling uncertain information: a review of
numeric and non-numeric methods In *Uncertainty in Artificial Intelligence*
(Kanal and Lemmer, eds.). North-Holland

Biggs S.F. and Mock T.J. (1983). An investigation of auditor decision processes in
the evaluation of internal controls and audit scope decisions. *Journal of
Accounting Research*, **21**(1)

Billingsley P. (1982). Navigation through hierarchical menu structures. Does it help
to have a map? In *Proc. Human Factor Society 26th Annual Meeting*, Seattle,
Washington

Blainbridge L. (1981). Verbal reports as evidence of the process operator's knowledge. In *Fuzzy Reasoning and its Applications* (Mamdani E.H. and Gaines
B.R.) eds. London: Academic Press

Bonczek R.H., Holsapple C.W. and Whinston A.B. (1981) *Foundations of Decision
Support Systems*. London: Academic Press

Bonini C.P. (1963). *Simulation of Information and Decision Systems in the Firm*.
Englewood Cliffs NJ: Prentice-Hall

Boose J.H. (1984). Personal construct theory and the transfer of expertise. In *Proceedings of AAAI-84*, 27–33

Boose J.H. (1985). A knowledge acquisition program for expert systems based on
personal construct psychology. *Int. J, Man–Machine Studies*, **23**(4)

Bouwman M.J. (1978). Financial diagnosis: A cognitive model of the processes
involved. *PhD Thesis* Carnegie-Mellon University, Pittsburg, Pennsylvania

Bouwman M.J. (1983). Human diagnostic reasoning by computer: an illustration
from financial analysis. *Management Science*, **29**(6)

Bouwman M.J., Frishkoff P.A. and Frishkoff P. (1987). How do financial analysts
make decisions? A process model of the investment screening decision.
Accounting, Organizations and Society, **12**(1)

Bower R.S. and Wipern R.F. (1969). Risk, return measurement in portfolio appraisal
models. *JFQA*, December 1969

Brans J.P., Vincke P.H. and Mareschal B. (1986). How to select and how to rank
projects: the PROMETHEE method. *European Journal of Operational
Research* **24**, 228–38. North-Holland

Breuker J.A. and Wielinga B.J. (1984). *Techniques for Knowledge Elicitation and
Analysis*. Report 1.5, Esprit Project 12, University of Amsterdam

Brigg R. (1986). How a complex numerical algorithm can be transformed into a
simple symbolic algorithm in *Coupling Symbolic and Numerical Computation
in Expert Systems* (Kowalin J.S., ed.). North-Holland

Briys E. (1987). Etude comparative des Systemes Experts en analyse financiere.
In *Compte Rendus dec JIIA-87* (Noel J.L.P., ed.). 6 rue Dufrenoy, 75116
Paris

Brooks F.P. (1977). *The Mythical Man-Month* 2nd edn, Reading MA: Addison-
Wesley

Buchanan B.G., Sutherland G.L. and Feigenbaum E.A. (1969). Heuristic

DENDRAL: a program for generating explanatory hypotheses in organic chemistry. *Machine Intelligence*, Vol 4 (Meltzer B. and Michie D., eds.). Edinburgh: Edinburgh Press

Buisine L. (1987). Intelligence artificielle et diagnostic d'entreprise. In *Actes de Colloque Systemes Experts et Gestion d'Entreprise*. Rue de la Gorenne, 92000 Nanterre, France

Bundy A., Silver B. and Plummer D. (1985). An analytical comparison of some rule-learning programs. *Artificial Intellience*, **27**(2)

Burgun J.J. (1988). Presentation du système FINSIM, SOREFI de Champagne Ardenne, Direction du Development, note interne. 9 bd de la paix, 51053 Reims Cedex, France

Butler Cox (1987). *Expert Systems in Business*. Research Report 60, Butler Cox & Partners Ltd, London

Carleton W.T. (1970a). An analytical model for long range financial planning. *Journal of Finance*, May 1970

Carleton W.T. (1970b). Linear programming and capital budgeting models: a new interpretation. *Journal of Finance*, December 1970

Carnap R. (1950). *Logical Foundation of Probability*. Chicago: The University of Chicago Press

Caroll D.C. and Zannetos Z.S. (1967). Toward the realization of intelligent MIS 1966. In *Information System Science and Technology* (Walter D.E., ed.), pp. 151–68. Washington DC: Thomson Book Company

Carter C. and Cartlett J. (1987). Assessing credit card applications using machine learning. *IEEE Expert*

Chambers, Zayay J.M.E. and Pregibon D. (1981). Expert software for data analysis: an initial experiment. In *proceedings of the 43rd Session of the International Statistics Institute*, Buenos Aires, Argentina

Chang C.L. and Walker A. (1984). PROSQL: A prolog programming interface with SQL/DS. In *Proc. First Int'l Workshop Expert Data Base Systems*, Kerschberg L. (ed.), Menlo Park, California: Benjamin Cummings

Chapuzot B. (1987) Un systeme expert de conseil en placement bancaire, communications. In *International Seminar on DSS and Knowledge Based DSS in Banking*, Centre HEC-ISA, F-78350 Jouy-en-Josas, France

Charniak E. and McDermott D. (1985) *Introduction to Artificial Intelligence*. Reading MA: Addison-Wesley

Charniawska B. and Wolff R. (1986). How we decide and how we act: on the assumption of Viking organization theory, Den X. *Nordiska Foretaksøkonomiske Konferanse*, NHH, Bergen, Norway

Checkland P. (1981). *System Thinking, System Practice*. Chichester: Wiley

Chi M.T.H. *et al.* (1981). Expertise in problem solving. In *Advances in the Psychology of Human Intelligence* (Sternberg R., ed.). Hillsdale NJ: Lawrence Erlbaum Associates

Chidan and Apté and S June Hong (1988). Using qualitative reasoning to understand financial arithmetic

Christensen G. (1987). Successful implementation of decision support systems; an empirical investigation of usage intentions and behavior, *PhD Dissertation*, University of California, LA

Clancey W.J. (1984). Knowledge acquisition for classification of expert systems. *Proc. ACM 1984 Annual Conference*, USA

Clarkson G.P.E. (1962) *Portfolio Selection: A Simulation of Trust Investment.* Englewood Cliffs NJ: Prentice-Hall

Cohen K.J., Gilmore T.G. and Singer F.A. (1966). Bank procedures for analyzing business loan applications. In *Analytical Methods in Banking* (Hammer ed.)

Cohen M.D., March J.G. and Olsen J.P. (1972). A garbage can model of organizational choice. *Administrative Science Quarterly*, **17**(1)

Condorcet, Marquis de (1785). *Essai sur l'application de l'analyse à la probabilité des decisions rendues à la pluralité des vois.* Paris

Cooper D. and Kornell J. (1986). Combining symbolic and numeric methods for automated induction in coupling

Cyert R.M. and March, J.G. (1963). A *Behavioral Theory of the Firm.* Englewood Cliffs NJ: Prentice-Hall

Davis G.B. and Olson M.H. (1985) *Management Information Systems*, New York: McGraw-Hill

Davis R. and Lenat D.B. (1982). *Knowledge-Based Systems in Artificial Intelligence.* McGraw-Hill

Delcambre L.M.L. (1988). RPL: An expert system language with query power. *IEEE-Expert*

Delgrande J.P. (1987). A formal approach to learning from examples, *Int. J. Man–Machine Studies*, **26**(2)

Drucker P.F. (1988). The coming of the new organization. *Harvard Business Review* (1)

Duchessi P., Shawky H. and Seagle J.P. (1988). A knowledge-engineered system for commercial loan decisions. *Financial Management*

Duda R.O., Gaschnig J.G. and Hart P.E. (1979). Model design in the PROSPECTOR consultant system for mineral exploration. In *Expert Systems in the Micro-electronic Age* (Michie D., ed.). Edinburgh: Edinburgh Press

Edwards W. (1983). Human cognitive capabilities, representativeness, and ground rules for research. In *Analyzing and Aiding Decision Processes* (Humphreys P., Svenson O. and Vari A., eds.). Amsterdam: North-Holland

Elam J.J. and Konsynski B. (1987). Using artificial intelligence techniques to enhance the capabilities of model management systems. *Decision Sciences*, **18**

Ericsson K.A. and Simon H. (1984) *Protocol Analysis.* Cambridge MA: The MIT Press

Europa: Management Report (1985). Digital Equipment Corporation International (Europe)

Express user manual (1980) Management Decision Systems Inc, Riverside Road, Weston, Mass, 02193 USA

Feigenbaum E. (1977). The art of artificial intelligence: themes and case studies of knowledge engineering. In *Proceedings of the Fifth International Joint Conference on Artificial Intelligence*, pp 1014–29, Cambridge MA

Feigenbaum E., Buchanan B.G. and Lederberg J. (1971). On generality and problem solving: a case study using the DENDRAL program. In *Machine Intelligence*, **6** (Meltzer B. and Michie D., eds.). Edinburgh: Edinburgh Press

DeFinetti B. (1974). *The Theory of Probability.* London: Wiley

FINSIM-EXPERT User Manual (1986). SIG, 4 bis rue de la Libération, 78350 Jouy-en-Josas, France

Fischhoff B. and M. (1981). *Acceptable Risk.* Cambridge: Cambridge University Press

Fischoff B. Goitein B.P., and Shapiro B. (1982). The experienced utility of expected utility aproaches. In *Expectations and Actions: Expectancy-value Models in Psychology*, (Feather N., ed.). Hillsdale NJ: Erlbaum

Følstad H. (1984). Thinking aloud protocols and protocol analysis. An attempt to apply this to a practical case of financial analysis (in Norwegian). *Termpaper*. NHH, Bergen, Norway

Forrester J.W. (1961). *Industrial Dynamics*. Cambridge MA: The MIT Press

Galbraith J.R. (1977). *Organizational Design*. Reading MA: Addison-Wesley

Gale W.A. and Pregibon D. (1983). *Building on Expert Interface*. Technical Memorandum Bell Telephone Laboratories

Gangneux P.H. and Rouxell C. (1988). A DSS to improve the link between the sale function and the manufacturing. In *Proceedings of the 5th International Seminar on Production Economics*, Elsevier

Gerrity T.P. Jr. (1970). The design of man–machine decision systems. *PhD Dissertation* MIT, Cambridge MA

Gerrity T.P. Jr. (1971). The design of man–machine decision systems: an application to portfolio management. *Sloan Management Review*, **12**(2), 59–75

Gilmore J.F. and Howard C. (1986). Expert system tool evaluation. In *Sixth International Workshop on Expert Systems*, Avignon, France

Ginzberg M.J. (1975). A process approach to management science implementation *PhD Dissertation,* MIT, Cambridge MA

Girault F. and Klein M. (1971). Le projet SCARABEE: une banque de données et de modèies pour la recherche en analyse financière et en gestion de portefeuille. *L'Analyse Financière*

Gorry G.A. (1967). *A System for Computer-Aided Diagnosis*. MAC-TM-44, Project MAC, MIT, Cambridge MA

Gorry G.A. (1969). Modelling the Diagnostic Process. In *Working Paper No. 370-69*, Sloan School of Management, MIT, Cambridge MA

Graham, I. (1987) Knowledge-based systems in the dealing room. In *IBM seminar on Expert Systems in Banking and Insurance* Jouy-en-Josas, France

de Groot M.H. (1970). *Optimal Statistical Decisions*. New York: North-Holland

Guilfoyle C. and Jeffcoate J. (1988). *Expert Systems in Banking and Securities*. Ovum Ltd, London

Gunton T. (1989). *Infrastructure. Building a Framework for Corporate Information Handling*. Hemel Hempstead: Prentice Hall International (UK) Ltd

Hacking I (1975). *The Emergence of Probability*. Cambridge: Cambridge University Press

Hajek P. (1982). Applying artificial intelligence to data Analysis: GURA, in context of expert systems. In *Proc ECAI-82*, Orsay, France

Hall R.H. and Quinn R.E. (1983). *Organizational Theory and Public Policy*, Sage CA

Hapek P. and Ivanek I. (1982). *Artificial Intelligence and Data Analysis*, COMPSTAT-82, Physica-Verlag, Vienne

Harmon P. and King D. (1985). *Expert Systems: Artificial Intelligence in Business*. New York: John Wiley

Harsanyi J.C. (1977). *Rational Behavior and Bargaining Equilibrium in Games and Social Situations*. Cambridge: Cambridge University Press

Hart A. (1986). *Knowledge Acquisition for Expert Systems*, London: Kogan Page Ltd

Haugeland, J. (1985). *Artificial Intelligence: The Very Idea*. Cambridge MA: The MIT Press

Hayes-Roth B. (1985). A blackboard architecture for control. *Artificial Intelligence,* **26**, 251–321, North-Holland, Elsevier

Hayes-Roth F., D.A. Waterman and Lenat D., eds. (1983). *Building Expert Systems.* Reading MA: Addison-Wesley

Helfert E.A. (1963). *Techniques of Financial Analysis.* Homewood Ill: Richard D. Irwin Inc

Henderson J.C. (1987). Finding synergy between decision support systems and expert systems research. *Decision Sciences,* **18**

Hiltz R. and Turoff M. (1978). The Network Nation, Human Communication via Computer, Reading MA: Addison-Wesley

Hogarth R.M. (1980). *Judgement and Choice,* New York: Wiley

Holsapple C.W. and Whinston A.B. (1986). *Expert Systems Using Guru.* Dow Jones-Irwin

Holsapple C.W. and Whinston A.B., eds. (1987). *Decision Support Systems: Theory and applications.* Springer Verlag NATO ASI Series, *Computer and System Science,* **31** (This volume contains the proceeding of the NATO Advanced Study Institute on Decision Support Systems Theory and Application, which took place at Maratea, Italy in June 1985.)

Holtzman S. (1989). *Intelligent Decision Systems,* Reading MA: Addison-Wesley

Howard R.A. (1968) The foundation of decision analysis, *IEEE-SSCA,* **3**

Howard R.A. (1980). An assessment of decision analysis. *Operation Research,* **28**(1), 4–27

Howard R.A. (1983). The Evolution of Decision Analysis. In *Readings on the Principles and Applications of Decision Analysis.* (Howard R.A. and Matheson J.E., eds.) Vol. 1, 5–16. Strategic Decision Group, Menlo Park CA

Howard R.A. (1988). Decision analysis: practice and promise, *Management Science,* **34**(6), 679–95

Howard R.A. and Matheson J.E. (1968). An introduction to decision analysis. In *Readings on the Principles and Applications of Decision Analysis.* Decision Analysis Group, SRI International

Howard R.A. and Matheson J.E. (1983). Influence diagrams. In *Readings on the Principles and Application of Decision Analysis* Vol II. (Howard R.A. and Matheson J.E., eds.), pp. 719–62. Menlo Park CA: Strategic Decision Group

Howard R.A., James E. and Matheson E. (1983). *Readings on The Principles and Applications of Decision Analysis,* Vols I and II. Strategic Decision Group, Menlo Park, CA

Huber G.P. and Mcdaniel R.R. Jr. (1986). Exploiting information technologies to design more effective organizations. In *Managers, Micros and Mainframes* (Jarke M., ed.) New York: John Wiley

Jäger K., Peemöller N. and Mohde M. (1988). A DSS for planning chemical production in a pharmaceutical company. In Proceeding of the Fifth International Seminar on Production Economics. Elsevier

Janis I.L. and L. Mann (1977). *Decision Making: A Psychological Analysis of Conflict, Choice, and Commitment.* New York: Free Press

Jarke M. and Radermacher F.J. (1988). The AI potential of model management and its central role in decision support in design aspects of advanced DSS. *DSS International Journal,* **4**(4)

Johansen *et al.* (1974). *Group Communication through Electronic Media: Fundamental choice and Social Effects.* Education Technology

Johnson P.E. (1983). What kind of an expert should a system be? *The Journal of Medicine and Philosophy*, **8**, 77–97

Johnson P.E. (1984). The expert mind: a new challenge for the information scientist. In *Beyond Productivity: Information Systems Development for Organizational Effectiveness* (Bemelmans, ed.) Elsevier Science Publications

Johnson T. (1984). The commercial application of expert system technology, *Knowledge Engineering Review*, **1**(1), 15–25

Kahl D., Klein M., Manteau A. and Perrin J.C. (1977). *Un Système d'Information et d'Aide à la Décision pour le contrôle financier des sociétés multinationales, Modélisation et Maîtrise des Systèmes*. Editions Hommes et Techniques tome 2

Kahnemann D., Slovie P. and Tversky A., eds. (1982). *Judgement under Uncertainty: Heuristics and Biases*. Cambridge: Cambridge University Press

Kaltenbach M. (1987). Computer representation and animation of mathematical proofs with dynaboard. *INRIA*. Le Chesnay Cedex, France

Kanal L.N. and Lemmer J.J., eds. (1986). *Uncertainty in Artificial Intelligence*. North-Holland: Elsevier Science Publishers BV

Kastner J., Apte C., Giesmer J., Hong S.J., Karnaugh M., Mays E. and Tozawa Y. (1986). A knowledge-based consultant for financial marketing. *The AI Magazine*

Keen P.G.W. (1981). Value analysis: justifying decision support systems. *Management Information System Quarterly*, **5**(1)

Keen P. (1986). Decision support systems: the next decade, In *Decision Support Systems: A Decade in Perspective* (McLean E.R. and Sol H.G., eds.) North-Holland: Elsevier Science Publishers BV

Keen P.G.W. and Scott Morton M.S. (1978). *Decision Support Systems, An organizational perspective*. Reading MA: Addison-Wesley

Keeney R. (1969). *Multidimensional Utility Functions: Theory, Assessment and Application*. Technical Report No. 73, Operations Research Centre, MIT

Keeny R. (1988). Value driven expert systems for decision support, in design aspects of advanced DSS. *DSS International Journal*, **4**(4)

Keeney R. and Raiffa H. (1976). Decisions with Multiple Objectives Preferences and Value Teedeoffs, New York: John Wiley

Kelly G. (1955). *The Psychology of Personal Constructs*. Norton

Kepner C.H. and Tregoe B.B. (1981). The New Rational Manager. Princeton: Princeton Research Press

Kerchberg L. (1986). Expert data base systems. In *Proceedings from the first International Workshop*, Menlo Park CA: Benjamin Cummings

Kerlinger F.N. (1973). *Foundations of Behavioral Research* 2nd edn. London: Holt, Rinehart and Winston

Keynes J.M. (1921). *A Treatise on Probability*

Kim J. and Courtney J.F. (1988). A survey of knowledge acquisition techniques *and* their relevance to managerial problem domains. *Decision Support Systems*, **4** (3)

King D. (1986). An explanation facility for decision support systems. *Sixth Journees Internationales, Les Systèmes Experts et leurs Applications*, Avignon, France

Kirkwood C.W. (1982). A case history of nuclear power plant site selection. *Journal of Operational Research Society*, **33**, 353–66

Kitzmiller C.T. and Kowalik J.S. (1985). Coupling symbolic and numeric computing in knowledge-based systems. *Proceedings of the Workshop Sponsored by the AAAI*, Seattle, Washington

Klein M. (1977). Systèmes question/réponse et aide à la décision en analyse financière. In *Proceedings of the International Seminar on Intelligent Question – Answering and Data Base Systems*, Bones 1977. (Simon J.C., ed.) INRIA

Klein M. (1986). Recent developments in PC-OPTRANS a KB-DSS generator. In *Euro VIII (8th European Conference on Operation Research)*. Fondation Calouste Gulbenkian, DSS and Expert System Session, (SIG)

Klein M. (1988). FINSIM Expert: a knowledge based DSS for financial analysis and planning. In *Proceedings Eurinfo'88*, North-Holland

Klein M. (1989). Experiment with FINSIM EXPERT a KB-DSS for financial analysis and planning. In *Proceedings 5th International Seminar on Production Economics*, Elsevier

Klein M. and Levasseur M. (1971). FINSIM: un outil d'aide à l'analyse financière. *Analyse Financière*

Klein M. and Levy J.P. (1974). SCARABEE, un langage d'aide à l'analyse financière. *01-Informatique, mensuel*

Klein M. and Manteau A. (1983). OPTRANS: a tool for implementation of decision support centers in *Process and Tools for Decision Support* (Sol H.G., ed.)

Klein M. and Pezier J., eds. (1975). *ARBRE, Manuel Utilisateur*. SIG, 4 bis, Rue de la Liberation, 78350 Jouy-en-Josas, France

Klein M. and Tixier V. (1971). SCARABEE: a data and model bank for financial engineering and research. In *Proceeding IFIP Congress*, North-Holland

Klein M. and Villedieu T. (1987). A KB-DSS for financial planning, application to French municipalities. *Engineering Costs and Production Economics*, **12**, North-Holland: Elsevier

Klein M., Levy J.P. and Limousin P. (1974) Projet SCARABEE. présentation, structure du système, aspects methodologiques. *Cahier de Recherche*, **10**, Centre HEC-ISA, Jouy-en-Josas, France

Klein M., Dussartre J.E. and Despoux F. (1987). Introducing AI in OPTRANS a DSS Generator in Decision Support Systems: Theory and Application (Holsapple C.W. and Whinston A.B., eds.). Springer-Verlag

Kolb D.A. and Frohman A.L. (1970). An organization development approach to consulting. *Sloan Management Review*, **12**(4), 51–65

Korsan R.J. and Matheson J.E. (1978). *Pilot Automated Influence Diagrams Decision Aid*. SRI International Technical report No. 7078 *SRI International*, Menlo Park, CA

Kosy D. and Wise B. (1984). Self explanatory financial planning models. In *Proc of the American Association for Artificial Intelligence* 1976–1981

de Langle C. and Michel S. (1985). Systeme Expert de placement bancaire pour les particulies. *Bancatique*, **5**

Laplace P. (1812). *Théorie analytique des probabilités*. Imprimerie Impériale

Larkin J.H. *et al.* (1980). Expert and novice performance in solving physics problems. *Science*, **208**, 1335–42

Laske O.E. (1986). On competence and performance notions in expert systems design: a critique of rapid prototyping. In *Proceedings of the 6th International Workshop on Expert Systems & Their Applications*. Avignon, France

Leavitt H.J. (1965). Applied organizational change in industry: structural, technological and humanistic approaches. In *Handbook of Organizations* (March J.G., ed.). Chicago: Rand McNally

Leavitt H.J. and Whisler T.L. (1958). Management in the 1980s. *Harvard Business Review*, **36**(6)

Lecot K. (1988). Using expert systems in banking: the case of fraud detection and prevention, *Expert Systems Review*, **1**(3) University of Southern California

Lee R.M. (1983). Epistemological aspects of knowledge-based decision support systems. In *Process and Tools for Decision Support* (Sol H.G., ed.), North-Holland: Elsevier

Lerner E.M. and Carleton W.T. (1966). *A Theory of Financial Analysis*. Harcourt, Brace & World, Inc

Levy J.P. (1973). Automatic handling of syntax errors in SCARABEE, an interactive system. *Centre HEC-ISA, Cahier de Recherche No. 2*

Lindblom C.E. (1959). The science of muddling through. *Public Administration Review*, **19**, 78–88

Lindblom C.E. (1979). Still muddling, not yet through. *Public Administration Review*, **39**, 517–26

Little J.D.C. (1970). Models for managers: a calculus of decision. *Management Science*, **16**(8)

Little J.D.C. (1979). Decision support systems for marketing managers. *Journal of Marketing*, **43**, 9–26

Lyngstad P.B. (1987). Knowledge modeling of expertise in financial diagnostics (in Norwegian). *PhD Thesis* NHH Bergen, Norway

McCarthy J. (1960). Recursive functions of symbolic expressions and their computation by machine. *Communications of the ACM*, **21**(12)

McCarthy (1984). *Private Correspondence to S. Holtzman*

McClelland J.L. and Rumelhart D.E., eds. (1986). *Parallel Distributed Processing; Explorations in the Microstructure of Cognition*. Cambridge MA: MIT Press, Bradford Books

McDermott D. (1982). Non-monotonic logic II: non-monotonic model theories. *JACM*, 33–57

McDermott J. (1982). R1: a rule-based configurer of computer systems. *Artificial Intelligence*, **19**, 39–88

McDermott D. and Doyle J. (1980). Non-monotonic logic 1. *Artificial Intelligence*, 41–72

McNamee P. and Celona S.J. (1987). *Decision Analysis for the Professional with SUPERTREE*. Redwood City CA: Scientific Press

March J.G., ed. (1965). *Handbook of Organizations*. Chicago

March J.G. (1978). Bounded rationality ambiguity and the engineering of choice. *The Bell Journal of Economics*, **9**

March J.G. and Simon H. (1958). *Organizations*. New York: John Wiley

Markowitz H. (1952). Portfolio selection. *The Journal of Finance*, 77–91

Markowitz H. *Portfolio Selection: Efficient Diversification of Investments*. New York: John Wiley

Matheson J.E. (1970). Decision analysis practice: examples and insights. In *Proceedings of the Fifth International Conference on Operational Research*, Venice and London, Tavistark Publications pp. 677–91

Mays E., Apte C., Giesmer J. and Kastner J. (1987). Organizing knowledge in a complex financial domain. *IEEE Expert* van Melle S. and Bennett P. (1981). *The EMYCIN Manual.* Computer Science Dept. Stanford University, Stanford CA

Merkhofer M.W. and Leof E.B. (1981). A Computer-aided Decision Structuring Process – Final Report. SRI International Technical Report, Menlo Park, CA

Methlie L.B. (1982). Data management techniques for DSS. *DATA Base,* **12**(1–2)

Methlie L.B. (1983). Organizational variables influencing DSS Implementation. In *Processes and Tools for Decision Support* (Sol H.G., ed.). North-Holland

Methlie L.B. (1987). On knowledge-based decision support systems for financial diagnosis. In *Decision Support Systems: Theory and Application* (Holsapple C.W. and Whinston A.B., eds.). Berlin: Springer-Verlag

Michalski R.S., Carbonell J.G. and Mitchell T.M. (1986). *Machine Learning: An Artificial Approach,* Vol. II. Los Altos, CA: Morgan Kaufman

Miller G.A. (1956). The magical number seven, plus or minus two: some limits on our capability for processing information. *The Psychology Review,* **63**(2)

Mills H.D. (1971). Top down programming in large systems, In *debugging techniques in large systems.* (Rustin R., ed.), pp. 41–55. Prentice-Hall

Minsky M. (1975). A framework for representing knowledge. In *The Psychology of Computer Vision* (Winston P., ed.). New York: McGraw-Hill

Mintzberg H. (1973). *The Nature of Managerial Work.* New York: Harper & Row

Mintzberg H., Raisinghani, D. and Theoret, A. (1976). The structure of the unstructured decision processes. *Administrative Science Quarterly,* **21**, 246–75

von Mises R. (1957). *Probability, Statistics and Truth.* New York: The Macmillan Corporation

Missikoff M. and Widerhold G. (1984). Towards a unified approach for expert and data base systems. In *Proc. First Int Workshop on Expert Data Base Systems* (Kerschberg L. ed.), Menlo Park CA: Benjamin Cummings

Mockler R.J. (1989). *Knowledge-Based Systems for Management Decisions.* Englewood Cliffs, NJ: Prentice Hall

Montgomery D.B. and Urban G.L. *Management Science in Marketing.* Englewood Cliffs, NJ: Prentice-Hall

Moore E.A. and Agongino M. (1987). INFORM: an architecture for expert-directed knowledge acquisition. *Int. J. Man-Machine Studies,* **26**(2)

Mottura P. (1988). *Problem-Solving and Decision-Making in Banks and the Opportunities of Knowledge Technology.* SDA-Bocconi, Milano, Italy

Mui C. and McCarthy W.E. (1987) FSA: applying AI techniques to the familiarization phase of financial decision making. *IEEE Expert*

Murphy G.L. and Wright J.C. (1984). Changes in conceptual structure with expertise: differences between real-world experts and novices. *Journal of Experimental Psychology: Learning, Memory and Cognition,* **10**, 144–55

Myers S.C. (1988). Notes on an expert system for capital budgeting. *Financial Management,* **17** (3)

von Neumann J. and Morgenstein O. (1944). *The Theory of Games and Economic Behavior.* Princeton: Princeton University Press

Newell A. and Simon H.A. (1963). GPS, a program that can simulate human thought. In *Computers and Thought* (Feigenbaum and Feldman, eds.), pp. 279–96

Newell A. and Simon H.A. (1972). *Human Problem Solving.* Englewood Cliffs NJ: Prentice-Hall

Newell A. and Simon H.A. (1976). Computer science as empirical inquiry: symbols and search. *Communications of the ACM,* **19**(3)

Nguyen T.A., Perkins W.A., Laffey T.J. and Pecora D. (1987). Knowledge base verification. *The AI-Magazine*

Olmsted, S.M. (1982). *SUPERTREE – decision tree processing program*. Menlo Park Ca: Strategic Decision Group

Olson M.H. (1982). New information technology and organizational culture. *MIS Quarterly*

Owen (1978). The use of influence diagrams in structuring complex decision problems. In *Readings on the Principles and Applications of Decision Analysis* Vol. 2 (1984) (Howard R.A. and Matheson J.E., eds.) Menlo Park, CA, Strategic Decision Example

Parfit D. (1986). *Reasons and Persons*. Oxford: Oxford University Press

Parnas D.L. (1972). On the criteria to be used in decomposing systems into modules. *Communications of the ACM*, **15**, 1053–58

PC-OPTRANS Expert User Manual. (1985). SIG, 4 bis rue de la Libération, 78350 JOUY-en-JOSAS

Pezier J. (1986). Real time financial trading systems. *SIAD Research Seminar*, Centre HEC-ISA, 78350 Jouy-en-Josas, France

Pezier J. and Klein M. (1973). *ARBRE Manuel d'utilisation* SIG, 4 bis rue de la Libération, 78350 Jouy-en-Josas, France

Pinson S. (1981). Representation des connaissances dans les Systems Experts *RAIRO*, **15**(4)

Politakis P.G. (1985). *Empirical Analysis for Expert Systems*. Boston: Pitman Publishing Inc

Pople H.E. (1982). Heuristic methods for imposing structure on ill-structured problems: the structuring of medical diagnostics. In *Artificial Intelligence in Medicine* (Szolovits P., ed.). Boulder CO: Westview Press

Popper K.R. (1963). *Conjectures and Refutation*. London: Routledge and Kegan Paul

Popper K.R. (1965). *The Logic of Scientific Discovery*. Harper Torchbooks

Pounds W.F. (1969). The process of problem finding. *Industrial Management Review* 1–19

Pracht W.E. (1987). A visual modeling acquisition and organization. In *Proc. of the Twentieth Hawaii International Conference on Systems Sciences*, Vol. I

Quade E.S. (1975). *Analysis for Public Decisions*. New York: North-Holland

Quade E.S. (1984). *Analysis for Military Decisions*. Chicago: Rand McNally

Quinlan J.R. (1979). Discovering rules by induction from large collections of examples. In *Expert Systems in the Micro-electronic Age* (Michie D., ed.), Edinburgh: Edinburgh University Press

Raiffa H. (1968). *Decision Analysis: Introductory Lectures on Choices Under Uncertainty*. Reading MA: Addison-Wesley

Ramsey F.P. (1931). Truth and probability. In *The Foundations of Mathematics and other Classical Essays*. (Braithwaite R.B., ed.). London: Kegan Paul

Raphael J., Klein M. and Manteau A. (1979). An investment and financial planning system for the road transport industry. *Engineering Cost and Production Economics*, **4**, 193–210

Reddy R. (1988). Foundations and grand challenges of artificial intelligence. *AI-Magazine*

Reiter R. (1978). On closed world data bases. In *Logic and Data Bases* (Gallaire H. and Minker J., eds.), 56–76. New York: Plenum Press

Ribe H. (1985). *A Study of Decision Processes in a Bank's Credit Department for*

Expert Systems Development (in Norwegian). Arbeidsnotat nr. 8/1986, Center of Applied Research NHH, Bergen

Rich E. (1983). *Artificial Intelligence*. New York: McGraw-Hill

Rich C. and Buchanan B. (1985). Expert systems – part 1, tutorial No. 5. *IJCAI 9*

Richter M.M. (1988). AI concept and OR tools in advanced DSS, in design aspects of advanced DSS. *DSS International Journal*, 4(4)

Rosch E., Mervis, C.B., Gray W.D., Johnson, D.M. and Boyes-Braem P. (1976). Basic objects in natural categories. *Cognitive Psychology*, 8, 382–439

Roy B. (1973). How outranking relation helps multiple criteria decision making. In *Selected Proceedings of a Seminar on Multi-criteria Decision Making*. Chapter Hill SL: University of South Carolina Press

Roy B. and Vincke P. (1981). Multicriteria analysis: survey and new directions. *European Journal of Operation Research*, 8(3)

Roy B. and Vincke P. (1984). Relational systems of preference with one or more pseudo-criteria: some new concepts and results. *Management Science*, 30(11)

Samuelson P.A. (1947). *Foundations of Economic Analysis*. Cambridge MA: Harvard University Press

Savage L.J. (1954). *The Foundation of Statistics* New York: Wiley

Schafer G.V. (1976). *A Mathematical Theory of Evidence*. Princeton: Princeton University Press

Schank R.C. and Abelson R.P. (1977). *Scripts, Plans, Goals, and Understanding*. Erlbaum, Hillsdale, NJ

Schoemaker P.J.H. (1980). *Experiments on Decisions Under Risk: The Expected Utility Hypothesis*. Boston: Nijhoff

Scott Morton M.S. (1971). *Management Decision Systems: Computer-based Support for Decision Making*. Cambridge, MA: Harvard Division of Research

Seaver D.A., von Winterfeld D. and Edwards, W. (1978). Eliciting subjective probability distribution on continuous variables. *Organizational Behavior and Human Performance*, 21, 379–91

Segal R. (1970). *Research in the Design and Management Decision System*. The Moore School of Electrical Engineering

Senicourt P. (1988). PREFACE-EXPERT: le simulateur expert pour lancer et piloter l'entreprise. In *Systemes Experts et Gestion d'Entreprise, Actes de Colloque EC2* ed., rue de la Garenne, 9200 Nanterre, France

Sharda R., Barr S.H. and McDonnell J.C. (1988). Decision support systems effectiveness: a review and an empirical test. *Management Science*, 34(2)

Sharpe W. (1963). A simplified model for portfolio analysis. *Management Sciences*, 9(2), 277–93

Shaw M.J. and Gentry J.A. (1988). Using an expert system with inductive learning to evaluate business loans. *Financial Management*

Shortliffe E.H. (1976). *Computer-Based Medical Consultations: MYCIN*. New York: Elsevier

Simon H.A. (1960). *The New Science of Management Decisions*. New York: Harper & Row

Simon H.A. (1969). *The Science of the Artificial*. Cambridge, MA: The MIT Press

Simon H.A. (1976). *Administrative Behavior*. New York: Free Press

Simon H.A. (1982). *The Science of the Artificial*. Cambridge MA: The MIT Press

Simon H. *et al.* (1987). Decision making and problem solving. *Interfaces* 17(5)

Slatter P.E. (1987). *Building Expert Systems: Cognitive Emulation*. New York: John Wiley

Smith E.E. and Medin D.L. (1981). *Categories and Concepts*. Cambridge MA: Harvard University Press

Smith J.M. (1986). Expert database systems: a database perspective. In *Expert Database Systems, Proceedings from the First International Workshop*. Menlo Park CA: Benjamin Cummings

Sowa J.F. (1984). *Conceptual Structures. Information Processing in Mind and Machine*. Reading MA: Addison-Wesley

Spetzler C.S. (1968). The development of a corporate risk policy for capital investment decisions. *IEEE Transactions on System Science and Cybernetics*. SSC-4, 279–300

Spetzler C.S. and Stael von Holstein C.A. (1975). Probability encoding in decision analysis. *Management Science*, **22**, 340–52

Sprague R.H. and Carlson E.D. (1982). *Building Effective Decision Support Systems*. Englewood Cliffs NJ: Prentice-Hall

Srinivasan V. and Kim Y.H. (1988). Designing expert financial systems: a case study of corporate credit management. *Financial Management*

Stabell (1974). Individual differences in managerial decision making processes, a study of conversational computer usage. *PhD Dissertation*, MIT, Cambridge MA

Stabell C.B. (1983). A decision oriented approach to building DSS. In *Building Decision Support Systems* (Bennet J.L., ed.), Reading MA: Addison-Wesley

Stansfield J.L. and Greenfeld N.R. (1987). Plan Power – a comprehensive financial planner, *IEEE Expert*

Stephens R.G. (1980). *Uses of Financial Information in Bank Lending Decision*. Ann Arbor MI: UMI Research Press

Stillings, N.A., Feinstein M.H., Garfield J.L., Rissland E.L., Rosenbaum D.A., Weisler S.E. and Baker-Ward L. (1980). *Cognitive Science: An Introduction*. Cambridge MA: The MIT Press

Suwa M., Scott A.C. and Shortliffe E.H. (1982). An approach to verifying completeness and consistency in a rule-based expert system. *The AI-Magazine*

Tener W.T. (1988). Expert systems for computer security. *Expert System Review*, **1**(2)

Thomas D. (1989). What is an object? *Byte*, McGraw-Hill

Tomlinson R. and Kiss I., eds. (1984). *Rethinking the Process of Operational Research and System Analysis*. Oxford: Pergamon Press

Toulmin S. (1972) *Human Understanding* Vol. 1. Princeton NJ: Princeton University Press

Tribus M. (1969). *Rational Descriptions, Decisions and Design* Oxford: Pergamon Press

Turban E. (1988). *Decision Support and Expert Systems*. New York: Macmillan

Vincke P. (1986). Analysis of multicriteria decision aid in Europe. *European Journal of Operational Research* **25**, 160–68. North-Holland

Waddington C.H. (1973). *OR in World War 2*. London: Elek Science

Warren J.M. (1974). An operational model for securing analysis and valuation. *JFQA*

Waterman D.A. (1986). *A Guide to Expert Systems*. Reading MA: Addison-Wesley

Watson S.R. and Buede D.M. (1987). *Decision Synthesis: The Principles and Practice of Decision Analysis*. Cambridge: Cambridge University Press

Weatherford R. (1982). *Philosophical Foundation of Probability Theory*. London: Routledge and Kegan Paul

Weingartner M.H. (1963). Mathematical Programming and the Analysis of Capital Budgeting Problems. Englewood Cliffs NJ: Prentice-Hall

Weiss S.M. and Kulikowski C.A. (1984). *A Practical Guide to Designing Expert Systems*. Totowa NJ: Rowman & Allanheld

Welbank M. (1983). A review of knowledge acquisition techniques for expert systems. *British Telecommunications*

Wick M.R. and Slagle J.R. (1989). An explanation facility for today's expert systems. *IEEE Expert*

Wielinga B.J. and Breuker J.A. (1984). Interpretation of verbal data for knowledge acquisition. *Proc. of ECA 84: Advances in Artificial Intelligence*. North-Holland: Elsevier

Williamson J.P. (1970). Computerised approaches to bond switching. *Financial Analyst Journal*, July–August 1970

Winograd T. and Flores F. (1986). *Understanding Computers and Cognition*. Reading MA: Addison-Wesley

Witte E. (1972). Field research on complex decision-making processes – the phase theorem. *International Studies of Management and Organization*, 156–82

Wittgenstein L. (1953). *Philosophical Investigations*. Oxford: Basil Blackwell

Woods D.D. (1984). Visual momentum: a concept to improve the cognitive coupling of person and computers. *International Journal Man–Machine Studies*, **21**, 229–44

Zadeh L. (1965). Fuzzy Sets. *Information and Control*, **8**

Zadeh L. (1965). Fuzzy Sets as a Basis for A Theory of Possibility. *Fuzzy Sets and Systems*, **1**(1)

Zadeh L.A. (1981). Possibility theory and soft data analysis. In *Mathematical Frontiers of the Social and Policy Sciences* (Cobb L. and Thrall R.M., eds.). Boulder Co: Westview Press

Zand D.E. and Sorenson R.E. (1975). Theory of change and the effective use of management science. *Administrative Science Quarterly*, **20**(4), 532–95

Zannetos Z.S. (1968). Toward intelligent management information systems. *Industrial Management Review* **9**(3), 21–38

Zeleny M. (1982) *Multiple Criteria Decision Making*. New York: McGraw-Hill

Zoeppritz A. (1986). Framework for investigating language-mediated interaction with machines. *International Journal Man–Machine Studies*, **25**, 295–315

Index